TRADE POLICY AND INDUSTRIALIZATION IN TURBULENT TIMES

The relationship between trade policy and industrialization has provoked much controversy. Can trade policy promote economic growth in developing countries? Those actively working in the area are becoming increasingly sceptical about the conventional advice given by international policy advisors and organizations.

The authors review the experience of fourteen developing countries with trade policy and industrialization in the 1970s and 80s. They employ current theory and empirical methodology to re-examine old controversies. Contrary to the accepted wisdom, the studies find that in this period, trade policy, narrowly defined, did not play a major role in growth and development experiences. The authors find that import substitution was only a limited and industry-specific phenomenon while industrial growth emanated primarily from expanding domestic demand and, increasingly, from exports.

Ultimately, the authors conclude that there are many routes to industrial expansion and that there can be no universal trade policy prescription that will generate improved economic performance everywhere. This volume builds upon earlier theoretical and empirical research on trade policy but is the first across-the-board attempt to review developing country experiences in this realm for twenty years. All of the country case studies are undertaken by nationals of the countries concerned, each of whom has a detailed understanding of their country's recent experiences.

Gerald K. Helleiner is Professor of Economics at the University of Toronto. He has vast experience in this area and currently coordinates the research of the group of Twenty-Four in the IMF and World Bank. He is also chairman of the Board of Trustees of the International Food Policy Research Institute. His most recent books are *The New Global Economy and the Developing Countries* and, as editor, *Trade Policy, Industrialization and Development*.

TRADE POLICY AND INDUSTRIALIZATION IN TURBULENT TIMES

Edited by G. K. Helleiner

London and New York

First published 1994
by Routledge
11 New Fetter Lane London EC4P 4EE

Simultaneously published in the USA and Canada
by Routledge
29 West 35th Street, New York NY 10001

© 1994 UNU/WIDER

Phototypeset in Garamond by Intype, London

Printed and bound in Great Britain by
Mackays of Chatham PLC, Chatham, Kent

British Library Cataloguing in Publication Data
A catalogue record for this book is available from the British Library.

Library of Congress Cataloging in Publication Data
Trade policy and industrialization in turbulent times /
edited by G. K. Helleiner
p. cm.
Includes bibliographical references and index.
ISBN 0–415–10711–3
1. Developing countries–Commercial policy.
2. Developing countries–Commerce.
3. Industrial promotion–Developing countries.
4. Developing countries–Economic policy.
I. Helleiner, Gerald K.
HF1413.T73 1994
382'.3'091724–dc20
93–26896
CIP
ISBN 0–415–10711–3

CONTENTS

CONTENTS

LIST OF FIGURES

LIST OF TABLES

CONTRIBUTORS

Isher Judge Ahluwalia is Research Professor at the Centre for Policy Research, New Delhi, India.

Narongchai Akrasanee is a Member of the Board of Directors, Thailand Development Research Institute.

Merih Celasun is Professor of Economics at the Middle East Technical University, Ankara, Turkey.

Gustavo H. B. Franco is Associate Professor of Economics at the Catholic University of Rio de Janeiro, Brazil and works at present for the Central Bank of Brazil in Brasilia.

Winston Fritsch is Professor, Department of Economics, Catholic University of Rio de Janeiro, Brazil and is at present Economic Policy Secretary in the Ministry of Finance, Brasilia.

Gerald K. Helleiner is a Professor of Economics at the University of Toronto, Canada.

Kwang Suk Kim is a Professor in the Department of Economics, Kyung-Hee University, Seoul, Korea. From 1972 to 1982 he was a Research Director and Vice-president of the Korea Development Institute.

Lim Teck Ghee is Professor of Land Use at the Institute of Advanced Studies, University of Malaya, Kuala Lumpur, Malaysia.

Patricio Meller is Executive Director of CIEPLAN, Corporacion de Investigaciones Economicas para Latinoamerica, Santiago, Chile.

Francis M. Mwega is Senior Lecturer at the Department of Economics, University of Nairobi, Kenya.

Benno Ndulu is Professor of Economics, University of Dar-es-Salaam, Tanzania, currently on leave while serving as Executive Director, African Economic Research Consortium, Nairobi, Kenya.

José Antonio Ocampo is Minister of Agriculture in Colombia, and previously was Senior Researcher at FEDESARROLLO and Professor of Economics at University de los Andes, Bogotá, Colombia.

Carlos E. Paredes is a Research Associate of the Group of Analysis for Development (GRADE) in Lima, Peru, and is, at present, at the Centre for Public Policy, Instituto de Estudios Superiores de Administración Caracas, Venezuela.

Sultan Hafeez Rahman is Senior Research Fellow at the Bangladesh Institute of Development Studies, Dhaka (currently on leave at the Asian Development Bank, Manila).

Jaime Ros, a Mexican economist, is Associate Professor of Economics and Fellow of the Kellogg Institute for International Studies at the University of Notre Dame.

Joseph J. Semboja is Senior Research Fellow, Economic Research Bureau, University of Dar-es-Salaam, Tanzania.

Moshe Syrquin is Professor of Economics at Bar Ilan University in Israel.

Toh Kin Woon is an Associate Professor attached to the Faculty of Economics, National University of Malaysia, Malaysia.

Paitoon Wiboonchutikula is Assistant Professor, Faculty of Economics, Chulalongkorn University, Bangkok, and Consultant, Thailand Development Research Institute.

Ganeshan Wignaraja is a Research Officer at the Oxford University Institute of Economics and Statistics.

PREFACE

This volume had its origins in an earlier research project of the World Institute for Development Economic Research (WIDER) which sought to assess the relevance of the 'new' trade theories to the developing countries. That project generated a summary volume (G. K. Helleiner, ed., *Trade Policy, Industrialization and Development: New Perspectives*, Clarendon Press, Oxford, 1992) and the conclusion that it was time for a major review of trade and industrialization experience in the developing countries over the 1970s and 1980s. This conclusion led to the creation of a new, much larger, WIDER research project.

The new project initially assembled prospective authors from seventeen developing countries and a select number of resource persons, some of whom were asked to write papers on designated research areas (David Evans, Howard Pack, Dani Rodrik, Jim Tybout, Yung Whee Rhee, Helen Shapiro and Lance Taylor), to consider how a review of the 1970s and 1980s might best be conducted. This consultation led to an agreed research plan, the first step in which was the preparation of country survey papers, a conference in which the papers were vigorously discussed, and, as its first major output, this volume. The project is now in a second stage in which more focused analysis of particular topics is being undertaken by the same set of authors.

Project participants are grateful to the Swedish International Development ment Authority (SIDA) for its financial support for the project and to WIDER for its sponsorship. They are also grateful to their conference hosts: the International Development Research Centre, Ottawa, in September 1990; and the OECD Development Centre, Paris, in September, 1991, and November 1992. Particular thanks are due to Lal Jayawardena, Director of WIDER, and Hema Perera, its Executive Officer, for their unflinching support for the project; to Louis Emmerij, President of the OECD Development Centre, and Giulio Fossi, its External Relations Director, for their warm hospitality; to Barbara Tiede, the project's secretary, at the University of Toronto, for her cheerful and efficient management of the details of the project's business and the final proof-reading of the manuscript; and to Rodney Schmidt, Claire Brenner, Jim Aikens and Nikela Hanko for their extensive assistance in preparing the project's papers for publication.

1

INTRODUCTION

G. K. Helleiner

This introduction has benefited greatly from comments on an earlier draft made by Manuel Agosin, Isher Ahluwalia, Alice Amsden, Merih Celasun, Philip English, David Evans, Gustavo Franco, David Glover, Sue Horton, David Kaplan, Mohamed Lahouel, Patricio Meller, Benno Ndulu, Akbar Noman, José Antonio Ocampo, Howard Pack, Carlos Paredes, Lant Pritchett, Dani Rodrik, Jaime Ros, Helen Shapiro, Hans Singer, Moshe Syrquin, Lance Taylor, Jim Tybout, Len Waverman and Ganeshan Wignaraja. Responsibility for this version rests, none the less, entirely with me.

TRADE POLICY AND INDUSTRIALIZATION: THE BACKGROUND

The role of international trade in industrialization processes and economic development has attracted a great deal of attention in the professional literature of economics. Trade policy features prominently in theoretical analyses of growth and development, in studies of economic history of both the industrial and developing countries, and in current normative and prescriptive writing on appropriate policies for the developing countries. Indeed, trade policy may have received disproportionate attention in the mainstream of the development economics literature relative to, say, the issues surrounding the means of increasing productivity in smallholder agriculture in low-income countries, or, in the industrial sector, other (non-trade) policies impacting upon the capacities of firms to respond to changing incentives or even upon incentive structures themselves.

Trade policy, in the currently dominant view, is a fundamental determinant of economic performance, and it functions best when it attempts the least. Domestic goods prices should closely approximate world prices, except in a narrowly limited range of cases, notably where countries possess market power (are not 'small') in the world markets for their principal exports. Government interventions should be few and, where they are made, should be unselective as between different areas of economic activity, leaving their impact as 'neutral' as possible. They should also, in general,

1

employ 'market-friendly' policy instruments, like subsidies or taxes, rather than administrative instruments, like quantitative controls. These trade policies are presumed to be universally appropriate and should be introduced everywhere as rapidly as possible. Liberal policies regarding the inflow of services, technology and capital are also recommended as part of this universally applicable set of appropriate policies. (Policies on services, technology and foreign capital may be more important to long-run development than policies on goods trade, but this volume, in accordance with much recent practice, confines itself primarily to the role of the latter.) Many developing countries are 'liberalizing' their trade policies on their own volition, having accepted the logic of the theoretical arguments for doing so, within the context of broad adjustments to development strategy following the disappointing experience of the 1980s. Many more are being pressed, in bilateral agreements with trading partners, in the GATT, and via external conditions on financial assistance, to 'liberalize' their trade and to 'disarm' themselves in respect of the potential for future more 'activist' trade and industrial policies (Agosin and Tussie, 1992). There are both theoretical and empirical reasons for doubt as to the universal validity of these general assessments and recommendations. Allowing for learning effects, scale economies, externalities, and less-than-perfectly competitive markets, it is easy, on the basis of standard economic theory, to posit alternative 'optimal' trade policies for development (each dependent on specific alternative assumptions regarding these matters). These issues were addressed in an earlier WIDER volume (Helleiner, 1992). Moreover, the historical record seems to offer remarkably few recent cases of rapid industrialization or development that can be associated with the currently recommended trade policies (Shapiro and Taylor, 1990). In a recent comprehensive empirical investigation of the sources of growth, in which the robustness of earlier results (including those relating to trade and trade policy) was subjected to systematic testing, the only variable that proved (robustly) correlated with economic growth was the investment rate (Levine and Renelt, 1992).

More particularly, many analyses of the East Asian successes of the 1970s and 1980s have called attention to the importance therein of governmental activism in trade and other spheres, much of which was quite selective in its intention and its impact (Westphal, 1982, 1990; Amsden, 1989; Wade, 1990). Previous approaches to lending in support of industrialization policies (in Korea, India and Indonesia) have recently been vigorously challenged even in the international financial institutions, within which there now appears to be some debate on these issues (World Bank, 1992a). There is widespread agreement that the strongest case for liberalized and neutral policies now rests not on economic theory but on political economy grounds, that is, on the risk that discretionary economic policy may be captured by political interests or, putting the point a little differently, the small likelihood of optimal policies in terms of economic theory emanating from discretionary political processes (e.g. Krugman, 1987).

The relatively heavy attention devoted to international trade and trade policy in the development literature (about which more below) may be attributable, at least in part, to the fact that the principal early contributors to the 'Western' literature were academics and policymakers in Northern (primarily US and UK) institutions, many of whom acquired their interest in development problems via their earlier interest in international economics. Also relevant is the traditional antipathy to 'industrial policy' in the US and the UK, which has left trade policy as the major instrument actually available in these economies for the pursuit of industrial sector objectives that other countries are comfortable pursuing more directly. Together with the fact that economists trained in English-speaking universities have continued to dominate the mainstream of the profession and the most influential international financial institutions, this may have further biased the literature on industrialization towards a heavy emphasis upon trade policy influences. ('Radical' analysts, whether reacting to the mainstream views or on their own, have also traditionally assigned great importance to trade and trade policy.)

The project of which this book forms an important part was motivated by the widespread expression of need for a balanced, independent and eclectic review of developing countries' overall experiences with trade policies and industrialization over the 1970s and 1980s. There have been no such across-the-board reviews since the influential studies of a much earlier period undertaken by the OECD Development Centre and the National Bureau of Economic Research (Little et al., 1970; Bhagwati, 1978; Krueger, 1978). The participants in the project agreed that since, as in many other branches of economics, the relevant theory (of the effects of trade and trade policy) is far more 'developed' than empirical analysis thereof, the most pressing research requirement was comparative analysis of recent experience, rather than further development of the underlying economic theory. While it obviously draws on such economic theory, this volume is therefore frankly empiricist in its orientation. It is also more concerned to describe recent experience accurately than to offer policy prescriptions for the future. It is positive, rather than normative, in its primary orientation.

The fourteen countries included in the study vary greatly in terms of size, per capita GDP, economic structure, degree of dependence on exports, and other characteristics.[1] Syrquin has categorized them broadly in chapter 2 according to size, the commodity specialization of their trade (primary/industry), and 'openness'.[2] In his terms, they include eight 'large' countries (population over 25 million in 1985: Bangladesh, Brazil, Colombia, India, Korea, Mexico, Thailand and Turkey) and six small ones (Chile, Kenya, Malaysia, Peru, Sri Lanka and Tanzania). In 1980, three were 'outward-oriented', of which one was a primary exporter and two were industrial

3

exporters; seven were 'inward-oriented', of which five were primary-oriented and two were manufacturing-oriented; and four were 'balanced', i.e. difficult to categorize. In terms of the World Bank's categorizations, the sample includes five low-income countries, eight lower-middle-income countries and one upper-middle-income country (Korea). Certainly, these countries' initial conditions (e.g. macroeconomic stability, external supports or constraints, etc.); boundary conditions (e.g. size, level of development, natural resource endowments, etc.); and indeed their entire histories – social, economic, political – show great variety. It is their very variety which buttresses the strength of whatever generalizations the studies of their experiences may generate; on the other hand, the same variety, as will be seen, makes it correspondingly more difficult to derive such generalizations.

The mandate given to the authors was a broad one – within the context of current theoretical understanding, to review the record of trade policies, and other policies relevant to industrial performance and industrial growth over, roughly, the last two decades. Any such analyses of the economic record and policy experience of the 1970s and 1980s in the developing countries must take full account of the fact that macroeconomic stability and overall economic performance in most of the developing world was much less satisfactory in this period than in the previous two decades. Severe global recessions, oil price 'shocks', interest rate volatility, rising protectionism in many industrial countries, and disorder in the global financial system all generated a degree of international economic turbulence not seen since the 1930s. These and other factors, often including deficient domestic economic policies, contributed to reduced growth (particularly in the 1980s), intensified balance of payments problems, and accelerated price inflation in the majority of the developing countries. Of the fourteen countries in our sample only two (India and Korea) experienced higher growth rates, and only two (Chile and Korea) had lower inflation rates, in the 1980s than the 1960s (see Table 1.1). (More details on countries' relative performance may be found in chapter 2.) Authors were therefore particularly asked to investigate the interactions between macroeconomic experiences and policies and the trade-industrialization issues that were the main focus of their studies.

The authors were also asked to devote particular attention to elements of policy and experience that have figured prominently in recent theoretical discussion – notably industrial productivity change, and its policy and other correlates,[3] including the roles of firm size, market structure and other dimensions of industrial organization. (Some of them were unable to report much on the latter issues.) They were also asked to investigate and, where possible, measure the role of non-trade (industrial) policies, and to assess their overall relative importance *vis-à-vis* trade and trade policies, in industrial performance. Individual authors, all of whom are nationals of the

4

Table 1.1 Macroeconomic performance indicators, 1960–89

	Real GDP growth rate (%)			Inflation rate[a] (%)		
	1960–70	1970–80	1980–9	1960–70	1970–80	1980–9
Brazil	5.3	8.2	3.1	46.1	36.7	227.8
Chile	4.4	1.4	2.2	33.2	185.6	20.5
Colombia	5.1	5.4	3.8	11.9	22.0	24.3
Mexico	7.3	6.4	0.7	3.6	19.3	72.7
Peru	4.8	3.8	0.4	10.4	30.7	160.3
Bangladesh	3.8	3.7	3.5	3.7	16.9	10.6
India	3.6	3.6	5.6	7.1	8.5	7.7
Korea (Rep. of)	8.9	9.1	9.7	17.4	19.8	5.0
Malaysia	5.9	7.9	4.9	−0.3	7.5	1.5
Sri Lanka	5.0	4.1	4.1	1.8	12.6	10.9
Thailand	8.3	7.1	7.1	1.8	9.9	3.2
Turkey	6.0	5.4	5.4	5.6	29.7	41.4
Kenya	8.2	5.6	4.2	1.5	11.0	9.0
Tanzania	7.8	3.1	2.6	1.8	11.9	26.1

Sources: GDP Growth: UNCTAD, Handbook of International Trade and Development Statistics, 1990: 434–41.
Inflation: World Bank, World Development Report, 1982: 110–11; World Bank, World Development Report, 1991: 204–5.
[a] Implicit GDP deflator.

countries they studied, were encouraged to emphasize whatever elements of their countries' experiences and policies they believed to be especially deserving of deeper (and WIDER) attention; further focused research on these questions is being undertaken in later stages of the research project. (They were specifically *not* asked, however, to explore the impact of *other* countries' trade policies, international trade agreements or the GATT upon their own trade and industrial performance or policies; that would require another whole volume.)

This introduction cannot begin to do full justice to the country studies that follow; the individual chapters are rich in both detail and insight, much of which is inevitably lost in any attempt to draw overall conclusions. It can highlight only a few of the studies' overall findings. There is, as always, no substitute for a complete read.

TRADE POLICY AND MACROECONOMIC POLICY: DEFINITIONS AND INTERACTIONS

The manner in which the studies in this volume seek to consider the interaction between trade (or commercial) policies and macroeconomic policies deserves some introductory discussion and clarification. Assessments of the nature and efficacy of a country's economic policies should, in our view, wherever possible, avoid confusing the issues of trade policy with those of macroeconomic (including exchange rate) policy. Trade policy relates, strictly speaking, to the overall structure of incentives to produce and consume, and hence import or export, tradable goods and services. It typically serves long-run objectives of growth and development. It is therefore usually closely linked to policies on both local and foreign investment, technology and particular sectoral objectives (industrial policy, agricultural policy, regional policies, etc.)

Macroeconomic policy, on the other hand, relates to the continuing (i.e. short-term as well as long-term) achievement of overall internal and external balance. Low rates of price inflation and high capacity utilization (especially of labour) are the primary objectives of internal balance. A current account in the international balance of payments that is sustainable in the sense that it is consistent with (expected) long-run capital flow is the objective of external balance. Both internal and external balance objectives are pursued, where possible, through means that are consistent with long-run development objectives and policies. Thus, for example, no matter whether the (longer-term) trade and development policy calls for an emphasis on export growth or for (efficient) import substitution, successful macroeconomic policy ensures that overall external and internal balance are maintained *en route*. Similarly, the attainment of short-term macroeconomic balance is not compatible with development objectives if it requires investment levels so low as to compromise future growth.

The two principal instruments of macroeconomic policy are aggregate demand (monetary and fiscal) policies and exchange rate policies. Nominal exchange rate policies typically seek to influence the relative price of tradables (to non-tradables). By altering the incentives to produce and consume these broad categories of goods and services, they influence the current account of the international balance of payments. Only changes in the *real* (i.e. inflation-adjusted) exchange rate can be expected to alter the relative price of tradables: other things being equal, real currency devaluation increases the relative price of tradables. Nominal devaluation has often proven difficult to translate into sustained real devaluation.[4]

The services of labour are broadly non-tradable; real currency devaluation therefore typically implies real wage reduction. (Where the consumption of wage-earners consists largely of non-tradables, this link is obviously weaker.) Indeed real wage reduction is often seen as an essential element of change within the overall restructuring of prices attendant on 'successful' real currency devaluation. Real wage reduction increases the competitiveness of non-traditional exports, cushions industrial firms against the increased costs of concomitant interest rate increases, and contributes to aggregate demand restraint (by redistributing income from lower to higher savers on the margin). The political management of changing wage and income distributional relationships is therefore critically important to the

6

success of macroeconomic management and, among other elements of performance, the sustainability of expanded industrial exporting.

Over the long run one can conceive of an equilibrium real exchange rate which is the product of such 'fundamentals' as the country's long-run productivity, terms of trade, sustainable external capital flow and trade policy regime. In the short to medium term, in which policies are made, however, the real exchange rate can be influenced by official policy on the nominal exchange rate (often buttressed by exchange restrictions) and aggregate demand, as well as by a variety of other shorter-term influences.[5] Although nominal exchange rate policy is usually directed at external balance objectives, it is also sometimes directed at the goal of internal balance, typically seeking to offer a nominal anchor in the pursuit of anti-inflationary objectives.

Since nominal exchange rate changes are frequently accompanied by changes in the trade regime, they are sometimes confused with, or even described as, trade policies (e.g. Thomas and Nash, 1992: 1–2). Elements of the import regime, particularly those that originated with balance of payments problems, are often removed at the same time as a currency devaluation. Sometimes long-run trade policies are also changed at the same time as the exchange rate. Such overall changes may be convenient to undertake 'in one go'. Indeed, some have actively fostered the idea that these separate issues are all of a single piece – to be dealt with by 'structural adjustment' reforms. Conceptually, however, it is still best, as argued above, to try to separate the macroeconomic (external) balance issues from longer-run trade and development policies and objectives. This conceptual distinction between alternative motivations for import barriers is clearly recognized in the GATT. It is also recognized in all careful theoretical analyses of trade and exchange rate phenomena (e.g. Edwards, 1989: 25–37, 81–2), and it is recognized throughout this volume as well.

However clear this conceptual distinction may be, the real world's taxation, control and licensing regimes in the sphere of international trade are frequently themselves murky in their motivation, and confusing and complex in their operation. Ministries of Commerce (or Trade) and Industry usually carry responsibility for such import licensing as may be associated with industrialization objectives. Finance Ministries, Treasuries and Central Banks are responsible for macroeconomic stability, and, in that connection, normally administer any foreign exchange controls and/or controls on credit systems. Customs duties, however, are collected by Finance Ministries or Treasuries, whose prime concern is the raising of revenue for the support of government activities. It is not always easy to discern whether particular governmental measures were undertaken primarily to address long-term development objectives, short-term macroeconomic targets, or both at the same time. During a period of great macroeconomic turbulence, such as that studied in this volume, it is often simply not possible – as it may be in calmer times – to isolate the role and impact of trade and industrial policies as distinct from those of macroeconomic policies. Moreover, consideration of the details of incentive structures at the micro-level always necessitates analysis of the joint effects of macroeconomic (especially exchange rate) policies, trade policies and a variety of other policies.

CHANGING SOURCES OF INDUSTRIAL OUTPUT EXPANSION: IMPORT SUBSTITUTION NO MORE

Import-substitution industrialization (ISI), defined as reduction in import shares of apparent consumption of manufactures, has been the usual route for early industrializers. Some has occurred, without governmental encouragement, through the natural evolution of market opportunities. Sometimes it was stimulated by such temporary 'shocks' as wars, sanctions and the Great Depression. Governmental encouragement of ISI through conscious protectionist policies was a prominent feature of development strategy in most developing countries in the 1950s and 1960s; and it has been heavily criticized (e.g. Little *et al.* 1970). Certainly ISI policies were at one time important elements of the development strategies of all of the countries studied in this volume.

During the 1970s and 1980s, very small shares of the overall expansion of manufacturing output in the developing countries studied in this volume could be attributed directly to import substitution in the sense of reduced import proportions of domestic manufacturing usage. When expansion of industrial output is decomposed, using Chenery's methodology, into its demand-side constituents, most of the industrial growth in the countries in this study was associated with growth in domestic demand.

Industrial growth associated with overall domestic demand expansion took place in industries that were developed in an earlier import-substituting period. Some of these industries were internationally competitive. Others, however, had originally been established with the help of protection against imports, much of which remained in place. To the degree that imports could have met some of the expanding domestic demand more efficiently, one could say that import-substituting industrial output under protection continued to expand along with domestic demand and, in an absolute sense, the static costs of protection grew; so, presumably, did any positive externalities, learning effects, employment creation or other desired effects of this protected output. Chenery's methodology for the measurement of import substitution is thus an imperfect indicator of the continuing role of import-substituting activities.

When changes in domestic demand dominate overall manufacturing growth, the pattern of change is primarily the product of differential income elasticities of demand for particular industries' outputs. The pattern

8

of export performance is also affected by differential domestic demand pressures on different industries as overall growth in demand varies. With few exceptions, industrial growth, when led by domestic demand (as is normal in large countries), followed the usual (large country) patterns. Heavy intermediate products, consumer durables and capital goods grew relatively more quickly in the 1970s and 1980s in such countries as Mexico, Brazil, Korea and Turkey. In India, however, where these 'late' industries were encouraged to make an early start in the 1950s and 1960s, consumer goods production enjoyed a relative spurt in the late 1980s.

Import shares of apparent consumption in manufacturing did sometimes change significantly in the countries in the sample during the 1970s and 1980s. For example, in Chile and in Sri Lanka, import liberalization in the 1970s increased import shares, reversing some of their earlier import substitution; and the manufacturing sector actually declined in size relative to the primary sector. Positive import substitution occurred in the 1970s in heavy and high-technology industries in Brazil, and in many industry-specific instances in other countries. In low-income Tanzania, the 'basic industry' strategy of the late 1970s even produced a temporary 'bulge' in the 'later' industries' share of manufacturing output. But, overall, the 1970s and 1980s cannot be characterized in terms of import-substitution phenomena.

Growth in exports, on the other hand, almost everywhere contributed an increased share of total manufactured output growth in the 1970s and 1980s, with particularly significant increases in many countries in the 1980s. In our sample of countries, export expansion rose to become a dominant source of industrial growth in the 1980s in Malaysia, Mexico, Turkey, and probably Brazil and Thailand, where the relevant data are not complete. It is generally anticipated that manufactured exports will continue to make a major contribution to developing countries' industrial growth in the 1990s. These changes in the manufacturing sector typically paralleled the changes at the level of the overall national economy where the share of exports (and, often to a slightly smaller degree, imports) in GDP rose as well.

When manufactured exports grew they did not do so equally across the whole range of domestic manufacturing activity. Even when the entire incentive structure was altered so as to offer new encouragement to all potential exporters, the initial response typically clustered in only a few segments of the manufacturing sector. The aggregate data on the sources of the manufacturing sector's output expansion may therefore be quite misleading. For instance, in Bangladesh, Sri Lanka, Malaysia and Thailand, garments (and, to a lesser degree in the latter two countries, electronics) totally dominated exports in the 1980s. Automobiles and, to a lesser extent, electronic equipment (computers) played a great role in Mexican (non-maquila) manufactured export expansion. In Turkey the textile industry dominated manufacturing for export. These response patterns reflect different domestic capacities, differential incentives to investors, and different comparative advantages, among other influences; these issues undoubtedly require more research (see p. 23).

THE ROLE OF MACROECONOMIC POLICIES

As noted above, the studies in this collection addressed the role of trade policies within the broad context of macroeconomic and other policies, only some of which were explicitly directed at industrialization and development, without prior assumptions as to their relative importance. When defined narrowly and, we believe, appropriately – as policies influencing the structure of incentives and influences upon the production and consumption of tradable goods and services – trade policies do *not* appear to have played a dominant role in these countries' industrialization and development experiences in the 1970s and 1980s.

Much more important have been macroeconomic policies and, in particular, policies in respect of the exchange rate. As noted above, during the 1970s and 1980s, much more than in the previous two decades, the macroeconomic environment in the developing countries was highly unstable. Two major oil price shocks, major global recessions, large international interest rate variations and the debt crisis all created severe external pressures that would have challenged the most astute of macroeconomic policymakers. Typically, these pressures, particularly the sharply increased external debt servicing obligations of the 1980s, reduced domestic savings available for productive investment. In some cases, as in that of the coffee boom in Colombia in the late 1970s or in those of the oil exporters, favourable shocks also created macroeconomic management difficulties.

Macroeconomic policymakers in the developing countries grappled with the new problems of this period as best they could. But balance of payments 'crises', large fiscal deficits, high rates of price inflation and, periodically, sharp currency devaluations and severe austerity programmes to deal with the latter problems, were characteristic of the period (see Taylor, 1988). Private investors and decisionmakers, both domestic and foreign, were understandably more anxious about the next macroeconomic policy moves of developing country governments than they might be in more economically stable times. The relative importance of microeconomic signals, reflecting trade, industrial and other policies, was bound to decline in such a macroeconomically turbulent period. The significance of policy reforms directed at the rationalization of micro-level incentives, and improved efficiency, was therefore almost certainly correspondingly less in the developing countries of the 1980s than it would have been, say, in the 1960s (when the Little–Scitovsky–Scott and Bhagwati–Krueger studies were undertaken).

Characteristic of all 'successful' manufactured export and/or overall growth experiences in these countries at this time (success in these two dimensions was highly correlated) was an 'appropriate' real (i.e. inflation-adjusted) exchange rate; that is, one that generated a relative price for tradables, both importables and exportables, sufficient to encourage enough domestic production and discourage enough consumption of tradables, to ensure sustainable external balance; or in terms of another perspective, one that generated real wages sufficiently low as to raise international competitiveness and lower domestic absorption, to achieve the same overall effect. 'Weak' performers all had overvalued currencies and unstable real exchange rates during the period under study, whatever else they may have been doing 'wrong'.

This evidence on the significance of the real exchange rate is consistent with the results of earlier empirical investigations (e.g. Cottani *et al.*, 1990; Dollar, 1992). The real exchange rate may be a more reliable predictor of longer term economic performance than any of the variety of measures of trade policy 'openness', which are not even highly correlated amongst themselves (Harrison, 1991; Pritchett, 1991a). In the very poorest countries, in one recent study, real exchange rate 'distortion' is the only variable significantly related to growth; even investment carried no explanatory power (Dollar, 1992: 537–8). Obviously, however, causality cannot easily be ascribed in these associations; when economies function well or badly, they tend to do so in many dimensions.

Stability in the real exchange rate has repeatedly been found to be associated positively with non-traditional export growth and indeed overall economic performance (e.g. Caballero and Corbo, 1989; Thomas and Nash, 1991: 53; Dollar, 1992)[6] The stability of incentives, and hence their credibility as guides to investment and other behaviour, may be as important as having the statically 'correct' ones, assuming (which may not always be easy) that one knows roughly what the latter are (Rodrik, 1991). If static optimum allocation is less important than ongoing productivity change, as is argued below, then whatever drives productivity change should carry greater importance than 'correct' prices. In the short- to medium-term, productivity is closely associated with macroeconomic performance. Macroeconomic performance, and particularly private investment, is typically highly sensitive to expectations, and not least to the expectation of stability in incentive structures. The evidence from the country studies in this volume provides some modest backing for the proposition that the stability of overall incentives is important – particularly from the Korean experience over the past two decades (during which there was remarkable stability not only in its real exchange rate but also in the degree of anti-export bias), and from shorter periods in the recent history of Colombia, Brazil, Chile, Malaysia, Thailand and Turkey.

For the purposes of understanding industrialization processes the longer

11

term structural consequences of real exchange rate behaviour (in particular, its level and stability) are far more important than its role in the maintenance of short-term external balance, or the often disruptive effects of changing it. As has been seen, these long-term exchange rate effects have been linked to trade policy in a general equilibrium framework of analysis; if such trade policy is reasonably stable, it can be regarded as one of the underlying determinants of the 'equilibrium real exchange rate', together with such other 'fundamentals' as long-term capital flow and the terms of trade. Observed (actual) real exchange rates can then be seen as the product of short-run macroeconomic policies, including those relating to the nominal exchange rate and short-term aggregate demand, and adjustment lags *en route* to (changing) equilibria; short-run macroeconomic policies thus can and do influence real exchange rates.

Quantitative restrictions (QRs) were often, in large part, also macroeconomic policy instruments employed for the objective of maintaining external balance. They were retained in the early 1990s, either as instruments of balance of payments policy or for protectionist purposes, or both, in more country cases in our sample than not; though they had often been significantly eased. Until the late 1980s, the easing of QRs was typically associated with favourable balance of payments circumstances, and conversely, their tightening reflected external imbalance. With the increased general pressure (and vogue) for trade liberalization in recent years, this association can no longer be so easily assumed as a pattern for the immediate future. Where QRs were used primarily as tools of balance of payments management they should presumably be assessed primarily on the basis of their efficacy in that regard, relative to alternative instruments of such policy.

Controls over capital movements were also employed by all of the sample countries in the 1970s and 1980s. Where the capital account of the balance of payments is freed of foreign exchange controls, or such controls are largely ineffective, the nominal exchange rate, rather than being a policy variable, acquires some of the characteristics of an 'asset price': potential volatility and extreme vulnerability to changing private expectations. Unless domestic circumstances are more stable than they usually can be in developing countries, there will be significant expectations-responsive international private capital flows. If the monetary authorities seek to modify consequent exchange rate fluctuations they must abandon some of their control over domestic monetary aggregates. Liberalized external accounts may thus reduce macroeconomic policymakers' autonomy and make it more difficult for them to achieve the stable and appropriate real exchange rates that have been associated with successful manufacturing for export.

What about the role of *internal* macroeconomic balance? Maintenance of an appropriate real exchange rate may be a necessary condition for sustained external balance but, it is often argued, it is not always consistent with internal balance and therefore not sufficient macroeconomic underpinning for growth. There has been considerable concern about the potential negative effects of price inflation, some of which may be implicit in a 'crawling peg' policy that seeks to retain a stable real exchange rate (e.g. Aghevli *et al.* 1991). By generating too much 'noise' in the signals emanating from the price system, rapid price inflation may seriously inhibit appropriate decisionmaking, particularly in the sphere of investment.

The studies in this volume shed little fresh light on these issues. (It was not intended that they should do so.) There is no obvious direct connection revealed, in these studies, between rates of price inflation and measures of industrial or overall economic performance. On the other hand, they do show that private industrial investment was typically low in the high inflation episodes of the 1980s in such sample countries as Brazil, Mexico and Turkey.

In recent years, aggregate demand restraint in developing countries has increasingly been directed at the reduction of inflation. Aggregate demand policies – with monetary and fiscal policies as the main instruments – were also clearly relevant to trade performance, the maintenance of external balance, and productivity growth, in the countries studied in this volume. Domestic demand compression, initiated for purposes of macroeconomic balance, played an important role in the stimulation of manufactured exports from existing industries in the 1980s in Mexico and Turkey, at the same time that it throttled some other domestic economic activity.[7] Aggregate demand restraint in these and other cases, to the degree that it reduced capacity utilization, investment and growth itself, however, reduced the short- to medium-term prospect for both industrial and total factor productivity growth.

Where substantial external financial support accompanied such macroeconomic restraint policy – as in Chile, Turkey and Tanzania – short-term setbacks were reduced or even offset. In previously 'import-strangled' economies, e.g. Tanzania, increased external finance made it possible to utilize industrial capacity more fully and thus to record short-term productivity improvement, as well as increased investment and the prospect of greater longer-term growth.[8]

It is also important to note that in some recent instances, for example, in Mexico, Turkey and Colombia in the late 1980s and in 1990, import liberalization appears to have been utilized as an instrument of anti-inflation policy, at the same time as traditional trade liberalization objectives were being pursued. It has even been suggested that radical trade liberalization may strengthen the credibility of government macroeconomic adjustment programmes and overall changes in the policy regime: the 'bigger the bang', so to speak, the more serious must be the reforming government (Rodrik, 1992b). In this connection, trade policy liberalization has sometimes also been accompanied by financial liberalization and consequently increased real interest rates, with further 'shock' effects, e.g. in Turkey, Chile and Mexico. Liberalizations that accompany, or precede, stabilization efforts may have the further advantages of avoiding inappropriate investments that have been influenced by 'distorted' incentive structures; and, to the extent that tariff revenues replace import quotas, easing the fiscal constraints (World Bank, 1992b).

There has been active debate about the appropriate pace of both macroeconomic stabilization efforts and trade policy reform. A major recent study of import liberalization experiences in middle-income countries concluded that such reforms most frequently 'held' when they were undertaken in quick and drastic fashion (Michaely *et al.*, 1991); but its assumptions and methodology have been vigorously challenged (Evans, 1991). The studies in this volume, while not set up specifically to test this conclusion, do not, on the whole, seem to support it. They include some cases of successful gradual trade policy change, notably Colombia (until 1991) and Korea;[9] and they suggest that some of the heavy costs of 'shock' liberalization in Chile, and, after periods of more gradual policy change, in Mexico and Turkey may have been unnecessary. (Wholesale import liberalization is not, in any case, seen as so central to policy reform by the authors in this volume as it is by many others.)

ASPECTS OF TRADE POLICY EXPERIENCE

Degrees of inward orientation/anti-export bias

The principal traditional summary measure of the orientation of trade policy is the degree of 'anti-export bias'. The details of measurement procedures vary but their essential feature is the comparison of the 'effective' exchange rate, allowing for all taxes and subsidies, for export activities with that for import-competing activities. When the incentives for exporting are the same as those for import-competing activity, the trade policy is 'neutral' in its encouragement to these two kinds of activity. When such neutrality exists or when exporting is favoured in the economy or, in studies of industrialization, for the industrial sector as a whole, the trade policy is generally said to be 'outward-oriented'. Otherwise, trade policy is said to be 'inward-oriented'. (Note that the usage of this terminology differs from that of Syrquin in chapter 2.) The ubiquity of barriers to imports unless they were offset by export subsidies, implies that, in most countries, there has been anti-export bias and 'inward-orientation'.

The studies in this volume indicate great variation in the degree of anti-export bias in manufacturing incentives across countries and within countries over time. All of the countries in our sample had a heavy anti-export bias as part of their import substitution strategy in the 1950s and

14

1960s.[10] Some retained it into the 1970s, e.g. Turkey, India, Sri Lanka, Peru, Bangladesh, Kenya and Tanzania. But many, by then, had significantly offset the effects of import protection with export promotion policies that left significantly lower degrees of overall anti-export bias, e.g. Colombia, Mexico and Brazil (and the rest did so thereafter). Typically, then, industrial anti-export bias declined in the sample countries in the 1970s and 1980s. In Korea, while there was wide variation across industries there was actually, on average, a pro-export bias in the manufacturing sector in the 1970s. These countries and others achieving improved manufactured export performance at that time typically also devalued their currencies in real terms and/or prevented their subsequent real appreciation. Import liberalization, except for imports destined directly or indirectly for use in manufactured exports, was *not* generally, however, an important means of reducing anti-export bias in the 1970s (or, in most cases, the 1980s). Typically, import-substitution policies were built upon, through the provision of new export incentives, rather than dismantled. Implicit in this experience was an overall structure of inter-industry incentives that was quite different from the relatively 'neutral' one that would have resulted from import liberalization.

The one exception to these generalizations about the usual means of reducing anti-export bias in manufacturing in the 1970s was the Chilean case. In Chile there was a massive across-the-board liberalization of imports over the 1974–9 period, with a consequent major reduction in overall anti-export bias. Initially, the import-substituting industrial sector was buffered against the effects of this import liberalization by real currency devaluation (although it suffered severely from the concomitant drastic demand restraint); but subsequent real currency appreciation then left it severely exposed. Manufactured exports and other non-traditional (primary) exports responded only moderately to Chile's drastic reduction in its previously high degree of anti-export bias. Non-traditional exports expanded much more rapidly in the 1980s with the initiation of a devalued and stable real currency value. Up until 1990 industrial exports had not materialized to any significant extent.

In the late 1970s and 1980s there were significant further moves to reduce manufacturing anti-export bias in Sri Lanka, Turkey, India, Mexico, Tanzania and Bangladesh. Sri Lankan policy toward the manufacturing sector actually created a pro-export bias following the major trade reforms of 1977. The sequence, again, was typically not so much to liberalize imports at the outset as to increase export subsidies, or create 'export-processing zones', first. Again, real currency devaluation was a concomitant of manufactured export success. Import liberalization, where it occurred, usually only came later. It was not until the late 1980s and early 1990s, in such cases as Mexico, Peru and Colombia, and, to a lesser extent, India and Korea, that import liberalizations themselves could be said to be 'leading' in the efforts to reduce anti-export bias in the manufacturing sector.

But the degree of anti-export bias or inward orientation is only one element of trade and industrial policy in the sample countries. The studies in this volume show that there was considerable variation of incentives *within* the export and import-competing sectors; and that there are important other dimensions to trade and industrial policy. In actual fact, governments typically have deployed a whole armoury of trade and industrial policy instruments, about which more below. The standard categorization of countries as either inward or outward oriented (even when modified so as to allow for 'moderate' or 'extreme' degrees of such orientations, e.g. in World Bank, 1987) seems much too crude either to describe trade and industrialization policies usefully or to explain divergent industrial performance.

Export subsidies

Among the most striking features of the trade policy of the developing countries in our sample was the important and continuing role of direct and indirect export subsidies. Despite discouragement of such subsidies in the GATT, and the prospect of countervailing duties in the importing countries to offset them, export subsidies on manufactured exports from the countries in our sample were very common and often very large. They took many forms – import and excise duty exemptions or drawbacks for inputs (often extended to local suppliers of inputs to exporters); subsidized credit; corporate tax concessions (reductions or refunds); preferential exchange rates; preferential foreign exchange retention rights or allowances; and direct cash subsidies. They are estimated by this volume's authors to have reached between 25 and 50 per cent of the relevant exports' value at various times in the last two decades in Brazil, Colombia, Turkey, India and Peru. Even Chile offered non-traditional exporters a flat 10 per cent subsidy after its major trade liberalization in the 1970s. The subsidies were often so generous that they induced over-invoicing of exports and even totally fictitious exports, with consequent overstatement of manufactured export 'success'.

Other accounts have highlighted the fact that there has usually been an anti-export bias in the overall structure of developing countries' incentives and, in particular, in that facing the manufacturing sector. As has been seen, that anti-export bias was found in almost all of the countries in our sample and almost all of the time, and it was frequently reduced in the 1970s and 1980s. Such reductions were achieved much more by export subsidies, however, than by (periodic) changes in the overall import regime. Export promotion policies during this period, while certainly variable, were much steadier and more similar across countries than import regimes, which were subject to constant 'tinkering' and periodic major changes. The tightening of GATT rules on export subsidies could, therefore, have profound implications for the developing countries' freedom for trade policy manoeuvre (although trade policies' influence upon export performance were, in any case, as noted above, usually dwarfed in importance by the behaviour of the real exchange rate).

There is virtually no evidence in these country studies of any direct link between the overall degree of protectionism in the import regime (as opposed to liberalized imports solely for exporters) and manufactured export performance. There is always, of course, a long-run link between the real exchange rate, which *is* associated with manufactured export performance, and the trade regime, in that the equilibrium real exchange rate reflects the trade flows that are influenced by the structure of trade barriers and subsidies. With real devaluations sufficient for external balance, export subsidies often were eliminated or reduced (e.g. Mexico and Korea) and import liberalization often followed.

Import duty exemptions

Another feature of the trade policy experience of the 1970s and 1980s in the countries studied in this volume is the major importance of exemptions from normal customs duties. Attempting to measure average tariff levels, virtually all the authors found enormous differences between scheduled tariff rates and actual tariff collections. Some of these differences were attributable to evasion, undervaluation and misclassification, particularly in high-tariff items. In some cases, where official development assistance was important, e.g. in Tanzania, they reflected external agencies' insistence on exemptions for their own trade. Most of the differences, however, were the product of various 'special regimes' for favoured activities, industries or firms. In Brazil in the mid–1980s, for instance, such special arrangements for duty exemptions covered nearly two-thirds of all imports; while scheduled duties averaged 90 per cent of Brazilian import value in 1984, import duties actually collected were only 19 per cent of imports. The difference between scheduled and collected duties was of a similar order in many other countries in this study. (Research elsewhere has found similar results: Kostecki and Tymowski, 1985; Pritchett and Sethi, 1992.)

Exemption of import duties for exporters was common, and carried a clear theoretical rationale. Most of the exemptions, however, were far more discretionary and *ad hoc* in their application. Moreover, they were often far from transparent: that is, the existence of specific exemptions was not public information. The importance of these exemptions makes it impossible to base analysis of tariff and incentive structures purely upon the legal tariff codes even where non-tariff barriers are few.[11] Changes in these exemption systems may also complicate analysis of tariff reforms. Tariff

17

reductions, accompanied by reduced exemptions, actually *raised* the ratio of tariff collections to imports in some import 'liberalizations', e.g. Colombia in 1985 and Chile in 1974–6. Others have found only weak correlation between scheduled and collected rates, with the relative import-ance of exemptions rising with the level of the scheduled rate (Pritchett and Sethi, 1992).

Evidently, the rules are not always what they seem. The apparently wide scope for discretionary exemptions from existing trade, tax (and presum-ably other) laws may make analysis of incentive systems and trade and industrial policies much more difficult than has been generally realized. These exemptions also imply enormous scope for rent-seeking activities; these socially costly activities would presumably have been reduced if the trade barriers from which exemptions were sought were lower.

Dispersion of incentives

The dispersion of the domestic prices of tradable goods (relative to their world prices) may be as important to industrial performance as the more aggregative measures that have so far featured in the literature. The disper-sion of such relative prices is not systematically related to any of the conventional indicators of 'openness' (which are, in any case, as noted, unrelated one to another) (Aitken, 1992; Pritchett, 1991a). Moreover, the same price structure may be the product either of direct governmental administrative controls or of taxes and subsidies. Since there is so much variety in the dispersion of incentives and in the instruments with which they are achieved, 'to characterize inward oriented countries as inter-ventionist and outward oriented countries as liberal . . . is simply wrong for developing countries' (Aitken, 1992: 29).

Which particular relative prices are high and which are low may also be at least as important as the degree of dispersion or the overall broad structure of relative prices. The prices of capital goods, especially machin-ery and equipment, have been singled out by some for particular attention (Aitken, 1992; DeLong and Summers, 1991). The non-tradable portion of the capital goods sector, i.e. the construction sector, is emphasized by others (Bevan *et al.*, 1990).

To understand changes in overall incentive structures at the industry or firm level, it is necessary to consolidate the effects of trade and exchange rate policies in measures of changing effective subsidies (or protection) or effective exchange rates. This is particularly the case when there have been official or *de facto* multiple exchange rate policies (e.g. varying rights of foreign exchange retention for exporters). Even when exchange rates have remained unified, changes in real exchange rates, frequently accompanied by changes in trade policies, have been major influences upon incentives for production and consumption of particular tradables. In turbulent times,

18

as shown repeatedly in these studies, changes in exchange rates usually dominated changes in trade policies, including those affecting the degree of dispersion of incentives. Moreover, where changes in the trade regime occurred they were frequently accompanied by compensating or partially compensating currency devaluations; typically, the principal effect of such combined policies was to reduce anti-export bias and encourage resources to flow from both the import-competing and the non-tradables sector into export activity.

Deriving 'tariff-equivalents' of import controls is a formidable task, involving problems of quality comparison, weighting and appropriate timing of product-by-product comparisons of domestic and world price levels. Where controls abound, it is therefore extraordinarily difficult to assemble micro-level data on incentive structures and to keep abreast of their change over time.

Even when one has acquired some micro-level data, it is difficult to characterize the degree of dispersion or selectivity in the incentive structure via any one summary measure. The studies in this volume use ranges, standard deviations, and the like; but these do not adequately portray the degree or direction of focus or targeting in trade or related industrial policies. For that, and for many other aspects of micro-level policy under-standing, a more qualitative and descriptive analysis is required, some of which is also provided in the country studies of this volume.

Except for the sharp interruption created by the debt crisis in many countries in the early 1980s, the 1970s and 1980s have seen fairly wide-spread (if usually moderate) simplification of trade policies, involving a shift from controls to tariffs, and reductions in the dispersion of protection-ism and incentive structures. By the early 1990s, this trend had become quite general and more pronounced. The country studies in this volume indicate a variety of means that countries have found to move in the direction of greater trade liberalization and more uniform incentives.[12] Liberalization usually began with imports employed as inputs to manufac-turing for exports. As far as the general range of imports is concerned, tariff structures were frequently significantly simplified, and sometimes average tariff levels were lowered, even while quantitative restrictions (QRs) were still fairly firmly in place, as in Tanzania and Bangladesh. Major tariffications of QRs, in which tariff rates obviously rose, took place in India (though, in this case, many QRs remained) in the late 1970s and early 1980s, and in Sri Lanka in the late 1970s.

In Chile the change, already realized in the 1970s, was particularly dramatic. The trade regime in Chile in 1973 (described in chapter 4) was surely among the most complex and unproductive anywhere. Tariffs aver-aged 105 per cent and ranged between zero and 750 per cent, but were subject to exemption or adjustment for particular regions, industries and (public) firms. In addition, there was a complex system of import licensing

19

and an extremely heavy (10,000 per cent) prior import deposit requirement, both with further discretionary exemptions and adjustments for firms, persons, industries or regions. At the same time there were eight different exchange rates with a 1,000 per cent differential between the extremes. By 1979, all of these complexities had been replaced by a modest uniform tariff, the level of which was subsequently altered from time to time in response to balance of payments experience. Chile was unique in our sample, not only in the degree of uniformity of its post-reform import tariff but also in its subsequent effective use of uniform tariff changes as a tool of balance of payments management.

Sharp reductions in the dispersion of protectionist incentives also occurred in Mexico and Turkey in the second half of the 1980s and in Colombia in 1990–1. A more gradual such reduction was registered in Korea, which had a remarkably high degree of dispersion about fairly low average import protection levels in the 1960s and 1970s. In some cases – e.g. India, Sri Lanka, Malaysia, Bangladesh, Brazil and Kenya – dispersion remained fairly high in the late 1980s even after conscious efforts, and even some success, at reducing it.

In Peru, however (as described in chapter 7), events in the 1980s moved in the reverse direction – towards greater complexity. By 1990, there were thirty-eight different tariff rates and fourteen types of surcharge, with gross tariff rates ranging from 10 per cent to 110 per cent. At the same time there were about fifty kinds of 'special' customs regimes for favoured enterprises or activities. Over 500 import items were banned and many of the rest (all the rest for a period) were subject to licensing. Massive simplification and liberalization began with the new administration in late 1990.

Selective promotion of particular industries was common in the sample countries. Many policy instruments were employed in these efforts, of which protection against imports was only one. They met with only mixed success. In the larger middle-income countries, support was usually directed at capital goods and intermediate goods producers, as in the cases of Brazil, India, Mexico and Korea. These countries also actively promoted the computer and automobile industries. Malaysia promoted petroleum refining and related industries with some success; its support for automobiles looked rather more problematic in terms of social returns. Where similar efforts were undertaken in lower-income or smaller countries, e.g. Tanzania and Peru, they were almost certainly even less successful in these terms. Careful social benefit–cost analyses of these various infant industry cases has not as yet, however, been done.[13]

The country studies in this volume offer no dramatic conclusions as to the importance (or unimportance) of the dispersion of incentives to industrial growth, relative to that of their average level, stability or other characteristics. Evidently, as, for instance, in the Korean case, dispersion and targeted incentives, if properly managed, can be conducive to successful industrial performance (see also Amsden, 1989; Westphal, 1982, 1990; Pack and Westphal, 1986). Equally clearly, when the state had limited implementation capacity and seemed easily manipulated by special interests, as for instance in Brazil, Bangladesh, and India, high dispersion could reflect gross mismanagement and resource misallocation. More research on the social efficacy of various kinds of selective policy and the circumstances required for success is still needed.

THE ROLE OF NON-TRADE POLICIES

Industrial policies

It takes considerable time to build capacities and institutions that are supportive and flexible, and that can be responsive to changing incentives for different kinds of industrial activity. 'Getting the prices right', through trade and other policies, however important, can achieve little in the absence of response capacity. Governments in many developing, indeed also industrialized, countries have played an important role in the long-run buildup of capacity to undertake efficient industrial production, not only through infrastructural and educational investments but also through support for research and development, encouragement of technological innovation, provision of finance, and a variety of other 'industrial policies' (Lall, 1990). Although there may be a theoretical preference for functional and 'neutral', rather than selective, governmental supports (and for factor market, rather than product market, 'interventions') such supports cannot, by their nature, always be totally neutral as between different kinds of industrial or other economic activities. Scarcity of governmental resources will often require choices as to where and how they are to be deployed (Lall, 1990; World Bank, 1992a). The immediate consequences for incentive structures may be quite small, but their ultimate consequences can be far-reaching. The impact of such governmental industrial policies comes through the increased response capacities and stronger institutions of the future.

Some governmental non-trade policies have more immediate effects upon micro-level industrial incentives. The authors of the studies in this volume call attention to the frequent important role of micro-level credit policy (in particular, interest subsidies and direct finance); direct industrial subsidies and encouragements; creation or reduction of domestic barriers to entry or exit, regulation and competition policy; state ownership; government procurement; supportive infrastructure; labour and management training; and research and development activities, etc. Many of these are, again, non-price interventions, suggesting that governments have normally doubted whether merely 'getting prices right' will suffice.

It is difficult to quantify the relative importance of these various policies and influences in the majority of cases. But the overwhelming impression derived from these studies is that, in terms of their influence upon the levels and character of industrial performance, they have usually been at least as important as trade policies, narrowly defined, and often more important. It seems that it may be as important to understand the disposition of government industrial and related 'support' expenditures as to know the overall structure of industrial input and output prices.

Policies on foreign direct investment and imported technology

Liberalized trade has brought increasing 'international production' and interpenetration of industrial firms' activities in the industrialized world. Foreign direct investments, technology agreements and various forms of strategic alliance among transnational corporations have become important determinants of international trading patterns and patterns of national manufacturing production. Developing countries have been largely on the periphery of the momentous process of global industrial integration that gathered steam in the 1970s and 1980s. In large part, this was through no fault of their own. Transnational manufacturing corporations have tended to concentrate their activities where the markets are largest and easiest to understand, and where economic and political conditions are more stable and familiar. But developing countries' own policies on foreign investment and imported technology have also played some role in the manner in which foreign firms have been involved in their industrialization processes.

As far as the manufacturing sector is concerned, foreign direct investment (FDI) can be expected to play a greater role when industrial growth is more export oriented and/or when it moves to 'higher-stage' (more technically demanding) import substitution. Changes in both of these directions have typified developing countries' industrialization experiences in the 1970s and 1980s. Policies toward FDI have therefore reflected, to a considerable degree, the changing stage and strategy of individual countries' industrializations. Generally, policies toward FDI in the developing countries in our sample, as well as elsewhere, were modestly liberalized over the past two decades, with a recent burst of more vigorous decontrol. The shift away from statist approaches to industrialization, in such countries as Chile, Peru, Bangladesh and Sri Lanka, has also 'opened up' foreign investment policies and thereby increased the potential role for FDI, and foreign firm activities more generally, in these and similarly changing countries. Foreign firms subsequently dominated the expansion of manufactured exports from Sri Lanka, as they also did in countries that had traditionally been more receptive to them, e.g. Malaysia, Thailand, Mexico and Brazil. ('Receptivity' in the latter two cases was accompanied by a considerable degree of regulation in particular sectors.) It is noteworthy, however, that Chile's dramatic expansion of non-traditional, resource-based exports in the 1980s was achieved largely, and especially in fruit, by local, rather than foreign, firms (though foreign firms were also involved – in wood, pulp and paper, and fish products).

Most of the country studies in this volume do not particularly highlight the role of FDI or imported technology. Where export processing zones have become important policy instruments, as in Bangladesh, Malaysia, Sri Lanka and the *'maquiladora'* sector in Mexico, FDI has obviously played a prominent role. In most of the other cases where FDI has been welcomed, it has played a relatively moderate role, though usually, as in Colombia, Mexico and Turkey, one that was larger in the 'later' stages of import substitution than in the 'easier' early ones. In Korea, after FDI policies were significantly eased in the early 1980s, FDI and technology imports rose sharply, especially in technology-intensive industries like electronics and electrical equipment, chemicals, and transport machinery and equipment. FDI still accounted, however, for a very small share of Korean industrial investment and total capital inflow.

In the Brazilian case, however, the role of transnational corporations, both in manufacturing production and in exporting, has long been major; and receptive policies toward it, except for selected sectors, have made this possible. While, in the 1980s, foreign investors have generally been skittish about directing further resources to debt-distressed countries, transnational corporations' trade, allocative and investment strategies have nevertheless been important to Brazilian industrial performance.

Policies on the acquisition and use of foreign technology and capital are likely to assume greater importance in the developing countries' industrialization processes as the emphasis in policy discussions shifts to productivity improvement and 'keeping up' with an increasingly integrated world economy. It is worth noting, for instance, that positive 'spillovers' from transnational corporate producers have been identified in the Mexican case study as significant contributors to total factor productivity growth in Mexican manufacturing. Trade policy that is designed purely to influence the incentives for the production and use of tradable *goods*, which is still how most (including the authors in this volume) think of it, may miss some of the most important issues and key determinants of industrial learning. Further research is required on the efficacy of alternative means of acquiring technology, critical services and capital from the global marketplace in support of industrial growth in the developing countries (see, for instance, Westphal, 1982, 1990; Lall, 1990).

ELEMENTS OF THE 'TRANSITION' TO MANUFACTURING FOR EXPORT

The 'transition' to manufacturing for export, where it occurred, took a variety of specific forms. In some cases, as in Colombia, Mexico and

Turkey (and in an earlier period, Korea), exports grew from previously (and often still) protected and originally import-substituting industries. (Mexico also experienced rapid expansion in its entirely export-oriented *maquiladora* sector.) Previous import-substituting production, much of which was encouraged by protection, thus apparently provided the base of experience, learning and, in some cases, scale economies that eventually made efficient manufactured exporting possible (though it can still be argued that without protection, export performance would have been stronger, and that protection necessitated larger incentives for exporting than would otherwise have been required). Real currency devaluation and/or stringent repression of domestic demand, typically in response to external shocks and debt crises, created strong incentives for producers to redirect output from domestic to external markets in these and other cases. In the late 1980s, a similar process emerged in India (which had also registered some manufactured export expansion in response to domestic demand restraint in the mid-1970s) and, to a lesser extent, in Kenya and Tanzania. When undertaken rapidly, as in Mexico and Turkey, these policies involved significant short-term income redistribution and unemployment and therefore socio-political stress that may call the sustainability of the transition to exporting into some question. In Colombia and Korea, where such manufactured exports from existing industrial capacity expanded more gradually and over a longer period, the sheer stability of incentives – offered mainly via the real exchange rate – appears, as noted above, to have carried considerable weight. In none of these cases did across-the-board import liberalization contribute significantly to the phenomenon of export expansion.

In Mexico, while the volume of (non-maquila) manufactured exports certainly has been influenced by short-term changes in the real exchange rate, it is difficult to ascribe its recent rapid increase solely to such changes in the incentive structure. In the 1970s and 1980s there was sharp variation in the real exchange rate; at times, the real value of the peso was even higher than in previous decades, implying reduced incentives for exporting. Moreover, the reduction in anti-export bias associated with the import liberalization of the second half of the 1980s cannot fully explain the rapid growth of manufactured exports either, since this export expansion started before liberalization. Other governmental programmes and foreign investors' responses were critically important to what transpired. In particular, specific export performance targets, or what the GATT negotiators term 'trade-related investment measures' (TRIMs), imposed by government in the (largely foreign-owned) automobile and computer industries, played a major role in the overall expansion of Mexican manufactured exports.

In other cases, manufacturing for export developed *de novo* in response to the creation of strong and stable incentives, usually in the form of appropriate real exchange rates and/or export subsidies. Frequently they took the form of export-processing or 'free' zones in which domestic taxes and other regulations were waived for foreign investors. Foreign investors brought international marketing experience and virtually automatic international market access, thus overcoming what were frequently critical barriers to local firms' entry to new exporting activities. In these cases, the foreign firms typically had no prior (or subsequent) experience selling in local markets; and there were usually fairly limited backward linkages to local suppliers of non-factor inputs. These highly import-dependent exporting activities, e.g. electronic components in Malaysia, garments in Bangladesh and Sri Lanka, and the *maquiladora* sector in Mexico, generated value added, overwhelmingly in the form of wages, that was much less than the gross value of recorded exports. While these exporting activities drew effectively upon these countries' unquestionable current comparative advantage in unskilled labour-intensive production, they generated criticism and raised doubts concerning their longer term developmental role, because of their limited development of efficient domestic linkages, training or other positive externalities.

The Chilean case of export expansion is unique in our sample. Its expansion of manufactured exports was based upon the processing of local primary products (forest products, fruits and vegetables, fish, etc.) for export. These processing activities built upon much earlier governmental investments in supportive infrastructure. When, in the 1980s, the real value of the currency, and (even before that) the real wage, were reduced, and imports liberalized, so as to provide strengthened incentives for the expansion of these resource-intensive exports the response came rapidly, from locally owned, as well as foreign, enterprises.

Evidently, there has been no single route to successful and efficient manufacturing for export. Governments have played an important role in manufactured exports' promotion; but, contrary to inferences one might draw from much of the recent literature, that role has *not* usually been the reduction of anti-export bias through across-the-board import liberalization. Rather, the most prominent governmental influences in the 1970s and 1980s were exchange rate policies, domestic demand restraint, real wage restraint, export subsidies, export-processing zones, and export performance 'requirements'. These policies built upon significant prior, and usually continuing, broad support for industrialization processes.

Have these policies created the basis for continued, sustained growth in exports of manufactures? Can these policies themselves be sustained? Manufacturing for export evidently frequently expanded in response to the short-term macroeconomic pressures and policies of the late 1980s rather than as part of a longer run reorientation of development strategies. Balance of payments pressures and debt crises in Mexico, Turkey and elsewhere led to significant real currency devaluation, real wage reduction, demand restraint, and increased efforts at export promotion, all of which had the desired effect of expanding export volume in the manufacturing sector as well as other sectors. It remains to be seen whether these new exports represent more than a temporary surge; in particular, whether they reflect the longer run 'entry' of exporting firms (see Roberts and Tybout, 1992) and thus constitute an important new element in sustained longer term industrial growth. Further WIDER research will explore these questions.

PRODUCTIVITY GROWTH, TRADE AND TRADE POLICY

In analysing developing countries' longer term growth and development, increasing attention has been devoted to the role of (total factor) productivity growth. Expanded inputs of capital, labour and other identifiable factors of production, while accounting for a much higher proportion of growth in output in developing countries than in industrial countries, still leave significant proportions unexplained, not only at the aggregate level (see chapter 2) but also at the level of the manufacturing sector as a whole, at the individual industry level and at the plant level. There is therefore a growing interest in the discovery of the determinants, or even the concomitants, of productivity change. Continuing improvements in productivity can obviously achieve more for overall sustainable growth, together with continuing expansion of factor inputs, than the primarily once-for-all gains that accrue from improved static efficiency of resource allocation or increased capacity utilization.

Much of the influential literature on trade policy of recent years presumes a positive association between openness in international relationships, defined in various ways, and the rate of productivity growth; and there is some modest evidence for this over the 1950–80 period (Syrquin and Chenery, 1989). Further, there is often a presumption that liberal trade policies and liberalization processes (variously defined) also generate productivity growth.

Why should productivity grow more quickly in 'open' economies than in 'closed' ones? The answer may be offered either in terms of externalities associated with alternative output-mixes or in terms of alternative incentive effects.

As far as output mix is concerned, some have argued that export activity can generate especially productive overall effects. Interaction with foreign buyers is frequently cited, for instance, as a source of dynamism, know-how, and marketing and production skills. Presumably, primary product exports, which are all some low-income countries can achieve in the fore-seeable future, would usually generate fewer such positive externalities than industrial exports; though adequate empirical support for this proposition is lacking. Some have formulated these arguments in terms of purported

26

positive externalities that are generated by the export sector to the benefit of the non-export sector (DeMelo and Robinson, 1990) and have sought to distinguish empirically between the (one-off) growth effects of reallocation and the (presumably continuing) growth effects of such externalities (Feder, 1983, 1986). It seems more plausible, however, to associate the main externalities associated with trade with *imports*, particularly those of capital goods and intermediate inputs (when they embody new technology) and technological and other non-factor services, rather than exports. Such imports bring the knowledge upon which long-term growth itself is now seen to be heavily dependent.

In the words of the *World Development Report*, 1991:

Openness – the free flow of goods, capital, people and knowledge – transmits technology and generates economic growth across nations.... First, increasing global competition raises the demand for new technology. Second, the supply of new technology for industrializing countries is determined largely by the degree to which they are integrated with the global economy. New products and processes are transmitted through imported inputs and capital goods, sold directly [or?] through licensing agreements, and transmitted through direct foreign investment or export contacts with foreign buyers.

(World Bank, 1991: 88)

By affecting the nature of inputs as well as production processes, trade could generate gains which greatly exceed the short-term benefits from improved resource reallocation.... The accumulated evidence suggests that the long-run gains from increased competition and the spillover of technology are likely to be much greater than the short-term gains.

(World Bank, 1991: 98)

Growth depends, in large part, according to this argument, upon the productivity-enhancing effects of particular kinds of imports, many of which are services. As with export staples, some kinds of imports are more 'valuable' than others. No doubt the technology embodied in some is wholly inappropriate. Policies on goods trade may therefore not be as important for growth as those relating to imports of foreign direct investment, intellectual property, and services. In this formulation exporting is important, above all, because it generates the foreign exchange with which to purchase productivity-enhancing imports.[14]

Others, however, have emphasized the knowledge-enhancing role of some kinds of production for the domestic market and the dependence of continuing growth upon them. Production of some tradables (whether import-competing or exportable) may generate learning or technological

27

spillovers (positive externalities) which also impact importantly upon growth. The unskilled labour-intensive activities in which developing countries usually have comparative advantage are often characterized as 'traditional', lacking in positive externalities, and stagnant in terms of productivity (e.g. Grossman and Helpmann, 1991: ch. 9). Whether welfare can be improved by subsidizing more 'dynamic' non-traditional activities certainly depends on a number of other influences, but the possibility, on these arguments, seems to exist. What is at issue is whether, or to what degree, productivity growth is influenced by the composition of output, or imports.

No less important to the related trade policy debate is the likelihood that particular governments will be able to identify the most 'productive' output mix and/or direct their policies so as to encourage economic decisionmakers to produce it. Evidently the 'correct' answers concerning the role of externalities are difficult to discern, even by the most objective and careful of analysts. How many governments are capable of selecting the most 'dynamic' industrial output mix? If the gains from choosing correctly are high enough, it may nevertheless be worth risking some mistakes in their pursuit. The prospect that weak governments, known by powerful interests to be amenable to selective interventions, may be driven, as in many instances in the past, to the encouragement of output mixes that owe much more to political pressures and corrupt influences than to any economic rationale must frequently be a source of deep concern. If manufactured exports truly *do* generally stimulate more learning than many other activities, say through the stimulus of contact with foreign buyers, it could be worth encouraging them *all* without trying to distinguish among them in terms of differential such effects.

Incentive effects are also ambiguous in their impact on productivity change. The usual presumption is that 'the brisk shower of competition', whether from imports on domestic markets or foreign rivals in export markets, sharpens performance and stimulates productivity change at more or less global rates. This proves to rest on some rather dubious assumptions as to prior entrepreneurial behaviour (Rodrik, 1992a).

Empirical research on the relationship between total factor productivity (TFP) growth and output mix, imports or the trade regime has been inconclusive. Comparisons across countries are often unpersuasive since there are so many other influences for which it is difficult to control. Typically, only growth in the labour force and in capital stock are controlled for in cross-section analysis; and even these are imperfectly measured. Nor are comparisons within countries over time always easy to interpret, since macroeconomic influences upon capacity utilization typically dominate the effects of changing output mix or incentive structure over the short- and medium-run; long-run data are rarely available for developing countries.

The impact of liberalization upon ongoing technical change is thus theoretically ambiguous and empirically uncertain. 'There is as yet no convincing empirical evidence for developing countries that shows liberalization to be conducive to industry rationalization' (Rodrik, 1992a: 170). For that matter, 'to date there is no clear-cut confirmation of the hypothesis that countries with an external orientation benefit from greater growth in technical efficiency in the component sectors of manufacturing' (Pack, 1988: 353). Even the World Bank, which vigorously promotes trade liberalization for its members, notes that 'the relation between imports and productivity growth is sometimes positive and sometimes negative', and concludes that 'the debate is not fully resolved' (World Bank, 1991: 99; see also Havrylyshyn, 1990; Tybout, 1991, 1992; Pack, 1992).

The evidence from the case studies in this volume is also, unsurprisingly, somewhat mixed. As always, detailed analysis is inhibited by the absence of data and the weak quality of much of the data there are. Interpretation of productivity data is also complicated by the need to take account of cyclical effects and compositional changes, and the difficulty of distinguishing these from learning or scale effects (Tybout, 1991, 1992). Sufficiently long time series to address long-term relationships are simply unavailable. It would certainly be difficult to infer any strong relationship between productivity growth and either trade or the trade policy regime from the evidence presented in the studies in this volume. Over the short- to medium-term periods analysed in these studies one finds the principal concomitant of manufacturing productivity growth to be the rate of growth of output itself.

Much of this association between productivity growth and output growth is attributable to the impact of variation in the level of capacity utilization. Particularly in times of great overall economic instability, the degree of utilization of existing installed capacity (and utilization of available labour) is highly variable. Conventionally, these variations are attributed to fluctuation in aggregate demand. In the 1980s foreign exchange 'scarcities' created severe import compression in many developing countries; the resulting shortages of inputs and spare parts created capacity underutilization from the supply side, as the more typical experience. As overall demand or supply constraints ease, the capital stock and labour that were previously underutilized are more fully employed and measured productivity rises; and conversely when they tighten output declines.

There are other well-known reasons, often associated with the names of Kaldor and Verdoorn, for anticipating more rapid productivity growth during periods of high investment and rapid growth in output. High investment rates are likely to generate technical advances through the embodiment of new technologies in freshly installed capital equipment and the reduced average age of the capital stock. Rapid output growth may also permit the realization of latent scale economies, positive externalities

29

and intensified learning experiences. These links between manufacturing productivity growth and the rate of macroeconomic growth are clearly evident in the high productivity growth realized at various times in the 1980s in such divergent countries as India, Turkey, Mexico, Colombia, Sri Lanka, Kenya and Tanzania and, for a brief period, in Garcia's Peru. Similarly, total factor productivity in manufacturing fell in Chile in the 1970s and Tanzania in the first half of the 1980s, times of severe macro-economic decline.

The case studies in this volume offer very weak, if any, support for the proposition that either import liberalization or export expansion are particularly associated with overall productivity growth. In Brazil, Turkey, Korea, Thailand, Kenya and Sri Lanka, manufacturing productivity increased at the same time as manufactured exports; but the latter success was also correlated with overall growth so the separate role of exports cannot easily be ascertained. In some of these cases, e.g. Thailand, TFP growth *was* greater in industries that were exporting than in protected import-competing industries.

On the other hand, the rapid growth in total factor productivity in India's manufacturing sector in the 1980s *preceded* its export boom in the latter part of the decade and the still later import liberalization. This TFP growth is attributed to more general domestic deregulation and to rapid overall economic growth that was, at least in part, the product of fiscal stimuli and, perhaps, the breaking of infrastructural bottlenecks through public investment. In Mexico, there was no clear link between increased productivity growth in manufacturing in the 1980s and the import liberaliz-ation which took place only in the second half of the decade; and such link as there may have been with export expansion was much more complex than that usually hypothesized by proponents of 'outward orientation'. Similarly, the period of most rapid productivity growth in Korea was not one of import liberalization. Nor was any such link with productivity visible in the Colombian experience with changing import regimes over the 1970s and 1980s. Import liberalization in Chile in the 1970s was accompanied by overall total factor productivity decline, although this decline was probably attributable, in large part, to the concomitant macro-economic decline. More micro-level investigation of possible links between Chile's import liberalization and productivity change found that, whereas technical efficiency improved most in the sectors that experienced the largest reductions in effective protection, the overall level of technical efficiency across all sectors did not change after import liberalization (Tybout *et al.*, 1991).

In some of the country case studies (Brazil, Colombia, India, Korea, Mexico and Peru) authors were able to conduct econometric investigation of some of the sources of inter-industry variation in total factor pro-ductivity growth. Scale and/or growth of own output were strongly positively related to productivity growth in Brazil, Colombia, India, Korea and Mexico, i.e. in every country for which there were data except Peru. Industrial concentration was associated positively with productivity growth in Brazil, Colombia and Korea.

The role of trade orientation of individual industries was mixed. In India those industries in which higher proportions of output growth were the product of import substitution experienced slower TFP growth. In Mexico, higher productivity growth was positively associated with (modest) protection against imports and also with the presence of transnational corporations. In Colombia, higher tariff and QR protection, and import substitution, were positively associated with productivity growth; export growth carried a negative, though insignificant, sign. Export growth was associated positively with TFP growth in Brazil in the 1970s, but in another formulation of the test, import-substituting growth was even more so. In Korea, greater import liberalization was associated with slower TFP growth, and the degree of export orientation was insignificantly related to productivity change. Export orientation was significantly negatively correlated with productivity growth in Peru in the 1980s although this was in the context of so adverse an economic environment that it is hard to know what to make of this result. Neither market concentration nor import dependence had significant effects in this country. It is difficult to find any overall pattern of relationship between trade and productivity growth in these inter-industry results.

It is possible that links between trade, trade policy and productivity growth take longer to manifest themselves than the relatively short periods analysed in this volume. In the long run, however, many other influences are also working more powerfully. On the basis of currently available evidence, it is difficult to escape the conclusion that trade policy has *not* been the major influence on productivity growth in manufacturing that many analysts have said that it should be. Such association as there has been between productivity growth and trade phenomena related to the probable positive role of manufactured export expansion, and *not* to import liberalization.

SUMMARY AND CONCLUSIONS

Industrial growth in the 1970s and 1980s in our sample countries was driven, above all, by expanding domestic demand and, increasingly in the 1980s, by exports. During this period import substitution, in the sense of reduced import shares of apparent consumption, was only a limited and industry-specific phenomenon. Governmental influences over industrial performance remained strong in the 1970s and 1980s, but they differed in their nature from their role in previous decades.

In the macroeconomically turbulent 1970s and 1980s trade policy, narrowly defined, did not generally play a major role in the growth and development experience of these countries. External shocks, debt crises and (sometimes related) internal imbalances necessitated macroeconomic policy responses; and these macroeconomic phenomena and policies dominated other determinants of industrial and overall economic performance. Industrial productivity growth was typically associated strongly with output growth; its relationship with the trade policy regime or the trade orientation of individual industries, however, was unclear. Real currency devaluation, associated real wage reduction and aggregate demand restraint, together with the perceived stability of the resulting incentives, contributed importantly to the rapid growth of manufactured exports in many countries. So did special encouragements to industrial exporting, in the form of significant direct and indirect export subsidies. Protectionist import regimes were frequently somewhat liberalized (in a few cases, radically so) but such import liberalizations were usually selective, slow and of limited impact on the overall degree of anti-export bias, relatively to export subsidies. Selective exemptions from import duties were of great and continuing importance. Non-trade industrial policies and policies on foreign direct investment and technology were also of major significance. The evidence on the effects of dispersion or non-uniformity of industry-level incentives is inconclusive.

The studies in this volume suggest that there are a great many routes to industrial expansion and, indeed to longer-run industrial productivity growth and successful manufacturing for export. The influences upon industrial performance have been many and varied. Governmental policies that have 'mattered' and 'worked' have also varied greatly. They include exchange rate policies, various kinds of direct and indirect export subsidies, and various industrial policies; and they include selective interventions. The policies that are appropriate for any particular time or place clearly depend upon initial conditions and constraints, not least the capacity of governments to implement them effectively. Needless to say, the longer run implications of alternative policies and growth patterns cannot yet be known; and they must be studied. On the basis of the evidence available, however, to suggest that there is a universal trade policy prescription that will generate improved economic performance for all is to ignore too much recent experience.

NOTES

1 Logistical difficulties, data problems and space constraints forced us to omit three other countries that were originally selected for study: Nigeria, Pakistan and Zimbabwe.
2 As will be seen, 'openness' and 'outward orientation' have proven to be particularly difficult concepts for economists to define or to measure in an agreed manner. Some use the term to describe observed features of an economy.

Others use it to describe the character of government policy. There are many alternative measures employed in each of these approaches; and they are unfortunately uncorrelated one with another (Pritchett, 1991a). Syrquin's measure relates to observed trade shares rather than to policy.

3 Economy-wide total factor productivity change is also addressed by Syrquin in chapter 2.

4 In this volume real or nominal currency devaluations are described as increases in measured exchange rates.

5 Where external capital flows have been liberalized or where they cannot be effectively controlled, short-term private capital movements may play a major role in the determination of actual real exchange rates.

6 There may be some doubt, however, as to whether the measure of instability usually employed accurately captures the type of short-term stability that is at issue (as opposed to periodic large 'corrections'). (Pritchett, 1991b; see also Roberts and Tybout, 1992.)

7 The substitution of foreign for domestic markets is obviously only possible when the products meet external demand standards.

8 Similar evidence is found in Khan and Knight, 1988.

9 The author of the Korean study in this volume was also the author of the Korean case study in the Michaely *et al.* study. His assessments of the Korean experience are similar in his contributions to the two projects.

10 Where there was 'water' in the import tariff, the traditional measures of this bias may have overstated its importance; but it was still certainly heavy.

11 The frequent existence of 'para-tariff import charges' – taxes on foreign exchange transactions; discriminatory application of domestic sales, excise or other taxes; 'service fees', special import surcharges, etc. – also significantly limits the value of such 'naive' analysis (Kostecki and Tymowski, 1985).

12 Transitional devices that can be employed include the raising of quota ceilings, the gradual product-by-product elimination of quotas, the auctioning of import licences or permits, and tariff quotas, each of which have advantages and disadvantages of their own (Takacs, 1990).

13 It had originally been hoped that at least a few such social benefit–cost analyses of governmental efforts to assist infant industries with targeted protection could be incorporated within some of the country studies in this project. Such studies, however, proved to be too demanding to be easily incorporated therein.

14 For related argumentation see Esfahani (1991). Foreign exchange may also break import bottlenecks and thus increase productivity over the short- to medium-run through increasing capacity utilization (see pp. 11–12).

REFERENCES

Aghevli, B. J., Khan, M. S. and Montiel, P. J. (1991) 'Exchange Rate Policy in Developing Countries: Some Analytical Issues', *IMF Occasional Paper* 78, Washington, DC.

Agosin, M. and Tussie, D. (1992) 'Globalization, Regionalization and New Dilemmas in Trade Policy for Development', Facultad Latinoamericana de Ciencias Sociales (FLACSO), Serie de Documentos e Informes de Investigacion, 126, June, Buenos Aires.

Aitken, B. J. (1992) 'Measuring Trade Policy Intervention, A Cross-Country Index of Relative Price Dispersion', World Bank, Policy Research Working Paper Series, 838, January.

Amsden, A. H. (1989) *Asia's Next Giant: South Korea and Late Industrialization*, Oxford: Oxford University Press.

Bevan, D., Collier, P. and Gunning, J.W. (1990) *Controlled Open Economies: A Neoclassical Approach to Structuralism*, Oxford: Oxford University Press.

Bhagwati, J. N. (1978) *Foreign Trade Regimes and Economic Development: Anatomy and Consequences of Exchange Control Regimes*, New York: National Bureau of Economic Research.

Caballero, R. J. and Corbo, V. (1989) 'The Effect of Real Exchange Rate Uncertainty on Exports: Empirical Evidence', *World Bank Economic Review* 3(2): 263–78.

Cottani, J. A., Cavallo, D. F. and Khan, M.S. (1990) 'Real Exchange Rate Behavior and Economic Performance in LDCs', *Economic Development and Cultural Change* 39(1): 61–76.

DeLong, B. and Summers, L. (1991) 'Equipment Investment and Economic Growth', *Quarterly Journal of Economics* 106(2): 445–502.

DeMelo, J. and Robinson, S. (1990) 'Productivity and Externalities: Models of Export-Led Growth', World Bank, PRE, Working Paper Series 387, March.

Dollar, D. (1992) 'Outward-Oriented Developing Economies Really Do Grow More Rapidly: Evidence from 95 LDCs, 1976–85', *Economic Development and Cultural Change* 40(3): 523–44.

Edwards, S. (1989) *Real Exchange Rates, Devaluation and Adjustment; Exchange Rate Policy in Developing Countries*, Cambridge, Mass.: MIT Press.

Esfahani, H. S. (1991) 'Exports, Imports and Economic Growth in Semi-Industrialized Countries', *Journal of Development Economics* 35(1,2): 93–116.

Evans, D. (1991) 'Institutions, Sequencing and Trade Policy Reform', Institute of Development Studies, University of Sussex, May.

Feder, G. (1983) 'On Exports and Economic Growth', *Journal of Development Economics* 12 (February–April).

Feder, G. (1986) 'Growth in Semi-Industrial Countries: A Statistical Analysis', in H. Chenery, S. Robinson and M. Syrquin, *Industrialization and Growth, A Comparative Study*, Oxford: Oxford University Press.

Grossman, G. M. and Helpmann, E. (1991) *Innovation and Growth in the Global Economy*, Cambridge, Mass.: MIT Press.

Harrison, A. (1991) 'Openness and Growth: A Time Series, Cross-Country Analysis for Developing Countries', World Bank, Policy Research, Working Paper Series 809, November.

Havrylyshyn, O. (1990) 'Trade Policy and Productivity Gains in Developing Countries, A Survey of the Literature', *World Bank Research Observer* 5(1): 1–24.

Helleiner, G. K. (1992) *Trade Policy, Industrialization and Development: New Perspectives*, Oxford: Clarendon Press.

Khan, M. and Knight, M. (1988) 'Import Compression and Export Peformance in Developing Countries', *Review of Economics and Statistics* 70(2): 315–21.

Kostecki, M. M. and Tymowski, M.J. (1985) 'Customs Duties versus Other Import Charges in the Developing Countries', *Journal of World Trade Law* 19(3): 269–86.

Krueger, A. O. (1978) *Foreign Trade Regimes and Economic Development: Liberalization Attempts and Consequences*, New York: National Bureau of Economic Research.

Krugman, P. (1987) 'Is Free Trade Passé?' *Journal of Economic Perspectives* 1(2): 131–44.

Lall, S. (1990) *Building Industrial Competitiveness in Developing Countries*, Paris: OECD Development Centre.

Levine, R. and Renelt, D. (1992) 'A Sensitivity Analysis of Cross-Country Growth Regressions', *American Economic Review* 82(4): 942–63.

Little, I. M. D., Scitovsky, T. and Scott, M., (1970) *Industry and Trade in Some Developing Countries*, Oxford: Oxford University Press.

Michaely, M., Papageorgiou, D. and Choksi, A. M. (1991) *Liberalizing Foreign Trade: Lessons of Experience from Developing Countries*, 7 volumes, Oxford: Basil Blackwell.

Pack, Howard (1988) 'Industrialization and Trade', in H. B. Chenery and T.N. Srinivasan (eds) *Handbook of Development Economics*, Amsterdam: North-Holland.

—— (1992) 'Learning and Productivity Change in Developing Countries', in G. Helleiner (ed.) *Trade Policy, Industrialization and Development: New Perspectives*, Oxford: Clarendon Press.

—— and Westphal, L. (1986) 'Industrial Strategy and Technological Change: Theory Versus Reality', *Journal of Development Economics* 22(1): 87–128.

Pritchett, L. (1991a) 'Measuring Outward Orientation in Developing Countries: Can It Be Done?' World Bank, PRE, Working Paper Series 566.

—— (1991b) 'Measuring Real Exchange Rate Instability in Developing Countries, Empirical Evidence and Implications', World Bank PRE, Working Papaer Series 791.

—— and Sethi, G. (1992) 'Tariff Rates, Tariff Revenue and Tariff Reform: Some New Facts', mimeo, World Bank, Washington, DC.

Roberts, M. and Tybout, J. (1992) 'Sunk Costs and the Decision to Export in Colombia', mimeo, North American Econometric Society.

Rodrik, D. (1991) 'Policy Uncertainty and Private Investment in Developing Countries', *Journal of Development Economics* 36(2): 229–42.

—— (1992a) 'Closing the Technology Gap: Does Trade Liberalization Really Help?', in G.K. Helleiner (ed.) *Trade Policy, Industrialization and Development: New Perspectives*, Oxford: Clarendon Press.

—— (1992b) 'The Limits of Trade Policy Reform in Developing Countries', *Journal of Economic Perspectives* 6(1): 87–105.

Shapiro, H. and Taylor, L. (1990) 'The State and Industrial Strategy', *World Development* 18(6): 861–78.

Syrquin, M. and Chenery, H. (1989) 'Patterns of Development: 1950 to 1983', World Bank Discussion Paper 41, Washington, DC.

Takacs, W. (1990) 'Options for Dismantling Trade Restrictions in Developing Countries', *World Bank Research Observer* 5(1): 25–46.

Taylor, Lance (1988) *Varieties of Stabilization Experience*, Oxford: Clarendon Press.

Thomas, Vinod, Nash, John and associates (1991) *Best Practices in Trade Policy Reform*, Oxford: Oxford University Press, for the World Bank.

Tybout, James (1991) 'Researching the Trade-Productivity Link: New Directions', World Bank, PRE, Working Paper Series 638, March.

—— (1992) 'Linking Trade and Productivity: New Research Directions', *World Bank Economic Review* 6(2): 189–211.

——, DeMelo, J. and Corbo, V. (1991) 'The Effects of Trade Reforms on Scale and Technical Efficiency: New Evidence from Chile', *Journal of International Economics* 31(3–4): 231–50.

UNCTAD, *Handbook of International Trade and Development Statistics, 1990*: 434–41.

Wade, R. (1990) *Governing the Market: Economic Theory and the Role of Government in East Asian Industrialization*, Princeton: Princeton University Press.

Westphal, L.E. (1982) 'Fostering Technological Mastery by Means of Selective

Industry Promotion', in M. Syrquin and S. Teitel (eds) *Trade, Stability, Technology and Equity in Latin America*, New York: Academic Press.

—— (1990) 'Industrial Policy in an Export-Propelled Economy: Lessons from South Korea's Experience', *Journal of Economic Perspectives* 4(3): 41–59.

World Bank (1982) *World Development Report*, New York: Oxford University Press.

—— (1987) *World Development Report*, New York: Oxford University Press.

—— (1991) *World Development Report*, New York: Oxford University Press.

—— (1992a) *World Bank Support for Industrialization in Korea, India and Indonesia*, Operations Evaluation Department, Washington, DC.

—— (1992b) *Trade Policy Reforms under Adjustment Programs*, Operations Evaluation Department, Washington, DC.

2

GROWTH AND INDUSTRIALIZATION SINCE 1965

A comparative study of fourteen countries

Moshe Syrquin

INTRODUCTION

Economic policymaking by its nature tends to be primarily oriented to the short run. In the decade of the 1980s analysis of the process of development shifted its concern from long-run growth and transformation to short-run issues related to real or perceived catastrophic situations. Recently there appears to be a renewed interest in long-run development in general and particularly in the process of industrialization. Even formal growth theory is having a comeback, this time incorporating factors that figured prominently in the development literature of the 1950s and 1960s.

Between the end of the Second World War and the oil shock of 1973 most developing regions embarked on a strong industrialization drive. In some cases, such as the larger or more advanced countries in Latin America, the postwar trends represented a continuation of an ongoing process dating back at least to the Great Depression. The difference was that the main policies pursued became now a strategy if not an ideology: inward-oriented industrialization based on import-substitution instruments.

During this inward-oriented period growth and structural change proceeded at a fast rate. By the late 1960s, however, the strategy was being attacked from the right and from the left. Market-oriented critics documented the excesses of the strategy of import-substitution industrialization (ISI) (Little *et al.* 1970; Balassa and Associates, 1971). On the left there was much disappointment with the achievements, summarized in Hirschman's felicitous phrase, 'Industrialization was expected to change the social order and all it did was to supply manufactures!' (1968: 32). The various reassessments were prodded by a slackening in the pace of growth in many of the ISI countries that suggested an exhaustion of the 'easy' phase of import

37

substitution based on light consumer goods. As important was the mounting evidence that spectacular achievements were possible with the alternative strategy of export-led development.

A reassessment of the debate about ISI two decades later cannot ignore the following points: (a) the strategy of ISI did lead to fast growth, at least for a while, but its implementation also resulted in distortions that reduced efficiency and productivity growth; (b) some of the policies had long gestation periods and the payoffs did not appear until well after the assault on the strategy; (c) the performance of the Southeast Asian economies that shifted early from ISI to export-led growth was spectacular. It also made their more open economies less vulnerable to the external shocks of the 1970s than was the case in the inward-oriented countries.

In this paper I will look at the experiences since the mid–1960s of fourteen countries in WIDER's study on trade and industrialization. Such a comparative framework should prove of help to evaluate specific results; what was unique and what was a more common experience. It is also essential to assess the importance of initial conditions or structural characteristics. For a long time growth theory focused on steady-state paths along which initial conditions were supposed to have washed out. Now that multiple equilibria are in vogue, growth theory has discovered initial conditions and hysteresis. Among the initial conditions influencing the path of development, this paper emphasizes those that affect the extent and nature of participation in international trade. Undoubtedly there is more to industrialization than trade policy, but nevertheless trade-related issues are given more emphasis because of their prominence in the debates about ISI of two decades ago, and because trade is believed by many to have been the main instrument used by governments to influence resource allocation.

THE SAMPLE: LEVELS OF INCOME AND WELFARE

The statistical information for placing the countries in a common framework will mostly refer to the period since 1970, going back in some cases to the 1960s as a background for subsequent developments.

The last two decades have been a very turbulent period, especially when compared to the preceding two decades which, when looked at from the present, appear to have been much calmer times. In the fourteen countries in this study the (unweighted) average of the annual growth rate in per capita income was 2.9 per cent during 1960–73, and went down to only 1.16 per cent for 1980–8. At the same time the coefficient of variation increased sharply from 0.5 in the first period to 2.1 in the 1980s. Furthermore, the country averages for the 1970s hide what has been at times enormous year-to-year variations in growth rates as, for example, in Chile and Peru. The instability has been the result of both severe external shocks and domestic policies. The principal external shocks were: the sharp increases in oil prices in 1973 and 1979 which represented an immediate severe blow to oil importers and, paradoxically, a no less severe blow in the longer run to some of the oil-exporting countries; the subsequent recession in the industrial countries; and the increase of interest rates in international markets to unprecedented levels.

A by-product of the internal and external shocks was an increase in inflationary pressures accompanied by substantial changes in exchange rates and other relative prices. These changes make more difficult any cross-country comparisons, particularly those that rely on exchange rate conversions, some of which I present below.

Table 2.1 presents some basic data on the sample of countries. Included in this sample are many of the very large developing countries in terms of population as well as some smaller economies, but none of them had a population in 1985 smaller than 10 million. This is appropriate in a study focusing on industrialization.

In all but the two African countries, population growth has begun to slow down in the 1980s or has not changed much from an annual rate lower than 3 per cent. The slowdown is particularly noticeable in Latin America and in Korea. By contrast, in the two African countries, in which per capita income was lower in 1988 than in 1980, population growth accelerated reaching extremely high levels, the consequences of which will be felt for decades to come.

According to the classification into income groups in the 1990 *World Development Report* (World Bank, 1990), the sample consists of five low-income countries, eight lower-middle-income countries and one (Korea) in the upper-middle-income group. The five low-income countries are the ones in South Asia and in Africa.

At official exchange rates we find in 1985 some association between per capita income and geographical regions. As a group, the poorest is the South Asia one with the three economies in the Indian subcontinent, followed by the two African economies. The use of exchange rates for converting local currencies has well known difficulties.

Also shown in the table are per capita income figures for 1985 converted by purchasing power parities (PPP) instead of exchange rates. The ratio between incomes converted at PPPs and at exchange rates appears as the 'exchange rate deviation index' (ERDI).[1] For 1985 the poor economies in South Asia show a much higher ERDI than the African economies. That is, real income was on average higher in South Asia than in Africa when using PPPs for conversion. Particularly noteworthy are the changes in rank for Bangladesh and Sri Lanka.

As mentioned before, the rate of growth of income per capita on the average slowed down considerably during the 1980s, even turning into

Table 2.1 Comparative indicators for sample countries[a]

Country	Population Millions 1985	Population Annual growth rate 1965–80	Population Annual growth rate 1980–8	Per capita GNP Level in 1985 US$ Exchange rate	Per capita GNP Level in 1985 US$ PPP	Per capita GNP Annual growth rate 1973–80	Per capita GNP Annual growth rate 1980–8	Exchange rate deviation index (ERDI) (5)/(4)	Infant mortality rate (per 1,000 live births) 1965	Infant mortality rate (per 1,000 live births) 1988
	(1)	(2)	(3)	(4)	(5)	(6)	(7)	(8)	(9)	(10)
Bangladesh	101	2.7	2.8	150	835	3.1	0.8	5.6	144	118
India	765	2.3	2.2	270	751	0.0	2.8	2.8	150	97
Kenya	20	3.6	3.8	290	885	0.4	−0.8	3.1	112	70
Tanzania	22	3.3	3.5	290	434	3.0	−0.5	1.5	138	104
Sri Lanka	16	1.8	1.5	380	1,869	2.1	3.1	4.9	63	21
Thailand	52	2.9	1.9	800	2,670	4.2	3.8	3.3	88	30
Peru	19	2.8	2.2	1,010	2,921	0.4	−1.4	2.9	130	86
Turkey	50	2.5	2.3	1,080	3,638	2.0	2.3	3.4	165	75
Colombia	28	2.5	2.1	1,320	3,889	2.8	0.9	2.9	86	39
Chile	12	1.7	1.7	1,430	4,440	1.1	−0.4	3.1	101	20
Brazil	136	2.4	2.2	1,640	4,406	4.0	−0.2	2.7	104	61
Malaysia	16	2.5	2.6	2,000	4,950	6.0	0.8	2.5	55	23
Mexico	79	3.1	2.2	2,080	5,239	3.7	−1.8	2.5	82	46
Korea	41	2.0	1.2	2,150	4,022	5.2	6.9	1.9	62	24

Sources: Columns (1), (4): World Bank (1987).
Columns (2), (3), (9), (10): World Bank (1990).
Column (5): World Bank (1990) except for Colombia, Peru, Chile, Brazil (World Bank, 1987); for Mexico and Malaysia the figure is based on the 'price level' for 1988 in Summers and Heston (1991).
Columns (6), (7): Summers and Heston (1991).
[a] In order of per capita GNP.

income falls in many of the countries. This trend, however, was not universal. Growth actually went up in South Asia (except Bangladesh) and Korea, and was sustained at respectable levels in Thailand and Turkey. This striking difference in growth performance cannot be solely blamed on external shocks. In relation to GDP, external shocks during the 1980s were most severe in Sub-Saharan Africa, but were also large and of similar magnitude in South Asia, in East Asia, and in Latin America (World Bank, 1990: 107). The last two columns in Table 2.1 show an alternative indicator of development: the rate of infant mortality (per 1,000 live births) at two points in time. From the figures it is apparent that there was substantial progress in reducing the rate of infant mortality from levels that were in some cases abysmal, although even by 1988 the rate is about or exceeds one hundred in three countries. Comparing the data on growth with those on the decline of infant mortality we observe an inconsistency between economic and social indicators. For Latin America such an inconsistency was underscored by Hirschman (1986), who observed the social indicators outperforming the economic ones particularly during temporary economic downturns.

Comparing the country rankings with respect to real income and to infant mortality in 1988 we observe a high correlation but with significant deviations from perfect correspondence. Countries that do better on infant mortality (and on other indicators not shown) than their income level would have suggested include Kenya, Sri Lanka and Thailand; while among the worse-than-expected performers we find Brazil, Peru and Turkey (but note the great improvement in the case of Turkey).

The same point can also be made within a much wider framework by contrasting rankings by per capita income with those by the human development index of the UNDP (1990). This index simply averages the position of a country on three indicators: life expectancy, adult literacy and real GDP per capita. The countries in this study that show a significantly higher ranking on the human development index are Sri Lanka, Chile, Thailand and Bangladesh. Lower rankings on this index were reported for Nigeria and Brazil.

TYPOLOGY

In the following sections I will summarize information about growth and structural transformation for the fourteen countries in this study. For this purpose the countries will first be placed in a simple typology of patterns of industrialization (see Table 2.2). This will facilitate comparisons among the fourteen countries and, by relying on the typology used in other studies for a much larger number of countries, will also provide a broader framework against which the country-specific experiences can better be studied.

41

Table 2.2 A typology of industrialization

Country	Y 1985	N 1985	D 1985	EL 1980	TO 1980	EM 1962	EM 1980
Outward, primary-oriented[a]							
Small							
Malaysia	2,000	16	50	217	2	1	10
Inward-oriented[a]							
Large, manufacturing							
India	270	765	230	120	−118	2	3
Bangladesh	150	100	700	62	−108	–	4
Large, primary							
Mexico	2,100	80	40	22[b]	14[b]	1	2
Brazil	1,650	135	16	58	−6	0	3
Turkey	1,100	50	64	37	8	0	2
Small, primary							
Chile	1,400	12	16	69	40	0	2
Peru	1,000	20	14	84	−15	0	3
Balanced[a]							
Large							
Colombia	1,300	30	25	72	23	0	3
Thailand	800	50	100	132	−11	1	6
Small							
Kenya	290	20	35	108	−30	2	3
Tanzania	290	20	23	80	−31	–	2
Outward, industry-oriented[a]							
Large							
Korea	2,150	40	400	157	−112	1	23
Small							
Sri Lanka	380	16	240	216	−37	1	5

Y, per capita income (GNP); N, population in millions; D, density (population per square kilometer): World Bank (1987).

EL, export level; TO, trade orientation index; EM, manufactured exports: database for Syrquin and Chenery (1989a).

[a] The inward-outward classification is based on data for 1980.

[b] Based on data for 1975.

The principal features associated with differences in patterns of growth and structural change in the last twenty years are measures of initial conditions related to size and natural resource endowments, and development strategies influencing the exploitation of those resources, and more generally the extent of participation in international trade (Chenery and Syrquin, 1986; Syrquin and Chenery, 1989a,b). This approach stresses the external dimension of a development strategy because it has been a key issue in policymaking and in the academic debates around it in the postwar period, and also because it explains some of the main differences in recent economic performance. A basic implicit hypothesis is that differences in initial structure and development strategy have affected the timing of the industrialization process and the sequencing of specific activities more than they have affected the overall pattern.

Three indicators are used to classify countries into more homogeneous groups: size as measured by population, commodity specialization of trade, and openness. The last two reflect the interaction of structural conditions with policy. Specialization is measured by a trade-orientation index (TO in Table 2.2) that compares the actual share of manufactured exports in total merchandise exports to the predicted ratio given the economy's income and size.[2] It partially reflects the relative abundance of natural resources that are economical to exploit at given prices and technology. A great abundance of resources is expected to lead to a high share of primary exports with corresponding effects on the structures of production and factor use. The relation between available resources and realized export composition is conditioned by policy decisions as to the exploitation of the natural comparative advantage. An additional simple proxy for the availability of resources in relation to population is the density of the population. It has been shown to be significantly associated with primary trade shares (inversely), and with the proportion of manufactured to total exports (Perkins and Syrquin, 1989).

Openness is measured by the observed share of merchandise exports in GDP relative to the share predicted from cross-country regressions, estimated separately for small and large countries. A country with a high relative export level (EL in Table 2.2) is classified as 'outward' whereas a low level results in an 'inward' classification. However, it has to be emphasized that the EL measure is not based directly on policy instruments but on realized levels of trade. It is also important to note that the data for the openness and trade orientation indicators refer to 1980. Changes during a ten-year period affecting the value of these indicators would in most cases not be big enough to affect the classification of a country. In exceptional cases a reassessment may be required. Finally, since the openness indicator is based on residuals from a regression, some observations will be classified as outward and others as inward, even if every single country were to increase its trade shares severalfold. The indicator is thus strictly a relative measure. Before proceeding to the classification a brief summary of the principal expected effects of the three criteria is now presented.[3]

Size

Large countries export a much smaller share of output than small ones. Small countries have relatively smaller domestic markets and the production structure tends to be more specialized than in larger countries. Smaller countries, being more specialized, are more subject to the commodity lottery. Within larger economies internal averaging masks extreme performance of specific regions. As a group therefore, small countries tend

43

to show a higher variance of growth than large countries (see Perkins and Syrquin, 1989).

Specialization

The effects of resources are interdependent with those of size. Unlike size, however, the pattern of trade specialization represents in part a strategy of development. Large countries have been prone to adopt inward-oriented policies. When natural resources have been abundant large countries have relied on (the artificially low) primary exports, while failing to develop manufactured exports. This is particularly the case for light manufactures and is reflected in the comparatively low share of light industries in GDP. By contrast, among large countries specializing in manufactures, the overall export share is still low but is made up predominantly of manufactured goods.

In small resource-poor countries, the absence of primary exports as a source of foreign exchange results in the need to develop light industry exports at an early stage, often supplemented by large inflows of foreign capital. Small resource-rich economies have tended to rely on primary exports as their source of foreign exchange for long periods of time. In the postwar period some small economies followed the large primary-oriented countries and adopted inward-oriented strategies of industrialization. Their narrower markets often turned this into a costly experience.

Export level

The impact of a higher export share on the degree of industrialization differs according to the type of specialization. Among primary-oriented economies higher exports are associated with higher mining shares and lower shares of manufacturing. This result reflects the combined effect of the import-substitution strategy in large inward-oriented countries (with relatively high industrial shares), and 'Dutch-disease' effects among mineral exporters.

When the country has a relative specialization in manufactures the higher the export share the larger the share of industry in output: light industry if the country is small, and heavy industry for a large country. There is some evidence that on average the more open economies have had higher rates of growth of output and factor productivity than the group of relatively more closed economies during the 1950–80 period (Syrquin and Chenery, 1989a).

In Table 2.2 the fourteen countries are classified into four general types according to their structural features and trade policies. However, since abundant natural resources are conducive to outward-oriented policies, whereas large domestic markets favour import substitution, it is not possible to make sharp distinctions between the influences of structure and of policy. The typology is identical to the one used to classify semi-industrial economies in Chenery and Syrquin (1986), and Syrquin and Chenery (1989a, b). The following brief description of the main features of the types is taken from the latter.

Outward, primary-oriented

The countries in this category have very high export shares made up predominantly of primary commodities. The continued primary specialization while entering into higher levels of per capita GDP can be characterized as a strategy of delayed industrialization. Large countries in this group, a category which is not represented in our sample, tend to be mineral exporters, while all agricultural exporters are small economies (Malaysia). The production and export of labour-intensive manufactures typically tends to lag in economies pursuing this strategy, but Malaysia, which maintained relatively neutral incentives among sectors, demonstrated substantial growth of manufactured exports with primary exports staying at a high level.

At low income levels the abundance of mineral resources typically dominates the effects of large size which would normally lead to low shares of trade and high shares of manufactured exports. In Perkins and Syrquin (1989) we focused on the experiences of the fifteen largest countries in terms of population. Four of these very large countries make up, together with Turkey, the group of inward-oriented large countries in our sample. The sample also contains three others of these largest countries.

Inward-oriented

The large countries in this type fall into two distinct groups. The first comprises the two very large countries in Asia with low income levels (China and Pakistan would have been classified in this group). The second includes large countries in Latin America and Turkey. Their incomes are significantly higher than in Asia and they have better endowments of natural resources. This is reflected in the substantially lower density of population in the second group and, in part, leads to the major difference between the two groups, namely their trade specialization. In the South Asia countries manufactures represent a high share of commodity exports while Latin American countries emphasize primary goods. The TO index highlights this difference, which would have been even more pronounced for earlier dates since by 1980 in the large Latin American countries manufactured exports had risen appreciably. It has been argued (Teitel and Thoumi, 1986) that the phase of inward-looking industrialization provided a preamble to the export stage during which the economy acquired a basic technological mastery required for exporting manufactures on a significant scale.

The two smaller economies in the inward-oriented group are somewhat similar in structure to the larger Latin American countries. They have very low density of population, have abundant natural resources, primarily minerals, and, in spite of their size, pursued an inward-oriented strategy for long periods of time. However, in the last fifteen years or so their development policies and performances have been very different from one another and from most other countries that could be classified in this type. Chile went from socialism to an extreme attempt at liberalization and integration in the international economy. Peru went through various half-hearted attempts to adopt a more outward-oriented strategy, followed by extreme populism. Average growth in both countries was low over the last fifteen years and subject to extreme fluctuations.

Balanced
This category contains countries that do not fit well in one of the other groups, often because during the period they have begun to shift from one type of strategy to another. Colombia and especially Thailand have increased their trade shares towards the average levels for their size while shifting their pattern of specialization toward manufactures.

The small economies in this group, all in Sub-Saharan Africa, were classified as industry-oriented in previous studies; outward in the case of Kenya, and inward for Tanzania. The reason was that, for their low income levels, they appeared to have relatively very high exports of manufactures. In recent times the proportion of manufactured exports has not continued to increase and the overall share of exports has fallen sharply in both countries. Given their low density of population a primary specialization is more likely at this stage of development.

Outward, industry-oriented
This strategy combines outward-oriented policies and a lack of comparative advantage in primary exports. The strategy has often been accompanied by large inflows of capital[4] and has usually followed an early phase of import substitution behind high protection. It manifests itself in rapid growth of exports with a marked emphasis on manufactures. Sri Lanka, previously classified as outward-primary, seems by now to fit better in this type.

The aims of the typology are to identify significant differences among broad groups and to provide relevant benchmarks for country analysis. For these purposes reclassifying a country among the types has only a marginal effect on the results. Clearly this is not the case when our interest rests on that particular country, but even then the detailed country analysis can usefully be done against the background of a general typology.

GROWTH OF OUTPUT AND FACTOR PRODUCTIVITY

During the three decades following the Second World War average growth of GDP in almost all regions of the world was significantly higher than in any comparable period in recent history. The only exception to this observation is the poor growth performance of the very low-income countries in Sub-Saharan Africa. Within that period numerous countries and regions experienced an acceleration of growth similar to the one identified by Kuznets (1966) in the early experience of today's developed countries. Growth acceleration in the distant past as well as in the postwar period resulted from increases in the rate of capital formation and of factor productivity growth. It was accompanied by, and was in part the result of, the rapid expansion of industry and the reallocation of resources from low-productivity to high-productivity activities.

This period saw the recovery of the network of international trade that had suffered severe blows during the depression of the 1930s and the war. World trade expanded at rates that had not been observed for decades. The main participants in the expansion were the advanced countries and a small group of semi-industrial economies that abandoned the inward strategy followed until then almost universally among developing countries.

As compared to previous decades, the 1970s were much more volatile. The various external shocks had different impacts on different countries and engendered a variety of responses. Although in general there was a certain slowdown in the rates of growth of output and productivity, relatively high rates of output expansion were maintained with the help of higher investment rates (Table 2.3). There is an interesting contrast between countries in Latin America and in Asia in the way they reacted and adjusted to the changes in external conditions. In Latin America growth in the 1970s was sustained by increased oil revenues (in some cases) and by borrowing in international markets. This last option reduced the urgency to design adjustment mechanisms to cope with the changed international economic environment (see Maddison, 1985). Countries in Asia adopted early adjustment measures and relied much less on foreign debt. The contrast becomes even sharper after 1980. In Latin America growth plummeted, turning the 1980s into the 'lost decade', while in South Asia and Korea growth accelerated (see Table 2.3). Using the labels of the typology, growth accelerated in industry-oriented countries and slowed down in those specializing in primary exports (including the 'balanced' group). Worst hit were the economies of Latin America and Sub-Saharan Africa. In the other three – Malaysia, Turkey and Thailand – growth either accelerated or was maintained at a relatively high rate. Of the fourteen countries in this study, these three and Korea were the only countries reporting real growth of merchandise exports during 1980–8 of 10 per cent per year or better (9.4 in Malaysia to be precise). The figures by income groups at the bottom of Table 2.3 show that on average among LDCs, growth of GDP fell during the 1980s.

How were these differences in performance related to differences in the accumulation of inputs and in the productivity of their use? Table 2.3

Table 2.3 Growth of output and productivity, 1960–89

Country	Annual growth rate of GDP			Rate of TFPG			Gross domestic share of GDP			Investment growth rate
	1960–70	1970–82	1980–9	1960–70	1970–82	1980–9	1960–70	1970–82	1980–9	1980–9
Malaysia	6.4	7.3	4.9	3.0	3.0	0.5	18	25	32	1.3
India	3.6	3.6	5.3	0.5	0.1	1.8	18	21	24	4.5
Bangladesh	3.7	4.2	3.5	1.4	1.7	0.7	10	8	14	-0.1
Mexico	7.3	5.9	0.7	3.6	1.6	-2.8	20	24	23	-5.0
Brazil	5.3	6.7	3.0	1.1	2.5	-0.2	25	27	22	0.7
Turkey	6.0	4.6	5.1	3.1	1.0	1.6	18	21	22	3.7
Chile	4.1	1.5	2.7	2.1	-0.9	0.2	13	13	18	2.7
Peru	4.7	2.5	0.4	1.3	-0.8	-3.5	19	15	26	-4.5
Colombia	4.8	5.0	3.5	0.9	0.9	0.4	19	19	20	0.3
Thailand	8.1	6.4	7.0	4.5	2.2	3.3	21	23	27	5.7
Kenya	5.6	5.7	4.1	2.5	2.0	-0.5	15	16	25	0.4
Tanzania	5.9	3.9	2.6	2.9	0.1	-1.6	16	21	22	2.1
Korea	8.3	7.8	9.7	4.9	2.9	6.2	16	31	31	11.6
Sri Lanka	4.5	4.7	4.0	1.6	0.6	0.7	15	25	26	-0.7
Country groups										
Low y	3.7	3.1	3.4	1.0	-0.2	-0.3	13	15	23	1.5
Lower mid-y	5.0	4.0	2.5	1.7	0.2	-1.3	18	21	26	-1.4
Upper mid-y	6.2	5.4	3.2	2.6	1.2	-0.6	21	27	30	0.6
Industrial	4.9	2.6	3.0	2.4	0.1	1.4	25	24	21	4.3

Sources: 1960–70 and 1970–82: World Bank tapes prepared for Syrquin and Chenery (1989a).
1980–9: World Bank, *World Development Reports*.

presents some rough estimates of the growth of overall productivity (TFP), calculated using a simple growth-accounting framework described in the appendix. The estimates are based on very crude assumptions and data, and more than the usual care is advised when drawing conclusions from them. The overall nature of the results however, was found to change only slightly under a variety of alternative assumptions.

During the 1960s factor productivity accounted for a substantial portion of output growth in all groups and regions. The picture changes drastically after that. In the 1970s productivity growth went down significantly almost everywhere. In the countries grouped by per capita income level, TFP growth was negligible except in the upper-middle-income group. This fall in productivity largely accounts for the slowdown in output growth, since the contribution of input expansion to output growth was no lower in the 1970s than in the 1960s. In fact, the real investment rate went up in most cases but its efficiency declined.

During the 1960s and 1970s middle-income countries outperformed both the low-income and the industrialized countries in terms of output and productivity growth. This implies that on average beyond a certain threshold there was a process of catching-up. This tendency becomes blurred after 1980.

For the 1980s it is more difficult to compute the conventional growth-accounting equation since some of the data are not available and some of the assumptions become even less tenable. The illustrative figures in Table 2.3 suggest a sharp deterioration in factor productivity in Africa and Latin America where TFPG comes out negative in most cases. The figures for Chile that indicate a mild recovery in growth and productivity in the 1980s are averages for the entire decade and thus do not yet fully reflect the strong performance in the latter part of this interval. Improvements in TFP during the 1980s are found in South Asia as well as in Korea, Thailand and Turkey.

A recent and more elaborate study of factor productivity from 1960 to 1987 shows basically the same overall pattern (World Bank, 1991: 43). The estimates of TFP by region for the periods 1960–73 and 1973–87 indicate an improvement in South Asia during the second period and a sharp decline in Africa and Latin America, the average TFPG coming out negative in both regions for the 1973–87 period.

The average investment rate for the 1980s is often higher than the average rate for earlier periods. This observation, however, tells us nothing about the trend of investment during the 1980s. In our sample once again we find a dichotomy: real investment stagnating or falling in Latin America and Africa and generally increasing in Asia and Turkey. In Tanzania the stagnation in investment followed a fall in saving. In Latin America this is not the case; significant trade surpluses were generated but a large share of saving had to be diverted from investment to service the debt.

The fall in investment was partly the result of attempts to correct domestic imbalances. In some cases it was also related to or due to a drastic import-reduction policy pursued to generate the surpluses in the trade balance needed to service the debt. The close association between investment and imports (at least in Latin America) reflects the success of previous import substitution in consumer goods and also the vulnerability of investment to shortfalls in income. Within countries in Latin America the simple correlation coefficient between investment and imports (in constant prices) during 1960 to 1980–2 exceeded 0.78 in 11 out of 17 countries (Syrquin, 1986). In our sample the correlation between the annual growth rates of real investment and real imports of merchandise for 1980–8 equals 0.83.

One problem in trying to compare factor productivity among countries for recent periods is the lack of comparative information on the growth of employment and its industrial composition. After publishing for many years employment data for the 1980s, the World Development Report stopped doing so temporarily until the 1990 round of census results becomes available. Since the growth of employment is clearly related to the growth of population with a lag, some interesting results emerge from comparing the rates of growth of population and of employment for 1965–80. Arranging the countries by the level of per capita income in 1988 we find three distinct groups. In countries in the middle of the range (e.g. Thailand) the difference between the two growth rates is negligible. In the lower-income group population growth exceeds the one for the labour force, all of which is assumed here to be employed, while at the higher income range the opposite is true – the growth of the labour force outstrips that of population. This pattern is what one would expect for countries going through the demographic transition during which population growth accelerates, reaches a peak rate and then slows down (assuming age-specific participation rates to remain unchanged). Two countries deviate from the pattern – Sri Lanka and Turkey. This conforms with the observations in Table 2.1 on socioeconomic indicators where Sri Lanka fares better than expected given her income and Turkey the opposite. Rapid growth of population and labour force pose a difficult challenge for a poor developing country. Undoubtedly those rapid growth rates open up new possibilities and can become an advantage, but often they do not, at least in the short run. One of the main differences in initial conditions between the richer nations when entering the process of modern economic growth and LDCs since 1950, one that it is claimed makes today's job much more difficult, is precisely the fact that the European nations and Japan did not have to contend with a population explosion. As seen in Table 2.1 in the richer countries in our sample population growth is slowing down. This already shows up in the growth of employment up to 1980 and will show up even more in the data for the 1980s (assuming again no big changes in participation rates). However, in Sub-Saharan Africa the worst is yet to come.

STRUCTURAL TRANSFORMATION

Comparative studies of structural transformation have established various uniform features of the process of development, commonly known as 'stylized facts'. These studies have also been useful in identifying the main reasons for departures from the uniform trends. The path of development is clearly not unique but depends on initial conditions and on 'planners' preferences' or policy.

Changes in the sectoral composition of economic activity are the most prominent feature of structural transformation. Shifts in the internal allocation of resources among sectors are the result of the interaction of changes in the composition of demand, and variations on the supply side. On the demand side the changes are derived from the pattern of income elasticities of demand, and on the supply side they are the effect of factor accumulation and productivity growth. The demand and supply effects are not totally independent from one another. Thus changes in demand between internal and external sources reflect changing comparative advantage, while aggregate productivity growth incorporates resource shifts from low-productivity to higher-productivity sectors.

Structural changes are a concomitant of modern economic growth but they may also be necessary for continued growth. Since policy influences the patterns of structural change a perennial and much debated issue has been its proper or optimal role. Obstructing or preventing change that otherwise would have occurred requires active intervention and can be extremely costly. A more moderate approach tries to anticipate structural change, facilitating it or accelerating it by removing obstacles and correcting for market failures. The policies pursued by the countries in this study covered this range between imposing structural change and trying to smooth the path for structural change to run its course.

Three aspects of structural transformation are discussed in this section: the level and composition of exports, the industrial composition of output and employment, and the effect on productivity of intersectoral factor shifts.

Exports

In a relatively closed economy the structure of production has to conform closely to the structure of domestic demand, but this no longer holds for the open economy. The extent of a country's participation in the international economy is only weakly related to the level of development across countries. The principal determinant of the share of trade in GDP across countries is the size of the economy. This comes out clearly in Table 2.4 where the first two columns give the export share in 1985 and the

Table 2.4 Export levels and composition

Country	E/Y 1985 (%)	Δ(E/Y) 1965–85	E_m/E 1985 (%)	Δ(E_m/E) 1965–85	E_p/N 1985 (US$)	E_m/N 1985 (US$)
Outward, primary-oriented						
Small						
Malaysia	55	13	27	21	697	258
Inward-oriented						
Large, manufacturing						
India	6	2	49	0	7	6
Bangladesh	6	−4	65	−	4	7
Large, primary						
Mexico	16	7	21	11	202	75
Brazil	14	6	41	33	112	77
Turkey	19	7	54	52	76	89
Small, primary						
Chile	29	15	7	3	290	22
Peru	22	6	12	9	137	19
Balanced						
Large						
Colombia	15	4	18	11	108	24
Thailand	27	9	35	30	89	48
Small						
Kenya	25	−6	13	3	43	6
Tanzania	7	−19	7	−6	11	1
Outward, industry-oriented						
Large						
Korea	36	27	91	31	67	672
Small						
Sri Lanka	26	−12	27	26	61	22
Country groups						
Low y	14	−5	24	15	18	6
Lower mid-y	23	7	30	21	95	40
Upper mid-y	28	10	47	22	210	240
Industrial	18	6	76	6	350	1,120

Source: World Bank (1987).
E, E_m, E_p, Y and N stand for exports, manufactured exports, primary exports, GDP and population.

change in that share between 1965 and 1985. One of the indicators for classifying countries in Table 2.2 was the relative export level (EL) showing the ratio of the actual share of exports to that predicted by cross-country regressions. Countries classified as 'outward' had around 1980 significantly higher than expected export shares, while the inward countries, especially the large ones, had significantly lower than expected shares. In some cases the 1980 (or 1985) position represents a shift from the situation in 1965. Thus in 1965 Korea would have been classified as inward while

Kenya and Tanzania were at that time significantly more open than in 1985. During those two decades export shares expanded in most countries. In part this is a by-product of the two oil shocks which automatically increased the shares (in current prices) of oil exporters and forced others to increase theirs to finance the higher import bills. In the large inward-oriented economies it represents an attempt to regain some of the ground lost during the more extreme import-substitution phases which coincided with the fast recovery of world trade after decades of disarray. Even large increases in exports during 1965–85 did not always suffice to move an economy into the outward category, because during that same period trade shares were rapidly expanding everywhere which means that its relative position might not have moved at all. The data for income groups in Table 2.4 show that the increase in exports was indeed quite universal except for the group of low-income countries.

As argued above, the commodity composition of trade and the type of specialization are largely determined by the availability of resources, by traditional factor proportions and by policy. In practice the evolution of comparative advantage and commercial policy have combined to create an export pattern that reinforces the shift from primary goods (agriculture and mining) to industry, implicit in the pattern of domestic demand. The nature and timing of the reorientation of exports have not been the same in all countries. Large countries have shifted away from primary specialization through import substitution. Small countries, poor in natural resources, have had to develop manufactured exports at an early stage. Resource-abundant countries have been able to postpone the shift to higher levels of manufactured exports, particularly in the case of mineral-rich countries. That such a shift has taken place is apparent in Table 2.4. The proportion of manufactured exports in exports increased substantially in all income groups and in most of the countries in this study. This increase in manufactured exports comes on top of the rapidly expanding share of total exports in GDP. The change in composition is particularly striking in the cases of Brazil, Korea, Malaysia, Sri Lanka, Thailand and Turkey. Since the composition of exports underlies the trade-orientation index (TO) used to divide countries into primary- or industry-oriented, it is not surprising to find relatively (for their income levels) low shares of manufactured exports in Latin America and quite high shares (again, given their income) in the large economies of South Asia. All this is in terms of shares in exports or in output. To supplement these share figures the last two columns of Table 2.4 show the dollar exports per capita of primary and manufactured goods. The income-related differences now appear forcefully. The large economies of Latin America have been rapidly increasing their exports of manufactures. On a per capita basis they export ten times as much as the poor and large countries of Asia. Particularly noteworthy is the impressive level of manufactured exports in Malaysia, especially when we also note the very high level of primary exports. A comparison with the averages for the higher income groups shows the vast potential for manufactured exports still ahead.

Changes in sector proportions

Changes in the sectoral composition of production are the most prominent feature of structural transformation. Associated with income growth are shifts in demand, trade and factor use. These interact with the pattern of productivity growth, the availability of resources, and policy to determine the pace and nature of industrialization.

The reallocation of economic activity from agriculture to manufacturing took place in all countries except for Chile and Tanzania where, over the complete period, agriculture increased its share and manufacturing went down, and Sri Lanka, in which structural change was negligible (see Table 2.5). As compared to the averages-by-income groups, the changes in the countries were quite substantial. This stands out in Korea, Malaysia, Thailand and Turkey – precisely the countries that, together with Sri Lanka, showed the largest reallocation of exports towards manufacturing. The averages for the group of industrial countries show a falling trend of manufacturing in both output and employment. This phenomenon of de-industrialization in industrialized countries has taken place in every single country in that group in the last two decades.

Changes in the composition of employment are similar to the shifts in value-added proportions but appear with a lag. Since (average) labour productivity in agriculture tends to be lower than in the rest of the economy, the lag in the employment shift implies a similar lag in the growth of labour productivity in agriculture behind that of other sectors, widening further the initial productivity gap. The data on employment in Table 2.5 show that as late as 1980 more than half of the labour force was still attached to agriculture in South Asia, Africa and Turkey. In some cases the share exceeds 80 per cent. In 1960 all countries except Chile had more than 50 per cent of the labour force in agriculture. During the 1960–80 period there was a significant reallocation of employment out of agriculture (mostly in relative terms) in the countries in our sample outside of South Asia and Africa, i.e. outside of the countries with lowest levels of development. As the average figures in the bottom of the table indicate, in middle-income countries only between 40 and 50 per cent of the decline in agriculture's share was taken up by industry (which includes mining, construction and public utilities). The middle-income countries in this study show a wider range of outcomes but remain, on average, around the 40–50 per cent mark. Elsewhere I have shown that this pattern has not been very different from the historical experience of today's advanced countries (Syrquin, 1988). In Latin American countries employment in services does

Table 2.5 Sectoral composition of output and employment

Country	1988		1980	1965–88		1980		1960–80	
	VA	VM	VN	ΔVA	ΔVM	LA	LI	ΔLA	ΔLI
Outward, primary-oriented									
Small									
Malaysia	23	19	8	–7	9	42	19	–21	7
Inward-oriented									
Large, manufacturing									
India	32	19	2	–12	3	70	13	–4	2
Bangladesh	46	7	0	–7	2	75	6	–12	3
Large, primary									
Mexico	9	26	7	–5	6	37	29	–18	9
Brazil	9	29	1	–10	3	31	27	–21	12
Turkey	17	26	2	–17	10	58	17	–21	6
Small, primary									
Chile	10	20	9	1	–4	17	25	–14	5
Peru	12	24	12	–6	7	40	18	–13	–2
Balanced									
Large									
Colombia	19	20	3	–8	1	34	24	–17	5
Thailand	17	24	2	–15	10	71	10	–13	6
Small									
Kenya	31	12	0	–4	1	81	7	–5	2
Tanzania	66	4	1	20	–4	86	5	–3	1
Outward, industry-oriented									
Large									
Korea	11	32	1	–27	14	36	27	–30	18
Small									
Sri Lanka	26	15	2	–2	–2	53	14	–3	0
Country groups	1985							1965–80	
Low y	36	12	–	–5	2	71	10	–8	2
Low mid y	22	17	–	–7	1	55	16	–10	4
Upper mid-y	10	–	–	–5	–	29	31	–16	8
Industrial	3	23	–	–2	–7	7	35	–7	–3

Sources: World Bank (1982, 1987, 1990).
VA, VM and VN are shares in value added of agriculture, manufacturing and mining.
LA and LI are shares in employment of agriculture and industry (= mining, + manufacturing + construction + public utilities).

appear to be relatively high, but even there this does not come about at the expense of industrial employment. It is made possible because of a relatively low proportion of employment in agriculture, which has as a counterpart a very high rate of urbanization. When we take into account the positive association of urbanization with income per capita, Latin America comes out as the most urbanized region of the world. Thus, the perception of a low rate of labour absorption in industry in Latin America

Table 2.6 Relative labour productivity and intersectoral reallocation

	Relative labour productivity[a]				Annual growth rate (1965–80) of $Y/L(g_y)$	Reallocation[b] (R)	R/g_y
	Agriculture		Non-agriculture				
	1965	1980	1965	1980			
Malaysia	47	57	176	131	3.8	1.1	29
India	64	44	197	231	2.1	0.3	14
Bangladesh	63	67	294	199	0.5	1.0	200
Mexico	28	30	172	141	2.5	1.1	44
Brazil	39	42	159	126	5.5	1.2	22
Turkey	45	33	265	193	4.5	2.1	47
Chile	33	41	125	112	–0.3	0.5	–
Peru	36	28	164	148	1.0	0.8	80
Colombia	67	59	127	121	2.9	0.4	14
Thailand	43	24	360	286	4.5	2.1	47
Kenya	41	38	462	364	2.7	1.2	44
Tanzania	50	67	675	303	1.1	1.6	145
Korea	71	39	135	134	6.5	1.0	15
Sri Lanka	50	51	164	155	1.8	0.2	11
Country groups							
Low y	52	51	281	220	1.0	1.0	100
Lower mid-y	45	40	202	173	3.8	1.0	25
Upper mid-y	33	34	155	127	3.9	1.1	28
Industrial	36	43	110	104	2.4	0.3	14

Source: World Bank (1987).
[a] Relative labour productivity is defined as $(V_i/V)/(L_i/L)$, where V is value added in constant prices, L is employment, and the i's refer to sectors (agriculture and non-agriculture).
[b] Reallocation (R) is estimated as:

$$\frac{1}{15} \ \Sigma \ 1_n \ \frac{1_i \ 1980}{1_i \ 1965} \left(\frac{V_i}{V} \right)$$

where $l_i = L_i/L$, and V_i/V is measured as the mean of the 1965 and 1980 values (to avoid interaction terms and to approximate a Divisia index).

is based on the composition of the non-agricultural labour force (see Syrquin, 1991).

Relative labour productivity

A partial indicator of differential returns across sectors is the pattern of relative labour productivity obtained by dividing a sector's share in value added by its share in employment. It is partial because it refers to average and not marginal products and considers only one input (labour).[5] Table 2.6 presents sectoral labour productivity relative to output per worker in the entire economy for agriculture and non-agriculture. Labour productivity tends to be significantly lower in agriculture than in the rest of the economy. In the process of development the growth of productivity in agriculture first tends to lag behind that in other sectors, further widening the pre-existing gap. Once migration and capital accumulation have significantly reduced the surplus of agricultural labour, the productivity gap tends to decline. The long-run pattern of relative productivity in agriculture traces out a curve that resembles, and in part underlies, the Kuznets curve of income inequality. The gap in output per worker among sectors is very much in evidence in Table 2.6. Over time a reduction has generally occurred in the productivity gap among sectors in the individual countries and in the country groups. The shift in the share of employment away from the low-productivity sector (agriculture) contributed to the increase in aggregate labour productivity. This contribution appears as the effect of reallocation in Table 2.6. It is an approximate measure of the efficiency increases resulting from an improved allocation of resources. Between 1965 and 1980 intersectoral labour shifts accounted for more than 25 per cent of average growth in output per worker in middle-income countries.

Comparing the contribution of resource reallocation to productivity growth in Table 2.6, with the estimates of TFP growth in Table 2.3, we find some interesting similarities. In most cases where TFP between 1960 and 1982 was relatively high, the contribution of resource shifts was also substantial.

APPENDIX

The estimates of total factor productivity growth (TFPG) were calculated using the following growth accounting equation:

$$g_y = MPK \cdot I/Y + E_L g_L + Y$$

where g_y is growth rate of GDP;

   MPK is marginal product of capital;

   I/Y is net domestic investment as a share of GDP;

   E_L is elasticity of output with respect to labour;

   g_L is growth rate of employment; and

   Y is residual or TFPG.

Because data are not readily available for all of these variables and in the right form, the following assumptions were made:

(a) The marginal product of capital was assumed to be 0.12 up to 1982 and 0.10 for the 1980s.

(b) For the 1980s, the labour force growth was assumed to be the same as the population growth rate.

To take into account the likelihood that the depreciation rate and the elasticity of output with respect to labour vary systematically with income, the following values of these rates were used:

Country groups	Depreciation rate (D/K)	E_L
Low–y	0	0.52
Lower mid–y	0	0.55
Upper mid–y	0.01	0.60
Industrial	0.03	0.64

NOTES

1 The reciprocal of the ERDI is the national level measured by the ratio of the PPP of the currency to the exchange rate.
2 The TO index compares actual trade bias to the one predicted from cross-country regressions. The trade bias is defined as TB = $(E_p - E_m)/E$ and the trade orientation index as TO = TB – $\hat{TB}$, where E_p, E_m and E stand for primary, manufactured and total exports and $\hat{TB}$ is the expected trade bias predicted from cross-country regressions. Taking total exports to refer to merchandise only, the TO can be shown to equal –2 $(E_m/E - \hat{E}_m/E)$. An extreme primary specialization gives a positive TO while an industry specialization results in a negative value (see Chenery and Syrquin, 1986: 114ff.).
3 The following draws liberally from Chenery and Syrquin (1986) and Syrquin and Chenery (1989a, b).
4 In previous studies that classified countries, we presented information on capital inflows and used it in designing the typology. In the 1980s the ratio of capital inflows to GDP reached very high levels in many of the countries in this study but the measure ceased to discriminate among strategies.
5 See Syrquin (1984) for a comparison of approaches to measuring the contribution of intersectoral resource shifts.

REFERENCES

Balassa, B. and Associates (1971) *The Structure of Protection in Developing Countries*, Baltimore: Johns Hopkins University Press.
Chenery, H. B. and Syrquin, M. (1986) 'The Semi-Industrial Countries' in H. Chenery, S. Robinson and M. Syrquin (eds) *Industrialization and Growth: A Comparative Study*, New York: Oxford University Press.
Hirschman, A. O. (1968) 'The Political Economy of Import-Substituting Industrialization in Latin America', *Quarterly Journal of Economics* 82: 2–32.
—— (1986) 'The Political Economy of Latin American Development: Seven Exercises in Retrospection', Center for U.S.–Mexican Studies, University of California, San Diego.
Kuznets, S. (1966) *Modern Economic Growth*, New Haven: Yale University Press.
Little, I. M. D., Scitovsky, T. and Scott, M. (1970) *Industry and Trade in Some Developing Countries: A Comparative Study*, London: Oxford University Press.
Maddison, A. (1985) *Two Crises: Latin America and Asia 1929–38 and 1973–83*, Paris: OECD Development Centre.

Perkins, D. H. and Syrquin, M. (1989) 'Large Countries: The Influence of Size', in H.B. Chenery and T.N. Srinivasan (eds) *Handbook of Development Economics*, vol. II, Amsterdam: North Holland.

Summers, R. and Heston, A. (1991) 'The Penn World Table (Mark 5): An Expanded Set of International Comparisons, 1950–1988', *Quarterly Journal of Economics* 106: 327–68.

Syrquin, M. (1984) 'Resource Reallocation and Productivity Growth', in M. Syrquin, L. Taylor and L. E. Westphal (eds) *Economic Structure and Performance: Essays in Honor of Hollis B. Chenery*, New York: Academic Press.

—— (1986) 'Growth and Structural Change in Latin America since 1960: A Comparative Analysis', *Economic Development and Cultural Change* 34: 433–54.

—— (1988) 'Patterns of Structural Change,' in H. B. Chenery and T. N. Srinivasan (eds) *Handbook of Development Economics*, vol. I, Amsterdam: North Holland.

—— (1991) 'A Comparative Analysis of Structural Transformation in Latin America' in M. Urrutia (ed.) *Long Term Trends in Latin American Economic Development*, Washington, DC: Inter-American Development Bank.

—— and Chenery, H. B. (1989a) 'Patterns of Development: 1950–1983', World Bank Discussion Paper 41.

—— and Chenery, H. B. (1989b) 'Three Decades of Industrialization', *World Bank Economic Review* 3: 145–81.

Teitel, S. and Thoumi, F.E. (1986) 'From Import-Substitution to Exports: The Manufacturing Exports of Argentina and Brazil', *Economic Development and Cultural Change* 34: 455–90.

UNDP (1990) *Human Development Report*, New York: Oxford University Press.

World Bank (1982) *World Development Report*, New York: Oxford University Press.

World Bank (1987) *World Development Report*, New York: Oxford University Press.

World Bank (1990) *World Development Report*, New York: Oxford University Press.

World Bank (1991) *World Development Report*, New York: Oxford University Press.

LATIN AMERICA

3

IMPORT COMPRESSION, PRODUCTIVITY SLOWDOWN AND MANUFACTURED EXPORT DYNAMISM

BRAZIL, 1975–90

Winston Fritsch and Gustavo H. B. Franco

With the usual caveats, the authors wish to thank the WIDER project participants, and very especially Gerry Helleiner, for a variety of comments and suggestions on an early draft of this paper.

INTRODUCTION

The record of Brazilian industrial growth and structural change up to the late 1970s, when looked at in a long-run perspective, seems quite impressive. Between the end of the Second World War and 1980, industrial output in Brazil grew at an average annual rate of nearly 8 per cent, while world industrial production rose at only about 5 per cent. Given Brazil's relatively large economic size, her share in total manufacturing value added of world market economies in 1980 reached 3.2 per cent, the sixth largest manufacturing sector of the capitalist world.[1]

This process of rapid industrial growth was far from uniform over time, notably showing a short interval of stagnation in the mid–1960s and a fall in average growth rates in the wake of the first oil shock. Following the second oil shock and the onset of the debt crisis, growth dramatically stalled and since the early 1980s industrial output has fluctuated widely around a stagnating trend.

During these four decades, the contribution of the industrial sector to total value added changed significantly: industry's share in GDP rose from under 25 per cent in the early postwar years to 35.5 per cent in 1985, replicating the classical patterns of transformation accompanying rapid economic development. Moreover, continuous structural change took place

63

within the manufacturing sector, increasing the weight of more capital-
and skill-intensive intermediate and capital goods in total manufacturing
value added.

This process of industrial growth and structural transformation was
accompanied by marked changes in the Brazilian trade regime and in the
import and export shares of its manufacturing output (or its 'tradability').
Three periods can be clearly identified in this regard. The first, which
lasted until the mid-1960s, was the heyday of classical import-substitution
(IS) policies. It was marked by a dramatic fall in import intensity and a
stagnation of the ratio of manufactured exports to total exports, as well as
that of exports to output in manufacturing, brought about by strongly
import- and, implicitly, export-repressive exchange rates. The second
period, which lasted until the first oil shock, was a period of slow import
liberalization, but decisive export promotion and stable real exchange rates.
As a result there was a noticeable recovery in both import and export
propensities. The third period, which started after the first oil shock and
lasts to the present, was one in which there was a return to import-
repressive policies but accompanied this time by the reinforcement of
export promotion instruments, helped, periodically, by resort to aggressive
real exchange rate devaluations. Although manufactured imports fell again
to a low share of domestic supply in this period, export propensities
continued to rise.

The aim of this paper is to describe this process of change and to explain,
with special emphasis on the post-1975 period, how, first, the evolving trade
and industrial policies interacted both with an unstable macroeconomic
environment and with developments endogenous to the process of industrial growth and maturation and, second, how they shaped productivity
growth and international competitiveness in Brazilian manufacturing. It is
divided into three sections. First, we briefly review the main 'phases' in
postwar Brazilian industrialization mentioned above, describe the evolution
of the regulatory framework and discuss how it helped to shape some
crucial features of industrial structure that influence competition and technological dynamism. Next we look at the performance of the Brazilian
manufacturing sector in terms of international competitiveness and productivity growth and their determinants. Finally, we offer some generalizations, based on the Brazilian experience, on the relative importance of
macroeconomic and microeconomic factors in the relationships between
trade policy, 'tradability', growth and macroeconomic instability.

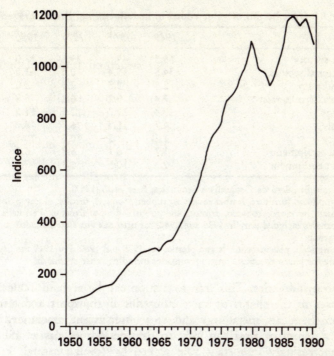

Figure 3.1 Industrial output, Brazil, 1950–89 (Abreu 1989)

THE EVOLUTION OF INDUSTRIAL STRUCTURE AND THE REGULATORY FRAMEWORK

Phases in Brazilian industrial development[2]

Figure 3.1 shows three long spurts of industrial output growth, followed by a decade of instability and stagnation. These three spurts reflect investment cycles, each of which had a different character and motivation. The first, which lasted until the stagflation crisis of 1962–6, was mostly a response to incentives to domestic production created basically by foreign exchange shortages experienced from the late 1940s onward, and corresponded to 'classic' import-substitution industrialization (ISI). The incentives to invest were mostly created by large cross-sectoral differences in rates of return produced by official manipulation of exchange rates and commercial policy and, after the mid-1950s, by explicit industrial promotion instruments, notably public long-term credit.

During this period the structure of industry was radically transformed: modern segments of consumer durables, the auto industry in particular, with important backward linkages to the mechanical and electrical equipment industries, were installed together with a number of basic input and

Table 3.1 Distribution of value added in manufacturing, Brazil, 1949–80

	1949	1967	1975	1980	1985
Traditional sectors[a]	65.5	44.6	39.6	37.0	35.9
Non-traditional sectors	34.5	55.4	60.4	63.0	64.1
Paper and pulp	2.1	2.9	2.5	3.0	2.9
Non-metallic minerals	7.4	5.2	6.2	5.8	4.2
Metallurgy	9.4	12.0	12.6	11.5	12.1
Chemicals[b]	4.7	10.9	16.7	18.7	21.1
Machinery	2.2	3.2	10.3	10.1	9.4
Electrical equipment	1.7	6.1	5.8	6.3	8.0
Transport equipment	2.3	10.5	6.3	7.6	6.4

Source: Instituto Brasilero de Geografia e Estatística; Baer *et al.* (1987).
[a] Includes wood and furniture, leather products, rubber products, textiles, clothing, footwear, food products, beverages, tobacco, printing and publishing, miscellaneous. Perfumes, soap and candles included only in 1975 and 1980; for previous years are included in the chemicals group.
[b] Includes chemicals, pharmaceuticals and plastics for 1975 and 1980. For 1949 the figures reported are for pharmaceuticals only, presumably including other chemicals.

capital goods industries. This transformation can be seen in Table 3.1 in the increases in the shares of such industries as transport and electrical equipment, chemicals, metallurgy and, to a lesser extent, machinery.

A crucial aspect of Brazilian industrialization in the 'classic' ISI years was the increasingly important role played by foreign capital. From a handful of assembly plants in 1946, mostly installed during the inter-war period, foreign-controlled firms came to account for nearly 19 per cent of total industrial capital by 1965 (cf. Malan and Bonelli, 1976: 395) and occupied leading positions in several of the most dynamic sectors of manufacturing. The importance of foreign capital during this period resulted from an unusual combination of protection against imports and a liberal treatment of foreign capital, two apparently contradictory policy stances explained by the continuous balance of payments problems brought about by grossly overvalued exchange rates. The maturation of investments associated with the 'classic' ISI phase created a reasonably integrated industrial sector in which the incentives available for import-substituting production tended to foster both industrial concentration in newer industries, and a system of inter-industrial links with great complementarities between firms with different patterns of ownership in existing ones. The great concern over the possibility of 'enclaves' in the establishment of modern industries in Brazil led to the imposition of heavy requirements with regard to national suppliers and downstream consumers, limiting vertical integration of multinational corporations (MNCs).

The second investment spurt – the so-called 'Brazilian economic miracle' of 1968–73 – was induced by the very rapid growth of industrial production (manufacturing output increased by 130 per cent in six years) and high rates of investment which were sustained to a significant extent by large

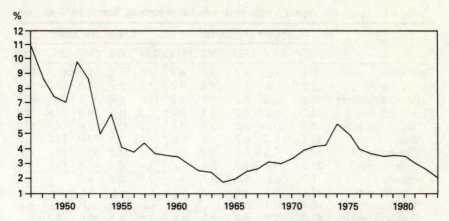

Figure 3.2 Ratio of imports to total supply in manufacturing, Brazil, 1949–83 (constant 1949 prices) (Malan and Bonelli, 1990)

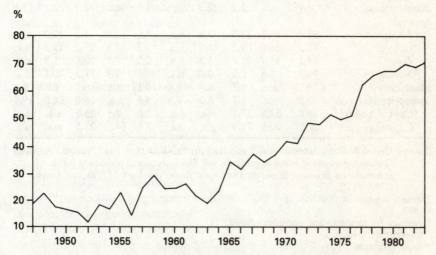

Figure 3.3 Ratio of manufactured exports to total exports, Brazil, 1949–83 (constant 1949 prices) (Malan and Bonelli, 1990)

government projects favouring capital goods and chemicals. As seen in Table 3.1, the joint share in Brazilian manufacturing (MVA) of these two industries increased from 14.1 per cent in 1967 to 27 per cent in 1975.

There was, however, a very significant difference in the trade orientation of the manufacturing sector between the 1968–73 boom period and the ISI-oriented investment spurt in the 1950s and 1960s, as can be seen in Figs 3.2 and 3.3, and Table 3.2. This stemmed from the more 'realistic' exchange rate policies of the later period – a crawling peg regime was

Table 3.2 Import and export coefficients, selected industries, Brazil, 1974–85 (%)

	Import coefficients					Export coefficients				
	1974	1978	1981	1983	1985	1974	1978	1981	1983	1985
Total trade	10.6[a]	n.a.	8.7	8.4	6.7	7.0	n.a.	8.5	10.7	11.3
Manufactures	11.2[a]	n.a.	5.3	4.8	4.9	7.4	n.a.	9.9	12.7	14.6
Light manufactures	1.8[a]	n.a.	1.2	1.5	2.0	15.8	n.a.	17.7	22.1	26.7
Heavy industry	11.1[a]	n.a.	4.8	3.9	3.6	2.2	n.a.	4.8	7.5	8.9
*Paper and pulp	6.3	n.a.	3.2	3.4	3.1	2.1	n.a.	7.6	8.9	12.0
*Steel	39.1	5.7	6.0	1.0	n.a.	2.2	5.4	13.9	37.8	n.a.
*Ferroalloys	7.5	1.2	2.0	0.2	n.a.	20.1	36.5	45.6	60.4	n.a.
*Refractories	25.3	4.8	14.9	5.1	n.a.	8.4	10.1	17.6	17.1	n.a.
Chemicals	11.7[a]	n.a.	5.6	5.1	4.8	2.4	4.8	6.5	7.9	n.a.
*Caustic soda	53.1	6.5	1.8	n.a.	n.a.	n.a.	n.a.	n.a.	n.a.	n.a.
*Fertilizers[b]	60.4	44.1	30.3	n.a.	n.a.	n.a.	n.a.	n.a.	n.a.	n.a.
*Petrochemicals[c]	41.0	22.0	6.0	2.0	n.a.	1.9	4.9	14.6	12.2	n.a.
*Petrochemicals[d]	14.0	11.0	0.4	0.6	n.a.	0.0	0.0	8.3	12.3	n.a.
*Thermoplastic resins	35.2	22.0	2.0	1.0	n.a.	2.0	2.0	17.0	30.0	n.a.
*Synthetic fibres	21.6	10.2	5.0	1.1	n.a.	1.3	2.2	12.3	9.6	n.a.
Non-metallic minerals	1.4[a]	n.a.	2.3	2.3	3.5	1.4	n.a.	2.3	2.3	3.5
*Aluminium	50.4	26.3	12.0	2.3	n.a.	1.6	2.0	8.2	40.0	n.a.
*Copper	72.2	80.0	79.2	40.4	n.a.	2.5	11.8	27.2	15.9	n.a.
*Zinc	64.2	49.7	21.7	3.3	n.a.	0.0	0.1	10.6	1.9	n.a.
*Silicon	94.2	0.5	0.0	0.0	n.a.	46.1	31.9	71.2	70.3	n.a.
Machinery	4.2[a]	n.a.	6.7	6.7	8.4	4.1	n.a.	6.7	6.7	8.4
Transport Material	9.3[a]	n.a.	6.7	8.3	7.9	5.3	n.a.	16.0	16.5	19.5
*Capital goods[e]	39.8	37.9	37.1[f]	n.a.	n.a.	3.0	8.9	15.9	n.a.	n.a.
*Capital goods[g]	27.0	20.5	24.9[f]	n.a.	n.a.	7.0	14.3	23.1	n.a.	n.a.

Sources: United Nations, *International Trade Statistics Yearbook*, vol. I and *National Accounts Statistics: Analysis of Main Aggregates*, vol. II; International Monetary Fund, *International Financial Statistics*; The World Bank, *Yearbook of 1988*, and Batista (1987: 73–5).
*Sectors targeted by PND-II.
[a] 1975.
[b] Average for nitrogen- and phosphate-based.
[c] Intermediate products.
[d] Basic products.
[e] 'On order'.
[f] 1980.
[g] 'In series'.

adopted in 1968 – and the development of export promotion schemes. Brazilian exports of manufactures grew at very impressive rates, reaching 15.4 per cent in constant dollar terms from 1965 to 1970, and 26.7 per cent between 1970 and 1975 (World Bank, 1983: 17). The country was hailed by many 'liberalizers' at the time as a textbook example of successful trade reforms, involving the abandonment of the inward orientation of the 1950s and 1960s.[3]

The period of the 'economic miracle' was cut short by the first oil shock but, in spite of Brazil's heavy dependence on imported oil, the recessionary effects of the import price shock were short-lived. The possibility of maintaining ample access to world capital markets made possible the financing of large current account deficits and thus allowed the adoption of a structural adjustment strategy – the Second National Development Plan (PND-II), announced in 1974 – that generated the third expansionary cycle in Brazil's industrial growth of the post war years.

The trade orientation this time reflected a return to the strategy of import substitution, especially in basic inputs and capital goods, but without the anti-export bias, or real exchange rate appreciations, that characterized such policies in the 1950s and 1960s. There was little structural change in industry in this period in terms of changes in shares of specific industries in total value added, but substantial changes in trade propensities of different industries could be observed. Table 3.2 shows a frequent combination of further deepening of import substitution and increasing export shares of output in the same industries in which import substitution was taking place.

The way in which Brazil's external balance problem was addressed after 1973 altered certain structural aspects of the country's relationship with the international economy, increasing its vulnerability to external shocks. On the one hand, the government's reluctance to alter relative prices or the availability of oil derivatives, the natural investment-production lags in oil prospecting and extraction, and the maintenance of high GDP growth rates combined to produce a 56 per cent rise in the volume of oil imports and a 7 per cent fall in the share of domestic supplies in total consumption between 1973 and 1979. The share of oil in total imports rose from 11.7 per cent, in 1973, to 37.5 per cent, in 1979. On the other hand, the quadrupling of the gross foreign debt between the same two years – with almost 70 per cent of the debt contracted with private banks in the form of foreign currency loans with floating interest rates – caused a serious deterioration in external indebtedness indicators and rendered the current account extremely sensitive to changes in dollar interest rates. This growing external vulnerability of the Brazilian economy became clear in the second half of 1979 when severe oil price and interest rate shocks threw the Brazilian economy into a decade of output instability and near stagnation of growth in productive capacity.

The initial response to the external shocks was an attempt to restore external equilibrium through a sudden and drastic tightening of both domestic credit and foreign capital inflows, coupled with large exchange rate devaluations. These policies were implemented in late 1980 but the curtailment of foreign lending in mid–1982 made the current account adjustment needs even more urgent. Between 1982 and 1984, a current account deficit of 8 per cent of GDP was turned into a small surplus.

The savage cut in domestic demand implemented between 1980 and 1983

69

Table 3.3 Average industrial output growth by user sector, Brazil (in % per annum)

	1968–73	1974–80	1981–3	1984–6	1987	1988	1989	1990
Industry	13.3	6.9	−5.6	8.5	0.9	−3.2	3.2	−8.9
Intermediate goods	14.0	8.3	−7.8	8.6	1.1	−2.1	2.7	−8.8
Capital goods	17.6	8.2	−17.8	16.3	−1.8	−2.1	0.5	−15.3
Consumer goods								
Durable	24.7	7.9	−5.9	9.5	−5.4	0.7	2.5	−5.8
Non-durable	9.6	4.9	0.4	6.2	1.6	−4.5	4.3	−5.4

Source: IPEA (1987: table A.2).

had a devastating effect on industrial activity levels, especially in the capital and durable consumer goods industries, as shown in Table 3.3. In 1984, however, the impacts of the rapid US recovery, further real exchange rate devaluation (undertaken in 1983) and depressed domestic demand levels combined to boost Brazilian exports. Although export prices remained depressed, a 23 per cent expansion in the volume of exports, plus the impressive reduction of real imports which had started in 1982 and was, to a large extent, associated with the maturing of investments initiated in the 1970s, eliminated the current account deficit. The stimulus given to aggregate demand by this sudden increase in net exports, coupled with the recovery of public investment, reversed the downward trend in activity levels, ending what was the most severe Brazilian depression of the post war period. By the end of the year, this unusual export-led industrial recovery had begun to trickle down to non-tradables as overall employment and real wages rose.

The success in restoring external balance was not matched by any success in reducing the rate of price inflation which accelerated during 1983 and was kept high by the inertial mechanisms associated with widespread indexation. These problems were exacerbated after 1985, the first year of a newly appointed civilian government, with the subsequent increase of the fiscal deficit. The steady growth of the fiscal deficit (operational concept) from an insignificant level in 1985 to a level of 10 per cent of GDP at the end of 1990 favoured economic growth at first (in 1984–7) but led eventually to a fiscal crisis which was at the root of the plunge into hyperinflation experienced by the Brazilian economy early in 1990. Several 'heterodox shocks' – that is, stabilization plans where the central policy measure was a mandatory wage and prices freeze – were implemented, starting in 1986 with the 'Cruzado Plan'. None of them, including the fifth and most recent, the Collor Plan 2 launched in 1991, addressed the fiscal fundamentals of inflation; all produced only short-lived reductions in inflation. The dismal industrial growth performance after 1987 (see Table 3.3) as well as the declining investment levels in manufacturing are directly associated with the extreme macroeconomic instability of this period. In this context, enormous political importance has been assigned to stabilization and, more specifically, to the restoration of fiscal equilibrium. Yet despite the fiscal commitments of the Collor government, which took office in early 1990, problems of political implementation have continued to block important initiatives towards fiscal reform. High rates of inflation persist and are likely to remain until political conditions are engineered for a serious stabilization attempt.

The anti-competitive regulatory framework

As reviewed above, up to the crisis of the early 1980s Brazilian trade and industrialization policies followed 'classic' ISI policies in which the main influence upon the sectoral pattern of resource allocation came from strong import protection. During this period, the usual interaction between inward-looking policies and small market size relative to best-practice optimum scales led to high levels of concentration in almost all new domestic industries from the outset.[4] The creation of a relatively stable oligopolistic structure was reinforced by the combination of (i) a high level of multinational penetration in response to restrictive import barriers coupled with relatively little interference in the FDI process; (ii) the creation of 'national champions' through the special protection-cum-domestic subsidies treatment given to domestic firms in some import substitution projects, frequently stimulated by local concern over the possible creation of industrial 'enclaves' by vertically integrated MNCs and their affiliates; (iii) state ownership in sectors requiring large initial investment outlays, which created, in fact, monopolistic public enterprises.[5]

The rapid output growth and the progress of trade liberalization in the 1968–73 period contrasted with the period following the first oil shock. The post–1973 period witnessed not only the return of high levels of import protection but also the consolidation of a regulatory framework which gave stability to the pre-existing non-contestable industrial structure.[6] This section describes the basic features of this regulatory framework, which began to be reformed only in 1990. Its main features were: (i) a peculiar system of import protection relying mainly on quantitative restrictions; (ii) active export promotion policies, which neutralized the strong distortions of the import regime; (iii) extensive domestic regulation with a clear pro-incumbent bias, reinforcing natural entry barriers, preventing exit by distressed firms and solidifying market positions.

Import protection

As mentioned above, the basic characteristics of the Brazilian protectionist import regime can be traced to the early postwar external shocks which affected the balance of payments position at a time when, as in many other developing countries, policymakers had a preference for quantitative restrictions (QRs) and multiple exchange rates over tariffs and real devaluations, under unified exchange rates. During the late 1960s, considerable progress was made towards a more balanced structure of incentives with export promotion schemes, exchange rate unification and the adoption of a crawling peg and, to a lesser extent, some import liberalization in the form of relaxation of QRs and further tariff cuts.[7]

However, the oil shocks reinforced the traditional balance of payments rationale for the maintenance of generalized QRs. Through the late 1970s and the 1980s, under the pressure of recurrent balance of payments stringencies, import prohibitions were introduced to a large number of tariff items as CACEX,[8] the agency responsible for issuing import authorizations, perfected its system of consultations with sectoral agencies and business associations, either in connection with the application of the 'law of similars', or on an *ad hoc* basis. Sectoral agencies and regulatory bodies, though still subject to CACEX scrutiny, were delegated powers to forbid and to authorize imports, which gave them great leverage in project approval and in the definition of sectoral industrial policies. This marked a significant diversification and decentralization of administrative obstacles to imports. Local content requirements proliferated – as an extraordinarily effective line of defence against imports – as conditions for access to fiscal incentives, credit from official institutions, and public procurement.

As a corollary of this decentralization of import controls many 'special import regimes' appeared. Favoured importing firms that needed to bypass local content requirements or other protectionist barriers invariably applied for tariff exemptions or reductions under such regimes, which were almost automatically granted either by specific legislation, or on an *ad hoc* basis, by the Federal Tariff Commission. The nature of the 'special regimes' was quite varied, comprising forty-two different types in 1989 including, for example, exporters' imports and purchases of food buffer stocks; in addition to which there were schemes administered by sectoral or regional agencies, state enterprises and *ad hoc* government bodies and councils. In each 'special regime' the exemptions from restrictive provisions on importing varied: they could involve any combination of tariff reductions; waiver from the 'law of similars', from submission of yearly 'import programmes' by firms, from external financing requirements or from 'negative lists'.[9] As a result of the proliferation of such 'special regimes', nearly two-thirds of Brazilian imports entered the country in 1985 with tariff reductions or exemptions. An interesting consequence of this was the large difference between the legal tariffs and the ones effectively collected, which can be gauged by calculating import tax revenues as a percentage of import value. In 1984, while the average tariff in manufacturing was 90.1 per cent, the 'true' level was 19.1 per cent; and while average effective rates of protection computed with legal tariffs reached 166 per cent, the 'true' rates averaged only 34.5 per cent. In 1989, when legal tariffs were brought down to an average of 49.4 per cent, 'true' tariffs, i.e. the effectively-paid rate, averaged 8.3 per cent.

Export promotion

The high levels of protection created a generalized anti-export bias which, in addition, displayed a large dispersion across industries (Tyler, 1983: 564). Interestingly, however, this bias was offset in many specific industries by export incentives that put them in a more or less 'neutral' regime. In 1984, for instance, the aggregate value of all export incentives reached 48.7 per cent of the FOB value of exports; 35.5 per cent was made up of rebates and exemptions of indirect taxes, 9.1 per cent came from benefits associated with draw-back operations and the rest (4.1 per cent) from subsidized credit and income tax reductions (Neves and Moreira, 1987: 484). Indeed, a positive and significant (rank) correlation was found, both in 1973 and 1977 (Neves, 1985: 67), between industry-level effective rates of protection and rates of export promotion (the value of incentives as a proportion of the value of exports), suggesting that export incentives were necessary to offset the prevailing structure of protection and thus were a *sine qua non* for sustained export performance. This phenomenon – of high protection together with high export subsidies – constitutes a double distortion in neoclassical terms; orthodoxy would require a devaluation cum removal (or reduction) of export subsidies and tariffs. The traditional obstacle to this simplification of the trade regime, as seen through Brazilian eyes, has been the inflationary consequences of real devaluation.

An important instrument conceived to bypass the structure of protection was the BEFIEX[10] programme. It consisted basically of tax exemptions on imports and freedom from 'similarity' examinations for inputs and capital goods in exchange for export commitments from the importers which were never below double the value of the allowed imports. The commitments were made in multi-year contracts that, initially, were mostly signed by MNC affiliates. Over the years the programme turned into a 'mechanism through which national firms seek to reduce import taxes on capital goods and to circumvent "similarity" examinations', i.e. a scheme through which exporting firms could get access to imports without which competitiveness would not be possible (Matesco, 1988: 15–16). As shown in Table 3.4, under this programme exports increased more than tenfold during the 1974–81 period, and fourfold during the 1982–9 period. There was a four-fold increase in the trade balance under the programme from 1978 to 1980, and another sevenfold increase from 1982 to 1989. The share of MNCs in the programme's exports fell significantly after the mid–1970s. Thereafter, the programme's share in total manufactured exports increased – from 16 per cent in 1975–9 to 23 per cent in 1980–4 (and approximately 3 per cent

Table 3.4 Exports and trade balance under BEFIEX and sale of foreign firms,[a]
Brazil, 1972–89

| Year | BEFIEX programme | | | | | Manufacturing exports | % BEFIEX |
	Programme exports[b]	% of foreign firms	Trade balance[b]	Contracts Total	MNCs		
1972	2	100	−10	2	2	898	0.0
1973	70	100	−100	3	3	1,434	4.9
1974	212	100	−72	3	2	2,263	9.4
1975	335	100	63	4	3	2,584	12.9
1976	456	98.5	174	11	4	2,776	16.4
1977	655	90.2	348	5	3	3,840	17.0
1978	865	88.4	222	10	5	5,083	17.0
1979	1,119	82.2	646	16	3	6,645	16.8
1980	1,793	74.3	1,068	35	12	9,928	17.9
1981	2,581	77.5	1,188	35	4	11,884	21.7
1982	2,343	70.6	1,031	79	25	10,253	22.4
1983	2,935	60.6	2,110	25	7	11,276	24.8
1984	3,872	58.0	2,865	44	11	15,102	26.1
1985	4,851	54.2	3,603	44	15	14,062	35.5
1986	5,128	n.a.	4,405	n.a.	n.a.	12,386	41.4
1987	7,629	n.a.	6,912	n.a.	n.a.	14,831	51.4
1988	9,573	n.a.	8,714	n.a.	n.a.	19,902	48.1
1989	8,979	n.a.	8,119	n.a.	n.a.	19,594	48.3

Sources: Neves and Moreira (1987: tables 5, 7 and 8); *Gazeta Mercantil*, 25 May 1990.
[a] The sample includes all exporting firms with foreign control.
[b] Millions of dollars.

of imports), reaching slightly over 50 per cent in 1987, where it has remained since (Neves and Moreira, 1987: 7; *Gazeta Mercantil*, 25 May 1990).

Industrial policy

The basic features of the framework of incentives and regulations created in the late 1950s were refined and consolidated by the very active policies followed in the late 1960s and thereafter, especially in the 1970s, in response to the perceived structural balance of payments problems created by the rise in oil price, as part of PND-II. Among these features it is important to emphasize: (i) the pervasiveness of fiscal incentives granted both in the form of credits from the state development bank, BNDES,[11] and directly by some government bodies; (ii) the regulations enhancing non-contestability of markets, particularly the direct investment licensing limitations imposed by sectoral or regional bodies or by the mechanism of 'sectoral agreements' coordinated by the Interministry Council on Prices (CIP[12]), the price control authority;[13] and (iii) most importantly, the imposition of local content requirements (*índices de nacionalização*) by BNDES – defined as the ratio between local cost components and total cost of a given product[14] – as a condition for access to its lines of subsidized credit for acquisition of capital goods, and also by other government bodies and state enterprises, especially in the context of public procurement contracts.[15] A 1988 decree actually made local content requirements enforceable in the production of all goods receiving any form of subsidy, purchased by any public body, or receiving any sort of financing from official institutions.[16] Table 3.5 provides a rough picture of the incidence of these dispositions.

Note that regulation is generally light in traditional industries, with the exception of price controls in sensitive products and in specific segments of industries. Wheat milling, for example, is subject to capacity regulation enforced through the rationing of imported wheat. Intermediate products are largely subject to price controls, given their weight in wholesale price indexes; these result in high entry barriers and constant complaints with regard to anti-competitive practices, as in the archetypal case of the cement industry.

In many industries the key source of regulation as regards the expansion of productive capacity and 'adequate' levels of minimum domestic content was the project evaluation activity carried out by the Industrial Development Council (CDI[17]) which was created in 1969 and closed in 1988. The Council also played an important role in coordinating the action of other key bodies such as the BNDES, some large industrial public enterprises and the Tariff Policy Commission (CPA[18]), which decided on concessions of trade-related tax exemptions on imported inputs. Although the resources granted as benefits under industrial promotion schemes on a discretionary basis were substantial – amounting to between 0.5 per cent and 0.8 per cent of GDP in the early 1980s (World Bank, 1990) – the bulk of these investment incentives were concentrated in a few targeted capital-intensive intermediate input industries: chemicals and pharmaceuticals accounted for 43.1 per cent of investments made under CDI; and non-metallic goods, including paper and cement, accounted for 34.2 per cent.[19] In consequence, as shown in Table 3.5, these sectors were subject to stringent local content requirements. In segments such as heavy (made-to-order) capital goods, electrical equipment and transport equipment, procurement rules on the part of public enterprises were the key source of local content requirements. The importance of local content requirements as an import restriction device for capital goods and parts cannot be underestimated. The share in manufacturing value added of industries shown in Table 3.5 as subject to some degree of local content requirement is slightly over 50 per cent, an astonishing figure (since it refers only to modern industries) that has crucial implications for the conduct of trade policy and, more particularly, for the process of liberalization planned for the 1990s.

75

Table 3.5 Regulation and promotion schemes in Brazilian manufacturing, 1989

Sector/subsector	Nature of regulation	Local content requirement	Price controls	Nature of incentives
Metal products (steel, rolled flats)	H; H (cap. licensing)	–	L; H	H (fiscal and credit); H
Machinery	H (access to Finame)	H (Finame, PSE)	H	H (fiscal and credit)
(made to order)	H (access to Finame and PSE)	H (Finame and particip. agreem.)	L	H (fiscal, credit and procurement)
Electric equipment (telecommunications equipment)	M; H (access to PSE)	H-M; H (PSE)	M-L; L	H (fiscal and credit); H (fiscal, credit and procurement)
(informatics products)	M (cap. licensing)	H (SEI)	L	M
(consumer electronics)	M (cap. licensing)	L (SUFRAMA)	M	M (fiscal)
Transport equipment (shipbuilding)	H (cap. licensing and access to PSE)	H-M (PSE)	L	H (fiscal, credit and procurement)
(aircraft)	M (access to PSE)	L	L	H (fiscal and procurement)
(cars, trucks, buses)	M (conditionality on incentives)	H (CDI)	H	H (fiscal)
(railway material)	M (access to PSE)	–	L	H (fiscal, credit and procurement)
Chemicals (petrochemicals)	M (conditionality on incentives); H (cap. licensing and conditionality on incentives)	H (CDI); H (CDI)	H; H	M (fiscal and credit); M (fiscal, credit and import prices)
(Camaçari petrochemical complex)	H (idem)	H (CDI)	H	M (idem plus income tax exemption)
Pharmaceuticals	M (access to govt market)	M	H	H (fiscal and procurement)
Non-metallic minerals (cement)	L; H (conditionality on incentives)	–; L	H-M; H	L; H (fiscal)
Paper products	M (conditionality on incentives)	M (CDI)	M	M (fiscal and credit)
Traditional[a]	L	L	M-H	L

Source: Based on World Bank (1990: 24–5).

The qualifications (H for high, M for medium and L for low) indicate the extent of government regulation, including barriers to entry, capacity limitations, conditionality on the access to incentives and others; the magnitude of requirements of local content (indication is provided as to the source of the requirement); the extent of price controls; and the magnitude of incentive available (with an indication of the nature of the incentive).

[a] Wood and furniture, rubber, leather and plastic products, perfumes and soaps, textiles and clothing, food and beverages, tobacco, printing and publishing, and miscellaneous. There are exceptional qualifications in some regulations (wheat milling) and incentives (wheat milling, textiles, and paper and printing).

BRAZILIAN COMPETITIVENESS

The substantial degrees of trade and industrial regulation and government interference with the competitive process, described in the previous section, were important supporting elements in the formative years of Brazilian industry. None the less, they seem to have had a fundamentally negative impact on entrepreneurial behaviour and industrial efficiency as they rewarded rent-seeking and inhibited managerial awareness of the strategic importance of the acquisition of technological capability. This shortcoming became particularly relevant at a time when there were very rapid changes in the post war technological paradigm upon which Brazilian industrial capability was built, and when continued manufactured export dynamism rested fundamentally on technological upgrading. For this reason the reforms in Brazilian trade and industrial policies undertaken in the early 1990s tended to emphasize industrial deregulation and sharpened competition policy, including, prominently, trade liberalization.

However, the relationship between the competitive regime and technological dynamism cannot be established purely on the grounds of a priori, theoretical, arguments. To probe this essentially empirical question this section follows two parallel, though by no means unrelated, paths: (i) investigation of the determinants of export performance; and (ii) investigation of the behaviour and, as far as possible, the determinants of productivity growth.

The sources of export growth in manufacturing

A crucial feature of the evolution of Brazilian competitiveness is that its improvement has been steady throughout the last two decades (see Nonnemberg, 1990) the recession and devaluations of the early 1980s, therefore, only reinforced long-term trends. This section explores the macroeconomic and microeconomic determinants of Brazilian competitiveness in manufacturing, which are mutually interdependent, in two separate subsections. The first subsection deals with macroeconomic influences on trade performance, particularly exchange rate policy, but also including fluctuations in domestic and external demand. It also devotes some attention to the impact of export incentives and mechanisms to bypass the very heavy structure of protection against imports. The next subsection considers determinants of competitiveness associated with market structure as well as with policies and other conditions favouring learning and technological innovation.

77

Table 3.6 Long-run manufactured export elasticities, Brazil

Price	Domestic demand	Foreign demand	Author	Period[a]
Manufactured export supply				
1.04[b]	−2.5[b]	−	Cardoso and Dornbusch (1980)	1960–77 A
1.19[b]	−2.1[b]	−	Markwald (1981)	1964–80 A
2.64	−4.5	−	Braga and Markwald (1983)	1959–81 A
1.10[b]	−1.3[b]	−	Rios (1986)	1964–84 A
1.39[b]	−1.6[b]	−	Zini (1988)	1970–86 Q
Manufactured export demand				
−0.68	−	2.53[b]	Lemgruber (1976)	1965–74 A
−1.12	−	2.19[b]	Pinto (1983)	1954–75 A
−2.82	−	2.59[b]	Braga and Markwald (1983)	1959–81 A
−1.38[b]	−	2.31[b]	Rios (1986)	1964–84 A
−0.31	−	4.92	Zini (1988)	1970–86 Q
Total export supply				
0.91	−1.0	−	Zini (1988)	1970–86 Q
Total export demand				
−0.17	−	0.75	Khan (1974)	1951–69 A
−0.41[b]	−	−1.97[b]	Lemgruber (1976)	1965–74 A
−0.95	−	2.89[b]	Zini (1988)	1970–86 Q

Source: Zini (1988: 650)
[a] A stands for annual and Q for quarterly data.
[b] Significant at a level of 5%.

Macroeconomic and policy factors in competitiveness

A survey of the extensive econometric work testing the links between the behaviour of aggregate manufactured exports and macroeconomic variables in the 1960s and 1970s reveals that, despite the variety of methodological approaches, the essential elements of all these exercises were very similar: a quantum index of manufactured exports, or their value in constant dollars, was regressed against variables such as the real exchange rate (adjusted for subsidies and tax incentives for exporters), world demand and cyclical influences, usually defined as shortfalls from a productive capacity (or potential output) variable (Braga and Markwald, 1983). More recent work uses a supply and demand equation specification. The estimates of price and world income elasticities of export demand, as well as price and domestic demand elasticity of export supply have displayed a fair amount of consistency, as shown in Table 3.6.

Manufactured export supply price elasticities are slightly above 1. Domestic demand was found to be an important negative influence on Brazilian manufactured exports, suggesting a clear 'vent-for-surplus' logic in Brazilian exports as is to be expected in a country with a large domestic market and in which exports represent a marginal activity for most exporting firms. Estimates of manufactured export price elasticities of demand are less homogeneous than the supply estimates, ranging from –0.31 to –2.82. Income elasticities of manufactured exports demand are consistently estimated as greater than 2, a very high value. The estimates for all elasticities of total exports are much lower than the ones for manufacturing.

The interpretation of these results involves some important issues. The influence of structural factors affecting export performance is not made explicit as, as far as capacity is concerned, these equations generally include only shortfalls from potential output; productive capacity increases in exporting industries, which are the result of the operation of structural factors, are hidden. A superficial reading of this literature could tend to associate export growth with domestic recessions, thus conveying the inappropriate impression of a contradiction between export-led and domestic-market-led growth.

On the price side it is important to distinguish between the effects of exchange rate policies and the effects of export subsidies. Most arguments emphasizing the 'artificiality' of Brazilian competitiveness underline the weight of the latter. It was already shown above that the value of export incentives in effect in Brazil from the late 1970s on was very substantial, which has constantly raised concern over the fiscal costs of export promotion.[20] Yet, the important point to observe is that, in a country in which the rate of effective protection is very high, the anti-export bias would also generally be very high if not offset by export promotion schemes attempting to place exporters into a more or less 'neutral' regime. Direct tax incentives as well as 'import-to-export' schemes, such as the BEFIEX which, as discussed above, played such an important role in manufactured export growth, are, thus, important to neutralize protection.

Structural influences

The debate about 'structural' elements that may explain the evolution of competitiveness over time has centred upon the relative importance of 'endogenous' mechanisms related to learning-by-doing and scale economies that accompany the process of 'maturation' of predominantly national firms in manufacturing,[21] and 'exogenous' influences, particularly those affecting the trade propensities of established foreign affiliates through processes of rationalization of global activities within MNCs.[22] The importance usually attached to 'endogenous' elements has been reinforced by the recent preeminence of the so-called 'new trade theories' which place great emphasis on the role of industrial organization features in creating competitiveness. More specifically, most models along these lines suggest an association between increases in size, or in rents connected to industrial concentration (or even to protection and 'market reserve policies'), and greater efficiency induced either by scale economies, learning-by-doing or R&D investment.[23] Yet this deterministic neo-Schumpeterian association

79

between size and competitiveness (efficiency) is very much open to question on empirical grounds.[24] Moreover, the empirical association between industrial organization features, including the trade regime, and competitiveness is not a clearcut one.[25]

The empirical literature addressing the relationship between export performance and industrial organization characteristics in the Brazilian case has devoted great attention to the association between export performance, firm size (or concentration), and foreign ownership. The methods used in controlling for other influences, or to purge multicollinearity problems from cross-section regressions, are crucial in establishing the existence of any meaningful correlation. The early entries to this literature use a 1978 income tax database including 15,122 reporting firms from which the first such study sought to investigate the distribution of export incentives according to firm size, ownership and regional location (Braga, 1981). It was found that incentives were appropriated mainly by larger firms, MNC affiliates (whose share of incentives was found to be larger than their share of exports) and richer regions, but the underlying multicollinearity problems were not adequately addressed.

These same data were later used to assert the lack of difference in export propensities between national and foreign firms (CEPAL, 1983). The authors' procedures were heavily criticized, however, for they did not control for firm size (Willmore, 1985: 620). A later, more careful study used an enlarged version of the same data set, to run regressions of export propensities on variables like industrial concentration, scale economies, capacity utilization, foreign ownership, tradability (proxied by geographical dispersion of production within the country), capital intensity, export incentives and R&D intensity (Braga and Guimarães, 1986). This study confirmed the relationships found in earlier macroeconomic studies, mentioned in the previous subsection, between export performance, incentives and domestic demand. The study also found positive relationships between export performance and industrial organization variables – market concentration, scale economies and R&D intensity – but failed to identify any significant influence of foreign ownership on export performance. A serious shortcoming in the identification of foreign firms in the 1978 data set resulted, however, in a very significant underestimation of their presence in Brazilian industry,[26] rendering some of the conclusions of the studies mentioned above, especially those relating to foreign ownership, quite questionable.

A more recent study, using the same 1978 data set but properly identifying foreign firms, conducted an extensive comparison of national and foreign firms using the methodology of matched pairs and obtained results substantially different from those of earlier studies (Willmore, 1985). It found that foreign firms exported a much larger proportion of their output than national firms of the same size even though they did *not* receive a

Table 3.7 Export performance and industrial organization, Brazil, 1980

Independent variable	Regressions	
	Probability of being an exporter	Exports
Constant[a]	−32.15	18.66
Foreign ownership[b]	1.32**	0.51**
State ownership	−0.76	0.25
R&D intensity (R&D expenditure as % sales)	0.06	0.26
Product differentiation[c]	28.17**	11.20**
Average wage	−0.09	−0.30**
Capital intensity[d]	−0.07**	0.29**
Vertical integration[e]	−0.69**	−0.88**
Size (value added)	2.53**	−1.09**
Size (value added) squared	−0.04**	0.06**
Tradability[f]	1.53**	–
Nominal protection	−0.44	–
Effective protection	0.12	–
R^2 (adjusted)	–	0.412
Degrees of freedom	–	3.584

Source: Willmore (1987: 315–18).
**Significant at level of 1%.
[a] Weighted average of intercepts.
[b] Foreign ownership defined as foreign equity share greater than 10%.
[c] Advertising intensity.
[d] Non-wage value added per worker in the first equation and fixed assets per worker in the second equation.
[e] Value added to gross output ratio.
[f] Geographical concentration of firms.

larger share of export incentives. In another study, Willmore (1987) used a sample of 17,053 firms in manufacturing in 1980, whose combined exports represented 74 per cent of Brazilian manufactured exports, and 652 of which were foreign. He estimated a recursive model in which the probability of a firm being an exporter was estimated through logit equations, and then export performance of exporters was explained. The main findings are summarized in Table 3.7.

Foreign ownership and product differentiation had significant positive influences both on the probability of being an exporter and on export performance. Interestingly, foreign ownership increased the odds of exporting by 3.75 (the anti-log of 1.32) times. The average wage, a proxy for skill intensity, had a weak influence on the probability of being an exporter and a negative impact on export performance. Capital intensity had a negative impact on the odds of exporting, but once the firm was an exporter it appeared with a positive sign. Vertical integration had a strong negative influence on both counts. Market concentration, which is not reported in the table, was not statistically significant in either equation. Nominal protection appeared, with a negative sign, as expected, whereas effective protection had a positive sign.[27] Finally, the influence of firm size was a complex one. Its influence was positive on the odds of exporting over the relevant size range but in terms of export performance its influence was negative when the firm was below the average size and positive when above it. Interestingly, the coefficient for size in the second equation was not statistically significantly different from 1, implying the absence of correlation between export propensity (exports/output) and size.

To sum up, the empirical evidence seems to show a positive influence of 'exogenous' determinants operating through foreign firms (foreign ownership) on export performance. Regarding other features of industrial organization, the evidence is clear on the positive influence of product differentiation and the negative influence of vertical integration on export performance. The precise nature of the relationship between size, other firm characteristics, or market structure features, on the one hand, and technological strategies and how firms evolve into export performers or, more generally, productivity growth, on the other, are much less clear. Between the rather general and exceedingly deterministic models of the 'new trade theory' and the many firm-specific case studies of successful technological acquisition,[28] there is vast unexplored territory for further research.

The sources of productivity growth in manufacturing

The previous section discussed the importance of macroeconomic influences and regulation-induced and/or industrial organization (structural) factors, to export behaviour. Presumably, these same factors should be determinants of yet another important aspect of firm performance, namely, productivity growth. In this section we compare the available estimates of TFP growth for Brazil in the last two decades and consider industrial organization and other influences, particularly trade orientation, on productivity growth.

The measurement of productivity growth is plagued with methodological and statistical problems,[29] as the dispersion of estimates generally seen in this literature shows. The work related to Brazil, summarized in Fig. 3.4, is no exception.

Differences between the several estimates are to be expected, given the variety of methodologies and databases employed by the authors. In these circumstances, comparisons between the estimates should be taken with a grain of salt. The magnitude of inconsistencies is very significant for some periods. Note, for example, that for 1960–5, when Brazil experienced a very sharp recession, a contrast is observed between the TFP growth estimates of Bonelli (1985) – 2.5 per cent for 1959–70 – and those of Elias (1978) – 0.2 per cent for 1960–5. The latter small figure is consistent with Verdoorn's law, given the growth deceleration in the first half of the 1960s.

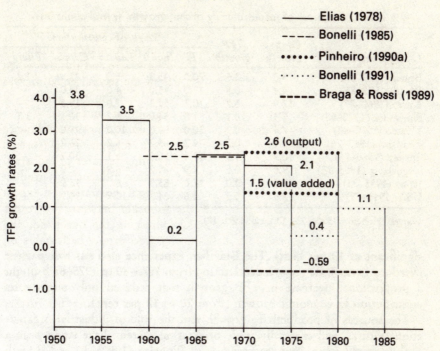

Figure 3.4 Estimates of TFP growth in manufacturing, Brazil, 1950–85

For the late 1960s and early 1970s some estimates showed positive rates (in the range of 2.1 per cent to 2.5 per cent.[30] Interestingly, Pinheiro (1990a) reported a lower rate for the 1970s on the basis of computations of residuals from factor contributions to manufacturing value added.[31] Braga and Rossi (1989) found a negative rate of TFP growth of 0.59 per cent for 1970–83,[32] signalling a sharp slowdown which, although probably exaggerated, seems to be confirmed by the low, though not as low, level of the more recent estimates of Bonelli. There appears to have been a productivity slowdown from the late 1970s onward which might be explained by the overall growth deceleration at this time; this influence should be controlled, however, in order to assess the precise relationship between TFP growth, increased competitiveness, and outward orientation since the second half of the 1970s.

The contribution of TFP growth to Brazilian economic growth is compared to that of other NICs, Japan and the USA in Table 3.8. Note that the Brazilian TFP growth performance is far superior to that of other countries, except for Korea. For all countries in the table, with the exception of Thailand, positive correlations were found between manufacturing output rates of growth and TFP growth, though only in three cases was this correlation significant at the 5 per cent level (another three cases were

Table 3.8 Sources of manufacturing output growth, several countries

Country/period	Output growth	TFP growth	Weighted contributions				
			TFP	Inputs	Labour	Capital	Energy
Brazil (1970–80)[a]	13.0	2.6	20.0	45.3	5.0	27.9	1.2
Brazil (1975–85)[b]	4.4	0.8	17.0	45.0	4.0	34.0	–
Korea (1960–77)	17.9	3.7	20.7	57.3	2.6	19.5	–
Singapore (1970–80)	8.3	0.1	1.0	54.9	9.7	30.1	3.3
Mexico (1970–80)	7.4	0.7	10.0	51.0	10.0	29.0	–
Thailand (1963–76)	16.4	0.7	4.2	63.4	6.2	26.2	–
Turkey (1963–76)	10.7	1.3	12.4	52.3	5.1	30.2	–
Yugoslavia (1965–78)	9.8	0.5	4.9	80.2	6.9	8.0	–
Japan (1955–73)	11.6	2.0	17.6	63.3	6.0	13.0	–
USA (1949–79)	3.8	0.5	13.6	64.7	10.9	10.9	–

Sources: [a]Pinheiro (1990a: 23); [b]Bonelli (1991: 17).

significant at 10 per cent). The Brazilian experience also fits this pattern (Verdoorn's law). Its growth deceleration from 1970–80 to 1975–85 brought a proportional decrease in TFP growth that reduced only slightly its contribution to economic growth (from 20 to 17 per cent).

The sources of productivity growth and the role of industrial organization features, and especially trade orientation therein, have lately been a hotly debated issue. The recent work of Pinheiro (1990a, b) and Bonelli (1991) address these issues directly. Both authors undertook a cross-section version of the exercise performed in Nishimizu and Robinson (1986), in which industrial TFP growth rates are regressed against the growth that is attributable to exports (EXP) and to import substitution (IS). The results were as follows:

$$\text{TFP GROWTH} = \quad 0.30 \quad + 0.55 \text{ EXP} + 0.80 \text{ IS} \quad R^2 = 0.59 \quad DW = 1.43$$
$$(1975\text{--}85) \qquad\quad (1.01) \qquad (2.13) \qquad (2.05)$$
$$\text{TFP GROWTH} = \quad 2.85 \quad - 0.01 \text{ EXP} + 0.34 \text{ IS} \quad R^2 = 0.07$$
$$(1970\text{--}80) \qquad\qquad\quad (-0.06) \qquad (1.54)$$

The first equation implies that both export-induced and import-substitution-induced output growth affect TFP growth positively, a result that seems consistent with the notion of 'efficient' import substitution, and, according to the authors, confirms 'the simple version of Verdoorn's Law, which implies that any expansion of the market, regardless of source, improves productivity performance' (Bonelli, 1991: 31–2). The second equation, which refers to an earlier period, shows the heterodox result that import substitution has a positive effect on productivity whereas export-induced expansion has a negative effect; however, none of the slope coefficients were statistically significant, which may have to do with the fact that in the 1970s by far the largest source of demand expansion for manufacturing was the domestic market.

According to Pinheiro (1990a: 30) domestic demand explained 83.4 per cent of manufacturing demand growth in the 1970s, with export expansion contributing 14.0 per cent and import substitution only 2.5 per cent. The second half of the 1970s saw much more significant efforts at import substitution, which showed their effects in the 1980s. Given the already small import coefficients Brazil had reached in the late 1970s, however, these efforts and effects meant a relatively small contribution to growth. Export expansion, on the other hand, increased significantly its contribution to total demand growth, accounting for nearly a quarter of overall output growth in 1975–85.

Table 3.9 shows that both import substitution and export expansion, especially the latter, were considerably more important in manufacturing that in total output. Export expansion represented 45.3 per cent of demand expansion in heavy industries and 36.8 per cent in high-tech industries; these estimates are consistent with the increases in export propensities in these industries that were documented in Table 3.2. In 'light' industries the contribution of export expansion was more modest, 21.2 per cent, though still substantial. Import substitution was undertaken primarily in the high-tech group and, within that group, in mechanical equipment. In broad terms, the figures in Table 3.9 confirm, again, the impression of a growing outward orientation, especially in the more sophisticated segments of manufacturing, though they had started from a situation in which export orientation was a marginal activity at best. With the growing importance of exporting, the question to be asked is what is the relationship, if any, between TFP growth and outward orientation, controlling for various industrial organization influences over TFP growth.

Indications along these lines are provided by the regression results in Table 3.10; the dependent variable in each of the regressions was industry-level TFP growth. These regressions were run on industrial census data for 1970 and 1980 using a three-digit classification, generating 112 different industries. Table 3.10 records three types of variables: (i) those related to trade performance, from which the increased commitment to exporting appears to be the most important (positive) influence on TFP growth, lending support to the 'orthodox' presumption of a positive correlation between exporting and efficiency; (ii) those associated with investment and growth, which show growth of firm size and investment rates both positively and highly significantly related to growth of TFP, consistent with expectations from Verdoorn's law; and (iii) those related to industrial organization features. Industrial concentration had a positive and significant, though small, impact on TFP growth, which confirms, for what it is worth, the neo-Schumpeterian presumption of a positive association between non-contestable markets and innovation. The regression coefficient for establishment age, a proxy for learning, was negative and insignificant.

Table 3.9 Sources of manufacturing demand growth, Brazil, 1970–85

	Weight in value added	Consumption expansion	Investment expansion	Export expansion	Import substitution
Memo: total output	–	83.4	–	14.0	2.6
Total manufacturing	100.0	47.5	4.4	33.6	15.0
'Heavy'	34.6	31.6	7.8	45.3	15.5
Non-metallic minerals	5.7	20.0	28.0	41.0	12.0
Metallurgy	11.8	12.0	4.0	57.0	27.0
Pulp and paper	2.7	37.0	2.0	48.0	13.0
Chemicals	14.5	51.0	4.0	37.0	8.0
'High-tech'	26.1	28.8	0.9	36.8	32.9
Mechanical equipment	10.2	14.0	0.0	25.0	62.0
Electric and communications equipment	7.0	41.0	4.0	31.0	24.0
Transport material	7.6	21.0	–1.0	62.0	15.0
Pharmaceuticals	1.6	111.0	2.0	17.0	–30.0
'Light'	39.2	72.9	3.8	21.2	2.4
Wood and furniture	4.4	27.0	17.0	48.0	8.0
Rubber	1.4	44.0	2.0	45.0	10.0
Leather	0.5	36.0	0.0	67.0	–4.0
Soaps and perfumes	0.9	86.0	0.0	10.0	5.0
Plastics	2.3	47.0	9.0	36.0	7.0
Textiles	6.2	60.0	1.0	36.0	3.0
Clothing and footwear	4.7	79.0	0.0	19.0	1.0
Food	11.7	110.0	3.0	–6.0	–6.0
Beverages	1.3	80.0	1.0	12.0	7.0
Tobacco	0.8	56.0	0.0	42.0	2.0
Printing and publishing	2.5	64.0	2.0	24.0	11.0
Miscellaneous	2.7	55.0	1.0	32.0	13.0

Source: Bonelli (1991: 25).

The main tenor of the results is that the key influence on TFP is that of growth and investment, i.e. the nexus usually associated with Verdoorn's law. The influence of the trade regime, as well as that of industrial organization variables, tends to be much weaker than that of growth-related variables. Nevertheless, it is possible to see that both greater trade involvement and industrial concentration appear to affect TFP positively. Note, however, that there were no controls for foreign ownership in this study.

Table 3.10 TFP growth, trade orientation and industrial organization, Brazil, 1970–80 (t-values in parentheses)

Independent variable	Regressions			
	1	2	3	4
Constant	1.848	2.462	–	–
Change in export propensties	0.447	0.390	0.493	0.503
	(2.31)	(1.99)	(3.12)	(3.20)
Change in import propensity (inputs)	–	0.082	−0.023	–
		(3.25)	(−0.80)	
Royalties as % of profits[a]	0.556	1.304	1.038	1.029
	(0.62)	(1.47)	(1.40)	(1.39)
Imports as % of investment[a]	0.022	0.016	0.012	0.011
	(1.39)	(0.99)	(0.86)	(0.79)
Import propensity for inputs[b]	0.068	–	–	0.024
	(3.68)			(1.01)
Average firm size (growth rate)	–	–	0.299	0.274
			(4.97)	(4.56)
% of skilled workers on employment[a]	–	–	0.189	0.051
			(1.52)	(0.35)
Industrial concentration[a]	–	–	0.032	0.025
			(2.56)	(2.03)
Relative TFP growth[c]	–	–	0.050	0.051
			(2.99)	(3.07)
Establishment age[d]	–	–	−0.034	−0.039
			(−1.12)	(−1.27)
Investment as % of capital stock[e]	–	–	5.914	4.726
			(2.20)	(1.95)
R squared	0.249	0.222	0.554	0.556
Degrees of freedom	75	75	69	69

Source: Pinheiro (1990a).
[a] 1970.
[b] 1980.
[c] TFP growth as % of the highest TFP rate of growth in the sample.
[d] Share of output of establishments founded in the five years preceding the two censuses, i.e. 1970 and 1980.
[e] Average 1970–80.

CONCLUSIONS: POLICIES FOR 'WHALES' AND 'TIGERS'

This paper has attempted to provide an assessment of the interrelationships between trade policy and economic performance. It was concerned to show that trade policy's influence on performance works through the modifications it engenders in an industrial structure of historically given characteristics, within which the competitive process has certain well-defined features. In addition, it showed that macroeconomic influences provide the framework within which firm level decisions are made, and thus affect, sometimes quite importantly, the outcome of otherwise microeconomic processes.

Against this backdrop, we offered an extensive review of the highly interventionist Brazilian trade and industrial policies and argued that such policies were crucial to the shaping of Brazilian industry. In order to assess more specifically the role of trade and industrial policies on performance, we reviewed three avenues of research: (i) the influence of macroeconomic and policy variables on export performance since the 1970s; (ii) cross-sectional econometric studies relating industrial organization features to export performance; and (iii) factors affecting TFP growth. The conclusions emerging from these reviews, especially when considered together, are quite revealing. The export equations (Table 3.7) show the important influence of macro variables, in particular, domestic and foreign levels of economic activity on export performance in as large and relatively closed a country as Brazil. Price variables, i.e. exchange rate and other incentives, are also shown to be important influences, though it seems clear that incentives, differentiated by industry or firm, had a clear role in offsetting some of the detrimental effects of the structure of protection on competitiveness. Cross-sectional and more industry-specific evidence tends to confirm the importance of incentives and other mechanisms, such as, for instance, the BEFIEX programme, in bypassing the negative influence of the structure of protection.

The key finding from our review of empirical work on the sources of productivity growth provides a synthetic view of these issues. Three types of influences on TFP growth – macro factors, industrial structure features, and the trade regime (or trade involvement related indicators) – may be grouped together and their relative importance evaluated. The key finding was the overwhelming importance of macro factors as against industrial structure or trade variables. This yields the challenging suggestion that trade regime and industrial policies may only be of secondary importance as determinants of productivity growth, especially during periods of high growth. Indeed, Brazilian TFP growth during the 1970s (2.6 per cent) was second only to that of Korea (3.7 per cent) despite (or because of!) the influences of prevailing trade and industrial competition regimes. When growth collapsed, so did TFP growth. This suggests the provocative conclusion that the policy agenda should have been more specifically geared towards restoring growth than to reforming the trade and industrial competition regime. While this should not be used as an argument for downgrading the importance of reforming the opaque and distortive import regime in Brazil, it may serve to reduce common illusions as to the likely effects of trade policy reforms on growth performance.

These conclusions regarding the overwhelming importance of macroeconomic performance for efficiency and TFP growth can hardly, however, be generalized. Country size is a very specific feature of the Brazilian economy on which such conclusions seem quite fundamentally to rest. But it does offer an explanation for good trade and productivity performance that frees one both from the presumed association between highly interventionist policies and good performance, so dear to earlier Brazilian policymakers, and from the liberal view that the move towards neutrality after the mid–1960s was responsible for the rapid export growth in the 1970s. There is much more therefore, to the interrelationships between policies and performance than is posited at either extreme of the ideological spectrum.

As already mentioned, once one accepts the Verdoorn nexus, alluded to above as a crucial element in the explanation of Brazilian competitiveness, one is led to a primarily macroeconomically based theory for the decline of productivity and competitiveness, whose key element is the growing macroeconomic instability experienced in the second half of the 1980s. But could the latter be attributable in some degree to the trade and industrial policies adopted in the years before? An interesting line of response is that such policies defined a 'model' of development and, in particular, created a number of structural features that enhanced external vulnerability to the kinds of shock that occurred in rapid succession in the early 1980s. In this connection, it is interesting to recall the purported, and much debated, 'contrast', especially regarding openness, between the 'models' of development of East Asia and Latin America. Since a cool look at the trade and industrial policies of, say, Brazil and Korea would hardly reveal much contrast,[33] the puzzle can be redefined as why (some) East Asians did well after 1982 and some Latin American countries, like Brazil, plunged into hyper-inflations and protracted recessions.

The suggested answer to the puzzle may be an unexpected one – trade openness. For many years *reduced* openness was sought in Latin America as a means to reduce external vulnerability. Indeed, the commonsense argument that high openness, *as such*,[34] increased vulnerability to external influences can be found in the work of historians of Latin American experience under the classical gold standard, and has been repeatedly raised as a justification for inward-oriented industrialization, or for 'autonomous' growth paths. History, on the other hand, repeatedly reported a paradox: low openness was associated with high vulnerability; 'the tail wagged the dog' and not the reverse. Interestingly, after import substitution projects in the 1974 adjustment plan (PND-II) were taken to their ultimate consequences, the Brazilian economy reached self-sufficiency, a degree of overall import penetration that was about as low as was feasible (4.5 per cent). According to the old structuralist argument, external vulnerability should no longer have been there. But, alas, the next external shock, in 1982, hit as hard as ever. The challenging proposition is that, in the presence of high levels of external indebtedness, low trade openness *increased*, rather than reduced, external vulnerability.

In order to illustrate this proposition consider the following exercise. Take two equally indebted countries (in terms of their debt to GDP ratios),

Table 3.11 Brazil and Korea, comparative macroeconomic indicators

	Brazil	Korea
Real effective exchange rates, 1985		
(1980/1=100)	143	112
GDP in 1985 (1980=100)	117	137
Inflation in 1985 (%)	226	2.5
Openness: in 1980/1 (%)		
Exports to GDP	7	38
Imports to GDP	7	36
Debt/GDP (1983/4) (%)	46	53
Debt service/exports (1983/4) (%)	44	19

Sources: Collins and Park (1989); Cardoso and Fishlow (1989).

both of which, in response to the 1982 crisis, are to produce a trade surplus of enormous proportions, say, 6 per cent of GDP. Now consider that one of these countries is large and fairly closed, having, before the shock, export (equal to import) shares of GDP of 7 per cent. Call this a 'whale' country and the other, with import and export shares equal to 30 per cent, a 'tiger'. Let us further assume unit export supply and import demand elasticities with respect to the real exchange rate. In these conditions, it is easily seen that the 'whale' country, to reduce import shares to 4 per cent of GDP and increase exports shares to 10 per cent of GDP, would need to undertake a real devaluation of 44 per cent, while the 'tiger' country, to reduce the import share to 27 per cent of GDP and raise the export share to 33 per cent of GDP, would have to devalue by only 10 per cent. The larger the required real devaluation (or required reduction in domestic activity levels), the larger macroeconomic instability is likely to be.

While this has obviously been a stylized and simplified account, the actual figures for Brazil and Korea, shown in Table 3.11, fit it quite well. The similarity of debt to GDP ratios and the difference in measures of openness are very much in line with what was suggested in the above exercise. The difference in the debt service ratio stems directly from the difference in openness. The differences in real devaluations are strikingly similar to the ones assumed in the exercise, and the fact that Brazil grew much less and exhibited a much higher inflation rate seems to confirm the basics of the 'whale' versus 'tiger' exercise: i.e. openness helped, rather than hindered, external adjustment. It should also be noted that Korea's higher trade openness, by averting a liquidity crisis, made it easier both to maintain short-term growth and to effect the distributive adjustments needed to increase domestic savings so as to sustain higher long-term growth.

The fact that Brazil was, indeed, a highly closed economy and was thus especially vulnerable to the 1982 crisis should not, however, be seen, as recently put, as 'a reflection of a God-given fact' but as the product 'of the policy option to pursue a largely inward-oriented import substituting development strategy during most of the post-World War period' (Bianchi, 1988: 196). If anything, the *key* lesson of the 1980s for a 'whale' country is that 'biological transformation' should be sought, i.e. increasing openness should be seen as desirable, not least because of its crucial importance in insulating growth from external shocks. Thus, trade liberalization makes sense as a policy proposition to increase competitiveness and productivity growth, though for reasons somewhat different from the microeconomic ones normally used to justify it. Its purpose is, rather, to enhance macroeconomic stability. To believe in this means to support the current drive towards liberalization throughout Latin America, for reasons divergent from the ones normally used to justify it. If this revisionist approach is correct, we may need to rethink such traditional liberalization issues as timing and sequencing in a new light. This, however, is a task for further research.

NOTES

1 Cf. OECD (1988). According to this study, comparable figures for the G7 countries were 27.7 per cent for the US, 14.3 per cent for Japan, 11.7 per cent for Germany, 7.2 per cent for France, 3.0 per cent for the UK, and 2.1 per cent for Canada. Mexico's share was 1.8 per cent and Korea's as well as Taiwan's share was 0.6 per cent.

2 This section draws upon Fritsch and Franco (1992b).

3 For example, in the classic study of J. Bhagwati (1978: 216).

4 For a discussion of the dynamics of such a process, see Merhav (1971).

5 For a more detailed discussion see Fritsch and Franco (1992b).

6 As forcefully argued in World Bank (1990) *passim*. Non-contestability is used here in the usual sense, namely, as an attribute of markets in which incumbents are not threatened by entry of potential competitors.

7 For an assessment of this liberalization episode see Coes (1991).

8 CACEX: Carteira de Comércio Exterior (Foreign Trade Department, Bank of Brazil).

9 'Import programmes' were required by CACEX to programme the issue of licences through the year. External financing requirements applied to imports with unit values above a given amount. For these imports, if external financing with maturities over a given duration were not available, the importation would not be authorized. Negative lists were enforced by CACEX and by the SEI (Secretaria Especial de Informática/Special Secretariat of Informatics). A detailed description of Brazilian QRs can be found in World Bank (1989).

10 BEFIEX: Comissão para a Concessão de Benefícios Fiscais e Programas Especiais de Exportação (Special Programme of Fiscal Incentives for Exports).

11 BNDES: Banco Nacional de Desenvolvimento Econômico a Social (National Economic and Social Development Bank).

12 CIP: Conselho Interministerial de Preços (Interministry Council on Prices).

13 On price control as a device to enforce entry barriers, see Fritsch and Franco (1989b).

14 In some cases imports were considered at CIF values, sometimes not, and the

ratios sometimes were computed in terms of weight, depending on the demanding agency.

15 For capital goods more generally, the access to FINAME (Agência Especial de Financiamento Industrial/Special Agency for Industrial Financing) credits – available to buyers of such goods at BNDES – depended on having the product registered in a FINAME listing with a predetermined local content requirement ranging between 70 and 85 per cent. For the informatics industry, local content requirements were imposed by SEI at very high levels – over 90 per cent. Interestingly, local content requirements were enforced on the substantially lower ratios – around 30 per cent – which was accepted by the industry as a quid pro quo for permission not to export more than 10 per cent of their output.

16 Article 16, Decree 2433, 19 May 1988.

17 CDI: Conselho de Desenvolvimento Industrial (Industrial Development Council).

18 CPA: Comissão de Política Aduaneira (Tariff Policy Commission).

19 Though together these two groups represented only 37 per cent of the projects approved by CDI. Cf. World Bank (1990: 41).

20 Concerns have also been voiced as to the possibility that benefits were distributed in a regressive fashion (Braga, 1981).

21 As hypothesized, for example, in Teitel and Thoumi (1986).

22 As explored, for example, by Fritsch and Franco (1992a).

23 Examples are Krugman (1984) and Rodrik (1992).

24 For a survey see Scherer (1984).

25 'There is no clear cut confirmation of the hypothesis that countries with an external orientation benefit from greater growth in technical efficiency in the component sectors of manufacturing; combined with the relatively small static costs of protection, this finding leaves those with a predilection towards a neutral regime in a quandary' (Pack, 1992). Indeed, the fact that the empirical arguments for defending export promotion vis-à-vis import substitution on the grounds of technical efficiency are simply not there was even admitted by Bhagwati (1988: 39–40). For a more recent discussion reaffirming these results see Tybout (1990).

26 Firms controlled by holding companies established in Brazil but controlled by foreign residents were considered national firms (see Willmore, 1985: 624–5).

27 Note that holding the price of the final product constant, an increase in the effective rate of protection, implies a reduction in the price of intermediate inputs, which is attainable via a production subsidy or a bypass of the structure of protection through a special import regime.

28 See Katz (1984) for a review.

29 For a review see Tybout (1990).

30 Pinheiro (1990a: 21) derives alternative estimates by using different measures for the inputs of labour and capital, obtaining numbers between 1.2 per cent and 3.1 per cent.

31 Alternative estimates, obtained through different measures for the inputs of labour and capital, are between 1.2 per cent and 2.7 per cent.

32 The adequacy of the database used by Braga and Rossi has been seriously questioned. Interestingly, in this connection, one of the authors in another paper, Braga and Hickman (1990), using the same database, reports sectoral TFP growth rates, defined as residuals on value added growth, which, using 1980 weights in value added, would indicate a positive rate of growth of TFP of 4.91 per cent.

33 See the review of Pack and Westphal (1986).
34 In addition to factors like commodity and geographical concentration of exports.

REFERENCES

Abreu, M. P. (ed.) (1989) *A Ordem do Progresso: 100 anos de política econômica republicana*, Rio de Janeiro: Campus Editora.

Baer, W. *et al.* (1987) 'Structural Changes in Brazil's Industrial Economy: 1960–1980', *World Development* 15.

Ballance, R.H. (1987) *International Industry and Business*, London: Allen & Unwin.

Batista, J.C. (1987) 'Brazil's Second National Development Plan and its Growth cum Debt Strategy', in *Instituto de Economia Industrial*, Rio de Janeiro: UFRJ.

Bhagwati, J. (1978) *Anatomy and Consequences of Exchange Control Regimes*, New York, Cambridge: NBER and Ballinger.

—— (1988) 'Outward Orientation: Trade Issues', in V. Corbo *et al.* (eds) *Growth Oriented Adjustment Programs*, Washington: International Monetary Fund and the World Bank.

Bianchi, A. (1988) 'Adjustment in Latin America, 1981–86', in V. Corbo *et al.* (eds) *Growth Oriented Adjustment Programs*, Washington: International Monetary Fund and the World Bank.

Bonelli, R. (1985) 'Além do Ajuste; uma nota sobre dilemas e limitações da industrialização brasileira na segunda metade dos anos 80', *Estudos Econômicos* 15.

—— (1991) 'Growth and Productivity in Brazilian Industries: Impacts of Trade Orientation', Departamento de Economia PUC–RJ, Texto para Discussão no. 258, June.

Braga, H. C. (1981) 'Aspectos Distributivos do Esquema de Subsídios Fiscais à Exportação de Manufaturados', *Pesquisa e Planejamento Econômico* 11/3, December.

—— and Guimarães, E. P. (1986) 'Exportações e Estrutura Industrial', *Pesquisa e Planejamento Econômico* 16(3), December.

—— and Hickman, E. (1990) 'A Produtividade Total dos Fatores', mimeo, IPEA/INPES, Rio de Janeiro.

—— and Markwald, R. (1983) 'Funções de Oferta e Demanda de Exportações de Manufaturados no Brasil: estimativa de um modelo simultâneo', *Pesquisa e Planejamento Econômico* 13(3), December.

—— and Rossi, J. W. (1989) 'A Produtividade Total dos Fatores de Produçao na Indústria Brasileira', *Pesquisa e Planejamento Econômico* 19(2), August.

—— *et al.* (1988) 'Proteção Efetiva no Brasil: uma estimativa a partir da comparação de preços', Série Epico no. 13, IPEA/INPES, Rio de Janeiro.

Cardoso, E. and Fishlow, A. (1989) 'The Macroeconomics of Brazilian External Debt', in J. D. Sachs (ed.) *Developing Country Debt and the World Economy*, Chicago: The University of Chicago Press and NBER.

CEPAL (1983) *Dos Estudios sobre Empresas Transnacionales en Brasil*, Estudios e Informes de la CEPAL 31, Santiago.

Chenery, H., Robinson, S. and Syrquin, M. (1988) *Industrialization and Growth: A Comparative Study*, Oxford: Oxford University Press.

Coes, D. V. (1991) 'Brazil', in M. Michaely, D. Papageorgiou and A. Choksi, *Liberalizing Foreign Trade*, vol.4, *The Experience of Brazil, Colombia and Peru*, Oxford: Blackwell.

Collins, S. M. and Park, W. A. (1989) 'External Debt and Macroeconomic Performance in South Korea', in J. D. Sachs (ed.) *Developing Country Debt and the World Economy*, Chicago: The University of Chicago Press and NBER.

Elias, V.J. (1978) 'Sources of Economic Growth in Latin American Countries', *Review of Economics and Statistics* 60(3), August.

Fajnzylber, F. (1983) *La Industrialización Trunca de America Latina*, Buenos Aires: Centro de Economia Transnacional.

Fritsch, W. and Franco, G. H. B. (1989a) 'Trade Policy, Trade Performance and Structural Change in Four Latin American Countries', a report prepared for UNCTAD.

—— and Franco, G. H. B. (1989b) 'Efficient Industrialization in a Technologically Dependent Economy: The Current Brazilian Debate', in *Competition and Economic Development*, Paris: OECD.

—— and Franco, G. H. B. (1992a) 'Foreign Direct Investment and Patterns of Industrialization and Trade in Developing Countries: Notes on the Brazilian Experience', in G. K. Helleiner (ed.) *Trade Policy, Industrialization and Development: New Perspectives*, Oxford: Clarendon Press.

—— and Franco, G. H. B. (1992b) *Foreign Direct Investment and Industrial Restructuring in Brazil: Issues and Trends*, Paris: OECD Development Centre.

Furtado, C. (1969) *Formação Econômica do Brasil*, Sao Paulo: Cia. Editora Nacional.

International Monetary Fund, *International Financial Statistics*.

IPEA (Instituto de Pesquisa Econômica Aplicada), *Boletim de Conjuntura*, several issues.

Katz, J. M. (1984) 'Domestic Technological Innovations and Dynamic Comparative Advantage: Further Reflections on a Comparative Case Study Program', *Journal of Development Economics* 16.

Krugman, P.R. (1984) 'Import Protection as Export Promotion: International Competition in the Presence of Oligopoly and Economies of Scale', in H. Kierzkonski (ed.) *Monopolistic Competition and International Trade*, Oxford: Clarendon Press.

Lafay, G. (1988) 'Les Indicateurs de Specialisation Internationale', Document de Travail CEP–II.

Malan, P. and Bonelli, R. (1976) 'Os Limites do Possível: notas sobre balanço de pagamentos e indústria nos anos 70', *Pesquisa e Planejamento Econômico* 6/2, August.

—— and Bonelli, R. (1990) 'Brazil 1950–1980: Three Decades of Growth Oriented Economic Policies', IPEA–INPES, Rio de Janeiro, Texto para Discussão Interna no. 187, março.

Matesco, V. (1988) 'As Novas Diretrizes da Política Industrial: relatório do seminário', Estudos de Política Industrial e Comércio Exterior, Série EPICO no. 14.

Merhav, M. (1971) *Technological Dependence Monopoly and Growth*, New York: Pergamon Press.

Neves, R.B. (1985) *Exportações e Crescimento Industrial no Brasil*, Rio de Janeiro: IPEA–INPES.

—— and H.C. Moreira (1987) 'Os Programs BEFIEX e Alguns Mitos a Respeito', mimeo, Brasília.

Nishimizu, M. and Robinson, S. (1986) 'Productivity Growth in Manufacturing' in Chenery, Robinson and Syrquin (eds) *Industrialization and Growth: A Comparative Study*, ch.10, pp. 283–308, London: Oxford University Press.

Nonnemberg, M. (1990) 'Vantagens Comparativas Reveladas, Custo Relativo de Fatores e Intensidade de Recursos Naturais: resultados para o Brasil, 1980–88', mimeo, IPEA–INPES, Rio de Janeiro.

OECD (1987) *Structural Adjustment*, Paris: Committee on International Investment and MNEs, OECD.
—— (1988) *The Newly Developing Countries: Challenge and Opportunity for OECD Industries*, Paris: OECD.
Pack, H. (1992) 'Learning and Productivity Change in Developing Countries', in G. K. Helleiner (ed.) *Trade Policy, Industrialization and Development: A Reconsideration*, Toronto and Helsinki: WIDER.
Pack, H. and Westphal, L. (1986) 'Industrial Strategy and Technological Change: Theory versus Reality', *Journal of Development Economics* 22(1): 87–128.
Pinheiro, A. C. (1990a) 'Measuring and Explaining Total Factor Productivity Growth: Brazilian Manufacturing in the 1970s', IPEA–INPES, Texto para Discussão Interna no. 189, March.
—— (1990b) 'Technical Efficiency in Brazilian Manufacturing Establishments: Results for 1970 and 1980', IPEA–INPES, Texto para Discussão Interna no. 190, June.
Rios, S.M.P. (1987) 'Exportações Brasileiras de Produtos Manufaturados: uma avaliação econométrica para o período 1964–84', *Pesquisa e Planejamento Econômico* 17(2), August.
Rodrik, D. (1992) 'Closing the Technological Gap: Does Trade Liberalization Help?', in G.K. Helleiner (ed.) *Trade Policy, Industrialization and Development: A Reconsideration*, Toronto and Helsinki: WIDER.
Scherer, F.M. (1984) *Innovation and Growth: Schumpeterian Perspectives*, Cambridge: MIT Press.
Teitel, S. and Thoumi, F. (1986) 'From Import Substitution to Exports: the Manufacturing Exports Experience of Argentina and Brazil', *Economic Development and Cultural Change* 34.
Tybout, J.R. (1991) 'Researching the Trade–Productivity Link: New Directions', World Bank, PRE, Working Paper Series 638.
Tyler, W. (1983) 'The Anti-Export Bias in Commercial Policies and Export Performance: Some Evidence from the Recent Brazilian Experience', *Weltwirtschaftliches Archiv* 119.
United Nations, *International Trade Yearbook* and *National Accounts Statistics*.
UNIDO (1985) *Industry in the 1980s: Structural Change and Interdependence*, New York: United Nations.
Willmore, L. (1985) 'Controle Estrangeiro e Concentração na Indústria Brasileira', *Pesquisa e Planejamento Econômico* 17.
—— (1987) 'Transnationals and Foreign Trade', Salvador, *Anais* XV° Econtro da ANPEC.
World Bank (1983) *Política Industrial e Exportação de Manufaturados*, Rio de Janeiro:, Fundação Getúlio Vargas.
—— (1987) *World Development Report*, New York: Oxford University Press.
—— (1989) *Trade Policy in Brazil: A Case for Reform*, Washington, DC: World Bank.
—— (1990) *Industrial Regulatory Policy and Investment Incentives in Brazil*, Washington, DC: Industry Development Division, World Bank.
Zini, Jr. A.A. (1988) 'Funções de Exportação e Importação para o Brasil', *Pesquisa e Planejamento Econômico* 18(3), December.

4

THE CHILEAN TRADE LIBERALIZATION AND EXPORT EXPANSION PROCESS 1974–90

Patricio Meller

The author acknowledges the helpful comments received from Gerry Helleiner, Lance Taylor, Juan Eduardo Coeymans, and CIEPLAN colleagues.

INTRODUCTION

Before 1974 Chile had a highly restrictive foreign trade regime which included quotas, prior import deposits, licences, foreign exchange budgets, forbidden import lists, special regimes for particular regions, for particular industries and for public firms, and quite high nominal tariffs. In a five-year period, 1974–9, all non-tariff barriers were eliminated and the average (highest) nominal tariff rate was reduced from 105 per cent (750 per cent) to a flat tariff structure of 10 per cent.[1]

It is a very complex analytical issue to examine the short- and medium-run implications and consequences of this drastic trade liberalization process. This is due to the fact that at the same time as the trade reforms, several other deep policy reforms were also implemented, such as price liberalization, fiscal reform, domestic financial market liberalization, capital account liberalization, labour market reform and privatization; furthermore, there was also an anti-inflation stabilization programme which reduced the annual rate of inflation from 605 per cent (1973) to 9.5 per cent (1981).

In this paper, the first section presents the basic facts of the Chilean trade reform, i.e. the stages of tariff and non-tariff barrier reduction, the movements of the exchange rate and the evolution of exports and imports. The next section gives the overall macroeconomic environment and the sequence of reforms which were implemented during the trade reform, including a special discussion about the interrelationship of the trade reform with the fiscal reform and with the liberalization of the capital account. Next we present some of the empirical issues relating to the effects of Chilean trade reform upon industry, before the final section provides some conclusions.

BASIC FACTS OF THE CHILEAN TRADE REFORM

There have been two separate stages in the recent evolution of Chilean international trade: first, the trade liberalization period of the 1970s, where the main feature was the great reduction of import barriers; and second, the export expansion period of the 1980s, after the external debt shock, where the real exchange rate constituted the main mechanism for export promotion.

For more than three decades (1940–73) the Chilean economy had been characterized by extensive price controls and highly restricted foreign trade. The rationale of the trade liberalization reform of the 1970s was to change the prevailing pattern of economic incentives, and in this way, it was complementary to concomitant price liberalization. Moreover, it pursued the rationalization of the complex Chilean trade regime, to eliminate the discretionary power of the bureaucracy. Tariff reduction was intended to be a clear signal of openness and the government's desire to equalize incentives across all types of goods (exportables, importables and non-tradables). During the 1970s, when the trade reform was being implemented, the exchange rate was used to counterbalance the effects of tariff reduction and, in the early days, the economic authorities were concerned about import competition. During the 1980s, however, there was an explicit new strategy. Following the external debt shock, exports were considered to be the engine of growth, deep real devaluations were implemented and a stable real exchange rate was sustained to promote exports.

In short, during the 1970s trade reforms followed the neutrality principle, equalizing incentives across goods. Given the prevailing anti-export bias, these measures were favourable to exports; however, towards the end of this decade there was a real appreciation of the currency. During the 1980s there was a clear shift towards exports using the general measure of depreciation of the domestic currency. (There were also special subsidies for minor exports and specific state measures which will be discussed later.)

Liberalization of the trade account

During the second quarter of 1973 the tariff structure was as follows (Behrman, 1976; Cauas and de la Cuadra, 1981; de la Cuadra and Hachette, 1986):

Table 4.1 Nominal tariffs during trade liberalization, Chile, 1973–9 (%)

| | Average tariff | Maximum tariff | | Mode |
		Level	Percentage of items subject to maximum tariff	
1973	105	750[a]	8.0	90
1974	75	160	17.1	60
1975	49	108	8.2	55
1976	36	66	0.5	35
1977	22	43	0.5	20
1978	15	20	22.0	10
1979[b]	10	10	99.5	10

Source: Central Bank and Ffrench-Davis (1980).
[a] Eight per cent of items were in the 220–750% range, with an average of 320% for this category.
[b] From June on.

(i) *Ad valorem* tariff rates ranged from 0 per cent to 750 per cent.
(ii) The average nominal tariff was 105 per cent and the mode was 90 per cent.
(iii) Eight per cent of the tariff lines had tariff rates equal to or higher than 220 per cent; 50 per cent of the tariffs were above 80 per cent.
(iv) Only 4 per cent of the tariff lines had tariff rates below 25 per cent.

In spite of the above characteristics of the tariff structure, import taxes were only 26 per cent of import value in 1971 (Behrman, 1976);[2] i.e. exemptions and special regimes (for particular regions, industries and public firms) played an important role.

In 1973 imports were also subjected to major non-tariff barriers: (i) For more than 60 per cent of imports there was a 90-day, non-interest-bearing prior deposit of 10,000 per cent of the import goods' CIF value. The Central Bank had discretionary power to suspend this restriction. (ii) Imports of more than 300 goods were expressly forbidden. (iii) Almost 50 per cent of the tariff lines required the Central Bank's approval for importing the goods. (iv) There were 290 import duty exemption measures which benefited firms, persons, productive sectors, geographic regions, etc. (v) Furthermore, in 1973 there were eight different exchange rates with a 1,000 per cent differential between the highest and the lowest one.

All non-tariff barriers were practically eliminated by August 1976;[3] all quotas and official approvals for starting an import operation were eliminated in 1974. Special import benefits for publicly owned firms were eliminated in 1974; most of the special import concessions were eliminated by 1979.

It is interesting to note that the time path of the actual tariff reductions shown in Table 4.1 does not correspond to an overall scheme announced at the beginning (1974).[4] The first stage (in 1974) was mainly focused on lowering the highest tariff levels (and elimination of bureaucratic official approvals for importing). Maximum tariff rates (ranging between 220 and 750 per cent) were reduced to a single rate of 160 per cent, tariffs between 35 and 215 per cent were reduced by 5–65 per cent, and tariff rates below 30 per cent remained unchanged. In the second stage (end of 1974 and 1975), the final tariff structure objective was to be defined; however, there were alternative proposals offered. The first had a threefold structure: 25 per cent for raw materials, 30 per cent for semi-manufactured goods, and 35 per cent for manufactured goods). However, this tariff structure implied that food, which had traditionally been exempted from duties and usually enjoyed preferential exchange rates, would have had a 25 per cent tariff rate. Therefore a second tariff structure was proposed with a 10–35 per cent range (10–15–20–25–30 and 35 per cent), with an average tariff of 20 per cent and a mode of 15 per cent; the level of tariffs was to increase according to the level of processing of the goods. The final 10–35 per cent tariff structure was to be achieved in five six-month stages (i.e. at the end of the first half of 1978). The tariff reduction process was to be as follows: (i) the target tariff structure of 10–35 per cent was multiplied by three, and then all existing tariffs exceeding these 'amplified' tariff levels were to be immediately adjusted to that level; (ii) the difference between the resulting tariff and the target tariff would be reduced by 20 per cent in each of the five (six-month) stages. At the end of 1977, however, a uniform and flat 10 per cent tariff structure was announced, which was to be reached in an 18-month period (by June 1979).

Table 4.1 provides the time evolution of the reduction and flattening of the tariff structure during the 1970s. By 1976 the average nominal tariff was 36 per cent, the maximum tariff was 66 per cent, and the tariff mode was 35 per cent; i.e. tariff levels were about one- third the level they had been in 1973. Three years later, the average, maximum (with the exception of cars) and mode tariffs were all 10 per cent.

The presence of 'water' in the tariff could be one factor which explains the fact that during the first stage of tariff reduction, there was practically no complaint from domestic producers (Cauas and de la Cuadra, 1981).[5] Table 4.2 shows that for the most important manufactured goods, nominal tariffs were in general higher in 1976 than implicit tariffs had been for the same goods in 1974. This situation was different, however, in 1977.

Having a flat tariff structure (10 per cent) gave the authorities, after the external debt shock, an easy-to-use tool, complementary to the exchange rate, with which to address external disequilibrium; moreover, it provided additional fiscal revenues to finance the fiscal deficit.[6] However, on the other hand, easy-to-see movements of the overall tariff structure constituted clear signals on the closing or opening of the economy. Table 4.3 shows the changes in import tariffs introduced to address the economic situation generated by the external debt shock.

Table 4.2 Implicit and nominal tariffs for selected manufactured goods, Chile (%)

	Implicit tariff	Nominal tariffs		
	1974	1974	1976	1977
Food products	21	83	30	18
Textiles	37	141	47	31
Shoes and clothing	47	160	49	32
Paper	26	97	35	21
Printing	5	114	36	26
Chemical	40	66	35	19
Basic metals	21	60	32	20
Metal product	38	91	47	31
Machinery	45	75	43	26

Source: Aedo and Lagos (1984).

Table 4.3 Average nominal tariffs after the external debt shock, Chile, 1982–90 (%)

1982	1983	1984	1985	1986	1987	1988	1989	1990
10	20[a]	20,35[b]	30,20[c]	20	20	15[d]	15	15

Source: Central Bank.
[a] Tariffs were increased to 20% in March 1983.
[b] Tariffs were increased to 35% in September 1984.
[c] Tariffs were decreased to 30% in March, and then to 20% in June 1985.
[d] Tariffs were decreased to 15% in January 1988.

Evolution of the exchange rate

The exchange rate is a key variable in the outcome of a trade reform. It is interesting to observe the evolution of the real exchange rate during and after the trade liberalization process (see Table 4.4). During the first couple of years, nominal tariff reduction was carried out with a compensating real devaluation; a passive crawling peg rule based mainly on past inflation was used to keep up the value of the real exchange rate (peso price of foreign exchange). This was facilitated by a sharp over-devaluation implemented during the last quarter of 1973 when the average official *real* exchange rate increased by 212 per cent. In this respect, the exchange rate was considered to be a tool complementary to commercial policies for achieving resource reallocation.

During 1976 and 1977 there were two sharp 10 per cent currency revaluations to break inflationary expectations. Moreover, from 1978 on, an active crawling peg rule was used (the so-called '*tablita*') ostensibly to guide price expectations; the exchange rate was then considered to be a tool more appropriate for anti-inflation stabilization objectives. From 1976 on, there began an appreciation of the real value of the currency while at the same

Table 4.4 Nominal tariffs and exchange rates, Chile, 1973–90

Year	Average nominal tariffs (%) (1)	Real exchange rate[a] ($/US$ of 1990) (2)	Indicator of level of real protection[b] (1990 = 100) (3) = [1+(1)] × (2)
1973	105	201.5[c]	117.8
1974	75	199.8	99.7
1975	49	273.8	116.4
1976	36	221.5	85.9
1977	22	184.7	64.3
1978	15	205.2	67.3
1979	11	200.5	63.5
1980	10	175.0	54.9
1981	10	148.8	46.7
1982	10	172.6	54.2
1983	18	207.2	69.7
1984	25	218.0	77.7
1985	26	264.9	95.2
1986	20	294.6	100.8
1987	20	305.1	104.4
1988	15	324.5	106.4
1989	15	313.6	102.9
1990	15	304.9	100.0

Source: Central Bank.

[a] Real exchange rate: Nominal official exchange rate (domestic currency price of foreign exchange) deflated by CPI (consumer price index) and inflated by an index of external inflation.

[b] Level of real protection: Real exchange rate times one plus the nominal tariff.

[c] The average value of the official and parallel exchange rate has been used for this computation. The average official real exchange rate increased 212% in the last quarter of 1973.

time nominal tariffs were reduced. By the time the flat 10 per cent tariff system was established (in 1979), the real (official) value of the currency had appreciated by 15.3 per cent with respect to its average value of 1974–5; from there, up to 1981, there was an additional appreciation of 25.8 per cent. In other words, by 1979, Chile had reduced its level of real protection by 40 per cent and it kept reducing it for the next three years (see Table 4.4).

After the balance of payments crisis of 1982, the main tool used to reduce the external disequilibrium was the exchange rate. During the 1982–4 period real devaluations were implemented to restore the real exchange rate level prevailing prior to 1979 (when a fixed nominal exchange rate had been established). However, because of the large external debt service payments now required, the 1982–4 devaluations were not enough, and additional real devaluations were implemented during and after 1985. The end result was that at the end of the 1980s Chile had a domestic protection level (of the productive sector competing with imports) close to that prevailing at the time when the trade liberalization process had begun (1974–6); but there had been a complete change in its components, because an undervalued currency had become the main component of the later level of overall protection.

The evolution of exports and imports

During the trade liberalization process of the 1970s, annual Chilean exports increased from US$1.3 billion (in 1973) to US$3.8 billion (in 1979). Moreover, there was an important diversification of the goods content of the export basket; in this respect, the export share of copper declined from 82.2 per cent (in 1973) to 48.8 per cent (in 1979). Non-copper exports rose from US$260 million (in 1973) to US$1,948 million (in 1979). The annual growth rate of total exports was 17.5 per cent for the 1973–9 period. (This average annual growth rate decreased to 13.5 per cent when the entire 1973–81 period is considered; see Table 4.5).

During the external disequilibrium adjustment process of the 1980s, annual Chilean exports increased from US$3.8 billion (in 1981) to US$8.3 billion (in 1990); non-copper exports rose from US$2.2 billion (in 1981) to US$4.7 billion (in 1990). The export share of copper fluctuated around 50 per cent of total exports. The annual growth rate of total exports was 7.4 per cent for the 1981–90 period, which increased to 9.5 per cent over the 1985–90 period. The 1982–5 period was a time of deep adjustment in the Chilean economy, in which the unemployment rate was over 24 per cent for four consecutive years.

Imports showed a moderate expansion in current price terms during the first stage (1973–6) of the trade liberalization process; in current dollars imports increased from US$1.3 billion (in 1973) to US$1.5 billion (in 1976). National accounts, however, showed a sharp decline of real imports of 33.9 per cent in the 1973–6 period; this decline is related to the severe shock adjustment policy implemented in 1975 when GDP fell by 12.9 per cent (see Table 4.5). However, by 1977 GDP had recovered the 1974 level. There was now a large expansion of imports again; in current dollars imports increased from US$1.5 billion (in 1976) to US$4.2 billion (in 1979) and they kept increasing up to US$6.5 billion (in 1981) (see Table 4.5). The (National Accounts) average annual growth rate of real imports for 1976–9 (1976–81) was 25.0 per cent (21.8 per cent). A breakdown by type of imports shows the following (real) average annual expansion rates for the 1976–9 period (Ffrench-Davis, 1980): 66.6 per cent for consumer durable goods (accounting for 16.3 per cent of total imports in 1979); 36.0 per cent for food (4.0 per cent);[7] 15.4 per cent for intermediate goods (59.2 per cent); and 14.7 per cent for capital goods (20.5 per cent).

In the first stage of the trade liberalization process (1973–6), the drastic shock adjustment (in 1975) explained the changes in the current account;

THE CHILEAN TRADE LIBERALIZATION

Table 4.5 Exports, imports, trade account and current account, Chile, 1970–9

	Exports (FOB)	Imports (FOB)	Trade account[a] (goods & services)	Current account	Rates of growth		
					Exports	Imports	GDP
						(Percentage)	
	(Millions of current dollars)						
	(1)	(2)	(3)	(4)	(5)	(6)	(7)
1970	1,112	956[b]	95	−81	2.1	0.9	2.1
1971	999	1,015[b]	−91	−189	0.8	8.5	9.0
1972	849	1,103[b]	−351	−387	−15.1	3.2	−1.2
1973	1,309	1,288	−197	−294	2.8	−5.4	−5.6
1974	2,151	1,794	−37	−211	45.9	3.4	1.0
1975	1,590	1,520	−217	−491	2.4	−38.7	−12.9
1976	2,116	1,479	−446	148	24.4	4.3	3.5
1977	2,185	2,151	−262	−551	11.9	35.5	9.9
1978	2,460	2,886	−669	−1,088	11.2	17.6	8.2
1979	3,835	4,190	−604	−1,189	14.1	22.7	8.3
1980	4,705	5,469	−1,144	−1,971	14.3	18.7	7.8
1981	3,836	6,513	−3,378	−4,733	−9.0	15.7	5.5
1982	3,706	3,643	−492	−2,304	4.7	−36.3	−14.1
1983	3,831	2,835	534	1,117	0.6	−15.1	−0.7
1984	3,651	3,288	−193	−2,111	6.8	16.5	6.3
1985	3,804	2,955	511	−1,329	6.9	−11.0	2.4
1986	4,199	3,099	666	−1,137	9.8	9.7	5.7
1987	5,223	3,994	766	−808	8.8	17.0	5.7
1988	7,052	4,833	1,576	−167	6.1	12.1	7.4
1989	8,080	6,502	944	−740	15.7	25.3	10.0
1990	8,310	7,065	794	−618	7.6	0.6	2.1

Sources: Central Bank.
    Columns (1)-(4) are from balance of payments; columns (5)-(7) are from National Accounts.
[a] Goods trade balance (FOB) plus non-financial services.
[b] CIF imports.

a US$491 million current account deficit in 1975 was transformed into a US$148 million surplus in 1976. From 1976 on, the current account started to show increasing deficits, from US$551 million (in 1977) to US$ 4,733 million (in 1981). Table 4.6 shows the evolution of the share of GDP accounted for by the current account deficits; during four consecutive years (1977–80) current account deficits were of the order of 5–11 per cent of GDP, reaching 14.5 per cent in 1981.[8]

During the 1980s, the required deep external adjustment had as a result a severe contraction of imports over an extended period. Imports were reduced from US$6.5 billion (in 1981) to US$2.8 billion (in 1983) and remained below US$4 billion up to 1987; in 1987 GDP recovered to the level of 1981.

The large (US$4.7 billion) current account deficit of 1981 (14.5 per cent

Table 4.6 Current account deficits, Chile, 1974–90 (% of GDP)

Current account deficit during import liberalization		Current account deficit during external disequilibrium adjustment	
1974	2.5	1982	9.5
1975	5.6	1983	5.7
1976	−1.5[a]	1984	10.7
1977	4.5	1985	8.3
1978	7.1	1986	6.5
1979	5.7	1987	4.3
1980	7.7	1988	0.8
1981	14.5	1989	2.9
		1990	2.2

Source: Central Bank.
[a] A minus sign implies the existence of a current account surplus.

of GDP) was reduced to a level below US$800 million from 1987 on (i.e. from 2 to 4 per cent of GDP) (see Table 4.6).

Let us look more closely at the timing and speed of the implementation of the Chilean trade reform. In general terms, it is often considered that, when an economy is affected by a serious balance of payments crisis and by a severe shortage of foreign currency, discretionary management and control of foreign exchange may temporarily be more efficient than retaining freedom for imports and/or applying a larger exchange rate devaluation; in other words, the best timing for starting a trade reform is considered to be when the economy is at the upper peak of the cycle with plenty of international reserves. Moreover, given the fact that a significant import liberalization may worsen a foreign exchange shortage, it is often suggested that there should be expansion of exports prior to the liberalization of trade. Once a sufficient trade surplus is achieved on the basis of a fairly diversified export basket, more ambitious stages of import liberalization can be applied.

In this respect, the Chilean experience was quite different. The trade reform was implemented simultaneously with a deep stabilization programme (GDP fell by 12.7 per cent in 1975); Chilean liberalization has been done by annexing external sector reforms to a stabilization programme. The severe contraction of aggregate demand reduced imports in 1975 and 1976. This could be interpreted in a positive way: the implementation of an import liberalization reform in the middle of a deep economic crisis provided exports with a two- to three-year (1974–6) headstart for expansion prior to the increase of imports. However, in spite of the fast initial expansion of exports (see Table 4.5), there was eventually an upper bound beyond which exports could not grow, which was in the 10–15 per cent annual growth range. On the other hand, once GDP recovered its prior level, import expansion occurred at more rapid rates; an annual growth

Table 4.7 Composition of total Chilean exports, 1970–90 (millions of dollars/% of total exports)

	Mining		Fish and sea products	Forestry and wood products	Agricultural products	Other	Total
	Copper	Non-copper mining					
1970	839.8	110.6	1.4	10.2	30.1	119.6	1,111.7
	(75.5)	(9.9)	(0.1)	(0.9)	(2.7)	(10.8)	(100.0)
1975	890.4	185.0	35.0	125.6	76.4	239.7	1,552.1
	(57.4)	(11.9)	(2.3)	(8.1)	(4.9)	(15.4)	(100.0)
1980	2,152.5	619.4	290.8	591.3	281.2	735.5	4,670.7
	(46.1)	(13.3)	(6.2)	(12.7)	(6.0)	(15.7)	(100.0)
1985	1,760.7	566.8	338.2	313.6	451.7	391.9	3,822.9
	(46.1)	(14.8)	(8.8)	(8.2)	(11.8)	(10.3)	(100.0)
1990	3,913.4	834.0	915.0	869.3	961.9	1,086.7	8,580.3
	(45.6)	(9.7)	(10.7)	(10.1)	(11.2)	(12.7)	(100.0)

Source: Central Bank.
These data are provided by customs authorities. They differ from those in Table 4.5, which come from the balance of payments.

rate of 15 per cent seemed to be a lower bound for the increase of imports (Table 4.5).

These asymmetric growth rates of imports and exports generated large current account deficits by the end of the 1970s; the Chilean experience suggests that to sustain an import liberalization programme would have required a level of financing of around 5 per cent of GDP per year for a five-year period (see Table 4.6).

The role of exports in the Chilean economy experienced a sharp change after the deep structural reform policies of the 1970s (see Table 4.7). There were several reasons for this: (i) The trade reforms of the 1970s eliminated the anti-export bias policies of the import-substitution industrialization regime. (ii) During the 1980s, a sustained real undervaluation of the currency provided clear and stable incentives to exporters. (iii) Exports from large copper mines, under state enterprise control,[9] significantly expanded output; Chile's share of world copper output (excluding centrally planned economies) increased from 14 per cent (at the end of the 1960s) to more than 20 per cent during the 1980s. (iv) The prevailing economic environment of free market prices, free trade, deregulation, debureaucratization, increased the overall efficiency of the economy.

However, there were also some specific factors explaining Chilean export expansion which are related to governmental measures: (i) During the 1960s, in the case of fruit exports, the state had invested in human capital (training and research) in local universities and in a large Chile–California programme through which many Chileans studied graduate-level agricultural economics. The fruit export boom was related to the introduction of the latest technology, and in order to use this type of technology, it was

Table 4.8 Exports and imports GDP shares, Chile, 1960–90 (%)

	Exports/GDP		Imports/GDP	
	Current prices	Constant prices	Current prices	Constant prices
1960	17.5	18.6	13.7	21.1
1970	19.0	15.9	13.9	24.3
1980	22.8	27.0	23.7	30.4
1985	29.1	26.3	26.4	20.1
1990	36.6	33.7	31.0	27.0

Source: Central Bank.

fundamental to have domestic know-how (Jarvis, 1991). Moreover, the agrarian reform (1965–73) created a market for land, encouraging a new type of entrepreneur to go into agriculture; these new entrepreneurs were more willing to introduce new techniques. (ii) In the case of forestry, there existed an old 'Forest Law' (1931) which made forestry an income-tax-free activity for thirty years after the trees had been planted. This law was replaced in 1974 by Decree 701, whic provided a direct subsidy of 75 per cent of the cost of planting and managing a forest; moreover, an income tax credit equal to 50 per cent of the tax on the income from forestry was provided. The fiscal cost of the special tax treatment for forestry has been estimated to be equal to 0.15 per cent of GDP per year. (iii) In the case of fishing, a state technical institute had been promoting investment in this sector since the 1960s. Chile has almost 5,000 k of coast and the fact that Peru (the northern neighbour) was one of the world's major fish exporters had a positive demonstration effect. Changes in sea currents and temperatures apparently induced a movement of the fish from Peruvian to Chilean coasts during the 1970s. During the 1980s, *laissez-faire* policies implied free access to fishing and, therefore, over-exploitation of the sea's resources for many years. The 1990s may witness a depletion of these resources. (iv) Special incentives were provided to small non-traditional exports (less than US$7.5 million) which involved a flat reimbursement of 10 per cent of the FOB export value; these subsidies benefited mostly industrial exports.

The export share of GDP (measured as a percentage of both current price and real GDP) increased significantly during the 1980s (Table 4.8). The export share of real (nominal) GDP reached 33.7 per cent (36.6 per cent) in 1990, roughly double the share in 1970, while the export share of GDP increased from 12 per cent in the 1960s to more than 30 per cent during the 1980s. Moreover, in spite of the important increase in copper exports, the share of copper in total exports declined from more than 75 per cent in the late 1960s and early 1970s to less than 50 per cent during the 1980s (Table 4.7).

In short, the present Chilean comparative advantage is structurally the same one as in the past, i.e. close to 90 per cent of the export basket depends upon Chilean natural resources. However, there are two important differences with respect to the past: (i) There has been a clear diversification of natural resource-based goods in the export basket. If world prices of basic commodities do not coincide in their fluctuation patterns, the Chilean economy will be exposed to smaller overall external shocks than those observed in the past. More important, the potential for total substitution of one of the commodities included in the export basket will not have the damaging effect that the appearance of synthetic nitrate had in the past. (ii) Most Chilean exports are now being produced by Chilean-owned enterprises; therefore, most of the surplus generated by export activities can be reinvested domestically.

MACROECONOMIC ENVIRONMENT AND REFORM SEQUENCE

It has been stated that the 'broad characteristics of any realistic sequence of reforms are no longer in doubt' (Blanchard, *et al.*, 1990). That is, there appears to be some consensus with respect to policy reform sequencing in developing and Eastern European countries. According to this consensus, macroeconomic stabilization has the first priority and is needed *before* structural reforms such as trade and capital market liberalizations (Rodrik, 1988; Fischer and Gelb, 1990). 'The importance of the sequence of reforms – reforms oriented mainly to reduce severe macro imbalances first and to improve resource allocation and restore growth later – has become increasingly clear with experience'; moreover, structural reforms 'undertaken in highly unstable macro conditions are typically unsuccessful' (Corbo and Fischer, 1990). It has been stated that this proposition has strong analytical underpinnings; structural reforms are oriented towards improving resource allocation by changing prevailing incentives (through changes in relative prices), and 'this would not work in a highly inflationary and balance of payments crisis environment' (Corbo and Fischer, 1990). However, it has been suggested that in economies having repressed inflation through price controls, domestic price reforms (i.e. price liberalization) are more likely to succeed if a trade reform has been implemented previously, because in that case, the appropriate set of world prices could serve as a guideline for domestic prices.[10]

The optimal sequence of reforms is practically impossible to define, especially in a second-best world. Therefore, it is important to learn from specific cases. The Chilean experience could be very useful in examining these sequencing issues. Contrary to some of the consensus propositions of the previous paragraph, the successful Chilean trade reform was implemented during a period with a three-digit inflation rate, and when the economy was experiencing a severe recession. As pointed out previously, from a purely theoretical point of view, the timing could not have been worse. Moreover, price liberalization (of an economy that had been almost fully price-controlled) preceded the trade reform.

In fact, macroeconomic stabilization is a process which can take many years. In the Chilean case it took three years to reduce inflation from a three-digit to a two-digit level, and it took four more years to reduce it to the one-digit level. Structural reforms, such as trade liberalization, were implemented during this anti-inflationary programme, and not afterwards, once inflation was under control. This has led Rodrik (1988) to assert that more attention should be paid to the sustainability of a structural reform package than to its liberalization characteristics; sustainability relates to the maintenance of such reforms in the future.

A full package of structural reforms was implemented in Chile during the 1970s; privatization, price liberalization, fiscal reform, trade reform, domestic financial and capital account liberalization, and labour reform (see Table 4.9). However, when these reforms were implemented, there was no overall scheme of appropriate sequencing, neither on how to implement each reform, and how far to go in each period. (This was pointed out previously with specific reference to the trade reform.) After the failure of the Unidad Popular Government (1970–3), which left a chaotic economic situation, most people were willing to see a move in the more market-oriented direction. At that time, there was only an overall guideline to the effect that the key parameters of the Chilean economy would be free markets, freer trade, a larger role for the private sector and higher protection for private property. This can be compared to the statement of Vaclav Klaus (Finance Minister of Czechoslovakia): 'Undertaking reforms is like playing chess: one needs to know the rules and have a sense of strategy, but it is not useful planning each specific move at the beginning' (cited in Fischer and Gelb, 1990).

Macroeconomic stabilization and trade liberalization

Table 4.10 provides information on the macroeconomic environment under which the Chilean trade liberalization reform was implemented. It can be observed that at the time that the level of tariffs was being reduced by two-thirds with respect to its original level, there prevailed a three-digit inflation rate; moreover, at the same time, there was a sharp reduction of the fiscal deficit from 13.8 per cent of GDP in 1973 to 2.3 per cent in 1976. Inflation and the fiscal deficit were further reduced during the 1976–9 period when the 10 per cent flat tariff structure was introduced.

In terms of the history of Chilean inflation, it could be said that inflation was at a 'normal' rate when it was below 40 per cent, a rate reached only in 1978. Therefore, according to some of the conventional wisdom noted above, the Chilean trade reform should not have started until that year; yet, in fact, by then the trade reform was almost completed.

Table 4.9 Chilean major structural policy reforms of the 1970s

Situation in 1972–3	Post–1973
Privatization	
More than 500 commercial firms and banks controlled by the state	By 1980, only 25 firms (including one bank) remained in the public sector
Prices	
Price controls	Market-determined prices except wages and exchange rate
Fiscal regime	
'Cascade' sales tax	Value-added tax of 20%
Large public payroll	Public employment reduced
Large fiscal deficits	Fiscal surpluses in 1979–81
Trade and exchange rates	
Multiple exchange rate system	Homogeneous, unified exchange rate
Prohibitions and quotas on imports	Flat import tariff of 10% (excluding automobiles)
High tariffs[a]	
Prior deposits for imports	Absence of other trade barriers
Domestic financial markets	
Controlled interest rates	Market-determined interest rates
State ownership of banks	Reprivatization of banks
Control of credit	Liberalization of capital markets
Capital mobility	
Total control of capital movements	Gradual liberalization of the capital account[b]
Government was the main external borrower	Private sector is the main external borrower
Labour regime	
Unions played a large role and had considerable bargaining power	No unions and no collective bargaining power
Worker dismissals prohibited	Relaxation of dismissals
High and increasing non-wage labour costs (40% of wages)	Prohibition and mandatory wage adjustments; severe cuts in real wages Reduction of non-wage labour costs (to 3% of wages)

[a] The average tariff was 105% and the maximum was 750%.
[b] Movements of long-term capital were liberalized in 1981, and those of short-term capital in 1982.

The Chilean anti-inflation (stabilization) programme also had stages:[11] First, there was almost complete price liberalization; it was argued that when free prices reached their equilibrium level, inflation would stop. At the beginning of 1974, slightly over thirty prices were controlled; by 1976, less than ten prices were controlled, and inflation was still at the three-digit level. In 1975, the closed economy monetary approach was used. Under this approach, because inflation is related to money growth which is caused by the fiscal deficit, fiscal discipline and monetary control are

Table 4.10 Macroeconomic environment of Chilean trade reform, 1973–9

	1973	1974	1975	1976	1977	1978	1979
	\multicolumn{7}{c}{Average nominal tariffs}						
Trade reform tariff:	105%	75%	49%	36%	22%	15%	10%
Inflation (%)	605[a]	369	343	198	84	37	38
Fiscal deficit (% GDP)	13.8	10.5	2.6	2.3	1.8	0.8	−1.5[b]
Unemployment (%)	7.2	9.2	15.7	18.8	17.6	17.4	17.2

Sources: Central Bank for inflation and fiscal deficit; Meller (1984) for unemployment.
[a] Cortázar and Marshall (1980); corresponds to the corrected CPI variation.
[b] A minus sign corresponds to a surplus.

the key means used to control inflation. A severe fiscal and monetary shock was implemented in 1975 (in 1973 and 1974 the fiscal deficit as a percentage of GDP reached two digits; see Table 4.10); GDP fell by 12.7 per cent and overt unemployment increased to over 15 per cent of the labour force. In spite of the large reduction of the fiscal deficit (to 1.8 per cent of GDP by 1977), inflation was still 84 per cent in 1977. In 1978, the open economy monetary approach was adopted. Under this approach, the exchange rate is seen as the nominal anchor to guide inflationary expectations. If the nominal exchange rate is fixed, the internal inflation rate tends to be equal to the external inflation rate; the nominal exchange rate is thus the main tool to fight inflation. In 1979 a fixed nominal exchange was established which lasted three years; the inflation rate fell to a one-digit level by 1981, but at the same time, the current account deficit reached 14.5 per cent of GDP. Almost seven years were eventually required (in the 1980s) to close the external disequilibrium gap, and the social costs incurred were heavy (see Meller, 1990, 1992).

It has been argued that import liberalization can help in the fight against inflation; tariff reduction reduces the domestic currency price of imports and this will generate downward pressure on the prices of domestic competing imports. In the Chilean case, there was declining inflation while tariffs were reduced; but even when tariffs got to their final 10 per cent level, inflation was still in the 40 per cent range. In other words, tariff reduction may have contributed to the reduction of inflation, but it was not the mechanism that could stop inflation.

A macroeconomic stabilization programme can have a severe impact upon a trade reform. First, the reduction of the fiscal deficit can lead to a decline in public investment, and this can affect the supply response of exports. This does not seem to have been a critical factor in the Chilean case because of the existence of unused capacity in infrastructure (roads, ports, etc.). More critical can be the impact of the stabilization programme upon the real exchange rate.

To ensure the success of a trade reform, there must be an increase of the real exchange rate (real devaluation), which should be sustained for a few years. In the presence of a steady rate of inflation a 'passive crawling peg' rule (mini-devaluations based on past inflation rates) can help to sustain the level of the real exchange rate. On the other hand, an anti-inflation programme may require a nominal anchor; as has been seen, a key instrument used for this purpose is the nominal exchange rate. In an environment of highly inflationary expectations, sharp revaluations are also used to break inflationary expectations, or sometimes an 'active crawling peg' (the *tablita*) is used to guide expectations.[12] A *tablita* system announcing future movements of the exchange rate is similar to a fixed nominal exchange rate in that money supply is in neither case any longer a policy tool subject to control by the Central Bank. If international reserves move according to supply and demand at the exchange rates specified in the *tablita*, the main monetary tool of the Central Bank is the control of domestic credit (Harberger, 1982).

In short, when the exchange rate is used as a tool to reduce inflation, there can be a real appreciation of the domestic currency; this erosion of the real exchange rate can generate an increasing external disequilibrium which will eventually produce pressures to stop or reverse the trade reform. In the Chilean case, the policy of fixing the nominal exchange rate, implemented in 1979, is considered by many as the main factor behind the severe balance of payments and overall economic crisis of 1982–3 in which GDP fell by 16 per cent and unemployment reached over 30 per cent.

Fiscal reform and trade liberalization

Trade taxes have been an important component of government revenues in Chile. Tariff reductions generate less import tax revenue, assuming a slow and price-inelastic response on the part of import demand. There may also be indirect revenue effects arising from the impact of trade reform upon the profitability of public enterprises; elimination of tariff exemptions has a negative effect on some public firms while, for others that previously were paying tariffs, the cost of imported inputs diminishes.

There are also factors which could lead to an increase of government revenues (World Bank, 1989): (i) A compensating devaluation accompanying a trade reform will have a positive effect on the revenue base of import taxes. (ii) Elimination or reduction of the number of exemptions from import duties will, other things being equal, increase revenues. (iii) Lowering very high tariffs can reduce customs evasion, and in this way increase the effective fiscal take from imports.

In the Chilean case the trade reform had the following impact upon fiscal revenues (see Table 4.11): (i) Import tariff revenues, which represented around 2.4 per cent of GDP at the end of the 1960s, increased significantly to 3 per cent during the first two years of the trade reforms (1974–5) because of the elimination of exemptions and special regimes. However,

Table 4.11 Tariff revenues, Chile, 1974–85

	Tariff revenues (million $, 1977) (1)	Tariff revenues as a % of GDP (%) (2)	Tariff revenues as share of total taxes (%) (3)
1974	11,148	3.6	17.4
1975	7,394	2.9	12.0
1976	6,235	2.3	9.5
1977	6,795	2.4	10.6
1978	6,427	2.0	9.3
1979	5,492	1.5	6.8
1980	5,389	1.4	6.4
1981	6,448	1.7	7.9
1982	3,601	1.1	5.2
1983	5,709	1.7	8.8
1984	9,549	2.8	13.0
1985	11,192	3.2	14.5

Source: Tesorería General de la República.

when the flat 10 per cent tariff rate was implemented (in 1980) import tariff revenues fell to around 1.5 per cent of GDP (1979–81). During the 1980s, tariff rates were increased to 20 per cent and more (see Table 4.11), generating revenues of 3 per cent of GDP (in 1984–5). (ii) Import tariff revenues constituted around 15 per cent of total tax revenues at the end of the 1960s; tariff reductions had reduced this percentage to 7 per cent by the final implementation of the trade reform.

In short, the trade reform generated a reduction of fiscal revenues of 0.9 per cent of GDP; however, this change was not an instantaneous one, since there were sharp increases of tariff revenues during its early years. An important tax reform in 1975, wherein a VAT (value-added tax) of 20 per cent was implemented, helped to accommodate the eventually lower revenues generated by the trade reform.

Trade account and capital account liberalization

In the Southern Cone liberalization experiences, while Argentina and Uruguay first liberalized the capital account, Chile first opened its commercial account.[13] It has been argued that the Chilean strategy was the more appropriate one; successful trade reform requires a sustained real devaluation of the currency to provide incentives for export expansion. Premature capital account liberalization can generate an appreciation of the currency, and thus an increasing trade deficit; overvaluation of the domestic currency could squeeze the tradable sector's profitability during a period when this sector has to incur major production adjustments. These results flow from the following phenomena: (i) The speed of adjustment of asset markets is much faster than that of goods markets; this generates 'overshooting' in short-run capital inflows with respect to their long-run equilibrium leading to an appreciation of the currency (Edwards, 1984). (ii) Asset prices are determined by the present value of expected future income streams; if there exist distorted relative prices (in particular, those of tradables versus non-tradables) there will be a distorted calculation of future incomes which will generate a misallocation of investment (Corbo and Fischer, 1990). (iii) Capital account liberalization exerts downward pressures on the domestic interest rate inducing expansion of domestic expenditure; this could generate an increasing trade disequilibrium. For these reasons, it has been suggested that capital inflows should be tightly controlled during a trade liberalization process.

On the other hand, it has been argued that the availability of external funds can help to minimize the adjustment costs associated with a trade reform programme. Therefore, the simultaneous reduction of external financial capital barriers could help to smooth the transition from a closed to an open economy. Liberalization of the trade account generates changes in domestic relative prices; local firms which previously had high protective barriers will require adjustment (e.g. technological change and labour training) to be able to face import competition. A gradual import liberalization process and funding to finance adjustment costs can ease adjustment processes. Moreover, there is typically a faster expansion of imports than exports during a trade reform. If a country does not have sufficient international reserves to handle the resulting trade deficit, simultaneous capital account liberalization may bring the finance that permits a trade reform to proceed.

In the Chilean case, there was a time interval between the implementation of the commercial and capital account liberalization processes; since neither of these processes were fully implemented overnight, it is difficult to measure the interval precisely, but it could be said that there was a period of about two to four years between the commercial and capital account liberalization reforms. The liberalization experiments nevertheless ended with a serious balance of payments crisis in 1982. It has been argued that one of the Chilean lessons is that 'it would have been advisable to distance even more in time the two reforms' (Edwards and Cox, 1987).

However, there have been different views expressed with respect to the main factors leading to the 1982 balance of payments crisis.[14] As has been pointed out previously, the fixed nominal exchange rate policy implemented in 1979 has been considered to be the main factor producing the large trade and current account deficits of 1980 and 1981. The erosion of the real exchange rate and corresponding loss of competitiveness of the tradable sector between 1979 (June) and 1982 (June) has been estimated to be about 30 per cent. The fact that there was an increasing deficit in the current account was not considered by the economic authorities to be a problem, given the fact that every year (from 1979 through 1981) there was a surplus in the overall balance of payments; this was taken as a signal that there was no overvaluation of the domestic currency. The fixed nominal exchange rate helped to bring inflation down to the one-digit level; however, the erosion of the real exchange rate was not undone once the convergence of domestic and external inflation was achieved (Balassa, 1985).

The large inflow of external credit had 'Dutch disease' effects. The real appreciation of the currency coincided with a large increase in domestic expenditure which stimulated output and employment; during the 1979–81 period the Chilean economy was booming with a strange combination of an overvalued currency, high growth rates, very high consumption levels especially of imported goods, large inflows of external capital and large increases in stocks and in real estate prices. The real appreciation of the currency was one of the factors which led to the increase of expenditure, and especially of imported durable goods. Other factors which contributed to higher expenditures during 1979–81 were: (i) easier access to consumer credit; commercial banks and 'financieras' (non-banking financial institutions which provide loans) were now competing in a market that had been previously controlled by wholesale and retail trade stores; and (ii) wealth effects – the increase of stock prices and real estate values coupled with the environment of euphoria led all agents to feel richer; people perceived that there had been an increase in their wealth, and this led them to higher consumption.

In short, the stimulation of higher expenditures, the liberalization of imports, and the overvaluation of the domestic currency generated increasing deficits in the commercial account of the balance of payments; and the liberalization of the capital account provided the resources to finance those deficits.[15]

In the above explanation, the origins of the 1982 crisis are related to the real economy, i.e. the current account deficit generated the capital account surplus. However, an alternative hypothesis states that the main cause of the 1982 crisis was the liberalization of the capital account: the large inflow of external credit generated the real appreciation of the currency and the expansion of domestic expenditure, i.e. the capital account surplus generated the current account deficit (Harberger, 1985; Edwards and Cox, 1987). In other words, according to this hypothesis, the fixed nominal exchange rate policy was not a mistake; the same huge inflow of capital with a floating exchange rate system would have produced a still larger real appreciation of the currency.[16]

In the 1977–81 period the Chilean economy had increasing net inflows of capital which reached US$3.2 billion in 1980 and US$4.7 billion in 1981; these figures were equivalent to 12.3 per cent (in 1980) and 15.9 per cent (in 1981) of GDP. In order to absorb this large inflow of foreign credit, real appreciation of the currency was required to generate a deficit in the commercial account, and to achieve equilibrium in the non-tradable sector.

Both demand and supply elements influenced the remarkable size of the inflow of capital. The reduction of restrictions in the capital account plus the persistent differential between domestic and international interest rates were the main elements on the demand side. On the supply size, the increase in international liquidity in the 1970s, plus the favourable attitude of international banks towards the evolution of the Chilean economy, provided increasing amounts of foreign credit. The Chilean external debt almost tripled in four years; it increased from US$5.6 billion in 1977 to US$15.6 billion in 1981. A slower rate of capital inflow would have induced a smaller real appreciation of the currency and a smaller increase in domestic expenditure; these would have implied a smaller burden of adjustment for the Chilean economy during the 1980s when the international banks decided on a drastic reduction in the flow of credit.

During the adjustment to external disequilibrium in the 1980s, controls were re-established in the capital account. It is interesting to see that even now (at the beginning of the 1990s), a long time after the implementation and consolidation of the other structural reforms, and when exports have expanded significantly, to over 30 per cent of GDP, there is a 'replay' of the earlier discussion about the liberalization of the capital account.

From 1985 on, exports have been considered to be the 'engine' of Chilean growth; the economic authorities have pursued a policy of maintaining a high and stable real exchange rate (see Table 4.4). However, in 1990–1, in order to reduce inflation (running at 30 per cent on an annual basis), the economic authorities increased the domestic interest rate to a level well above the international rate; this increased differential generated a relatively large inflow of capital. On the other hand, in order to maintain its real exchange rate policy, the Central Bank had to increase its stock of international reserves to US$6 billion (a level equivalent to ten months of imports).

The recent economic policy discussion has focused on two issues: (i) the need to sustain a high real exchange rate, and (ii) the most appropriate tools to do so. The new inflow of financial capital is considered by some economists to be a long run phenomenon, i.e. Chile has merely recovered its access to international capital markets; moreover, the higher level and degree of diversification of exports suggests that there already exists a solid export foundation. This means that some fundamentals have changed and therefore it is no longer necessary to keep the high real exchange rate. This type of argument leads to the recommendation of a liberalized capital account; it has also been said that a modern economy has to be fully integrated in all respects to the world economy. It is argued by others that a large proportion of the financial capital inflow is of a short-term nature, much of it speculative, and responsive to the interest rate differential.

Given the relatively large existing stock of international reserves, they ask, why should Chile pay such rent to short-run speculative financial capital? Moreover, the fact that around 90 per cent of Chilean exports are basically natural resources implies that their continued export expansion will require increasing availability of new natural resources. They then question whether Chile has a solid export basis for the future. In this respect it is said that Chile has successfully achieved the first and easy stage of export expansion; now it is necessary to enter into a second stage where more value is added to natural resources and/or where other types of goods, not necessarily based on domestic natural resources, are exported.

It has also been suggested that liberalization of the capital account may help to sustain the high real exchange rate. If domestic financial capital is allowed to leave the country, that outflow could counterbalance the inflow of capital and thus reduce the monetary expansion, international reserves and downward pressures upon the real exchange rate. However, the recent experience of external debt shock has shown that international financial capital is quite volatile; it enters into a country in excess amounts when it is least required and leaves the country when it is most needed.

The policies recently implemented by the Chilean authorities to maintain the high real exchange rate were the following: (i) Discrimination between long-term and short-term capital movements. Restrictions on long-term capital movement, to Chile and out of Chile, have been significantly reduced; thus, foreign investment in Chile and foreign investment abroad by domestic firms is encouraged. On the other hand, taxes are imposed upon short-term capital entering into the country, while short-term movements of domestic financial capital out of the country are forbidden. (ii) Nominal tariffs were reduced from 15 to 11 per cent (in 1991) to encourage expansion of imports; at the same time, other taxes were increased to counterbalance the fiscal impact of tariff reduction (estimated as US$200 million, or 0.7 per cent of GDP).

There remain some key questions. When is the export basis sufficiently solid that it does not require the maintenance of a real exchange rate? When is the right time for a developing country to liberalize the capital account?

The issue of credibility

Policy reforms that start with low credibility about their permanence will not last very long because they will be destabilized by economic agents' actions. Authorities should therefore provide clear and steady signals from the beginning; the availability of funding and institutional support by multilateral organizations can help to increase the credibility of reforms.

It has been suggested that international financial institutions should be more concerned, in the application of conditionality, with the sustainability

Table 4.12 Indicators of the decreasing importance of the Chilean state, 1973–80

	1973	1974	1975	1976	1977	1978	1979	1980
Number of controlled prices	3,000	33		<10[a]				
Number of firms privatized	–	251	67	32	13	10	8	6
Share of government credit in total domestic credit (%)	88	81	85	75	59	40	29	10
Credit to private sector (% GDP)	1.6	2.5	5.4	4.7	8.8	15.7	19.2	24.6

Sources: Edward and Cox (1987); Harberger (1982); Wisecarver (1985).
[a]See Wisecarver (1985) for detailed discussion on price deregulation.

of the policy reforms they advocate than with the degree of liberalization (Rodrik, 1988). Credibility is fundamental to the sustainability of a policy change like a trade reform. In its absence there is a coordination failure, the end-result of which is that private-sector expectations are self-fulfilling. To sustain the trade reform an increase of investment is required; given the irreversibility of investment, investors delay until they perceive that there will be no policy reversals. On the other hand, sustainability requires signals of the early success of the reform such as are conveyed by increases of investment; if all investors believe in the sustainability of the trade reform and increase their investment very quickly, this will help to create momentum and help to sustain the reforms through time. But if each investor separately adopts the 'wait and see' attitude and is sceptical about the maintenance of the reform, this could lead to a policy reversal.

As mentioned previously, in Chile many reforms and stabilization programmes were implemented simultaneously during the 1970s (Table 4.9). It has been noted that overall guidelines stating the main role of the free market, free trade and the private sector were provided through explicit and often repeated statements. General Pinochet and the Chicago economists provided the credibility component while the long-run prospect of the military regime (1973–90) generated the sustainability ingredient; no matter the possible social costs, the reforms were there to stay. This experience could be taken as very pessimistic for developing countries trying to implement a full spectrum of policy reforms. However, there are also some Latin American examples, e.g. Bolivia and Mexico, where deep trade reforms were recently implemented in a much shorter time than in the Chilean case, and under democratic regimes.

Words are not enough for economic agents; there were some clear actions taken by the military regime to back up their statements of economic principle. Table 4.12 shows the evolution of some indicators showing the reduction of the role of the state in the economy, both as a productive agent and as an interventionist agent. The number of controlled prices diminished very quickly and significantly; privatization of firms (including banks) was quite large for the first two years (almost 80 per cent of the firms were privatized during 1974–5). The share of government credit in total domestic credit was reduced from 88 per cent (in 1973) to 10 per cent (in 1980), while credit to the private sector increased, as a percentage of GDP, from around 2 per cent (in 1973–4) to almost 25 per cent (in 1980).

It is said that inconsistent policies generate a lack of credibility. However, it is sometimes not easy to identify an inconsistent programme in a developing country; this is illustrated by the difficulty in establishing the 'right' level of the real exchange rate in the Chilean case during the 1970s and even today. Only when a crisis explodes is the (*ex-post*) explanation usually related to the existence of inconsistent policies. Future failure of a trade reform could be anticipated from an explosive import boom such as happened in Chile in 1979–81 (see Table 4.5). It has been argued that this import boom constituted a sort of 'capital flight' prior to an anticipated balance of payments crisis (Edwards and Cox, 1987); people bought imported goods because they anticipated a bleak future and perceived that those goods would not be available or would become much more expensive in the future. However, during that same period there was a completely opposite explanation of the import boom – that people really believed in a highly promising future due to the fact that the trade reform had moved the Chilean economy to a higher growth path, and therefore, they had adjusted their expenditure pattern to their new permanent income and wealth status.

In this specific case, different agents had different perceptions about the future, but they were generated by the same phenomenon, the low exchange rate; however, the end-result was the same, a balance of payments crisis which left winners and losers.

EFFECTS OF THE TRADE REFORM UPON INDUSTRY

De-industrialization

The Chilean foreign trade regime prevailing prior to 1973 provided high relative protection to the industrial sector; industry should have been the most damaged sector, then, with the reduction and removal of external trade barriers. Furthermore, Chilean comparative advantage is generally believed to rest upon natural resources (mining, fishing, forestry, fruits). A neutral price incentive structure would, therefore, not encourage industrial production. However valid such conceptual arguments might be at the aggregate level, it is important to examine their validity at a disaggregated industry level since effective protection varied significantly across industries and some manufacturing activities involving the processing of natural

Table 4.13 Industry shares of GDP and employment, Chile, 1970–90 (%)

	1970	1974	1977	1979	1981	1985	1990
Industry share of GDP	24.7	25.1	21.7	21.8	21.9	20.9	20.6
Industry share of employment	18.0	19.4	17.9	16.7	15.2	14.2	n.a.

Sources: GDP, Central Bank; employment, Jadresic (1986).

Table 4.14 Export share of domestic production and import share of apparent consumption in selected Chilean industries, 1967–89 (%)

	Natural resources-based industries[a]			Import-substituting industries[b]		
	1967	1979	1989	1967	1979	1989
Exports/gross value of production	6.5	12.8	23.1	0.6	2.9	4.4
Imports/apparent consumption	6.9	9.9	7.4	26.8	40.5	48.1

Source: Central Bank and Manufacturing Census (INE).
[a] Including manufacturing sectors (ISIC) 311–313–331–341–371.
[b] Including manufacturing sectors (ISIC) 321–322–324–381–382–383–384.

resources could experience expansion. The key questions remain. If import-substitution industrialization policies had generated a highly inefficient industrial sector, how did domestic manufacturing adjust to increased import competition? How severe has the de-industrialization process been?

Industry was indeed the sector most affected by the liberalization of the trade account; during the import boom years, 1976–81, while (real) imports increased at 21.8 per cent per year, industry exhibited a 4.2 per cent annual growth rate.[17] In short, there has been some degree of de-industrialization in the Chilean economy. The industry share of GDP decreased from over 25 per cent at the end of the 1960s to around 20 per cent during the 1980s. The industry share of employment decreased from 18–19 per cent prior to the trade reform to around 14 per cent during the 1980s (Table 4.13).

There are two different channels through which imports affect the level of domestic production: (i) direct substitution of domestic goods and inputs by imports, (ii) the substitution of imported intermediate inputs for domestic value added via the elimination of whole stages of domestic production; in other words, a domestic industrial firm may have the same physical industrial output but use a much smaller quantity of domestic productive factors.[18]

Trade liberalization had a large impact upon intra-industry reallocation; manufactured exports and imports significantly increased their role in domestic production and consumption. The manufactured export share of gross value of production in the natural resource processing industries increased significantly, reaching 23.1 per cent (in 1989); even in the import substituting industries, exports acquired increased importance (Table 4.14). At the same time, the import share of apparent consumption increased greatly in

Table 4.15 Industrial employment during the trade reform, Chile, 1974–81

	Industrial employment index	
	SOFOFA (1)	INE (2)
1974	110.4	107.5
1975	100.0	100.0
1976	92.6	94.3
1977	92.1	95.9
1978	92.0	94.1
1979	91.0	92.8
1980	87.1	87.8
1981	84.6	81.6
Average annual growth rates (%)		
1974–81	–3.7	–3.9
1975–80	–2.7	–2.6
1976–81	–1.8	–2.9
1977–80	–1.8	–2.9

Sources: Column (1): SOFOFA, Síntesis Económica, Departamento de Estudios.
Column (2): INE, Anuario de Industrias Manufactureras; establishments employing 50 or more persons.

the import-substituting industries; the quite low import share of the 1960s reached almost 50 per cent by the end of the 1980s.

There has been controversy about the impact of trade liberalization upon industrial employment. In 1975–6, due to the shock policy adjustment, unemployment increased to 18.8 per cent[19] and stayed over 15 per cent up to 1981. According to Tokman (1984) trade liberalization implied an 'absolute destruction of the industry jobs without any job creation elsewhere'; on the other hand, Sjaastad and Cortés (1981) point out that 'trade liberalization had a negligible impact upon the level of industrial employment', since most of the unemployment was generated before, by the 1975 recession. According to Meller (1984), the industrial sector generated increasing employment during the 1960s at a rate of 2.9 per cent per year; during the trade liberalization process there was an annual rate of industrial 'job destruction' of almost 2 per cent per year (see Table 4.15).

Table 4.16 shows the evolution of GDP for selected manufacturing industries during and after the trade reform. Given that the final tariff structure achieved (in 1979) was a flat 10 per cent across the board, it would have been expected that those industries having the highest initial protection would have been the ones which had the biggest adjustment problems. Thus, the textiles and clothing industry, which had quite high nominal tariffs (150 per cent) in 1974, had negative annual growth rates of 5 per cent to 6.6 per cent during the 1974–85 period; the share of textiles and clothing in overall manufacturing value added fell from 13.7 per cent (in 1974) to 7.7 per cent (in 1985). However, manufacturing industries like

Table 4.16 Evolution of value added for selected manufacturing industries, Chile, 1974–85 (%)

Manufacturing industry	Nominal tariff 1974[a]	Annual growth rates		Share of total manufacturing industry		
		1974–81	1974–85	1974	1981	1985
Food[b]	83	3.8	2.7	28.8	34.8	38.3
Textiles and clothing	150	–6.6	–5.0	13.7	7.9	7.7
Paper and printing	105	2.5	1.1	8.7	9.6	9.8
Chemicals	66	0.4	–0.8	16.7	16.2	15.3
Metal products and machinery	83	0.6	–3.8	19.1	18.6	12.4

Source: Central Bank.
[a] Average values from Table 4.2 have been used.
[b] Including food, beverages and tobacco.

Table 4.17 Composition of industrial exports, Chile, 1970–89 (million $/% of total industrial exports)

	Fish meal and food products	Paper, wood and wood products	Basic metal products	Other industrial products	Total
1970	0.0	8.9	23.5	0.0	32.4
	(0.0)	(0.8)	(2.1)	(0.0)	(2.9)
1975	101.8	121.9	58.6	111.3	393.6
	(6.6)	(7.9)	(3.8)	(7.2)	(25.4)
1980	375.7	589.7	279.0	320.8	1,565.2
	(8.0)	(12.6)	(6.0)	(6.9)	(33.5)
1985	406.3	313.1	60.4	189.6	969.4
	(10.6)	(8.2)	(1.6)	(5.0)	(25.4)
1989	507.8	714.0	80.2	453.1	1,755.1
	(6.2)	(8.7)	(1.0)	(5.5)	(21.4)

Source: Central Bank.

food and machinery which had similar nominal tariffs (83 per cent) in 1974 had quite different post-reform performance; the share of food in manufacturing increased from 28.8 per cent (in 1974) to 38.3 per cent (in 1985) while that of machinery (and metal products) decreased from 19.1 per cent (in 1974) to 12.4 per cent (in 1985).[20]

In short, besides the reduction of industry's share of GDP, there were important compositional changes within the manufacturing sector. Generally, those manufacturing industries depending on domestic natural resources increased their relative importance.

The composition of industrial exports shows a similar pattern; industrial goods that are the result of the processing of basic resources constitute the main part of Chilean industrial exports. Fish meal, paper, wood and wood products, and basic metals represent around 80 per cent of total industrial exports (Table 4.17).

Table 4.18 Basic data for Chilean industry, 1967 and 1979 (1967=100)

	1967	1979
Average gross output per plant	100	101
Value added per plant	100	75
Workers per plant	100	88
Efficiency labour per plant	100	98
Capital per plant	100	195

Source: Tybout et al. (1990).

Table 4.19 Average industrial labour productivity, Chile, 1970–85 (1974 = 100)

1970	1974	1977	1978	1979	1980	1981	1985
101.7	100.0	90.2	94.2	101.4	103.4	103.8	110.6

Source: Manufacturing value added, Marcel and Meller (1986); employment, Jadresic (1986).

Changes in industrial productivity

The increase of foreign competition resulting from a trade reform should increase domestic industrial efficiency. This could be due to a reallocation of resources according to comparative advantage, to an increase in scale and/or to technical efficiencies (X-efficiency).

A comparison of plant-level information from the 1967 and 1979 Chilean industrial manufacturing censuses showed the following results (see Table 4.18): (i) 'Output per plant remained surprisingly stable between 1967 and 1979'; (ii) 'value added per plant fell more rapidly than workers per plant (however measured), so labour productivity dropped'; (iii) 'value added per unit capital fell'; (iv) 'taken together (the last two items), these results suggest an unequivocal fall in total factor productivity for the manufacturing sector as a whole between 1967 and 1979' (Tybout et al., 1990: 5). In short, according to these figures, industrial productivity was higher during the high protection period than right after the implementation of the trade reform. Tybout et al., suggest that the 'productivity drop probably reflects the relatively slack demand for manufactured products in 1979' (p. 5). However, the figures show that annual manufacturing growth was 7.9 per cent in 1979 while it was only 2.8 per cent in 1967.[21]

According to aggregate information, average industrial labour productivity has tended to follow the economic cycle (see Table 4.19); in 1974–85 it is therefore difficult to isolate the impact of the trade reform from the impact of the economic cycle. This fact explains the strange type of results provided previously. Table 4.20 shows the evolution of sectorial unused capacity; the figures for industry provide further evidence in this respect.

Other results relating to the impact of the trade reform upon industrial

Table 4.20 Sectorial unused capacity, Chile (%)

Year	Agriculture[a]	Fishing[c]	Mining[a]	Industry[a]	Construction[a]	Transport[b]
1974	8.4	38.7	−0.9	6.1	8.9	12.7
1975	5.3	48.6	14.0	30.4	33.8	22.4
1976	9.4	37.7	7.2	26.5	45.6	21.8
1977	1.4	34.1	8.2	20.6	47.0	16.4
1978	7.4	28.3	10.1	13.7	43.6	12.4
1979	3.5	24.0	8.5	7.3	31.3	7.6
1980	1.4	23.7	7.0	2.0	16.1	0.0
1981	0.0	15.5	3.1	0.0	0.0	4.3
1982	5.6	13.0	0.0	23.2	25.2	20.0
1983	12.2	10.6	4.7	23.0	37.3	26.7
1984	8.4	3.6	2.1	18.4	37.3	27.3
1985	5.5	2.7	1.4	18.4	27.8	27.2
1986	4.5	0.8	5.0	14.7	20.2	23.5
1987	3.5	12.9	7.3	12.2	13.6	19.5
1988	1.4	14.5	5.6	6.9	10.1	14.0
1989	1.6	0.0	0.0	0.0	0.6	5.7
1990	0.0	13.9	2.9	2.2	0.0	0.0

The method of trend-through-peaks has been used. The years chosen for each sector are:
[a] 1971, 1981 (1982 for mining), 1989 (1990 for agriculture).
[b] 1971, 1980 to 1990.
[c] 1971, 1989.

efficiency, obtained through the use of establishment data, are the following: (i) There may have been an improvement in scale efficiency since (a) entering firms were larger than exiting firms (Tybout, 1989); and (b) as protection fell, small plants either dropped out or increased production levels toward minimum efficient scale (Tybout et al., 1990).[22] (ii) Using three-digit ISIC industry-level data, 'there is no evidence of overall improvements in productive efficiency for the manufacturing sector'. 'Of the 21 manufacturing industries analyzed, only 10 showed reductions in estimated returns to scale, only nine showed evidence of Hicks neutral productivity improvements, and only five registered reductions in the index of efficiency dispersion' (Tybout et al., 1990: 17).

In spite of the above results, there is a widespread perception that Chilean industry has experienced a large increase in efficiency as a result of the implementation of the free pricing/free trade system.

Chilean entrepreneurs

At the beginning of the twentieth century Encina (1911: 67) stated: 'The Chilean entrepreneur has the same psychology as the Spanish conqueror; the obsession of making a quick fortune in one stroke or in a strange venture'. In fact, for more than fifty years there was the popular image that Chilean entrepreneurs were adventurers who wanted to get rich over-

Table 4.21 Number of export firms, by value of exports, Chile, 1986–9

Value of exports	Number of firms			
	1986	1987	1988	1989
More than US$100 million	4	6	8	8
From US$10 million to US$100 million	38	50	66	76
From US$1 million to US$10 million	193	248	303	341
From US$100,000 to US$1 million	661	772	854	892
Total	896	1,076	1,231	1,317

Source: Central Bank, unpublished data.

night, and had neither the work ethic nor the savings propensities of the developed countries' entrepreneurs.

During the 1960s there was a different type of criticism. Chilean entrepreneurs were considered to be inefficient, with no innovative abilities, and with rent-seeking attitudes that led them to look for state subsidies and/or protection. Moreover, wealth was seen as the main requirement for becoming an entrepreneur; the high executive positions in firms were seen as mainly going to relatives or friends of the entrepreneurs.

Prior to 1970, the lack of entrepreneurship was considered to be one of the key factors explaining slow growth in Chile. During the 1980s, there was a complete reversal of perceptions; Chilean entrepreneurs achieved a positive social evaluation and were considered the main factor contributing to the successful export expansion. Recent studies show the appearance of a new type of entrepreneurial climate in which professionalism is more important than wealth; these new entrepreneurs are biased towards the use of modern technology, are risk-takers, are outward-looking ('our market is not the Chilean one, it is the world'), and have an expansionary attitude (Montero, 1990).

It is very difficult to prove that this new generation of aggressive entrepreneurs has emerged as a result of the deep policy reforms introduced in the 1970s (Table 4.9); however, it is interesting to observe the recent sharp increase in the number of exporting firms in an economic environment in which macroeconomic equilibrium, high real exchange rates and explicit stimulus to private investment have prevailed. The number of Chilean firms (including joint ventures and majority foreign-owned firms) exporting more than US$100,000 per year increased from almost 900 to more than 1,300 in only four years (from 1986 to 1989) (Table 4.21). This is a quite different picture from the 1960s and 1970s when two foreign firms (Anaconda and Kennecott) exported around 70 per cent of total exports.

However, it should be pointed out that the new Chilean entrepreneurs are not innovative Schumpeterians; they are really imitators rather than innovators. They have developed a managerial capacity, i.e. the ability to coordinate and manage all the distinct and complex features of modern enterprises; they are managers with organizational abilities, who select responsible and qualified personnel, and who are well informed about the latest technologies and the development of industrial countries. In semi-industrialized economies it is more important to do these things well rather than to be an innovator – incompetence and inefficiency in entrepreneurial ability have been major barriers to their firms' expansion to foreign markets (Ray, 1988). Union leaders have pointed out that present Chilean entrepreneurs have a modern attitude toward the introduction of twenty-first century technology, but inside of the firm they retain the same labour relations as in the nineteenth century, i.e. entrepreneurs deal with workers much as the landed oligarchs treated their peasants.

FINAL REMARKS

In the Chilean case, the credibility of the trade reform was more related to the overall macroeconomic and policy reform environment than to the specificity of the stages and content of the trade reform itself. The planned time path of the tariff reductions and the final tariff levels of the Chilean trade reform were changed many times. At first (1974), there was only a general indication of the intention to lower tariff levels; later on (1975), a 10–35 per cent tariff structure scheme was scheduled to be implemented in four years; finally, this objective was changed (1977) and a flat 10 per cent tariff was scheduled, to be reached in two years. These changes did not meet the requirement of stability and predictability of the rules over time (Rodrik, 1990); however, it would seem that once there had been some important initial changes, it became easier to implement further changes later on.

Another interesting aspect of the stability and predictability question is the fact that the flat (10 per cent) tariff structure seems to have been less stable than a non-flat tariff structure would probably have been. During the 1980s, when the Chilean economy had to face balance of payments crises, it was quite easy to change the flat level of the tariff structure. With tariff levels moving frequently, to 20 per cent (1983), 35 per cent (1984), 20 per cent (1985), 15 per cent (1988) (see Table 4.3), there was a clear violation of the principle of stability; on the other hand, local authorities had an additional easy-to-use and easily reversible mechanism for responding to balance of payments disequilibria and fiscal deficits. During the severe external disequilibrium problems of the 1980s, there was no resort to quantitative restrictions, non-tariff barriers or multiple exchange rates. External problems were met with large real devaluations, increases of the flat nominal tariff rate and maintenance of foreign exchange controls.

Trade liberalization generates a reallocation of resources in the direction of comparative advantage; both at intersectorial and intrasectorial levels. In the Chilean case, at the intersectorial level, there was a substitution within tradables towards exports of natural resources (mining, forestry, fish, fruit) which displaced industry. At the intrasectorial level, there was a restructuring within industry involving an expansion of manufacturing related to the processing of (Chilean) natural resources and a contraction of manufacturing competing with imports.

As expected, industry was the sector most affected by the trade liberalization. At the overall level, there was some de-industrialization involving a reduction of the GDP share of industry from 25 per cent to 20 per cent, and industrial employment decreased by 10 per cent during the trade reform years (1974–9). There were different types of adjustment on the part of industrial firms: (i) There was some industrial restructuring according to comparative advantage relating to the processing of domestic natural resources; deeper research is required on this subject. (ii) Some firms went into bankruptcy right away, while others were able to postpone bankruptcy by acquiring heavy financial debts. The specific causes of the large number of bankruptcies observed in 1982 are not clear – some were related to high interest rates and some to the loss of domestic competitiveness due to the overvaluation of the Chilean currency – but the end-result was a catastrophe for the industrial sector. (iii) Some firms adjusted their production processes by substituting imported inputs for domestic stages of production; in this way, they may have increased physical output but with much lower domestic value added content. Other firms may have gone further by becoming importers of the same types of goods that they were formerly producing. In this way, they took advantage of their existing merchandise distribution systems and achieved a sort of portfolio diversification in which they combined domestic production with imports in their sales. Other firms specialized in the production of goods in which they found they had comparative advantage.

Trade liberalization can have positive effects: resource reallocation according to comparative advantage, increases in consumer welfare via access to better quality and lower priced goods, increased efficiency of domestic import-competing producers, and introduction of the latest technology to the domestic economy. However, it is important to be aware of problems that can arise during the implementation of a trade reform. From Chilean experience the following should be mentioned:

(i) Tariff reductions can generate a drop in fiscal revenues (close to 1 per cent of GDP in the Chilean case). Therefore, a previous or concomitant fiscal reform that offsets the negative fiscal impact of the trade reform may be desirable.

(ii) Unilateral trade opening can generate a significant current account disequilibrium. Consumer good (non-food) imports are highly elastic; in the Chilean case income and price elasticities close to 2 and −2, respectively, have been observed. The external resources required to

126

finance the Chilean deficit after the import liberalization amounted to 5 per cent of GDP every year for five consecutive years.

(iii) Keeping the 'right' level of the real exchange rate is the key to the 'success' of a trade reform. To achieve this objective is not easy in an inflationary environment.

(iv) The Chilean trade reform generated a reduction of industrial employment close to 10 per cent.

(v) Export expansion is a very slow process. Specific measures taken by the state during a previous period (in the 1960s) were crucial to the achievement of the increase of exports in the 1970s (under a neutral incentive system), even in those sectors where Chile had a natural resource comparative advantage. Moreover, in the Chilean case, the real exchange rate was a key variable in the encouragement of exports. Therefore, there should be special care with the liberalization of the capital account (even long after the trade reform has been implemented) in order to avoid pressures which might erode the level of the real exchange rate. Moreover, in the formulation of exchange rate policy, there is likely to be a difficult choice between the short-run objective of reducing inflation and the long-run objective of export expansion. A key issue at this point is the degree to which a country has established a solid export basis, i.e. when its future competitiveness is not fully dependent upon the high level of the real exchange rate.

NOTES

1 Cars over 850 cc were the only exception. For a detailed description of the Chilean foreign trade regime prevailing prior to 1974 see Behrman (1976) and World Bank (1979).

2 Import taxes as a percentage of imports averaged 21 per cent in the 1960–4 period, and 17 per cent in the 1965–70 period (see Behrman, 1976). See also Cortés et al. (1981).

3 In August 1976 the list of forbidden imports contained only *six* goods; this list was completely eliminated in 1981. The 10,000 per cent prior deposit was legally eliminated only in 1976, but it stopped being applied before that.

4 For more details see Ffrench-Davis (1980) and de la Cuadra and Hachette (1986).

5 However, it should be pointed out that in the Pinochet dictatorship, even for entrepreneurs, complaining was a highly risky enterprise.

6 In addition, countervailing duties were imposed during 1982 to counter what were considered to be dumping prices of some import goods; these duties covered 6 per cent of total imports. The surcharge plus the tariff had a 36 per cent ceiling. Furthermore, three important agricultural goods (wheat, sugar and oil) have had, from 1984 on, a compensatory mechanism to offset external price instability. See Ffrench-Davis and Vial (1990) for further details.

7 Bracketed figures indicate the share of each import category in total imports in 1979.

8 However, overvaluation of the domestic currency in the 1979–81 period led to

an underestimation of the relative GDP share of the current account deficits; i.e. overvaluation hid the increasing external disequilibrium. Using the real exchange rate prevailing in 1984, the GDP shares of the current account deficits of 1980 and 1981 increased to 12.5 per cent and 25.5 per cent respectively (see Meller, 1990); i.e. these corrected gap figures for the current account deficits would have provided a clearer warning about balance of payments problems in 1980, two years before the 1982 balance of payments crisis.

9   Large copper mines were completely nationalized in 1971.

10 For a detailed discussion of this subject see Corden (1990), Dornbusch (1990) and Selowsky (1990).

11 For a deeper analysis see Foxley (1983), Ramos (1984), Edwards and Cox (1987).

12 When there are declining inflation rates, it is possible to reconcile the use of an appropriate *active* crawling peg rule with the maintenance of the real level of the exchange rate.

13 For a survey and references on this subject see Edwards (1984).

14 For more detailed discussions see Ffrench-Davis (1982), Zahler (1983), Sjaastad (1983), Ramos (1984), Harberger (1985), Balassa (1985), Corbo *et al.* (1986), Edwards and Cox (1987), Morandé and Schmidt-Hebbel (1988), Meller (1992).

15 In Meller (1986) it is estimated that the 'over-expansion' of imports of non-food consumer goods in the 1977–81 period increased Chilean external debt by US$6.4 billion; this figure represents 30 per cent of the level of the 1985 Chilean external debt.

16 Edwards (1986) estimated that the nominal exchange rate in mid-year 1981 would have been 30 to the dollar instead of the nominal fixed rate of 39 to the dollar.

17 This is a revised figure for industry growth; see Meller *et al.* (1984).

18 The usual procedure used in Latin American countries of measuring industrial GDP through the use of physical output indicators does not capture this substitution mechanism; and official figures may show increasing figures of industrial output while in fact there may be a decrease in the value added of the industrial sector (see Meller *et al.* 1984).

19 The normal rate of unemployment of the Chilean economy had been 6 per cent during the 1960s.

20 For a disaggregated analysis of the Chenery type at three-digit ISIC level see Vergara (1980) and Corbo and Pollack (1982).

21 Other factors mentioned by Tybout *et al.* (1990) are a gradual change in the mix of products, the nature of technology, and measurement errors.

22 However, in another study using Chilean data, Roberts and Tybout (1991) conclude that 'increased exposure to import competition appears to clearly *reduce* the size of all plants in both the short run and the long run'; 'it appears that models that predict trade liberalization will increase average plant size in import-competing sectors do not describe recent Chilean and Colombian experiences' (p. 27).

REFERENCES

Aedo, C. and Lagos, F. (1984) 'Protección efectiva en Chile 1974–1979', *Documento de Trabajo* no.94, Instituto de Economía, Universidad Católica de Chile.

Balassa, B. (1985) 'Policy Experiments in Chile, 1973–1983', in G. Walton (ed.) *The National Economic Policies in Chile*: London: JAI Press, pp. 203–38.

Behrman, J. (1976) *Foreign Trade Regimes and Economic Development: Chile*, NBER, Columbia University Press.

Blanchard, O., Dornbusch, R., Krugman, P., Layard, R. and Summers, L. (1990) 'Reform in Eastern Europe', mimeo, WIDER, November.

Cauas, J. and de la Cuadra, S. (1981) 'La política económica de la apertura al exterior en Chile', *Cuadernos de Economía* 54–5: 195–230, December.

Corbo, V. (1985) 'Chilean Economic Policy and International Economics Relations Since 1970' in G. Walton (ed.) *The National Economic Policies of Chile*, London: JAI Press, pp. 107–44.

—— and Fischer, S. (1990) 'Adjustment Programs and Bank Support: Rationale and Main results', mimeo, World Bank, November.

——, De Melo, J. and Tybout, J. (1986) 'What Went Wrong With the Recent Reforms in the Southern Cone?', *Economic Development and Cultural Change* 34(3): 607–40, April.

Corbo, V. and Pollack, M. (1982) 'Fuentes de cambio en la estructura económica chilena: 1960–79', *Estudios de Economía* 18: 55–96, Santiago, 1st semester.

Corden, M. (1990) 'Macroeconomic Policy and Growth: Some Lessons of Experience', in *Proceedings of the World Bank Annual Conference on Development Economics*, World Bank, Washington, DC, pp. 59–84.

Cortázar, R. and Marshall, J. (1980) 'Indices de precios al consumidor en Chile: 1970–78', *Colección Estudios CIEPLAN* 4: 159–201, Santiago, November.

Cortés, H., Butelmann, A. and Videla, P. (1981) 'Proteccionismo en Chile: Una visión retrospectiva', *Cuadernos de Economía* 54.5: 141–94, December.

de la Cuadra, S. and Hachette, D. (1986) 'The Timing and Sequencing of a Trade Liberalization Policy', Working Paper, Instituto de Economía, Universidad Católica de Chile, December.

Dornbusch, R. (1990) 'Policies to Move From Stabilization to Growth', in *Proceedings of the World Bank Annual Conference on Development Economics*, World Bank, Washington, DC, pp. 19–48.

Edwards, S. (1984) 'The Order of Liberalization of the External Sector in Developing Countries', Princeton Essays in International Finance, New Jersey.

—— (1986) 'Monetarism in Chile, 1973–83: Some Economic Puzzles', *Economic Development and Cultural Change* 34(3): 535–60, April.

—— and Cox, A. (1987) *Monetarism and Liberalization. The Chilean Experiment*, Cambridge: Ballinger.

Encina F. (1911) *Nuestra Inferioridad Económica*, 7th edition, 1990, Santiago: Editorial Universitaria.

Ffrench-Davis, R. (1980) 'Liberalización de importaciones: la experiencia chilena en 1973–79', *Colección Estudios CIEPLAN* 4: 39–78, Santiago, November.

—— (1982) 'El experimento monetarista en Chile: una síntesis crítica', *Colección Estudios CIEPLAN* 9: 5–40, Santiago, December.

—— and Vial, J. (1990) 'Trade Reforms in Chile: Policy Lessons for the Nineties', paper presented at the World Bank Seminar 'Latin America Facing the Challenges of Adjustment and Growth', Caracas, July.

Fischer, S. and Gelb, A. (1990) 'Issues in Socialist Economy Reform', mimeo, World Bank, July.

Foxley, A. (1983) *Latin American Experiments in Neo-Conservative Economics*, Berkeley: University of California Press.

Harberger, A. (1982) 'The Chilean Economy in the 1970's: Crisis, Stabilization, Liberalization, Reform', in K. Brunner and A. Meltzer (eds) *Economic Policy in a World of Change*, Carnegie-Rochester Conference Series on Public Policy, vol. 17, New York: North-Holland, pp. 115–52.

—— (1985) 'Observations on the Chilean Economy, 1973–1983', *Economic Development and Cultural Change* 18, August.

Jadresic, E. (1986) 'Evolución del empleo y desempleo en Chile, 1970–85. Series anuales y trimestrales', *Colección Estudios CIEPLAN* 20: 147–94, Santiago, December.

Jarvis, L. (1991) 'The role of Markets and Public Intervention in Chilean Fruit Development Since the 1960s: Lessons for Technological Policy', mimeo, CIEPLAN, October.

Larrain, F. (1991) 'Public Sector Behaviour in a Highly Indebted Country: The contrasting Chilean Experience 1970–85', in F. Larraín and M. Selowsky (eds) *The Public Sector and the Latin American Crisis*, San Francisco: International Center for Economic Growth.

Marcel, M. and Meller, P. (1986) 'Empalme de las Cuentas Nacionales Chile 1960–1985. Métodos alternativos y resultados', *Colección Estudios CIEPLAN* 20: 121–46, December.

Meller, P. (1984) 'Análisis del problema de la elevada tasa de desocupación chilena', *Colección Estudios CIEPLAN* 14: 9–42, Santiago, September.

—— (1986), 'Un enfoque analítico-empírico de las causas del actual endeudamiento externo chileno', *Colección Estudios CIEPLAN* 20: 19–60, Santiago, December.

—— (1990) 'The Chilean Case', in J. Williamson (ed.) *Latin American Adjustment: How Much Has Happened?*, Washington, DC: Institute of International Economics, pp. 54–85.

—— (1992) *Adjustment and Equity in Chile*, Paris: OECD.

——, Livacich, E. and Arrau, P. (1984) 'Una revisión del milagro económico chileno (1976–81)', *Colección Estudios CIEPLAN* 15: 5–109, Santiago, December.

Montero, C. (1990) 'La evolución del empresariado chileno: ¿Surge un nuevo actor?', *Colección Estudios CIEPLAN* 30: 91–122, Santiago, December.

Morandé, F. and Schmidt-Hebbel, K. (eds) (1988) *Del auge a la crisis de 1982*, Santiago: ILADES.

Ramos, J. (1984) 'Estabilización y liberalización económica en el Cono Sur', Estudio de la CEPAL no. 38, United Nations, Santiago.

Ray, D. (1988) 'The role of entrepreneurship in economic development', *Journal of Development Planning* 18.

Roberts, M. and Tybout, J. (1991) 'Size Rationalization and Trade Exposure in Developing Countries', in R. Baldwin (ed.) *Empirical Studies of Commercial Policy*, Chicago: University of Chicago Press for NBER.

Rodrik, D. (1988) 'Liberalization, Sustainability, and the Design of Structural Adjustment Programs', mimeo, World Bank, November.

—— (1990) 'Conceptual Issues in the Design of Trade Policy for industrialization', mimeo, WIDER Conference on Trade and Industrialization Reconsidered, Ottawa, September.

Selowsky, M. (1990) 'Preconditions for the Recovery of Latin America's Growth', *Finance and Development* 27(2): 28–31, June.

Sjaastad, L. (1983) 'The Failure of Economic Liberalism in the Southern Cone', *World Economy* 6: 5–26, March.

—— and Cortés, H. (1981) 'Protección y empleo', *Cuadernos de Economía* 54–5: 317–60, August.

Tokman, V. (1984) 'Reactivación con transformación: el efecto empleo', *Colección Estudios CIEPLAN* 14: 105–28, Santiago, September.

Tybout, J. (1989) 'Entry, Exit, Competition and Productivity in the Chilean Industrial Sector', mimeo, World Bank, May.

——, De Melo, J. and Corbo, V. (1990) 'The Effects of Trade Reforms on Scale and Technical Efficiency. New Evidence From Chile', Working Papers WPS 481, World Bank, August.

Vergara, P. (1980) 'Apertura externa y desarrollo industrial en Chile: 1974–78', *Colección Estudios CIEPLAN* 4: 79–118, Santiago, November.

Wisecarver, D. (1985) 'Economic Regulation and Deregulation in Chile 1973–1983', in G. Walton (ed.) *The National Economic Policies of Chile*, Connecticut: JAI Press, pp. 145–202.

World Bank (1979) 'Chile: An Economy in Transition', Report no. 2390-Ch, World Bank, Washington, DC.

—— (1989) 'Strengthening Trade Policy Reforms', mimeo, Washington, DC, November.

Zahler, R. (1983) 'Recent Southern Cone Liberalization Reforms and Stabilization Policies. The Chilean Case, 1974–1982', *Journal of Interamerican Studies and World Affairs* 25(4): 509–62.

5

TRADE POLICY AND INDUSTRIALIZATION IN COLOMBIA, 1967–91

José Antonio Ocampo

I am grateful to participants in the WIDER Project for comments, and to Luz Marina Monroy and Jesus Alberto Cantillo for their assistance.

INTRODUCTION

As in other Latin American countries, Colombia adopted an import-substitution industrialization (ISI) policy in the 1930s. As a result of the need to reduce the excessive dependence on coffee foreign exchange earnings, since the late 1950s, ISI was combined with an explicit export promotion strategy. This 'mixed model', as we will call it in this paper, was enriched by the trade and exchange reform of 1967, leading to one of the most successful periods of industrial and export growth in Colombian history.

Since the mid–1970s, this process has been interrupted. The turning point can be traced to the abandonment of the mixed model as a reflection of the 'Dutch disease' effects of the booms in international coffee prices and foreign indebtness which took place between 1975 and 1982. As industrial growth slackened, total factor productivity (TFP) levelled off, export coefficients declined and structural change ceased. Since the mid-1980s, the return to the central features of the mixed model has been reflected in the renewed dynamism of the industrial sector. None the less, the falling returns from the import-substitution elements of the model, together with the radical change in external conditions facing the country, led to a radical turnaround in economic policy in 1990–1, by which the country adopted a more explicit outward-oriented strategy.

This paper analyses the relations between trade policy and industrial performance in Colombia since 1967. It is divided in six sections, the first of which is this introduction. The second overviews events prior to 1967. The third reviews foreign exchange and trade policies since 1967. The fourth considers the demand aspects of manufacturing growth since 1967, including the determinants of export performance. The fifth takes a look at the supply aspects, particularly the determinants of total factor productivity growth. Finally, the sixth draws some major conclusions of the analysis.

TRADE AND INDUSTRIALIZATION PRIOR TO 1967

ISI took off in the 1930s. Starting in that decade, the share of manufacturing in Colombia's GDP grew rapidly for half a century as the industrial sector underwent a steady structural transformation. Three distinct phases can be differentiated in this process. During the first wave of import substitution, which took place during the Great Depression and the Second World War, industrial growth was led by beverages, oil derivatives, non-metallic minerals and, in particular, textiles. During a transitional phase, which covers the first decade of the postwar period, these sectors continued to expand and, indeed, peaked as a share of manufacturing value-added in the early 1950s, but the contribution of 'late' industries to manufacturing activity started to increase. Since the 1950s, the central feature has been the rise of 'late' industries (paper and printing, chemicals and rubber, basic metals and metal products), in what may be called the second phase of import substitution (Ocampo, 1991, 1994).

As in most LDCs, the employment creation effects of factory manufacturing remained limited. Factory employment peaked at slightly over 10 per cent of non-agricultural employment from the mid-1950s to the mid-1960s, but then started to decline (Ocampo, 1994). The scarcity of skilled labour was a major characteristic of industrialization up to the mid-1960s and was reflected in rising relative industrial wages. Educational efforts undertaken on a massive scale since the 1950s interrupted this process and reversed it in the following decade (Londoño, 1990).

In the early stages of industrialization, capital and entrepreneurship came mainly from domestic sources. In the second phase of import substitution, both public-sector firms and multinationals played an increasing role. None the less, the global scope of industrialization remained limited. Berry (1983) estimated that in 1969 8 per cent of industrial production came from public-sector firms, whereas 16 per cent of capital invested in manufacturing came from multinationals. Although detailed calculations for later years are not available, the share of MNCs in the manufacturing capital stock may have declined in recent decades.

Stock issues (by both corporations and limited-liability companies) and the reinvestment of profits were the major sources of capital accumulation up to the mid-1950s. The share of stock issues as a source of funds of industrial firms has experienced a long-term downward trend since the mid-1950s, as the reinvestment of profits and, particularly, bank lending filled the gap in different periods (Sandoval, 1983; Ocampo, 1994). Since the early stages of development, industrial concentration has been relatively high in most sectors (Echavarría, 1989). Detailed studies for 1968 and 1984 indicate that concentration has been rising in recent decades; by the latter year, close to 60 per cent of industrial production came from sectors characterized by the prevalence of highly concentrated oligopolies – those with four-firm ratios of 50 per cent or higher (Misas, 1989).

Import substitution, as it took place in Colombia, has been characterized by many authors as a relatively efficient process. TFP grew at an annual rate of some 2 per cent (faster if the decline of cottage-shop employment is included in the calculations) and was reflected in falling relative manufacturing prices (Berry, 1983; Posada and Rhenals, 1988; Ocampo, 1994). The country did not incur high costs associated with the excessive development of 'late' industries, where high capital intensity and economies of scale are important. In 1967–74, the share of many traditional sectors in GDP remained larger than the Kuznets–Chenery pattern, while some late sectors, particularly basic metals and metalmechanic activities, were considerably 'underexpanded' relative to such standards (Echavarría et al., 1983; Syrquin, 1987). On the other hand, in 1969, effective protection really utilized by the traditional manufacturing industries was relatively low compared to other developing countries (Hutchenson, 1973, and Table 5.2).

The traditional instruments of state promotion of industrialization were designed in the 1930s, but most of them came to play an important role only in the second phase of import substitution in the mid–1950s. Protectionism has been firmly embedded in domestic policies since the late nineteenth century but it played a rather secondary role during the first phase of import substitution. Indeed, a generalized system of high *ad valorem* duties was only established in 1959 and 1964. By then, tariffs were fixed at fairly high levels – a weighted average of 65.6 per cent (Martínez, 1986).

Early in the Great Depression, the country adopted stringent foreign exchange controls, and controls on current transactions have been constantly maintained since 1931. Quantitative import restrictions (QRs) were introduced in 1937, but they were used on a large scale only much later, when the collapse of coffee prices in the mid–1950s generated a period of endemic foreign exchange shortage. In 1948, exchange controls on capital movements were replaced by a freely floating exchange rate for capital transactions. This innovation was part of a transition to a multiple exchange rate system, which prevailed for two decades.

Prior to the large-scale use of tariffs and QRs in the mid-1950s, real exchange rate fluctuations played a more important role in providing price signals to industrial entrepreneurs. Indeed, since the 1920s, the real exchange rate has depicted two basic features: a long-run upward trend and a cyclical pattern opposite to that of the (mainly coffee-determined) terms of trade (Ocampo, 1991). Real depreciation has thus provided a signal to deepen import substitution when coffee prices have collapsed – the 1930s, the second half of the 1950s, and the 1960s. In the intermediate period of high coffee prices, appreciation played an alternative role: it provided relatively cheap foreign exchange to accelerate capital accumulation (Ocampo, 1994).

The intensive use of both tariffs and QRs induced by the collapse of coffee prices in the mid-1950s also led the government to introduce a complete set of policies to promote the diversification of exports. Preferential (capital market) exchange rates for non-traditional exports were granted for the first time in 1948. Since the mid-1950s, such preferential exchange rates have been complemented by tariff exemptions for imports used in the production of non-traditional exports, known in Colombia as the Vallejo Plan (1957), tax incentives (1960), and special credit facilities, including access to external credit free of exchange rate risks (1962 and 1964). Up to 1967 such incentives were very high (an average of 35 per cent in 1953–66) but unstable (Diaz-Alejandro, 1976: ch. 2).

The anti-export bias generated by intensive protectionism has thus been eased by devaluation and aggressive export promotion policies since the mid-1950s. The policy package followed since then can be characterized as a 'mixed' strategy of import substitution *cum* export promotion. Since the late 1950s rapid import substitution has, in fact, been accompanied by export diversification, particularly in agricultural activities (Ocampo, 1991).

The incentives generated by the trade regime were reinforced by direct public-sector investments and by the design of appropriate instruments to finance the industrial sector. The Industrial Development Institute (IFI) was created in 1940 to advance risk capital on a temporary basis to new import-substitution sectors. The IFI played a leading role in the diversification of industrial production during the second phase of ISI. Simultaneously, the government oil company, ECOPETROL, created in 1951, played a crucial role in oil refining and petrochemical developments in the 1960s. Since the early 1970s, the role played the by IFI and ECOPETROL in the channelling of public risk capital to new manufacturing sectors has been considerably downgraded.

On the other hand, development financing was given a central role in economic policy in the 1950 Financial Reform. Investment banks (*Corporaciones Financieras*) were created in the late 1950s as new instruments to channel private risk capital and long-term financing to the industrial sector. However, the large-scale provision of directed credit to manufacturing and other priority sectors – agriculture in particular – came much later, in the mid-1960s, when a series of Development Funds managed by the Central Bank (Banco de la República) were created. These funds were financed by loans from multilateral agencies, forced investments by financial intermediaries, explicit taxes and, to a lesser extent, by high-powered money creation.

TRADE AND MACROECONOMIC POLICIES, 1967–91

The golden age (1967–74)

The year 1967 is generally regarded as a turning point in the history of foreign trade and exchange policies in Colombia. In that year, the Lleras Administration, in confrontation with the major multilateral institutions and the US Agency for International Development (AID), put an end to a liberalization episode which had taken place since 1965 under severe pressures from the donor agencies (Diaz-Alejandro, 1976: ch. 7). The government refused to devalue, as these agencies demanded, and adopted instead the crawling peg and stringent import and exchange controls. In addition, it adopted a stable export promotion policy, which incorporated into a coherent framework the incentives for non-traditional exports which had been used in previous decades.

This policy package was a prelude to the period of fastest growth and export diversification in postwar Colombian economic history. From 1967 to 1974 GDP grew at an average of 6.3 per cent, as manufacturing boomed, reaching an impressive 9.6 per cent a year (Fig. 5.1a).[1] Controls kept the current account deficit of the balance of payments initially low. As controls eased (see below), the deficit increased, peaking in 1971, but subsequently fell, as exports increased and the demand for imports normalized. Inflation accelerated at the end of the boom and by 1974 had reached some 25 per cent, a high level by Colombian historical standards (Fig. 5.2a). Industrial inflation lagged up to 1972 but then led the acceleration of inflation in 1973 and 1974.

The 1967 package may be seen as a consolidation and rationalization of the 'mixed' strategy followed since the late 1950s. In 1969, the Cartagena Agreement, which created the Andean Group, added a new element to the strategy: ISI in a regional context, conceived as a mechanism to reduce the costs of advanced import substitution. In the early 1970s, dissatisfaction with ISI spread in Colombia and the region, as the mechanisms adopted by the Andean Group proved inoperative. In fact, during the Pastrana Administration, inaugurated in August 1970, ISI became a villain and emphasis was placed on the export growth component of the 'mixed' strategy. Criticism of ISI was indeed incorporated in the development plans of succeeding administrations. It did not lead, however, to a dismantling of the protectionist mechanisms established in previous years, but rather to an open disregard for new IS initiatives and to a gradual import liberalization.

In any case, and contrary to what the donor agencies argued in 1965, import liberalization was not a precondition for either export diversification or rapid economic growth. Rather, the causal link ran in the opposite direction. The success in easing the severe foreign exchange bottleneck

136

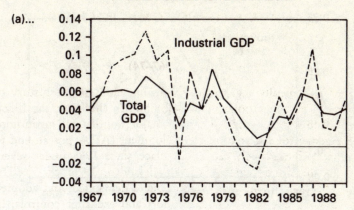

Figure 5.1(a) GDP and industrial growth, Colombia, 1967–90

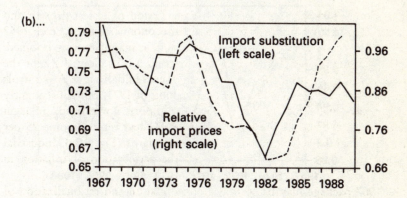

Figure 5.1(b) Import substitution versus relative industrial import prices

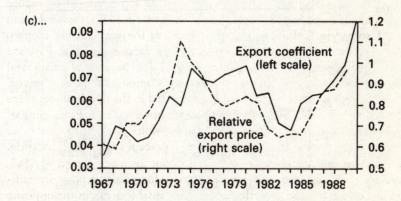

Figure 5.1(c) Manufacturing export coefficient versus relative export prices

Figure 5.2(a) Inflation: GDP deflator versus industrial prices

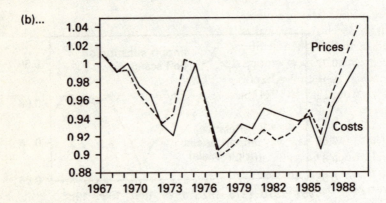

Figure 5.2(b) Relative industrial prices and unit costs

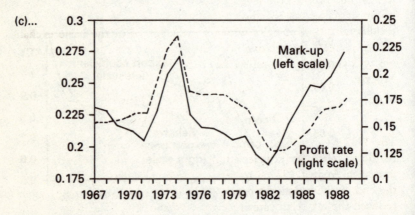

Figure 5.2(c) Industrial mark-up and estimated profit rate

138

which the country had faced since the mid–1950s and the resumption of rapid economic growth were the bases for the gradual liberalization which took place in the early 1970s.

In the first years of that decade, the process took the form of reducing red tape and delays in the approval of licences for non-competitive imports and in reducing the 'water' in the 1964 tariff. However, as we will see below (p. 146), this tariff reform, and its successors in the following years, maintained the traditional escalated tariff structure, which granted high protection to the traditional consumer good industries. Liberalization was thus initially consistent with the preservation of high tariffs and a generalized system of QRs, including a substantial list of goods for which imports continued to be totally prohibited. Explicit liberalization was adopted only late in the process, at the end of 1973 and early 1974, as part of a programme to fight rising inflation (Table 5.1).

The system of export incentives designed in 1967 included four major mechanisms: (i) a tax rebate certificate, which replaced the exchange rate and tax incentives typical of the 1960s; (ii) tariff exemptions for imports used in the production of non-traditional exports (the Vallejo Plan); (iii) the prefinancing of exports free of exchange rate risks; and (iv) export financing by the new Export Promotion Fund, PROEXPO. As Table 5.1 shows, from 1967 to 1974 the subsidy element of these incentives fluctuated between 19 and 27 per cent. The global incentive was smaller than that typical of the two decades prior to 1967 but considerably more stable.

The crawling peg was initially successful in generating a substantial real devaluation. The joint effect of devaluation and stable export incentives was thus a rapid increase of the real effective exchange rate applicable to non-traditional exports (Table 5.1). In the early 1970s the real effective exchange rate for imports also depreciated. However, the real rate was revalued in 1973 and 1974, as liberalization accelerated. By the mid-1970s it was thus back to the levels typical in the late-1960s. If the period of the boom is taken as a whole, the authorities were able to compensate the liberalization of QRs with the devaluation of the basic exchange rate and to increase the relative price incentives for non-traditional exports. As we will see, this was reflected in the rapid expansion of manufacturing exports.

From boom to crisis (1975–82)

The 1967–74 expansion came to an end as the result of the contractionary fiscal and monetary policies adopted by the Lopez Administration – inaugurated in August 1974 – to reduce the high inflation rates experienced at the end of the boom. As part of the stabilization package, the government reduced the tax certificates received by exporters. The attempt to compensate for this reduction with a temporary acceleration of the crawl of the

139

Table 5.1 Trade policy, Colombia, 1967–91

Year	Average nominal tariff[a]	Basic surcharge[a]	Collected average tariffs and surcharges	Distribution of items in the tariff schedule[c]			Imports under prior licensing as % of total imports	Excess demand for licences[d]	Tariff equivalent of QRs	Weighted real import exchange rate (1986=100)	Average export subsidies	Weighted real exchange rate for non-traditional exports (1986=100)
				Free licensing	Prior licensing	Prohibited						
1967	65.6[b]	3.0	14.7				96.2	41.0	36.2	75.1	23.1	73.4
1968			15.1				83.0	19.4	25.0	76.6	21.2	80.1
1969			16.2				82.8	21.6	25.7	78.9	19.1	79.9
1970	51.9		17.5				81.0	8.9	20.9	81.0	19.8	84.7
1971			16.4	3.4	80.4	16.2	71.7	12.7	19.9	82.6	22.6	90.0
1972			16.5				71.9	12.9	20.0	85.8	26.8	96.6
1973			16.7	20.2	79.8	0.0	68.8	6.0	17.0	82.6	26.6	95.0
1974		5.0	13.4	29.6	70.4	0.0	56.4	3.4	13.3	76.2	23.5	90.9
1975	32.6	6.5	15.3	34.1	65.9	0.0	57.2		13.3	79.3	13.0	85.1
1976			16.1				60.2		14.0	79.3	10.2	81.9
1977			17.2				58.8		13.7	71.7	9.9	73.4
1978	30.5		15.7	52.8	47.2	0.0	57.2		13.3	70.4	14.1	76.0
1979	28.2		16.4	66.7	33.3	0.0	55.6	1.1	12.4	67.1	14.1	72.6
1980	26.0		14.9				56.0	1.4	12.6	67.8	15.1	74.8
1981	25.9	6.5	14.8				47.8	3.4	11.3	65.4	16.4	73.9
1982			14.8	70.8	29.2	0.0	45.3	3.7	10.8	60.4	18.8	70.0
1983			14.5	41.9	58.1	0.0	58.6	19.5	18.9	62.9	23.7	70.9
1984	41.7	7.0	14.8	0.5	83.0	16.5	71.9	23.8	23.6	71.1	27.0	79.0
1985	31.4	15.0	19.3	27.0	71.6	1.4	85.2	35.4	31.1	89.7	26.4	89.9
1986			23.9	36.2	62.7	1.1	57.6	19.2	18.6	100.0	18.4	100.0
1987	24.9	18.0	24.9	37.8	61.1	1.1	54.7	22.5	18.9	103.7	15.6	100.1
1988			24.1	38.7	60.3	1.1	52.8	18.0	17.0	101.5	14.1	98.9
1989	26.6		22.4	38.8	60.1	1.1	55.3	2.3	12.7	98.3	14.8	101.5

| 1990 | 21.1 | 13.0 | 18.1 | 96.7 | 3.3 | 0.0 | 38.3 | 0.0 | 9.2 | 103.1 | 13.3 | 112.5 |
| 1991 | 6.1 | 8.0 | 13.3 | 98.6 | 1.4 | 0.0 | 11.8 | 0.5 | [c] | 88.0 | 10.9 | 106.9 |

Sources: Ocampo (1990a) and author's estimates using information from Banco de la República, INCOMEX, PROEXPO and DANE. Real effective exchange rates are estimated using the series of FEDESARROLLO up to 1975 and that of Banco de la República since then. The real effective import exchange rate includes average collected import duties and the tariff equivalent of QRs. The latter is calculated using the coefficients of a regression on the demand for imports in 1967–90, which includes as explanatory variables GDP, real import prices (including import duties), the proportion of imports under prior licensing and the percentage of licences rejected. The real effective exchange rate for non-traditional exports includes export subsidies.

[a] End of year. Unweighted.
[b] 1964.
[c] August 1971 and 1973; June 1974; February 1975 and 1978; September 1979. End of year since 1982.
[d] Partial information for 1974–84 (except in 1980).
[e] Assumed to be zero in 1991.

peso and with increasing credit from PROEXPO was only partly successful and thus resulted in a real appreciation of the exchange for non-traditional exports (Table 5.1).

When the stabilization programme was just starting to bear fruit in terms of inflation, particularly of industrial goods (Figure 5.2a), the Colombian economy was faced with the favourable terms of shocks generated by the 1975 frosts in the coffee regions of Brazil. The major preoccupation of the economic authorities was then how to manage five consecutive years of booming coffee prices and current account surpluses. Since it had been decided from the onset that the coffee sector would not play the leading role in the stabilization effort (real domestic coffee prices were significantly raised in the early part of the boom, largely to accelerate the renovation of plantations), a harsh monetary and fiscal policy was adopted, together with strong controls on external indebtness.

The inauguration of the Turbay Administration in August 1978 led to a radically different strategy: an expansionary fiscal policy, accompanied by a contractionary monetary policy and import liberalization. The expansion of public expenditure was justified on developmental grounds: the need to integrate the domestic market and to face the energy crisis. As a result of expenditure increases and tax reductions decreed in 1979, the virtual fiscal equilibrium typical of the coffee boom years turned into a 7.1 per cent consolidated public sector deficit in 1982. A corollary of fiscal expansion was massive borrowing abroad by the public sector. Simultaneously, controls on private capital flows were lifted and the economy thus experienced a debt boom – sufficiently late, however, to avoid the devastating effects which similar processes had in other Latin American countries. Foreign indebtness maintained the excess supply of foreign exchange after the coffee boom came to end in 1980 and the economy started to run record current account deficits.

Although in the initial years of the coffee boom the authorities tried to avoid its real exchange rate effects, the attempt was finally abandoned in 1977, when nominal devaluation was temporarily suspended. Real appreciation deepened during the debt boom of the early 1980s. As a result of its adverse effects on non-traditional exports (see below), subsidies were increased again from 1978. The real effective export exchange rate stagnated, in any case, at fairly low levels (Table 5.1). Import substitution having been abandoned as an explicit development strategy since the early 1970s, the second component of the 'mixed' model, export diversification, was equally left aside in the mid–1970s, but as the result of short-term macroeconomic conditions rather than a long-term strategy of any sort.

On the other hand, the effects of revaluation in the late–1970s and early 1980s were reinforced by import policies (Table 5.1). As part of the series of anti-inflationary programmes adopted during these years, further liberalizations of QRs and tariff reductions took place in 1976 and, particularly, in 1979–81. As a result, by 1982, 71 per cent of the tariff schedule had been transferred to the free licensing regime and tariffs had declined by some 20 per cent of the levels typical in the mid-1970s (Table 5.1). Simultaneously, increasing public investment was reflected in a boom of non-oil public-sector imports.

The stabilization programme adopted in late 1974 generated a recession in 1975, which was particularly severe in the manufacturing sector. In the following years, growth resumed, but the rate of expansion of industrial production remained significantly below that of the 1967–74 boom (Figure 5.1a). Starting in 1980, conditions faced by the manufacturing sector further deteriorated and, in the following years, the economy entered the worst recession of the postwar period. Moreover, despite persistent stabilization efforts, price shocks and the spread of indexation practices were reflected in persistent inflation (Fig. 5.2a). By the early 1980s, the Colombian economy was thus faced with recession, inertial inflation, record fiscal deficits, booming balance of payments disequilibria and rapidly increasing external liabilities.

Shifting external strategies (1983–91)

The deterioration of economic conditions led the Betancur Administration, inaugurated in August 1982, to a sharp turnabout in trade policy. The new administration rapidly reversed more than a decade of gradual import liberalization. A series of tariff increases decreed from 1982 to 1984 raised the average nominal rate of protection from 32 to 49 per cent, including tariff surcharges. None the less, existing and newly decreed exemptions significantly diminished the effect of tariff rises, as the evolution of the average collected tariff indicates (Table 5.1).

QRs thus played a more important role in the protectionist backlash. The first transfer of items in the tariff schedule to the prior licensing regime, which took place in September 1982, was moderate. As the drain of international reserves gained momentum in 1983 and 1984, the process accelerated. At the end of the process, in April 1984, the free licensing regime had virtually disappeared and one-sixth of the tariff schedule was back in the reborn prohibited list. Simultaneously, the government recreated and progressively tightened the 'import budget', generating a rapid increase in the excess demand for licences.

Export subsidies were simultaneously increased, by 1984 reaching levels typical to the early 1970s, as the crawl of the peso accelerated. The global package thus had many similarities with the 'mixed' strategy which the country had followed up to 1974. It was successful in generating an important recovery of industrial production (Fig. 5.1a) and simultaneously reducing current account disequilibria; however, the attempt to devalue the currency in real terms was checked by continued revaluation of the dollar.

This fact, together with the severe loss of foreign exchange reserves and the increasing difficulties faced by the authorities in negotiating new international loans led to a radical change in economic policy in the second semester of 1984. In 1985 restrictive aggregate demand policies and a rapid crawl of the peso replaced the role which had been assigned since 1982 to QRs as the mechanism of balance of payments adjustment (Ocampo and Lora, 1987).

Devaluation was extremely successful in generating a strong effect on relative prices. It thus facilitated the moderate liberalization of the trade regime agreed with the World Bank in 1985. As in the early 1970s, most of the liberalization initially concentrated in reducing red tape and delays in approving licences for non-competitive imports of intermediate and capital goods. After mid–1985, the prohibitive list was reduced to a few items and the free licensing regime progressively expanded to encompass one year later 36 per cent of the tariff schedule (Table 5.1). The import budget was gradually increased, particularly in 1986, when the country experienced a short coffee boom. However, the proportion of import licences rejected remained historically high up to 1988; in 1989, it finally returned to the levels typical of the late 1970s and early 1980s. Despite a significant liberalization, at the end of the process, in 1989, less than 18 per cent of the domestic production of tradable goods was subject to competition from imports under the free licensing regime (Ocampo, 1990a).

As part of the policy shift, tariffs were significantly cut in 1985 (Table 5.1). However, as many exemptions were simultaneously eliminated, average collected tariffs were actually raised (Cubillos and Torres, 1987). Increases in the import surcharge decreed for fiscal reasons in 1985 and 1987 also enhanced aggregate tariff protection. Thus, a moderate liberalization of QRs, mostly for non-competitive goods, was accompanied by higher import duties, generating a net protectionist effect. None the less, as had been true during the 1967–74 boom, import liberalization was not a *precondition* for export expansion but rather a *result* of the normalization of balance of payments conditions.

As part of the reforms adopted in 1985, the Vallejo Plan was widened, to allow the importation of intermediate and capital goods for non-traditional export activities, even if goods were produced domestically. As a compensation, 'indirect' exporters were also allowed access to the system. Other export incentives were cut from 1985 to 1989, partly as a reflection of policy decisions (the reduction of tax certificates and the increase in the interest rate charged by PROEXPO), but largely as the result of the inadequate growth of PROEXPO credit in the face of a new boom of non-traditional exports. In any case, despite the reduction of export subsidies and the liberalization of QRs, exchange rate policy was extremely effective in generating a devaluation of the effective exchange for both exports and imports. By 1986, both rates had amply surpassed their historical peaks (Table 5.1).

The 1984–5 stabilization package had moderate contractionary effects, particularly on industrial activities. Under the favourable conditions created by the 1986 coffee boom, the economy returned to a more steady growth path. However, industrial growth remained unstable and both GDP and industrial growth kept significantly below their 1967–74 record. Finally, inflation tended to accelerate, with the industrial sector playing a leading role in the process (Fig. 5.1a and 5.2a).

Frustration with the inability to return to rapid rates of growth with price stability generated a perception of the authorities that trade policy required a radical change towards an explicitly outward-oriented strategy. More important than this factor was the ideological swing towards a classical market-oriented ideology and its rapid and somewhat unexpected penetration in Latin America. The new trade policy thus formed part of a larger package of reforms, which included the partial liberalization of exchange controls, the privatization of port services, open access to direct foreign investment and a moderate liberalization of the labour market. The emphasis placed by the defenders of the new model on the exhaustion of 'import substitution' was, none the less, misplaced, as the traditional ISI model had long been abandoned in Colombia and even the import-substitution component of the 'mixed' strategy had been downgraded since the early 1970s (see pp. 133 and 149).

A series of decisions taken since February 1990 by the Barco Administration, and followed by the Gaviria Administration, after its inauguration in August 1990, thus led to a rapid turnabout in trade and, particularly, import policy. By November of that year, QRs had been virtually eliminated, as tariffs and the import surcharge were significantly cut. By December, the government announced a tariff reduction schedule, which would bring the consolidated tariff and surcharges to an average slightly under 15 per cent by 1994 (Ocampo, 1990a; Garay, 1991: ch. 1; Hallberg and Takacs, 1991). As a result of strong inflationary pressures, the government decided in June and July to speed up the reductions planned for 1992, and in August those expected for 1993 and 1994. This meant that import duties were cut by two-thirds in 18 months. Export incentives were adjusted more gradually. However, credit subsidies were virtually eliminated in October 1990, and a reduction of the tax rebate was initiated in May 1991 (Table 5.1), with the purpose of bringing it to an average level consistent with estimates of incidence of indirect taxes on non-traditional exports.

Simultaneously, in the meeting of the Andean presidents at Galapagos in December 1989, and their later rendezvous at La Paz in November 1990, the Andean Group experienced an equally radical change. In particular, the long-postponed liberalization of intra-regional trade was accelerated and was virtually completed in January 1992 (July 1992 for Ecuador and Peru). They also decided, in Cartagena, in December 1991, that a Customs Union should be in place in 1992, with tariffs slightly lower than those adopted by Colombia in August 1991.

To pave the ground for import liberalization, the crawl of the peso was accelerated from mid-1989, generating by 1990 a significant real devaluation, which undoubtedly facilitated the trade reform at a political level. However, acceleration of inflation led to a new stabilization programme in 1991, which included a moderate real appreciation of the peso and, as we have seen, the acceleration of tariff reductions programmed for 1992–4, and a stringent fiscal and monetary policy. The combined effect of revaluation, liberalization and tariff reduction has been a massive revaluation of the import exchange rate and a more moderate revaluation of that applicable to non-traditional exports, which still stands, however, at a historically high level (Table 5.1).

The structure of effective tariff protection

Despite swings in import policy, the traditional escalated structure established by the 1959 and 1964 tariff reforms remained relatively unchanged in the following decades (Martínez, 1986). The effective protection granted by the tariff and its evolution over time is difficult to assess on the basis of existing studies, for four different reasons: (i) few studies have tried to measure the 'water' in the tariff; (ii) few have estimated the effect of existing exemptions on protection; (iii) studies usually exclude tariff surcharges from the calculations; and (iv) effective protection rates are generally estimated using the whole tariff schedule, regardless of the fact that domestic production covers 40 per cent or less of all items in the schedule.

Table 5.2 summarizes existing estimates of effective protection to manufacturing activities. Sectoral rates have been weighted by 1979 values added to generate totals for traditional and late industries. Despite obvious differences in the methodologies used to estimate effective protection, several features stand out.

First, legal effective protection – i.e. that granted independently of exemptions and 'water' in the protection system – has been generally high. This fact is clearer when import surcharges are included and the calculations and the analysis is restricted to domestically produced goods. Moreover, although time comparisons are not reliable, effective tariff protection may have stood at a historical peak just before the recent liberalization. Even after the massive reductions decreed in 1990 and 1991, it still remained at a moderate 35 per cent.

Secondly, legal effective protection has been generally higher for the traditional manufacturing sectors. However, a large proportion of the apparent dispersion between and among traditional and 'late' industries is

Table 5.2 Effective protection, Corden method, Colombia

ISIC	Sector	Effective protection used 1969	Using legal tariffs, complete tariff schedule									Using legal tariffs and surcharges, domestically produced goods	
			Using collected tariff rates			Tariffs only				Tariffs and surcharges			
			1974	1984	1985	1979	1984	1985	1989	1989	1991	1989	1991
311/12	Foodstuffs	8.9	54.0	41.3	37.9	75.1	124.6	108.3	146.5	185.7	60.0	179.9	59.0
313	Beverages	103.3	75.2	55.3	26.1	79.9	136.2	92.5	95.0	119.2	31.4	108.7	30.5
314	Tobacco	83.6	97.6	17.9	48.1	50.6	86.1	87.5	100.1	123.2	36.4	91.2	31.0
321	Textiles	7.6	16.0	70.0	71.8	129.0	209.6	104.8	102.3	134.3	36.2	149.9	37.8
322	Apparel	12.7	49.3	-11.0	-17.2	108.2	185.2	109.6	116.9	143.3	38.1	143.3	39.3
323/24	Leather goods	4.1	14.8	32.5	28.7	63.9	133.7	87.5	57.2	88.0	20.9	108.4	27.7
331	Wood, excl. furniture	1.1	17.8	31.4	30.1	71.6	117.3	80.9	80.9	109.2	30.9	118.0	32.6
332	Furniture	-10.9	57.8	16.4	-16.3	67.8	125.9	67.0	66.2	93.7	38.4	92.0	39.3
34	Paper and printing	8.0	40.8	8.1	41.7	38.4	61.0	51.4	56.1	81.5	24.8	92.5	30.3
351/52	Basic chemicals	22.6	7.3	35.9	37.5	25.3	41.3	34.7	23.0	44.4	16.5	64.9	21.8
353/54	Oil refining	4.1	6.7	49.4	49.1	23.6	27.0	30.2	31.7	59.2	27.6	73.3	30.8
355	Rubber	-25.8	18.1	60.4	68.5	75.7	99.1	71.7	58.9	88.3	28.6	99.7	31.8
356	Plastics	89.2	n.a.	62.6	57.7	73.8	126.3	88.6	88.6	118.6	33.9	131.0	38.9
36	Non-metallic minerals	0.0	5.3	37.3	43.1	43.0	71.7	53.6	49.3	75.6	25.7	75.0	26.1
37	Basic metals	32.1	8.8	28.2	38.1	28.8	42.7	32.4	24.7	53.1	18.0	69.8	23.7
381	Metal products	42.9	47.0	55.9	58.5	63.9	99.7	75.6	58.3	84.8	31.0	87.4	32.6
382	Non-electrical machinery	11.9	27.4	28.7	31.4	25.8	39.8	24.8	20.8	44.2	13.1	52.3	18.2
383	Electrical machinery	668.1	28.4	30.2	31.1	51.0	75.2	50.6	40.7	67.2	23.8	80.1	28.3
384	Transport equipment	319.0	70.9	29.7	22.9	72.5	99.1	61.5	71.3	96.3	29.0	117.5	38.7
385/90	Scientific equipment	0.0	24.1	44.6	37.6	101.1	76.7	58.0	41.1	69.9	24.8	77.3	31.2
	Traditional sectors[a]	6.7[c]	41.7	46.9	40.8	81.1	134.6	90.1	98.9	129.2	38.7	129.7	39.0
	Late industries[a,b]	104.5	28.4[d]	40.3	40.3	45.9	67.4	50.0	43.8	68.8	22.8	83.4	28.1
	Total manufacturing[a]	53.3[c]	36.5[d]	44.3	40.6	67.0	107.6	74.0	76.8	105.0	32.3	111.1	34.7

Sources: Hutchenson (1973); Cubillos and Torres (1987); Departamento Nacional de Planeación.
[a] Weighted by 1979 values added.
[b] Sectors 351/352, 355, 356, 37 and 38.
[c] Excludes beverages and tobacco.
[d] Excludes plastics.

associated with goods which are not produced in the country. Thus, the relative effective protection of late industries is significantly higher when estimates refer only to domestically produced goods. After the August 1991 reform, the theoretical average effective protection for those industries was 28 per cent versus 39 per cent for traditional industries.

Thirdly, protection is significantly smaller if exemptions are taken into account; for such purpose, effective rates are estimated with average collected rather than with legal tariffs. Such exemptions include those benefiting the public sector (eliminated in 1991), a variable list of 'priority' private activities, imports from the Andean Group and the Latin American Integration Agreement, and inputs for non-traditional exports (Vallejo Plan).

Finally, throughout the period of analysis, there has been substantial 'water' in the tariff, particularly in traditional manufacturing sectors. In contrast, it is likely that for some 'late' industries, QRs have kept domestic/foreign price ratios above nominal tariff protection. Since many late industries produce intermediate goods, this has traditionally reduced even further the effective protection granted to traditional industries. The relation between price ratios and nominal protection has probably followed fluctuations of the real exchange rate. Thus, when the exchange rate has depreciated, the 'water' has increased; when the exchange rate has appreciated the 'water' has decreased. This implies that domestic industrial prices have a strong non-tradable component. Domestic dollar prices of traditional manufacturing goods do, in fact, show a strong negative correlation with the real exchange rate (Ocampo, 1990a).

Few studies have tried to measure the magnitude of 'water' in the protection system. The study by Hutchenson (1973) for 1969, summarized in Table 5.2, indicated that tariff protection contained substantial 'water' for traditional industries, but very little for a few late industries. In contrast the study by Fernandez et al. (1985), with data for 1983, a year of substantial currency overvaluation and harsh QRs, indicated that domestic/foreign price ratios were generally higher than those allowed by tariffs. The study concentrated, however, on late industries and did not carefully correct for commercial margins involved in the comparisons.

The most recent (unpublished) study, undertaken by Banco de la República in early 1989, concluded that there was considerable 'water' in the tariff. However, the analysis concentrated on a few sectors. The study found that domestic/foreign price ratios fell substantially short of the nominal tariff for foodstuffs (8 versus 53 per cent), paper products (3 versus 59 per cent) and pharmaceuticals (–25 versus 38 per cent) and was only similar for auto parts (37 versus 43 per cent). This evidence is consistent with the lack of demand for most consumer goods when an auction system was temporarily adopted in 1990 as a transition to full import liberalization (Ocampo, 1990a; Hallberg and Takacs, 1991).

DEMAND ASPECTS OF MANUFACTURING GROWTH

General links between domestic demand, external policy and industrial growth

Figures 5.1b and c show the major links between external policies and industrial performance in Colombia since 1967. Table 5.3 reproduces, in turn, the usual demand decomposition of sources of growth popularized by Chenery. As a whole, import substitution has not been an engine of manufacturing growth during this period. On the contrary, the aggregate import-substitution coefficient (the ratio of domestic production for the domestic market to apparent domestic demand) has shown a generally downward trend. Exports have been a moderate engine, as reflected in the upward trend in the ratio of exports to production.

Both indices show, in turn, a strong cyclical pattern, closely associated with shifts in trade and exchange rate policies. In the early part of the 1967–74 boom, domestic demand, and imports in particular, grew rapidly, largely as a result of the repressed demand for non-competing goods accumulated during the years of severe import and exchange controls. In the later part of the boom, the import substitution coefficient normalized. This factor, together with booming manufacturing exports, helped to sustain rapid manufacturing growth.

The mid-1970s experienced a radical change in the relation between external policies and industrial performance. Thus, as import substitution fell back, the export boom came to an end. The strongest impacts were felt, however, in the early 1980s, when the accumulated effects of exchange rate revaluation, import liberalization and the reduction of export subsidies were combined with a strong world and Latin American recession and collapsing terms of trade for most Colombian exports. In 1980–2, the direct contribution of external variables was an annual reduction of close to 4 per cent in industrial production, most of it associated with the rapid reversal in import substitution.

It is important to notice that the strongest contractionary effects of trade polices coincided with the collapse of international coffee prices. Thus, they can hardly be associated with the 'Dutch disease' effects of the coffee boom as such, which were rather mild, as the evolution of the industrial sector in 1975–9 indicates. A stronger 'Dutch disease' was thus a result of exchange rate and trade policies induced by the debt boom of the early 1980s.

The radical change in external policies adopted by the Betancur Administration led to a rapid change in the contribution of external policies to industrial growth. In 1983–5, manufacturing growth was basically associated with the rapid reversal of adverse trends in the import-substitution

Table 5.3 Sectoral sources of growth, demand side, Colombia (gross value of production)

	Foodstuffs	Beverages	Tobacco	Textiles, apparel and leather	Wood and products	Paper and printing	Chemicals	Non-metallic minerals products	Metals and products	Machinery	Transport equipment	Total
A. Domestic demand												
1967–70	3.43	10.98	17.43	5.80	4.71	14.77	15.33	9.51	15.19	21.37	14.64	11.20
1970–4	6.37	6.13	0.32	6.84	2.37	9.93	14.41	6.44	6.96	3.90	4.73	7.62
1974–9	5.78	6.55	−2.46	2.55	0.16	3.34	1.81	3.75	4.50	6.76	9.76	4.23
1979–82	2.87	1.94	1.93	−2.51	−3.06	2.34	1.99	4.01	6.09	7.64	6.10	2.76
1982–5	0.13	2.45	2.06	0.10	5.40	2.85	4.88	1.42	−2.49	−6.99	−11.07	−0.49
1985–9	2.98	1.46	−7.11	3.19	8.96	3.66	3.13	6.74	1.41	11.02	5.36	3.74
1989–91	−0.93	−1.18	7.63	0.43	−3.47	5.26	1.34	−0.57	1.34	−4.59	−8.38	−0.31
B. Import substitution												
1967–70	1.08	−1.81	−10.43	0.04	−0.51	−1.99	−5.49	−2.07	−5.53	−3.01	11.17	−2.96
1970–4	−0.16	0.17	4.28	−0.95	0.19	2.31	−0.08	−0.55	2.26	8.63	12.02	1.12
1974–9	−1.11	0.13	−1.84	−0.34	−0.13	0.68	1.01	−0.03	−1.54	−3.08	−3.03	−0.78
1979–82	−1.11	−0.06	−0.73	−1.51	−1.54	−2.15	−1.88	−0.39	−8.64	−11.23	−12.84	−3.53
1982–5	2.37	1.06	7.05	0.86	2.23	1.37	−0.39	1.24	1.71	9.50	10.82	3.44
1985–9	0.50	0.13	0.06	−0.71	−0.61	1.46	0.42	0.13	3.82	−4.45	3.90	0.03
1989–91	−0.43	1.20	−0.60	−1.78	0.35	0.41	0.40	−0.83	−1.51	−1.21	−3.58	−0.14
C. Exports												
1967–70	0.18	0.00	0.00	1.52	1.17	−1.01	0.20	1.13	0.54	0.67	0.28	0.50
1970–4	0.25	0.01	0.04	1.50	2.35	0.35	1.18	2.03	0.77	1.29	0.46	0.90
1974–9	0.79	0.00	0.08	0.79	−0.26	0.81	0.41	1.54	−0.08	1.19	0.31	0.58
1979–82	0.11	0.01	−0.02	−1.23	−1.38	0.17	−0.35	−2.10	−0.25	−0.14	−0.21	−0.41
1982–5	0.14	0.03	−0.08	−0.53	−0.51	0.61	0.84	−0.14	−0.28	−1.61	−0.39	0.03
1985–9	0.26	0.01	0.08	2.75	−0.82	0.19	0.75	0.89	−0.06	0.98	0.02	0.73
1989–91	2.11	0.11	1.59	4.62	2.76	2.14	2.73	5.09	0.80	4.68	0.88	2.60

D. Total growth

1967–70	4.69	9.17	7.00	7.36	5.37	11.77	10.04	8.57	10.20	19.03	26.09	8.74
1970–4	6.46	6.31	4.64	7.39	4.91	12.59	15.51	7.92	9.99	13.82	17.21	9.64
1974–9	5.46	6.68	-4.22	3.00	-0.23	4.83	3.23	5.26	2.88	4.87	7.04	4.03
1979–82	1.87	1.89	1.18	-5.25	-5.98	0.36	-0.24	1.52	-2.80	-3.73	-6.95	-1.18
1982–5	2.64	3.54	9.03	0.43	7.12	4.83	5.33	2.52	-1.06	0.90	-0.64	2.98
1985–9	3.74	1.60	-6.97	5.23	7.53	5.31	4.30	7.76	5.17	7.55	9.28	4.50
1989–91	0.75	0.13	8.62	3.27	-0.36	7.81	4.47	3.69	0.63	-1.12	-11.08	2.15

Sources: Estimates based on DANE National Accounts. The gross value of production and imports include commercial margins. Imports also include duties. 1991 according to preliminary estimates of FEDESARROLLO.

coefficient typical of the early 1980s. As the coefficient normalized, the new export boom was felt, helping to sustain the new phase of industrial expansion. Moreover, despite a dramatic contraction of the domestic demand for manufactures in 1991, the export boom which the Colombian economy experienced in 1990 and 1991 helped to sustain moderate industrial growth. Indeed, according to preliminary evidence, in 1991 the export coefficient of the manufacturing sector reached 12 per cent, significantly above the 7.3 per cent peak of the mid-1970s (Tables 5.3 and 5.4).

Despite the close association between external policies and industrial performance, domestic demand has continued to be the major determinant of manufacturing growth in the period under analysis. Thus, the significant slowdown of manufacturing production since the mid-1970s must be associated basically to the deceleration of domestic demand, as a reflection of the slowdown in the rate of economic growth.[2] In fact, although the income elasticity of demand for intermediates has shown a small but statistically significant decline in the period under analysis, the demand for all producer goods has been income-elastic since 1967 (1.2 for intermediates and 1.5 for capital goods).

In contrast, the household demand for manufactures has been characterized by a unitary elasticity. Such a global estimate hides, however, contrasting trends of different consumer goods. The share of processed foodstuffs and beverages in household consumption has remained fairly constant over the past quarter century; that for tobacco, textiles, apparel and leather products has shown a strong downward trend, particularly in the 1980s, whereas the demand for the other manufactured consumer goods (paper and printing, chemicals and durables) has been income-elastic. Overall, the share of manufactures in household consumption increased from 36.3 per cent in 1967 to over 39 per cent in 1976–8, indicating that the growth in the demand for income-elastic manufactures overwhelmed the contraction in that for income-inelastic goods. Since the late-1970s, the latter prevailed, and such share declined to 36.9 per cent in 1989. This evolution indicates that household consumption patterns have matured, reaching an Engel's turning point in the late 1970s. This fact has enormous implications for those manufacturing sectors for which, in contrast to historical patterns prior to 1967, domestic demand has ceased to be a driving force of industrialization.[3]

The downward trend of the relative price of industrial goods was interrupted in the late 1960s or early 1970s (Posada and Rhenals, 1988; Ocampo, 1994). Since then, relative industrial prices have shown a strong cyclical element with a slightly upward trend. Given the relatively high price-elasticity of the household demand for manufactured goods (–0.9 in 1967–89), such a trend has also had adverse effects on domestic demand and, thus, on industrial growth. These fluctuations have been closely associated with the evolution of unit costs of production (Fig. 5.2b), and indus-

Table 5.4 Sectoral features, Colombia

	Foodstuffs	Beverages	Tobacco	Textiles, apparel and leather	Wood and products	Paper and printing	Chemicals	Non-metallic minerals	Metal and products	Machinery	Transport equipment	Total
A. Share of value added												
1967	15.23	9.11	5.66	23.09	3.62	6.30	15.35	6.68	9.32	3.51	2.13	100.00
1974	13.41	10.76	4.85	21.44	2.90	7.57	15.19	6.17	8.93	4.71	4.07	100.00
1979	15.25	11.64	2.87	19.42	2.54	8.32	15.48	6.53	8.10	5.40	4.45	100.00
1983	17.24	13.07	3.05	16.16	2.49	8.78	15.88	7.08	7.51	4.90	3.84	100.00
1989	16.63	11.47	2.28	16.83	2.84	9.36	16.40	7.69	7.07	5.37	4.07	100.00
1991	16.18	11.02	2.58	17.20	2.70	10.43	17.15	7.92	6.86	5.03	3.08	100.00
B. Share of exports												
1967	37.96	0.00	0.00	21.02	5.24	10.37	7.54	7.74	7.28	2.41	0.07	100.00
1974	17.29	0.05	0.05	34.19	6.22	3.03	15.18	8.51	7.32	4.50	1.12	100.00
1979	20.67	0.02	0.12	31.22	3.68	5.47	14.78	9.13	4.32	6.25	1.53	100.00
1983	32.21	0.12	0.07	22.57	1.88	7.24	20.73	5.17	2.90	4.21	1.12	100.00
1989	20.44	0.15	0.10	34.56	1.06	6.84	22.17	6.05	1.94	4.46	0.45	100.00
1991	19.64	0.26	0.38	31.58	1.43	7.06	22.92	7.42	2.16	6.39	0.76	100.00
C. Exports coefficient[a]												
1967	5.80	0.00	0.00	3.57	6.39	6.59	1.77	7.07	3.44	2.98	0.12	3.70
1974	5.18	0.04	0.14	10.19	15.47	2.48	4.34	12.94	5.11	5.67	1.57	5.75
1979	7.35	0.02	0.60	12.43	14.33	5.48	5.59	16.65	4.05	9.63	2.37	7.31
1983	6.98	0.06	0.23	7.29	5.24	4.67	5.09	5.88	1.96	4.96	1.41	4.95
1989	7.11	0.14	0.64	16.87	3.91	6.20	7.91	9.40	2.16	7.25	0.80	7.54
1991	11.41	0.37	3.34	23.78	9.02	9.09	12.47	17.92	3.74	16.91	2.81	12.08
D. Import substitution[b]												
1967	93.45	97.53	99.50	97.88	97.70	77.22	78.34	96.13	66.77	33.34	26.38	79.56
1974	95.92	93.81	92.24	94.63	97.03	79.21	68.61	89.03	63.22	42.68	50.50	76.68
1979	91.24	94.33	83.45	92.95	96.30	81.77	72.11	88.90	58.89	37.17	44.81	73.91
1983	91.27	94.59	86.31	89.20	90.04	77.78	68.33	90.61	49.99	27.51	37.82	69.32
1989	97.15	96.40	99.77	87.98	95.39	84.75	68.99	91.72	56.04	33.16	53.24	74.44
1991	96.22	98.76	98.68	84.23	96.14	85.44	69.58	89.99	54.35	32.21	48.93	74.21

Sources: See Table 5.3.
[a]Exports as a proportion of the gross value of production.
[b]Production for the domestic market as a share of apparent domestic demand.

trial mark-ups have also exhibited significant cyclical variations (Fig. 5.2c). Strong upward pressures have been characteristic of the end of the 1967–74 period and the post-1983 recovery. Econometric evidence (not reported here) indicates, however, no important links between mark-ups and domestic demand and, on the contrary, a somewhat stronger effect of protection through price mechanisms (real exchange rate and tariffs) and QRs on the former variable. None the less, the latter effects are much weaker than those of costs on industrial prices.[4]

Sectoral effects of external policies

The effects of domestic demand, import substitution and exports have varied considerably among sectors (Table 5.3). The slowdown in the rate of growth of domestic demand since the mid-1970s had an adverse effect on many industrial branches, particularly textiles, paper, chemicals and non-metallic minerals. Since the late-1970s, this factor became widespread and most sectors actually experienced a significant contraction of domestic demand in either 1979–82 or, particularly, the years of balance of payments adjustment, 1982–5. Since then, demand has generally recovered but it has not reached yet the rates of growth typical of the 1967–74 boom.

On the other hand, import substitution had been completed by 1967 in foodstuffs, beverages, tobacco, textiles, wood and non-metallic minerals; it was fairly advanced in paper, chemicals and metals and still very limited in machinery and transport equipment. Significant contributions of import substitution to economic growth were obtained in 1967–74 in the latter two sectors, especially in transport equipment (Table 5.3). Since 1967 and especially since 1974, there has been a general reversal of import substitution, notably in textiles, chemicals, metals and machinery. Most sectors also experienced a sharp cycle of the import-substitution coefficient in 1979–85; such movements were particularly strong, however, for machinery and transport equipment (Tables 5.3 and 5.4).

Among the traditional manufacturing sectors, exports made the most significant contribution to growth in 1967–74 in textiles, wood and non-metallic minerals. The latter two sectors show a disappointing export performance since the mid-1970s, except in very recent years. Textiles have, in contrast, shown a strong cycle with an upward trend and by 1989 had the highest export ratio of the Colombian manufacturing sector. Foodstuffs and paper and printing also show a moderate contribution of exports to sectoral growth in different periods. Among late industries, there are contrasting trends between chemicals and machinery, on the one hand, and metals and transport equipment, on the other. Exports have shown an important dynamism in the former two sectors, particularly in the case of chemicals. This is, thus, the sector where late import substitution – particularly in the 1960s – has been combined with export growth in the 1970s

154

and 1980s. In contrast, metals and transport equipment show a disappointing export performance.

Quantitatively, manufacturing exports have been dominated by foodstuffs, textiles and chemicals. Overall, these sectors made up two-thirds of industrial exports from 1967 to 1979 and three-quarters in the 1980s. Exports of foodstuffs have been the most stable but the least dynamic. Their share in total manufacturing exports has thus been anti-cyclical: it has tended to increase when the aggregate export coefficient declined, indicating that it has been less sensitive to shifts in domestic policies and international demand. Textiles display, in contrast, an upward trend and a strong pro-cyclical performance. Finally, chemicals exhibit a strong upward trend and a less marked pro-cyclical pattern (Table 5.4).

Existing studies indicate that both short-term and structural factors have had significant effects on non-traditional export performance. The short-term determinants are relative price shifts and the dynamics of international markets, with the emphasis on one or the other depending on the author (Echavarría, 1982; Villar, 1983; Botero and Meisel, 1988).[5] On the other hand, three structural factors are particularly important. Overall, manufacturing exports are relatively natural resource and unskilled labour-intensive (Thoumi, 1979; Villar, 1983). However, exporting firms are relatively larger and more capital-intensive than non-exporting firms in each sector (Echavarría and Perry, 1981; Villar, 1983). Finally, a few capital-intensive and human capital-intensive sectors have, none the less, been successful in combining import substitution with an important penetration in regional markets.

Factor-intensity is also closely associated with the destination of manufacturing exports. Thus, most of the natural resource-intensive exports (foodstuffs, wood and basic metals) depend strongly on markets from developed countries (78 per cent in 1990). Also, more than half of all textile and non-metallic mineral exports are destined to DCs. Paper and printing exports are in an intermediate position, with DCs and regional markets absorbing an approximately equal share of exports. Finally, in the case of chemicals and machinery, regional markets are dominant (70 per cent in 1990).

To explore the short-term determinants of manufacturing export performance, Table 5.5 summarizes the results of eclectic export functions. Sectoral export coefficients are the dependent variable in all cases. Following traditional estimations, both current and lagged relative export prices are included as explanatory variables. Given the market fragmentation typical of manufactured goods, the growth of world trade is also included as an independent variable in the regressions; the index used is a weighted average of real imports of OECD and Latin America. The dynamic economies of scale emphasized by new trade theories are captured by an index of 'export experience', which is defined as accumulated exports since 1951,

Table 5.5 Determinants of export coefficients, Colombia (t-statistic in parenthesis; long-run standardized coefficient in square brackets)

Sector[a]	Constant	Relative prices		Growth of world trade		Export experience	Average tariffs	Tariff equivalent of QRs	First order autocorrelation	R²	DW
		Current	Lagged	Current	Lagged						
Foodstuffs[b] (1967–89) [0.0623]	0.0780				0.0113 (0.227) [0.004]		-0.0519 (-0.841) [-0.002]	-0.0242 (-0.559) [-0.002]		0.1741	2.383
Beverages (1972–89) [0.001]	-0.0002		0.0003 (0.860) [0.000]		0.0001 (1.001) [0.000]	0.0002* (1.672) [0.000]			0.6199* (1.832)	0.7710	1.635
Tobacco (1972–89) [0.003]	0.0046				0.0084 (0.797) [0.003]	0.0006 (1.365) [0.001]	-0.0045 (-0.227) [0.000]	-0.0173* (-1.652) [-0.001]		0.1197	1.661
Textiles, apparel and leather (1967–89) [0.099]	-0.0508	0.0798* (1.936) [0.014]	0.0753* (1.655) [0.013]		0.1107 (1.443) [0.035]	0.0007 (0.068) [0.000]		-0.0708 (-0.652) [-0.005]		0.7517	1.613
Wood and products (1967–89) [0.094]	0.1603	0.0223 (0.323) [0.003]		0.2713* (1.441) [0.085]		0.0251 (0.528) [0.007]	-0.4292* (-2.327) [-0.019]	-0.1741 (-1.079) [-0.011]		0.1618	2.122
Paper and printing (1967–89) [0.055]	0.0165		0.0151 (0.484) [0.002]	0.0583 (0.860) [0.018]		0.0109 (0.801) [0.008]			0.5796* (2.736)	0.3947	1.485
Chemicals (1967–89) [0.050]	-0.0436	0.0593* (3.065) [0.007]		0.0941* (2.864) [0.030]	0.0732* (2.315) [0.023]	0.0307* (8.469) [0.022]		-0.0395 (-1.422) [-0.003]		0.8274	2.069

Industry (period) [mean]							
Non-metallic minerals (1968–89) [0.118]	-0.0304	0.2125* (4.431) [0.029]	0.1560* (2.497) [0.049]		-0.0566* (-1.875) [-0.004]	0.8066* (5.855)	0.8504	1.148
Metals and products (1967–89) [0.035]	0.0694		0.0777* (2.227) [0.024]	-0.1384* (-3.182) [-0.006]			0.3731	1.837
Machinery (1968–89) [0.065]	-0.0589	0.1575* (2.228) [0.008]	0.2025* (3.423) [0.064]	0.0175* (3.459) [0.016]	-0.3191* (-4.477) [-0.021]	0.2979* (1.625)	0.7485	1.961
Transport equipment (1967–89) [0.020]	-0.0002	0.0339* (2.320) [0.006]	0.0327 (0.717) [0.010]		-0.0908* (-2.264) [-0.006]		0.3226	2.324
Non-oil manufacturing (1967–89) [0.059]	0.0119	0.0459* (2.782) [0.006]	0.0507* (1.921) [0.016]	0.0111* (3.073) [0.005]	-0.0351 (-0.953) [-0.002]		0.7202	1.421

a Period covered by regression in parenthesis; mean value of dependent variable in square brackets.
b Regression included a dummy variable for 1977.
* Significantly different from 0 at 90% confidence level.

assuming a 10 per cent annual depreciation of 'experience' (20 per cent coefficient was also tried, with somewhat poorer results); experience is measured relative to current exports. Finally, to capture the 'anti-export bias' generated by import policies, both the average collected tariff and the tariff equivalent of QRs are also included as explanatory variables.

For non-oil manufacturing as a whole, relative prices, the growth of world trade and export experience make statistically significant contributions to export performance. In contrast, import policies do not play any important role. Among the three dominant sectors, foodstuffs show an inertial pattern with no sensitivity to any of the variables included in the estimations. Textile exports depend basically on relative prices and world demand, with experience playing no role. Chemicals show a strong dependence on world trade and experience and a somewhat weaker dependence on relative prices.

Relative prices also play an important role in the dynamics of the exports of non-metallic minerals, machinery and transport equipment, and the dynamics of world trade in those of wood, non-metallic minerals, metals and machinery. Export experience also influences the exports of machinery (this is also true of beverages and tobacco, but they have insignificant export ratios). This result, together with the important role which this variable plays in chemical exports indicate that dynamic scale economies are primarily important for late industries heavily dependent on regional markets.

In contrast, the role of the 'anti-export bias' of the trade regime on export performance is limited. As indicated, they do not come out as a statistically significant determinant of total non-oil manufacturing exports. They play a significant role only in sectors which are relatively secondary for aggregate export performance. Thus, high tariffs deter exports of wood and metals, and QRs those of tobacco, metals, machinery and transport equipment. There is also a statistically weak effect of QRs on the exports of chemicals.

As a result of demand factors affecting sectoral performance, the industrial structure of the country has experienced some important changes since 1967. During the 1967–74 boom, the sectors which increased their share in industrial value added were those which underwent additional import substitution – paper and printing, machinery and transport equipment – and beverages. From 1974 to 1983, the rising share of late industries in value added was interrupted and, in some sectors, particularly metals, experienced an important retrogression. Affected by the slow growth in domestic demand and falling export coefficients, textiles faced an ever more pronounced relative decline. Curiously enough, as a result of a better domestic demand performance, some of the most traditional industries, foodstuffs and beverages, increased their share in industrial production. Finally, since 1983, those sectors experiencing rising export coefficients have been shown to increase their share in production. In particular, the relative decline of textiles has been reversed, as chemicals have resumed their long-run rising share in industrial production (Table 5.4).

SUPPLY DETERMINANTS OF INDUSTRIAL GROWTH

Productivity performance

A Verdoorn association between industrial growth and productivity performance is shown in Table 5.6. At an aggregate level, TFP increased at a rate over 1.2 per cent a year during the 1967–74 boom. The slowdown of industrial growth during the coffee bonanza of the 1970s and the recession which followed was reflected in a moderate decline of TFP. Since 1983, the partial recovery of industrial growth has been reflected in a new phase of TFP growth, at 0.9 per cent a year. Although this rate is slower than that achieved during the industrial boom of the late 1960s and early 1970s, its contribution to total growth has been higher (23 per cent versus 13 per cent during the boom).

Changes in capacity utilization have reinforced the effects of TFP, with an even clearer association with industrial growth. Increases in utilization during the 1967–74 boom were particularly strong.[6] The joint effect of these two factors was an impressive growth of productivity during this period – 3.3 per cent a year. In contrast, falling utilization rates (particularly in the early 1980s) magnified the moderate fall of TFP in 1975–82, leading to an aggregated productivity reduction of 1.0 per cent a year. Since 1983, the effects of rising capacity utilization have been positive but moderate.

At a sectoral level, TFP shows a more erratic pattern, with major sectoral differences across all subperiods of analysis. None the less, it also reflects the global Verdoorn trend. Thus, 1967–74 was a period of rising productivity in all sectors. The 1974–82 period shows, in contrast, a mixed pattern, with about half the sectors showing positive and half negative productivity growth. Since then, productivity performance has been positive again in most sectors.

Few studies have explored the determinants of productivity growth in the Colombian manufacturing sector. The early work by Dudley (1983) found evidence of strong learning effect on labour productivity in the metal-products sector in the 1960s, with this variable explaining annual productivity increases of 2–3 per cent a year. On the other hand, Sandoval (1982) with data for 51 firms in the period 1966–75 found a close association between labour productivity and production and no relation with (a relatively poor indicator of) R&D. The more recent work by Roberts (1988) explored the determinants of TFP growth with sectoral data for 1977–83. He also found a strong Verdoorn effect (with a 1 per cent growth

Table 5.6 Sources of growth, supply side, Colombia (value added at market prices)

	Foodstuffs	Beverages	Tobacco	Textiles, apparel and leather	Wood and products	Paper and printing	Chemicals	Non-metallic minerals products	Metal and products	Machinery	Transport equipment	Total
A. Total factor productivity												
1967–74	0.14	4.10	3.66	0.37	0.23	2.22	0.27	2.67	0.05	2.28	8.32	1.23
1974–82	-2.24	1.00	0.24	-1.41	-1.20	-0.55	-0.76	1.17	0.07	0.26	-1.66	-0.24
1982–9	1.36	2.05	0.78	0.95	5.29	0.06	2.66	1.10	-0.67	1.71	1.42	0.93
B. Capacity utilization												
1967–74	1.88	2.81	2.29	2.29	0.09	3.51	0.90	1.26	1.26	2.39	3.88	2.05
1974–82	0.79	-1.06	-2.70	-0.54	0.72	1.11	-0.31	-1.27	-1.45	-0.98	-1.14	-0.79
1982–9	-0.96	0.38	0.74	0.74	-1.51	1.57	0.13	0.26	0.66	0.22	2.12	0.28
C. Labour												
1967–74	1.89	1.74	0.64	3.42	2.46	2.79	3.60	1.72	4.09	7.00	1.33	2.89
1974–82	0.89	2.21	-0.75	-0.37	-0.97	0.37	1.18	0.29	0.02	0.63	0.97	0.45
1982–9	0.19	-1.17	-2.24	0.48	1.89	0.31	0.03	0.20	-0.78	1.35	0.35	0.27
D. Capital												
1967–74	3.43	2.89	0.37	2.02	3.20	3.27	4.26	2.38	3.15	1.67	4.88	2.96
1974–82	5.53	2.28	-0.54	1.55	0.41	2.78	2.49	3.55	1.80	2.95	2.92	2.69
1982–9	3.26	1.06	0.68	1.70	1.66	3.30	1.74	3.78	3.40	1.78	1.32	2.58
E. Total growth												
1967–74	7.35	11.54	6.96	8.11	5.99	11.79	9.02	8.02	8.56	13.34	18.40	9.12
1974–82	4.97	4.43	-3.76	-0.76	-1.04	3.72	2.61	3.74	0.44	2.86	1.09	2.12
1982–9	3.85	2.31	-0.05	3.87	7.32	5.23	4.57	5.33	2.61	5.06	5.21	4.06

Sources: See text and appendix.

being reflected in an increase of TFP of over 0.4 per cent), as well as a positive impact of rising import shares on TFP and adverse effects of higher concentration ratios. The latter two effects were, however, quantitatively weaker than the growth–productivity link.[7] In contrast, Ocampo (1990b) found no statistically significant relation between import penetration and labour productivity with quarterly data for nine industrial sectors in 1976–87, except in chemicals.

A more recent study by Echavarría (1990) explored these and other relations with cross-section data for close to 2,600 firms in 1974–9 and 1979–87. For both periods, he found a very high Verdoorn coefficient (in the order of 0.9) and evidence that productivity growth is higher for older, national firms. For 1974–9, he also found results similar to those of Roberts regarding the effects of import competition and industrial concentration on productivity, as well as a positive link between exports and the latter variable. However, for 1979–87, some of these relations came out with the opposite sign. For the earlier period, Echavarría also found evidence of a positive link between capital intensity and productivity. The effects of all these additional variables is, none the less, quantitatively weak, as a simple Verdoorn relation explains close to 88 per cent of the variance in productivity performance across firms.

The close relation between economic growth and productivity is confirmed in Table 5.7. This table shows the econometric determinants of TFP using pooled data for the eleven sectors considered in this study in six of the subperiods examined in Table 5.3 (excluding 1989–91 for lack of data). The exercise explores the effects of economic growth, industrial concentration and trade policies on TFP. The second of these variables is measured as the weighted four-digit concentration ratio in 1984, according to Misas (1989). Trade policies are measured alternatively by the real exchange rate for imports (including tariffs and surcharges, but excluding QRs) and indicators of QRs, and by the contribution of import substitution and exports to growth according to the Chenery growth exercise.

The results confirm the central role played by Verdoorn effects on TFP performance in the Colombian manufacturing sector. A simple regression using value added as the only explanatory variable explains, by itself, most of the variance in TFP growth. The estimated coefficients for this variable indicate that a 1 per cent growth in value added is reflected in TFP growth of 0.3 per cent. This coefficient is, thus, lower than those estimated by Echavarría and Roberts. The difference can be explained, however, by the fact that neither of these authors adjusted capital stocks by capacity utilization; the problem may be particularly severe in the study by Roberts, which refers to a short period of high instability of industrial growth. Indeed, using the same data but estimates of TFP unadjusted by capacity utilization, the estimated coefficient fluctuates between 0.5 and 0.6 – i.e. in the intermediate range between those of the aforementioned authors.

Table 5.7 Determinants of total factor productivity growth, Colombia, 1967–89 (t-statistic in parenthesis; standardized coefficient in square brackets)

	1967–70	1970–4	1974–9	1979–82	1982–5	1985–9
Constant	−0.006	−0.035*	−0.047	−0.003	−0.027*	−0.026
	(−1.49)	(−2.09)	(−1.54)	(−0.78)	(−1.66)	(−1.59)
Growth of value	0.355*	0.360*	0.332*	0.297*	0.307*	0.338*
added	(6.48)	(6.70)	(5.39)	(5.19)	(5.38)	(5.37)
	[0.020]	[0.020]	[0.018]	[0.017]	[0.017]	[0.019]
Four-digit		0.049*	0.049*		0.041	0.038
concentration		(1.79)	(1.75)		(1.50)	(1.41)
ratio		[0.005]	[0.005]		[0.004]	[0.004]
Real import			−0.001			
exchange rate			(−0.05)			
			[−0.000]			
Tariff equivalent of			0.084			
QRs			(1.24)			
			[0.004]			
Contribution of				0.169*	0.155*	0.139*
import substitution				(2.49)	(2.27)	(2.00)
				[0.008]	[0.007]	[0.006]
Contribution of						−0.415
exports						(−1.15)
						[−0.004]
R²	0.420	0.451	0.467	0.458	0.497	0.509

Sources: Pooled data results. See text. Productivity estimates have been adjusted by capacity utilization.
*Statistically different from 0 at 95% confidence level.

In contrast, the effects of trade variables and domestic concentration are contrary to Roberts' results for 1977–83. In particular, both import substitution and the four-digit concentration ratios have *positive* effects on TFP, which are particularly strong for import substitution. The tariff equivalent of QRs also come with a similar sign, but its statistical significance is weak. Finally, the contribution of exports comes out with a negative but statistically insignificant coefficient.

These results, together with those of former studies, indicate that Verdoorn effects dominate TFP performance in the Colombian manufacturing sector. This may be interpreted in the sense that TFP is largely a *dependent* rather than an independent variable, with the demand variables analysed in the previous section playing the dominant role in industrial growth. It also means that trade policy will only have a positive effect on productivity if it also has an expansionary effect on domestic production. In contrast, the direct effects of trade variables and domestic concentration on TFP are weaker and have the opposite sign to that suggested by defendants of domestic and external competition as a source of productivity enhancement.

Labour and capital

Industrial employment grew at a very healthy rate during the 1967–74 boom (6.6 per cent a year – fig. 5.3a). As a result, employment contributed with a 2.9 per cent growth, according to the usual Solow growth exercise (Table 5.6). Wages also increased in real terms in the early part of the boom, but then lagged in the face of rising inflation in 1973 and 1974 (Fig. 5.3b). In contrast, since the mid-1970s, employment performance in the Colombian industrial sector has been dismal. It increased by only 15 per cent between 1974 and 1979, declined sharply to 1985 and then partly recovered in the following years. By 1989, however, it was only 10 per cent above 1974 levels. As a result, the contribution of employment to industrial growth has been very low since the mid-1970s. Real wages show the opposite trend: they rose from the mid-1970s to the mid-1980s, but then stagnated, if deflated by the CPI, and declined in terms of industrial prices. Since the elasticity of the demand for labour to real wages is low (−0.1 to −0.2 according to existing studies – Misión de Empleo, 1986; Reyes, 1987), real wages have only exercised a weak effect on employment relative to the traditional Keynesian effect of economic activity on the latter variable.

Both the evolution of industrial employment and detailed analysis of labour market conditions (see, for example, Misión de Empleo, 1986) indicate that, despite unionization and legal restrictions on mobility, the industrial labour market is relatively flexible in Colombia. Moreover, unionization in the large-scale manufacturing sector has experienced a long-term decline in the period under analysis: from more than 60 per cent in the mid-1960s to 27 per cent in the second half of the 1980s.[8] On the other hand, the 1990 labour reform eliminated the major legal restrictions on labour mobility.

Whereas the contribution of labour to industrial growth has been secondary since the mid-1970s, that of capital has been larger and steadier – from 2.6 to 3.0 per cent throughout the period of analysis (Table 5.6). Capital accumulation shows, none the less, two discernible peaks, in the early 1970s and in the early 1980s (Fig. 5.3c). The natures of these investment booms were, however, quite different. The earlier one was clearly a reflection of the accelerator mechanism, and was thus consistent with falling capital–output ratios. In contrast, that of the early 1980s was induced by the low relative price of capital goods and thus led to a sharp increase in the global capital–output ratio (Fig. 5.3d).

Given the high import content of industrial machinery and equipment, the low relative price of capital goods in the early 1980s was largely associated with the real appreciation of the peso. Thus, the high costs of revaluation on the demand side (see p. 149) were somewhat compensated by its favourable effects on capital accumulation. To a large extent, the

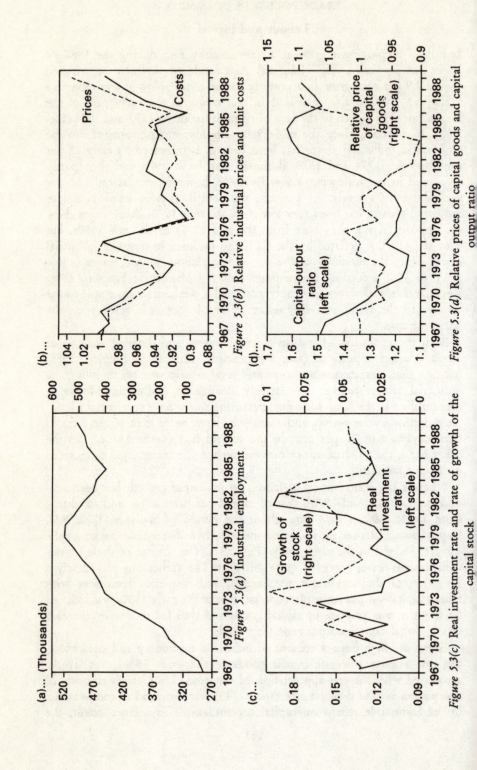

Figure 5.3(a) Industrial employment

Figure 5.3(b) Relative industrial prices and unit costs

Figure 5.3(c) Real investment rate and rate of growth of the capital stock

Figure 5.3(d) Relative prices of capital goods and capital output ratio

most recent industrial recovery was facilitated by investment in previous years. Indeed, real devaluation has had an adverse effect on industrial investment. None the less, the rate of capital accumulation showed a renewed upward trend from 1986 to 1989 (Fig. 5.3c) which, according to FEDESARROLLO's Entrepreneurial Surveys, was only interrupted by the severe domestic recession of 1991.

Investment financing also experienced substantial changes in the period under analysis. Three major phases in the evolution of the financial structure of industrial firms can be differentiated (Sandoval, 1983; Chica, 1984–5; Ocampo, 1989; Acosta, 1991). The first, which coincides with the 1967–74 boom, was a period of rising dependence on development financing. To a large extent, this period can be regarded as a continuation of trends which were discernible in the 1960s (see p. 133). The second is a phase of high debt financing and risky financial deepening on both sides of the balance sheets of productive firms. This process was to a large extent determined by the moderate financial liberalizations of 1974 and 1979, the financial innovations induced by harsh monetary control during the coffee boom years and the collapse of the household demand for equity in the mid-1970s. As this process implied increasing reliance on short-term commercial financing, recession in the early 1980s was accompanied by a severe financial crisis of manufacturing firms. This process was, in fact, part of a larger financial collapse, which led to a wave of nationalizations of banks and other intermediaries.

As a result of the crisis, a major financial restructuring of manufacturing firms has take place since 1983. Reliance on debt financing has experienced a considerable decline. Tax legislation and rising interest rates on development credits have encouraged this but it is unclear whether they have been the major determinants of this trend. As reduced debt financing has not been accompanied by a recovery in equity financing, reinvestment of profits has become the major source of investment financing. Indeed, the increase in profit margins since 1983 may be seen as the way by which industrial firms have been able to reduce debt financing without a recovery in the demand for equity.

CONCLUSIONS

The evidence presented in this paper indicates that import substitution has played a moderate role in industrial development in Colombia since 1967. The unique reliance on ISI was abandoned more than three decades ago and IS actually became a villain of economic policy from the early 1970s. Up to the 1991 tariff reform, this policy stance did not lead, however, to major reductions in the high effective tariff protection rates inherited from the period of ISI.

Throughout the past two decades, both IS and exports have followed a similar cycle, associated with shifts in external conditions and accompanying exchange rate movements, with trade policies playing a reinforcing role. Neither high tariff protection nor QRs have been a major obstacle to rapid manufacturing export growth when exchange rate policies have been favourable (1967–74 and since 1985). Major exports have also been strongly affected by fluctuations in world market demand and, for those with heavy dependence on regional markets (chemicals and machinery), by important dynamic scale economies.

Over the past quarter century, manufacturing production has, none the less, continued to depend mainly on domestic demand fluctuations generated by macroeconomic events. Engels' turning points were also experienced by some sectors in the late 1970s. Finally, productivity performance has been subject to a strong Verdoorn pattern, with positive links to import substitution and domestic industrial concentration. Employment was dynamic during the 1967–74 boom but has played a rather secondary role in industrial growth since the mid-1970s. Capital accumulation has shown a steadier contribution, subject, none the less, to a strong cyclical pattern associated with economic activity and relative prices.

APPENDIX: A BRIEF NOTE ON SOURCES AND DEFINITIONS

For the purpose of this paper, the industrial sector excludes coffee hulling, meat processing and oil derivatives. Production is measured alternatively by GDP at market prices or the gross value of industrial production. Prices are measured by the implicit deflator of the latter variable. Productivity changes are estimated with translog production functions and adjusted by capacity utilization. Employment refers to permanent employment up to 1985 and to the permanent equivalent of total employment since then. Capital stocks are calculated using capital–output ratios estimated for 1951 by CEPAL (1957) and real investment series, assuming a depreciation rate of 4 per cent a year.

Data used combine three different sources. Production, value added and cost estimates come from Departamento Administrativo Nacional de Estadística (DANE) National Accounts, whereas employment and investment series are taken from DANE Annual Manufacturing Surveys. Capacity utilization rates for 1973 and since 1980 are taken from FEDES-ARROLLO's Entrepreneurial Surveys (see the several issues of *Coyuntura Económica* for the surveys of the 1970s, and *Indicadores de la Actividad Productiva* for those of the 1980s); the utilization rate for beverages, tobacco and transport equipment in 1973 is taken from Thoumi (1978). Rates refer to utilization during the fourth quarter of each year (the peak seasonal rate), weighted by the production of each firm. With original data from the surveys, such weighted utilization rates were estimated for 1980 and 1987 and the published unweighted series adjusted accordingly. Prior to 1973 and for 1974–79, utilization rates are estimated on the basis of sectoral output–capital ratios, adjusted for their trends during the period of analysis.

NOTES

1 As pointed out in the appendix, the 'industrial sector' as defined in this paper excludes coffee, meat processing and oil derivatives.
2 It should be emphasized, however, that the usual Chenery decomposition exercises tend to overestimate the role of domestic demand by excluding from the calculations the multiplier effects of export growth and import substitution. Ocampo (1990b) estimated the multiplier effects of import policies to have fluctuated between 1.6 and 2.1 in the late 1970s and in the 1980s.
3 The downward decline in the demand for textiles, apparel and other income-inelastic manufactured consumer goods may be partly associated with the increasing demand for smuggled foreign goods. Evidence on the evolution through time of (the relatively widespread) smuggling activities is, however, imprecise; none the less, there is strong qualitative evidence that large-scale smuggling of consumer goods in the late 1970s and early 1980s reinforced the adverse effects of trade policy and external events on industrial production.
4 One standard deviation of the import exchange rate (including tariffs and surcharges but excluding QRs) leads to a 1.8 per cent rise in industrial prices (5 per cent for metals and machinery). On the other hand, one standard deviation in the tariff equivalent of QRs leads to a 1.6 per cent rise in prices (4 per cent for chemicals and transport equipment).
5 A brief summary of earlier estimations can also be found in the latter study.
6 For the industrial sector as a whole, capacity utilization is estimated to have increased from 66.9 per cent in 1967 to 75.8 per cent in 1970 and 87.5 in 1974. Evidence of considerable excess capacities in the 1960s and their rapid reduction during the boom are summarized in Thoumi (1978). See also estimates for 1970 in Departmento Nacional de Planeación (1971).
7 Thus, according to the results of this author, slower economic growth can explain a difference in TFP of 4 per cent a year when comparing 1977–80 and 1980–3, whereas rising imports shares can only explain a difference in TFP growth of 0.2 per cent a year in the same period.
8 For the figure on workers affiliated to unions according to union censuses of 1984 and 1990, see Ministerio del Trabajo, *Boletín de análisis y estadísticas laborales*, no. 41, July–December, 1989. These figures have been compared with factory employment according to DANE Manufacturing Surveys.

REFERENCES

Acosta, O. L. (1991) 'Situación de las empresas privadas', mimeo, Banco de la República, May.
Berry, A. (1983) 'A Descriptive History of Colombian Industrial Development in the Twentieth Century', in A. Berry (ed.) *Essays on Industrialization in Colombia*, ch.2, Temple: Arizona State University.
Botero, C. H. and Meisel, A. (1988) 'Funciones de Oferta de las Exportaciones Menores Colombianas', *Ensayos sobre Política Económica*, no. 13, June.

167

CEPAL (1957) *Análisis y Proyecciones del Desarrollo Económico. Vol. III, El Desarrollo Económico de Colombia*, Mexico: CEPAL.

Chica, R. (1984–5) 'La Financiación de la Inversión en la Industria Manufacturera Colombiana', *Desarrollo y Sociedad*, no. 15–16, September–March.

Cubillos, R. and Torres, L. A. (1987) 'La Protección en Colombia en un Régimen de Exenciones', *Revista de Planeación y Desarrollo*, June.

Departamento Nacional de Planeación (1971) 'Comentarios Preliminares de los Resultados de la Encuesta sobre Utilización de la Capacidad Instalada en la Industria Manufacturera Fabril Colombiana', mimeo, August.

Diaz-Alejandro, C. F. (1976) *Foreign Trade Regimes and Economic Development: Colombia*, New York: NBER.

Dudley, L. (1983) 'The Effects of Learning on Employment and Labor Productivity in Colombian Metal Products Sector', in A. Berry (ed.) *Essays on Industrialization in Colombia*, Temple: Arizona State University.

Echavarría, J. J. (1982) 'La Evolución de las Exportaciones Colombianas y sus Determinantes: Un Análisis Empírico', *Essayos sobre Política Económica*, no. 2, September.

—— (1989) 'External Shocks and Industrialization in Colombia, 1920–50', mimeo, Oxford University.

—— (1990) 'Cambio Técnico, Inversión y Reestructuración Industrial en Colombia', *Coyuntura Económica*, June.

—— and Perry, G. (1981) 'Aranceles y Subsidios a las Exportaciones: Análisis de su Estructura Sectorial y de su Impacto sobre la Industria Colombiana', *Coyuntura Económica*, July.

—— Caballero, C. and Londoño, J. L. (1983) 'El Proceso Colombiano de Industrialización: Algunas Ideas sobre un Viejo Debate', *Coyuntura Económica*, September.

Fernandez, J., Bello, C. I., O'Byrne, A. and Roldán, J. (1985) 'Protección Aduanera e Inceantivos a las Exportaciones: Experiencia Colombiana Reciente', *Revista de Planeación y Desarrollo*, December.

Garay, L. J. (1991) *Apertura y Protección: Evaluación de la Política de Importaciones*, Bogotá: Tercer Mundo-Universidad Nacional.

Hallberg, K. and Takacs, W. (1991) 'Trade Reform in Colombia, 1990', Paper presented to Conference on 'The Colombian Economy: Issues of Debt, Trade and Development', Lehigh University, April.

Hutchenson, T. L. (1973) 'Incentives for Industrialization in Colombia', PhD dissertation, Michigan University.

Londoño, J. L. (1990) 'Income Distribution during the Structural Transformation: Colombia 1938–88', PhD dissertation, Harvard University.

Martínez, A. (1986) *La Estructura Arancelaria y las Estrategias de Industrialización en Colombia, 1950–82*, Bogotá: Universidad Nacional.

Misas, G. (1989) 'Estructura de Mercado y Conducta de las Empresas', research report presented to the World Bank, January.

Misión de Empleo (1986) *El Problema Laboral Colombiano: Diagnóstico, Perspectivas y Política, Economía Colombiana*, document no. 10, August–September.

Ocampo, J.A. (1989) 'El Proceso Ahorro-Inversión y sus Determinantes en Colombia', in C. Caballero (ed.) *Macroeconomía, Mercado de Capitales y Negocio Financiero*, Bogotá: Asociación Bancaria de Colombia, pp. 103–55.

—— (1990a) 'La Apertura Externa en Perspectiva' in F. Gomez (ed.) *Apertura Económica y Sistema Financiero*, Bogotá: Asociación Bancaria de Colombia, pp. 40–97.

—— (1990b) 'Import Controls, Prices and Economic Activity in Colombia', *Journal of Development Economics* 32(2): 369–88.

—— (1991) 'The Transition from Primary Exports to Industrial Development in Colombia' in M. Blomstrom and P. Meller (eds) *Diverging Paths*, Baltimore: Johns Hopkins University Press, pp. 213–40.

—— (1994) 'El Proceso Colombiano de Industrialización' in E. Cárdenas (ed.) *Historia de la industrialización en América Latina*, Mexico: Fondo de Cultura Económica,.

—— and Lora, E. (1987) 'Colombia', in *Stabilization and Adjustment Policies and Programmes*, Country Study no. 6, Helsinki: WIDER.

Posada, C.E. and Rhenals, R. (1988) 'La Dinámica Económica Colombiana: el Caso de los Crecimientos Industrial y Global entre 1950 y 1985', *Perfil de Coyuntura Económica*, no. 3, March.

Reyes, A. (1987) 'Ingresos Laborales y Empleo', in J.A. Ocampo and M. Ramírez (eds) *El Problema Laboral Colombiano*, vol. I, Bogotá: Contraloría General–DNP–SENA, pp. 265–83.

Roberts, M. J. (1988) 'The Structure of Production in Colombian Manufacturing Industries, 1977–85', World Bank, October.

Sandoval, D. (1982) 'Fuentes de Crecimiento en la Productividad de la Industria Manufacturera Colombiana, 1966–75', *Desarrollo y Sociedad*, no. 7, January.

—— (1983) 'Política Económica y Financiamiento de la Industria Manufacturera Colombiana, 1945–82', mimeo, CCRP, August.

Syrquin, M. (1987) 'Crecimiento Económico y Cambio Estructural en Colombia: Una Comparación Internacional', *Coyuntura Económica*, December.

Thoumi, F. E. (1978), 'La Utilización del Capital Fijo en la Industria Manufacturera Colombiana', *Revista de Planeación y Desarrollo*, September–December.

—— (1979) 'Estrategias de Industrialización, Empleo y Distribución del Empleo en Colombia', *Coyuntura Económica*, April.

Villar, L. (1983) 'Las Exportaciones Menores en Colombia: Determinantes de su Evolución y su Composición', MA thesis, Universidad de los Andes.

6

MEXICO'S TRADE AND INDUSTRIALIZATION EXPERIENCE SINCE 1960

A reconsideration of past policies and assessment of current reforms

Jaime Ros

I am indebted for comments to Ernie Bartell, José Casar, José Luis Estrada, Claudia Schatan and the participants at the WIDER conference held at the OECD Development Centre, Paris, 31 August – 3 September 1991. Special thanks are due to Gerry Helleiner for his many comments and suggestions on an earlier version. All remaining errors are entirely my own responsibility.

As many other developing countries in Latin America and elsewhere, but perhaps faster and farther than most of them, Mexico has been moving in the 1980s towards a liberalized trade regime after a long period of import-substitution industrialization. Compared to the experiences of other countries, especially those which are also well advanced in this process such as Chile and Bolivia in Latin America, the Mexican case shows a number of singular features which, over a longer time span, will probably make it a unique example of economic and political success in terms of the smoothness of its transition, given the small adjustment costs involved and the virtual absence of political tensions and resistance to change.

This paper argues that – besides the critical role of non-economic factors, including geography and politics – this outcome can largely be attributed to the no less successful experience that Mexico had with import-substitution industrialization and, perhaps more paradoxically, to the very adverse macroeconomic conditions under which trade reform was undertaken in the 1980s. At the same time, and for related reasons, the paper is sceptical about the long-term benefits that the particular form of trade liberalization adopted is likely to bring.

The development of this argument requires a reconsideration of the industrial development experience before the 1980s. This is the task addressed in the first section, which looks at Mexico's trade and industrial policies since 1960, focusing in particular on the dynamic costs and benefits of its particular policy regime. This analysis is followed by an overview of macroeconomic adjustment and trade policy reform in the 1980s, and a preliminary assessment of the multiple impacts of trade liberalization. A concluding section summarizes the paper's main findings.

INDUSTRIALIZATION EXPERIENCE: THE POLICIES AND THEIR OUTCOME

The trade and industrial policy regime: an overview

The evolution of industrial and trade policies since 1960 and the macro-economic environment in which they operated, is summarized in Table 6.1.

Table 6.1 Macroeconomic and trade policy indicators, Mexico, 1960–90

	1961–70	1971–5	1976–81	1982–90
Annual growth rates (%)				
GDP	7.0	6.5	6.9	0.8
Consumer prices	3.5[a]	12.1	22.3	69.8
% of GDP				
Investment	18.7	20.3	22.2	17.7
Operational fiscal deficit	1.4[b]	3.4	4.6	1.1
Indices (1978=100)				
(initial/end of period values)				
Real value of the peso:				
Consumer/wholesale prices[c]	95.5/111.5	113.9/124.5	111.4/126.7	84.2/109.8
Relative wholesale prices[d]	96.2/103.2	104.1/109.3	103.1/121.5	79.4/100.6
Effective-Banco de México[e]	NA/124.1	123.0/131.6	120.0/136.6	99.8/100.5
Relative unit labour costs[f]	NA/96.7	102.1/124.0	119.0/128.2	83.1/83.9
Import value under licences (%)				
(initial/end of period values)	53.8/68.3	67.7/68.4	90.4/85.5	100.0/19.7[g]

Sources: Banco de México, *Indicadores económicos*, various issues; Presidencia de la República, Criterios Generales de Política Económica para 1992; US unit labour costs supplied by OECD.
[a] Based on the private consumption deflator.
[b] 1965–70.
[c] Mexico's consumer prices/US wholesale prices.
[d] Mexico–US.
[e] Based on consumer prices.
[f] Mexico's manufacturing sector/US business sector.
[g] 1988.

During the 1960s, when import substitution had already been completed in most non-durable consumer goods and light intermediates, industrial and trade policies laid an almost exclusive emphasis on the local development of the durable consumer, heavy intermediate and capital goods industries.[1] The protectionist regime relied increasingly on import licences – granted essentially on criteria of availability of domestic supplies – and tariff protection became thus less important than it had been in the previous two decades. These instruments were combined with a number of other policies to promote local industrial integration, including the establishment of domestic content requirements (DCRs) in the automobile industry (1962), the yearly publication of lists of industrial products with potential for import substitution, and 'fabrication programmes' in the heavy intermediates and capital goods sectors, comprising sector- or firm-specific fiscal incentives and import licences.[2] Export promotion policies, on the other hand, were virtually absent in this period, except for the establishment in the mid-1960s of the 'maquiladora' programme, a special free trade and investment regime for export-processing plants along the northern border region.

The exchange rate regime had been characterized since 1954 by a fixed nominal rate (which was to last until August 1976) and a rather stable real exchange rate up to 1973. During the 1960s the value of the peso rose slowly in real terms at less than 1 per cent per year. More generally, prudent macroeconomic management successfully oriented fiscal and monetary policies to the achievement of price stability and fast economic growth. Thus, this decade of 'stabilizing development' ('desarrollo estabilizador') – the golden age of Mexico's postwar development experience – recorded an average inflation rate of 3.5 per cent per year and unprecedented rates of overall economic growth.

In the early 1970s, industrial policy diversified its objectives to include export promotion and the strengthening of international competitiveness, the development of capital goods industries, regional decentralization of industrial activities and foreign investment regulation (see, in particular, CEPAL, 1979; Solís, 1980; and the Plan Nacional de Desarrollo Industrial 1979–82). The new priorities were reflected in a number of policy reforms. Export promotion policies included the establishment of export subsidies (Certificados de Devolucion de Impuestos, CEDIS) in 1971, and of tariff rebates on imported inputs of exporting firms, the expansion of short-term export credits provided by Fondo para el Fomento de las Exportaciones de Productos Manufacturados (FOMEX), and the creation in 1972 of Fondo de Equipamiento Industrial (FONEI) for the financing of export-oriented investments, as well as of Instituto Mexicano de Comercio Exterior (IMCE) in 1970 to strengthen export promotion efforts and facilitate access to international markets. From 1977 to 1981, a number of trade reforms replacing import licences by tariffs were also undertaken with the aim of reducing the anti-export bias of the protection regime and increasing industrial efficiency. In addition, a second generation of fabrication programmes and other sector-specific policies – such as the 1977 automobile industry programme and the 1981 programme for microcomputers – tended to condition import protection and fiscal incentives to the achievement of domestic price and export targets, a move that was often accompanied by the relaxation of DCRs and their replacement with foreign exchange budgets (see p. 187).

The concern for promoting a domestic capital goods industry[3] inspired the 1973 tariff reforms, which increased the level of protection for that industry, and led to the replacement in 1975 of Rule XIV of the tariff legislation – which had traditionally provided subsidies on imported machinery and equipment – with subsidies on imported machinery for the production of new capital goods. Fiscal incentives were also revised and, through a unified framework (Certificados de Promoción Fiscal, CEPROFIS), afforded preferential treatment to the production and purchase of domestic capital goods, as well as to small firms and regionally decentralized activities. The period also witnessed a reactivation of the role of development banks in industrial financing and of public investments in the oil, petrochemicals, steel and some capital goods industries. The 1973 Law on Foreign Investment redefined the rules for the participation of foreign investors, including a general 49 per cent restriction on foreign ownership.[4]

The macroeconomic environment, however, became highly unstable in the 1970s and often destroyed the incentives provided by industrial policy. The re-emergence of inflation and periodic episodes of foreign exchange difficulties made the real exchange rate highly volatile compared to the previous decade. The peso appreciated strongly in real terms during the fiscal expansion from 1972 to 1975 and again during the oil boom from 1977 to 1981. These periods induced an increased use of quantitative import restrictions (1974, 1976–7, and 1981–2), and were followed by exchange rate crises, sharp devaluations and recession-led adjustments in the balance of payments.

A comparison with the import-substitution regime of the 1960s suggests that the reforms of the 1970s transformed the old arrangements into a hybrid three-tier system which comprised:

(i) A scheme of export promotion through import protection in sectors under specific industrial programmes (automobiles, microcomputers and a number of heavy intermediates and capital goods). These industries were protected through import licences in the domestic market and, at the same time, were given partial and increasing access to inputs at international prices and quality in exchange for export commitments. They enjoyed, generally, the highest levels of effective protection in the economy (see below).

Table 6.2 Effective protection rates, Mexico, 1960–90 (%)

	1960	1970	1980
Agriculture	3.0	−1.4	18.5
Mining	−0.2	−12.3	
Oil	−7.9	5.3	−82.0[a]
Manufacturing	46.6	36.9	33.1
Consumer goods	40.1	28.4	5.2
Light intermediates	42.7	15.1	39.4
Heavy intermediates	38.1	41.4	53.2
Consumer durables and capital goods	85.2	77.1	108.9
Average nominal protection[b]	15.1	13.1	9.0–14.0[c]

Sources: Bueno (1971) for 1960; Ten Kate and Wallace (1980) for 1971; Ten Kate and de Mateo (1989) for 1980.
[a] Oil extraction.
[b] All tradables.
[c] Excludes oil.
Figures refer to implicit rates without exchange rate adjustment. Treatment of non-tradables follows Balassa's modified method for 1960 and 1970 (value added of non-tradables is assumed not to change) and Balassa's original method for 1980 (prices of non-tradables are assumed not to change).

(ii) An export-oriented system for the *maquiladora* plants in the northern border region – the expansion of which to other regions was facilitated throughout the 1970s – under a *de facto* free trade regime for the imported inputs to be processed and exported, albeit with restrictions on selling in the domestic market.[5] This sector was thus virtually de-linked from the rest of the Mexican economy, with a share of value added in gross output of the order of 23 per cent and importing over 98 per cent of its material inputs. Labour-intensive, low-paid assembly of electronic components and apparel are the quintessential *maquiladora* industries.

(iii) A traditional import-substitution regime in the rest of manufacturing (mostly consumer goods and light intermediates) modified only by the presence of some export promotion incentives. These sectors generally enjoyed lower effective protection rates, sometimes negative, than those of the first group.

The changing structure of incentives associated with evolving industrial and trade policies is summarized in the estimates in Table 6.2 of nominal and effective protection rates, those available on a broadly comparable basis, for 1960, 1970 and 1980. As shown in the table, protection levels escalated significantly with the degree of manufacturing, especially among consumer durables and capital goods,[6] and did so increasingly over time both between the manufacturing and the primary sectors and within the industrial sector itself, where the position of consumer goods worsened and that of consumer durables and capital goods improved. The main bias against the primary activities has not been suffered by agriculture – largely as a consequence of guaranteed prices and input subsidies – except from the mid-1960s to the mid-1970s when effective protection turned from positive to negative in this sector and apparently contributed to its economic slow-down. Rather, since the mid-1970s, it has been the mining and especially the oil sector which have subsidized heavily, through low energy prices, the rest of the Mexican economy.

It has often been noted that Mexico's protection rates have been relatively moderate when compared to most Latin American countries as well as other developing economies (see Little et al., 1970; Balassa et al., 1971; Ten Kate and Wallace, 1980). This feature has been attributed to the fact that, in spite of an extensive use of quantitative restrictions, a degree of domestic price discipline has been enforced by the threat of smuggling and potential competition through a several thousand kilometre border with the US economy, as well as by the role of price controls in manufacturing and guaranteed prices in agriculture.

This evidence on protection rates is consistent with the rather low but increasing estimates of the static costs of Mexico's protectionist policies. The costs of protection in 1960 were estimated by Bergsman (1974) at 2.5 per cent of GDP, with only 0.3 percentage points having its origin in resource misallocation effects (the rest, 2.2 percentage points, being attributed to 'X-inefficiency' plus monopolistic rents). In a subsequent study, the World Bank (1977) suggested that the policy changes since 1960 may have increased the sum total of these costs by 2.5 percentage points of the manufacturing value added.

We shall leave a detailed analysis of the period since 1982 for the next section, but it is worth emphasizing here that, among its main features, the decade has witnessed the emergence of a new trade policy regime in the midst of severe adjustments to the 1982 debt crisis and the 1986 collapse of the international oil market. These adjustments led to historically unprecedented weakness of the real value of the peso (together with a rather high variability), the collapse of the real and dollar value of domestic wages, very high rates of inflation and a deep and prolonged economic slowdown.

The Pattern of Industrial Growth

Trade and industrial policies provided a number of incentives to the expansion of manufacturing industries, especially those which in the early 1960s were infant industries in the heavy intermediates, consumer durables and capital goods sectors. These incentives are embodied in the structure of protection presented in Table 6.2 and reflect the influence of energy and agricultural price policies together with overall macroeconomic management as much as the role of the trade regime. We now focus on how the

175

Table 6.3 Manufacturing growth, Mexico, 1960–89

	Percentage of manufacturing output (1980 prices)				Annual rates of growth (%)		
	1960	1970	1980	1989[a]	1960–70	1970–80	1980–9
Manufacturing output	100	100	100	100	8.1	6.3	1.4
Imports[b]	19.7	12.3	16.9	15.7	2.6	10.3	0.0
Exports[b]	6.3	5.1	4.6	13.1	5.4	5.6	13.4
Consumer goods	56.2	49.0	40.9	40.0	6.5	4.4	1.1
Light intermediates	10.0	9.7	9.7	9.6	7.7	6.3	1.2
Heavy intermediates	21.3	24.0	28.0	31.5	9.3	7.9	2.7
Consumer durables/ capital goods	12.5	17.3	21.3	18.9	11.5	8.5	0.1

Source: Instituto Nacional de Estadística, Geografía e Informática (INEGI), Sistema de Cuentas Nacionales de México, various issues.
[a] Preliminary.
[b] Percentage of gross manufacturing output.

Table 6.4 Sources of growth in manufacturing output, Mexico

Year	Domestic demand	Export expansion	Import substitution
1960–70	87.4	2.3	10.3
1970–4	102.2	2.5	–4.7
1974–80	105.0	2.2	–7.2
1980–9	–54.9	154.1	0.8

Source: Instituto Nacional de Estadística, Geografía e Informática (INEGI), Sistema de Cuentas Nacionales de México, various issues.

industrial sector responded to them by looking at the sources of demand and supply expansion and the evolution of the industrial structure.

Sources of market expansion

Tables 6.3 and 6.4 show the growth of manufacturing output and its main sub-sectors, together with the sources of demand expansion since 1960. From 1960 to 1980, industrial expansion proceeded at a fast and sustained pace, continuing and even exceeding the high growth rates achieved in the previous two decades. The speed and stability of the growth process is outstanding among postwar developing country experiences and placed Mexico, together with Brazil, at the top in terms of growth among the larger Latin American economies.

Mexico followed a large country pattern of industrialization (see Chenery et al., 1986), i.e. the rapid expansion of domestic markets was the major source of industrial growth,[7] and the changing structure of industrial output – showing a rapidly increasing share of heavy intermediates, consumer durables and capital goods – has to be interpreted in this light. However, the 1960s also recorded an intense import-substitution process which significantly contributed to the expansion of those sectors. Among them, those showing the largest reductions in import coefficients and the highest growth rates were the automobile industry, machinery and electrical appliances, rubber and chemicals. Although export markets made a much smaller contribution and the export–output ratio tended on average to decline, the decade also witnessed the beginning of a process which was to become more important in the first half of the 1970s, i.e. a substantial increase of export coefficients in the consumer durables and capital goods sectors, and the development of the 'maquiladora' assembly plants in the northern border region. Transnational companies were prominent in the expansion of the leading sectors, particularly in three of the four fastest growing industries (automobiles, non-electrical machinery and electrical appliances) and significant and increasing in the fourth one (chemicals). The contribution of public enterprises became, in contrast, less important compared to previous decades, even though they participated in some of the fast growing sectors as well as in the rapid development of the fertilizer and heavy petrochemicals industries.[8]

The contribution of import substitution to industrial growth declined sharply during the 1970s and became even negative, particularly in the late years of the decade when the oil boom triggered a rapid import expansion. Nevertheless, significant import-substitution processes – which become apparent in a more detailed analysis – continued to take place in the heavy intermediates (petrochemicals and steel) and capital goods sectors. The small aggregate contribution of export expansion also hides the rapid increase in the first half of the 1970s of the export coefficients in these sectors (as well as in the automobile industry) which were the major beneficiaries of the export incentives introduced throughout the decade.

Both of these processes, import substitution and export expansion, contributed to the continuously rising share of heavy intermediates, consumer durables and capital goods from 1970 to 1980. The pace of structural transformation is even more evident in the composition of manufacturing exports. By 1980 those sectors accounted for nearly half of all manufacturing exports; the consumer durables and capital goods sector alone, whose exports were virtually non-existent two decades earlier, represented 20 per cent of the total. These trends also meant an increasing share in foreign trade of capital-intensive manufacturing exports, giving rise to the paradox – first noted in 1970 and much discussed since then – that Mexican manufacturing exports were more capital-intensive than imports.[9]

Industrial structure and trade orientation in 1980

The end result of these long-term trends is summarized in Table 6.5. The table aggregates four-digit manufacturing industries according to trade orientation, distinguishing the following sectors:

Table 6.5 Industrial structure and trade orientation, Mexico, 1980

	Intra-industry trade	Import competing	Export oriented	Non-traded	Share in total value added
Commodity composition					
Consumer goods and light intermediates	23.3	20.0	73.4	73.0	47.0
Heavy intermediates	24.4	49.0	15.6	20.0	28.8
Consumer durables	37.1	8.6	0.0	4.9	12.8
Capital goods	15.4	22.4	11.0	2.1	11.4
Total	100.0	100.0	100.0	100.0	100.0
Shares in total (%)					Total
Value added	22.5	28.1	6.6	42.9	100.0
Foreign trade[a]	35.7	53.1	9.1	2.1	100.0
Exports[a]	51.4	8.7	36.4	3.6	100.0
Imports[a]	30.6	67.3	0.4	1.6	100.0

Source: Ros (1991).
[a] Average share for the period 1978–83.

(i) the intra-industry trade sector, showing a relatively high share (more than 50 per cent) of intra-industry trade in its total foreign trade;[10]
(ii) the import-competing (i.e. net importing) sector, with a low share of intra-industry trade;
(iii) the export-oriented or traditional exportable (i.e. net exporting) sector, with a low share of intra-industry trade;
(iv) the non-traded sector, showing, in contrast to the previous three groups, very low shares (less than 5 per cent) of foreign trade in the industry's gross output.

The table shows the weight of each of these sectors in manufacturing value added and foreign trade, together with its commodity composition.[11] By 1980 the intra-industry trade sector had not only reached a large share in overall manufacturing trade (of the order of 35 per cent) but even dominated manufacturing exports with a share (51.4 per cent) significantly larger than that of export-oriented sectors (36.4 per cent). The composition of the intra-industry trade sector was heavily biased towards consumer durables and capital goods, with a substantial share of heavy intermediates (although the share of the latter in the intra-industry trade sector was lower than its share in manufacturing as a whole). Intra-industry trade-oriented consumer durables included automobiles and auxiliary industries, while the corresponding capital goods and intermediates comprised business machines, basic chemicals, non-ferrous metals and non-metallic minerals. The presence, in this sector, of consumer goods is limited to some alcoholic beverages, textiles and printing.

When we consider the following two categories, a sharp contrast stands between the composition of the import-competing sector – dominated by capital goods and heavy intermediates – and that of the export-oriented industries, strongly biased towards consumer goods and light intermediates. In the importing sector, capital goods are, indeed, of major importance. As much as 55 per cent of capital goods production is generated in this sector, and when the latter is considered together with the intra-industry trade sector, they comprise more than 80 per cent of the capital goods industries. At the same time, almost half of the production of heavy intermediates originates in the importing sector. The paper industry and a large proportion of the steel and aluminium metallurgy industries stand as the major ones among them. The presence of consumer goods in these import-competing sectors is limited to some final products of the industries just mentioned, as well as to some basic products (powdered milk and sugar) that Mexico had to import in large amounts during the period considered. The overall importance of inter-industry trade (with a share of over 60 per cent in total manufacturing trade) is largely accounted for by the importing sector, which represents almost 70 per cent of manufacturing imports – many of which are strictly not competing with domestic production – and have traditionally determined Mexico's structural trade deficit in manufactures. In contrast, the export-oriented sector shows a very limited importance in both manufacturing value added (6.6 per cent) and foreign trade (9.1 per cent). This sector includes essentially natural resource intensive activities, the processing of some of the main exportable agricultural inputs (fish and shellfish, cotton, fruits, coffee and tobacco) as well as some wood products, porcelain, and marble.

Just as in the case of traditional exportables, the composition of non-traded goods is also strongly biased towards consumer goods and light intermediates. These industries – many of which are really early import-substituting industries – consist by and large of the bulk of the food, textiles, clothing and wood industries, and account for a large share (43 per cent) of manufacturing value added. This importance stands in sharp contrast to the very limited weight of the export-oriented sector, and both of these features are linked to the prominent role that the domestic market has played in Mexico's industrial development, partly reflecting, as we shall discuss below, the inhibiting effects that trade policies have had on international competitiveness and the development of export potential.

An extensive pattern of growth?

Table 6.6 looks at the growth process from the perspective of sources of supply expansion, summarizing the available evidence on factor inputs and total factor productivity (TFP) growth. It focuses, in contrast to Table 6.7, on aggregate performance on the assumption that industrial growth, as we

Table 6.6 Growth of output, inputs and total factor productivity in various countries (average annual growth rates, whole economy)

Country	Years	Output	Capital	Labour	TFP	Source
Mexico	1950–75	6.2			2.2[a]	Syrquin (1986)
	1960–74	6.8	6.7	3.3	2.0	Elías (1978)
	1960–75	6.4	6.2	2.4	2.6	Reynolds (1980)
Developing						
Argentina	1960–74	4.1	3.8	2.2	0.7	Elías (1978)
Latin America[b]	1960–74	5.3	4.7	2.7	1.3	Elías (1978)
Brazil	1960–74	7.3	7.5	3.3	1.6	Elías (1978)
Colombia	1960–74	5.6	3.9	2.8	2.1	Elías (1978)
Turkey	1963–75	6.4	6.8	1.0	2.1	Krueger and Tuncer (1980)
Korea, Rep.	1960–73	9.7	6.6	5.0	4.1	Christensen et al. (1980)
Developed[c]	1960–73	5.7	6.3	0.8	2.7	Christensen et al. (1980)
US	1960–73	4.3	4.0	2.2	1.3	Christensen et al. (1980)
Germany	1960–73	5.4	7.0	–0.7	3.0	Christensen et al. (1980)
Japan	1960–73	10.9	11.5	2.7	4.5	Christensen et al. (1980)

[a] Derived from the rates of change of output per worker and capital-labour ratio assuming a capital elasticity of 0.48.
[b] Average of six Latin American countries (excluding Mexico) (see Elías, 1978).
[c] Average of eight developed countries (see Christensen et al. 1980).

Table 6.7 Growth of TFP and labour productivity in manufacturing, Mexico (average annual growth rates)

Years	TFP	Labour Productivity	Source
1960–80	1.1	3.4/6.6[a]	Velasco (1985); Hernandez Laos and Velasco (1990)
1960–73	0.8	3.4/7.8[a]	Velasco (1985); Hernandez Laos and Velasco (1990)
1973–80	1.5	3.3/4.5[a]	Velasco (1985); Hernandez Laos and Velasco (1990)
1970–80[b]	0.9	3.8	World Bank (1986)
1950–75	2.0	3.0	Syrquin (1986)
1963–81[c]	3.6	6.0	Samaniego (1984)

[a] Value added per man-hour in manufacturing firms with more than 100 employees.
[b] Mean growth rates of 20 two-digit manufacturing industries.
[c] Mean growth rate of 17 four-digit manufacturing industries.

shall see below, is likely to have affected the overall productivity performance of the economy.

Estimates of long-term trends in total factor productivity growth per year fall in the 2.0–2.6 per cent range, thus 'explaining' around 35 per cent of the increase in total output. This performance could suggest a rather extensive pattern of growth, largely based on a high rate of capital accumulation (of the order of 6.2–6.7 per cent per year). This may well be the case when Mexico's record is compared to those of developed economies or to the Korean experience, where over 40 per cent of output expansion is attributable to TFP growth. But the growth pattern also appears to be significantly more intensive than the rest of Latin America (with a 25 per cent contribution of TFP growth), and compares favourably with other fast-growing developing economies such as Brazil, in terms of productivity performance, or Turkey, in terms of employment absorption.

The performance of the manufacturing sector itself appears, however, to have been less satisfactory. Table 6.7 presents the available estimates and makes clear the considerable differences between them. These can be explained by the methods followed as well as by differences in coverage and time periods; at the risk of some oversimplification, one could say that the lower estimates for TFP growth in the table exclude the productivity effects of factor reallocation within manufacturing (Hernandez Laos and Velasco, 1990; World Bank, 1986), the intermediate ones include these reallocation effects (Syrquin, 1986), while the higher estimates are representative of large and medium-size firms (Samaniego, 1984, as well as Velasco, 1985, for labour productivity). Overall, however, they suggest that for manufacturing as a whole (including large and small firms) and for the two decades since 1960, the Mexican industrial sector showed a slow rate of TFP growth (of the order of 1 per cent per year). The contrast with the higher estimates in the table suggests in turn the presence of divergent trends in productivity growth between large-scale and small-scale establishments in manufacturing.

This high productivity performance of the modern large-scale segment of manufacturing compares favourably with other developing and developed country experiences (see Samaniego, 1984). This finding is consistent with international comparisons of output per worker, indicating that the labour productivity gap between Mexico and US manufacturing has been diminishing since the 1960s. One such comparison (Blomstrom and Wolff, 1989) shows a convergence of productivity levels between 1965 and 1984 in all industries for which data are available, with the biggest catch-up taking place during the second half of the 1960s. This study also found the smaller productivity gaps occurring in the modern TNC-dominated sectors of manufacturing. Bacha (1966) compared productivity levels for 1960 and Maddison and van Ark (1989) did it for 1975, carefully adjusting real output levels following an 'industry of origin approach'. A comparison of their findings also suggests a reduction in the US–Mexico productivity gap between 1960 and 1975 (see Estrada, 1991).

These features – the slow TFP growth in manufacturing as a whole and the more satisfactory performance of large-scale manufacturing and the overall economy – suggest, taken together, that the main contribution of manufacturing expansion to aggregate productivity performance must have taken place through the reallocation effects of industrial growth rather than through rapid increases of factor productivity in manufacturing itself.[12] This overall positive impact of industrial growth qualifies again the notion of an extensive growth pattern in the Mexican experience. For, given the initially very large labour surpluses in traditional agriculture and services and the very fast rate of demographic expansion during the period (of the order of 3–3.5 per cent per year) – both of which tended to moderate the overall productivity effects of resource reallocation towards manufacturing[13] – it is not easy to see how, given the actual rate of capital accumulation, the growth pattern could have been much more intensive. The reason is that the slow productivity growth in manufacturing can be largely attributed to the lack of productivity increases in the small-scale sector, a feature which in turn reflects a high rate of employment absorption from other sectors. There is thus a trade-off between the reallocation effects of industrial growth and the productivity increases within the industry; a trade-off which was aggravated by very fast rates of population growth and could not be easily overcome except by means of higher rates of capital accumulation.

The question remains, however, as to which other factors, the policy regime in particular, played a role in the slow productivity growth of manufacturing and the divergent trends of its different sectors. We turn now to this issue.

Industrial productivity growth and the policy regime

Besides the importance attributed to educational levels and training of the work force, three main hypotheses have been advanced on the determinants of industrial productivity growth. First, the Smithian or market competition hypothesis emphasizes the incentives to technical change, to the adoption of best-practice techniques and the reduction of 'X-inefficiency' provided by competitive market structures and openness to international competition. The case for trade liberalization on dynamic efficiency grounds relies heavily on this view of technological progress (see, for example, Bhagwati, 1978). The Schumpeterian approach underlines, in contrast, the means necessary to generate and introduce technological progress and the incentives provided by protection of innovative activity, both of which are most likely to emerge in large-scale manufacturing industries and oligopolistic market structures. A recent restatement of the Schumpeterian approach can be found in Nelson and Winter (1982); for its application to international trade analysis, see Dosi et al. (1990). Finally, Verdoorn's law, or the Kaldor–Verdoorn hypothesis, focuses on the mechanisms linking endogenous productivity growth to the rate of market expansion: a faster rate of output growth enhances productivity increases by facilitating the adoption of new technologies embodied in new capital goods, reducing the average age of the capital stock and intensifying learning processes, together with the productivity improvements resulting from increasing returns to scale (see Schmookler, 1966; Kaldor, 1970). As pointed out by Nishimizu and Robinson (1986), Verdoorn's law suggests a positive link between productivity growth and export expansion as well as import substitution, to the extent that both of these processes tend to increase the size of the market.

These different hypotheses have all been present in the empirical literature on productivity growth differentials within Mexico's manufacturing sector. Blomstrom and Wolff (1989) explained productivity growth rates across industries (as well as the rate of convergence between Mexico and US industries) by the degree of foreign ownership and the initial Mexico–US productivity gap, and emphasized the spillover effects of TNCs, including in particular the competitive stimuli on domestic firms in TNC-dominated sectors. Vázquez (1981) and Casar *et al.* (1990) identified positive Kaldor–Verdoorn effects modified by market structures and firm size distribution, including the role of competitive pressure in dualistic structures and significant 'Schumpeterian' effects in sectors dominated by large firms (both national and foreign). The World Bank study on Mexico's trade policy and industrial performance (1986) also found positive effects of output growth on productivity growth performance across industries, together with negative effects from quantitative restrictions reflecting the lack of external competitive pressure.

Unfortunately, most of these studies (all, in fact, with the exception of the latter) have limited themselves to labour productivity indicators and neglected the role of industrial and trade policies, while, on the other hand, research on TFP growth (summarized above in Table 6.6) has focused on measurement rather than explanation.[14] In what follows, using some of the data and results from these studies, this section examines the determinants of TFP growth differentials in manufacturing, including among them the influence of trade policy. Table 6.8 presents the Hernandez Laos and Velasco (1990) estimates of TFP growth and TFP growth differentials with the US for 1962–80 in an eight-sector decomposition of manufacturing. The table also includes the rate of output growth for the same period, the shares of TNCs and large private national firms in 1980, and two indicators related to the trade regime, effective protection in 1970 and dominant trade orientation in 1980.

The table suggests, first, a positive, but not strong, association between TFP and output growth. The three worst performing industries (all of them with negative TFP growth differentials with respect to the US) show the three slowest rates of output growth, but the two top TFP performers (the paper industry and non-metallic mineral products) are not the fastest growing industries. Firm size and the degree of foreign ownership also

Table 6.8 Productivity growth differentials in manufacturing, Mexico (annual growth rates, 1962–80 (%)

	TFP growth		Output growth	Share of TNCs 1980 (%)	Share of LNFs[a] 1980 (%)	Effective protection 1970 (%)	Trade orientation[b] 1980
	Mexico	Mexico-US differential					
Consumer goods							
Food processing[c]	1.0	-0.7	5.9	19.5	25.0	20.1	NT-EO
Textiles, apparel and leather	0.7	-2.4	6.7	9.1	35.8	38.6	NT
Light intermediates							
Lumber, wood, furniture	-2.3	-3.3	6.9	8.9	26.8	12.2	NT
Paper	3.6	2.5	7.7	17.0	48.3	16.1	MC
Heavy intermediates							
Chemicals	2.5	0.9	9.7	55.6	24.7	94.4	MC-II
Stone, clay and glass	2.5	1.6	8.6	12.2	46.9	5.5	EO-NT
Basic metals	1.4	1.1	8.1	14.2	39.0	22.9	MC-II
Consumer durables and capital goods							
Fabricated metals, machinery and equipment	2.2	0.6	10.6	51.7	29.1	77.2	MC-II
Mean values	1.5	0.04	8.0	23.5	34.5	35.9	

Sources: TFP Growth: Hernandez Laos and Velasco (1990).
Output growth: Instituto Nacional de Estadística, Geografía e Informática (INEGI), Sistema de Cuentas Nacionales, various issues.
Share of TNCs and LNFs in gross output: Casar et al. (1990).
Effective protection: Ten Kate and Wallace (1980). Weighed by value added at foreign prices.
Trade orientation: Ros (1991).

[a] LNFs = Large private national firms (more than 100 employees and less than 15% foreign ownership).
[b] NT, non-traded; EO, export-oriented; MC, import-competing; II, intra-industry trade.
[c] Includes beverages and tobacco.

have significant effects on productivity growth which may contribute to explain this asymmetry. The top performers are large-scale sectors where large domestic firms coexist and compete with TNC affiliates (they show, in fact, the highest shares of large domestic firms within manufacturing), in contrast to the three slow-growing industries, all dominated by small firms (accounting for 55–70 per cent of these sectors' gross output) and showing below-average shares of TNCs. These features convey the importance of competitive stimuli and spillover effects of TNCs, stressed by Blomstrom and Wolff (1989). But even more, they highlight the role of 'Schumpeterian' effects: productivity growth is highest when the local producers are large enough to respond effectively to the competitive challenge from TNCs.[15] In more fully TNC-dominated sectors (chemicals, consumer durables and capital goods), productivity performance, especially with respect to their US counterparts, is below that of more mixed structures.

The links between productivity growth and trade regime are more complex. Output growth shows a fairly high association with effective protection rates, a result that was first established by Ten Kate and Wallace (1980) in a cross-section analysis of two-digit manufacturing industries.[16] This close association is probably a consequence of the structure of incentives having favoured the development of sectors with a high income elasticity of demand and substantial import-substitution potential (such as consumer durables, chemicals and capital goods), as well as having hindered the growth of industries that had exhausted their import-substitution potential by 1960 and could not harness their export potential from then onwards (consumer goods and light intermediates), a feature that may explain why these sectors are also largely dominated by non-traded goods. To this extent, the prevailing dispersion of effective protection rates can help explain the huge productivity growth differentials between, say, the chemicals, consumer durables and capital goods sectors, on the one hand, and the wood industry, on the other. In the latter, the structure of incentives probably aggravated the effects of the lack of competitive stimuli arising from the absence of TNCs and large domestic firms, as well as of the relatively slow growth of domestic demand given by the low income elasticities of demand and the exhaustion of its import-substitution potential. In the former, in contrast, the high protection rates are likely to have enhanced the productivity increases stemming from output growth effects.

The fact, however, that these highly protected sectors show, in spite of higher rates of output expansion, slower productivity increases than the top performers (paper and non-metallic minerals) with much lower protection rates, suggests indeed that protection may well have been excessive in those sectors by inhibiting the external competitive pressures on technical change. The explanation of productivity–trade links that emerges from Table 6.8 appears thus to draw on all three hypotheses reviewed earlier. For, one would expect from that discussion to find, other things being equal, the highest rates of productivity growth in sectors with moderately positive protection rates, i.e. not too high as to eliminate the stimuli from international competition, and not too low as to hinder excessively output growth and, thus, investment and technical modernization through Verdoorn-type effects (as has happened in some primary activities and light manufacturing industries). The *ceteris paribus* clause – which refers to the role of firm size and domestic market structure – is important, however, as the very different productivity performance of similarly protected sectors (such as wood and non-metallic minerals, or food processing and paper, or textiles and basic metals) clearly suggests.

This explanation of productivity growth differentials therefore suggests that productivity–trade links are far from clear-cut. The effect of trade protection on productivity growth depends on whether its negative direct influence (through the lack of external competition) is more than offset by the indirect effects through faster output growth which depend on a given industry's market demand, technological characteristics and import-substitution potential. More precisely, a positive net effect on productivity growth becomes more likely to the extent that: (i) the structure of protection favours the domestic development of industries with a high income elasticity of demand, strong economies of scale and substantial import-substitution potential;[17] (ii) the dispersion of effective rates across industries is bounded by the criteria just mentioned, which implies its changing structure through time with, in particular, declining rates in infant industries as their import-substitution potential is being exhausted.

The first feature applies broadly to the Mexican case, and probably explains the catching-up process that has taken place in several infant industries in the heavy intermediates, consumer durables and capital goods sectors as well as what is, after all, a comparatively successful experience of import-substitution industrialization. The structure of protection appears indeed to have worked in the right direction, in the sense that it provided greater incentives to industries with high income elasticities of demand, increasing returns to scale and large potential for import substitution. The second feature fits less well, particularly with respect to the evolution through time of infant industry protection. The dispersion of the incentives structure has probably been greater than what was warranted by market demand and technological differences among industries, and the incentives provided to several infant industries persisted for too long, even increasing, as shown in Table 6.2.

TRADE LIBERALIZATION IN THE 1980S: A PRELIMINARY ASSESSMENT

Macroeconomic adjustment since 1982: a brief overview

Since 1982, the Mexican economy has been subject to a number of external and policy shocks. External macroeconomic conditions have been dramatically adverse as a consequence of the debt crisis in 1982 and of declining real oil prices, affecting Mexico's major export product, after the price hike in 1979–80. Table 6.9 shows the impact of the debt crisis on the current and capital accounts of the balance of payments. Declining oil prices, especially during the 1986 collapse, are reflected in the sharp terms of trade deterioration and in the fall to almost one-third (compared to their 1980 values) of the country's oil revenues.

The policy responses to the 1982 debt crisis and the 1986 oil price collapse both involved drastic exchange rate and fiscal adjustments. The real value of the peso, which had reached record peaks by late 1981 – when the oil boom since 1978 was coming to an end – has since then remained, on average, well above historical levels with, however, a significant variability as a result of successive external shocks and the often conflicting stabilization and structural adjustment objectives of the government's economic strategy.

Three large devaluations took place in 1982. They were associated with the February policy package designed to regain fiscal control and cut a widening and unsustainable deficit in the balance of payments, with the interruption of international lending to Mexico in August, and with the attempt by the new De la Madrid Administration in December to reduce the spread with the black market rate. Taking into account all these adjustments, the nominal devaluation from February to December had been approximately 250 per cent for the controlled rate (for foreign trade transactions) and 450 per cent for the free rate (other transactions). In real terms, the peso also reached record lows; in the controlled market, its value in mid-1983 was still over 35 per cent below its 1981 level, and around 20 per cent below its mid-1978 level (before the real appreciation during the oil boom), which is also approximately the historical average during the period of high and stable growth of the 1960s.

After the December adjustments, the rate of daily, preannounced, nominal mini-devaluations was set in such a way as to contribute to the deceleration of inflation while at the same time keeping a real exchange parity appropriate to the achievement of the long-term (structural change) objectives, particularly the promotion of a (non-oil) export-led economic recovery. The appropriate parity was, initially, considered to be the mid-1983 level of the controlled rate. This approach required thus that, from then onwards, actual inflation followed, approximately, the percentage rate of

Table 6.9 Macroeconomic indicators, Mexico, 1981-90

	1981	1982	1983	1984	1985	1986	1987	1988	1989	1990
GDP growth rate (%)	8.8	-0.6	-4.2	3.6	2.6	-3.8	1.7	1.3	3.1	3.9
Investment/GDP ratio (%)	26.5	22.2	16.6	17.0	17.9	16.4	16.1	16.8	17.4	18.9
Consumer price inflation (%)[a]	28.7	98.9	80.8	59.2	63.7	105.7	159.2	51.7	19.7	29.9
Real average earnings[b] (index 1980 = 100)	103.5	102.2	80.7	75.4	76.6	72.3	72.8	72.1	75.8	78.0
Operational fiscal deficit (% GDP)	10.0	5.5	-0.4	0.3	0.8	2.4	-1.8	3.6	1.7	-1.8
Indices 1978 = 100										
Real value of the peso										
Consumer/wholesale prices[c]	126.7	84.2	80.3	92.9	96.1	77.5	78.2	97.8	102.7	109.8
Relative wholesale prices[d]	121.5	79.4	77.7	92.5	93.2	76.0	78.0	94.7	96.2	100.8
Effective-Banco de México[e]	136.6	99.8	91.7	111.9	116.1	79.6	73.0	88.4	97.2	100.5
Relative unit labour costs[f]	128.2	83.1	64.0	69.8	67.8	51.9	53.5	67.6	77.3	83.9
Terms of trade (index 1971 = 100)	124.3	108.4	99.0	97.1	91.9	66.2	73.1	66.1	70.5	73.8
Debt/export ratio (%)	288	337	346	322	357	459	371	346	289	258
Balance of payments (US$ billion)										
Exports (goods)	20.1	21.2	22.3	24.2	21.7	16.0	20.7	20.6	22.8	27.0
Oil	14.6	16.5	16.0	16.6	14.8	6.3	8.6	6.7	7.9	10.1
Non-oil	5.5	4.8	6.3	7.6	6.9	9.7	12.0	13.9	15.0	16.8
Imports (goods)	23.9	14.4	8.6	11.3	13.2	11.4	12.2	18.9	25.4	31.1
Current account	-16.1	-6.2	5.4	4.2	1.2	-1.7	4.0	-2.4	-6.0[g]	-6.3[g]
Capital account[h]	17.4	2.9	-2.3	-0.9	-3.6	2.3	2.1	-4.3	6.4	9.6
Change in reserves	1.3	-3.3	3.1	3.3	-2.4	0.6	6.1	-6.7	0.4	3.2

Sources: Banco de México, *Indicadores Económicos*, various issues; CEPAL, *Balance Preliminar de la Economía de America Latina, 1990*; Presidencia de la República, *Criterios Generales de Política Económica*; OECD (for US unit labour costs).

[a] December-December rate.
[b] Manufacturing sector. Includes wages, salaries and fringe benefits.
[c] Mexico's consumer prices/US wholesale prices.
[d] Mexico-US.
[e] Based on consumer prices.
[f] Mexico's manufacturing/US business sector.
[g] The figures for 1989 and 1990 are not comparable with previous years due to an upward adjustment in workers' remittance (approximately 1.9 billion). (See Banco de México, 'Methodological note on the balance of payments'.)
[h] Includes errors and omissions.

announced mini-devaluations (in turn decided on the basis of government's inflation targets). Such was not the case, however, and increasing tensions appeared between the stabilization and the structural adjustment objectives of the strategy and the associated criteria for exchange rate management.

During this first adjustment period, fiscal adjustment relied on sharp cuts in public investment, real salary reductions of government employees, increases in indirect taxes and public prices, and no less important, on the strong revaluation, due to peso depreciations, of the real peso value of the government's foreign exchange balance – a balance in surplus broadly equal to oil export revenues minus external debt service. As a result, the public sector operational balance (i.e. the inflation adjusted budget), which had reached a record deficit of 10 per cent of GDP in 1981, was brought into a small surplus in 1983, while at the same time the primary surplus was over 4 per cent of GDP.

The exchange rate and fiscal adjustments led in 1983 to an improved performance of non-oil exports and a favourable balance of trade position; to an 'overkill', in fact, of the original targets which was reflected in a much sharper than expected economic recession. These conditions, together with difficulties in regulating other key prices, contributed to the prevalence of short-term criteria and objectives in exchange rate management. From mid-1983 to mid-1985 the peso appreciated significantly in real terms, even though, during this first phase, the controlled rate remained on average well above 1981 levels and even above 1978 levels. But real appreciation since early 1983 weakened export performance substantially from the last quarter of 1984 and led to a sharp decline of the trade and current account surpluses achieved in 1983 and the first half of 1984. In the first semester of 1985, the trade surplus was nearly half its level of a year before. These difficulties were aggravated by financial speculation, stimulated by the prospect of a large overshooting of the inflation targets for 1985 and declining oil prices in the international markets over 1985. In July–August 1985 a new collapse of the foreign exchange market followed. The controlled rate was devalued by about 20 per cent and then allowed to crawl down, while a complete 'free' rate was legalized. Fiscal adjustment – which this time relied on both investment and current expenditures cuts – and the pace of peso depreciation, were both accentuated when in early 1986 international oil prices collapsed, leading to a loss of export and fiscal revenues of the order of 7 per cent of GDP during 1986. The real value of the peso would reach new unprecedented low levels in 1986–7 when its average level was even lower than in 1983 (and 40 per cent lower than in 1981). The operational fiscal balance, which had turned into a deficit as a result of the loss of oil revenues in 1986, was again brought into a surplus of almost 2 per cent of GDP in 1987.

This time, circumstances had tilted the balance between the conflicting policy objectives in favour of structural adjustment and the maintenance

189

of a low real value of the peso. The severity of the balance of payments and fiscal constraints, as a result of the oil price collapse, probably left no alternative but to sacrifice the stabilization objectives and accept a sharp acceleration of the inflation rate in order to offset the loss of government revenues and keep the current account position within sustainable limits. The real appreciation that had taken place over 1983 and 1984 after the exchange rate adjustments to the debt crisis, was now avoided, and for most of 1986 and 1987 the real value of the peso was kept broadly stable at mid-1983 levels, and thus well below the average levels of the previous phase.

The cost of the strategy was, of course, a higher rate of inflation and, from mid-1987, at an accelerating pace. The restoration of current account surpluses, a comfortable position in international reserves – as a result of those surpluses and new lending from the IMF and international banks – together with the prospect of an uncontrolled inflation turning into hyperinflation, were to lead in late 1987 to a new change of policy. In December 1987, an agreement was reached between the government, labour unions and business confederations on a comprehensive attack on inflation comprising a deindexation programme, a tight monetary and fiscal stance and a set of import liberalization measures. Deindexation involved, after a once-and-for-all devaluation, a freeze on wages, prices and the exchange rate.

Since March 1988, the exchange rate has been allowed to crawl at a preannounced rate. The success of the programme in bringing down inflation (from 160 per cent in 1987 to 30 per cent in 1990) together with the turnabout in the capital account of the balance of payments since 1989, has enabled the government to meet its exchange rate targets and, in fact, to reduce over time the percentage rate of mini-devaluations, in spite of the continuing real appreciation of the peso since 1988. By 1990–1, the real exchange rate was well below the average levels since 1982 and, in some measures, even below those of the previous lows of the 1984–5 period (which had contributed to the mid-1985 foreign exchange crisis). At the same time, the recent period has recorded a debt relief agreement with international commercial banks and an acceleration of structural economic reforms in areas other than trade policy – privatization and economic deregulation, including foreign investment flows – which, as discussed below, appear to have contributed to the strengthening of the capital account position that has made recent trade reform and exchange rate policy sustainable.

Trade and industrial policy reform

Those have been the macroeconomic conditions and adjustments under which the reform of past industrialization and trade policies was

Table 6.10 Import licence coverage, Mexico

Year		As percentage of tariff items	As percentage of import value	As percentage of 1986 production
1977		80	90	
1980		24	60	
1981		26	85.5	
1982		100	100	
1983		100	100	
1984		65	83.5	
1985	June			92.2
	August	11	37.5	
	December			47.1
1986	February	10	35	
	June		31	46.9
	December			39.8
1987	May	6	26	
	June			35.8
	December		20	25.4
1988	April		20	23.2

Sources: Banco de México, *Direccion de Investigaciones Económicas*, cited by USITC (1990); Balassa (1985); de Mateo (1988); Zabludovsky (1990).

undertaken. The history of trade policy changes in the 1980s starts, however, with the growing balance of payments strains experienced during the oil boom from 1978 to 1981. These difficulties were eventually to lead to the reversal of the import liberalization measures adopted under the 1976–8 stabilization programme. Direct import controls were fully re-established in mid-1981, and this policy stance prevailed during the difficult 1982–3 period following the debt crisis (see Table 6.10). At that time, tariffs ranged from 0 to 100 per cent, with a production-weighted average of 23.5 per cent. Tariffs were often reinforced by a system of reference prices that formed the basis for establishing the actual tariffs to be paid.

In 1984 moderate import liberalization measures were undertaken as part of the structural change strategy of the De la Madrid Administration. Licensing import requirements were relaxed and partially replaced by tariffs. Thus, the percentage of import value subject to permits fell to 83.5 per cent, while tariffs increased and the percentage of import value exempt from tariffs declined to 36 per cent. Additional steps were announced in early 1985. In the context of a medium-term plan prepared by the Ministry of Industry and Trade, a programme was launched for the gradual elimination of import licences between 1985 and 1989, together with a series of steps towards the establishment of a more uniform structure of effective protection. At the same time, a US–Mexico bilateral trade agreement was signed, reaffirming the commitment to liberalization and pledging the elimination of export subsidies; in exchange, Mexico obtained from the US some of the advantages normally reserved for members of GATT.

Table 6.11 Import tariff structure, Mexico, 1982–9

End of year	Tariff mean (unweighted)	Dispersion	Trade-weighted average tariff	Number of tariff rates
1982	27.0	24.8	16.4	16
1983	23.8	23.5	8.2	13
1984	23.3	22.5	8.6	10
1985	25.5	18.8	13.3	10
1986	22.6	14.1	13.1	11
1987	10.0	6.9	5.6	5
1988	10.4	7.1	6.1	5
1989[a]	13.1	4.3	9.8	5

Source: Zabludovsky (1990), based on data from Direccion General de Política de Comercio Exterior, SECOFI (Secretaria de Comercio y Fomento Industrial)
[a] To 9 March 1989.

The July 1985 reform and GATT membership

The disappointing performance of non-oil exports in the first half of 1985, and the increasingly influential view in government circles attributing the failure to meet the 1983–5 inflation targets to the sluggishness of import liberalization,[18] led to additional trade reforms in mid-1985. As part of the devaluation and fiscal correction package in mid-1985, the removal of import licences and the reform of the tariff system were thus further accelerated.

Licensing requirements decreased to 37.5 per cent in August 1985 as a percentage of import value (and to 47 per cent of production by the end of the year), and continued to be removed throughout 1986 and 1987. Intermediate goods were heavily liberalized, together with selected consumer goods. Liberalization also emphasized capital goods imports which fell, as a percentage of the licensed import bundle, from 19 to 10 per cent (having represented 31 per cent in 1982; see Zabludovsky, 1990). At the same time, tariff rates were increased, the trade-weighted average rising from 8.6 per cent in 1984 to 13.3 per cent by the end of 1985 (see Table 6.11). This was followed by further steps towards reducing tariff dispersion; by 1986, 90 per cent of the dutiable import bundle was subject to three rates (10, 22.5 and 37 per cent; see Zabludovsky, 1990).

A GATT membership agreement was negotiated and signed in July 1986. Mexico pledged to continue the replacement of direct controls by tariffs (which by then was well advanced), followed by tariff reductions,[19] and a system to assess anti-dumping and countervailing duties was introduced. Mexico maintained the right temporarily to exclude from licence removal agriculture and some manufacturing sectors, such as automobiles, pharmaceuticals and electronics, under specific industrial promotion programmes (see below for further analysis of these programmes). In addition to obtaining the advantages of GATT membership, the agreement was viewed by the Mexican administration as a means of strengthening the private sector's confidence in the government's long-term commitment to trade liberalization.

The December 1987 reforms and the current state of trade liberalization

Additional major steps were undertaken in late 1987, in the context of the 'Economic Solidarity Pact' – the stabilization programme adopted at the time by the government with the cooperation of labour unions and business organizations. Licensing requirements dropped further to 20 per cent (as a percentage of import value), the removal involving this time most consumer manufactures. Tariff dispersion was reduced to the 0–20 per cent range, with only five rate categories (0, 5, 10, 15 and 20 per cent). The average tariff rate fell to 10 per cent (unweighted) and 5.6 per cent (import-weighted) (see Table 6.11), while the average production-weighted import tariff declined to 12 per cent (from a level of 23.5 in 1982). Practically all remaining reference prices were removed. These changes in the tariff system went far beyond the schedule of the 1986 tariff reform programme. Subsequent tariff reforms included the elimination in 1988 of the 5 per cent import surcharge (which had been introduced in stages since 1985) and import tariff reductions in support of the stabilization programme, with a view to selectively increasing competitive pressure on goods which had been experiencing above-average price increases since the introduction of the counter-inflation programme of December 1987. In January and March 1989, concerns about making effective protection more uniform and, probably even more, about the surge of consumer goods imports during 1988, led the new Salinas Administration to close the dispersion in nominal tariffs through an upward adjustment in tariff rates for most goods previously exempt or subject to a 5 per cent rate.

Thus by late 1989 the import-weighted average tariff was 9.8 per cent. The sectors that remained protected under import licences accounted for around 25 per cent of tradable output, and included mainly agricultural goods and a few manufacturing industries under industrial promotion programmes. Continuing reforms and removal of import licences are currently taking place in these sectors, as discussed below. These current trends are likely to accelerate again in the event of a Free Trade Agreement with the US and Canada, which for Mexico – with over two-thirds of its overall foreign trade and around 90 per cent of its manufacturing trade being carried with the US – may simply mean free trade *tout court*.

Although trade reform since 1983 has focused mainly on the import regime, significant changes have also taken place in export promotion policies (besides the effects on them of changes in the import regime and exchange rate policy). Export restrictions are now less important than in

1982, and those remaining are largely determined by the presence of domestic price controls and international and bilateral trade agreements. Export licences affect agricultural goods with controlled prices and products subject to international agreements (such as coffee, sugar, steel, textiles) – accounting together for 24.4 per cent of non-oil exports (242 tariff items). Export tariffs (of up to 5.5 per cent) affect largely a number of agricultural products subject to export licensing and representing 6.7 per cent of non-oil exports. At the same time, traditional export subsidies (through tax refunds to exporters) have been eliminated. The present export incentives scheme includes mainly a programme exempting tariffs on 'temporary' imports and a programme which exempts exporting firms from import licences on inputs.[20]

Industrial promotion policies and the experience of two survivors

As discussed earlier, besides the conventional instruments of trade policy, Mexico's industrial development strategy had relied since the 1960s on sector or firm-specific programmes designed to promote local industrial integration, foster manufacturing exports and develop national firms. These industrial programmes (or *programas de fabricacion*') provided import licences and fiscal incentives in exchange for the achievement of increasing degrees of local integration. They were generally subject to an agreed schedule and a maximum domestic to import price differential, and included in some cases the meeting of export targets. The number of these programmes increased throughout the 1960s and most of the 1970s, especially in the heavy intermediate and capital goods industries.[21] They had turned, in effect, into the major industrial policy instrument during the second and more difficult stage of import-substitution industrialization.

The shift since 1978, and even more so since 1983, towards a more outward-oriented industrial strategy was accompanied by a sharp reduction in the use of this policy instrument, as the replacement of import licences by tariffs liberalized the importation of the products included in the programmes themselves. At the same time, this shift led to greater selectivity in industrial promotion, and so the programmes established (or reformed) during the 1980s focused on a small number of priority industries – essentially the automobile, microcomputer and pharmaceutical sectors[22] – while greater emphasis was given to export promotion, price competitiveness and the improvement of technological and product standards in the design of these programmes.

The Automotive Industry

The industrial policy set out in the 1962 decree on automobile production – prohibiting the importation of assembled vehicles, starting in 1964, establishing a minimum degree of local integration, and obliging the firms producing auto parts to have a minimum of 60 per cent Mexican capital – marked the transformation of the automobile sector from an assembly industry into a manufacturing activity. It marked also the beginning of a rapid local development by which the industry became a leading sector in industrial growth.[23] A common feature of this and subsequent decrees (1969, 1972, 1977 and 1983) has been the establishment of domestic content requirements aimed at the reduction of the industry's trade deficit and the strengthening of the local auto parts industry based on national firms.

The 1977 and 1983 decrees introduced, however, a significant shift in approach to the industry's regulatory framework.[24] The 1977 decree established foreign exchange budgets for each producer of finished vehicles but gave greater flexibility to firms with respect to the means to achieve them (more exports or greater local integration), while, at the same time, eliminating the system of production quotas and price controls with a view to increasing competition and encouraging productivity gains. The 1983 decree ratified the focus on foreign exchange balances, allowing a lesser degree of integration to be offset by more exports. It also introduced new regulations with a view to promoting a fuller use of economies of scale and the rationalization of the industry's supply structure, essentially through a reduction in the differentiation of models and product lines.[25]

As we shall see in detail below, when discussing the impact of trade policy, the 1977 and 1983 reforms were successful in meeting their export promotion and trade balance objectives; having been for decades a large net importer, the industry now ranks second, after the export of crude oil, in generating foreign exchange. The other major objective of the 1983 decree – the rationalization of industry supply through a reduction of product differentiation – was not achieved. The average scale on which the Mexican automobile industry worked in 1987 was only 14,800 units per line, a decline from 1981 levels and far from the scale considered minimum in the 1983 reform (50,000). Two major factors account for this failure. First, the contraction of the domestic market created a very adverse environment for the achievement of the goal: the 1982–3 recession alone brought down the average number of cars per line to 11,000 (compared to 18,000 in 1981). A second factor was the option offered in the 1983 decree which permitted additional lines on condition that they be self-sufficient in foreign exchange and that they export more than 50 per cent of their output (or the equivalent value in assembly material for each line).

Further deregulation and trade liberalization measures were introduced by the Salinas Administration in late 1989, including the removal of import licences in the auto parts industry, a relaxation of foreign exchange requirements and the elimination of restrictions on lines and models introduced by the 1983 decree. It is still too early to evaluate the impact of the December 1989 decree, especially the extension of trade liberalization to the automobile industry. The reforms are likely to strengthen current trends towards a greater intra-industry specialization in foreign trade, by allowing terminal firms to specialize in the production of some models while importing others. At the same time, and despite its recent export performance, strong reservations have been expressed on the current state of the industry's competitiveness given, in particular, the failure to achieve the rationalization of domestic supply. This accounts for the industry's still high domestic pre-tax prices, in both the terminal and auto parts sectors. In addition, the likelihood that such prices partially reflect a cross-subsidy of exports casts doubts on the impact of trade liberalization on future exports and trade balance performance.

The Computer Industry

The computer equipment industry – unlike the automotive sector or other sectors in the electronics industry – was virtually absent in Mexico by the late 1970s. The 1981 Computer Industry Programme set the goals and policy guidelines that (with the exception of a major change in 1985) were to govern the development of this infant industry for the rest of the decade. This industrial programme included goals concerning: (i) import substitution, to be achieved through the establishment of DCRs, so that by 1986 local production would supply at least 70 per cent of domestic demand;[26] (ii) export development, setting foreign exchange balances (as in the automotive industry) stipulating that an increasing share of payments abroad would be covered by exports; (iii) domestic–import price differential reduction, so as to keep domestic prices only slightly above (not more than 15 per cent) those of the firm's home country; (iv) technology transfer and national technological development, by setting a minimum of 5 per cent of sales to be spent on R&D, as well as the provision of technical training; (v) development of national enterprises by reserving the production of microcomputers for firms with a majority of Mexican capital (51 per cent at least).[27]

In exchange for their commitments, firms were granted tax incentives (mainly a 20 per cent tax credit calculated on the basis of new investments, wages or domestic purchases of components) and trade protection, including import licences for finished equipment as well as tariffs (initially set at 30 per cent for microcomputers and lower levels for minis, mainframes, peripherals and components). The programme also used government procurement to favour firms adhering to the programme guidelines.

A major policy change took place in 1985 regarding the limits on foreign ownership, following IBM's request to set up a production plant with 100 per cent foreign capital. After an initial rejection by the National Commission on Foreign Investment, the request was later accepted in exchange for a substantial increase in IBM's investment and export commitments.[28] The policy change – which was then extended to other foreign firms that had previously developed joint ventures with Mexican capital – meant that foreign companies in the microcomputer sector could now choose between keeping within the framework of the 1981 rules (a position adopted by Unisys) or request permission to operate with 100 per cent foreign capital in exchange for larger export requirements (i.e. an export-- import ratio of the order of three to one instead of one to one).[29]

Further policy changes took place in April 1990. A new decree for the computer industry then removed import licences and replaced them with a 20 per cent tariff on imports of micros and peripherals (the maximum rate in the current tariff structure). An agreement was also reached at the time between the government and industrialists for a gradual phasing-out (to be completed by 1992) of domestic content and foreign exchange requirements.

The results of the 1981 programme have been mixed. As in the case of the automobile industry, its major successes took place in areas where the strategies of foreign firms and the government's policy objectives coincided. The sector has been one of the fastest growing export industries of the 1980s (albeit from very low initial levels). By 1985–7 more than half of production was exported (and the corresponding share of exports rises to nearly 80 per cent in the case of PCs). By 1987 national supply covered about 56 per cent of domestic demand, only 14 percentage points below the 1981 programme target for 1986. As a result, the trade deficit in computer products has been decreasing – from nearly 100 per cent of imports in 1981–2 to around 30 per cent in the first half of 1987 – a significant achievement during a period when the stock of computers per thousand inhabitants expanded from 0.14 to 1.5. Similarly, the reduction of domestic and import price differentials seems to have been largely achieved. Different estimates suggest that the domestic retail prices of best-quality micros are around 15–20 per cent higher than US prices (Peres, 1990) or 25 per cent higher according to the World Bank (1990), which estimates the price differential in 1982 at 200 per cent. In contrast to these achievements, less progress appears to have been made in technology transfer and development (especially in product technology, see Peres, 1990) while, as already indicated, the goal of reserving production of microcomputers for firms with national majority ownership was abandoned after the 1985 policy change.

In sum, the results of the more flexible and selective approach to the automobile and computer industries, while mixed, appears to be a considerable improvement over past policies of infant industry protection. In the case of the automobile industry it strengthened ongoing trends towards greater intra-industry and intra-firm specialization in foreign trade, with a clearly positive impact on export performance and probably also, as seen below, on productivity growth. The experience of the computer industry compares favourably (in terms of export performance and price differentials) with older sectors with similar characteristics, such as consumer electronics, and the difficulties faced by the latter during the recent trade liberalization experience sharpen this contrast.

Compared to a fuller liberalization of these industries, the benefits of this sectoral and certainly discriminatory approach may be criticized on two grounds. The international strategies of TNCs and Mexico's cost and locational advantages played a major role in the recent successful performance of these industries, and thus it is difficult to disentangle the specific contribution of the sectoral programmes themselves. In addition, the programme regulations lacked transparency. Both of these are valid arguments. However, as we shall see later, the performance of these sectors under specific industrial programmes compares favourably, especially in terms of exports and trade balances, with fully liberalized industries with similar characteristics. And the degree of discretion provided by the programme regulations also left a certain amount of national leverage in these TNC-dominated sectors, which the government used quite effectively to strengthen the achievement of some of the programme objectives, as the export experience of the computer industry suggests.

The effects of trade policy reform

Prices and employment

Trade liberalization had several aims, one of them being, especially in late 1987, to strengthen price discipline in the manufacturing sector by opening it to greater international competition. Yet, although the counter-inflation package in late 1987 has been successful to this date, economists of different persuasions agree that trade liberalization made no significant contribution to it (see Brailovsky et al., 1990; Ize, 1990). The evidence even suggests that profit margins, rather than being squeezed by international competition, have actually increased since 1987. The real peso appreciation that was a key factor in the deceleration of inflation in the recent period was accompanied by declining public-sector prices in real terms and stagnant real wages, rather than by increasing real wages and reduced profit margins.

To explain this behaviour, it is necessary to consider separately the long-term structural effects of trade liberalization on price discipline from those of the initial macroeconomic conditions under which it was undertaken. From a long-term perspective, the presumption that a more open economy may well weaken the market power of domestic firms and labour unions, and thus reduce the inflationary bias built into highly oligopolistic market structures, seems a plausible one. In the short term, however, exchange rate policy will have a major influence on profit margins in the tradable goods sector since domestic prices are likely to adjust with a lag to exchange variations. The heavy depreciations in 1986 and 1987 created – as shown in the estimates by de Mateo (1988) and Ten Kate and de Mateo (1989) – a large foreign/domestic price differential across all sectors producing tradable goods in the Mexican economy. The ensuing upward adjustment of profit margins that was slowly taking place during the trade reform period thus prevailed over the structural effects of trade liberalization on competition and market structures.

The fact that the elimination of import licences was being effectively compensated for by 'exchange rate protection' – most forcefully expressed in the evolution of relative unit labour costs in Mexico's manufacturing sector (see Table 6.9) – also accounts for the hardly visible adverse impact of trade liberalization on overall industrial employment. The latest industrial census data show that from mid–1985 to mid–1988 the country's traditional industrial centres – the metropolitan area of Mexico City in the Federal District and Estado de México, and Monterrey in the State of Nuevo Leon – suffered severe job losses (of almost 250,000) and plant closures. At the same time, however, new jobs and industrial plants were rapidly being created in the rest of the country – the central and eastern regions of Puebla and Veracruz and, especially, the northern border states of Chihuahua, Coahuila and Nuevo Leon (excluding Monterrey). The net result of these opposed trends was a reduction of industrial employment in the order of 4 per cent together with an increase in the number of industrial establishments (by 4.5 per cent).

The net job losses can be largely explained by the severity of the contraction of industrial demand in 1986 and the first half of 1987 – which resulted from the fiscal austerity package that followed the early 1986 oil price collapse[30] – rather than from import penetration in a stagnant or expanding domestic market. This conclusion is strengthened by the fact that employment losses, according to preliminary census information, were concentrated in highly pro-cyclical industries (basic metals, steel, electrical appliances) and consumer goods with a relatively high income elasticity of demand (meat and some textile products).[31] Since 1988, the additional liberalization measures, combined with an appreciating real peso, have strengthened the extent of import penetration. However, the adverse effects of these developments on industrial employment have been partially offset by more favourable domestic demand conditions since then, as the success of the counter-inflation programme of late 1987 has been accompanied by a moderate recovery of economic activity and private investment.

Table 6.12 Growth of non-oil exports, Mexico, 1982–8

	1982	1988	Annual growth rate (%)	Contribution to overall increase (%)
	(US$ billion)			
(i) Automobiles and computers	0.5	3.8	40.4	31.1
Automobiles	0.5	3.5	38.8	27.9
Computers	0.002	0.340	135.5	3.2
(ii) Maquiladoras	0.9	2.3	18.3	13.9
(iii) Other non-oil exports	4.3	10.2	15.5	55.1
Manufacturing	2.5	7.9	21.1	49.4
Metallic products	0.076	0.818	48.6	6.9
Steel	0.112	0.759	37.6	6.1
Cement	0.013	0.146	49.6	1.2
Other	2.3	6.1	17.4	35.2
Agriculture	1.2	1.7	5.2	4.1
Mining	0.50	0.66	4.7	1.5
(iv) Total	5.6	16.3	19.5	100.0

Source: Banco de México, Indicadores del Sector Externo, various issues.

Export performance and resource reallocation

The major goal of trade reform was, however, to eliminate the anti-export bias of past protectionist policies and thus improve the economy's export performance sector as well as its overall efficiency in resource allocation. Mexico's strong export performance in the 1980s – non-oil exports have recorded an unprecedented boom, rising from around US$5.5 billion in 1981 to over $16 billion in 1990, an almost threefold increase[32] – is sometimes taken as a major outcome of trade liberalization (see, for example, Zabudovsky, 1990), i.e. a consequence of the greater access by producers of exportable goods to inputs at international prices and quality as well as of the shift in the relative profitability of producing for export markets.

While these factors have undoubtedly played a role, a close look at the sectoral and time pattern of export growth clearly suggests that trade liberalization as usually understood – i.e. the policy reforms introduced in the 1985–8 period – has not been the main force behind the fast growth of manufacturing exports. Table 6.12 shows the expansion of non-oil exports from 1982 to 1988 grouped according to policy regime: (i) those under specific industrial programmes and corresponding to the type (i) regime on p. 171 (ii) the maquiladora industries; (iii) the rest of non-oil exports including those from manufacturing industries which effectively recorded a shift in trade regime during the period from import-substitution policies to liberalized trade, and those from primary activities which were also affected by the policy change.

As shown in the table, the fastest growing exports originate from sectors under specific industrial programmes: the automobile industry (which alone accounts for 35 per cent of the total increase in non-maquiladora exports) and the computer industry. As discussed above, these are precisely the industries where liberalization measures were temporarily waived, and whose finished products have been fully protected by import licences during the whole period under consideration. Here, a fortunate combination of international factors and the industrial policy reforms of the late 1970s and early 1980s appear to be the major causes of rapid export growth. Following the 1977 automobile decree, and from 1978 onwards, all the automotive firms in the terminal industry began to set up plants making engines and assembling vehicles largely for export and, from 1977 to 1987, the share of exports in total sales increased tenfold, from 3.9 to 39.7 per cent. Certainly, this increasing importance of foreign markets partly reflects the sharp contraction of domestic demand since the 1982 crisis and a shift of domestic supply towards exports in order to offset declining domestic sales. But more important was the fact that the concern for improved competitiveness and export performance expressed by the 1977 and 1983 reforms was in harmony with the international strategies of foreign enterprises in the terminal industry.[33] The rapid advances of the Japanese automobile industry in international competition – at the expense, in particular, of American corporations – had forced the latter to redefine its productive strategies, including a shift of new investments towards lower cost countries. Mexico's advantages in terms of proximity to the US market, experience in automobile production, and costs and subsidies made it an attractive location for the new, export-oriented investments. By relaxing domestic content requirements, the 1977 regulatory changes facilitated this process by reducing the disadvantages that might have arisen from the use of less efficient locally produced parts, thus allowing firms to take full advantage of Mexico's cost and locational advantages.

The other major contribution to export increases has its origin in the maquiladora assembly plants in the northern border region – a sector which has traditionally been subject to a free trade regime for the processing of imported materials and its re-exporting abroad, and which therefore did not record a change in trade regime during the period. Here, the role of the real exchange rate has been decisive. The very dynamic and improved performance of this sector in the 1980s, compared to previous periods, can be explained by the abnormally low dollar value of domestic wages – which resulted from peso depreciations – together with its locational advantages given by its proximity to the large and expanding US market, during a period of increased global competition.

When these two groups of industries are excluded from the total, we are left with those that effectively recorded a change in trade regime. The annual growth rate of non-oil exports then drops from 23.8 per cent to a less impressive 15.5 per cent. This is, nevertheless, a very respectable rate and an encouraging sign, especially if one looks at the manufacturing component of this group (21.1 per cent). It is not easy, however, to disentangle the specific contribution of trade liberalization from that of real exchange rate movements and the contraction of domestic demand during the period, and one such exercise assigns a predominant role to the latter (see Brailovsky *et al.*, 1990). In any case, it seems clear that there are no firm grounds for great optimism and that the contraction of the domestic market played a major role, making these export increases rather vulnerable to a future economic recovery. Three factors point in this direction. First, export increases in this third group have been mostly concentrated in several heavy intermediate goods (petrochemicals, steel, cement) which under normal demand conditions suffer from a structural trade deficit, but have recorded an export boom during the period following the sharp contraction of the domestic market and the large underutilization of their productive capacities. The same probably explains a second worrying feature, the fact that industries showing high export growth did not seem to have had a significantly better investment performance than other sectors (Lopez, 1988; World Bank, 1988). Moreover, a detailed consideration of the pattern through time of export growth points to the same conclusion (see Table 6.9). Manufacturing exports grew rapidly both before and after the major liberalization measures were introduced in mid-1985. And since 1988, after the additional reforms of late 1987, the pace of export growth has slowed down significantly in the midst of a moderate economic recovery.

The export performance of some heavy intermediate industries also reflects, however, a dynamic response of some Mexican conglomerates to the new competitive conditions of the 1980s. This response went, in fact, well beyond a redirection of their sales towards foreign markets and involved a whole redefinition of competitive strategies by some domestic leading firms (see Peres, 1990, on this subject). An emerging trend – fairly clear in at least the glass and cement industries – is, indeed, the internationalization of Mexican firms which, besides an enhanced export activity, are advancing deeply into the US market by taking over American firms. The first successful hostile takeover of an American company was done in 1989 by the Monterrey-based Vitro conglomerate, a holding company which is a leading producer in the glass industry (with sales of US$1,100 million in 1989).[34] In the cement industry, another Mexican conglomerate – Cemex, controlling 66 per cent of the Mexican market and a leading exporter to the US – also went abroad. Cemex initially took over the UK Blue Circle's affiliate in Mexico to increase by 20 percentage points its domestic market share and to protect its own export market in the American South. Then Cemex bought Blue Circle cement properties in the US, thus becoming the fourth largest producer in the world.[35]

The end result of these trends in manufacturing exports is summarized

Table 6.13 Composition of manufacturing exports, Mexico (constant 1980 prices, % of total)

	1980	1985	1989[a]
Consumer goods	47.7	27.3	26.2
Food processing	32.6	18.6	15.6
Textiles	13.0	6.2	8.1
Other industries	2.1	2.5	2.5
Light intermediates	3.3	3.4	5.4
Wood and furniture	1.3	1.9	3.3
Paper	2.0	1.5	2.1
Heavy intermediates	29.0	43.3	35.0
Chemicals	24.0	34.3	23.1
Stone, clay and glass	3.2	5.0	4.5
Basic metals	1.8	4.0	7.4
Consumer durables and capital goods	20.0	26.0	33.4
Total	100.0	100.0	100.0

Source: Nacional Financiera, 1990, based on Instituto Nacional de Estadística, Geografía e Informática, Sistema de Cuentas Nacionales de México, various issues.
[a] Preliminary.

in Table 6.13, which compares the export structure in 1980, 1985 and 1989, in terms of the broad components of manufacturing. For those expecting a large, painful, but greatly beneficial reallocation of resources in favour of traditional exportable goods, and labour – and natural resource-intensive goods, the experience with trade liberalization to date will have been greatly disappointing. For, beyond a few encouraging signs – the growing export shares of the wood industry and, since 1985, of the textiles and apparel industries – the 1980s have witnessed an extrapolation of past trends in the trade and industrial patterns marked by the increasing importance of heavy intermediates, consumer durables and capital goods. Since 1985, the first year of radical trade reform, these trends have continued unabated[36] and, in the case of consumer durables and capital goods, have, if anything, accelerated.

A major factor explaining these developments is, in our view, the advanced stage, reviewed earlier, that intra-industry (and intra-firm) processes of specialization and trade had reached already by 1980, precisely in those capital-intensive, large-scale manufacturing industries which have been responsible for most of the export boom of the decade[37]. The industrial policy reforms of the late 1970s in some of these sectors gave further impulse to those processes. The incentives provided later by a very attractive exchange rate, and to a lesser extent by the mid-1980s trade reforms, fell on already fertile ground. The outstanding export performance of Mexico's manufacturing sector in the 1980s is thus, to a large degree, a

Table 6.14 Output and productivity growth in manufacturing, Mexico, 1980–9

	Annual growth rates				Percentages					
	Labour productivity		Output		Import ratios[a]			Export ratios[b]		
	1980 –5	1985 –9	1980 –5	1985 –9	1980	1985	1989	1980	1985	1989
Food processing[c]	0.7	1.3	2.5	1.8	12.9	4.4	10.2	12.0	11.8	15.5
Textiles, apparel and leather	0.3	–0.9	–0.3	–1.8	5.5	2.4	8.5	8.6	8.1	19.1
Lumber, wood and furniture	3.3	0.4	–0.5	–0.7	6.0	3.1	6.1	2.9	8.2	24.2
Paper	2.4	1.2	2.4	2.6	28.4	14.8	25.9	3.4	4.3	9.1
Chemicals	1.7	1.5	4.6	2.8	43.7	36.9	46.4	14.6	32.6	33.0
Stone, clay and glass	–0.2	0.5	1.1	1.7	6.2	3.1	5.2	4.1	12.1	17.0
Basic metals	–0.1	6.4	0.1	1.8	81.1	37.4	42.3	2.6	11.4	31.7
Fabricated metals, machinery and equipment	0.9	4.2	–1.6	2.2	99.2	56.1	93.9	8.5	23.4	46.3
Automobiles[d]	1.2	5.6								
Other manufacturing	0.3	–1.2	1.3	–1.2	67.6	48.2	75.4	7.3	16.0	38.3
Total manufacturing	1.2	1.8	1.2	1.6	40.5	22.9	36.4	9.0	16.7	26.3

Source: Instituto Nacional de Estadística, Geografía e Informática, *Sistema de Cuentas Nacionales*, various issues.
[a] Ratio of imports to sector GDP (1980 constant prices).
[b] Ratio of exports to sector GDP (1980 constant prices).
[c] Includes beverages and tobacco.
[d] Terminal industry.

legacy of the import-substitution period and highlights in a very real sense its success: it led, indeed, to an irreversible change in the economy's structure of comparative advantages.

Productivity–trade links in the 1980s

If trade liberalization has not much to show in terms of intersectoral reallocation of resources, what about its dynamic effects on productivity performance? An attempt to answer this question at this stage must be considered tentative and preliminary. The time period elapsed is still too short to draw any definite conclusions and the data required to construct adequate indicators are still unavailable. It is with these strong qualifications in mind that we can look at the available evidence.

Table 6.14 shows, for the main component sectors of manufacturing, the output and labour productivity growth rates for 1980–5 and 1985–9, together with indicators of import penetration and export performance in those periods. Overall labour productivity growth in the 1980s, at 1.4 per cent per year, has been clearly below historical trends (of the order of 3.5 per cent per year, see Table 6.7), but this is surely attributable to the sharp industrial slowdown during the decade. More interestingly, productivity growth shows a recovery in the post-trade liberalization period since 1985 compared to the first half of the decade which is more than proportional to the recovery of output and in fact proceeds at a higher rate than output growth itself. This development, indicating a reduction of employment levels in the midst of a slight recovery of output levels, suggests the presence of industry rationalization processes within manufacturing since 1985. A closer look reveals that these processes are largely concentrated in two sectors – consumer durables and capital goods and basic metals – which show the best productivity performances and are responsible for most of the acceleration of productivity growth during the second half of the decade.

Within the consumer durables and capital goods sector, the terminal automotive industry shows the highest rate of productivity growth and is also the one, given its weight, that has probably made the largest contribution to the sector's performance. The extraordinary expansion of the industry's exports and the rapidly increasing import ratios since 1985 suggest, in turn, that productivity gains are most likely the result of a process of increasing intra-industry (and intra-firm) specialization in foreign trade, associated with its special policy regime and the international developments already discussed. In particular, the export-oriented investments of the late 1970s and early 1980s, following the 1977 reform of the automotive decree, must have made a significant contribution to the technical modernization of the industry, whose effects were only fully felt well into the 1980s as the new plants created by those investments came into operation and rapidly expanded their share in the industry's output (on the subject, see Moreno, 1987).

In the second case, basic metals, the sector's fast export expansion must also have contributed to its high productivity performance. However, the sector's rationalization appears to be more closely related to a government programme with precisely that goal; a part of a broader policy of state disengagement in the economy, which included the shut-down and privatization of many public enterprises in a sector where the latter have traditionally shown a relatively high share of output (29.5 per cent compared to 7.2 per cent on average for manufacturing). The timing of the programme, which started in 1985 with a major shut-down (the Fundidora Monterrey steel mill employing 8,000 workers) taking place in 1986, and the pattern of accelerating productivity growth precisely in the second half of the decade strengthen the presumption that this has been the major factor in the improved productivity performance of the sector during this period.

Another sector making a significant contribution to the acceleration of productivity growth is food processing. The fact that productivity increases have taken place here in the midst of a slowdown of the sector's output growth also suggests a process of rationalization – albeit less intense and without the absolute reductions in employment levels of the previous two and, as we shall see, of a different nature altogether. In this case, rationaliz-ation is probably associated with the rapid import penetration in the sector in the recent period (in fact, only since 1988) by which the import ratio by 1989 had more than doubled compared to its 1985 level. This rapid expansion of imports in the domestic market has probably led to the shake-out of some parts of the industry, with the elimination of less efficient producers explaining its rising average productivity levels, while at the same time accounting for the deceleration of output growth in the midst of an overall economic recovery in manufacturing.

The benefits of import penetration in terms of productivity performance become much more doubtful, however, when we look at the rest of manu-facturing. The expansion of imports in the domestic market has been generalized across all manufacturing industries during the post-trade lib-eralization period, especially since the late 1987 acceleration of trade reform. As shown in Table 6.14, despite the overall improvement in pro-ductivity growth, five out of the nine broad component sectors of manufac-turing[38] have, in fact, recorded a decline in productivity growth rates after 1985 compared to the first half of the decade. Two of them, textiles and other manufacturing industries, show, in addition, negative rates in the more recent period. Moreover, the three worst performers (the two just mentioned and the wood industry) have all of them declining output levels since 1985, reflecting a displacement of domestic production by imports which more than offset the effects on output of a quite outstanding export expansion. Together with food processing, they show the fastest rates of import penetration within manufacturing, with the almost fourfold increase in the textiles import ratio standing out as the most remarkable.

It is possible that, in these industries, TFP growth would show a better performance than output per worker if there has been a change in their output mix towards more labour-intensive products and processes; but, given the contraction of output, this is unlikely to make much difference. It is also possible that current developments are transitory and that the benefits of import penetration will only be felt over a longer time span; but it is impossible to resolve this issue at present. Whether current trends are likely to be reversed, and are simply the prelude to the technological revival and modernization of these light manufacturing industries or, on the contrary, these sectors are set in a downward spiral of stagnation, declining productivity performance and increasing import penetration, remains to be seen. In any case, their recent experience, and the interesting contrast that it provides with the more positive developments in food processing, clearly indicate that the short-term productivity effects of import penetration can easily turn from positive to negative – even in the context of a fast export expansion – when it proceeds at an excessive pace.

Policy credibility and medium-term macroeconomic effects

The surge in imports that followed the 1987–8 acceleration of the trade liberalization programme had other impacts of doubtful value. The results of a survey by the World Bank (1988) on enterprise perceptions of credibility and consistency of trade policy indicate that after an improvement in policy credibility during 1985 and 1986 – possibly as a result of Mexico's entry into GATT in 1986 as well as of the heavy peso depreciations at the time – there was a clear deterioration in enterprise perceptions in 1987 and again in 1988. The latter probably reflects the impact of the recent import boom, especially acute in 1988, when imports increased at a spectacular rate (see Table 6.9). At the same time, as argued by Rodrik (1990), the surge in imports was also partly a consequence of the lack of credibility, i.e. a sign of speculation against the exchange rate freeze and the acceleration of trade liberalization that were part of the 'Economic Solidarity Pact', the stabilization package of late 1987.

As we have already seen, the additional trade liberalization measures in late 1987 do not appear to have made any significant contribution to the deceleration of inflation achieved by the stabilization programme. Its inclusion in this package, particularly in combination with an exchange rate freeze, is therefore very controversial as it may well have worsened the trade-off between the price stabilization objectives and the external balance constraints under which the 'Economic Pact' operated (see Ros, 1992). For it exacerbated the conflicting pressures on the exchange rate – upwards in order to compensate for the adverse effects of trade liberalization on the trade balance, downwards in order to guarantee the deceleration of inflation – and reduced (by up to one-half) the share of trade taxes in government revenues (see Rodrik, 1990). Equally important, these circumstances forced the monetary authorities to increase domestic real interest rates to unprecedented levels, and the higher burden of domestic debt service in government expenditures magnified in turn the required fiscal retrenchment. The result was, indeed, to complicate unnecessarily the task of macroeconomic management.

Recent import trends have also left the country's current account balance in a very vulnerable position. Combined with the export slowdown in recent years, the rise in imports has led to a declining trade surplus which turned later into a widening deficit. These developments are also partly explained by the peso real appreciation in recent years and by the moderate recovery of domestic demand. But the fact that the import boom appears to be clearly linked to the trade liberalization measures of late 1987, and given that those measures have not substantially improved overall export performance, provide a strong indication that trade liberalization since then has, in fact, had a negative impact on the structural trade balance (i.e. the trade balance at constant utilization and exchange rates). By tightening

207

foreign exchange constraints, the overall effect of the trade liberalization on medium-term economic growth could well turn out to have been negative.[39]

In the longer term, the impact and sustainability of trade liberalization relates to two main issues. First, to whether the initially dominant and negative effects on import functions will be gradually offset by a spurt of productivity growth and a change in the structure of investments and productive capacity toward exportable goods, with its positive sequel on export functions. Second, to the permanent or temporary nature of the turnabout of the capital account since 1989 which has made trade liberalization sustainable to this date. Casual observation suggests that the recent and massive capital inflows are related to a revival of business confidence – determined, in chronological order, by inflation stabilization, the debt relief agreement with commercial banks, massive privatization of public enterprises and, more recently, by the prospects of a Free Trade Agreement with the US and Canada.[40] But a part of these capital inflows – capital repatriation and a fraction of portfolio foreign investment – is clearly of a once and for all nature, and its future exhaustion raises a macroeconomic adjustment problem in a longer term horizon.

CONCLUSIONS

Mexico's industrial development was nurtured in a rather typical import-substitution policy regime which provided, however, moderate levels of effective protection to manufacturing with a limited, albeit increasing through time, dispersion of protection rates across industries; the policy regime also included a number of sector-specific programmes in infant industries which gave increasing emphasis to export targets and price competitiveness. Manufacturing, especially its heavy intermediates, consumer durables and capital goods sectors, benefited from three main mechanisms of resource transfer: high prices for their products arising from protection of domestic industrial markets; lower input costs resulting from energy subsidies, export taxes and licences on some agricultural raw materials and minerals; and low prices for imported capital goods as a consequence of low exchange rates and high tariff exemptions on imports of machinery and equipment which facilitated the financing of industrial investments. Of these different mechanisms, the first (high product prices) was generally limited and important only in a few sectors, while the influence of the other two changed over time: resource transfers from agriculture increased in the mid-1960s but disappeared by the late 1970s, while energy subsidies and a low exchange rate became increasingly important throughout the 1970s.

The industrial response to these incentives was highly dynamic in terms of output growth and its resource allocation effects generated a rather good productivity performance in the economy as a whole, even though productivity growth in manufacturing itself was less satisfactory. By 1980, the expansion of manufacturing industries, especially fast in the heavy intermediates, consumer durables and capital goods sectors, had radically transformed Mexico's industrial structure and its pattern of foreign trade. The latter, in particular, was becoming increasingly marked by rapid processes of intra-industry trade and specialization in capital-intense, large-scale manufacturing sectors under specific industrial programmes. These developments contrasted with the limited and declining importance in foreign trade and industrial structure of consumer goods and light intermediates, with the only exception of the processing of some agricultural inputs constituting the bulk of traditional exporting sectors.

The 1980s witnessed the overhaul of trade and industrial policies. The transition towards a liberalized trade regime has been strikingly smooth in terms both of the microeconomic processes of resource reallocation and the macroeconomic adjustments dependent on overall industrial competitiveness. This paper has argued that two main economic factors account for this. First, Mexico's successful import-substitution experience in the past – in the sense that this strategy effectively modified the economy's pattern of comparative advantages in favour of manufacturing and the initially infant industries – a feature manifested in the fact that current trends in the trade pattern and industrial structure are with no major exceptions an extrapolation of the past. Second, and perhaps paradoxically, the adjustment to the debt crisis and declining terms of trade during the 1980s forced macroeconomic policy to provide unprecedented levels of 'exchange rate protection' which also facilitated the adjustment of industrial firms to a more open economy and subsumed the specific dislocation costs of trade liberalization into the broader and more apparent costs of overall macroeconomic adjustment. In this way, the latter also contributed to lessen resistance to change, and created a mistaken evaluation of the role of trade policy in the manufacturing exports boom during the decade, followed by exaggerated expectations about its benefits in terms of long-term productivity performance. In the end, all this further contributed to radicalize the reform process.

In this paper's view this process has gone too far. Mexico is currently abandoning trade and industrial policy instruments that worked successfully in the past. While their use clearly required reform, and some policy schemes are less necessary and beneficial today, the economy runs the risk of freezing, or changing too slowly, its present structure of comparative advantages, getting stuck in relatively unskilled and low-paid tasks of the production processes of capital-intensive industries, a far-from-desirable prospect for a country that needs to grow fast and to rapidly increase the living standards of its nearly 90 million people. Moreover, as the real exchange rate returns to historical levels, the macroeconomic adjustment costs of trade liberalization are reappearing. Their potential effects could be highly adverse in the future unless substantial capital inflows, well above historical levels, can permanently finance a current account deficit that by now appears to be in the order of 6 per cent of GDP if historical growth rates are to be resumed. It is here that a paradoxical qualification to the paper's main argument comes in. For one way of addressing this problem involves more, rather than less, trade liberalization in the form of a Free Trade Agreement with the US and Canada. To the extent that such an arrangement can provide the necessary capital inflows to shift the growth-balance of payments trade-offs, it could make possible the resumption of a fast rate of economic development that would otherwise be prevented by an unsustainable current account deficit. Exploring this issue would lead us, however, well beyond the scope of the present paper.

NOTES

1 For a description of industrial policy during this period, see King (1970), Commission Económica para America Latina–Nacional Financiera SA (CEPAL–NAFINSA) (1971), Villarreal (1976) and Solís (1980).
2 General fiscal incentives, provided in the framework of the 1955 Law for the Development of New and Necessary Industries, also played a role, albeit a relatively minor one and secondary to trade protection. Another feature of the period was the reduction of the state's promotion action in the field of industrial financing and public enterprises, both of which had been decisive in the earlier industrialization phases. These roles were increasingly taken over by domestic private banks in long-term financing and by direct foreign investment in the fastest growing manufacturing industries.
3 Mexico's production of capital goods lagged considerably behind other semi-industrial economies. As the Nacional Financiera–Organización de Naciones Unidas para el Desarrollo Industrial (NAFINSA–ONUDI) (1985) study found, over 90 per cent of Mexico's market for machine tools was supplied from abroad, compared to only 20 per cent in Brazil and 44 per cent in Korea, countries which in addition exported 27 per cent and 20 per cent respectively of their local production of machine tools.
4 The National Foreign Investment Commission (NFIC) – a regulatory agency established by the Law – was empowered, however, to modify this general rule and to grant authorization for a higher percentage when such an investment was considered beneficial for the economy. In practice, the Law was to apply to new foreign investment projects since the NFIC allowed those businesses that were wholly foreign-owned prior to the adoption of the Law to retain their existing capital structure. In approving new investment projects, and waiving the 49 per cent limit, the NFIC was to consider a number of criteria including their complementarity with national capital, technology transfer, balance of payments and employment effects.
5 Permission to market up to 40 per cent of the product in Mexico is granted in some cases. These products fall into the '807' Section of the US Tariff Schedule which allows products assembled abroad to re-enter the US without tariffs on the US-made components.
6 Escalation within the manufacturing sector in 1960 and 1970 is, however, almost

fully explained by the high protection rates for the automobile industry. In 1980, it also reflects the increase in effective protection for the capital goods industry that took place in the 1970s.

7 The 1980s were no exception since the contraction of domestic demand meant a prolonged period of industrial stagnation. For a detailed analysis of the 1980s, see pp. 187–90.

8 For the source of this more detailed analysis, see Ros and Vázquez (1980).

9 For a review of the literature on this issue, see Ros (1991).

10 The share of intra-industry trade (I_j) in industry j is defined as: $I_j = 1 - (iX_j - M_{ji})/(X_j + M_j)$. The index I_j has a minimum at O (when the industry exports without importing or imports without exporting) and increases towards 1 as the products of the industry are exported and imported simultaneously. See Ros (1991) for the construction and estimation of these indices.

11 The aggregation in the table is not identical but is broadly comparable with that of Tables 6.2 and 6.3 and subsequent ones. Since the relative shares of each type of good in manufacturing are very different – consumer goods and intermediates have large shares and capital goods have little significance – the discussion that follows compares the composition of each sector to that of manufacturing as a whole.

12 The importance of these reallocation effects in Mexico's development experience and productivity performance is examined and highlighted in Reynolds (1980) and Syrquin (1986).

13 We mean here the direct effects of resource reallocation towards higher productivity industries as well as the indirect effects on agriculture and services productivity levels occurring as a result of the reduction of labour surpluses and the induced reorganization of methods of production. The latter may be no less important than the former as the postwar development experience of developed countries clearly suggests (see Cripps and Tarling, 1973; Syrquin 1986).

14 Samaniego's estimates (1984) show, however, a fairly high association between output and TFP growth across industries, although this correlation is not made explicit in the text. Hernadez Laos and Velasco (1990) also found a positive impact of output growth – in time series analysis for aggregate manufacturing – together with relative factor price effects.

15 The glass industry, within the non-metallic minerals sector, is illustrative of the innovative activity of large national firms; in fact, one of the few examples of significant research and development efforts in manufacturing. This industry stands as the top performer (with an average TFP growth rate of 13.4 per cent per year) in Samaniego's (1984) study of 17 four-digit manufacturing industries in the period 1963–81.

16 The Spearman rank correlation coefficient between output growth rates in 1960–70 and effective protection rates in 1970 was found at 0.778 (see Ten Kate and Wallace, 1980).

17 See Ros (1986) which examines also the role of the country's overall rate of economic growth. A related approach is Pasinetti's analysis of 'comparative productivity-change advantage' as a criterion of specialization in international trade (see Pasinetti, 1981).

18 In this view, the absence of foreign competition explained the downward rigidity, during a recession, of profit mark-ups in manufacturing, which in turn accounted for the relatively slow deceleration of inflation. Import controls should, therefore, be eliminated as fast as possible in order to force down inflation.

19 This involved tariff concessions on approximately 16 per cent of the 1985 import bundle, a reduction of the maximum tariff to 50 per cent, and the elimination of official import reference prices (see de Mateo, 1988, and Zabludovsky, 1990).

20 These are respectively PITEX (Programa de Importacion Temporal para la Produccion de Artículos de Exportacion) and DIMEX (Derechos de Importacion para la Exportacion). Both were set up in 1985.

21 According to CEPAL (1979) over 750 programmes were established between 1965 and 1970, and over 1,200 between 1971 and 1978.

22 A programme for the petrochemicals industry was also issued in 1986, but this was intended essentially to regulate the increasing privatization of this sector.

23 Entry regulations limiting the number of firms in the terminal industry (assembly activities), and aimed at promoting use of economies of scale, was another important aspect of the policy approach in the early 1960s. Since then the industry has been characterized by a broadly stable and dual market structure: an oligopoly of seven multinational corporations in the terminal industry (five at present) together with a more fragmented structure of small and medium-sized suppliers of auto parts, consisting of national firms or joint ventures with national majority ownership.

24 For a detailed discussion of the 1977 and 1983 reforms, see Moreno (1987) and Peres (1990). This section relies heavily on these studies.

25 In 1981, the seven terminal companies produced an average of 18,000 cars per line, well below Brazil (45,000) or South Korea (more than 100,000). Through a gradual reduction in the number of models and product lines, the 1983 decree aimed at an average of 50,000 units per line by 1987, the minimum considered necessary to take advantage of economies of scale.

26 These requirements were later reduced to about 30–40 per cent (from up to 60 per cent) as firms found compliance difficult.

27 This requirement was waived in the case of mini-computers and mainframes where technological sophistication meant greater dependence on a few international suppliers. Although similar, Mexico's policy towards microcomputers differs from Brazil's 'market-reserve' policy in that foreign enterprises (through joint venture) could participate in the sector. This decision was made in the hope that such firms would contribute to technical progress and to greater access to foreign markets. After 1985, the policy was to differ even more from Brazil's, as we shall see below.

28 IBM increased its investment project from US$7 million to $91 million and agreed to export at least 92 per cent of production.

29 This was the choice made by IBM as well as, reversing earlier decisions, by Apple and Hewlett Packard. Apple's failure to meet the export requirements led it, however, to stop producing microcomputers in Mexico in late 1987.

30 As a result, manufacturing production declined by 5.7 per cent in 1986 and grew by only 2.6 per cent in 1987.

31 Employment in the basic metals industry was also affected by government divestments in this sector, as discussed below. Some of the other industries, such as consumer electronics in Monterrey and Mexico City and the clothing and footwear industry in the central region of Guanajuato appear to have also been affected by import penetration, but mostly after 1987.

32 Most of it (over 80 per cent) is due to manufacturing. When the gross exports of the border assembly plants (maquiladoras) are included, Mexico's manufacturing exports rise to over $21 billion in 1988, placing Mexico ahead of Brazil as an exporter of manufactures, and just behind the four leading East Asian NICs.

33 Most of the export supply clearly stemmed from the newly installed capacity after 1978 rather than from a mere reorientation of production towards exports. Thus, for example, while domestic sales of vehicles fell by 180,000 units between 1981 and 1985, exports of engines increased by more than one million units in the same period (see Moreno, 1987).

34 Vitro acquired, through a tender offer, 95 per cent of the Anchor Glass Container Corporation, the second largest glass container manufacturer in the US. According to Vitro's executives, the conglomerate went abroad because, in the context of a more open Mexican economy, it could no longer be satisfied with having a strong domestic base and some export activity (actually 25 per cent of its total sales in 1989) if it wanted to continue to be a glass company (see *Expansion*, 6 December 1989, cited by Peres, 1990).

35 In accounting for the firm's new strategy, Cemex's executives argued that the mergers will increase cost-efficiency through economies of multi-plant operation, improved distribution channels and reduced transportation costs (see *The News*, Mexico City, 10 January 1990, cited by Peres, 1990).

36 The declining share of heavy intermediates between 1985 and 1989 is largely due to the falling share of petrochemicals, whose export boom was concentrated in the first half of the decade as the large expansion of productive capacity undertaken during the oil boom found no outlet in the domestic market. The share of heavy intermediates in 1989 was, nevertheless, well above 1980 levels.

37 Another possibility worth exploring is provided by the interesting finding of Ten Kate and de Mateo (1989) that up to late 1987 (their most recent estimate) the pattern of effective protection had not changed much. In particular, its dispersion had not declined, despite all the changes that occurred since the early 1980s in licensing requirements and tariff structure. They attribute this puzzling development to time lags and to the many other factors, including domestic and international market structures and arrangements, which affect effective protection besides trade policy instruments.

38 The other four are the three just discussed and non-metallic minerals which shows a more moderate acceleration of productivity growth and, unlike food processing, in the context of an improved output performance.

39 In other words, given domestic savings rates and the present current account deficits (or foreign savings), the Mexican economy should have been growing in recent years at higher rates than it has. The fact that it has not may well be due to the adverse impact of trade liberalization on import functions and capacity utilization.

40 The specific contribution of trade liberalization to this process is, however, more uncertain and, if anything, probably negative. In fact, the sequence of events suggests that the (not necessarily desirable) acceleration of reforms in some of these areas, including also deregulation of foreign investment, was triggered as a means to alleviate, through capital inflows, a balance of payments position that was otherwise unsustainable precisely as a result of recent trade and exchange rate policies.

REFERENCES

Bacha, E. (1966) 'Comparación entre la productividad industrial de México y los Estados Unidos', *El Trimestre Económico* 33/32: 657–73.

Balassa, B. (1985) 'Trade Policy in Mexico', in R. Dávila and A. Violante (eds) *México, una Economía en Transición* pp. 12–34, Mexico: Limusa.

Balassa, B. and Associates (1971) *The Structure of Protection in Developing Countries*, Baltimore: Johns Hopkins University Press.

Banco de México, *Indicadores del Sector Externo*.

Banco de México, *Indicadores Económicos*.

Bergsman, J. (1974) 'Commercial Policy, Allocative Efficiency and X-Efficiency', *Quarterly Journal of Economics* 88(3): 409–33.

Bhagwati, J.N. (1978) *Foreign Trade Regimes and Economic Development: Anatomy and Consequences of Exchange Control Regimes*, Cambridge: Ballinger.

Blomstrom, M. and Wolff, E. (1989) 'Multinational Corporations and Productivity Convergence in Mexico', National Bureau of Economic Research Working Paper no. 3141.

Brailovsky, V., Clarke, R. and Warman, N. (1990) *La Política Económica del Desperdicio*, Mexico: Universidad Nacional Autónomia de México.

Bueno, G. (1971) 'The Structure of Protection in Mexico', in B. Balassa *et al.*, (eds) *The Structure of Protection in Developing Countries*, ch. 8, Baltimore: The Johns Hopkins Press.

Casar, J., Marquez, C., Marván, S., Rodriguez, G. and Ros, J. (1990) *La Organización Industrial en México*, Mexico: Editorial Siglo XXI.

CEPAL (1979) *Principales Rasgos del Proceso de Industrialización y de la Política Industrial de México en la Década de los Setenta*, CEPAL/MEX/1011/Rev.1.

—— (1990) *Balance Preliminar de la Economía de America Latina*, Santiago, Chile: Naciones Unidas.

CEPAL–NAFINSA (1971) *La Política Industrial en el Desarrollo Económico de México*, Mexico: Nacional Financiera S.A.

Chenery, H., Robinson, S. and Syrquin, M. (1986) *Industrialization and Growth: A Comparative Study*, London: Oxford University Press.

Christensen, L. R., Cummings, D. and Jorgenson, D. W. (1980) 'Economic Growth, 1947–73: An International Comparison', *Studies in Income and Wealth* 44: 595–698.

Cripps, T. and Tarling, R. (1973) *Growth in Advanced Capitalist Economics 1950–1970*, London: Cambridge University Press.

de Mateo, F. (1988) 'La Política Comercial de México y el GATT', *El Trimestre Económico* 55(217): 175–216.

Dosi, G., Pavitt, K., and Soete, L. (1990) *The Economics of Technical Change and International Trade*, New York: New York University Press.

Elías, V. J. (1978) 'Sources of Economic Growth in Latin American Countries', *Review of Economics and Statistics* 60(3): 362–70.

Estrada, J. L. (1991) 'A Comparative Study of Manufacturing Productivity in Mexico and South Korea, 1960–1985', dissertation proposal, New School of Social Research.

Hernandez Laos, E. and Velasco, E. (1990) 'Productividad y Competitividad de los Manufacturas Mexicanas, 1960–1985', *Comercio Exterior* 40(7): 658–66.

Instituto Nacional de Estadística, Geografía e Informática, *Sistema de Cuentas Nacionales de México*, various issues.

Ize, A. (1990) 'Trade Liberalization, Stabilization and Growth: Some Notes on the Mexican Experience', mimeo, Fiscal Affairs Department, International Monetary Fund.

Kaldor, N. (1970) *Strategic Factors in Economic Development*, New York: Cornell University Press.

King, T. (1970) *Mexico, Industrialization and Trade Policies Since 1940*, London: Oxford University Press.

Krueger, A. O. and Tuncer, B. (1980) 'Estimates of Total Factor Productivity Growth for the Turkish Economy', World Bank Research Paper.

Little, I. M. D., Scitovsky, T. and Scott, M. (1970) *Industry and Trade in Some Developing Countries*, London: Oxford University Press.

Lopez, J. (1988) 'Apertura Comercial y Desempeño de la Industria en México', mimeo, CIDE.

Maddison, A. and van Ark, B. (1989) 'International Comparison of Purchasing Power, Real Output and Labour Productivity: A Case Study of Brazilian, Mexican and US Manufacturing, 1975', *Review of Income and Wealth* 35(1): 31–55.

Moreno, J. C. (1987) *The Motor-Vehicle Industry in Mexico in the Eighties*, Geneva: International Labor Organization.

Nacional Financiera SA. (1990) *La Economía Mexicana en Cifras*, Mexico: Nacional Financiera SA.

NAFINSA–ONUDI (Nacional Financiera SA–Organizacíon de Naciones Unidas para el Desarrollo Industrial) (1985) *Mexico: los Bienes de Capital en la Situación Económica Presente*, Mexico: Nacional Financiera SA.

Nelson, R. and Winter, S. (1982) *An Evolutionary Theory of Economic Change*, Cambridge, Mass. The Belknap Press of Harvard University Press.

Nishimizu, M. and Robinson, S. (1986) 'Productivity Growth in Manufacturing', in H. Chenery, S. Robinson and M. Syrquin (eds) *Industrialization and Growth: A Comparative Study*, ch. 10, London: Oxford University Press.

Pasinetti, L. L. (1981) *Structural Change and Economic Growth: A Theoretical Essay on the Dynamics of the Wealth of Nations*, Cambridge: Cambridge University Press.

Peres, W. (1990) *Foreign Direct Investment and Industrial Development in Mexico*, Paris: OECD.

Presidencia de la República (1991) *Criterios Generales de Política Económica para 1992*, Mexico.

Reynolds, C. W. (1980) 'A Shift–Share Analysis of Regional and Sectoral Productivity Growth in Contemporary Mexico', International Institute for Applied Systems Analysis.

Rodrik, D. (1990) 'How Should Structural Adjustment Programs be Designed?', *World Development* 18(7): 933–47.

Ros, J. (1986) 'Trade, Growth and the Pattern of Specialization', *Political Economy* 2(1): 55–71.

—— (1991) 'Industrial Organization and Comparative Advantage in Mexico's Manufacturing Trade', Working Paper No. 155, Kellogg Institute, University of Notre Dame.

—— (1992), 'Capital Mobility and Policy Effectiveness under a Credit Run: The Mexican Economy in the 1980s', in T. Banuri and J. Schor (eds) *Financial Openness and National Autonomy* London: Oxford University Press.

Ros, J. and Vázquez, A. (1980) 'Industrialización y Comercio Exterior, 1950–1977', *Economía Mexicana* 2: 27–56.

Samaniego, R. (1984) 'The Evolution of Total Factor Productivity in the Manufacturing Sector in Mexico, 1963–1981', Serie Documentos de Trabajo, El Colegio de México.

Schmookler, J. (1966) *Invention and Economic Growth*, Cambridge, Mass: Harvard University.

Secretaria de Patrimonio y Fomento Industrial (1979) *Plan Nacional de Desarrollo Industrial 1979–1982*, Mexico.

Solís, L. (1980) 'Prioridades Industriales en México', *Prioridades Industriales en*

Países en Desarrollo, New York: Organización de Naciones Unidas para el Desarrollo Industrial.

Syrquin, M. (1986) 'Productivity Growth and Factor Reallocation', in H. Chenery, S. Robinson and M. Syrquin (eds) *Industrialization and Growth: A Comparative Study*, ch. 8, London: Oxford University Press.

Ten Kate, A. and de Mateo, F. (1989) 'Apertura Comercial y Protección', *Comercio Exterior* 39(4): 312–29.

Ten Kate, A. and Wallace, R. B. (1980) *Protection and Economic Development in Mexico*, New York: St. Martin's Press.

US International Trade Commission (1990) *Review of Trade and Investment Liberalization Measures by Mexico and Prospects for Future United States–Mexican Relations, Phase I*, Washington, DC.

Vázquez, A. (1981) 'Crecimiento Económico y Productividad en la Industria Manufacturera', *Economía Mexicana* 3: 65–78.

Velasco, E. (1985) 'El Ciclo de la Productividad de la Gran Industria en México (1950–1982)'. Paper presented to the Conference on Cycles and Crisis in the Mexican Economy, The Long View, La Jolla, California.

Villarreal, R. (1976) *El Desequilibrio Externo en la Industrialización de México (1929–1975): Un Enfoque Estructuralista*, Mexico: Fondo de Cultura Económica.

World Bank (1977) *Mexico: Manufacturing Sector: Situation, Prospects and Policies*, Washington, DC: World Bank.

—— (1986) *Mexico: Trade Policy, Industrial Performance and Adjustment* Washington, DC: World Bank.

—— (1988) *Mexico: Trade Policy Reform and Economic Adjustment*, Washington, DC: World Bank.

—— (1990) *Mexico: Industrial Policy and Regulation*, Washington, DC: World Bank.

Zabudovsky, J. (1990) 'Trade Liberalization and Macroeconomic Adjustment' in D. S. Brothers and A. E. Wick (eds) *Mexico's Search for a New Development Strategy*, Boulder: Westview Press.

7

TRADE POLICY, INDUSTRIALIZATION AND PRODUCTIVITY GROWTH IN PERU

An overview of the 1970s and 1980s

Carlos E. Paredes

I am thankful to Rossana Polastri for her valuable contributions to this paper and to Helen Chin for excellent research assistance. In addition, I am grateful to Mario Tello for providing me with disaggregated industrial data for this study.

INTRODUCTION

Compared to other countries in Latin America, Peru was a latecomer to industrialization via import substitution. The country pursued export-led growth, based on primary commodity exports, until the late 1950s. Since the early 1960s, however, trade policy has been aimed explicitly at supporting industrialization. Even by regional standards, the level of protection in Peru for manufacturing activities during this period was very high.

Initially the new industrialization strategy spurred high rates of industrial and aggregate economic growth; nevertheless, increasingly protectionist measures in the late 1960s and early 1970s led to an overprotected industrial sector and introduced severe anti-export and anti-agricultural biases into the economy. These policy-induced distortions, compounded by extreme macroeconomic mismanagement, led to a stagnation in exports and in agriculture. Industrial and aggregate economic activity slowed down and then plummeted at the end of the 1980s. The results were so disastrous that by the 1990 presidential campaign a strong political consensus had formed around the position that Peru needed to liberalize its economy. In late 1990, the newly elected government of Alberto Fujimori launched a far-reaching trade reform, which may turn out to be the epitaph of the ISI strategy in Peru.

217

The purpose of this paper is to analyse the effects of trade and industrial policies on the pattern of industrialization in Peru over the last two decades, with particular emphasis on the performance of manufactured exports. The first section reviews the main trade and industrial policies, as well as the macroeconomic policy framework of this period. The next section describes the main characteristics and trends of the Peruvian manufacturing sector in light of the major changes in policy previously identified. A more detailed analysis of the performance of manufactured exports during this period is presented in the third section, followed by a brief conclusion.

TRADE AND INDUSTRIALIZATION POLICY IN PERU, 1970–90[1]

The Peruvian economy can be characterized as a small and semi-open one, whose role in world trade has traditionally been that of an exporter of primary products. Indeed, until the late 1950s, successive governments pursued a commodity export growth strategy, fostered foreign direct investment and exercised fiscal discipline. This policy framework allowed the country to achieve high rates of growth and low inflation. In the early 1960s Peru began to move towards an increasingly protectionist trade regime with the aim of promoting import-substitution industrialization. During this phase fiscal discipline gradually dissipated, the economy endured two severe balance of payments crises and by the late 1970s economic activity stagnated. Between 1979 and 1982, an important attempt at trade liberalization was carried out but failed, mainly because of its inconsistency with macroeconomic policy. As a result, trade policy once again resumed a protectionist stance. By 1990 unprecedented macroeconomic chaos in the country and sweeping economic reforms around the world eased the way for a new and much more far-reaching trade liberalization programme in Peru. The sustainability of the current programme, however, is still open to question and not enough time has passed for an assessment of its effects on domestic industry.

Figure 7.1 shows the evolution of the average tariff rate from 1950 to 1991. Peru had an average tariff rate of over 60 per cent in the protectionist periods, which dropped to levels below 40 per cent in the liberalization episode of the early 1980s. This lower average tariff rate, however, was still much higher than the rates which prevailed during the 1950s. Only since the current trade reform has the average tariff rate fallen to levels close to those that prevailed during the export-led growth period.

Background: the first two decades of ISI in Peru

Many authors have used the passing of the Industrial Promotion Law in 1959 to mark the start of the import-substitution industrialization (ISI)

218

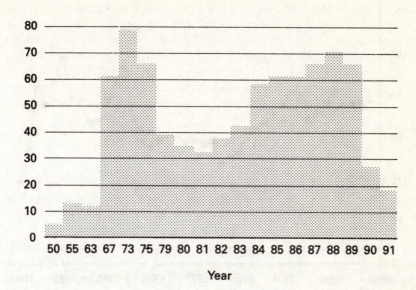

Figure 7.1 Average tariff rates for selected years, 1950–91 (Armas *et al.* 1989 and author's calculations)
Note: Specific import duties, which existed up to 1973, were converted into equivalent *ad valorem* rates

strategy in Peru. This legislation established tariff exemptions on imports of intermediate and capital goods for the steel, metals, fertilizers and explosives industries. In other sectors import duties on intermediate and capital goods were reduced by 50–100 per cent. In addition, tax incentives for industrial firms were so generous that they amounted to complete exemption from corporate income taxes. However, it was not until 1964, with the introduction of a new tariff code, that a clearly protectionist trade strategy was established: 'tariffs then became effective instruments of industrial development' (Rossini and Paredes, 1991: 277).

In the beginning, this policy promoted industries which already existed; these fell into two groups of activities. The first group was involved in the processing of export products (sugar, for example) and, in this sense, did not conform to the definition of an import-substituting industry. The second group included textiles and foodstuffs (Pinzás, 1981: 40).

New sectors also flourished during these years, especially chemicals, automobile assembly plants and electrical and non-electrical machinery. However, the greatest rate of industrial growth during the decade was registered in the fish meal and fish oil subsector, which was mainly oriented

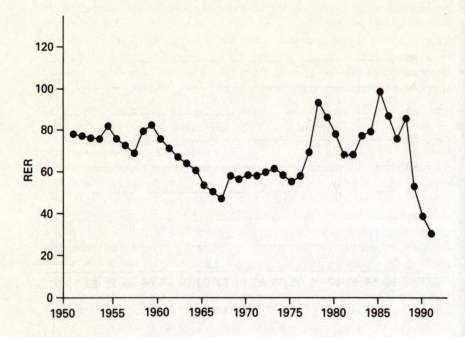

Figure 7.2 Real exchange rate index, 1950–91 (July 1985 = 100)

towards export markets. The growth in fish meal exports was so remarkable that it actually provided a push for the rest of the economy.[2] It could be said then that import substitution was working and, moreover, that its anti-export bias did not prevent the growth of resource-based export activities.

Import substitution in the Peruvian case was limited to consumption goods and as pointed out by GIECO (1972), the tariff structure granted a high rate of effective protection to products consumed by the higher income strata. Changes in the structure of tariffs throughout the 1960s systematically strengthened the bias against the production of intermediate and capital goods. At the same time, while encouraging intensive use of imported intermediate and capital goods, the industrialization strategy resulted in oversized industrial facilities and the adoption of capital-intensive technologies.

Throughout the 1960s an increasingly lax fiscal stance was accompanied by the inappropriate management of exchange rate and monetary policies, leading to a progressive real appreciation of the Peruvian currency. Between 1959 and 1967 the real exchange rate index fell by more than 30 per cent (Figure 7.2).[3] Increasing fiscal imbalances and exchange rate misalignment led to a severe balance of payments crisis in 1967. The crisis was initially dealt with by increasing tariffs – particularly on consumption goods – and by banning some imports outright. However, despite these measures, the defence of the Peruvian sol, which had been fixed to the US dollar since February 1961, became unsustainable and the Central Bank had to withdraw from the foreign exchange market. This led to a 37 per cent depreciation of the sol in September 1967 and to the launching of an IMF-supported stabilization programme.

Pushing ISI to its limits: 1968–75

In October 1968, a military coup ousted the civilian administration. During its first years, the military government carried out a series of economic reforms that deeply affected the structure of ownership, marginally improved income distribution and significantly increased the role of the state in the economy. The initial reforms were carried out while the new government continued to implement the orthodox stabilization package launched by the previous administration. In fact, 1969 saw the first central government budget surplus in 8 years. In the early 1970s, the country experienced a favourable external shock; terms of trade improved significantly and international reserves almost tripled. This, however, proved to be a mixed blessing. As soon as balance of payments difficulties were overcome, the government abandoned fiscal restraint (fiscal expenditures increasingly depended on foreign financing) and implemented a series of measures that pushed the process of import substitution to its limits.

During these years import substitution was pursued not only with the government's encouragement but with direct government intervention. The legal framework of the military government's industrial strategy was specified in the General Law of Industries of 1970. In order to start a second phase in the country's industrialization process – characterized by the substitution of imports of intermediate and capital goods by domestic production – a priority list of industries for protection was established. Basic industries, producers of intermediate goods (steel, basic chemicals, fertilizers, cement, paper, etc.) and capital goods industries (machinery and equipment, transportation, aeronautical material, naval construction, etc.), were identified as having first priority. Moreover, in the interventionist environment prevailing at the time, production and trade activities in basic industries were reserved for state-owned enterprises. Traditional manufacturing activities (food, textiles and small industries) were assigned second and third priority.

Technically, the main objective of the ruling was to promote domestic production of intermediate and capital goods. However, in practice, tariff rates continued to favour the production of consumption goods. This contradiction was heightened by the effects of the main quantitative restriction introduced by the aforementioned law: the National Register of Manufactures (NRM). Under this system, if a product was listed in the register,

Table 7.1 Non-tariff restrictions on imports, Peru

	Dec. 1973	Dec. 1978	Dec. 1979	Jul. 1980	Dec. 1980	Jul. 1984	Jul. 1985	Dec. 1985	Dec. 1988	Dec. 1989
Number of items:										
Non-restricted	2734	1753	3745	4745	4990	5120	4757	3259	0	4192
Restricted[a]	386	1038	1258	348	107	116	350	1553	4724	535
Prohibited	1395	1852	9	9	7	8	8	525	539	539
Temp. prohibited	0	369	0	0	0	51	188	0	0	0
Total	4515	5012	5012	5102	5104	5295	5303	5337	5263	5266
Percentages:										
Non-restricted	61	35	75	93	98	97	90	61	0	80
Restricted[a]	9	21	25	7	2	2	7	29	90	10
Prohibited	30	37	0	0	0	0	0	10	10	10
Temp. prohibited	0	7	0	0	0	1	3	0	0	0
Total	100	100	100	100	100	100	100	100	100	100

Source: Central Reserve Bank, *Memoria* (several issues).
[a] Restricted items were subject to import licences, quotas and other quantitative restrictions (excluding import prohibitions).

it meant that imports of similar products were banned, provided that domestic producers could prove that they could satisfy domestic demand with goods of similar quality. The producers' claims were usually evaluated generously, so that in effect they enjoyed almost limitless protection.

Another important change in trade policy occurred in December 1972, when a new tariff code was approved. This change led to a significant increase in the average tariff rate (Fig. 7.1) and in tariff dispersion. Among the protectionist measures introduced by the military government, however, even more important than tariff barriers were quantitative restrictions (QRs) on trade. For example, in 1973, out of a total of 4,515 tariff items, only 2,734 were not subject to QRs; 386 required import licences, 786 were subject to import prohibitions, an additional 537 were included in the NRM, and 72 were under government monopoly control (Table 7.1).

These protectionist trade policies were accompanied by the introduction of labour legislation that significantly increased labour market rigidities. Indeed, the General Law of Industries of 1970 mandated the creation of 'industrial communities' within medium and large manufacturing firms. These entities represented the interests of workers, and would have a progressively increasing share of the profits, management and ownership (initially up to 50 per cent) of the firm. Later that year a job security law was passed. The law established that after a three-month probation period workers would acquire job security, meaning they could not be fired unless they committed a 'serious offence' (as defined by the law). Although on paper it did not prevent layoffs for justifiable economic reasons (e.g. a fall in the demand for the firm's output), in practice it meant that labour became a quasi-fixed factor of production. Altogether, these measures had the effect of diverting resources toward the use of capital-intensive technologies at notably low levels of capacity utilization (Abusada, 1976).

Despite the objectives of the 1970 industrial law and the changes in the tariff code of late 1972, the existence of QRs and multiple exemptions to the tariff code resulted in a protective structure that continued to favour the production of consumer goods. For example, in 1973, while foods and beverages benefited from an effective protection rate (EPR) of 312 per cent, the EPRs for chemical products and machinery and equipment were 46 per cent and 56 per cent, respectively (Torres, 1976). In a comprehensive analysis of the Peruvian industrial sector in the mid-1970s, Torres concluded that protection to the industrial sector was 'exaggerated; a comparison with other Andean countries confirms this conclusion. The protection structure discriminates against basic intermediate industries, including the majority of agricultural products.' Consumer goods were almost entirely domestically produced but 'exports are not feasible because inefficient industries have been granted exaggerated protection'.

Towards 1974 rapidly growing fiscal and monetary imbalances led to a real appreciation of the currency. Given the pervasiveness of QRs protecting domestic manufactured goods, this real appreciation may in fact have increased the rate of effective protection for import-substituting industries,[4] but it had a negative effect on export and unprotected import-competing activities (agriculture, in particular). This, compounded with the effects of macroeconomic mismanagement and a poorly implemented land reform, led to the stagnation of exports and agriculture during these years. The vulnerability of the industrialization strategy became quite evident when primary commodity exports, a major source of foreign exchange, began to decline and capital inflows dried up in the mid-1970s.

Balance of payments crisis and promotion of non-traditional exports: 1976–8

The increase in domestic absorption, the real appreciation of the Peruvian sol and the decline in the terms of trade led to a severe balance of payments crisis in the mid-1970s. As in the preceding crisis, the initial policy response was to increase protection, including further curtailment in the foreign exchange allowances for imports and the establishment of minimum financing periods for them. However, by then, the major contradictions in the economy could no longer be ignored; the industrial sector's increasing trade deficits, the strategy's anti-export bias and recurrent foreign exchange crises had to be dealt with.

Among the policy instruments used to tackle the crisis were incentives to promote the growth of non-traditional exports, in particular those of manufactures. In 1976 the coverage and magnitude of fiscal and credit subsidies for non-traditional exports (Certificado de Reintegro Tributario, CERTEX, and Fondo de Exportaciones No Tradicionales, FENT, respectively) were expanded significantly. The maximum CERTEX rate (as a percentage of the value of exports) was increased from 15 to 40 per cent, an additional 10 per cent was granted to firms producing outside Lima, and an extra 2 per cent was allowed for products not previously exported. Moreover, the law established a time horizon of ten years during which these rates would be applicable. Similarly, the subsidy channeled though the promotional FENT credit line expanded and averaged 2 per cent of the value of non-traditional exports during the second half of the 1970s.

As a result of these export subsidies and the large real depreciation of the currency and decline in domestic sales which resulted from the stabilization attempts of 1976–8, exports of manufactured goods increased significantly. During this period the value of manufactured exports (in constant dollars) increased at an annual rate of 52.4 per cent and their share in total exports grew from 8.7 per cent in 1976 to 15.8 per cent in 1978.[5] External balance, on the other hand, was still far from realization; the current account showed large deficits and net international reserves continued to be negative. In this context, a law to promote non-traditional exports was passed. The law maintained the CERTEX rates that had been set in 1976 and established a new time horizon of ten years (starting in November 1978) during which these rates would be in effect. In addition, the Job Security Law was modified in 1978 to allow greater flexibility in formal labour markets and non-traditional exporters were allowed to hire personnel who were not subject to job security requirements.

Trade liberalization: 1979–82

The reduction in domestic absorption and the large real depreciation of the currency, brought about by the stabilization attempts of 1976–8, and the rapid growth in the country's traditional exports[6] subsequently led to a significant improvement in the country's trade balance. This caused a dramatic increase in international reserves, permitted a recovery in the level of economic activity, and contributed to a reduction in the fiscal deficit. Paradoxically, the export boom also jeopardized the government's stabilization efforts due to its effects on money growth. Because the Central Bank was not able to sterilize such a large foreign exchange inflow, the government's policy response was to liberalize the current account of the balance of payments.

The trade reform of the late 1970s and early 1980s initially concentrated on the elimination of non-tariff barriers to imports. The NRM was eliminated in March 1979; between then and July 1980, the percentage of import items that were not subject to QRs rose from 37 to 93 per cent. Similarly, the percentage of import items which were banned was reduced from 40

Table 7.2 Tariff levels and structure, Peru[a]

	Dec. 1975	Dec. 1979	Jul. 1980	Dec. 1980	Dec. 1981	Dec. 1984	Aug. 1985	Dec. 1989
Average[b]	66	39	39	34	32	57	63	66
Standard deviation[c]	26	n.a.	n.a.	18	18	22	24	25
Maximum level	355	155	155	60	60	76	86	84
Tariff surcharge	0	0	0	0	0	15	17	19
Effective tariff	15.8	13.8	n.a.	15	18	21	n.a.	15
Hypothetical tariff[d]	n.a.	n.a.	n.a.	n.a.	n.a.	n.a.	n.a.	45
Number of items:								
(1) At 0%			30	31	37	5	5	10
(2) Over 0% and up to 10%			390	388	594	458	177	683
(3) Over 10% and up to 20%			773	755	1297	451	611	298
(4) Over 20% and up to 30%			1535	1577	1223	529	574	530
(5) Over 30% and up to 40%			773	768	647	1456	753	689
(6) Over 40% and up to 50%			440	436	380	759	1213	1143
(7) Over 50% and up to 60%			455	1149	1029	266	579	562
(8) Over 60% and up to 70%			209	0	0	360	129	126
(9) Over 70% and up to 80%			175	0	0	1017	312	285
(10) Over 80%			317	0	0	0	967	940
Total			5097	5104	5207	5301	5320	5266

Source: Central Reserve Bank of Peru, *Memoria* (several issues).
[a] Information is available for the end of each period.
[b] Arithmetic average of nominal tariffs including tariff surcharges.
[c] Does not take into account tariff surcharges.
[d] Tariff rate plus surcharge weighted by the level of 1988 FOB imports.

to 0 per cent (see Table 7.1). A new tariff code was approved in September 1979 and implemented in December of that year. The new structure was discussed with representatives of the business community, who accepted a significant reduction in tariffs (the maximum rate was reduced from 355 to 155 per cent, while the average tariff rate decreased from 66 to 39 per cent; see Table 7.2).[7] However, the relative disparities in tariffs did not change much, and high rates continued to be maintained on products such as garments, alcoholic beverages, footwear, packages and boxes, and plastic products, among others.

The second phase of the liberalization process began in September 1980, during President Belaunde's second term in office (1980–5). The maximum tariff was lowered from 155 to 60 per cent and an announcement was made (with no clear time schedule) that a uniform tariff of 25 per cent was the goal. However, the average tariff decreased by only 5 percentage points, from 39 to 34 per cent, because rates below 60 per cent were left virtually unchanged. This phase of the reform basically involved 701 import items with tariff rates ranging between 61 and 155 per cent, and led to a reduction in the dispersion of tariff rates. The standard deviation of the

C.E. PAREDES

tariff schedule decreased from 26 per cent in December 1975, to 18 per cent in December 1980 (Table 7.2).

This was the only important trade liberalization measure during President Belaunde's second administration. From the very beginning it encountered strong resistance from industrial interests, opposition parties, as well as some members of the party in government. The arguments against tariff reduction were varied, among them that it had been carried out without prior consultation or warning and that it did not take into account huge distortions prevailing in domestic factor markets.

The main problems of this experiment were the lack of coordination between trade liberalization and macroeconomic policy and factor market reforms that would have supported the opening of the economy. Indeed, the first years of the 1980s were characterized by growing fiscal deficits, largely financed by monetary expansion, and by an exchange rate policy which led to a real appreciation in the national currency of 10 per cent during 1980 and 13 per cent in 1981 (Fig. 7.2). This reflected the use of the nominal exchange rate as an anti-inflationary instrument, a policy inconsistent with the lack of fiscal discipline and with unchecked monetary expansion. Not surprisingly, the overvaluation of the domestic currency sharply reduced the degree of protection for domestic industry. Rossini and Paredes (1991) estimated effective protection rates for twenty import-substituting manufacturing sectors for the periods immediately before and after the tariff reduction and found that, when the real appreciation of the currency is taken into account, the average rate of effective protection for these sectors fell from 44 to 17 per cent. Moreover, they conclude that the real appreciation of the currency actually contributed more to the decrease in protection than the tariff reduction itself.

As liberalization continued in an unsuitable macroeconomic environment and without reforms in the factor markets that would have allowed a rapid mobilization of resources towards the more profitable sectors under the new trade regime, consensus began to emerge in favour of increased protection. Proponents of this position prevailed in 1982 when fiscal and balance of payments problems once again led to the adoption of restrictive trade policies.

The return to protectionism in the 1980s

The slow reversal of the liberalization process began in January 1982 with the establishment of a temporary 15 per cent tariff surcharge (it was reduced by 5 percentage points in March 1983 and then increased again to 15 per cent in April 1984). In July 1984, the *ad valorem* duties of the tariff schedule were significantly increased (increases in tariff rates varied between 5 and 40 percentage points). As a result the average tariff rate rose from 41 per cent at the end of 1983 to 57 per cent in December 1984.

226

Moreover, because it was scaled, this measure increased the dispersion of tariffs. A further tariff increase was put into effect in January 1985, with tariffs rising between 1 and 8 percentage points, and the tariff surcharge was increased from 15 per cent to 17 per cent. As a result, the average tariff rate (inclusive of tariff surcharges) increased from 57 to 63 per cent between December 1984 and August 1985. On the non-tariff barriers side, the number of QRs was increased again in 1984. Initially, fifty-one import items were temporarily banned and near the end of the year the list was expanded to 172 items, consisting primarily of apparel, tobacco products and footwear. Liberalization had, therefore, been completely reversed.

The switch back to protectionist policies during the last three years of Belaunde's second term was so striking that by the end of his administration trade barriers were greater than those which were in effect when he took office. For example, the average tariff rate increased from 39 to 63 per cent between July 1980 and August 1985, the number of import items not subject to QRs dropped from 93 per cent of the total number of tariff items to 90 per cent, and the number of banned items (including those temporarily banned) increased from 9 to 196.

The administration of Alan García, which was inaugurated in July 1985, continued the protectionist trends begun in 1982, although it placed greater emphasis on the use of QRs. Initially, a series of import bans were introduced and soon thereafter, import licences became of general use in the context of a deteriorating balance of payments. The list of banned items grew from 196 to 525 by December 1985, and by the end of García's term in office the list totaled 539 items (Table 7.1). In October 1985, the administration also increased the maximum tariff rate to 120 per cent (it was subsequently reduced to 84 per cent in August 1989). The tariff surcharge was increased in 1987 from 17 to 21 per cent and in 1988 to 24 per cent.

By the end of the García Administration the most important feature of the tariff structure was the multiplicity of rates and their wide dispersion. The combination of 38 different tariff rates and 14 types of surcharges led to 56 different gross tariff rates ranging from 10 to 110 per cent. Many of the tariffs had been made for particular interest groups, although these 'custom-made' benefits were not in accordance with the main objectives of trade or industrialization policies. Rent-seeking activities by industrial interests proved to have high payoffs in Peru.[8]

A second important feature was the multiplicity of exemptions – about fifty types of special customs regimes existed for public sector enterprises and specific economic activities. Although there is no estimate of the fiscal losses incurred as a result of these exemptions, or an overall analysis of their economic rationality, simple calculations confirm that the reduction in tax collection was significant and that these measures may also have had adverse effects on domestic production. For example, in 1989, while the average tariff rate (weighted by the value of imports, which approximately indicates how much could have been collected) was 45 per cent, the effective tariff rate, calculated as duties actually paid (as a percentage of the total value of imports) was only 15 per cent.

In addition, tariff exemptions, along with an overvalued currency, disproportionately increased the competitiveness of foreign goods, particularly foodstuffs imported by the state trading enterprises, thereby hurting domestic production. Tariff revenues were also curtailed because many of the items with the highest tariff rates were subject to import bans. Rossini and Paredes (1991: 286) estimate the fiscal revenue loss caused by import prohibitions for 1989 at 0.8 per cent of GDP.

Evidence of the highly distorting resource allocation effects of the protective structure prevailing at the end of the García Administration is presented in Table 7.3. First, the estimated rates of effective protection at the end of 1989 varied significantly across sectors. Second, these rates showed an obvious bias against export and agricultural activities (the negative numbers in the table). In comparison, high effective protection rates existed for manufacturing industries such as apparel, footwear, tobacco and beverages, and other manufactures (column 2 of the table). But, some of these high rates must be discounted because of differences between the various exchange rates and the parity exchange rate level at the end of 1989.[9] Indeed, the massive overvaluation of the currency prevailing at the time meant much lower rates of effective protection, in particular for agricultural and export activities (column 3 of the table). However, to the extent that the currency overvaluation was accompanied by an increase in non-tariff import barriers (which are not properly reflected in these calculations), the last column in Table 7.3 underestimates the effect of protection. This observation is particularly relevant for import-substituting activities but not for the agricultural or export activities, which were hurt by the overvaluation of the currency but were not or could not be compensated through non-tariff barriers.

High levels of protection and oligopolistic market structures made it possible for domestic producers in certain industrial sectors to have a considerable degree of control over price setting. This is reflected by the fact that these sectors took the lead in domestic price increases during the 1980s. For example, between 1981 and 1988 the relative price index for manufacturing jumped from 80 to 125 (the highest in the economy) and it took place despite the appreciation of the currency which occurred during this period. In contrast, relative prices for primary goods sectors went down (Rossini and Paredes, 1991: 288).

As for the effect of protection on output growth, employment and wages in various sectors of the economy, the evidence presented in Table 7.4 indicates that the unprotected sectors recorded the greatest reductions in real wages. Likewise, the unprotected export sector (mining, fish meal and

Table 7.3 Effective protection rates, Peru, 1989

	Nominal protection on final good	Effective protection	Total effective protection[a]
Agriculture	46.7	−0.6	−40.2
Forestry and hunting	0.0	−5.3	−60.0
Oil	0.0	−21.7	−78.7
Mining	0.0	−11.9	−74.2
Non-metallic minerals	72.3	77.5	−25.5
Dairy products	60.8	77.1	−22.3
Canned fish	27.0	14.5	−59.9
Fish meal and oils	0.0	−10.1	−73.0
Other food products	61.6	100.3	−14.7
Tobacco and beverages	112.4	178.8	20.9
Textiles	14.9	−16.1	−73.9
Apparel	143.8	254.3	52.6
Leather products	31.8	31.1	−38.7
Footwear	127.9	200.0	24.0
Furniture	96.4	131.4	−3.1
Paper and allied products	72.9	91.0	−20.0
Printing and publishing	45.4	33.8	−43.2
Basic chemicals and fertilizers	38.4	47.4	−39.6
Pharmaceutical	3.5	−22.4	−66.9
Other chemical products	89.2	142.1	0.7
Rubber and plastic products	52.1	68.4	−28.9
Non-metallic mineral products	48.5	50.5	−36.6
Steel foundries	20.2	17.6	−50.6
Non-ferrous metal prod. transport	0.0	−3.2	−69.2
Fabricated metal products	68.2	127.7	−6.5
Machinery except electrical	30.5	19.6	−53.5
Machinery, equipment and supplies	78.5	135.2	3.8
Household appliances	116.6	156.0	8.2
Transportation equipment	72.9	87.6	−20.1
Other manufactured products	82.3	131.5	0.4
Average	53.8	69.4	−29.6
Coefficient of variability	74.8	104.5	−111.7

Source: Rossini and Paredes (1991: 287).
[a]Includes the effect of currency overvaluation.

textiles) experienced heavy reductions in production levels and in its capacity to generate employment. But the converse is not true, protection does not necessarily lead to greater levels of activity; production in many protected sectors did not increase.

Thus, the protectionist scheme of the late 1980s, particularly as reflected in the protective structure prevailing at the end of the García Administration, was inconsistent with the achievement of sustained growth for the economy as a whole, because of its bias against exports and its strong dependence on imports. Moreover, it had regressive income distribution

Table 7.4 Evolution of real wages, employment and production, Peru

	GDP % change 1979–88	Employment % change 1979–87	Employment % share 1987	Real wages % change 1979–87
Protected sectors:				
Milling and bakery	33	21	0.6	−5
Apparel and clothes	−4	11	1.9	−3
Leather products	−20	1	0.1	−34
Footwear	−31	−3	0.3	−43
Other chemical products	65	21	0.2	9
Rubber and plastic products	1	17	0.2	2
Steel	−11	22	0.2	17
Household appliances	1	−10	0.1	−6
Transportation equipment	84	12	0.3	10
Other manufactured products	−2	26	0.4	−49
Unprotected sectors:				
Agriculture	26	12	33.7	−20
Dairy products	17	11	0.2	−27
Mining	−13	2	0.9	−22
Fish meal	−37	−62	0.1	−56
Textile exports	−2	15	1.1	−16
Mineral refining	−27	−9	0.2	−34
Fertilizers	26	−16	0.2	−22

Source: Rossini and Paredes (1991: 290).

effects (due to its negative impact on agriculture, where most of the poor are employed).[10]

Peru's import-substitution industrialization, which had already been pushed to its limits in the early 1970s, was stubbornly pursued during the past decade and finally derailed in the late 1980s, as the economy sank into its deepest and longest recession. Extreme protectionist policies, which responded more to particular interest groups and short-term balance of payments problems, rather than to a long-term growth strategy for the Peruvian economy as a whole, had led to a progressive closing of the economy. Figure 7.3 shows that since the adoption of the ISI strategy in Peru in the early 1960s, the ratio of foreign trade to GDP fell (the only exceptions being the periods of active promotion of manufactured exports and import liberalization, 1976–82).

In September 1990 the recently elected government of Alberto Fujimori launched a sweeping overhaul of the trade regime. The majority of the quantitative restrictions to trade were removed, the number of tariff rates was reduced from fifty-six to three (15 per cent, 25 per cent and 50 per cent),[11] most tariff exemptions were eliminated, and the maximum CERTEX rate was reduced to 10 per cent and then eliminated altogether. Although the sustainability and eventual success of this reform are still

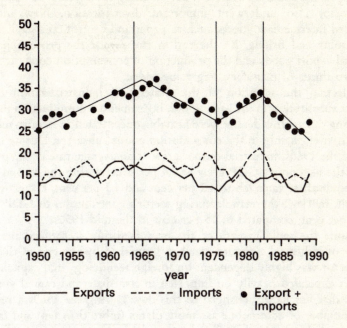

Figure 7.3 Export and import shares of GDP, 1950–89. 1950–63: Outward growth based on commodity exports. 1964–75: Import-substitution industrialization. 1976–82: Promotion of non-traditional exports and import liberalization. 1983–9: Adjustment to the fall in terms of trade, to the debt crisis and to García's populism. (Author's calculations based on data in constant 1986 intis from Webb and Fernandez-Baca, 1990)

open to question – as in the previous liberalization episode, macroeconomic policy is not supporting the opening of the economy – the reform may well constitute a major change in the country's trade and industrialization patterns.

GROWTH AND STAGNATION OF THE PERUVIAN MANUFACTURING SECTOR[12]

Background

Despite the *laissez-faire* nature of economic policy and, in particular, the lack of protectionist trade policies, the Peruvian manufacturing sector registered a significant expansion during the 1950s. During this decade manufacturing output grew at 7.2 per cent per year while GDP grew at an average annual rate of 5.1 per cent. This expansion was strongly related to the processing of export products, such as sugar and minerals. In fact, industrial growth in the early 1950s was more export-supporting than import-substi-

231

tuting (Thorp and Bertram, 1978: 261). During these years the manufacturing sector also underwent important diversification. New industries included intermediate goods, such as paper and cement, and capital goods for mining and fishing. By the end of the decade the processing of traditional export goods and the production of consumption goods accounted for two-thirds of manufacturing value added.

Reflecting the adoption of the strategy of industrialization through import substitution in the early 1960s, investment and production in manufacturing during this decade were heavily concentrated in import-substituting activities, mainly in the consumption goods subsector. During the first half of the 1960s, industrial output grew at an average rate of 8.9 per cent, while the economy's GDP grew at 7.4 per cent; during the second half of the decade these rates fell to 4.2 per cent and 4.3 per cent, respectively. As a result, in 1969, the manufacturing sector's contribution to GDP peaked at 25 per cent, compared to 15 per cent in the mid-1950s.

Despite the rapid growth of the manufacturing sector and the multiplicity of industrial activities that had flourished by the end of the 1960s, this sector was highly dependent on foreign technology and capital. Moreover, it depended heavily on imported intermediate and capital goods, an aspect that has hardly changed to this day. During the 1960s a relatively large number of automobile assembly plants (more than ten) and factories for household electrical appliances were built, all of them subsidiaries of foreign companies. These firms produced exclusively for the domestic market and were among the most dynamic in the economy.[13]

The limitations of the new industrialization model were evident by the late-1960s. The easy phase of import-substitution (characterized by the substitution of imported consumption goods) was nearly complete, the domestic market was saturated and, since this strategy had discouraged exports,[14] rapid growth of export-oriented manufacturing activities was unlikely. Moreover, given the very small size of the domestic market, it was difficult to foresee that important intermediate and capital goods sectors would develop to support the domestic consumption goods industry. Not surprisingly, investment in manufacturing began to decline: it decreased from an average of 5.2 per cent of GDP in 1960–4 to 2.2 per cent in 1965–70 (Fitzgerald, 1981).

In the 1970s and 1980s manufacturing was the most important sector of the economy in terms of its contribution to GDP (23.4 per cent on average). Its share in GDP, however, did not increase during this period. On the contrary, a slight declining trend has been observed since 1975 (Table 7.5). This decline occurred despite the fact that during these years manufacturing activities operated in an environment characterized by high protection and widespread subsidies.

In contrast with this sector's large contribution to GDP, manufacturing activities accounted for only 11.5 per cent of employment over the past

Table 7.5 Manufacturing sector shares of GDP and employment, Peru (%)

	1970–5	1975–9	1979–82	1982–5	1985–9	1970–89
Share of GDP	25.1	24.4	23.2	21.7	22.8	23.4
Share of employment	12.6	12.5	11.4	10.6	10.4	11.5

Source: Author's calculations based on Instituto Nacional de Estadística (1989).

twenty years (Table 7.5). Moreover, this share declined from 12.6 per cent in 1970–5 to 10.4 per cent in 1985–9.[15] This was the result of an industrialization strategy which did not properly take into consideration the relative factor endowment of the Peruvian economy and, therefore, led to a manufacturing sector with a limited capacity for labour absorption.

In addition to its relative stagnation and modest employment-generating capacity, during the past two decades this sector displayed a permanent imbalance between its export capacity and import dependence. Table 7.6 shows that manufactured exports accounted for only a small share of manufacturing output (10 per cent on average), despite the fact that this sector heavily depended on imports of intermediate and capital goods (the latter were equivalent to 38 per cent of manufacturing value added). Moreover, the last two columns of the table show that, even when exports of fish meal are included in the definition of manufactured exports, the manufacturing sector's trade deficit absorbed a large share of the foreign exchange generated by non-manufactured exports (37 per cent on average for the period).[16]

The large dependence of manufacturing on foreign exchange generated by other sectors has made this activity extremely vulnerable to foreign exchange shortages. Therefore, it should not be surprising that the slump of traditional export activities that resulted from the anti-export bias of policies implemented during this period significantly contributed to the stagnation of this sector. Moreover, as documented by Hamann and Paredes (1991), these factors not only led to long-term stagnation but to the intensification of the business cycle in Peru (in particular, that of manufacturing): its average duration shortened and the difference in the growth rates corresponding to recession and expansion phases increased. These amplified stop–go cycles made manufacturing a much more unstable and risky activity.

Structural characteristics

Changes in the manufacturing structure have not been very significant over the past two decades. Indeed, the dependence on imported intermediate and capital goods has not been reduced, while both the composition of manufacturing output and the degree of industrial concentration have remained unchanged.

233

Table 7.6 Export orientation and import dependence of the manufacturing sector, Peru

Year	Manufactured exports[a]		Imports of manufacturing sector		Manufacturing sector trade deficit	
	Million US$	% of manufacturing GDP[b]	Million US$	% of manufacturing GDP[b]	% of non-manufactured exports [c]	[d]
1970	87	3.1	1,012	35.8	31.8	2.3
1971	76	2.4	1,230	38.9	47.7	24.2
1972	118	3.5	1,201	35.4	44.7	27.0
1973	238	6.3	1,357	35.9	46.5	38.2
1974	278	7.0	2,232	56.2	71.6	66.9
1975	152	3.9	2,365	60.9	97.0	96.5
1976	205	5.1	1,776	44.3	73.4	69.1
1977	327	8.3	1,491	37.8	46.2	38.8
1978	476	10.4	1,304	28.4	32.6	23.6
1979	974	19.6	1,724	34.6	18.7	11.0
1980	904	20.0	1,912	42.3	26.8	22.0
1981	685	17.1	2,214	55.4	53.4	50.8
1982	741	18.3	2,030	50.1	46.3	41.8
1983	527	14.9	1,422	40.0	33.6	31.4
1984	673	16.5	1,269	31.1	23.1	18.7
1985	644	11.9	1,154	21.4	20.9	16.7
1986	612	8.7	1,538	21.9	44.3	37.7
1987	649	8.5	1,903	25.0	59.2	54.2
1988	650	7.9	1,628	19.8	47.8	36.8
Period average	475	10.2	1,619	37.1	45.6	37.2

Source: Author's calculations based on Instituto Nacional de Estadística (1989).
[a] Estimated as the total value of non-traditional exports minus the value of agricultural non-traditional exports. Does not include fish meal exports.
[b] Figures in intis were converted into 1988 dollars using the PPP exchange rate.
[c] Does not include fish meal exports as manufactured exports.
[d] Includes fish meal exports as manufactured exports.

Table 7.7 Imports of the manufacturing sector as a percentage of Peru's total imports (period averages)

	1970–5	1975–9	1979–82	1982–5	1985–9	1970–89
Intermediate goods	51.2	52.9	42.4	44.0	50.9	48.3
Capital goods	24.2	25.2	26.1	26.1	22.2	24.8
Total imports of the sector	75.4	78.1	68.6	70.2	73.1	73.1
Share of imports in the sector's intermediate demand	33.4	33.8	33.3	32.4	29.4	32.5

Sources: Author's calculations based on data from the Ministry of Industries and from the Statistical Office of the Ministry of Finance (OFINE).

Dependence on imports of intermediate and capital goods

Despite policy goals to increase the backward linkages of Peruvian manufacturing activities, the country's manufacturing sector still exhibits a heavy dependence on imports of intermediate and capital goods. Table 7.7 shows that about 33 per cent of the intermediate goods consumed by the manufacturing sector was imported and that this ratio remained remarkably stable during the past two decades.

The top three rows of Table 7.7 present imports for the manufacturing sector as a percentage of the country's total imports. Although imported intermediate goods only represented one-third of the manufacturing sector's intermediate demand, it accounted for close to half of the country's total imports. Similarly, imports of capital goods for this sector amounted to 25 per cent of total imports.[17] Thus, the manufacturing sector's imports of intermediate and capital goods represent about three-quarters of the country's total imports. These ratios emphasize the problems posed by the low export capacity of this sector and by policies that hindered export growth.

Composition of output

Given the small size of the domestic market and more than thirty years of policies that fostered import-substitution industrialization, it is not surprising to find that Peruvian manufacturing activities are highly concentrated in the production of consumer goods. Despite the fact that the initial and easy phase of this strategy was exhausted long ago, in the late 1980s the share of consumer goods in manufacturing value added was still slightly above 50 per cent. However, over the last two decades, Peru's manufacturing structure registered a small shift from the production of consumer goods to that of capital goods. Table 7.8 shows that during the 1970s, the production of capital goods slightly increased its share in total manufacturing value added. As discussed, this was the result of protectionist policies, large government investment[18] and the processing of mineral exports.

Table 7.8 Manufacturing output by type of goods, Peru (percentage shares)

	1970–5	1976–9	1979–82	1982–5	1985–9	1970–89
Consumer goods	52.9	49.5	47.2	49.6	50.6	50.0
Intermediate goods	26.2	23.8	23.6	22.8	24.0	24.1
Capital goods	20.9	26.7	29.2	27.7	25.4	26.0
Total manufacturing	100.0	100.0	100.0	100.0	100.0	100.0

Source: Author's calculations based on data from the Ministry of Industries.

Table 7.9 Output concentration index of four largest firms, by sector

	1971	1974	1982	1983	1984	1985
Agricultural products	53	50	33	44	43	41
Cooking oils	45	46	48	57	58	58
Food, beverages and tobacco	59	55	51	53	52	51
Minerals products	59	52	52	55	60	57
Chemical products	58	56	58	57	59	57
Plastics	61	59	74	70	69	68
Leather and fur	46	38	33	37	47	34
Wood and coal	40	24	31	26	24	21
Paper	65	64	56	54	56	57
Textiles	48	43	37	36	46	45
Footwear	66	62	48	36	32	33
Construction materials	68	68	58	66	65	63
Jewellery	58	54	46	64	43	77
Basic metals	48	50	49	50	46	46
Machinery	66	67	45	54	47	50
Transport equipment	73	74	75	67	68	74
Other industrial products	72	61	56	44	41	42
Non-exporting industries	63	60	55	57	56	56
Exporting industries	48	45	43	42	46	46
Manufacturing average	59	56	52	53	52	54

Source: Tello (1988).

Industrial concentration

The high degree of protection of the domestic market and its rather small size have led to high concentration ratios within the manufacturing sector. Table 7.9 show that since the early 1970s, in most industries more than half of the output was produced by the four largest firms, Moreover, this degree of concentration has not changed since the mid-1970s (Tello, 1988). By the mid-1980s concentration ratios varied between one-third and nearly four-fifths.

The rows at the bottom of Table 7.9 indicate that non-exporting sectors were more concentrated than exporting sectors.[19] This reflects the relative sizes of the domestic and international markets. While the small size of the domestic market puts a natural limit on the number of firms that

Table 7.10 Growth in GDP and in manufacturing, Peru, 1971–89[a]

	1971–5	1975–9	1979–82	1982–5	1985–9	1971–89
Gross domestic product	5.1	2.3	3.7	−1.5	−0.2	1.7
Total manufacturing	5.0	1.0	2.3	−2.8	0.1	0.9
Consumer goods	3.0	−1.7	1.0	−1.4	1.2	0.2
Intermediate goods	9.4	0.4	3.3	−4.4	−0.7	1.7
Capital goods	6.0	6.9	3.7	−4.0	−1.4	2.0

Source: Author's calculations based on data from the Ministry of Industries.
[a]Average annual growth rates (%).

can operate in it, the size of world markets does not lead to 'natural oligopolies'.

Manufacturing output performance in the 1970s and 1980s

Following a period of rapid growth, which lasted until the mid-1970s, Peru's manufacturing sector entered a prolonged recessionary phase (Table 7.10). Starting in 1977, manufacturing activity, which had previously led economic growth, trailed behind the other economic sectors.

The poor performance of the manufacturing sector over the past fifteen years is explained not only by government attempts to push the industrialization strategy beyond its limits, but also by macroeconomic mismanagement. Never before had the Peruvian economy been subject to such a prolonged period of inconsistent and unstable macroeconomic policies. Stop–go policies, repeated and unwarranted efforts to postpone economic adjustment, and severe economic and social costs when adjustment finally had to be made, contributed to the stagnation of the Peruvian economy, and in particular of the manufacturing sector. Moreover, due to the inward orientation of the industrial sector and its dependence on imported intermediate and capital goods, manufacturing activity was severely depressed during periods characterized by balance of payments problems and by adjustment policies (1976–8, 1982–5 and 1988–90). Not surprisingly, then, manufacturing production cycles were more pronounced than those of the overall economy (Fig. 7.4).

In contrast to what some analysts expected and what many industrialists feared, the opening of the economy in the late 1970s did not lead to the collapse of domestic manufacturing. Although during the trade liberalization period (1979–82) manufacturing growth trailed behind overall GDP growth, it was significantly higher than the rates of manufacturing growth registered in the preceding period and during the rest of the 1980s (Table 7.10). This is not to say that increased foreign competition actually spurred domestic manufacturing activity, but should be taken as evidence of the crucial roles of foreign exchange availability and domestic expenditure on

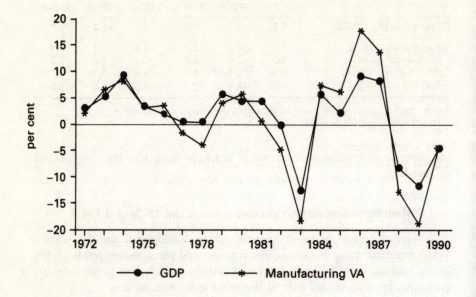

Figure 7.4 GDP and manufacturing value added (growth rates)

manufacturing performance. Indeed, during the trade liberalization episode, abundant international reserves and increased domestic absorption (fuelled by expansionary fiscal and monetary policies) allowed the manufacturing sector to grow, despite the reduction in protection.[20]

As reviewed above, the protectionist policies of the 1980s responded more to short-term balance of payments problems than to a consistent growth strategy. Furthermore, these policies were used to facilitate the implementation of unsustainable expansionary programmes that led to the depletion of the country's international reserves and to severe adjustment processes (such as that under García during the second half of the 1980s). The result was a severe anti-export bias, which did not facilitate the transition to an export-oriented manufacturing sector. The protectionist trade policies of the 1980s were not supportive of the country's industrialization process and, not surprisingly, failed to repeat the manufacturing sector's previous performance.

Intrasectoral differences

Table 7.10 also presents a breakdown of manufacturing growth by types of goods produced. These data indicate that, consistent with what the industrial law of 1970 tried to accomplish, the intermediate and capital goods subsectors did lead manufacturing growth during 1971–5. The consumer goods subsector was affected most by adjustment policies and the recession during the second half of the decade, and by the liberalization of the economy at the end of the 1970s. This subsector is more obviously identified as import-substituting, and it enjoyed higher rates of protection before the liberalization episode. Thus, it is not surprising to find that it was the most vulnerable to increased foreign competition and that it benefited from the return to protectionism by outperforming the other two subsectors in the 1980s.

In sharp contrast to the consumer goods subsector, the production of capital goods significantly expanded during the second half of the 1970s and led manufacturing growth during the trade liberalization episode. Moreover, this sector fell into a severe recession between 1982 and 1989, and displayed negative rates of growth, on average declining more rapidly than the other two subsectors. This behaviour may be explained by the fact that a large number of the 'capital goods' produced were traditional mineral export products that underwent some degree of manufacturing processing in the late 1970s in order to benefit from the subsidies granted to non-traditional exports (Hunt, 1985). This explains the boom in this sector in the late 1970s and its decline in the 1980s, when international market conditions for these goods worsened and non-traditional export incentives were curtailed.

After a period of rapid growth in the early 1970s (reflecting mainly large public investment), the intermediate goods subsector stagnated in the 1980s. This was due to the change in the pattern of public investment (towards housing and infrastructure), the return to a trade policy of overprotecting domestic consumer goods industries at the expense of intermediate and capital goods industries, and to the fact that the domestic market for intermediate goods was too small and probably saturated.

Table 7.11 provides information on the growth of eleven selected manufacturing activities that accounted for about 70 per cent of manufacturing value added during this period. The first five correspond to the consumer goods subsector, the sixth (industrial chemicals) to intermediate goods, and the last five are classified as capital goods. In general, the growth of these activities mirror the respective trends of the sectors under which they are classified (Table 7.10). The disaggregation provides information on the behaviour of industrial activities with varying degrees of vulnerability to foreign competition. As shown, the trade reform of the late 1970s and early 1980s brought about a significant deceleration in industrial activities such as textiles and apparel. In comparison, activities which are shielded from foreign competition by high transportation costs, such as beverages and food processing, were not significantly affected by trade liberalization. A rather surprising result, however, was the large increase in the production

Table 7.11 Growth in major industries, Peru

	1971–5	1975–9	1979–82	1982–5	1985–9	1971–89	
						Growth	Productivity share
Fish meal	–22.4	–0.1	–1.7	–11.9	21.2	–7.7	3.4
Food processing	7.8	–0.0	2.2	–0.6	0.4	2.3	17.1
Beverages and tobacco	9.7	0.0	5.3	0.1	0.6	2.8	8.7
Textiles	3.3	0.0	–2.1	2.2	4.5	1.7	9.0
Apparel	7.2	–0.0	–0.5	–1.3	2.8	0.6	5.8
Industrial chemicals	13.1	0.1	3.0	–0.3	–3.5	4.4	2.7
Basic ferrous metals	20.5	0.0	–5.4	–3.9	–1.3	3.9	2.3
Non-ferrous metals	–5.9	0.2	3.7	–2.3	–1.6	2.5	13.6
Non-electrical machinery	20.9	0.0	4.0	–21.4	10.2	3.9	1.0
Electrical machinery	21.6	–0.0	–0.6	–6.7	–0.7	2.8	2.7
Transport equipment	12.8	–0.1	20.1	–24.5	–0.8	–0.9	2.8

Source: Author's calculations based on data from the Ministry of Industries.

of transportation equipment during this period. This can be explained by the elimination of foreign exchange quotas which severely constrained this activity in the previous period, the reduction in the relative prices of these goods (both domestically produced and imported) brought about by the import liberalization, and the increase in domestic income registered during this period.

The return to protectionist policies in the 1980s permitted those industrial activities that had been hurt by the trade liberalization experiment to resume modest rates of growth, but was also associated with a significant deceleration in the production of capital goods. Moreover, since increased protection was also accompanied by adjustment policies to deal with the external sector crisis and by a reduction in real incomes, most industrial activities fell into recession during this period.

The initial protectionist reaction to the debt crisis proved to be ineffective in spurring manufacturing growth. Indeed, within a context of macroeconomic adjustment it was difficult to foresee that industrial recovery could be inward-oriented. However, Alan García was elected president and launched a populist economic programme in 1985, which consisted of expansionary fiscal and monetary policies, a unilateral cap on foreign debt service, price controls and protectionist trade measures. This heterodox policy mix and the existence of large foreign exchange reserves led to a significant reactivation of the economy, in particular of the manufacturing sector, and to an abrupt reduction in inflation. The inconsistency and unsustainability of these policies, however, inexorably led to a balance of payments crisis and to a traumatic and prolonged recession starting in

1988. The logical policy response to the economic environment of the 1980s (perfect hindsight notwithstanding), would have been an aggressive promotion of manufactured exports. Such a programme was not pursued and the sector stagnated. Some manufacturing activities, however, such as textiles, which had flourished under the umbrella of import substitution, were able to grow (although at modest rates) in this environment of domestic recession. Not surprisingly, they were exporting part of their production, albeit under the umbrella of export subsidies.

Productivity growth in Peruvian manufacturing

Having documented the stagnation of the manufacturing sector over the past fifteen years, we now turn to the issue of the underlying changes in productivity. Table 7.12 presents estimates of rates of growth in factor input, labour productivity, capital productivity, total factor productivity (TFPG) and in output for the manufacturing sector as a whole, for manufacturing activities classified by the types of goods produced and for the three-digit ISIC sectors which experienced the fastest and slowest TFPG during the 1976–87 period.[21] The top part of the table indicates that for the manufacturing sector as a whole total factor productivity (TFP) declined at an annual rate of 0.56 per cent during this period.[22] Productivity losses were higher in the capital goods sector while the intermediate goods sector was the only one that did not display negative rates of growth in productivity. The latter reflects the extraordinary productivity performance of the petroleum refining industry, which can be considered as the 'outlier' of the sample.[23] In fact, if petroleum refining is excluded, this sector's TFPG estimate is reduced to –1.66 per cent.

The bottom part of Table 7.12 presents the distribution of industries according to TFPG (a complete listing of productivity growth estimates by industries is presented in the appendix). As shown, there was only one case with a rate of TFPG larger than 1.5 per cent and, out of 27 industries, only 6 (accounting for less than 30 per cent of manufacturing value added) displayed positive rates of growth in TFP. Moreover, of the 21 industries with negative TFPG rates, 14 (which accounted for 55.5 per cent of output during this period) displayed rates below –1.5 per cent, meaning that their cumulative loss in TFP during this period was over 17 per cent (for the seven industries with TFPG rates below –3 per cent, the cumulative productivity loss was over 30 per cent).

The appendix also presents TFPG estimates for the first and second half of the period. In terms of policy, the first half (1976–81) covers the phases of adjustment and promotion of non-traditional exports (1976–8) and the opening of the economy (1979–81), while the second half includes the return to protectionist policies and the initial years of García's populist programme. The data presented in the table indicate that productivity

Table 7.12 Output and productivity growth in Peruvian manufacturing, 1976–87

	Factor input	Labour productivity	Capital productivity	Total factor productivity	GDP	Share in manufacturing output (%)
		(Percentage growth rates)				
Total manufacturing	0.45	-1.44	-0.22	0.56	-0.10	100.0
Consumer goods	0.55	-2.44	-0.67	-1.16	-0.61	42.3
Intermediate goods	0.38	0.20	2.11	1.63	2.01	35.4
Capital goods	0.27	-1.84	-2.49	-2.28	-2.02	22.3
Industries with the fastest TFP growth						
353 Petroleum refining	-2.75	10.95	15.22	14.64	11.89	13.0
313 Beverages	2.24	0.77	1.19	1.13	3.37	9.7
361 Pottery, chinaware	-6.13	-2.22	3.84	1.05	-5.07	0.4
Industries with the slowest TFP growth						
383 Electrical machinery	6.42	0.88	-8.40	-5.88	0.54	4.3
385 Scientific equipment	1.21	-7.96	-4.37	-6.20	-4.99	0.3
372 Non-ferrous metals	8.83	-2.51	-9.87	-8.78	0.05	5.0

Frequency distribution of TFP growth

	Number of industries	Share in output (%)
TFP > 1.5	1	13.0
1.5 > TFP > 0.0	5	16.7
0.0 > TFP > -1.5	7	14.8
-1.5 > TFP > -3.0	7	39.2
-3.0 > TFP	7	16.3

Mean TFP growth for 27 industries (%) -1.47
SD of TFP growth for 27 industries (%) 3.97

Source: Author's calculations based on data from the Ministry of Industries.

performance was significantly superior during the second half – the TFPG rate for the manufacturing sector as a whole went from –6.3 per cent to 5.4 per cent and 23 of the 27 industries under consideration showed an improvement in TFP. Clearly, this behaviour is dominated by short-term changes in aggregate demand and highlights the crucial role played by domestic expenditure on manufacturing performance in a country where the manufacturing sector is essentially oriented towards the domestic market. In fact, while the government pursued adjustment-oriented policies (although with varying degrees of effectiveness) during most of the first period (1976–80), the second period includes years of severe policy mismanagement (1982–3 and 1986–7), in which the budget deficit soared and deficits in the current account of the balance of payments were financed either with new external loans or by running down the Central Bank's stock of international reserves. In this respect, if the last two years of the sample are excluded, the aggregate TFPG estimate for the second sub-period is reduced to 0.56 per cent and, in this case, 17 of the industries considered showed losses in TFP.[24]

Clearly, the productivity record during this period was disastrous. Moreover, it may be hypothesized that these figures underestimate the real fall in productivity due to accounting practices and very high rates of inflation observed during these years (which lead to an underestimation of the value of the capital stock). In any case, the across-the-board nature of the fall in productivity suggests that growing macroeconomic chaos and pervasive policy-induced market distortions play a much larger explanatory role in the poor productivity performance than sector-specific factors.

Sector-specific characteristics, however, may help explain differences across sectors. For example, it may be hypothesized that sectors that were more export-oriented, depended less on imported intermediate goods (and thus were less vulnerable to foreign exchange shortages) or displayed a more competitive market structure were more likely to show a better TFPG performance.[25] In order to test these hypotheses, the sectoral TFPG rates were regressed on each sector's ratio of exports to total sales (EXPO), the share of domestic inputs in each sector's total intermediate demand (DINP), and the sectoral output concentration index (CONC) discussed above. In addition, the average rate of growth of output (OUTGR) was included as an explanatory variable (Verdoorn's law or economies of scale provide a rationale for including this variable).[26] The regression was run with data for the period as a whole and with data for each of the subperiods discussed above. Given that the case of the petroleum refining industry is considered an outlier in the sample, this sector was excluded from the regression.[27]

The regression results presented in Table 7.13 need to be interpreted with caution and further analysis is required if inferences about the direction of causality are to be made. As expected, the constant term is negative

Table 7.13 Cross-section regressions for TFPG, Peru (t-statistics in parentheses)

Period	CONST	EXPO	DINP	CONC	OUTGR	Rbar²	F-test[d]
1976	−0.02	−0.12[b]	0.01	0.01	0.09	0.14	3.14
−87	(−0.72)	(−2.76)	(0.21)	(0.52)	(0.63)		
1976	−0.12[c]	0.09	0.08	0.02	0.71[a]	0.39	0.46
−81	(−1.86)	(0.95)	(1.06)	(0.57)	(3.54)		
1982	0.06	−0.42[a]	−0.02	−0.03	0.43	0.29	0.02
−7	(0.59)	(−3.07)	(−0.21)	(0.43)	(1.57)		

[a] Significant at the 1% significance level.
[b] Significant at the 5% significance level.
[c] Significant at the 10% significance level.
[d] F-test for heteroscedasticity based on regressing the squared residuals on the squared fitted values. The critical level for the test is 7.8.

(although statistically significant only for the first subperiod) and output growth is positively correlated with TFPG. Moreover, the link between these two variables is stronger in the shorter periods, reflecting the fact that in the short run changes in TFP are dominated by changes in demand. These findings and the fact that 21 out of the 26 sectors included in the regression registered negative rates of growth in output during 1976–87 support the hypothesis that the poor performance in TFPG was to a large extent explained by the inadequate macroeconomic environment that prevailed during this period.

However, contrary to what was hypothesized, neither dependency on domestic inputs nor market concentration appear to be correlated with TFPG.[28] Moreover, the most salient and surprising feature of these results is the negative correlation between export orientation and TFPG. Apparently, this finding is inconsistent with hypotheses such as: (i) a higher rate of TFPG increases the international competitiveness of a sector and thus makes it more likely to export; and (ii) export-oriented sectors benefit from large markets that provide the opportunity for high rates of output expansion and, hence, for large TFPG rates.[29] However, it is crucial that during the first subperiod the sign of this coefficient was positive (although not significantly different from zero) while in the second subperiod it was negative, large and statistically significant.[30] Furthermore, the correlation coefficient between EXPO and OUTGR drops from 0.38 in the first subperiod to 0.03 in the second.[31] In fact, these changes – in particular, that of the relationship between export orientation and TFPG – may reflect some perverse factors that negatively affected the performance of Peruvian manufactured exports during the second subperiod, and therefore had a larger toll on export-oriented industries.

THE STAGNATION OF MANUFACTURED
EXPORTS: FURTHER ANALYSIS

As discussed above, the adoption of import-substitution industrialization policies in the early 1960s led to rapid growth of the Peruvian manufacturing sector during that decade and the first half of the 1970s. Although the expansion of manufacturing output capacity can be considered as a prerequisite for the growth of manufactured exports, clearly it is not a sufficient condition. The high protection levels at the time did not encourage domestic firms to produce goods to meet international standards of quality and thus they were not competitive in world markets. Moreover, the real appreciation of the currency that accompanied the adoption of protectionist trade policies constituted a further disincentive to the development of a manufacturing-export base. Not surprisingly then, by 1975 less than 4 per cent of total manufacturing output was exported (see Table 7.6).

Recent performance of manufactured exports

The policy changes discussed earlier (pp. 223–4), coupled with the effects of domestic recession and favourable external market conditions, brought about a significant expansion of manufactured exports during the second

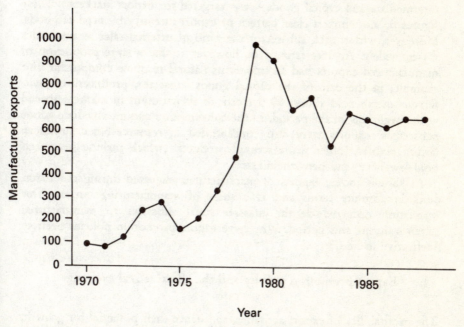

Figure 7.5 Manufactured exports, 1970–88 (millions, 1988 dollars)

245

Table 7.14 Manufactured exports as a percentage of manufacturing output, Peru

	1982	1983	1984	1985	1986	1987	Average
Consumption goods	6.29	7.75	9.96	9.89	6.43	5.44	7.63
321 Textiles	18.61	26.08	27.20	28.52	18.00	16.74	22.52
390 Other manufacturing	11.17	31.19	25.86	42.01	29.78	16.10	26.02
Intermediate goods	9.15	14.02	14.11	13.45	10.72	11.06	12.08
351 Industrial chemicals	11.20	17.12	19.80	4.50	15.58	12.05	13.38
352 Other chemicals	3.03	2.70	2.79	3.12	3.34	3.31	3.05
Capital goods	16.97	25.46	26.16	6.27	3.70	9.43	14.67
372 Non-ferrous metals	81.45	81.86	72.00	5.98	5.68	39.47	47.74
Total industries	10.1	14.56	15.01	11.14	7.48	8.26	11.08

Source: Author's estimates based on data from the Ministry of Industries.

half of the 1970s.[32] As shown in Fig. 7.5, however, after reaching their peak in 1979, manufactured exports declined during the first half of the 1980s and stagnated during the second half of the decade. Consequently, after ten years of explicit policies aimed at promoting the growth of non-traditional exports, the share of manufacturing output that was exported was still quite low in the mid-1980s (see Table 7.6).

The figures in Table 7.14, based on survey data, are consistent with those of Table 7.6, based on national accounts and customs data. They indicate that in the 1980s a very low share of manufacturing output – consumer, intermediate and capital goods – was targeted for export markets.[33] These figures do not show a clear pattern of export intensity by type of goods. Moreover, within each sub-sector the ratio of external sales to total sales varied widely. An interesting fact, however, is that a large proportion of manufactured exports had an important natural resource component. For example, in the case of the capital goods subsector, producers of non-ferrous metals sold almost 80 per cent of their output in markets abroad at the beginning of the period. In the consumption and intermediate goods subsectors, exports were also concentrated in resource-based products: cotton textiles, 'other manufactured products' (which include silver and gold jewellery) and petrochemicals.

As shown above, exports of manufactures stagnated during the 1980s, both in absolute terms and as a share of manufacturing output. This stagnation occurred despite massive fiscal subsidies to manufactured exports during this period. Why have export promotion policies been so ineffective in Peru?

Export promotion policies and the effective real exchange rate

The profitability of export activities, and hence their potential for growth, is affected by numerous policy instruments: from the various trade policy

Table 7.15 Export subsidies through CERTEX and FENT, Peru

	1980	1981	1982	1983	1984	1985	1986	1987	1988	1989
CERTEX rate[a]	23.3	26.8	29.5	28.3	27.5	26.0	26.2	26.6	26.5	21.4
FENT subsidy rate	n.a.	0.5	0.6	1.1	1.9	1.5	1.7	2.1	n.a.	n.a.

Source: Escobal (1991).
[a] Calculated as the CERTEX effectively received by exporters as a percentage of exports eligible for this subsidy.

tools – such as direct export subsidies or import restrictions – to the different components of macroeconomic policy, which help determine the economy's real exchange rate. Therefore, it is necessary to assess the *net* effect of the management of these various policy instruments on export growth. The effective real exchange rate (ERER) index constitutes a simple and traceable indicator which summarizes the impact of the policy environment on the profitability of exports through time.[34] It is defined as the real exchange rate index multiplied by 1 plus the *ad valorem* export subsidy rate and can be shown to be equivalent to a constant plus the profit rate of export activity. Accordingly, an increase (fall) in this index reveals a higher (lower) rate of return for exports.

The export incentives included in our definition of the ERER are direct fiscal and financial subsidies, the CERTEX and the FENT, respectively. As shown in Table 7.15, the resources channeled to exporters through these mechanisms were significant; on average, they represented about 25 per cent of the value of non-traditional exports during the 1980s.[35]

The other component of the ERER, the real exchange rate index, has been extremely unstable and has displayed cyclical behaviour during the past three decades (see Fig. 7.2). The introduction of export subsidies did not dampen the swings in the real exchange rate. On the contrary, the management of export subsidies mirrored the behaviour of the real exchange rate and therefore resulted in a highly unstable ERER index.[36] During the 1960–88 period, this index fluctuated within a range of 36.75 to 103.42, with a mean of 65.35 and a median of 62.5. Therefore, the ERER fluctuated within a band of plus 58 per cent and minus 44 per cent around its mean (or of plus 65 per cent and minus 41 per cent around its median). Clearly, this level of instability has been too high and may have hampered export growth. An international comparison will help to underscore this point.

Table 7.16 presents data on real exchange rates for Peru and four other countries in the region.[37] During the debt crisis period (post-1982) all of these countries, except for Peru, were able to increase their real exchange rates (depreciate their currencies). Moreover, during the last two periods shown in the table, Peru displayed a very high coefficient of variability of the real exchange rate (in both periods it was the second highest, below

Table 7.16 The real exchange rate and its variability, 1960–88

	1960–72	1973–81	1982–8
Real exchange rates[a]			
Brazil	70.61	77.88	105.65
Chile	33.00	94.41	144.39
Colombia	86.89	107.02	115.20
Mexico	100.56	102.18	128.93
Peru	68.12	84.41	80.63
Coefficients of variability[b]			
Brazil	63.14	52.70	98.52
Chile	54.48	168.78	96.04
Colombia	54.18	40.56	72.36
Mexico	11.00	69.76	124.87
Peru	45.07	85.81	114.89

Source: Author's estimates based on data from the IMF.
[a] The base year for the RER index is 1980.
[b] The coefficient of variability of the RER index was estimated for overlapping eight quarter periods and then multiplied by 1000.

Table 7.17 Annual regressions for manufactured exports, Peru, 1970–88 (t-statistics in parentheses)

Constant	ERER	RERVAR	EXPCAP	Rbar^2	DW
−32.97[a]	2.34[a]	−3.80[b]	3.50[a]	0.80	1.78
(−4.54)	(4.32)	(−2.32)	(3.49)		

[a] Significant at the 1% significance level.
[b] Significant at the 5% significance level.

another country that had secured a significant real depreciation of its currency). Therefore, it can be concluded that economic policy in Peru during the 1980s was not consistent with the expansion of the manufactured exports sector. Economic policy did not increase the profitability of this sector (by failing to secure a higher real exchange rate) and instead increased the risk of this activity (through high variability in the real exchange rate).

Regression results for the supply of Peruvian manufactured exports confirm these hypotheses. The econometric estimates presented in Table 7.17 indicate that the supply of manufactured exports is highly sensitive to movements in the effective real exchange rate (ERER); the estimated supply price elasticity is over 1.3 and statistically significant at the 1 per cent level of significance.[38] Similarly, these results show that manufactured exports are supply-constrained; therefore, an increase in export capacity (EXPCAP) has a positive effect on export performance. Finally, the estimates also indicate that real exchange variability (RERVAR) has significantly hindered the growth of manufactured exports in Peru.[39]

These results, together with the behaviour of the ERER in the 1980s discussed above, help explain the pathetic performance of Peruvian manufactured exports during the decade. The appreciation of the currency and the increased variability in the real exchange rate observed during the post-1981 period (Table 7.16) had a clear negative impact on the supply of manufactured exports. Given the fact that the behaviour of the ERER reflected domestic policy options more than the external shocks that affected the economy's equilibrium real exchange rate,[40] it can be concluded that the domestic policy framework of the 1980s was incompatible with the promotion of a dynamic manufactured export sector. Moreover, if negative external demand shocks are taken into account – such as the recession and increased protectionism in the industrial world at the beginning of the period, and the collapse of Latin American markets resulting from the debt crisis – the negative trend in the country's manufactured exports observed during this period should not be surprising. These developments help explain the negative correlation observed during this period between productivity growth and export orientation.

FINAL COMMENTS

The performance of the Peruvian manufacturing sector since the mid-1970s can be aptly described as catastrophic. During this period (1975–90), manufacturing output fell at a rate of 0.7 per cent per year (a cumulative decline of almost 40 per cent in per capita terms), TFP in manufacturing fell at an even higher rate, and none of this sector's structural problems – high dependence on imports of intermediate and capital goods, low export capacity, capital intensive bias and high concentration of output – were effectively tackled. Although this sector's performance was by no means an exception – the economy as a whole stagnated during these years – it was the sector with the worst growth record. Certainly, the inappropriate macroeconomic policy environment of these years, characterized by growing disorder and frequent policy reversals, helps explain this poor record (in particular, through its effects on aggregate domestic expenditure, foreign exchange availability and the real exchange rate). However, it does not explain the whole story.

As stated earlier, the import-substitution industrialization strategy was pushed to its limits during the first half of the 1970s. For all practical purposes, the easy phase of import substitution had been completed by the mid-1970s. Domestic producers enjoyed almost infinite rates of protection but the internal market was already saturated. Moreover, the relatively small size of domestic producers of consumer goods and the prevailing structure of protection hindered the growth of inward-oriented intermediate and capital goods subsectors. Therefore, the progress of industrialization in the country required policies that fostered the growth of export-oriented manufacturing activities. Indeed, as suggested in World Bank

(1983), both the low share of exports in manufacturing output and the huge growth of manufactured exports during the second half of the 1970s indicated 'their high potential as a continued source of industrial growth' (p.iv).

However, the promotion of manufactured exports in Peru has neither been part of an overall industrial growth strategy nor a new conception of how to integrate the country into the world economy. Rather, the episodes of active manufactured exports promotion have been short-term policy responses to balance of payments crises. The episodes of manufactured exports promotion (1967–9, 1976–8, 1984–5, 1987–8) were accompanied by non-selective increases in tariff and non-tariff barriers and were certainly not part of any new industrial strategy aimed at restructuring the manufacturing sector through a reduction in the excessive protection of the domestic market. It is not surprising that the manufacturing sector, and manufactured exports in particular, stagnated during the last decade.

NOTES

1 This section's discussion of trade policy builds on Rossini and Paredes (1991).
2 Fish meal exports grew at 20.4 per cent during the 1960s and in 1970 they accounted for 30 per cent of the country's total export revenues.
3 The exchange rate is defined as the domestic price of foreign currency, i.e. a reduction in the rate indicates an appreciation of the domestic currency.
4 The appreciation of the currency reduced the price of imported intermediate and capital goods for these industries, and did not affect the price of the final goods they produced because foreign competition was absent.
5 These figures do not include exports of fish meal as manufactured exports.
6 The latter was due to the large increase in the volume of oil exports which followed the opening of an oil pipeline in the northern area of the country and to the improvement in the international prices of the country's main export commodities beginning in late 1978.
7 Nogués (1989) interprets this as an indication that the previous protection levels were far too high. Although this is indisputable, it should also be noted that towards the end of the 1970s the real exchange rate index reached unprecedentedly high levels (by historical standards the currency was undervalued) and thus counterbalanced the reduction in tariffs.
8 In this regard, it is interesting to note that out of fifty-six gross tariff rates, four key rates applied to 46 per cent of the total number of import items.
9 The exchange rate that would have permitted the maintenance of purchasing power parity with respect to the rate prevailing in July 1985, when García came into office.
10 Moreover, in Peru there seems to be a direct relationship between the level of protection and the share of profits in GDP. Rossi and Paredes (1991: 289–90) indicate that this may be the result of failing to protect labour-intensive sectors and overprotecting capital-intensive ones.
11 In March 1991 the number of tariff rates was further reduced to two: 15 per cent and 25 per cent, although a special rate of 5 per cent was maintained for imports by the state-owned steel company.
12 This section was written in collaboration with Rossana Polastri.

13 For example, between 1960 and 1965, the transportation subsector grew at an average annual rate of 14 per cent and the electrical machinery subsector grew at 30 per cent, both well above the rates of growth registered by the manufacturing sector as a whole (Shimabakuro, 1990).

14 The growth of exports decelerated significantly from 8.8 per cent during 1950–62 to 3.0 per cent during 1963–8.

15 These figures may underestimate this sector's real contribution to output and employment due to the growth of informal (underground) manufacturing activities during this period.

16 Although this net import bias varies across subsectors, most manufacturing activities displayed trade deficits in the 1980s. For example, Jiménez (1987) found that during 1985–8, only the textiles, apparel, leather and footwear subsectors showed positive net export capacities.

17 During the 1970–88 period, 85 per cent of investment in industrial machinery and equipment for the manufacturing sector were purchases of imported equipment.

18 In fact, during 1971–78, 49.9 per cent of public investment was directed towards the production of basic metals.

19 The former also displayed higher ratios of imported inputs to total inputs and are more capital-intensive.

20 In comparison, the periods immediately preceding and following trade liberalization were characterized by balance of payments problems and macroeconomic policies aimed at reducing domestic expenditure. Despite the much higher levels of protection prevailing in these periods, the performance of the manufacturing sector was extremely unsatisfactory.

21 The data cover twenty-seven three-digit ISIC sectors for the 1975–87 period. The figures reported in the table are period averages of annual translog estimates of TFPG. In all cases the sector-specific period average share of labour income in value added was used to generate the TFPG measures.

22 This negative rate of TFPG differs from the large and positive TFPG rates estimated by Correa (1970) and Elías (1978) for the Peruvian economy as a whole in previous periods. Correa, using data from nine Latin American countries during the 1950–62 period, found that Peru had the second largest annual rate of TFPG (2.6 per cent) and that gains in TFP accounted for almost half of the Peruvian economy's growth during that period. Elías, on the other hand, estimated the economy's TFPG rate at 2.3 per cent during the first half of the 1960s and at 0.6 per cent during the second half of that decade.

23 TFPG in the petroleum refining industry (14.6 per cent per year) was well above the manufacturing sector's average (1.47 per cent or 2.09 per cent if petroleum refining is excluded). This performance is mainly explained by two factors: (i) petroleum refining is a state monopoly that benefited from the large increase in domestic prices of refined fuels registered during this period; and (ii) in the late 1970s a new oil pipeline started operating and allowed the refining industry to significantly increase its activity level.

24 Moreover, although no data on the manufacturing sector's capital stock and employment are available for the 1988–90 period, the huge fall in manufacturing output registered during these years (a cumulative loss of 33 per cent) allows one to conclude that this sector's TFPG performance during the 1976–90 period was even worse than is discussed in the text.

25 Refer to Nishimizu and Robinson (1984), Pack (1988) and Havrylyshyn (1990) for a rationale of the links between TFPG and trade policies.

26 In addition to these variables, an index of capital-intensity (stock of capital per

worker in each sector) was also tried as a regressor. However, it did not prove to be statistically significant.

27 This sector was the one with the highest TFPG and output growth rates (see Table 7.12), displayed an export ratio three times as large as the sample's mean, and had the second largest concentration index in the manufacturing sector.

28 The latter finding is not consistent with Clague's (1970: 204) conclusion that, in the case of Peruvian industry, one can 'observe a loose positive relationship between relative competitiveness and relative efficiency'.

29 While both hypotheses provide a rationale for a positive link between export orientation and TFPG, the direction of causality is the opposite in each case.

30 The correlation coefficient between EXPO and TFPG falls from 0.46 during the first sub-period to −0.49 in the second one.

31 In its analysis of the sources of industrial growth, World Bank (1983) finds that export expansion accounted for about 29 per cent of output growth during 1976–81. Although the authors only had data up to 1981, they singled out the deterioration of the real exchange rate beginning in 1979 as a major cause for the reversal of the contribution of manufactured exports to this sector's growth during the last two years of their sample period (pp. 4–8).

32 Manufactured exports (excluding fish meal) as a share of total exports rose from 2.9 per cent in 1970 to 19.5 per cent in 1979.

33 The Ministry of Industries' survey, on which this table is based, does not cover sectors such as fish meal, fish processing and copper products. These industries were able to export a much larger share of their production, mainly because of their comparative advantage based on natural resources.

34 However, to the extent that this indicator is also influenced by non-policy variables, such as the terms of trade, the behaviour of these exogenous variables should also be taken into account when analysing this indicator.

35 Although other export incentives were available during this period, such as a temporary duty-free import regime (imports of intermediate goods for export activities were not subject to tariffs under this regime), few exporters took advantage of this system. See Hanel (1987).

36 Paredes (1988, 1989) argues that the instability of the ERER was mainly due to the counter-cyclical and short-term nature of export promotion policy in Peru.

37 The comparison is based on the real exchange rates and not on the ERER due to lack of cross-country data on the latter variable.

38 The theoretical considerations behind this regression specification can be found in Paredes (1989). The dependent variable and the regressors are expressed in log-levels; therefore, their coefficients are elasticity estimates. The only exception is given by RERVAR, which was measured as the annual coefficient of variability of the quarterly observations of the real exchange rate. Given that the value of manufactured exports (in constant dollars) was used as the dependent variable, the supply price elasticity is equal to that presented in the table minus 1. EXPCAP is an instrumental variable for total manufacturing output (in constant dollars). The instrumental variable corresponds to the fitted values of the regression of manufacturing value added on a constant, a time trend, and two lags of itself.

39 The export promotion policy, aside from not successfully fostering a strong and dynamic export sector, created problems in other ways. The financing of this policy created pressures on the fiscal and on the Central Bank accounts (due to the CERTEX and FENT, respectively), and thereby contributed to

monetary expansion, which was the basis for the high rates of inflation recorded throughout the 1980s.

40 Moreover, it can be argued that the country's declining terms of trade and the cutback in external financing observed during this period contributed to the increase in the equilibrium real exchange rate.

REFERENCES

Abusada, Roberto (1976) 'Utilización del Capital Instalado en el Sector Industrial Peruano', Centro de Investigaciones Sociales, Económicas, Políticas y Antropológicas (CISEPA) Working Paper, Pontificia Universidad Católica del Perú.

Armas, A., Palacios, L. and Rossini, R. (1989) *El Sesgo Anti-Exportador de la Política Comercial Peruana: Un Estudio de Protección Efectiva a la Minería*, Lima: Instituto de Estudios Económicos Mineros.

Bruton, Henry (1967) 'Productivity Growth in Latin America', *American Economic Review* 57(5): 1099–116.

—— (1989) 'Import Substitution', in Hollis Chenery and T. N. Srinivasan (eds) *Handbook of Development Economics*, vol. 2, ch. 30, Amsterdam: Elsevier Science Publishers.

Caller, Jaime y Rosario Chuecas (1989) *Estrategia de Desarrollo Industrial: Algunas Reflexiones*, Lima: Fundación Friedrich Ebert.

Central Reserve Bank of Peru (1983) 'El Proceso de Liberalización de Importaciones: Perú 1979–1982', mimeo.

—— *Memoria*.

Clague, Christopher (1970) 'The Determinants of Efficiency in Manufacturing Industries in an Underdeveloped Country', *Economic Development and Cultural Change* 18(2): 188–205.

Correa, Hector (1970) 'Sources of Economic Growth in Latin America', *Southern Economic Journal* 37(1): 17–31.

De La Cruz, Jorge (1989) 'Situación de la Industria de Bienes de Capital en el Perú', Instituto Nacional de Planificación and Deutsche Gesellschaft für Technische Zusammenarbeit, Lima.

Elías, Victor J. (1978) 'Sources of Economic Growth in Latin American Countries', *Review of Economics and Statistics* 60/3: 362–70.

Escobal, Javier (1988) 'Las Condicionantes de las Exportaciones No Tradicionales: Un Análisis Sectorial', Grupo de Análisis para el Desarrollo (GRADE).

—— (1991) 'Marzo de 1991: el Mes de las Reformas Estructurales en el Perú', Grupo de Análisis para el Desarrollo (GRADE).

Fitzgerald, E. V. K. (1981) *La Política Económica del Perú 1956–1978*, Lima: Instituto de Estudios Peruanos.

(GIECO) Grupo de Investigaciones Económicas (1972) 'Industrialización y Política de Industrialización en el Perú, con Énfasis en el Periodo 1950–1968', Universidad Nacional de Ingeniería, Project UNI/KTH/INP, Working Paper no. 20.

Hamann, Javier and Paredes, Carlos (1991) 'Economic Characteristics and Trends', in Carlos Paredes and Jeffrey Sachs (eds) *Peru's Path to Recovery: A Plan for Economic Stabilization and Growth* Washington, DC: Brookings Institution, pp.41–79.

Hanel, Peter (1987) 'Efectos de la Protección al Mercado Interno en la Actividad Exportadora No Tradicional del Perú 1979–1986', Grupo de Análisis para el Desarrollo (GRADE).

Havrylyshyn, Oli (1990) 'Trade Policy and Productivity Gains in Developing Countries. A Survey of the Literature', *World Bank Observer* 5(1): 1–24.

Hunt, S. (1985) 'Peru's Non-traditional Exports: The Present and the Future', mimeo, Inter-American Development Bank.

Instituto Nacional de Estadística (1989) *Cuentas Nacionales*.

Jimenez, Felix (1987) 'Reactivación y Crecimiento de las Importaciones: Análisis y Propuestas de Política', Centro de Estudios para el Desarrollo y la Participación (CEDEP).

Ministry of Industries (various years), 'Survey of Establishments with Five or More Employees'.

Nishimizu, M. and Robinson, Sherman (1984) 'Trade Policies and Productivity Change in Semi-Industrialized Countries', *Journal of Development Economics* 16(1–2): 177–206.

Nogués, J. (1985) 'The Timing and Sequencing of Peru's Trade Liberalization Policy: Analysis of Peru's Trade Liberalization Episode', Mimeo, World Bank.

—— (1989) 'An Historical Perspective of Peru's Trade Liberalization Policies of the 80s', World Bank Discussion Paper DRD168.

Pack, Howard (1988) 'Industrialization and Trade', in Hollis Chenery and T.N. Srinivasan (eds) *Handbook of Development Economics*, vol. 1, ch. 9, Amsterdam: Elsevier Science Publishers.

Paredes, Carlos (1988) 'Política Económica, Industrialización y Exportaciones de Manufacturas en el Perú', Working Paper, Grupo de Análisis para el Desarrollo (GRADE).

—— (1989) 'Inflation, Devaluation, The Real Exchange Rate and Export Performance: Three Essays on Latin America', unpublished PhD Dissertation, Yale University.

Pinzás, Teobaldo (1981) *La Economía Peruana, 1950–1978*, Lima: Instituto de Estudios Peruanos.

Revilla, Víctor C. (1990) 'El Proceso de Liberalización Comercial 1978–1983: Lecciones de una Experiencia Frustrada', Fundación Friedrich Ebert, Lima.

Rivera, Iván (1983) 'Política Industrial Peruana', Conference Paper for the High-Level Expert Group Meetings Preparatory to the Fourth General Conference of UNIDO, Industrial Development Strategies and Policies for Developing Countries, Lima, Peru, 18–22 April.

Roemer, Michael (1970) *Fishing for Growth, Export-led Development in Peru, 1950–1967*, Cambridge, Mass.: Harvard University Press.

Rossini, R. and Paredes, C. (1991) 'Foreign Trade Policy', in Carlos Paredes and Jeffrey Sachs (eds) *Peru's Path to Recovery: A Plan for Economic Stabilization and Growth*, ch. 9, Washington, DC: Brookings Institution.

Schydlowsky, D., Hunt, S. and Mezzera, J. (eds) (1983) *La Promocion de Exportaciones en el Perú*, Lima: Asociación de Exportadores No Tradicionales (ADEX).

Shimabukuro, Iris (1990) 'Proceso de Industrialización 1950–1988. Pautas para el Diseño de una Nueva Política Industrial', Instituto Nacional de Planificación and Deutsche Gesellschaft für Technische Zusammenarbeit Lima.

Syrquin, Moshe (1989) 'Patterns of Structural Change', in Hollis Chenery and T.N. Srinivasan (eds) *Handbook of Development Economics*, vol. 1, ch. 7, Amsterdam: Elsevier Science Publishers.

Tello, Mario (1988) 'Organización Industrial, Características de la Industria y Política Comercial en el Perú: 1971–1985', Centro de Investigaciones Sociales, Económicas, Políticas y Antropológicas (CISEPA) Working Paper 73, Pontificia Universidad Católica del Perú.

—— (1990) 'Exportaciones y Crecimiento Económico en el Perú, 1950–1987', Fundación Friedrich Ebert, Lima.

Thorp, Rosemary and Bertram, Geoffrey (1978) *Peru 1890–1977: Growth and Policy in an Open Economy,* London: Macmillan Press.

Torres, Jorge (1976) *Estructura Económica de la Industria en el Perú,* Lima: Editorial Horizonte.

Vega Centeno, Maximo (1983) *Crecimiento, Industrialización y Cambio Técnico: Perú 1955–1980,* Lima: Pontificia Universidad Católica del Peru, Fondo Editorial.

Webb, Richard and Fernandez-Baca, Graciela (1990) *Perú en Números 1990. Almanaque Estadístico,* Lima: Editorial Navarrete.

World Bank (1983) 'Peru. The Manufacturing Sector: Performance and Policy Issues', mimeo, Projects Department, Latin America and the Caribbean Regional Office.

ASIA

8

TRADE AND INDUSTRIALIZATION IN BANGLADESH

An assessment

Sultan Hafeez Rahman

I owe a great debt to Professor G. K. Helleiner for his comments on an earlier draft. The content and presentation of the paper have benefited immensely from these and other comments received from participants at the UNU/WIDER Conference on 'Trade and Industrialization Reconsidered' held in Paris from 31 August to 3 September, 1991. I should also like to thank Dr Mustafizur Rahman of Dhaka University and Mr M. S. Emran, Research Associate, Bangladesh Institute of Development Studies, for their support. Mr Rafiqul Hassan and Mr A.A. Masud Chowdhury deserve special mention for excellent research assistance. Thanks are due to Mr Fariduddin Ahmed for his sincere help with word processing.

INTRODUCTION

Bangladesh became independent in 1971 following a nine-month-long War of Liberation which devastated the material economic base of the country. Reconstruction efforts began immediately following the war and were consolidated within the framework of the First Five-Year Plan launched in 1973. The country consists of 144,000 square kilometres of low deltaic land in the confluence of two major rivers of the world, the Ganges and Brahmaputra. The area is highly disaster-prone, being subject to recurrent floods and cyclones. It is the most densely populated country in the world with a population of 70 million in 1971 and 108 million in 1991. The population density at present is 750 persons per square kilometre. The country has a poor natural resource base: except for limited gas and coal reserves, it has no other known natural resource. With a per capita income of US$180, a very low domestic saving rate and a large external debt, Bangladesh faces an extremely difficult development challenge.

In the 1980s in particular, the industrial sector has received priority attention among macro-sectors, and has been recognized as the sector that holds the key to growth, employment and poverty alleviation. This preferential treatment is reflected in high relative government allocations and industrial, fiscal, financial and trade policies that have biased the structure of incentives significantly in favour of the industrial sector. Faced with serious external payments imbalances at its inception, the country formulated policies aimed at promoting import substitution, including high protection rates, foreign exchange rationing, quantitative trade restrictions, fixed multiple exchange rates, etc. Furthermore, in 1972, despite the objectives of equity and social justice stated in the Constitution, 92 per cent of the fixed assets of the formal manufacturing sector were nationalized.

The country's reliance on concessional external assistance from the World Bank and International Monetary Fund (IMF) has shaped the evolution of its economic policies. The violent overthrow of the first elected government of Bangladesh in a military coup in 1975 paved the way for a retreat from past policies which favoured a domestic market-based industrialization strategy, equity and social justice. A major overhaul of the trade policy regime was initiated in 1979. A 'managed' floating exchange rate system replaced the fixed exchange rate system and the scope of import licensing was reduced. Denationalization of the state-owned sector began in the early 1980s. The new policy orientation was strengthened and its pace accelerated as Bangladesh came under the purview of policy-based lending of the World Bank, its prime donor, in 1980. The most significant shift in economic policy, however, came with the initiation of the three-year IMF structural adjustment facility (SAF) in 1986. The lending facility provided an economy-wide policy framework which Bangladesh was obliged to follow. The move towards an open, liberalized, market-based and decentralized economic regime has, however, proved to be protracted and arduous. The transition continues, with the IMF enhanced structural adjustment facility (ESAF) having taken effect in 1990.

In spite of the reforms, economic growth was very low in the 1980s and nothing significant was achieved in terms of reducing the external and fiscal deficits, increasing the saving rate, or alleviating poverty (Rahman, 1991). The modern manufacturing base remains narrow and its growth performance has been particularly unsatisfactory. The overall economic growth and manufacturing sector growth rates were 5.1 per cent and 4.9 per cent per annum respectively, from 1974–5 to 1980–1. In the 1980s there was a significant deceleration of overall and sectoral economic growth rates. The overall economic growth rate dropped sharply to 3.8 per cent per annum while the growth rate of the manufacturing sector was only 2.5 per cent per annum. During this period population growth was 2.1 per cent per annum. Consequently, the share of manufacturing GDP in the total has stagnated at around 10 per cent virtually throughout the country's existence.

This paper provides an overview of trade and industrial policies and the performance of the manufacturing sector in Bangladesh. The first section presents the initial conditions and the major trade, financial, fiscal and institutional policies relating to the industrial sector. The next sections are devoted to a discussion of the export policy regime and performance of the export sector, followed by a discussion of the trade policy regime and performance of the industrial sector. Finally, the last section contains the conclusions.

INITIAL CONDITIONS AND THE EVOLUTION OF TRADE, EXCHANGE RATE AND INDUSTRIAL POLICIES

Initial conditions

At its inception, Bangladesh was a predominantly agricultural economy with agriculture contributing 60 per cent of the total GDP and absorbing 77 per cent of the total employed labour force. The share of agricultural GDP has declined to 38 per cent at present. The sector, however, still accounts for 56 per cent of total employment. The decline in the share of agriculture in total GDP was compensated for by an increase in the share of the service sector. The share of manufacturing has stagnated at around 10 per cent of total GDP throughout the last two decades.

A striking feature of Bangladesh's macroeconomic reality is the low domestic saving rate and its resilience to change. The large internal and external resource gap (Table 8.1) made it imperative for Bangladesh to rely on concessional external assistance, particularly from the World Bank and the IMF, on a large scale from the very beginning. The country's inability to accelerate the domestic resource mobilization effort and achieve major structural change in the external sector, e.g. significantly increase the export: GDP ratio, has kept the country excessively dependent on external assistance to finance development. Until 1980–1, 75 per cent of development expenditure was financed by foreign aid. The contribution of foreign aid to development expenditure increased to 90 per cent in 1991.

Bangladesh inherited very little by way of modern manufacturing activity except for the jute textile industry and a few cotton textile industries. As East Pakistan, i.e. a peripheral province in the pre-independence period, Bangladesh was shut out of the rapid industrialization experienced by West Pakistan. The centre of trade and commerce was also in West Pakistan. Bangladesh even lacked critical personnel with manufacturing and related skills, e.g. technicians, mechanics, electricians, etc., at the time of independence in 1971. The situation was greatly aggravated by the large-scale migration of the non-Bangladeshi entrepreneurs and businessmen on the one hand and skilled workers and managers on the other after independence, virtually forcing the country to start from scratch. The supporting infrastructure and services were also highly inadequate.

Table 8.2 shows the structure of manufacturing output and the share of

Table 8.1 Basic indicators, Bangladesh (%)

	Real GDP growth	Domestic savings: GDP	Investment: GDP	Government revenue: GDP	Fiscal deficit: GDP	Export: GDP	Import: GDP	External (trade) deficit: GDP	Debt service ratio	Inflation rate
1974–5	3.3	2.0	7.3	5.2	−8.4	2.5	8.7	−6.2	9.0	20.6[a]
1980–1	6.8	3.2	10.5	9.3	−9.1	5.0	17.7	−12.7	12.8	10.3
1984–5	3.7	2.3	12.4	8.6	−7.2	6.5	18.3	−11.8	19.4	14.9
1989–90	5.5	1.9	12.0	9.1	−7.4	6.9	17.5	−10.6	26.3	7.7

Source: Rahman (1991).

[a] Average of 1973/74–1975/76 was taken because 1974–5 was an abnormal year with a famine.

Table 8.2 Trade and manufacturing output in Bangladesh, 1976–7

Sectors [a]	Manufac- tured exports	Manufac- tured imports	Gross manufacturing output[b]	Exports/ output[c]	Imports/ output[c]
Consumer goods	166.10	7,016.60	20,233.16 (54.3)	0.01	0.26
Intermediate goods	3,805.70	11,309.10	14,760.32 (39.6)	0.26	0.43
Capital goods	23.20	7,186.60	2,279.08 (06.1)	0.01	0.76
Total	3,995.00	25,512.30	37,272.56	0.11	0.41

Source: Based on twenty-three manufacturing sectors of the input-output table for 1976–7.

[a] Consumer goods: food products, beverages, tobacco products, textiles, paper and paper products.
Intermediate goods: iron and steel, chemicals and chemical products, petroleum products, non-metallic minerals, jute baling and processing, rubber products, ice making.
Capital goods: non-electric machinery, electric machinery, transport equipment.
[b] Figures in parentheses are shares of total gross output.
[c] For exports: weighted average share of sectoral exports in gross manufacturing output. Weights are shares of each sector's export in total gross manufacturing output.
For imports: weighted average share of imports in total manufacturing supply (gross output plus imports). Weights are shares of each sector's import in total manufacturing supply.

manufactured exports and imports in total manufacturing output and supply in 1976–7. The share of manufactured exports in total gross output was negligible, except in the case of intermediate goods in which jute, a major export, is included. The share of manufactured imports in the total supply of manufactured goods was large, particularly in the case of capital goods and intermediate goods, showing the country's dependence on imported manufactured products. The shares of exports and imports in manufactured output had not changed significantly by 1988.

Bangladesh, having been left out of both Pakistan's development experience in the pre-1971 period and, prior to that, colonial India's development experience, was not endowed with a well-developed entrepreneurial class or culture. Eastern Bengal had neither a wealthy middle class nor a landed aristocracy that could provide the basis for the growth of an entrepreneurial class. The rich Hindu landed aristocracy had mostly migrated to India after partition in 1947 (Rahman, 1950) and the little commerce, trade and industry that existed in Bangladesh was dominated by West Pakistani entrepreneurs who had migrated from India at the time of its partition.

The exploitation of Bangladesh's economic resources during the Pakistan era created a deep sense of frustration with a private enterprise-led development strategy in the minds of the political leadership of the Awami League, the party that led Bangladesh to independence and formed the first government. This, combined with the extreme radicalization of the political leadership through an armed struggle for liberation and the decisive US government 'tilt' in favour of the Pakistan military junta in 1971, changed the basic character of the Awami League from a political party of the East

Pakistani middle class led by its nascent entrepreneurs demanding a fair share of Pakistan's increasing fortunes to a populist party with socialist aspirations. Thus, in 1972, 92 per cent of the fixed assets of the formal manufacturing sector was nationalized and brought under state ownership. The nationalization of manufacturing units abandoned by non-Bengali entrepreneurs was, at least initially, a necessity, but the nationalization of industries owned by Bangladeshi entrepreneurs profoundly shook their confidence in the first political regime. Later political regimes attempted to nurture an entrepreneurial class but the process degenerated into a 'patron–client' relationship characterized by massive corruption and rent-seeking.

Apart from being poor in material resources and human skills, Bangladesh was an impoverished country at birth and continues to be so. Socioeconomic indicators still reveal conditions of abject poverty prevalent on a large scale. The human resource development (HRD) index is only 0.32 for Bangladesh (ranked twenty-third lowest in the world) and there are great inequities in the distribution of income and assets in the country. In 1973–4 the bottom 40 per cent of all households received only 18.3 per cent of total income and the top 10 per cent received 28.4 per cent. The corresponding figures for the bottom 40 per cent and top decile of households were 18 per cent and 30 per cent respectively in 1988–9. Thus, income inequality has remained unchanged (Bangladesh Bureau of Statistics, 1991). The situation with respect to the distribution of land is worse, with the bottom 40 per cent of households owning only 2.8 per cent of the land, while the top 10 per cent own 45 per cent (Rahman et al., 1991). The low per capita income growth has constrained the growth of the domestic market while poor socioeconomic conditions and a highly unequal distribution of income have constrained the size of the domestic market for mass consumer goods. It has also kept labour productivity very low.

Trade and exchange rate policies

Until recently, import substitution was the cornerstone of the Bangladesh industrial strategy. The choice of this strategy was dominated by macroeconomic concerns about the balance of payments and the fiscal balance. The industrial sector was heavily protected through high tariffs and extensive use of quantitative restrictions on imports in the 1970s. High tariffs on imports has been the single largest source (35 per cent) of revenue for the government. The policy of high protection to domestic industry was complemented by a policy of fixed exchange rates. The entire trade and industrial policy regime was excessively regulated: more than a dozen permits and licences were required to operate an industrial unit. Private foreign investment was discouraged.

By the mid-1970s it was apparent that the strategy of one-sided reliance on the domestic market to promote industrialization needed a major over-haul. The task of liberalization of the trade and industrial policy regime, however, was left to the second political regime, which came to power after the military coup of August 1975. The pace of reform was very slow initially but accelerated after the second successful military coup of 1982. The slow pace of reforms at that stage, however, cannot be attributed to recalcitrance of the government machinery alone. The full force of the new 'orthodoxy' emphasizing export-oriented industrial, trade and exchange rate policies was not felt in the 1970s.

Trade policy reforms were aimed at import liberalization, tariff rationali-zation and export promotion. Along with complementary reforms relating to exchange rate management, the regulatory framework, public enterprises and the financial sector, the trade policy reforms were aimed at accelerating production, export, employment, increasing factor productivity and improving allocative efficiency. A major objective of the trade and exchange rate policy reforms has been to neutralize the incentive structure which was traditionally biased in favour of import-substituting industries.

Export policies

Major export policy reforms were formulated in the 1980s. These reforms were aimed at providing (i) unrestricted and duty-free access to imported inputs; (ii) economic assistance mainly to non-traditional exports through the Export Performance Benefit (XPB) scheme; (iii) easy access to credit and credit subsidies; and (iv) tax rebates on export income and concession-ary duties on imported capital machineries. Thus the policy reforms in the export sector included trade, exchange rate, monetary and fiscal policy incentives aimed at increasing effective assistance to exports.

Incentives were provided to the export sector through access to banned and restricted imported inputs, duty drawback arrangements, and bonded warehouse facilities. The XPB scheme was introduced to provide assistance mainly to non-traditional exports. Three coefficients – 40 per cent, 70 per cent and 100 per cent – were used to represent the domestic content of value-added of exports and their priority status in determining the magni-tude eligible for XPB. The spread between the official and secondary foreign exchange rate was then applied to the eligible magnitude to deter-mine the export bonus. The XPB coverage was extended significantly in 1986 to include all exports except raw jute and unprocessed leather. In 1988, seventy-six export items with value added greater than or equal to 70 per cent were eligible for 100 per cent XPB and thirty-eight items with value added of over 50 per cent were eligible for 70 per cent XPB. In 1987, XPB coverage was extended further to include indirect exports, i.e. domestic inputs to export industries, in order to promote backward linkage. Exporters of ready-made garments and processed leather are eligible for

100 per cent XPB if domestic raw materials are used, compared to 40 per cent if raw materials are imported.

Major monetary and credit policy instruments introduced to support export industries were: (i) a back-to-back letter of credit (BBLC) facility for imported and domestic raw materials and inputs, (ii) a concessional rate of interest on working capital, i.e. 8.5–11.5 per cent per annum compared to the commercial rate of 16 per cent per annum, and (iii) export insurance through introduction of the Export Credit Guarantee Scheme (ECGS). However, while the BBLC facility has proven highly successful in the case of ready-made garments, foreign exporters have been reluctant to accept BBLCs on a deferred payment basis due to the long periods involved (120 days or more).

Fiscal incentives to exporters include rebates on income taxes and concessionary duties on imported capital machinery. The tax rebate system provides for a reduction of the usual rates to a maximum of 60 per cent in the case of export sales exceeding 40 per cent of the gross value of export production. While traditional exports, e.g. jute and tea, are excluded from the system, handicrafts are completely exempted from income taxes. Export industries which export 70 per cent or more of total production, and small and cottage industries are eligible for importing capital machineries at an initial tariff rate of 2.5 per cent of CIF value. Another important fiscal incentive includes excise tax refunds on domestic intermediates. However, there remain serious difficulties in the implementation of the proclaimed policies, undermining the credibility of the policy initiatives (Rab, 1989).

Import policies

On the import side, policy reforms were aimed at (i) decreasing tariff levels, (ii) rationalizing the tariff structure, (iii) removing quantitative restrictions (QRs), and (iv) simplifying trade procedures.

In January 1985, the import control system was changed significantly. The Positive List (specifying items which could be imported) was changed to a Negative List (which specified items that could not be freely imported), the implication being that any item that was not on the list could be imported, either freely or by fulfilling specified requirements. The Restricted List was left intact. Targeted reduction of tariffs and rationalization of the tariff structure took place along with rapid phasing-out of the QRs through an amendment to the Import Policy Order (IPO) in May 1988. Two major changes in the IPO of 1989–90 and 1990–1 took place: the IPO would henceforth remain in force for two years instead of one and the Negative and Restricted Lists of imports were amalgamated into one Control List. Thus, policy continuity and much greater ease in import procedures were provided. The number of categories containing banned items was reduced by 20 per cent per year, with priority for removing bans in the steel, chemicals, textiles and light engineering sectors. From July 1986 to July 1990, four-digit categories in the Negative and Restricted Lists were reduced from 648 to 343. The remaining items include many products which compete with domestic production. Although the ambitious target of phasing out all QRs by 1990–1 was not achieved, the number of four-digit items subject to controls has been reduced by about 25 per cent and, allowing for some new restrictions, there has been an effective reduction of about 18 per cent in the Control List.

Taxation of imports in Bangladesh has included a combination of customs duties, sales taxes, development surcharges (DSC) and licence fees. Sales taxes are imposed on the duty-paid value of imports, while tariffs, DSC and licence fees are levied on the CIF value of imports. Sales taxes are levied only on imports in Bangladesh and, hence, are import taxes. Tariffs are the most important of the taxes. In regard to tariffs, the government publishes a series of statutory rates which are the highest rates that can be legally levied although the operative rates are in many cases much lower because of various exemptions and concessions (for example, to stimulate investment in priority sectors, promote export-oriented industries and induce business in less developed areas). Reforms in connection with tariff rationalization and reduction have aimed specifically at: (i) reducing maximum tariff rates to 100 per cent (with the exception of luxury goods); (ii) limiting customs duties to a maximum of 20 per cent on raw materials, 75 per cent on intermediate products and materials, and 100 per cent on final products; and (iii) restructuring import tariffs in the textiles, steel and engineering sectors so that nominal tariffs in these sectors fall within the 0–85 per cent range. These objectives, however, have not been achieved as yet.

To assess the effects of trade policy liberalization relating to imports, statutory tariff rates in 1982–3 were compared to those of 1989–90, i.e. one year after the significant import policy changes relating to tariffs and QRs began. The distribution of statutory tariff rates shown in Table 8.3 is based on 106 imported manufactured products covering approximately 60 per cent of total import value and 95 per cent of manufacturing output. There are significant increases in the headings in 40 per cent and 50 per cent duty slabs in 1989–90. The 75 per cent duty slab was withdrawn and rates of 100 per cent and above applied to only 29.25 per cent of the items covered in 1989–90 compared to 52.83 per cent in 1982–3. Although the weighted average tariff rate increased somewhat over the period, the dispersion of the tariff rates measured by the coefficient of variation decreased from 0.70 in 1982–3 to 0.59 in 1989–90. Thus, significant trade policy reforms have taken place.

Operative tariffs, the actually-charged tariff rates, differ from the statutory rates due to duty concessions and exemptions provided by the govern-

Table 8.3 Distribution of tariffs, Bangladesh

Tariff rate (%)	Percentage of import items	
	1982–3	1989–90
20	13.21	10.38
40	5.66	28.30
50	18.87	31.13
75	6.60	–
100	27.39	22.64
150	18.87	1.89
300	5.66	4.72
Average rate	92.88	103.11
Coefficient of variation	0.71	0.59

ment to imported commodities. Nearly 25 per cent of imports currently enter duty-free on raw material for the ready-made garments sector alone. The actual tax revenue collections from imports shown in Table 8.4 are, therefore, much lower than the level suggested by statutory tariffs.

Exchange rate policies

Bangladesh started with a fixed exchange rate system. In August 1979, the fixed exchange rate policy was replaced by a 'managed' flexible exchange rate policy in which the taka was pegged to a basket of currencies of Bangladesh's major trading partners, weighted according to their bilateral foreign exchange transactions with Bangladesh. The weights have been changed a few times in the 1980s to reflect changing trade weights. The intervention currency has been the US dollar since early 1983, prior to which it was the UK pound sterling. Since 1985, a policy of frequent adjustment of the nominal exchange rate was adopted in concert with

Table 8.4 Average import revenue collection, Bangladesh (value in core taka)

Year	Sales tax[a]	Customs duties	Total import tax revenue	Import value	Average tax rate
1974–5	61.88	151.20	213.08	1,084.00	19.66
1980–1	340.00	710.70	1,050.70	5,216.00	20.14
1981–2	350.00	765.20	1,115.20	5,236.00	21.30
1982–3	316.00	899.30	1,215.30	5,489.00	22.14
1983–4	345.00	993.10	1,338.10	5,869.00	22.80
1984–5	410.00	1,104.42	1,514.42	6,874.00	22.03
1985–6	440.00	1,193.90	1,633.90	7,065.00	23.13
1986–7	550.00	1,537.40	2,087.40	8,026.00	26.01
1987–8	525.00	1,618.00	2,143.00	9,329.00	22.97
1988–9	540.00	1,807.30	2,347.30	10.848.00	21.64

Source: Bangladesh Bureau of Statistics, *Statistical Yearbook*, various issues.
[a] The sales tax is an import tax in Bangladesh.

overall macroeconomic policy reform under a three-year IMF SAF programme which was to become operative the following year. The primary objective of the frequent exchange rate depreciation was to prevent overvaluation of the exchange rate. The exchange rate policy was aimed at making exports more price competitive, eliminating budgetary subsidies for exports and helping to restrain import growth without reimposing quantitative restrictions. Combined with the trade policy reforms stated earlier, the policy was expected to reduce smuggling, induce reallocation of resources in sectors of export orientation and import substitution, and encourage diversification and rapid growth of non-traditional exports.

Two exchange rate markets – the official primary exchange rate market (OEM) and a secondary exchange rate market (SEM) – have been operative since the mid-1970s. The SEM comprises the Wage Earners Scheme (WES) and the Export Performance Benefit (XPB) Scheme. Foreign exchange remittances of overseas Bangladeshis, tourists and other service earnings are channelled for sale through the WES. A band for the WES rate is determined by a committee of authorized foreign exchange dealers comprised of commercial banks with the Bangladesh Bank participating as an observer. The actual WES market rate is then determined within the predetermined band through auction. The spread between the WES and the official exchange rate was 12 per cent in June 1985 but dropped sharply to 4.5 per cent in June 1988 due to the frequent exchange rate adjustments in the 1985–90 period. The spread in 1991 was around 2 per cent. Thus, the foreign exchange market has been almost unified. The scope of the SEM has been enlarged greatly since 1986–7. The share of imports transacted through the SEM increased from 12 per cent in 1980–1 to 45 per cent in 1988–9. Around 70 per cent of the non-aid imports are currently transacted through the SEM.

Industrial policies

The most significant feature of the evolution of industrial policies in Bangladesh is the change in the status of state-owned enterprises. At the time of independence, 34 per cent of the fixed assets of the formal manufacturing sector was owned by a specialized industrial corporation (EPIDC), i.e. the state, 47 per cent by non-Bangladeshi (Pakistani) entrepreneurs, and the remaining 19 per cent by Bangladeshis (Harvard Institute for Industrial Development/Employment and Small Scale Enterprise Policy Planning [HIID/ESEPP], 1990). The non-Bangladeshi entrepreneurs abandoned their enterprises in the aftermath of independence. The government nationalized 92 per cent of the total fixed assets of the manufacturing sector through an ordinance in 1972. Included in this were a great many local Bangladeshi enterprises. Private sector participation was seriously restricted to medium, small and cottage industries (Sobhan, 1990) with an investment ceiling of

$2\frac{1}{2}$ million takas. This ceiling was increased to 30 million takas under the 1974 Industrial Policy.

The stage for a major reversal of the 1972 nationalization ordinance was set with the military coup of 1975 in which the incumbent government was violently overthrown. An Industrial Investment Policy was declared in December 1975 in which the private investment ceiling was further increased to 100 million takas, the restriction on private sector participation in large-scale manufacturing was withdrawn, direct foreign investment lending to the private sector was permitted, and the Dhaka stock exchange was reactivated. However, the pace of denationalization was remarkably slow. Up to June 1981, only 7 per cent of the total fixed assets of the manufacturing sector were divested.

Denationalization and liberalization were stepped up severalfold with the seizure of state power by the military coup led by General H.M. Ershad in 1982. The emphasis of industrial policy clearly shifted towards private-sector development at a rapid pace. By 1986, the fixed assets of the manufacturing sector under state ownership were reduced to 40 per cent. Several supporting policy measures pertaining to bank finance, corporate taxes, concessionary imports, export benefits, etc. to liberalize the industrial regime were undertaken. These policies were proclaimed through the New Industrial Policy of 1982 (NIP–1982) and the Revised Industrial Policy of 1986 (RIP–1986). The NIP–1982 provided a Reserved List (for public investment only) and Discouraged List for industrial investment. All industries not on the two lists were opened to private investment. The RIP–1986 further committed the government to sell 49 per cent of the shares of public-sector enterprises (PSE) to the public. However, this could not be executed as envisaged due to strong trade union and political opposition. Only six out of sixteen PSEs were sold.

Discrimination against private foreign investment (PFI) was withdrawn in 1975. An act to protect PFI was promulgated in 1980 and an export-processing zone (EPZ) was set up in Chittagong to attract PFI. Fiscal, financial, trade and infrastructural facilities, e.g. duty-free imports of capital goods and raw materials in bonded warehouses, roads, water, power, telecommunications, long tax holidays, profit repatriation benefits, etc., have been provided in the EPZ and 100 per cent foreign ownership is permitted.

The most recent biennial Industrial Policy (1991–2 and 1992–3) has declared export-oriented industrialization as one of its prime objectives. Biennial export and import policy statements have also been proclaimed in concert with the Industrial Policy to support private sector-led industrialization through a more liberalized, deregulated trade policy regime based on world prices.

EXPORT POLICIES AND PERFORMANCE

Exchange rate policy and export performance

The export sector of Bangladesh has undergone significant changes in the 1980s. The average annual real growth rate of total exports in US dollars in the 1980s was 7.7 per cent per annum. Real growth of non-traditional exports and traditional exports was 20.4 per cent and 0.7 per cent, respectively, between 1981–9. Trends in exports are shown in Table 8.5. Export growth was very strong in the latter half of the 1980s, particularly in non-traditional products. Non-traditional exports experienced a growth rate of 20.4 per cent per year in the 1980s. The share of non-traditional exports in total exports was 26 per cent in 1980–1, 35 per cent in 1984–5, and increased sharply to 67.5 per cent in 1988–9. The shares of the three main non-traditional groups, i.e. ready-made garments, frozen fish and leather, in total exports increased from 0.04 per cent, 5.6 per cent and 8 per cent, respectively, in 1980–1 to an estimated 37 per cent, 10.3 per cent and 11 per cent, respectively, in 1989–90. The non-traditional export base of the country is, however, narrow. No significant diversification beyond these three categories of exports took place in the 1980s. There is also no significant evidence of strong growth of backward linkages in these export sectors, keeping domestic value added low. These non-traditional export industries were based on the work market from inception and did not mature into export industries through a dynamic process of change from import-substituting industries.

At the time of independence, Bangladesh's primary commodity concentration in total exports was high. In 1972–3 the share of primary commodities in total exports was 43 per cent, declining to 31 per cent by 1979–80. In the 1980s this proportion declined to 23 per cent. The major part of the structural change of the export base towards manufactured exports, therefore, had already taken place in the decade of the 1970s. Bangladesh, unlike countries such as the Philippines and Malaysia, is not endowed with an adequate primary commodity resource base. It must, therefore, rely on manufactured goods to expand its export base. However, the manufacturing export sector suffers from a difficult structural problem. A large part of this sector comprises jute goods, leather goods and frozen fish exports. The prices of these manufactured goods are strongly influenced by their respective raw material prices, i.e. raw jute, fish, shrimp, hides and skins. Prices of these raw materials are subject to excessive fluctuations which show up in the manufactured products. Thus, although the share of the manufactured exports sector in total exports is high (77 per cent in 1989–90), in the case of Bangladesh it remains vulnerable to primary commodity price instability in the world markets.

Table 8.6 shows trends in relevant exchange rates. Though there is a

271

Table 8.5 Trends in exports, Bangladesh, 1980/81 to 1989/90 (US$ million)

	1980/81	1981/82	1982/83	1983/84	1984/85	1985/86	1986/87	1987/88	1988/89	1989/90ᵃ	% of exports 1980/81	% of exports 1988/89
Traditional exports	526	432	475	543	602	450	436	421	417	493	74.0	32.5
Raw jute	119	102	110	117	151	124	104	81	97	124	16.7	7.5
Jute goods	366	292	318	357	390	293	302	301	280	326	51.5	21.9
Tea	41	38	47	69	61	33	30	39	40	43	5.8	3.1
Non-traditional exports	185	195	211	268	332	369	638	810	869	982	26.0	67.5
Ready-made garments	3	7	11	32	116	131	299	434	471	550	0.4	36.6
Leather	57	63	58	85	70	61	135	147	137	163	8.0	10.6
Fish and shrimp	40	53	72	77	87	113	136	140	141	152	5.6	11.0
Others	85	72	70	74	59	64	68	89	120	117	12.0	9.3
Total exports	711	627	686	811	934	819	1,074	1,231	1,286	1,475	100.0	100.0
Export price index (1980/81=100)	100.0	84.8	88.6	101.3	119.3	94.1	101.6	108.0	112.7			

Source: World Bank (1990).
ᵃ World Bank estimates.

Table 8.6 Nominal, real, effective exchange rates and trade policy bias, Bangladesh

Year	OER	PPPI	EX	EM	RER	RERX	RERM	TPB
1973–4	7.97	2.07	11.18	22.00	16.51	23.18	45.59	0.51
1974–5	8.88	1.82	12.80	18.73	16.13	23.26	34.04	0.68
1975–6	15.05	1.83	16.98	21.83	27.54	31.06	39.93	0.78
1976–7	15.43	1.89	18.52	23.36	29.21	35.07	44.25	0.79
1977–8	15.12	2.02	18.72	22.63	30.49	37.77	45.66	0.83
1978–9	15.22	2.02	16.75	19.40	30.80	33.90	39.25	0.86
1979–80	15.49	2.07	15.80	22.61	32.02	32.67	46.74	0.70
1980–1	16.26	1.84	17.10	23.43	29.89	31.44	43.07	0.73
1981–2	20.07	1.56	21.44	27.34	31.25	33.39	42.57	0.78
1982–3	23.80	1.41	24.52	34.53	33.48	34.51	48.58	0.71
1983–4	24.94	1.25	27.46	41.38	31.14	34.28	51.65	0.66
1984–5	25.96	1.09	32.16	40.03	28.18	34.91	43.44	0.80
1985–6	29.89	1.00	31.95	40.09	29.89	31.95	40.09	0.80
1986–7	30.63	0.99	30.77	37.97	30.36	30.49	37.64	0.81
1987–8	31.24	0.96	32.02	41.10	30.12	30.87	39.62	0.78
1988–9	32.14	0.90	32.84	39.88	28.82	29.45	35.76	0.82

Source: Rahman (1992).
OER: Official exchange rate.
PPPI: Purchasing power parity index (trade weighted WPI of major trading partners/ domestic CPI).
EX: Nominal effective exchange rate for exports.
EM: Nominal effective exchange rate for imports.
RER: Real exchange rate.
RERX: Real effective exchange rate for exports.
RERM: Real effective exchange rate for imports.
TPB: RERX/RERM (trade policy bias or anti-export bias).
A rise in the exchange rate is a depreciation. All real exchange rates are in 1985–6 prices.

significant depreciating trend in the nominal exchange rate, the real exchange rate (RER) changed very little throughout the 1980s. The nominal exchange rate depreciation policy has basically served to prevent over-valuation of the real exchange rate, and had a favourable impact on nominal export growth. It provided continuity and demonstrated strong government commitment to the policy of promoting exports (Balassa, 1989). Though frequent exchange rate adjustments helped export growth, the trade policy bias (last column of Table 8.6) against exports as reflected in the higher effective exchange rate to imports (RERM) relative to exports (RERX) has remained.

Some factors other than exchange rate depreciation were, perhaps, more important determinants of the high export growth observed in the post-1984 period in Bangladesh. As shown above, export growth performance was led by ready-made garments. International marketing intermediaries faced with binding quota restrictions in their own country relocated part of their trade to Bangladesh. The industrial technology required for entry into the trade was labour-intensive, simple and well-known in Bangladesh (a 'greenhorn' worker could qualify as a semi-skilled worker in three months), capital cost was low, and the trade was undisrupted due to opening up of the European markets when quotas were imposed on the nascent sector in the US market. Quick government support in the form of bonded warehouse facilities, back-to-back letter of credit facilities for raw material imports, export-performance benefit (XPB) entitlement, and access to subsidized credit from banks helped enormously to create the needed incentives, all of which were transparent. Continued government support lent credibility and continuity to the stated export-promotion policies. No less important, at least until 1988, was the additional income (often abnormally high) made possible by selling 'surplus' cloth and accessories (raw material imported duty-free by exporters) in the domestic market. This, however, constituted smuggling. The market for textiles being highly protected (over 150 per cent nominal tariffs) at the time permitted abnormal rents to be extracted from the illegal sale of duty-free cloth in the domestic market. This provided a steady source of income augmentation to the otherwise low value-added industry.

Thus rapid export growth in Bangladesh was the result of a combination of factors, including the normal exchange rate adjustment policy. The exchange rate policy alone does not help to explain the strong export performance. Reliance on this policy alone in the future would focus attention away from other critically important considerations.

Effective rates of assistance to export industries

In order to measure the net incidence of both trade and industrial policies, the HIID/ESEPP Project[1] computed effective rates of assistance (ERA) for different industrial sectors across time. The ERA is similar to, but broader in its coverage of incentives than the effective rate of protection (ERP), and quantifies the impact of various concessions as well as costs to producers by computing the effect of taxes, implicit subsidies, etc. and other price distortions. Table 8.7 shows that while the ERAs for export-oriented (EP) industries ranged from 0.01 to 0.17 from 1974–5 to 1987–88, the ERAs for import-substituting (IS) industries ranged from 0.54 to 0.76. These ERAs were recomputed by us according to the two broad groups based on the HIID/ESEPP (1990a,c) ERA computations for twenty-one industrial sectors of the 1986–7 input-output table for Bangladesh. The average ERA for the IS group is 0.78, whereas it is only 0.09 for the export industries, i.e. on average the import-substituting industries group enjoyed effective assistance rates that were several times higher than those for the export-oriented industries. Though the discrimination against export sectors decreased in the 1980s, it was still very high.

Rab (1989) investigated the overall ERAs received by nine sample firms from all existing export incentives and those of ERA received with and

Table 8.7 Effective rates of assistance in the manufacturing sector, Bangladesh

Years	ERAIS[a]	ERAEX[b]
1974–5	0.623	0.014
1975–6	0.712	0.022
1976–7	0.693	0.025
1977–8	0.715	0.035
1978–9	0.682	0.032
1979–80	0.700	0.032
1980–1	0.694	0.055
1981–2	0.682	0.091
1982–3	0.738	0.169
1983–4	0.932	0.172
1984–5	0.941	0.156
1985–6	0.964	0.152
1986–7	0.901	0.151
1987–8	0.914	0.161
Average	0.778	0.091

Source: Rab (1989).
[a] ERAIS, Effective rate of assistance to import-substituting activities.
[b] ERAEX, Effective rate of assistance to export-promoting activities.

Table 8.8 Estimates of the ERAs received by firms, Bangladesh (%)

Product	Overall ERA	ERA without XPB subsidy	ERA without XPB subsidy and income tax rebate
Ready-made garments	25.42	13.92	−1.31
Finished leather	72.99	25.54	−13.89
Frozen fish	−16.38	−21.24	−25.40
Glycerin	9.08	6.65	−4.24
Porcelain tableware	6.67	3.28	−1.58
PVC pipes	8.49	3.16	−9.00
Textile fabric and household linen	6.92	0.07	0.07
PVC cables and conductors	Negative	Negative	Negative

Source: Rab (1989).

without XPB, interest subsidies and income tax rebates taken together. His estimates are shown in Table 8.8. The existing export policies provide positive assistance to all export products examined except processed frozen fish, PVC cables and conductors (in the first case mainly due to the high percentage of locally purchased fuel without being compensated for the taxes imposed and in the case of the latter mainly due to a shortfall in the duty drawback received and the imputed cost of the long delay). The assistance received by the positively assisted export products show that finished leather (73 per cent of value added) and ready-made garments (25 per cent of value added) are the most highly assisted activities. All other

275

activities except frozen fish, which receives negative assistance, are moderately assisted. It is important to note the XPB policy alone provides the largest assistance to the most assisted sectors, i.e. ready-made garments and leather. Assistance to the ready-made garment industry is reduced by nearly 50 per cent if the XPB benefit is excluded, while in the case of finished leather it is reduced by nearly two-thirds. However, the unification of the primary (official) and secondary foreign exchange markets due to the flexible exchange rate adjustment policy has greatly reduced the net XPB benefit.

Rab (1989) found from his case studies that: (i) existing policies do not fully assure unrestricted and duty-free access to inputs; (ii) the incentives provided, such as XPB, interest subsidies and income tax rebates, work only in part to compensate for the inadequate offset provisions on taxes on imported inputs; (iii) in cases where domestic purchases of inputs with a high protection content are involved, even all the incentives together may not suffice to assure non-negative assistance (as in the case of processed frozen fish); (iv) the general level of assistance received by most export activities is moderate, only a few percentage points above zero. This, in contrast to a much higher general level of assistance received by import-substitution activities, suggests the existence of a significant bias of the existing policies against exporting activities; (v) current incentives seem to be biased in favour of low value-added activities, despite some differentiation maintained in XPB rates to provide a higher benefit to higher value-added export producers. Export firms who are not fully export-oriented are relatively disadvantaged compared to the direct export producers as they seem unable to fully avail themselves of the existing incentives for one reason or the other.

Most statements of public policy reflected in documents such as the Export Policy, Import Policy, Industrial Policy, etc., remain mere pronouncements of intentions. Strong commitment to implementation of trade and industrial policies towards the industrial sector in general and export-oriented industries in particular is critical to the creation of an investment climate conducive to rapid industrialization.

The assessment of incentives to exports shows that while exchange rate policies taxed the export sector, overall economic assistance was still positive and sometimes significantly so. Policy reforms undertaken till the late 1980s have, however, had little effect in terms of neutralizing economic incentives between export and import-substituting activities. It is the relative incentive to the export sector vis-à-vis the IS sector that would influence growth of the export sector. The relative incentive (ERA) to the ready-made garments sector was only 32 per cent of the ERA for the group of IS industries. Thus the strong growth of the ready-made garments industry cannot be explained in terms of the absolute level of economic incentives enjoyed by it. The export sector in Bangladesh evolved directly in response to world market demand. In other words, it did not emerge through a process of dynamic learning and maturity of import-substituting industries ultimately permitting them to graduate into export industries.

ECONOMIC INCENTIVES AND PERFORMANCE OF THE INDUSTRIAL SECTOR

Structure of trade policy incentives

Trade, macroeconomic and sectoral policies in any policy regime have very strong implications for resource allocation and efficiency. Measures such as nominal and effective rates of protection have been widely used in the literature to represent the levels and structure of a given protection regime. However, the ERP may not be an adequate indicator of the degree of assistance to the industrial sector when other non-trade policies exist. A more relevant measure, which includes both trade and non-trade policies, would be the ERA. The ERP and ERA for different industry categories at the four-digit level of disaggregation, based on Census of Manufacturing Industries (CMI) data for twenty-one manufacturing sectors of the 1986–7 input–output tables for Bangladesh, were computed by the HIID/ESEPP project. Apart from these estimates, some other estimates of the ERA are also available for selected manufacturing activities in Bangladesh for certain years (e.g. Ahmed and Islam, 1989). But for reasons just stated, we use only the estimates of the HIID/ESEPP project, presented in Table 8.9.[2]

Table 8.9 shows that the industrial sector has been highly protected. There was a sharp rise in the effective protection and assistance rates shown in Table 8.9 with the initiation of the New Industrial Policy (NIP) in 1983–4. The average ERP was 0.86 from 1974–5 to 1982–3 which increased sharply to an average of 1.14 during the New Industrial Policy period (1983–4 to 1985–6). During the Revised Industrial Policy (RIP) period (1986–7 onwards), the ERP declined somewhat to an average of 1.05 but remained well above the average of the pre-NIP period. It may be noted that the RIP was launched to support the economywide policy framework which Bangladesh was obliged to follow under the IMF SAF programme initiated in 1986–7. The objective of reducing protection through trade liberalization policies discussed earlier clearly did not materialize until 1987–8. The trade liberalization measures, however, were greatly stepped-up in 1988 and their expected impact would be observed in later years, which are beyond the period covered in this study. The ERA also shows similar time behaviour. Average ERAs were 0.69, 0.94 and 0.85 in the three periods, respectively.

The ERP as an index of incentives reflects the effects of trade policies, while the ERA captures the effects of domestic policies in addition to trade policies. It is important to note that the ERA has always been lower than

Table 8.9 ERP and ERA estimates for manufacturing, Bangladesh, 1974–5 to 1988–9

Years	ERP	ERA
1974–5	0.80	0.63
1975–6	0.86	0.69
1976–7	0.83	0.66
1977–8	0.85	0.68
1978–9	0.82	0.65
1979–80	0.86	0.69
1980–1	0.92	0.75
1981–2	0.91	0.75
1982–3	0.91	0.73
1983–4	1.10	0.91
1984–5	1.15	0.96
1985–6	1.17	0.97
1986–7	1.04	0.84
1987–8	1.06	0.86

Source: HIID/ESEPP (1990d).
ERP: Effective rate of protection.
ERA: Effective rate of assistance.

the ERP, implying that some of the incentives created by trade policies were offset by the negative assistance created by domestic policies.

Consumer goods, capital goods and intermediate goods

The ERA estimates reported in the HIID/ESEPP study (1990a) for forty-seven sectors of the 1976–7 input–output table were aggregated into three sectors by using value-added weights from the 1976–7 input–output table. An aggregate ERA estimate, ERAA for the manufacturing sector as a whole, was also computed using the same weights. These are reported in Table 8.10. The ERA indices show that, through most of the period, consumer goods industries received the highest assistance, followed by capital goods industries. Intermediate goods industries received the lowest assistance. The strength of the bias in favour of consumer goods industries (relative to capital and intermediate goods industries) is more transparent from the indices of bias shown in Table 8.10. The bias against capital goods industries declined remarkably after 1980–1. The next three years, i.e. 1981–2 to 1983–4, in fact represent a reversal of the bias. But the bias is observed again after 1983–4. In the case of consumer goods industries relative to intermediate goods industries, the bias in favour of the former was much greater and consistently higher. Thus, the nature of the assistance regime has remained strongly inclined towards consumer goods industries.

Table 8.10 Effective rates of assistance and relative policy bias for manufacturing industries by economic classification, Bangladesh, 1974–5 to 1987–8

Year	ERAA[a]	ERAC	ERAK	ERAR	ERAC/ ERAK	ERAC/ ERAR
1974–5	0.50	0.65	0.59	0.31	1.08	2.05
1975–6	0.51	0.75	0.63	0.35	1.19	2.16
1976–7	0.49	0.73	0.64	0.33	1.13	2.23
1977–8	0.51	0.76	0.63	0.34	1.21	2.23
1978–9	0.48	0.69	0.62	0.35	1.11	1.96
1979–80	0.50	0.71	0.61	0.36	1.15	1.95
1980–1	0.52	0.74	0.54	0.37	1.35	1.98
1981–2	0.53	0.65	0.68	0.40	0.97	1.62
1982–3	0.58	0.68	0.81	0.48	0.84	1.44
1983–4	0.72	0.88	0.92	0.50	0.94	1.76
1984–5	0.72	0.91	0.90	0.49	1.00	1.85
1985–6	0.73	0.95	0.82	0.49	1.14	1.90
1986–7	0.66	0.86	0.82	0.48	1.04	1.90
1987–8	0.69	0.89	0.80	0.49	1.11	1.81

Source: Computed from data in HIID/ESEPP (1990a).
ERAA: Effective rate of assistance to the manufacturing sector as a whole.
ERAC: Effective rate of assistance to consumer goods industry.
ERAK: Effective rate of assistance to capital goods industry.
ERAR: Effective rate of assistance to intermediate goods industry.
[a] ERRA is computed using value-added weights for the 21 manufacturing sectors of the 1976–7 input-output table. Hence, it is not strictly comparable to the ERA series reported in table 8.9, which is based on value-added weights of the 1986–7 input-output table.

Domestic resource costs

Empirical evidence on the impact of different policy regimes on allocational decisions in the Bangladesh economy is scarce. Only one study by Islam (1979) estimates domestic resource costs (DRC) covering a broad range of manufacturing activities in Bangladesh. The study used two measures of DRC for sixty-two manufacturing activities in 1979. The first measure, short-run DRC (SDRC), estimated DRC under the assumption of a fixed capital stock. The second measure, which allowed for capital accumulation, estimated long-run DRC (LDRC). The Trade and Industrial Policy study (1986) computed DRCs for only a few manufacturing industries.

The major findings of the study by Islam (1979) were: (i) for eighteen activities LDRCs were negative, implying a net drainage of scarce foreign exchange; (ii) for nineteen other activities, estimated LDRCs were positive but greater than the shadow price of foreign exchange, indicating a lack of comparative advantage; (iii) for only twenty-five activities did the value of long-run DRC estimates imply long-run comparative advantage of those manufacturing activities.

Measures of dispersion among DRCs of different activities have been widely used to indicate the degree of allocative efficiency. Coefficients of variation were calculated by us for SDRC and LDRC based on all the

Table 8.11 Dispersion of domestic resource costs, Bangladesh

	Mean	Standard deviation	Coefficient of variation
LDRC (65 manufacturing sectors)	0.65	3.71	5.72
SDRC (65 manufacturing sectors)	1.28	5.54	4.34
Consumer goods industries	−0.49	8.48	−17.33
Capital goods industries	0.92	1.96	2.13
Intermediate goods industries	0.32	1.43	4.50

Source: Computed from data in Islam (1979).

sixty-two manufacturing activities and separately for SDRC of the consumer, capital and intermediate goods industries (Table 8.11). Reclassification of DRCs according to the broader categories were also done by us. All the measures of relative dispersion of DRCs were high. The dispersion is highest in the case of the consumer goods industry, i.e. the group of manufacturing activities which enjoyed the highest protection. It was lowest in the capital goods industry. Estimates of DRC for a large number of manufacturing activities for any other year are not available in the case of Bangladesh. Though both the levels of protection and wide dispersion of the protection structure were directly targeted for reform under the IMF SAF programme, protection levels and their dispersion continue to remain high (World Bank, 1990).

Wide dispersion in DRCs need not, however, indicate a high degree of allocative inefficiency. The jute and textile industries accounted for 24 per cent of industrial output value in 1987–8. The most significant changes in the structure of the manufacturing sector have been the phenomenal growth of 100 per cent export-oriented ready-made garments and pharmaceuticals, mostly based on imported raw material, and fertilizer production based on Bangladesh's domestic gas resources. These manufacturing sectors plus food-processing industries together accounted for 40 per cent of the total output value of the manufacturing sector in 1987–8. There can be little debate about whether Bangladesh has comparative advantage in these products. However, one point about the jute manufacturing industry in this context deserves mention. The jute industry based on domestic raw material mushroomed in the period 1960–8 supported by a highly subsidized export policy regime known as the Bonus Voucher System (BVS). Under the BVS, exporters were provided import entitlements which they could transfer freely to importers at premia of up to 140 per cent in a regime of high overvaluation of the exchange rate. The result was the emergence of an oversized jute manufacturing industry in the late 1960s when synthetic substitutes for jute were already making inroads into the jute products markets. Bangladesh thus inherited an oversized jute industry relative to world demand.

Domestic manufacturers would be eligible for tariff protection only *after* establishment of their units, at which time the National Board of Revenue (NBR) would determine the level of tariff on the competing imported commodity. Imports could even be banned if the NBR was convinced of the existence of significant domestic manufacturing capacity.[3] The practice of providing protection to manufacturing units only after establishment so that the investor, while being assured of high protection prior to establishment of the unit, could not know its precise level, particularly in relation to protection of other industries, appears to have prevented serious allocative inefficiency in an otherwise highly protected sector. Thus, the wide dispersion in DRCs probably did not engender excessive misallocation of resources.

Performance of the manufacturing sector

We now turn to the performance of the industrial sector, given the backdrop of the incentives structure discussed in the previous subsection. Growth of value added, capacity utilization and total factor productivity (TFP) are examined as performance indicators. Unfortunately, the empirical evidence in these areas is scarce.

Growth of manufacturing

The trend growth rate of manufacturing value added from 1974–5 to 1988–90 was 3.5 per cent. Real growth of manufacturing value added in the second half of the 1970s was 4.9 per cent per annum. The growth rate slowed down sharply to an average of 2.5 per cent per annum in the 1980s. In the first five years of the 1980s the real growth rate of the manufacturing sector was a dismal 1.7 per cent per annum. Two features of the manufacturing value added growth performance may be noted. First, the growth rates have been low throughout the past two decades in spite of a heavy policy bias in favour of the sector. Second, there was a serious slowing down of the growth rate in the 1980s in spite of the pronouncement of two successive industrial policies (NIP–1982 and RIP–1986), privatization and liberalization of the trade and industrial policy regimes. However, the recent trade policy reforms, i.e. post-1987 and the NIP–1991, consisting of significant reduction of import tariffs and QRs noted earlier, are not reflected in the growth performance under review here. The share of manufacturing value added in total GDP has remained virtually unchanged at approximately 10 per cent in the last two decades.

Output, employment and real wage indices for consumer goods, capital goods and intermediate goods industries are reported in Table 8.12. These indices were computed based on Bangladesh Bureau of Statistics and World Bank data. The output index for consumer goods depicts stagnation while that of capital goods shows a sharp decline in the 1980s.[4] However, there

Table 8.12 Output, employment and wages in the manufacturing sector, Bangladesh (1973–4 = 100)

	1973–4	1982–3	1987–8
Consumer goods			
Output[a]	100	123	100
Employment[b]	100	114	121
Real wages[c]	100	138	136
Intermediate goods			
Output	100	134	252
Employment	100	90	99
Real wages	100	161	164
Capital goods			
Output	100	731	360
Employment	100	317	386
Real wages	100	143	163

[a] Output indices were computed from Bangladesh Bureau of Statistics and World Bank data.
[b] Employment indices are simple ratios of the average daily employment of production workers aggregated according to the three manufacturing categories in each year to the base year, 1973–4.
[c] Value-added weights were applied to real wage indices reported by the Bangladesh Bureau of Statistics by disaggregated manufacturing sectors to obtain real wage rate indices for the three manufacturing categories shown.

is an upward trend for capital goods for the period 1973–4 to 1987–8 as a whole. Estimated growth rates of output in the period 1973–4 to 1988–9 for consumer, capital and intermediate goods industries were 1.4 per cent, 11.1 per cent and 5.4 per cent respectively over the period. In 1988–9 the contributions of these three categories of industries to gross output value were estimated at: consumer goods, 55 per cent; capital goods, 6 per cent; and intermediate goods, 39 per cent. While the consumer goods industry enjoyed the highest effective protection (in all years except for three years from 1982–3 to 1984–5) its output growth performance has been the poorest. Intermediate goods industries received the least protection – half the level of assistance compared to consumer goods industries – but experienced much higher growth. Both real wages and employment in the most protected industries, i.e. consumer goods, stagnated in the 1980s. Though there was some growth in the intermediate goods sector, employment and real wages stagnated. Relative to the other two sectors, employment and real wages increased most in the capital goods sector which was second-ranked in terms of protection. High protection has not resulted in high growth rates in the manufacturing sectors. Moreover, the most protected sector did not experience the highest growth in output, employment or real wages.

There are alternative estimates of output and value added growth for the manufacturing sectors of Bangladesh. Growth rates of value-added obtained by HIID/ESEPP (1990b) are, in fact, lower than those obtained

Table 8.13 Summary sources of output growth by subgroups of industries, Bangladesh (%)

	Domestic demand	Export growth	Import substitution	Total
1976–7 to 1982–2				
Consumer goods manufacturing industry	94.03	–0.08	6.05	100
Intermediate goods manufacturing industry	323.44	120.35	–343.79	100
Capital goods manufacturing industry	146.25	0.33	–46.58	100
Total	128.89	16.65	–45.54	100
1981–2 to 1988–9				
Consumer goods manufacturing industry	76.57	2.30	21.13	100
Intermediate goods manufacturing industry	46.97	7.61	45.42	100
Capital goods manufacturing industry	119.64	0.57	–20.21	100
Total	64.17	4.89	30.94	100

by us. The picture that emerges for the Bangladesh manufacturing sector over the past two decades is one of low growth of value added and output in spite of the significant economic policy bias in favour of the sector. Whether the experience of industrial stagnation constitutes an indictment of the highly protectionist policy regime is nevertheless difficult to say.

Sources of output growth

Table 8.13 shows the sources of output growth in the manufacturing sector. The analysis of growth is based on the twenty-one manufacturing sectors of the input–output tables of 1976–7, 1981–2 and 1988–9. The contribution of import substitution to output expansion was, in fact, negative in the 1977–82 period for the overall manufacturing sector. It contributed somewhat to output expansion only in the consumer goods sector in this period. The contribution of import substitution increased significantly in the 1980s, with 31 per cent of output expansion of the overall manufacturing sector being contributed by it. Domestic demand remains the major source of output growth, while export growth has contributed very little to overall output growth.

Capacity utilization

There is a great dearth of data and empirical evidence on capacity utilization rates in the Bangladesh manufacturing sectors. The Bangladesh Bureau of

Table 8.14 Deviations from trend output in the manufacturing sector, Bangladesh

Year (1)	Actual (2)	Trend value (3)	CU index[a] (3/2)
1972–3	82.4	82.4	100.0
1973–4	81.6	83.9	97.3
1974–5	71.3	85.4	83.5
1975–6	79.8	86.8	91.9
1976–7	78.9	88.3	89.4
1977–8	86.3	89.8	96.1
1978–9	78.7	92.2	86.2
1979–80	92.4	92.8	99.6
1980–1	94.2	94.2	100.0
1981–2	93.8	94.2	99.6
1982–3	91.5	94.2	97.1
1983–4	94.2	94.2	100.0
1984–5	88.1	92.5	95.3
1985–6	84.4	90.8	93.0
1986–7	85.9	87.2	98.5
1987–8	87.3	87.3	100.0
1988–9	82.3	83.8	98.2

[a] CU index is a capacity utilization index computed as the percentage shortfall from trend-through-peak estimated from Bangladesh Bureau of Statistics output data.

Statistics reports an industrial output index each year. We computed the percentage shortfall from trend-through-peaks estimated from the available annual output indices as a rough indicator of capacity utilization in the absence of better measures. These are reported in Table 8.14. The actual output index has fluctuated without showing any significant trend between 1972–3 and 1988–9. However, there was a positive trend up to 1980–1 which remained unchanged between 1983–4, followed by a negative trend. The percentage shortfall from trend was, however, lower in the 1980s compared to the 1970s. The maximum shortfall from trend in the 1980s was 7 per cent in 1985–6 compared to 21 per cent for the 1970s in 1978–9.

Data on capacity utilization in only two major manufacturing sectors of the Bangladesh economy – jute and cotton textiles – are available since 1974–5. Information for a few other important sectors are available for only two years. There is evidence of large excess capacity (20–40 per cent) in the manufacturing sectors, viz. for jute, cotton yarn and textiles, fertilizer, sugar, chemicals, etc. (Planning Commission, 1991).

Efficiency and factor productivity

We now turn to the evidence on the efficiency of resource use in the manufacturing sector. The data and evidence in this regard are inadequate. However, to obtain some impression of the status in this respect, we looked at available information on total factor productivity.

Table 8.15 Technical efficiency of manufacturing sectors, Bangladesh

Industries	Technical efficiency (%)	
	Minimum	Median
Fish and seafoods	4.5	67.9
Grain milling (flour)	6.9	10.7
Cigarettes	17.3	39.1
Cotton textiles	14.4	57.4
Jute textiles	24.2	34.7
Handloom textiles	8.6	23.2
Knitting mills	59.3	73.6
Tanning and finishing	44.2	65.7
Allopathic medicines	16.5	50.9
Soaps and detergents	18.1	72.1
Match manufacturing	35.6	61.0
Miscellaneous plastic products	72.7	90.0
Iron and steel, rerolling	38.9	66.8
Utensils – aluminium	16.7	24.6
Umbrellas and walking sticks	17.4	61.2

Source: Krishna and Sahota (1991).

Krishna and Sahota (1991) computed technical efficiency at the firm level for thirty industries at the four-digit level of disaggregation. Table 8.15 shows the technical efficiency parameters for fifteen four-digit industries derived from estimated translog frontier production functions. The efficiency parameters are derived as percentages of efficiency of the 'best practice' technology of the industry. The second column of Table 8.15 shows that for 40 per cent of the industries, median firm efficiency was 50 per cent or less and all but *one* industry category (miscellaneous plastic products) operated at less than 75 per cent median efficiency level. Thus, the evidence indicates a high degree of inefficiency in the manufacturing sector.

Total factor productivity (TFP) indices were calculated in the HIID/ESEPP Project for a large number of manufacturing activities both at the establishment and four-digit industry levels and reported for six years (HIID/ESEPP, 1988, 1990b). The overall results show that only 35 per cent of the establishments experienced a positive cumulated TFP growth over the entire reference period (1975–6 to 1983–4).

Table 8.16 shows cumulated TFP indices for selected manufacturing sectors and the percentage of industries experiencing positive cumulated TFP growth in the consumer, capital and intermediate goods industries. Since it would be more useful to identify the industries experiencing better productivity growth rates over the entire reference period, cumulative rather than year-to-year TFP indices have been used. The capital goods sector turns out to be the best performer in this respect, with 56 per cent of the industries yielding a cumulated TFP greater than 1. There is no

Table 8.16 Cumulated total factor productivity (TFP) growth in selected
manufacturing sectors, Bangladesh, 1975–6 to 1983–4

Code	Sector	Cumulated TFP growth
3116	Edible oil	1.4386
3119	Rice milling	1.5859
3126	Tea and coffee processing	0.3638
3141	Cigarettes	0.4828
3201	Cotton textiles	0.2313
3206	Handloom textiles	0.0712
3219	Textile manufacturing	0.6985
3221	Ready-made garments	0.2590
3233	Leather products	1.6200
3241	Leather footwear	0.3150
3501	Allopathic medicine	0.6415
3523	Soap and detergent	0.7351
3203	Jute textiles	0.3992
3411	Pulp and paper	0.6463
3519	Industrial chemicals	0.0838
3529	Chemical products manufacturing	1.2052
3530	Petroleum refining	1.6776
3541	Petroleum products	0.3948
3693	Cement manufacturing	0.7657
3719	Iron and steel industries	0.7495
3821	Engines and turbines	1.4733
3822	Agri machinery and equipment	0.8050
3823	Metal and woodwork machine	1.0738

	Consumer goods	Intermediate goods	Capital goods	Total
Number of industries	48	43	16	107
TFP > 1	15	13	9	37
Percentage	31.25	30.23	56.25	34.58

Source: HIID/ESEPP (1988).

significant difference between the performances of the other two sectors
in this respect, i.e. consumer and intermediate goods industries, with about
30 per cent of industries showing cumulated TFP growth exceeding 1.

It may be expected that the most protected industrial sector would
demonstrate the highest productivity growth. However, the evidence shows
that in the consumer goods industry, which received the greatest protection,
only 34 per cent of the firms experienced positive factor productivity
growth. There is little evidence of dynamic learning and maturity in the
manufacturing sectors.

Within the HIID/ESEPP Project (1990d,e) the relationship between economic incentives (ERAs) and performance given by value-added growth

and TFP growth at the four-digit level of industrial classification was extensively investigated, but no systematic relationship was found.

CONCLUSIONS

In spite of large incentives, particularly to the import-competing sector, the manufacturing sector has experienced low growth rates, low capacity utilization, inefficiency and low factor productivity. The growth rate of the manufacturing sector declined sharply from 4.9 per cent per year in the 1974–80 period to a mere 2.5 per cent in the 1980s. Growth of value added in the manufacturing sector was historically the lowest, at 1.7 per cent per year, in the 1980–5 period. The picture does not change no matter what classification of industries is chosen. Even with primary emphasis on import substitution, better results could have been achieved. The failure to redress the large inequities in the distribution of income and assets, especially in the early years after independence when the political climate for land reforms was favourable, has kept effective demand heavily depressed and acted as a drag on industrial growth.

The inappropriate sequencing of trade, industrial and financial policy reforms has also contributed to poor industrial performance in a major way. Financial reforms should have been undertaken prior to trade and industrial policy reforms. However, financial sector reforms received serious attention only in the late 1980s, i.e. nearly a decade after the other policy reforms were initiated. Privatization of SOEs with the predominant nationalized banking sector untouched simply transferred the financial burden of the government from the fiscal account, i.e. the budget, to the nationalized banking sector, resulting in a massive debt-default problem which has threatened the viability of the entire financial sector.

The financial sector which controls the life of the industrial sector remains predominantly state-owned. Financial allocations (investment and working capital) by the nationalized banks have largely been determined by the degree of access to state power of individuals or groups of individuals seeking bank loans rather than by market signals. Successive political regimes have used the nationalized banking system to extend political patronage and indulge in large-scale corruption. The result has been the growth of a debt-default culture which has threatened the existence of the entire banking sector. A total of Tk.60 billion (or US$1.64 billion in 1991) in industrial loans are now in default, being classified as bad debt, out of Tk.220 billion (US$6.03 billion) in outstanding loans. Fifty-five per cent of the loans were provided to only seven powerful individual firms, all directly connected to the top echelons of state power in Bangladesh by the major DFI, Bangladesh Shilpa Bank, while 85 per cent went to eight business groups in the case of the other major DFI, Bangladesh Shilpa Rin Sangstha. The essence of liberalization, i.e. the promotion of competition, has been defeated as the public-sector monopoly has been replaced by private-sector monopolies. The privatization process in Bangladesh has been grossly mismanaged (Sobhan, 1990). Loan default had become common practice by the mid-1980s and the recovery rates on loans extended by DFIs declined from 16 per cent in 1982–3 to 8 per cent in 1985–6 (Sobhan, 1990). The average recovery rate on industrial loans in the banking sector as a whole is around 16 per cent, i.e. equal to the interest rate on short-term lending. The industrial loan disbursement process shows how the role of economic incentives in guiding investment decisions and promoting growth in the industrial sector has been seriously undermined. Massive reforms in the financial sector to modernize and commercialize their orientation have been greatly delayed, slowing down growth of trade and industrialization in the country.

Trade and exchange rate policy reforms in the 1980s were associated with improvement in both the fiscal and external deficits. This was in no small measure due to complementary contractionary fiscal and monetary policies. However, the deficits are still very large. The pace of trade liberalization has been greatly stepped-up since 1988. With large initial deficits, the liberalization process could increase the deficits further in the short run. In the case of Bangladesh, the entire increase would have to be financed almost entirely by foreign aid, further increasing dependence on external resources.

While nationalization of industrial assets abandoned by non-Bangladeshi owners at the time of the country's independence in 1971 was necessary, extending state ownership to cover industrial assets owned by Bangladeshi owners was *not* essential. The record of managing SOEs has been poor. With firm political commitment better results could have been achieved even with nationalization of the industrial sector. However, it was clear at the very outset that even the first political regime had neither any serious commitment nor the motivated machinery required to manage and implement a strategy of rapid industrialization based on state-owned enterprises. The decision created enormous difficulties, contributing in a major way to the poor industrial performance. First, the nationalization order alienated the nascent Bangladeshi entrepreneurs, destroying their confidence in the political leadership. Their alienation was a major source of instability in an already difficult political situation and contributed to a poor investment climate. Second, the continuity of the process of development of an entrepreneurial class and culture, which began in the late 1950s and was so critical to rapid industrialization of the country, was broken. Third, the state ownership of industrial assets concentrated enormous powers in the hands of the bureaucracy, which developed into a strong vested interest. Public-sector corporations managed by administrative fiat and arbitrary political decisions have been a major source of unproductive rent-seeking in the economy. This vested interest later became a major obstacle to reforms and restructuring of this sector and caused the reform process to be painfully slow. In spite of their repeated proclamations, the post-1975 BNP regime was unable to carry out any significant denationalization. Even the Ershad government could not dismantle the SOEs in nearly one decade. It is clear, therefore, that the SOEs served the interests of all the organs of state power, including the political regimes and bureaucracy. On the whole, nationalization retarded technical change and maturation of infant industries.

Military coups and counter-coups up to the early 1980s followed by large-scale political agitation throughout the 1980s, leading finally to the ousting of President Ershad in 1990, along with continuous labour unrest in the industrial sector, has seriously undermined investment in the manufacturing sector. Such political instability throughout the country's existence has encouraged short-term trading, speculative activities and capital flight.

The policy implementation and reform process in Bangladesh has been very slow. The bureaucratic state machinery has functioned as a retarding juggernaut, slowing down economic growth and structural change in every sector. In addition, successive political regimes have showed little commitment to economic growth and poverty alleviation objectives. Poor governance, reflected in massive corruption, inability to manage rents, the existence of organized smuggling syndicates, gross abuse of the nationalized industrial and financial sectors, macroeconomic mismanagement, etc., has consistently undermined the credibility of the policy formulation and implementation process. Institutional reforms in these crucial areas are as critical as other policy reforms in a low-income country like Bangladesh in order to regenerate and maintain a high growth rate in the manufacturing sector.

NOTES

1 ESEPP: 'Employment and Small Scale Enterprise Policy Planning' Project. The project was executed by the Harvard Institute of International Development (HIID) in Bangladesh from 1986 to 1989.
2 The study used value-added weights of the 1986–7 input–output table to compute the annual average ERP and ERA for the manufacturing sector as a whole. However, the 1986–7 input–output table to has not yet been finalized by the Planning Commission. Therefore we used value-added weights of the 1976–7 input–output table to compute average ERAs in every case in this study.
3 This point has been made by Naqvi and Kemal (1983), Lewis and Soligo (1965), Hamid and Kemal (1991) and Noman (1991), in the case of Pakistan. Until recently, Bangladesh followed the same procedures for extending protection to newly set-up domestic industries.
4 The severalfold increase in the capital goods output index reported by the Bangladesh Bureau of Statistics *Statistical Year Book* and World Bank (1989), in 1982–3 from which the output indices were computed by us is the result of a

massive increase in iron and steel production in that year. The domestic small iron and steel rerolling sector based on shipwrecking suddenly proliferated in the early 1980s. However, the capital goods sector is insignificant within the manufacturing sector.

REFERENCES

Ahmed, M. and Islam, M. (1989) 'Nominal and Effective Rates of Protection in the Bangladesh Textile Economy', *Bangladesh Development Studies* 17 (1–2):57–75.
Balassa, B. (1989) 'A Conceptual Framework for Adjustment Policies', PPR Working Paper, World Bank.
Bangladesh Bureau of Statistics (BBS), *Statistical Year Book*, various issues.
—— (1991) *Report on the Household Expenditure Survey 1988–89*, Dhaka: Bangladesh Bureau of Statistics.
Hamid, N. and Kemal, A.R. (1991) 'Pakistan Industrial Sector Policy Review', mimeo, Asian Development Bank, Manila.
HIID/ESEPP (Harvard Institute of International Development/Employment and Small Scale Enterprise Policy Planning Project). (1988) 'Total Factor Productivity and Efficiency by Size–Class of Manufacturing Enterprises', Working Paper no. 3, Planning Commission, Dhaka.
—— (1990a) 'Effective Rates of Assistance (ERAs) in Bangladesh', Working Paper no. 14, Planning Commission, Dhaka.
—— (1990b) 'Productivity and Economic Development in Bangladesh', Working Paper no. 15, Planning Commission, Dhaka.
—— (1990c) 'A supplement to Working Paper 14: ERAs' Planning Commission, Dhaka.
—— (1990d) 'An Assessment of the Impact of Industrial Policies in Bangladesh', Working Paper no. 16, Planning Commission, Dhaka.
—— (1990e) 'An Identification of Dynamic Industrial Subsectors (HIID/IN Survey Data)', Working Paper no. 20, Planning Commission, Dhaka.
Islam, A. (1979) 'Comparative Advantage of Bangladesh Within the Manufacturing Sector', *Bangladesh Development Studies* VII (4): 43–68.
Krishna, K.L. and Sahota, G.S. (1991) 'Technical Efficiency in Bangladesh Manufacturing Industries', *Bangladesh Development Studies*, IX (1–2): 89–105.
Lewis, S. (1969) *Economic Policy and Industrial Growth in Pakistan*, London: George Allen & Unwin.
Lewis, S. and Soligo, R. (1965) 'Growth and Structural Change in Pakistan Manufacturing Industry, 1954–64', *Pakistan Development Review* 5(1): 94–139.
Mubin, A. (1989) 'Industrial Regulatory and Promotional Policies', unpublished report to the World Bank.
Naqvi, S.N. and Kemal, A.R. (1983) 'Structure of Protection in Pakistan, 1980–81', Pakistan Institute of Development Economics, Islamabad.
Noman, A. (1991) 'Growth-Oriented Industrialization in Pakistan – An Overview and Assessment', paper presented at the UNU/WIDER Conference on Trade and Industrialization Reconsidered, Paris, July.
Planning Commission (1990a) 'Input-Output Structure of the Bangladesh Economy 1981–82', Planning Commission, Government of Bangladesh, March 1990.
—— (1990b) 'Input-Output Structure of the Bangladesh Economy 1988–89', mimeo, Planning Commission, Government of Bangladesh, October 1990.
—— (1991) 'The Fourth Five-Year Plan of Bangladesh, 1990–95', General Economics Division, Planning Commission, Government of Bangladesh.

Rab, A. (1989) 'Value of Bangladesh's Policies to Promote Exports', unpublished report to the World Bank.

Rahman, H. (1950) 'Chittagong Since Partition', *Pakistan Economic Journal* 1(3): 65–81.

Rahman, H.Z., Sen, Binayek and Hossain, M. (1991) 'Rethinking Poverty: Dimensions, Process, Options', APT Project, Bangladesh Institute of Development Studies, Dhaka.

Rahman, S.H. (1991) 'Macroeconomic Stabilization and Adjustment: The Experience of Bangladesh in the 1980s', mimeo, March.

—— (1992) 'The Impact of Trade and Exchange Rate Policies on Agriculture in Bangladesh', Agriculture Diversification Project Working Paper, International Food Policy Research Institute – Bangladesh Institute of Development Studies.

Sobhan, R. (1982) 'The Crisis of External Dependence – The Political Economy of Foreign Aid to Bangladesh', UPL, Dhaka.

—— (1990) 'The Development of the Private Sector in Bangladesh: A Review of the Evolution and Outcome of State Policy', Research Report no. 124, Bangladesh Institute of Development Studies, Dhaka.

World Bank (1984) 'Bangladesh: Economic Trends and Development Administration', vol.II, Statistical Appendix, 27 February, Report no. 4022.

—— (1989) 'Bangladesh: Recent Economic Developments and Short-Term Prospects', Report no. 7596-BD, Asia Country Dept 1, 13 March 1989.

—— (1990) 'Bangladesh: Managing the Adjustment Process – An Appraisal', Report no. 8344-BD, Asia Country Dept 1, 16 March 1990.

9

THE ROLE OF TRADE POLICY IN INDIAN INDUSTRIALIZATION

Isher Judge Ahluwalia

I am grateful to Ms Shelly Gupta for her able research assistance for this project.

Trade policy is only one element, albeit an important one, in the overall industrial policy regime in India. This study begins with a review of the original premises of planning for industrialization and the subsequent evolution of the policy regime with special reference to trade policy changes. This is followed by an analysis of the long-term trends in growth and productivity in the industrial sector as well as the long-term trends in exports and imports. The relationship between trade policy and productivity performance is explored within an econometric framework. The new government which took office in June 1991 has since announced major changes in both industrial policy and trade policy which fall beyond the scope of this paper.

Policy was designed to pursue a multiple set of objectives, for example, growth, diversification, employment generation, regional dispersal, development of the small scale sector, etc. The industrial policy framework was governed not so much by considerations of compensating for perceived market failures but by a strong belief in wide-ranging state intervention designed to guide the destiny of the industrial sector. The regulatory industrial policy framework and the protective trade regime were often interrelated through a complex policy network. In many cases trade distortions were introduced and trade policy was tailored specifically to support inefficient investment decisions which were ordained in pursuit of a multiple set of domestic policy objectives.

THE BROAD STRATEGY

The basic elements of the Indian strategy of industrialization were first put in place at the time of formulating the Second Five Year Plan and were subsequently articulated in the Industrial Policy Resolution of 1956.

A central role for the public sector

Apart from the considerations of bulky investments and long gestation lags in the core infrastructure sectors, e.g. transport, power, coal, etc., which were naturally seen as the exclusive responsibility of the public sector, and the motivation of 'strategic control' of the key sectors, e.g. atomic energy, arms and ammunition, etc., the desire to socialize profits was an additional powerful argument in favour of a central role for the public sector in the industrialization strategy. It was also expected to play a major role in fostering indigenous technological development.

The public sector in India has actually grown over the years, not only in the core or strategic sectors but also in a variety of other sectors, such as hotels, tourism, textiles and baked goods. In many cases the proliferation of the sector resulted from nationalization of unsuccessful units in the private sector. In view of the severe fiscal crisis and the resultant inability of the government to harden the soft budget constraint that these enterprises have become accustomed to, calls for the reform of the public sector have repeatedly been made in recent years.

Emphasis on heavy industries

The emphasis on heavy industries was a second major anchor of the Indian strategy of industrialization, also known as the Mahalanobis strategy after the name of its architect. The emphasis was largely derived from the quest for modern industrial power. Heavy industries such as steel and machine building were seen as prime symbols of modernity. A structural view of growth implied that a higher investment rate at the margin was expected to generate a greater rate of growth of output. Productivity considerations were subsumed in the assumption of a constant capital–output ratio. It was only in the 1980s that some attempts were made to redress this imbalance, as we shall see later. The employment consequences of the heavy industries strategy were sought to be moderated through parallel emphasis on the small-scale sector, at least in the short run. The latter was also expected to meet the increasing demand for consumer goods.

Self-reliance and export pessimism

Self-reliance has long been a principal objective of Indian industrial planning, although the concept of self-reliance was explicitly introduced for the first time only in the Third Five Year Plan (1961–6); it became firmly entrenched in the Fourth Five Year Plan (1969–74). In India self-reliance has in practice been interpreted to mean a strong import-substitution orientation in the development strategy because of the assumption of export pessimism. Even while interpreting self-reliance as import substitution, the aspects that were ignored related to the degree of protection and phasing of protection for different industries in order to establish some limits on the extent of economic inefficiency to be tolerated in the process. The Sixth Plan (1980–5) was the first to make reference to the importance of 'efficient' import substitution.

As for export pessimism, there is no doubt that this assumption dominated the thinking and strategies of many developing economies in the immediate post-Second World War period. Prebisch and Nurkse were two of the most influential prophets of export pessimism. But as events unfolded in the 1960s and the 1970s, many of the developing economies adjusted their course to tap the potential offered by the growth of exports. India, along with some Latin American economies, however, persisted in export pessimism until, for India, it became a self-fulfilling prophecy.

THE POLICY REGIME

The second half of the 1970s stands out as a period of 'official reflection' on the ineffectiveness of the policy instruments in achieving their targets.[1] Emerging from this introspection a process of reorientation of the policy framework began in the late 1970s/early 1980s but for a variety of reasons it seemed to be losing momentum towards the end of the decade. The new decade has brought with it new zeal for liberalization partly derived from confidence that the policies of deregulation and rationalization of the 1980s have had perceptible effects on productivity and growth and partly because the current unprecedented fiscal crisis in the economy has made the need for structural reforms that much more urgent.

The trade policy regime

The overriding principle behind trade policy in the economy has been the desire to provide protection to domestic industry from foreign competition while also conserving scarce foreign exchange. As the import-substitution oriented policies created anti-export biases, attempts were made to offset these biases through export subsidies in various forms. Also, as the process of industrialization led to the creation of an industrial base with a substan-

294

tial demand for a wide variety of intermediate inputs and components, import policy was also guided by the need to provide access to such inputs to meet the production requirements of domestic industry.

Beginning with the late 1970s, easier access to imported inputs was provided through loosening somewhat the quantitative restrictions, while tariffs increased over the same period as did the non-transparency in the tariff regime because of the proliferation of exemptions from custom duties. It was only in the second half of the 1980s that trade policy focused on liberalizing the import of capital goods in the context of giving a thrust to technological upgrading for specified export industries. The exchange rate was not generally used as an instrument of policy although, through most of the decade of the 1970s and again in the late 1980s, there is evidence of real effective depreciation and it is associated with a significantly better performance of exports.

Quantitative restrictions

Quantitative restrictions typically take the form of import licensing, involving physical rationing of imports. The system of import licensing basically caters to capital goods and intermediate goods since imports of consumer goods have been largely banned all along, except for mass consumption goods, e.g. foodgrains, edible oils, kerosene, etc. The latter, as well as 'crucially essential' products such as petroleum and fertilizers, are subject to 'canalization' or monopoly import through designated public-sector agencies, such as the Indian Oil Corporation and the State Trading Corporation. The share of established importer (trader) licences has declined over the years, and the actual user licences (for intermediate goods) and capital goods licences (for investment) have come to dominate the licensing regime.

For intermediate goods, i.e. raw materials and components, the import policy contains lists of items that are (i) banned; (ii) restricted, i.e. very rarely allowed under licences; (iii) permissible, i.e. relatively easily allowed against licence; and (iv) on Open General Licence (OGL). For capital goods, policy is generally one of protecting indigenous production through the mechanism of CG (capital goods) licences. The industrial licensing framework has also provided an additional instrument for the quantitative control of imports of capital goods because industrial licences are frequently not given where imports of capital goods would be high.

In a review of the import control regime as it stood at the end of the 1960s, Bhagwati and Desai (1970) highlighted how the twin criteria – the essentiality criterion and the indigenous availability criterion – imparted considerable inflexibility to the pattern of utilization of imports. Bhagwati and Srinivasan (1975) show how strict quantitative import restrictions were imposed during the period from 1956 to 1962 and were followed in the subsequent five-year period by export subsidies to offset anti-export biases of the import control regime, on the one hand, and customs duties to mop up part of the increased premia on the imports within the restrictive regime, on the other.[2]

When the exchange value of the rupee was lowered in June 1966, the scope of the export subsidies was substantially reduced and import duties were also lowered. As a result, the net devaluation on the (visible) trade account was estimated by Bhagwati and Srinivasan (1975) to be 21.6 per cent for exports and 42.3 per cent for imports when gross devaluation of the rupee was of the order of 57.5 per cent. The abortive attempt at liberalization following the ill-timed devaluation (in-between the two major agricultural droughts of the decade) is by now part of history.

Much of the decade of the 1970s basically witnessed a relapse into a regime of quantitative restrictions supplemented by tariff protection and export subsidization. The trade policy regime became increasingly non-transparent and complex. Many of the anomalies of the regime were brought to light by a number of official committees which submitted their reports in the late 1970s and early 1980s: i.e., the Alexander Committee (1978), Tandon Committee (1980) and Hussain Committee (1984).

In an attempt to simplify the procedures in the late 1970s, not only were the raw material imports made easier but also the range of readily importable (i.e. OGL) items was increased. For the first time, what was not specified on the banned or the restricted list of imports could be imported automatically on OGL. With a view to facilitating technological upgrading there was also some easing of administrative constraints on the imports of capital goods within the discretionary framework.

In the mid-1980s an element of stability was injected into the policy regime by switching over to the announcement of trade policy every three years instead of every year. While there was some backtracking after the attempt in 1985 at lowering the duty on certain capital goods imports, the gradual shift away from quantitative controls was more durable.

The trade policy for 1985–8 focused on the liberalization of the import of capital goods by placing them on OGL with a view to facilitating the process of technological upgrading of Indian industry, particularly for exports. In the Import–Export Policy of 1988–91 the liberalized access to machinery and equipment for selected export industries was extended to more industries, e.g. electronics, tea and silk. Moreover, for the first time, some selected capital goods for exporting industries were allowed to be imported without clearance from the indigenous availability angle.

A profile of import licensing in India prepared by the World Bank (1989) at the end of the 1980s shows that as much as 21 per cent of the items of manufactured goods imports cannot be classified, suggesting a lack of transparency in the system. Based on output-weighted items on HS codes (i.e. harmonized system classification used to report imports and tariffs), 80 per cent of the imported items are in restricted categories, 9 per cent in canalized categories, and only 11 per cent on OGL. The analysis in this study also shows that the distribution of actual imports by licensing categories tends to understate the degree of restrictiveness. This is because many items on the restricted list are not imported.

Notwithstanding the complexity and the non-transparency of the import control regime, the evidence points towards some loosening of the quantitative restrictions during the decade of the 1980s. A major exception to this process of loosening was the introduction of the phased manufacturing programme (PMP) which required indigenization of certain newly set-up domestic industrial units, although this programme itself is now being phased out.

The tariff structure

Tariffs on Indian imports consist of three parts: the basic customs duty (mostly *ad valorem*) applied to the CIF price of the import, an auxiliary duty applied to the CIF price[3], and an 'additional' countervailing duty (CVD) which is equal to the excise duty levied on the locally produced product and applied to the CIF price plus the basic customs duty plus the auxiliary duty. The basic customs duty plus the auxiliary duty together constitute a protective tariff, while the 'additional' CVD represents the non-protective part of the tariff.

The loosening of the import licensing regime after the late 1970s was associated with an upward trend in tariff rates. A recent analysis by the World Bank (1989) based on comparisons of forty-six chapters of the Tariff Schedule in 1977 and 1982 shows that during this period the average protective tariff (i.e. basic plus auxiliary duty) increased in every case when weighted by imports.

The customs tariff structure for a number of sectors of the Indian economy is presented in Table 9.1. The average nominal protective tariff for 1989–90 is 116.5 per cent, while the non-protective element of the tariff amounts to 25 per cent. Manufacturing sectors, with the exception of machinery and transport equipment, have protective rates of much more than 100 per cent. As one would expect, the import-weighted tariffs are lower than the nominal tariffs. The variance among the different subsectors is also greater for import-weighted tariffs than for nominal tariffs, implying that the goods that are allowed to be imported have significantly lower tariffs.

The large difference between the nominal tariff rates and the actual duty collection rates reflects the proliferation of the exemptions and of duty-free imports for export production. As Table 9.2 shows, average duty collection rates on total imports increased from 21 per cent in 1969–70 to 31 per cent in 1979–80 and then almost doubled to 60 per cent in 1987–8. The

Table 9.1 Customs tariff structure, India, 1987–8

| | % Distribution of | | Tariffs | | | | Collection rates | |
| | Imports | Customs duties | Nominal[a] | | Trade-weighted | | | |
			P	T	P	T	P	T
Total	100.0	100.0	116.5	141.7	78.7	92.0	54.1	61.2
Agriculture	4.3	1.6	87.8	90.3	37.5	39.7	21.6	21.9
Energy	14.8	14.2	92.6	115.1	60.7	60.7	54.6	55.5
Minerals	1.9	0.8	99.5	103.6	24.3	27.8	20.7	23.1
Manufacturing	79.9	83.4	119.2	146.6	85.6	102.2	56.6	65.3
Food, beverages, etc.	3.9	4.1	135.1	147.1	79.6	87.4	59.5	60.7
Textiles and leather	1.1	1.4	136.1	158.4	121.0	171.9	43.8	72.1
Petroleum and coal products	4.9	2.7	128.1	176.3	104.8	131.6	12.6	32.6
Chemicals	13.5	20.4	118.3	156.4	94.0	124.0	70.0	87.2
Non-metallic minerals	9.5	0.8	126.3	171.0	49.6	52.7	3.8	4.7
Metals	11.2	15.6	117.2	132.9	88.9	101.4	70.7	80.2
Metal products	1.2	1.1	131.0	167.9	99.1	130.9	45.3	56.8
All machinery	21.3	24.8	92.0	109.3	89.3	100.6	62.6	67.3
Electrical appliances and electronics	3.8	3.9	105.1	144.6	96.3	128.7	48.3	58.3
Transport equipment	2.2	2.2	95.7	125.7	74.5	90.7	50.4	58.0
Others	6.5	6.4	115.4	147.4	81.6	93.7	49.7	56.1

Source: Directorate General of Commercial Intelligence and Statistics, Ministry of Commerce, Government of India and World Bank estimates.
P, Protective; T, Total.
[a] The nominal tariff structure relates to the year 1989–90. There has been only marginal change in the nominal tariff structure between 1987–8 and 1989–90.

three subsequent years have clearly seen a decline in the collection rates, but this has only brought the incidence of custom duties at the end of the 1980s to about the level of the mid-1980s. For the decade as a whole, there has been a clear increase in the incidence of custom tariffs.

Import duties have become an increasingly important source of revenue for the budget. From an average of 11–11.5 per cent of total current revenues all through the 1960s and the 1970s, customs revenues increased their share in the total to 15 per cent in the first half of the 1980s and almost 20 per cent in the second half of the 1980s (see Bagchi and Nayak, 1993). The potential revenue loss from tariff reform therefore causes concern to policymakers unless alternative means are found for maintaining the growth of revenues.

Effective protection

A few studies are available for India reporting effective rates of protection (ERPs) at different points in time, some depending upon the prevailing

Table 9.2 Import duty collection rates, India (%)

Year	Total imports	Manufactures			Intermediate materials
		Capital goods			
		Machinery	Transport	Total	
1960–1	13.8	7.3	3.8	6.5	21.2
1965–6	38.9	35.8	25.3	34.3	60.2
1969–70	20.7	26.5	25.9	26.4	27.4
1975–6	25.8	45.7	44.0	45.4	50.6
1979–80	31.2	63.3	28.3	54.7	54.8
1985–6	48.4	60.7	52.7	59.6	75.4
1986–7	55.8	71.5	56.9	69.7	56.9
1987–8	60.3	88.6	44.4	81.9	57.7
1988–9	55.1	86.3	52.1	81.4	49.8
1989–90	49.9	65.9	30.4	59.6	50.1
1990–1	47.0	64.0	42.0	60.4	7.3

Source: World Bank estimates up to 1985–6, Ministry of Finance data after 1985–6.

tariff rates to measure differences between domestic and world prices of inputs and outputs and others depending upon direct international price comparisons. In situations where quantitative restrictions are widespread, the price comparison method is clearly superior since the actual level of protection may be much higher than implied in the tariff. Equally it is possible that there is 'water' in the tariff in the sense that tariff levels are much higher than is really needed for protection.

Bhagwati and Desai (1970) estimated the average rate of effective protection due to tariff and non-tariff factors in 1961 and 1962 to be in the range of 80–100 per cent for eighteen industries. Panchamukhi's (1978) disaggregated estimates of ERP based on tariff rates and premia rates on import licences for 1968–9 were 91 per cent and 165 per cent for food and non-food consumer goods, respectively, 143 per cent and 106 per cent for agro-based intermediate goods and other intermediate goods, respectively, and 78 per cent for capital goods. Nambiar (1983) estimated ERPs for 1968–9 using the two alternative methods and found the difference to be very large. The average rate of effective protection for manufactured goods for 1968–9 as estimated by Nambiar was 140 per cent when based on the tariff route and only 41 per cent when based on the direct price comparison route.

Table 9.3 presents the frequency distribution of manufacturing industries by their degree of effective protection as estimated in a recent World Bank (1989) study using direct price comparisons. Effective protection is high (i.e. 70 per cent or more) for 39 per cent of manufacturing; moderate (i.e. between 30 and 70 per cent) for only about 6 per cent; and low (i.e. 30 per cent or less) for about 55 per cent. The relatively low rates of protection

Table 9.3 Approximate nominal and effective protection of manufacturing industries in India

Protection category	Number of sectors	Gross, value added (% share)	Fixed capital per person (Rs'000)	Average wage (Rs'000)
Nominal, inputs				
H	28	39.9	33.3	14.8
M	8	9.4	33.8	10.8
L	20	50.4	31.3	8.8
?	3	0.3	15.7	9.8
Nominal, outputs				
H	27	33.0	56.4	14.5
M	13	39.1	50.8	14.9
L	16	27.6	12.9	7.3
?	3	0.3	15.7	9.8
Effective				
H	21	39.0	92.5	15.8
M	5	5.6	32.4	18.0
L	30	53.0	17.8	9.4
?	3	0.3	15.7	9.8

Source: World Bank (1989).
H: High – 70% protection rate or more.
M: Moderate – between 30 and 70% protection rate.
L: Low – 30% protection rate or less.

resulting from the World Bank study are in line with Nambiar's earlier estimates.

One possible explanation for this phenomenon may be that in many large labour-intensive sectors such as food processing, sugar, textiles, garments and bicycles in which domestic competition is substantial, the latter may well have been sufficient to keep prices below the levels that they might otherwise reach because of tariffs. In effect, there is tariff redundancy in these cases. More generally, the apparently low ERP levels need to be seen together with non-price factors when judging the competitiveness of these industries. This is because long years of insulation have led to product types and qualities in many sectors which are out of line with those prevailing abroad and they would not be able to stand product quality competition very easily even if they were pricewise competitive.

An important aspect of the nature of trade distortion is the extent of variation in nominal and effective protection rates across industries. A common criticism of the Indian tariff structure, and one that is borne out by the data in Tables 9.1 and 9.3, is that rates of protection vary substantially over sectors. A recent study for the Asian Development Bank by Kelkar, *et al.* (1990) also reports effective rates of protection for selected industries estimated during the late 1980s which range from 0–40 per cent for some metal-based industries at one end to as much as 500 per cent for urea.

Bias against exports

The effect of the protective regime in discriminating against exports has been analysed at length in the Indian literature, although quantification of this bias is not easy. The Tandon Committee (1980) highlighted the nature of these biases. Estimates made for 1980–1 by the Industrial Credit and Investment Corporation of India (ICICI, 1989) for fourteen industries also show that in eleven of the fourteen industries the effective protection coefficient (EPC) for domestic sales exceeded that for export sales by a substantial margin. The unweighted average EPC for export sales in the ICICI study was 0.74, indicating negative protection of 26 per cent, while the average EPC for domestic sales was 2.04, indicating effective protection of 104 per cent.

In recognition of the need to compensate exporters for the anti-export biases created by the trade policy regime, several policy interventions evolved over time. Some examples are advance licences to provide duty-free access to specified inputs, drawback of customs and excise duties on materials, cash compensation payments to offset the effect of other indirect taxes, and subsidy schemes in some industries for refunding to exporters the difference between the world prices and the domestic prices of locally produced inputs, e.g. steel and rubber. There has also evolved a system of replenishment (REP) licences which enables exporters, on the strength of their export realization, to import raw materials or components which they need or to sell the licence to others who need to import. Other measures to promote exports have also included the development of free trade zones and bonded manufacturing, assistance in the development of export markets, interest subsidies, and income tax waivers. In more recent years, efforts have also been made to provide access to modern capital goods at lower rates of customs duty.

It is possible that the discriminatory effect on exports was reduced over the 1980s, but no verifiable estimates are available of such a trend. The increasing budgetary burden of these subsidies, however, is ambiguous. Total export subsidies (not including the gems and jewellery sector) increased from US$130 million in 1970–1 to US$922 million in 1980–1 and further to US$1,594 million in 1987–8 (Table 9.4). As a proportion of exports, these subsidies almost doubled from 12.7 per cent in 1970–1 to 22.1 per cent in 1980–1 and further to 24.5 per cent in 1987–8. The growing burden of these subsidies on the budget has been a matter of considerable concern in recent years. As part of the new policy initiatives of July 1991, a significant step was taken to abolish the cash assistance to exporters and

Table 9.4 Incentives for manufactured exports, India

	1970–1	1980–1	1981–2	1982–3	1983–4	1984–5	1985–6	1986–7	1987–8
Total subsidies (in US$ millions)	129.9	922.2	993.5	883.7	850.5	894.1	950.8	1223.2	1594.1
Total exports (in US$ millions)	1026.1	4177.7	4315.5	3740.1	3649.6	4253.4	4047.9	4577.7	6490.3
Subsidies as a % of exports									
Total	12.7	22.1	23.0	23.6	23.3	21.0	23.5	26.7	24.5
Export promotion	5.4	12.1	12.4	13.2	12.3	10.2	12.2	13.5	11.0
Of which cash assistance	(n.a.)	(11.4)	(11.7)	(12.5)	(11.4)	(n.a.)	(n.a.)	(n.a.)	(n.a.)
Duty drawbacks	4.2	5.0	5.3	3.5	3.5	3.0	3.2	3.1	2.9
Advance licence	0.0	3.4	3.7	5.1	5.7	6.0	6.1	8.2	8.6
REP premia	3.1	1.6	1.6	1.8	1.8	1.8	1.9	1.9	2.0

Source: World Bank.

also withdraw the interest subsidy for exports. Offsets were provided by substantially widening the scope of REP licences and by devaluing the rupee.

Policies towards foreign investment and import of technology

As a general principle, foreign investment in Indian industry has been acceptable only as a means of transfer of technology, and the policy has tended to be discretionary and rather restrictive. In 1973 the Foreign Exchange Regulation Act (FERA) laid down certain guidelines for the dilution of foreign shareholdings of equity to a maximum of 40 per cent with a view to restricting foreign exchange outflows arising out of dividend and royalty payments. The companies which diluted their holdings were then supposed to be treated on a par with Indian companies and the rest were known as FERA companies.

Approvals for investments and technology were subsequently governed by the Technology Policy Statement of 1983. The emphasis has been on selectivity and filling technological gaps. In May 1990 there was some deregulation allowing an entrepreneur to conclude an agreement with a collaborator without consulting the government, provided the royalty payment did not exceed 5 per cent of domestic sales and 8 per cent of exports. In selected areas, investments with up to 40 per cent foreign equity have been allowed on an automatic basis. Investment flows in India even at the end of the 1980s, however, continue to be very small – about US$200 million per year compared with US$2.3 billion for China, US$1.1 billion for Thailand, US$700 million for Indonesia and US$500 million for the Philippines.

Industrial Policy Regime

The import-substitution oriented trade policy regime was buttressed by a heavily regulated domestic industrial policy framework. Its principal instrument – the Industries Development and Regulation (IDR) Act of 1951 – was designed to channel industrial investments in 'socially desired directions'. It controlled both entry into an industry and expansion of existing capacity.

Apart from the administrative hurdles, the more serious economic consequence of the industrial licensing system was its contribution towards creating barriers to entry into individual industries and thereby severely limiting the degree of competition within the domestic industrial sector, which was already highly insulated from foreign competition through the restrictive trade policy regime.[4] As demands from the small-scale sector became more pressing in the late 1960s, supplementary instruments were devised to meet these demands. The move from promotional policies (development of physical and institutional infrastructure) up to the late 1960s to protective policies (reservation in production for small-scale sector and fiscal concessions) in the subsequent period represented a significant change in instrumentality.

As for industrial dispersal, the industrial licensing framework as well as policies of freight equalization for certain major inputs, e.g. iron and steel, cement, etc., were used with a view to promoting industries in areas located away from major sources of raw materials and production centres. In the course of time, industrial dispersion also relied increasingly on financial incentives and concessions. There was a tendency to license a number of plants of suboptimal scale in different regions as opposed to one large plant which would exploit the economies of scale. Problems were further compounded by the fact that this happened even when the necessary preconditions of infrastructure development in these regions were not met.

A parallel development in the late 1960s was the emphasis placed on checking the concentration of economic power. The Monopolies and Restrictive Trade Practices (MRTP) Act was passed in 1969 and came into force from 1 June 1970. This Act sought to regulate the expansion of large industrial houses and/or 'dominant' undertakings by subjecting investment and expansion proposals of such undertakings to separate scrutiny over and above the industrial licensing approvals required under the IDR Act.[5] The MRTP Act managed to accentuate the already slow and cumbersome functioning of the system by subjecting the MRTP cases to stringent and long enquiries.

If barriers to entry into the Indian industrial sector were many, the exit

303

routes were also blocked by labour legislation which was designed to protect the interests of those who are employed in the organized sector. Under the Industrial Disputes Act it is not possible to retrench workers and close an establishment that employs one hundred or more workers without the permission of the government. Other laws and procedures also make it practically impossible for a non-viable industrial unit to close down.

Following an extensive phase of 'official reflection', a process of reorientation of industrial policies began in the late 1970s and gathered some momentum in the 1980s. The most important changes have related to reducing the domestic barriers to entry and expansion to inject a measure of competition in domestic industry, simplifying procedures, and obtaining more flexibility in the use of installed capacity with a view to facilitating supply responses to changing demand conditions. Large business houses have been allowed to play a larger role in industrial development. Recognizing the need for technological upgrading, policies have also sought to provide a thrust to the modernization of the capital stock in Indian industry. However, conspicuous by their absence in the domestic policy reform package have been the steps needed to reduce if not eliminate the barriers to exit.

Price and distribution controls of 'essential' or 'crucial' products, e.g. coal, fertilizers, cement, aluminium, sugar and steel, also formed an important part of the industrial policy regime up to the end of the 1970s. However, the extent of their control was liberalized significantly in the 1980s.

Another significant development during the 1980s was the long overdue emphasis placed on infrastructure sectors, e.g. electricity, railways and coal. Following a decade of neglect, there was some improvement (from 4 per cent per annum to 5 per cent per annum) in the growth of infrastructure investment in the second half of the 1970s, even when the growth of public investment showed very little pick-up. This was followed by a stronger resurgence in infrastructure growth at the rate of 10 per cent per annum during the Sixth Plan period and the first few years of the Seventh Plan.

The revival of investment in the infrastructure sectors was also associated with discernible improvement on the efficiency front. For example, against the past performance of a steadily declining load factor in thermal power plants from 55.9 per cent in 1976–7 to 44.6 per cent in 1980–1, there was a distinct turning around so that the plant load factor reached a level of 56.5 per cent in 1987–8, a little above the earlier peak achievement of 1976–7. The subsequent years, however, have seen some deterioration in the plant load factor, while the regional variation in the power situation has also persisted throughout. Efforts to streamline railway operations and measures towards technological upgrading have also helped in bringing about better efficiency in this sector. Net tonne kilometres per tonne of wagon capacity experienced a strong and sustained improvement after 1980–1.

While it would be far-fetched to conclude that the infrastructure constraint to industrial growth was overcome in the 1980s, it is reasonable to argue that a new beginning was made after the cumulative neglect of a decade and a half.

PERFORMANCE OF INDUSTRIAL GROWTH, PRODUCTIVITY AND EXPORTS

The performance of industrial growth, productivity and exports over the three decades 1960–90 needs to be analysed against the background of overall macroeconomic developments during this period. Such a perspective is provided in Table 9.5 which presents the trends in the major economic indicators.

An overview of saving-investment trends and growth trends shows, on the one hand, that the increase in saving and investment rates in the 1970s was associated with a slowdown in the growth of GDP from 3.8 per cent per annum in the 1960s to 3.3 per cent per annum in the 1970s. In the 1980s, on the other hand, stagnation in the overall savings rate and a small increase in the investment rate were associated with a significant acceleration in GDP growth to 5.6 per cent per annum. Industrial growth showed much the same pattern over the three decades.

The slowdown in growth in the 1970s was associated with an increase in the inflation rate, while the growth revival of the 1980s was associated with some slowing down of inflation as measured by increases in the wholesale price index and the implicit GDP deflator. Another significant development during the 1980s was the emergence and continuance of a deficit on the revenue budget (i.e. current fiscal account). The process of dissaving began as early as 1982–3 and got steadily worse so as to reach a level of 3.4 per cent of GDP for the Centre, States and Union Territories taken together in the year 1989–90. The overall fiscal deficit during the same year stood at 11.3 per cent of GDP.

A more interesting and useful analysis of the trends in growth and productivity can be obtained by reviewing the performance with reference to a different periodization. The period from 1960–1 to 1987–8, for which consistent data on value added and factor inputs in the manufacturing sector are available, can be divided into three sub-periods: (i) the first half of the 1960s which was the heyday of the Mahalanobis strategy of industrialization; (ii) the period from the mid-1960s to the end of the 1970s which can be characterized as the period of 'industrial drift' although it includes the second half of the 1970s when reflection and some action on policy reorientation began; and (iii) the subsequent period which was marked by a clear move towards deregulation and liberalization. The per-

Table 9.5 Macroeconomic indicators, India

(*a*) Selected ratios (% of GDP)

Year	Saving	Investment	Trade in goods and services		Current account BOP	Fiscal deficit[a]	
			Exports	Imports		Current	Overall
1960–1	12.7	15.7	4.8	7.6	−2.4	0.5	n.a.
1970–1	15.7	16.6	4.1	4.2	−1.0	0.3	n.a.
1980–1	21.2	22.7	6.5	10.0	−1.2	0.1	−9.4
1981–2	20.9	22.6	6.4	9.4	−1.5	0.6	−8.1
1982–3	19.1	20.6	6.7	9.2	−1.3	−0.2	−8.8
1983–4	18.8	20.0	6.5	8.6	−1.1	−1.1	−9.4
1984–5	18.2	19.6	6.9	9.1	−1.2	−1.9	−11.1
1985–6	19.7	22.1	6.0	8.9	−2.3	−1.9	−11.3
1986–7	18.4	20.6	6.0	8.5	−2.0	−2.6	−12.2
1987–8	20.3	22.4	6.3	8.6	−1.9	−3.0	−11.4
1988–9	21.1	23.9	6.6	9.6	−2.6	−3.1	−10.8
1989–90	21.7	24.1	7.8	10.6	−2.3	−3.4	−11.3

(*b*) Selected growth rates (% per annum)

	1960–1 to 1970–1	1970–1 to 1980–1	1980–1 to 1989–90	1960–1 to 1965–6	1965–6 to 1979–80
GDP (at constant prices)	3.8	3.3	5.6	4.2	3.6
GDP in industry (at constant prices)	5.0	4.8	7.1	7.3	4.8
Prices					
Implicit GDP deflator	7.0	8.4	7.8	6.4	7.3
Wholesale price index	7.1	9.1	6.6	6.0	8.1
Consumer price index	7.2	7.8	8.5	6.6	7.2

Sources: Economic Survey, Ministry of Finance, Government of India, and National Accounts Statistics, Central Statistical Organization, Ministry of Planning, Government of India.
[a] For Centre, States and Union Territories taken together.

iodization essentially reflects differences in performance with respect to growth and productivity in the manufacturing sector.[6]

The picture that emerges is one of rapid growth during the first half of the 1960s and again during the 1980s, separated by a long period of stagnation. This is as much true for manufacturing (Table 9.6) as for industry (Table 9.5). There is a difference in the growth performance in the two 'rapid growth' periods, however (Table 9.6). The rapid growth of the earlier period was associated with high rates of growth of factor inputs and poor productivity growth. By contrast, the resurgence of rapid growth in the more recent period was marked by a moderate growth of investment, a decline in employment and strong productivity growth. A remarkable feature of the fifteen-year period from 1965–6 to 1979–80 is that

Table 9.6 Trends in productivity and growth, India, 1959–60 to 1987–8

	Total factor productivity			Labour productivity			Capital productivity			Value added			Capital stock			Employment		
	I	II	III	I	II	III	I	II	III	I	II	III	I	II	III	I	II	III
Manufacturing	0.2	-0.3	2.5	4.9	1.4	7.3	-3.8	-1.9	-0.8	9.1	5.0	6.5	13.4	7.0	7.4	4.0	3.5	-0.7
Intermediate goods	-0.9	-0.9	-1.8	4.4	1.5	6.4	-5.0	-2.7	-0.8	10.9	4.4	6.3	16.8	7.4	7.2	6.2	2.9	-0.1
Consumer non-durables	0.4	-0.5	3.8	4.2	0.3	8.9	-2.9	-1.2	-0.2	5.0	4.7	6.8	8.2	6.0	7.0	0.7	4.4	-2.0
Consumer durables	2.5	0.9	3.0	4.8	3.2	8.2	-0.4	-2.0	-0.9	14.0	8.0	10.6	14.5	10.2	11.6	8.8	4.7	2.2
Capital goods	2.7	1.7	2.0	6.2	4.3	5.4	-1.2	-0.9	-0.6	15.6	6.7	6.1	17.0	7.7	6.7	8.8	2.2	0.6

Source: Ahluwalia (1991).
Figures relate to semi-log trends of the indices of total factor productivity (translog index derived by using the growth accounting method), average labour productivity and average capital productivity. For details on methodology, see Ahluwalia (1991). Periods I, II and III denote 1959–60 to 1965–6, 1965–6 to 1979–80, and 1980–1 to 1987–8, respectively.

while growth of the capital stock declined *pari passu* with the slowdown in the growth of value added, growth of employment did not record a slow-down on a similar scale. After a long period of indifferent performance, productivity growth picked up during the 1980s. This is true whether we analyse total factor productivity growth or growth in partial productivities (Table 9.6). It is worth noting that the consumer goods sectors were the leaders in the turnabout in productivity growth after 1979–80.

The resurgence in growth and significant improvement in productivity performance of the industrial sector during the period from 1980–1 to 1987–8, however, were not associated with an export boom which came in the late 1980s (Table 9.8). In order to explore the factors underlying the performance of exports, it is important to analyse export trends at a disaggregated level. Table 9.7 presents the structure of exports and imports at four different points in time, while Table 9.8 presents the growth of total exports, total imports and their major categories.

The share of agricultural exports declined from 44 per cent in 1960–1 to less than 18 per cent in 1989–90, while that of manufactured products increased from 45 per cent to 75 per cent (Table 9.7). Much of the latter

Table 9.7 Structure of exports and imports, India

	1960–1	1970–1	1980–1	1989–90
A. Exports				
Agriculture and allied products	44.2	31.7	30.6	17.6
Iron ore	2.6	7.6	4.5	3.3
Petroleum products	0.6	0.3	0.1	2.5
Manufactured goods	45.3	50.3	55.8	74.6
Gems and jewellery	0.1	2.8	9.6	19.1
Ready-made garments	0.1	1.9	8.4	11.6
Engineering goods	2.0	12.0	13.0	8.5
Chemicals and allied products	1.1	2.3	3.5	7.8
Leather and leather manufactures	3.9	4.7	5.0	7.0
Jute manufactures	21.0	12.3	4.9	1.1
Other manufactures	17.0	14.2	11.3	19.4
Other exports	7.2	10.0	8.9	1.9
Total exports	100.0	100.0	100.0	100.0
B. Imports				
Petroleum oil and lubricants	6.1	8.3	41.9	17.8
Fertilizers	1.1	5.1	5.2	5.0
Cereal and cereal preparation	16.1	13.0	0.8	1.1
Edible oils	0.3	1.4	5.4	0.6
Capital goods	31.7	24.7	15.2	24.9
Other imports	44.6	47.4	31.4	50.5
Total imports	100.0	100.0	100.0	100.0

Source: Directorate General of Commercial Intelligence and Statistics, Ministry of Commerce, Government of India and World Bank estimates.

Table 9.8 Growth of exports and imports, India (% per annum)

	1960–1 to 1969–70	1970–1 to 1979–80	1980–1 to 1989–90	1980–1 to 1985–6	1985–6 to 1989–90
A. Exports					
Agriculture and allied products	5.5	15.5	8.7	8.6	10.9
Iron ore	23.9	12.6	11.3	12.4	12.2
Petroleum products	13.9	7.3	26.2	127.0	4.0
Manufactured goods	10.3	17.1	19.7	11.5	34.9
Gems and jewellery	62.5	38.5	25.1	18.2	39.0
Ready-made garments	42.8	40.0	20.7	14.0	30.6
Engineering goods	36.3	24.1	7.9	2.7	22.5
Chemicals and allied products	17.5	24.1	25.6	18.0	45.2
Leather and leather manufactures	16.1	19.7	23.2	18.3	26.6
Jute manufactures	6.3	0.9	0.1	–1.3	2.2
Other manufactures	7.2	13.3	22.6	10.5	45.6
Other exports	12.9	14.5	–0.6	–17.5	21.2
Total exports (Rs)	10.2	19.3	14.9	11.3	26.5
(US$)	3.2	18.1	7.2	3.3	15.9
(volume index)	3.6	7.3	3.6	1.1	11.5
Non-petroleum exports (US$)	3.2	18.1	7.7	1.1	16.9
B. Imports					
Petroleum oil and lubricants	3.8	41.0	–1.8	–0.8	9.3
Fertilizers	33.7	17.8	12.9	23.8	0.5
Cereal and cereal preparation	13.4	–2.8	5.0	–3.4	56.0
Edible oils	18.9	51.5	–3.4	6.9	–21.3
Capital goods	4.5	16.5	19.7	17.5	16.4
Other imports	4.8	17.4	16.9	13.2	23.9
Total imports (Rs)	7.2	21.6	11.2	9.1	16.4
(US$)	0.5	19.3	5.4	1.4	10.5
(volume index)	1.9	4.5	5.9	4.8	6.2
Non-petroleum imports (US$)	0.7	15.4	10.4	6.4	12.5

Source: Directorate General of Commercial Intelligence and Statistics, Ministry of Commerce, Government of India and World Bank estimates.

actually took place in the 1980s. There was also a massive increase in the export of petroleum and products in the first half of the 1980s, after the major discovery of oil in the offshore fields off the west coast of India (commonly known as Bombay High), but with the development of the refinery capacity, these exports tapered off as fast as they had surged (Table 9.8).

Total export growth in US dollars had accelerated from 3.2 per cent per annum in the 1960s to 18 per cent per annum in the 1970s and then

Table 9.9 Real effective exchange rate of Indian rupee

Years	I	II	III
1971	88.31	–	78.56
1972	90.15	–	80.53
1973	95.12	–	83.93
1974	92.74	–	83.33
1975	100.00	–	80.59
1976	111.20	–	92.87
1977	110.55	–	102.15
1978	120.66	–	103.14
1979	120.98	–	111.41
1980	110.72	–	108.05
1981	105.89	125.08	100.00
1982	108.29	124.80	99.95
1983	105.10	119.90	101.76
1984	–	122.38	98.79
1985	–	129.38	100.33
1986	–	145.22	106.34
1987	–	158.03	123.49
1988	–	165.48	–
1989	–	182.91	–

Data in column I are from Joshi (1984) and are a ten-country export-weighted index. Data in column II are from National Institute of Bank Management (1990) and are a thirteen-country export-weighted index. Data in column III are from World Bank and are a twenty-three country export-weighted index.

experienced a major slowdown so as to grow again by only 3.3 per cent per annum in the first half of the 1980s. In fact, if petroleum exports are excluded, the first half of the 1980s experienced export growth of only 1 per cent per annum. By contrast, non-petroleum exports grew at almost 17 per cent per annum and total exports at almost 16 per cent per annum between 1985–6 and 1989–90.

The phenomenon of sluggish export growth in the first half of the 1980s, in spite of the turnabout in growth and productivity during that period, can partly be attributed to the appreciation of the real effective exchange value of the Indian rupee during the period from 1979 to 1983 or thereabouts, which adversely affected the competitiveness of Indian exports (Table 9.9). The slowdown in the growth of world markets was also a factor.

In a recent study Virmani (1991) explored the demand and supply factors in India's trade within an econometric framework. He first estimated an inverse supply function for manufactured exports and found that the quantum of exports has no effect on the supply price, thereby indicating 'a flat or elastic supply function with respect to export price'. He then proceeded to estimate a demand function for India's manufactured exports. Estimating the demand function for India over the period 1963–4 to 1985–6 with the real effective exchange rate as one of the explanatory variables, Virmani finds a significant relationship which shows

> that a 10 per cent depreciation of the rupee relative to our trading partners will result in a 29 per cent increase in the quantity of exports, and a 19 per cent increase in the foreign currency value of exports. The response of exports to changes in the exchange rate is much higher than the response to changes in the measured rupee price of exports.
>
> (Virmani, 1991)

Rangarajan (1991) finds a similar relationship in his econometric estimation of an export demand function over the period 1977–90.

Among the manufactured goods, gems and jewellery and ready-made garments were by far the fastest growing exports during the 1960s and the 1970s. Their growth decelerated in the first half of the 1980s only to bounce back in the second half of the decade. Engineering goods exports recorded a marked slowdown to grow by less than 3 per cent per annum in the first half of the 1980s after a very rapid growth (36 per cent per annum) in the 1960s and a slower though still rapid (24 per cent per annum) growth in the 1970s. Exports of leather and leather products and chemical products experienced a milder slowdown in the first half of the 1980s.

It is possible to argue on the basis of the trends at the disaggregated level that the newer non-traditional products such as gems and jewellery, ready-made garments and leather with simpler technologies and less governmental thrust showed better export performance than engineering goods. The latter, with their forward and backward linkages which were rooted in the regulatory policy regime, became a victim of the cost-push effects of the regime. As the import regime was made easier for exports, and as the real effective exchange rate depreciated in the second half of the 1980s, the effect could be seen in the pick-up in export growth of engineering goods and chemicals.

As regards imports, even excluding petroleum imports which had suffered a marked slowdown, growth of non-petroleum imports decelerated from 15.4 per cent per annum in the 1970s to 10.4 per cent per annum in the 1980s. The thrust on modernization and consequent loosening of imports of capital goods in the 1980s was reflected in an increase in capital goods imports, as a percentage of total investment, from 6.2 in 1980–1 to 7.4 in 1988–9. By contrast, imports of intermediate goods as a percentage of the value of output in manufacturing declined from 8.1 in 1980–1 to 7.5 in 1988–9.

AN ECONOMETRIC SEARCH

An overall assessment of the impact of the complex policy regime on the inter-industry differentials in productivity growth within the manufacturing sector is not an easy task. A preliminary attempt is made here within an econometric framework to determine the effect of certain quantifiable variables, which may be few but which have important implications for policy, e.g. the degree of import substitution, the level of capital-deepening and the rate of growth of value added.

The results of the ordinary least squares regressions explaining the variations in total factor productivity growth for sixty-two industry groups of manufacturing are presented in Table 9.10. The explanatory variables include growth in value added (GV), the Chenery measure of import substitution (MS), the capital–labour ratio (K/L), growth in the number of factories (GF) over the period, and a scale variable (SC) measured as the size of the capital stock per factory (an average of four points in time during the period).

Apart from testing for the Verdoorn (1949) effect, the inclusion of the growth of value added in the equation serves to purge movements in total factor productivity growth from those in the growth of value added, and allows us to explore the effect of other variables, e.g. the degree of import substitution and the degree of domestic competition. In fact it is the net effect of the market-expanding forces and the protectionist forces that determines the direction of the relationship between import substitution and overall productivity growth.

Ideally, one would require a measure of effective import substitution which will not only take into account the tariff protection on a value-added basis, but would also quantify the effect of import licensing. In fact, because of data constraints we have only been able to compute the Chenery (1960) measure of the contribution of import substitution to growth for the sixty-two industries. This variable measures the differences in the contribution to growth due to changes in the import ratio without any explicit identification of whether the change in the import ratio is the result of deliberate promotion of import substitution by policy or simply shifting patterns of trade. Nevertheless we use the measure as the only one available.

If import substitution was one important plank in the development strategy in India, another equally important plank was the emphasis placed on heavy industries and the major role to be played by the public sector in their development. It is possible to argue that industries with relatively high capital intensity would be the industries with more chances of embodied technical progress and more scope for learning-by-doing. Should one therefore be expecting higher productivity growth in such industries? An answer to this question is not easy to provide because the industries

Table 9.10 Explaining inter-industry differences in TFP growth

Equation	C	Intercept dummy	GV	MS	K/L	GF	SC	Multiplicative dummy GV	MS	K/L	GF	SC	R^2
1	-2.502 (4.4)	0.109 (0.1)	0.370 (4.9)	-0.034 (2.3)	-	-	-	0.303 (3.4)	0.013 (0.6)	-	-	-	0.71
2	-2.155 (3.6)	-0.300 (0.4)	0.383 (5.1)	-0.030 (2.0)	-1.594 (2.0)	-	-	0.289 (3.3)	0.008 (0.4)	1.714 (1.7)	-	-	0.72
3	-1.830 (3.2)	0.968 (1.1)	0.425 (5.7)	-0.030 (2.1)	-1.409 (1.9)	-11.120 (1.7)	-	0.253 (3.0)	0.020 (0.9)	1.582 (1.7)	-34.222 (2.8)	-	0.76
4	-2.317 (4.0)	-0.500 (0.6)	0.389 (5.3)	-0.026 (1.8)	-2.440 (2.4)	-	0.008 (1.2)	0.319 (3.7)	-0.008 (0.4)	1.085 (0.9)	-	0.005 (0.7)	0.74
5	-1.993 (3.5)	0.721 (0.8)	0.430 (6.0)	-0.026 (1.9)	-2.225 (2.30)	-10.850 (1.7)	0.007 (1.3)	0.280 (3.4)	0.004 (0.2)	1.071 (0.9)	-32.055 (2.7)	0.004 (0.6)	0.78
1a	-2.517 (4.4)	0.060 (0.1)	0.356 (4.9)	-0.028 (2.5)	-	-	-	0.320 (3.9)	-	-	-	-	0.72
2a	-2.426 (4.2)	0.178 (0.2)	0.356 (4.9)	-0.025 (2.2)	-0.437 (0.9)	-	-	0.325 (3.9)	-	-	-	-	0.72
3a	-2.042 (3.5)	1.219 (1.5)	0.397 (5.5)	-0.020 (1.9)	-0.289 (0.7)	-12.991 (1.9)	-	0.293 (3.6)	-	-	-30.293 (2.5)	-	0.76
4a	-2.618 (4.7)	0.147 (0.2)	0.384 (5.5)	-0.027 (2.5)	-1.798 (3.0)	-	0.011 (3.5)	0.324 (4.1)	-	-	-	-	0.74
5a	-2.246 (4.1)	1.175 (1.5)	0.420 (6.0)	-0.021 (2.1)	-1.583 (2.9)	-12.263 (1.9)	0.011 (3.6)	0.295 (3.8)	-	-	-29.867 (2.6)	-	0.78

The dependent variable is the trend growth in total factor productivity (TFP) for the 62 industries of manufacturing. The independent variables GV, MS, K/L, GF and SC represent growth in value added, Chenery measure of import substitution, capital-labour ratio, growth in factories and scale (capital stock per factory). The number of observations is 124. The first 62 observations relate to cross-section data for the period 1959–60 to 1979–80 and the next 62 observations relate to cross-section data for the period 1980–91 to 1987–88. The dummy variable D has values equal to zero for the first set of 62 observations and 1 thereafter. The capital-labour ratio relates to 1970–1 for the first set and to 1984–5 for the second set. The scale variable is an average of the values for 1959–60 and 1975–6 for the first set and the same of 1982–3 and 1985–6 for the second set.

with relatively high capital intensity were also the industries which received more effective protection through the trade regime, and they were also the industries in which the public sector presence was dominant. The capital–labour ratio for the sixty-two industry groups was used as an explanatory variable in the equations.

The nature and stringency of the regulatory framework has varied from time to time and from industry to industry. In the absence of a composite measure of domestic regulation (encompassing the effect of the multiple policy instruments) of the different industry groups, we have attempted to use some partial measures, e.g. scale, growth of economic units in an industry, etc. Their effect on productivity growth is analysed within the cross-section framework.

The equations were estimated by pooling cross-section data for sixty-two industries in two periods (i.e. sixty-two observations relating to the period from 1959–60 to 1979–80 and sixty-two observations relating to the period from 1980–81 to 1987–88). An intercept dummy variable and multiplicative dummy variables were used to allow the coefficients to be different in the two periods. The first set of five equations has multiplicative dummy variables on all the explanatory variables, while the second set includes only those which are statistically significant.

Equation 1 shows the simple relationship between total factor productivity growth, on the one hand, and growth in value added and the degree of import substitution for the sixty-two industries, on the other. Equation 2 adds to this the effect of capital intensity. In equation 3 growth of factories in the different industries is added as a proxy variable for the degree of competition. As an alternative, in equation 4 scale is used as a proxy to measure the effect of fragmentation on productivity growth. Equation 5 is estimated including all the explanatory variables.

As expected, growth in value added has a positive and statistically significant impact on productivity growth. The elasticity of total factor productivity with respect to value added is 0.37. It is almost twice as high in the 1980s as in the earlier two decades (equation 1a). As for import substitution, the coefficient is 0.03 and this is statistically significant at the 5 per cent level. It appears that the protective impact of import substitution dominates any market expanding impact on productivity growth. There is no significant difference between the two periods in this respect. On the domestic regulatory front, some limited exercises in equations 3a to 5a reveal a positive link between the scale of operations and productivity growth and a tendency towards fragmentation of firms, possibly because of certain distortions created by the policy regime.

In conclusion, we must highlight the major findings of our analysis of the role of trade policy in Indian industrialization. The analysis clearly establishes that the decade of the 1980s was, on the one hand, a time of domestic deregulation, loosening of the quantitative restrictions on imports, and providing partial offsets to the anti-export biases of the policy regime, but, on the other hand, also a period of some increases in tariffs and reductions in the transparency of the tariff regime. These trends were associated with a significant positive turnabout in productivity and growth in the industrial sector. While fiscal deficits of the 1980s created expansionary demand conditions, the policy reorientation provided a supply-side framework within which to respond to the stimulus. Emphasis on the infrastructure sectors in the 1980s was another significant factor which helped in the turnabout.

As far as export growth is concerned, it was more a phenomenon of growth-led exports, as exports picked up only in the late 1980s. One possible explanation for the sluggish performance of exports in the first half of the 1980s may well lie in the appreciation of the real effective exchange rate from 1979 to 1983. The constraint imposed by the restrictive import-substitution regime on productivity growth is also established in our econometric analysis, which finds total factor productivity growth to be negatively associated with the degree of import substitution. The analysis at a disaggregated level also suggests that industries with more backward linkages, e.g. engineering industries, which are more prone to the constraining effects of the restrictive regime, have done relatively poorly in exports.

NOTES

1 See Dagli (1979), Alexander (1978), Rajadhyaksha (1980), and Pande (1980).
2 Bhagwati and Srinivasan (1975) estimated the effective exchange rate facing importers during the 1950s and 1960s. However, their compulsion for making simplifying assumptions about the export subsidy rates during the different years in the absence of the actual information make their exact quantitative estimates that much less reliable, as does the fact that such analysis for imports in a regime dominated by quantitative restrictions can at best only be incomplete.
3 The concept of auxiliary duty on imports was introduced in the early 1970s as a temporary measure after the India-Bangladesh war in 1971. In the event, the measure has come to stay, and there is little to distinguish the auxiliary duty from the basic customs duty on imports.
4 For a detailed discussion of the policy framework, see Ahluwalia (1985).
5 Large houses were defined as industrial houses with gross assets in interlinked undertakings exceeding Rs200 million until 1985 and Rs1 billion since then, while dominant undertakings were defined as undertakings with a market share exceeding 33 per cent until 1982 and 25 per cent since then.
6 Ahluwalia (1991) searches statistically for the turnabout in growth of value added and productivity after the mid–1970s and establishes the turnabout after 1979–80.

REFERENCES

Ahluwalia, I. J. (1985) *Industrial Growth in India, Stagnation Since the Mid-1960s*, Delhi: Oxford University Press.

—— (1991) *Productivity and Growth in Indian Manufacturing*, Delhi: Oxford University Press.

Alexander, P. C. (1978) 'Report of the Committee on Imports–Exports Policies and Procedures', Ministry of Commerce, Government of India.

Bagchi, A. and Nayak, P. B. (1993), 'Public Finance and the Planning Process: The Indian Experience' in N. Stern and A Bagchi (eds) *Public Finance Planning*, Delhi: Oxford University Press.

Bhagwati, J. N. and Desai, P. (1970) *India: Planning for Industrialization, Industrialization and Trade Policies Since 1951*, Delhi: Oxford University Press.

—— and Srinivasan, T. N. (1975) *Foreign Trade Regimes and Economic Development: India*, Delhi: Macmillan.

Chenery, H.B. (1960) 'Patterns of Industrial Growth', *American Economic Review*, 50: 624–54.

Dagli, V. (1979) 'Report of the Committee on Controls and Subsidies', Ministry of Finance, Government of India.

Hussain, A. (1984) 'Report of the Committee on Trade Policies', Ministry of Commerce, Government of India.

ICIC (Industrial Credit and Investment Corporation of India), (1989).

Joshi, V. (1984) 'The Nominal and Real Effective Exchange Rate of the Indian Rupee 1971–83', *Reserve Bank of India Occasional Papers* 5(1): June.

Kelkar, V., Kumar, R. and Nangia, R. (1990) 'India's Industrial Economy: Policies, Performance and Reforms', Asian Development Bank, Manila, September.

Nambiar, R. G. (1983) 'Protection to Domestic Industry Fact and Theory', *Economic and Political Weekly*, 1 January: 27–32.

National Institute of Bank Management (1990) 'Statistical Tables', *Journal of Foreign Exchange and International Finance* IV(4): October–December: 7–9.

Panchamukhi, V. R. (1978) *Trade Policies of India: A Quantitative Analysis*, Delhi: Concept Publishing Company.

Pande, B. D. (1980) 'Report of the National Transport Committee', Planning Commission, Government of India.

Rajadhyaksha, V. G. (1980), 'Report of the Committee on Power', Ministry of Energy and Coal, Government of India.

Rangarajan, C. (1991) 'Recent Exchange Rate Adjustments: Causes and Consequences', *Reserve Bank of India Bulletin*, September: 905–09.

Verdoorn, P. J. (1949) 'Fattori che Regolano lo Sviluppo della Productivita del Lavoro', *L'Industria*.

Virmani, A. (1991) 'Demand and Supply Factors in India's Trade', *Economic and Political Weekly*, 9 February: 309–14.

World Bank, (1989) *India: An Industrializing Economy in Transition*, Washington, DC: World Bank.

10

TRADE AND INDUSTRIALIZATION POLICIES IN KOREA

An overview

Kwang Suk Kim

INTRODUCTION

Trade and industrialization policies in the Republic of Korea (hereafter referred to as Korea) have undergone four distinct phases over the post-Korean war period. The first phase, which covers the postwar reconstruction period from 1953 to 1960, may be characterized as the phase of easy import substitution. The second phase covered only a short period from 1961 to 1965, and was a transitional one in which major policy reforms were undertaken to institute an export-oriented industrialization strategy. The period from 1966 to the end of the Park regime (1979) can be taken as the third phase in which the export-oriented strategy was promoted in earnest to maximize industrial output growth without paying much attention to domestic price stability. In the fourth phase beginning in 1980, the government pursued the same export-oriented strategy while emphasizing domestic price stability and structural adjustment.

This historical evolution of Korea's trade and industrialization policies has accompanied rapid growth of GNP and structural transformation, particularly since the transitional phase. During the past twenty-eight years, from 1962 to 1990, the country's GNP grew at an average annual rate of about 9 per cent, and per capita GNP increased nearly seven times, from about US$520 to $3,494 in 1985 constant prices. This GNP growth was led mainly by the manufacturing sector, which grew at an average annual rate of 15 per cent during the same period. The manufacturing sector's share in GNP more than doubled, increasing from 14 to 30 per cent over the same period, whereas the agriculture–forestry–fishery sector's share declined sharply from 37 to 9 per cent.

This paper makes an overview of the country's trade and industrialization policies and experience since the shift of industrialization strategy in the first half of the 1960s. Initial conditions and the reforms of trade and industrial policies in the transitional period (1960–5) are, however, discussed before dealing with the evolution of the policies after the reforms and their impacts on the country's patterns of industrialization.

INITIAL CONDITIONS AND REFORMS IN THE TRANSITIONAL PERIOD (1961–5)

Initial conditions in the early 1960s

South Korea, separated from North Korea by a demilitarized zone, has a land area of about 98,000 square kilometres. The country is quite mountainous and its arable land accounts for a little over 20 per cent of the total land area. Total population in 1960 was 27 million and was growing at nearly 3 per cent a year. Population density as of the early 1960s was roughly 255 people per square kilometre, already one of the highest in the world. The overall rate of urbanization, measured in terms of the ratio of urban population to the total, was only 28 per cent as of 1960, although the population in the capital city of Seoul and other major cities began to increase more rapidly than in other areas.

South Korea lacked economically important natural resources, since most of the mineral resources available in Korea before 1945 were left to North Korea. The country was only endowed with abundant human resources. In 1963, the first year in which a labour force survey was conducted in Korea, the total labour force exceeded 8.3 million, about one-third of the total population, although the country's labour participation rate was relatively low at that time (Economic Planning Board, 1967: 164–5). Of this total labour force, more than 60 per cent were farm workers as of 1963. The nation's average unemployment rate in the early 1960s was 8.2 per cent, but the non-farm unemployment rate was as high as 16.4 per cent. On the other hand, the average educational level of the labour force was relatively high compared with other LDCs with a similar level of per capita income. The average education level for both sexes in terms of the number of years in school turned out to be 5.6 years in 1960. The educational level of the male labour force was 6.4 years, much higher than that of the female labour force which was only 3.8 years (Kim, K.S., 1991a: 17).

Korea's per capita GNP in 1960 was equivalent to US$495 in 1985 constant prices, or about US$80 in current prices (using the exchange rate for 1960). As shown in Table 10.1, value added in the agriculture–forestry–fishery sector accounted for about 37 per cent of GNP in the

Table 10.1 Macroeconomic indicators for initial years, compared with the recent year (1989), Korea

Categories	1960	1965	1989
1. Mid-year population ('000s)	25,012	27,984	42,380
2. GNP and per capita GNP (1985 constant prices)			
GNP (billion won)	10,813[a]	14,797[a]	119,535
Per capita GNP ('000 won)	432	529	2,821
Per capita GNP (US$)	495	607	3,235
3. GNP by industrial origin (percentage share in current prices)			
Agriculture, forestry and fishery	36.8	38.0	10.2
Mining and manufacturing	15.9	20.0	31.9
(manufacturing)	(13.8)	(18.0)	(31.3)
Electricity, gas, water and construction	4.1	4.7	12.1
Other services	43.2	37.3	45.8
4. Expenditures on GDP (percentage share in current prices)			
Private consumption	85.3	84.1	53.2
Government consumption	14.6	9.4	10.3
Gross investment	11.0	15.1	34.5
Exports of goods and non-factor services	3.4	8.6	34.2
Imports of goods and non-factor services (less)	12.8	16.0	31.5
Statistical discrepancy	−1.5	−1.2	−0.7
5. Financing investment (percentage ratio to GNP)			
Gross domestic saving	0.8	7.4	36.0
Foreign saving	8.6	6.4	−1.9
Statistical discrepancy	1.5	1.2	0.7
Total	10.9	15.0	34.8
6. Trade and balance of payments (current million US$)			
Commodity exports (FOB)	33	176	61,409
Commodity imports (FOB)	365	416	56,812
Trade balance	−332	−240	4,597
Current account balance	13	9	5,055
Foreign debt outstanding (gross)	0	206	29,400

Sources: Bank of Korea, *National Accounts,* 1990; *National Income Accounts,* 1984; *Economic Statistics Yearbook,* 1963, 1966, 1990; Economic Planning Board (1990).
[a] Adjusted to make the GNP figures consistent with the new national account series available only for the period after 1970.

early 1960s, while the mining and manufacturing sectors produced 16 per cent. The share of manufacturing in GNP, which measures the degree of industrialization for a country, was only about 14 per cent in 1960.

In the early 1960s Korea could barely save for domestic investment. The meagre gross domestic investment, which was 11 per cent of gross domestic product, had to be financed mostly by foreign saving (net foreign transfers). The country's exports of goods and non-factor services were only about 3 per cent of GDP while imports of goods and non-factor services were nearly 13 per cent, indicating a large deficit in the net foreign balance on goods and services. However, the current account balance in the early 1960s was in minor surplus because the large deficits in the net foreign balance were more than offset by the large receipt of foreign transfers, mainly from the United States. It should also be noted that Korea did not have any repayable foreign debt in the early 1960s since the inflow of foreign resources had taken place in the form of grant aid until that time.

The country's commodity exports amounted to only US$33 million in 1960, a little over one-tenth of its imports. The exports mainly consisted of such primary goods as fish, rice, raw silk, mineral ores, agar-agar, seaweed, etc. Manufactured goods only accounted for 15 per cent of total commodity exports.

Domestic prices, which had been stabilized in 1958–9 for the first time since 1945, started to rise again in 1960 due mainly to the political and social instability caused by the student revolution in that year. The rate of inflation measured in terms of the national wholesale price index rose from 2 per cent in 1959 to about 11 per cent in 1960 and then to 18 per cent in 1961. At the same time, the growth rate of GNP decelerated from 5 per cent to 2 per cent between 1959 and 1960, and remained at a 2–4 per cent level until 1962.

In the early 1960s the country maintained a complicated system of multiple exchange rates. The official exchange rate was devalued to 65 won to the dollar in February 1960, but it was not really important because practically all trade and other commercial activities were conducted at exchange rates that were significantly higher than the official rate in terms of won per US dollar. Exporters and others with foreign exchange earnings were given transferable rights to use their exchange earnings for importing.[1] Government allocations of foreign exchange were also made under a system of foreign exchange bidding, by imposing a foreign exchange tax, or by other methods to increase the *de facto* value of the won currency (Frank, *et al.*, 1975: 29–36).

No positive measures were taken for export promotion in the early 1960s. The government policy was mainly to prevent the disincentive effects of restrictive foreign exchange and trade regimes on exports by adopting the system of multiple exchange rates. Indeed, the government was more concerned about maximizing the receipt of foreign aid rather than trying to increase foreign exchange earnings by means of export promotion.

On the other hand, imports were strictly controlled by means of both tariffs and non-tariff barriers in the early 1960s. The tariff schedule which had been effective since its revision in 1957 specified tariff rates ranging from zero to 100 per cent on 1,269 commodity items in total. The simple average of the tariff rates was about 30 per cent (Kim, K. S., 1991a: 40). In addition to the legal tariffs, a foreign exchange tax was imposed on the commercial uses of foreign exchange for importing until 1962. In 1960, for instance, the foreign exchange tax collections reached about 23 per cent of the won value of actual imports. This implies that the average rate of legal tariffs and tariff equivalent in 1960 was around 53 per cent. The average rate of actual tariffs and tariff equivalent was, however, about 46 per cent since tariff exemptions were granted for imports of machinery and equipment for key industries and for some other imports (Kim, K. S., 1991a: 41).

Despite the high rate of legal tariffs and tariff equivalent, the government also controlled imports by means of quantitative restrictions (QRs). The government used a 'positive list', a semi-annual trade programme that listed only those commodity items which might be imported with or without prior approval of the government (see Kim, K. S., 1991a: 35).

Finally, the political situation of Korea in the early 1960s was very unstable, partly reflecting the general public's discontent arising from sluggish economic activities. Immediately following the student revolution in April 1960, the Chang Myon regime came into power but was again overthrown by a military coup led by General Park in May 1961. After about three years of rule by the military government, the nominal civilian government under President Park and the Democratic Republican Party emerged from a general election in early 1964. Despite this political turmoil in the early part of the 1960s, the country has had a tradition of strong government, owing probably to its Confucian cultural background. The Korean government has had the ability and willingness to carry out its policy decisions once such decisions were made.[2]

Policy reforms in the transitional period

The military government that managed the Korean economy during 1961–3 began to shift economic policy from stabilization and inward-looking industrialization to a programme of rapid industrialization based on export expansion. This policy shift, of course, reflected the changing conditions of the economy in the early 1960s. By that time, Korea had almost completed the postwar reconstruction and the early stage of import substitution, so that domestic production might now replace the previous imports of non-durable consumer goods and the intermediate goods used in their manufacture. The country's poor growth performance was, however, quite frustrating to both policymakers and the people. A growth strategy based on further import substitution of heavy and chemical industrial products was found to be inappropriate owing to the small domestic market and the large capital requirements for such ventures. Korea's poor natural resource endowment had also to be taken into account. Moreover, the policymakers had to find a source of foreign exchange for resolving the balance of payments difficulties arising from the phase-out of US assistance programmes. The availability of a low-wage labour force with a high educational level gave the country a comparative advantage in labour-intensive exports in the early 1960s.

The military government first attempted to unify the exchange rate and undertake reforms of the exchange control, currency, budget and tax systems. Some of these early attempts, however, failed or turned out to be even deleterious because they were poorly designed and not consistent with other government policies. It also started to take positive measures to increase exports and restrict imports in order to deal with the problem of foreign exchange shortages arising from a rapid decline in foreign assistance. But most of the export promotion measures, including the export–import link system adopted in 1963, had the characteristic of *ad hoc* measures to offset the disincentive effect of an overvalued won currency on exports. Even import controls were further tightened in 1963 by means of both the export–import link system and QRs.

The exchange rate reform of 1964–5 then marked a turning point not only in the unification of the foreign exchange rate but also in the transition to export-oriented industrialization policy. In May 1964, the government devalued the official exchange rate from 130 to 256 won per US dollar and announced that the existing fixed exchange rate system would be changed to a unitary floating exchange rate system.[3] An actual adoption of the unitary floating exchange rate system was, however, delayed until March 1965, by which time the government became more confident in maintaining a stable rate of foreign exchange. But after allowing a clean floating of the exchange rate for about 3 months, the Korean monetary authorities tended to peg the exchange rate at around 270 won to the dollar by continuously increasing the supply of foreign exchange on the market. Despite the government intervention in the foreign exchange market the exchange rate was thereafter allowed to change by market forces or by periodic government adjustments so that roughly the same level of the PPP-adjusted, real exchange rate might be maintained after 1965.

Immediately following the announcement of the exchange rate reform in May 1964, the Ministry of Trade and Industry (MTI) abolished the export–import link system and prepared a comprehensive plan for export promotion, consistent with the new exchange rate system after discussions with the business community, as well as with other government agencies. The export incentive measures listed in the plan were: (i) a preferential export credit; (ii) tariff exemptions on imports of raw materials for export production (drawback system); (iii) indirect domestic tax exemptions on intermediate inputs used for export production and on export sales; (iv) direct tax reductions on income earned from exports (abolished in 1973); (v) wastage allowances for raw materials imported for export production; (vi) a system of linking import business to export performance; (vii) tariff and indirect tax exemptions for domestic suppliers of intermediate goods used in export production; and (viii) accelerated depreciation allowances for fixed assets of major export industries (Frank et al. 1975: 40–51).

After the interest rate reform of 1965 the preferential export credit became an important incentive for exporters since the reform substantially widened the interest rate differential between export credit and ordinary bank loans. The various export incentive measures, other than the preferential export credit and the direct tax reduction on export income, were intended mainly to ensure that exporters, who must sell their products at world market prices, could purchase intermediate goods for export products at world market prices. This indicates that most of the incentive measures served primarily to offset the disincentive effect on exports that the trade regime would otherwise have created. These incentive measures were supposed to be applied to all exporters on a non-discriminatory basis.

In addition to these incentive measures, the government started to use three administrative instruments for export promotion. One was government support for overseas marketing activities of Korean exporters through the expansion of the overseas network of the Korea Trade Promotion Corporation (KOTRA). The second was the government export targeting system which was used to set annual export targets by major commodity groups and by destination, and to monitor export performance very closely. The last was the instrument of the Monthly Export Promotion Conference which was renamed the Monthly Trade Promotion Conference in the early 1970s. The conference, which was usually attended by the president himself, all cabinet members and other influential people from both the government and the private business circles, essentially served to disseminate the president's emphasis on export promotion and also to quickly solve problems encountered by exporters through the final decisions of the president (Rhee et al., 1984: 29–35).

On the import side, only minor progress in import liberalization was made in the sense that the import control by QRs was somewhat replaced by tariffs immediately following the exchange rate reform. Beginning in 1964 the government introduced special tariffs to soak up excess profits accruing to importers of selected commodities.[4] However, the government also lessened non-tariff import barriers by gradually increasing the number of import permissible items in the MTI's semi-annual trade programmes during 1964–5.

Unlike the early attempt of the military government, the exchange rate and other reform programmes undertaken in 1964–5 were accompanied by the price stabilization programme that was being implemented again after a nearly four-year suspension.

Finally, a quantitative assessment of the effects of the major policy reforms is made on the basis of the time series estimates of nominal and PPP-adjusted (real) effective exchange rates for exports and imports in the first half of the 1960s, which are shown in Frank, *et al.* (1975: 70–3).[5] The PPP-adjusted effective exchange rate for exports, which is the nominal effective exchange rate adjusted by a PPP index, increased in terms of the number of won per dollar between 1962 and 1964, indicating that the exchange rate reform of 1964–5 increased net incentives to export. A really important point is, however, that the exchange rate reform substantially reduced the gap between the official and the effective rates for exports by largely replacing *ad hoc* export subsidies with the official devaluation of the won. The PPP-adjusted effective rate for imports also increased in terms of the number of won per dollar. The gap between the official and the effective rates for imports was similarly reduced by the reform. All these indicate that the policy reforms of 1964–5 did bring about some increase in the measurable incentive to export, as well as in the level of protection for domestic industry. What was more important than these increases was that the reforms replaced a complicated, largely *ad hoc* system of incentives based on multiple exchange rates and direct cash subsidies with a simplified and more stable system.

EXPORT POLICY AND PATTERNS OF INDUSTRIALIZATION (1966–90)

Export incentives and export performance

After 1965, the simplified export incentive system, which had been institutionalized by the exchange rate reforms of 1964–5, was adjusted in the direction of reducing trade-distorting effects on the export side. With a more realistic official exchange rate in place since 1965, the government could gradually reduce the value of net export subsidies per US dollar of exports over time without a discernible negative impact on export performance. For instance, the direct tax reduction on export income was dropped in 1973, and interest-rate subsidies implicit in the preferential export credit significantly declined from 1972 and were completely eliminated after 1982. This indicates that as from 1983, the effective exchange rate for exports, which was supposed to include net export subsidies, became identical to the official exchange rate in Korea.

This evolution of the country's export incentive system since 1965 is reflected in the nominal and PPP-adjusted effective exchange rates for exports and imports during 1965–90, as shown in Table 10.2. Although Korea had experienced substantial price inflation, particularly before 1982, the PPP-adjusted official exchange rate did not show any wide fluctuation

Table 10.2 Nominal and purchasing-power-parity-adjusted effective exchange rates for exports and imports, Korea, 1965-90

Year	Nominal exchange rate (won per US$)			WPI and PPP index 1965=100			PPP-adjusted exchange rate (won per US$)			Anti-export bias
	Official rate (1)	Effective rate for Exports[a] (2)	Effective rate for Imports[b] (3)	WPI, Korea (4)	WPI, major trade partners[c] (5)	PPP Index (6=100×5/4)	Official rate (7=1×6/100)	Effective rate for Exports (8=2×6/100)	Effective rate for Imports (9=3×6/100)	(10=8/9)
1965	265.4	275.3	293.1	100.0	100.0	100.0	265.4	275.3	293.1	0.94
1970	310.7	331.5	336.4	145.9	112.8	77.3	240.2	256.2	260.0	0.99
1971	347.7	370.5	369.5	158.5	115.4	72.3	253.1	269.7	269.0	1.00
1972	391.8	404.3	415.2	180.7	126.8	70.2	275.0	283.8	291.5	0.97
1973	398.3	407.0	417.7	193.3	155.6	80.5	320.6	327.6	336.2	0.97
1974	407.0	415.6	425.5	274.7	188.4	68.6	279.2	285.1	291.9	0.98
1975	484.0	496.9	508.9	347.4	197.0	56.7	274.4	281.7	288.5	0.98
1976	484.0	496.3	515.4	389.4	206.7	53.1	257.0	263.5	273.7	0.96
1977	484.0	493.4	519.7	424.5	226.8	53.4	258.5	263.5	277.5	0.95
1978	484.0	495.0	526.9	473.4	266.1	56.2	272.0	278.2	296.1	0.94
1979	484.0	495.0	520.0	562.5	284.1	50.5	244.4	250.0	262.6	0.95
1980	607.4	628.0	641.8	781.3	323.7	41.4	250.1	260.0	265.7	0.98
1981	681.0	696.0	715.1	940.6	341.8	36.3	247.2	252.6	259.6	0.97
1982	731.1	734.0	772.9	984.4	332.9	33.8	247.1	248.1	261.2	0.95
1983	775.8	775.8	831.7	986.7	336.9	34.1	264.5	264.5	283.6	0.93
1984	806.0	806.0	858.0	993.6	337.6	34.0	274.0	274.0	291.7	0.94
1985	870.0	870.0	920.3	1,002.5	334.6	33.4	290.6	290.6	307.4	0.95
1986	881.4	881.4	942.9	987.5	379.1	38.4	338.5	338.5	362.1	0.93
1987	822.6	822.6	888.3	992.4	410.2	41.3	339.7	339.7	366.9	0.93
1988	730.6	730.6	780.3	1,019.2	445.5	43.7	319.3	319.3	341.0	0.94
1989	671.5	671.5	705.6	1,034.5	440.6	42.6	286.1	286.1	300.6	0.95
1990	708.6	708.6	748.0	1,077.9	440.3	40.8	289.1	289.1	305.2	0.95

Source: Kim (1991a: 24).

[a] Official exchange rate plus net export subsidies per US dollar of export.
[b] Official exchange rate plus actual tariffs and tariff equivalents per US dollar of import.
[c] An average of WPIs for the United States and Japan, weighted by the average shares of the United States and Japan in Korea's total trade volumes with the two countries during 1963–80. The Japanese WPI was, however, adjusted by the index of the exchange rate of the yen to the dollar.

over more than two decades, indicating that the nominal exchange rate was often adjusted to prevent any significant overvaluation of the won currency. If two unusual periods are excluded (1973 and 1985–8, during which the won became undervalued due mainly to an effective devaluation of the US dollar in international markets), the country's real exchange rate was even more stable over the same period. In addition, since the net export subsidies accounted for a small proportion of the effective exchange rate and were completely eliminated after 1982, the PPP-adjusted effective exchange rate for exports was also very stable over a long period, again except for the two unusual periods. The real effective exchange rate for imports was a little higher (in terms of the number of won) than the rate for exports, because the value of actual tariff collections per US dollar imports was not only higher than the net export subsidies when such subsidies existed, but also persisted even after the abolition of export subsidies. As a result, an indicator showing the degree of anti-export bias in the country remained at around 0.95–1.00 throughout the period (see column 10, Table 10.2).

The relative stability in the PPP-adjusted effective exchange rate since 1965 made continuous rapid growth of Korea's merchandise exports possible after that year. The country's exports actually started to increase during the transitional period owing to some *ad hoc* measures for export promotion, but that increase might be considered as a 'catch-up' to a normal level from the abnormally low level of the early 1960s. The export expansion, however, continued and proceeded at an unusually rapid rate after the mid-1960s. Total merchandise exports, which were only at the level of US$175 million, or 5.8 per cent of GNP, in 1965, increased to about $17.5 billion, or 23.9 per cent of GNP, in 1980, and then to $65 billion or about 27 per cent of GNP by 1990. Although the rate of increase in exports started to decelerate in the late 1970s, the nominal value of exports has expanded at an average annual rate of about 27 per cent during the past two and a half decades. Even discounting for the rise in export prices, the total export volume increased by about 22 per cent annually during the same period. As a result, the country's exports, which had accounted for only 0.1 per cent of world exports in 1965, occupied about 2.1 per cent by 1988.

What made this rapid expansion of exports possible in Korea? The export expansion was not primarily a result of direct financial incentives, since exchange premia, exchange rates and export subsidies did not change much before and after the exchange rate reform of 1964–5. Mason *et al.* (1980) suggest that one of the main reasons for the change was the disappearance of the rich opportunities for profit from import substitution provided by the foreign exchange regimes before the reform. In addition, the fact that Korea could maintain a stable level of the real effective exchange rate after 1965 was very important for export expansion.

Balassa *et al.* (1989) suggest, on the basis of their empirical estimates of Korea's export supply and demand functions for the 1965–79 period, that Korean exporters respond more strongly to changes in the nominal effective exchange rate than to changes in the foreign prices of exports and non-export domestic prices. They suggest, 'The relatively high elasticity obtained with respect to the nominal effective exchange rate reflects expectations on the part of businessmen that changes in exchange rates and in export incentives will not be reversed', while the prices of exports and domestic goods fluctuate, involving reversible changes (p. 11). Their estimates of Korea's export demand function indicate that the income elasticity of demand for Korean exports was extremely high, about 5.3–5.4 during 1965–79, while the price elasticity of demand was about −1.0 to −1.1.

The rapid expansion of total exports was accompanied by a substantial change in the commodity composition of exports. The manufactured goods which had accounted for about 61 per cent of total exports in 1965[6] increased to about 94 per cent by 1990, while the share of primary products, including mineral fuels, in total exports declined from 39 per cent to only 6 per cent over the same period. Within the category of manufactured exports, the 'manufactured goods classified chiefly by material' showed a relative decline from about 39 per cent of total exports to 22 per cent between 1965 and 1990, while 'machinery and transport equipment' marked a continuous increase from 3.1 per cent of the total to nearly 40 per cent. On the other hand, the shares of 'chemicals' and 'miscellaneous manufactured goods' in total exports increased between 1965 and 1980, but thereafter declined slightly (Bank of Korea, *Economic Statistics Yearbook*, various years).

The structural change in export commodities was accompanied by a significant diversification of export markets. In 1965, about 60 per cent of Korean exports went to two rich countries, the United States and Japan. This percentage gradually declined to about 55 per cent in 1975 and to 50 per cent during 1985–90, as sales to Europe, the Middle East, and other areas outside Asia expanded (Bank of Korea, *Economic Statistics Yearbook*, various years).

The diversification of export commodities and markets was mainly a consequence of the Korean efforts to diversify export commodities and to penetrate important foreign markets. Since foreign direct and joint investments in the country have been relatively small compared with both annual gross investment and annual inflows of foreign capital, foreign investors have not been the major promoters of Korean exports and market diversification. Really the major promoters of the country's export marketing have been the domestic private enterprises with the profit motivation. The overseas marketing activities of such enterprises have, of course, been assisted by the overseas network of the government-supported KOTRA.

Among the domestic enterprises, which ones are the major contributors to the country's export expansion? Korean Foreign Trade Association (1990a: 15–16) shows that between 1978 and 1983 the share of large enterprises' exports, including the exports of General Trading Companies (GTCs), in total exports showed a continuous increase from about 64 per cent to 80 per cent, while the share of small-scale enterprises declined from 36 per cent to 20 per cent. After 1983, however, the trend reversed. The large enterprises' exports showed a relative decline to reach 62 per cent of the total by 1989 while the small enterprises' exports increased to 38 per cent. This recent increase in the share of small-scale enterprises in total exports seems consistent with the increasing share of such enterprises in total mining and manufacturing production in the 1980s (Economic Planning Board, 1990: 53–4).

The export share of large enterprises, in general, moved together with the share of GTCs in total exports. Exports by the GTCs were only about 13.3 per cent of total exports in 1975, the first year in which such companies were created in Korea imitating the Japanese model (Jo, 1991: 511–25). Thereafter, the export share of GTCs rose continuously to reach about 48 per cent by 1983 but then the trend reversed. In 1989 the exports by GTCs accounted for about 38 per cent of total exports, which was still substantially higher than the 10 per cent share of Japanese GTCs in its total exports.

Exports and patterns of industrial growth

Due to the rapid expansion of exports since 1965, the manufacturing sector grew at an average annual rate of nearly 15 per cent during 1965–90, compared with the average GNP growth rate of about 9 per cent. The GNP share of manufacturing at current domestic prices therefore rose from 18 per cent in 1965 to 30 per cent by 1990. The structural change in industrial output is also revealed in a time series study of Korean input–output (I–O) data, deflated to constant domestic prices, as shown in Table 10.3.[7]

As shown in the table, the manufacturing production which had accounted for about 33 per cent of total domestic production in 1963 rose to 57 per cent in 1975 and then to about 63 per cent by 1985. Manufactured exports rose from about 39 per cent of total exports of goods and services in 1963 to 82 per cent in 1975 and to 84 per cent by the mid-1980s. The extent to which industrialization is linked to exports is shown by the rapid increase in manufactured exports as a share of total production. The manufactured exports which had comprised only 4 per cent of total manufacturing production in 1963 increased rapidly to about 24 per cent in 1975 and then to 31 per cent by the mid-1980s.

The relationship between exports and the patterns of industrial growth can also be discussed in terms of structural changes in production and

Table 10.3 Changes in the structure of manufacturing production and exports, and the ratio of exports to production by major sector, Korea, 1963–85 (%)

	Processed food	Textiles	Finished consumer goods	Intermediate products	Machinery and transport equipment	All manufacturing	Manufacturing share in all industry total[a]
A. Structure of production							
1963 (1968 prices)	27.8	15.4	18.0	30.0	8.8	100.0	33.2
1975 (1968 prices)	15.7	14.9	18.3	32.2	18.9	100.0	57.2
1975 (1975 prices)	16.7	12.1	16.8	40.8	13.6	100.0	53.0
1985 (1975 prices)	10.5	9.5	12.7	38.3	29.0	100.0	62.6
B. Structure of exports							
1963 (1968 prices)	20.7	20.8	13.9	38.6	6.0	100.0	38.8
1975 (1968 prices)	4.2	15.5	33.6	18.3	28.4	100.0	81.7
1975 (1975 prices)	8.6	12.7	31.9	28.0	18.8	100.0	74.9
1985 (1975 prices)	1.5	9.6	20.7	27.9	40.3	100.0	83.8
C. Ratio of exports to production (%)							
1963 (1968 prices)	3.1	5.5	3.2	5.3	2.8	4.1	—
1975 (1968 prices)	6.3	24.5	43.1	13.3	35.3	23.5	—
1975 (1975 prices)	12.4	25.5	45.8	16.6	33.4	24.2	—
1985 (1975 prices)	4.6	31.8	51.0	22.8	43.5	31.3	—

Source: Kim and Hong (1990: 27–31).

[a] Indicates the manufacturing sector's share in the total production and exports of industry, including the primary sector, social overhead and services, and unclassifiables.

exports within the manufacturing sector. The relative importance of 'early industries' such as processed food and textiles in total manufacturing production consistently declined during the period 1963–85, while that of intermediate products and machinery gained considerably. The share of finished consumer goods in total production remained almost unchanged between 1963 and 1975 but thereafter showed a decline. The structural change in manufacturing exports generally followed the patterns of change observed in the case of manufacturing production, with two exceptions. One is that the share of intermediate products in total manufacturing exports was unusually high in 1963 and showed a decline between 1963 and 1975. The other is that the share of finished consumer goods in total manufacturing exports sharply increased from 14 per cent to 4 per cent between 1963 and 1975, although it thereafter showed a declining trend. On the other hand, reflecting the overall rise in the ratio of exports to manufacturing production discussed above, the export ratios for all major sectors except processed food increased continuously during the period of observation.

Table 10.4 gives the sources of industrial output growth for 1955–85, which are quoted from Kim and Hong (1990). The table attempts to explain the degree to which domestic demand, exports, import substitution and technological change have each contributed to the growth of industrial output.[8] The decomposition of the sources of industrial output growth is actually based on the five I–O tables for 1955, 1963, 1970, 1975 and 1985, which are all made consistent over time and deflated into 1968 or 1975 constant domestic prices.

As shown in the table, the relative sizes of total (direct plus indirect) contributions of various autonomous factors to aggregate output growth for the whole economy changed considerably between the 1955–63 period and the later two periods (1963–75 and 1975–85). The total contribution of export expansion (EE), for instance, was about 9 per cent of aggregate national output growth during the 1955–63 period, but it increased to 32 per cent and 45 per cent during the later two periods, respectively. In contrast, the total contribution of import substitution (IS) declined from 16 per cent in the early period to around 6 per cent in the later two periods. The total contribution of domestic demand expansion (DDE) showed a continuous decline over the three periods. The contribution of technological change (TC), or more specifically changes in I–O coefficients, however, remained unchanged between the two earlier periods (1955–63 and 1963–75) but showed a minor increase in the later period (1975–85).

The increase in manufacturing output over the last three periods was much greater than the increases in other sectoral outputs. The growth of manufacturing output was mainly attributable to DDE and IS in the earlier period, and to DDE and EE in the later two periods. Thus, DDE was the most important factor for the growth of manufacturing output in all

Table 10.4 Sources of industrial output growth, Korea, 1955–85
(total, direct plus indirect, % contribution)

	DDE	EE	IS	TC	Change in gross output (billion won)
1955–63					
Primary sector	97.8	7.2	–20.2	15.2	125
Manufacturing					
Processed food	64.6	6.5	16.1	12.9	63
Light industry	78.9	16.1	52.3	–47.3	97
Heavy industry	45.4	8.9	28.6	17.1	83
Machinery	43.9	6.6	32.7	16.8	30
Manufacturing total	61.6	10.6	34.6	–6.8	272
Social overhead	136.1	14.9	23.9	74.9	31
Other services	81.1	4.8	3.8	10.3	70
All industry total	78.0	9.2	15.9	–3.1	497
1963–75					
Primary sector	119.9	26.2	–3.3	–42.9	445
Manufacturing					
Processed food	88.2	12.1	2.8	–2.9	572
Light industry	47.2	52.9	1.8	–1.5	1,537
Heavy industry	42.9	33.8	19.9	3.5	1,228
Machinery	42.0	43.9	10.5	3.6	802
Manufacturing total	50.4	39.9	8.9	0.8	4,139
Social overhead	88.1	15.9	1.7	–5.8	748
Other services	78.9	17.9	3.1	0.2	1,083
All industry total	64.4	32.4	6.3	–3.1	6,415
1975–85					
Primary sector	93.9	17.1	0.7	–11.7	1,661
Manufacturing					
Processed food	80.6	5.7	5.0	8.7	3,113
Light industry	30.1	64.4	2.9	2.6	8,877
Heavy industry	35.6	64.4	11.1	–11.1	12,550
Machinery	30.9	55.3	9.7	4.1	11,988
Manufacturing total	36.6	56.4	8.1	–1.1	36,529
Social overhead	75.4	23.6	0.6	0.4	7,361
Other services	74.3	20.9	1.1	3.7	8,875
All industry total	49.7	45.0	5.7	–0.4	54,426

Source: Kim and Hong (1990: 39) based on Syrquin's (1976) total method, using first differences.
DDE, domestic demand expansion; EE, export expansion; IS, import substitution; TC, technological change. The sources-of-growth decompositions for the periods 1955–63 and 1963–75 are based on the Korean input-output tables for respective years which were deflated to 1968 constant domestic prices, while the decomposition for the 1975–85 period is based on the I-O data deflated to 1975 constant domestic prices. All estimates are arithmetic averages of estimates derived from Laspeyres and Paasche indexes.

the periods although its relative contribution gradually declined over the three periods. On the other hand, trade effects shifted greatly between 1955–63 and the latter two periods, reflecting the policy change discussed in the previous section. For instance, the total IS contribution, which explained about 35 per cent of the increase in manufacturing output in 1955–63, declined to about the 8–9 per cent level in the later two periods. In contrast, the total EE contribution, which was 11 per cent in the earlier period, rose with the trend of acceleration to 40 per cent and 56 per cent, respectively, in the latter two periods.

Examining the sources of growth by major industry within manufacturing it appears that DDE also contributed greatly to the growth of almost all major industries during the three periods of observation, while the trade effects were again reversed in all major industries between the 1955–63 period and the later two periods. On the one hand, the total IS contributions to the growth of individual industries' outputs generally declined during the later two periods, but those contributions to the growth of heavy industry and machinery were quite substantial. That is, the total IS contributions to the growth of heavy industry and machinery were 20 per cent and 11 per cent, respectively, during the 1963–75 period, while those contributions to the growth of other industries were generally less than 3 per cent. Even during the 1975–85 period, both heavy industry and machinery industry continued to show a relatively high IS contribution, reaching about 10–11 per cent, while the other industries' IS contributions ranged from 3 to 5 per cent. On the other hand, all major industries, except processed food, recorded very high total EE contributions during the later two periods.

These results support our hypothesis that export expansion was substantially more important to Korea's industrialization during the period 1963–85 than import substitution, although the situation in the preceding period had been the other way around. They also indicate that the policy reforms made in the first half of the 1960s were quite effective in altering the pattern of industrialization. It is also noted that the role of exports in Korea's industrialization has continuously expanded since the mid–1960s.

Export policy and industrial organization

This section makes a brief overview of the evolution of the country's industrial organization in the course of rapid industrialization based on export expansion. Industrial or market concentration and economic power concentration have been the two main issues of the country's industrial organization, and the trends in these concentration measures are discussed.

Table 10.5 shows the trend in commodity market concentration, based on the seven-digit level of manufactured commodity classification for the 1970–87 period. As shown in the table, monopoly and duopoly markets accounted for about 48 per cent of total manufactured commodity markets in terms of the number of commodities, and about 25 per cent in terms of the value of shipments in both 1970 and 1977. Between the two

Table 10.5 Trends in commodity market concentration, Korea, 1970–87

	Monopoly	Duopoly	Oligopoly	Competitive market	Total
1970					
No. of commodities	442	279	495	276	1,492
Share of commodities (%)	29.6	18.7	33.2	18.5	100.0
Share of shipments (%)	8.7	16.3	35.1	39.9	100.0
1977					
No. of commodities	475	279	528	264	1,543
Share of commodities (%)	30.8	17.0	34.9	17.2	100.0
Share of shipments (%)	12.7	12.6	48.6	26.1	100.0
1987					
No. of commodities	533	277	1,173	655	2,638
Share of commodities (%)	20.2	10.5	44.5	24.8	100.0
Share of shipments (%)	7.8	7.7	40.2	44.3	100.0

Source: Lee and Lee (1990: 24); and 1970 data are from Lee, K.U. (no date).
Monopoly is defined as $CR1 > 80\%$ and $S1/S2 > 10.0$; duopoly is $CR2 > 80\%$ and $S3 < 5.0$; oligopoly is $CR3 > 60\%$ (excluding monopoly and oligopoly); and competitive market is $CR3 < 60\%$. CRi and Si represent the ith-firm shipment concentration rate and the market share of the ith firm, respectively.

years, however, the share of oligopoly markets in terms of shipment values increased substantially, while that of competitive markets declined, although the shares of both oligopoly and competitive markets in terms of the number of commodities did not show any significant change. Between 1977 and 1987, the share of both monopoly and duopoly markets significantly declined in terms of both the number of commodities and the value of shipments, while the share of competitive markets rose substantially in both terms. The share of oligopoly markets also showed a decline in terms of shipment values during the same period, although that in terms of the number of commodities continued to rise. On the whole, it can be said that the overall degree of market concentration was very high in the 1970s, reflecting the small size of the domestic market, but has shown a gradual decline since then as new commodities have emerged and domestic markets have become larger in the course of rapid industrialization. In other words, the general trend has been toward a more competitive market structure, since the 'speedy oligopolization' that took place in the 1970s shifted to the new phase of 'moderate competitivization' in the 1980s (Lee and Lee, 1990: 24).

Another major issue of the country's industrial organization concerns the concentration of economic power in the hands of a small number of large business groups called *jaebols*. The jaebol, which resembles in many respects the Japanese *jaibatsu* in the pre-war period, consists of a number of large firms that are operating in diverse markets but are practically owned or controlled by a particular individual and his kin. On the basis

of the thirty largest jaebols ranked in the order of their assets, the
number of subsidiaries, which had been only 126 in 1970, increased continuously to reach 575 by the end of 1990. Lee and Lee (1990: 28) report
that the thirty largest jaebols' share in the nation's manufactured goods
shipments continuously increased from 34 per cent to 41 per cent between
1977 and 1982 but then showed a gradual decline to reach 37 per cent by
1987. Even the share of the five largest jaebols in the nation's manufactured
goods shipments, which had rapidly increased from 15.7 per cent to 22.6
per cent during the earlier period, showed a minor decline to reach 22 per
cent by 1987. The thirty largest jaebols' share in total commodity exports,
which increased from 38.5 per cent to 41.3 per cent during 1977–85, was
only slightly higher than their share in manufactured goods shipments.

All the subsidiaries of the jaebols are effectively owned by the particular
individuals holding the largest share of equities, their kin, and the subsidiaries under their control. As of April 1989, the largest shareholders, their
kin and subsidiaries under their control held about 46 per cent of all
equities in the ten largest jaebols. In addition, the subsidiaries of the ten
largest jaebols opened to public ownership accounted for only 27 per cent
in terms of the number of subsidiaries and 56 per cent in terms of equity
values (Lee and Lee, 1990: 53–4). This indicates that the equity ownership
of the subsidiaries is still highly concentrated in a small number of individual shareholders. An increase in the dispersion of such ownership is
therefore becoming the major policy issue for the country's future
industrialization.

It seems that the growth of jaebols and the concentration of economic
power are a result of both government policy and the ambitious entrepreneurship in the country. The government gave preference to large enterprises in the course of promoting industrialization since they were believed
to enjoy economies of scale and to be more efficient than the smaller ones.
In addition, the larger ones could promote their profit-making ventures
more effectively than the smaller ones because the former have many
advantages in terms of manpower, the capacity to mobilize financial
resources, and so forth. Despite the rapid expansion of jaebols and the
consequent concentration of economic power in the hands of a small
number of business groups, the government did not act to contain their
expansion until the early 1980s. Even monopoly and oligopoly firms had
not really been regulated until the Anti-trust and Fair Trade Law became
effective in 1981. In the 1980s, however, the government began to discourage the further expansion of jaebol groups mainly by means of imposing
an annual ceiling on outstanding domestic credit to each of the thirty
largest jaebols and restricting intercompany shareholding within a jaebol.

Exports and employment

Exports have played an increasingly important role in Korea's industrialization since the mid-1960s. It would then be interesting to examine the effects of export expansion on the country's employment, which may be influenced by the patterns of factor use under the export-oriented strategy of industrialization. Korea had the typical characteristics of a labour surplus economy in the 1960s and at least until the mid-1970s. It can therefore be safely assumed that it had a comparative advantage in labour-intensive as opposed to capital-intensive activities, although a country's comparative advantage is determined not only by its factor endowment but also by many other conditions. Were the patterns of factor use in Korea consistent with this factor endowment theory of comparative advantage? How did these patterns affect employment and income distribution?

In order to address these questions, Korean data on the factor intensity of trade are first discussed. Westphal and Kim (1977) estimated Korea's factor intensity of trade for the 1960–68 period using factor input coefficients for 1968 and other data for various years. Their estimates indicate that the direct, as well as the total (direct plus indirect) labour intensity of manufactured exports was substantially greater than that of imports over the period from 1960 to 1968.

Hong (1979, 1988) provides more recent estimates for selected years from 1960 to 1985, although they are not directly comparable with Westphal and Kim's estimates due to a difference in price terms. Hong (1988) shows that the total capital intensities of both exports and competitive import replacements increased rapidly during the two and a half decades, but manufactured exports were less capital-intensive than competitive import replacements throughout the period. In the case of all goods and services, exports had been more capital-intensive only in 1960, and were less capital-intensive during the later period. These results indicate that exports have been more labour-intensive than imports (specifically competitive import replacements) since the mid-1960s, although there were some exceptional years.

This discussion on the factor intensity of trade seems to indicate that Korea's export-oriented growth, in general, accompanied a relatively efficient allocation of primary factors in line with the country's factor endowment. It also suggests that Korea's rapid export expansion should have accompanied a rapid growth of employment. An estimate by Hong (1979: 22) indicates that the direct and indirect employment generated by manufactured exports rose from about 6 per cent of total manufacturing employment in 1963 to 30 per cent by 1975. Hong's estimate of the total employment generated by all exports (including service exports) indicates that it rose from a mere 2 per cent of total employment in 1963 to 11 per cent by 1975. According to a recent KFTA report (1990b: 5),

335

the direct and indirect employment generated by manufactured exports in 1985 was about 38 per cent of total manufacturing employment, while the total employment generated by all exports was 16 per cent of the nation's employment.

Owing to the increased contribution of exports to employment generation, total employment grew very rapidly during the 1965 to 1990 period, thereby gradually reducing the nation's unemployment rate from 7.4 per cent to 2.4 per cent. In particular, manufacturing employment increased at an average annual rate of 7.6 per cent, far exceeding the increasing rate of total employment which averaged 3.2 per cent a year (see Table 10.6). The rapid increase in manufacturing employment was accompanied by concurrent rises in labour productivity and real wages in the same sector over the 1965–90 period. Although the real wages of manufacturing increased rapidly over the whole period, the increasing rate of real wages was only slightly higher than the growth rate of labour productivity measured in terms of value added per worker until the mid-1980s. It became much higher than that of labour productivity by the latter half of the 1980s, however, reflecting strengthened labour union activities and some labour shortages in the manufacturing sector. For this reason, Korea's unit labour costs in terms of both local currency and US dollars showed the most rapid rise among the twenty-three major trading nations listed in the OECD survey during 1987–90 (OECD, 1991).

IMPORT POLICY AND LIBERALIZATION EXPERIENCE (1966–90)

Import liberalization

Until the mid-1960s imports had been strictly controlled by the government using both high tariffs and QRs. In fact, a production-weighted average rate of legal tariffs, including special tariffs, in 1965 was about 53 per cent, while the semi-annual trade programme for the first half of the year announced by MTI listed only 1,447 import items out of a total 30,000 tradable items as automatic approval (AA) items. Since that year, however, the government has undertaken a gradual liberalization of the import regime. To show the trend in Korea's import liberalization, the overall degree of import liberalization estimated for the period 1965–90 is shown in Table 10.7. Average legal tariff rates and the degree of import QRs are taken into account in the estimation of the overall degree.

First, the degree of import liberalization in terms of tariffs is taken to be represented by the annual series of a reciprocal of the average legal tariff rate, which is estimated by adding the average actual rate of special tariffs to the average legal rate of regular tariffs (see Kim, K.S., 1991a: 39–43, for statistical data). This series indicates that the degree of import

Table 10.6 Trends in employment, manufacturing productivity and wages, Korea, selected years

	1965	1975	1985	1990	Average annual rate of increase (%)			
					1965–75	1975–85	1985–90	1965–90
A. Total employment (thousand persons)	8,206	11,692	14,970	18,036	3.6	2.5	3.8	3.2
B. Manufacturing employment (thousand persons)	772	2,175	3,504	4,847	10.9	4.9	6.7	7.6
(share in total employment)	(9.4)	(18.6)	(23.4)	(26.9)				
C. Value added in manufacturing (1985 constant billion won)	1,572	7,648	24,530	43,954	17.1	12.3	12.4	14.3
D. Value added per worker in manufacturing (1985 constant thousand won) (C/B)	2,036	3,516	7,001	9,068	5.6	7.1	5.3	6.2
E. Average monthly wage of manufacturing workers								
1. Nominal value (thousand won)	4.7	38.4	269.6	590.8	23.4	21.5	17.0	21.3
2. National CPI (1985=100)	9.3	32.1	100.0	130.2	13.2	12.0	5.4	11.2
3. Real wage (1985 constant thousand won)	50.5	119.6	296.6	453.8	9.0	8.5	11.0	9.2

Source: Bank of Korea, Economic Statistics Yearbook, various years.

Table 10.7 Estimate of overall degree of import liberalization for Korea, 1965–90 (%)

Year	Average rate of legal tariffs		Inverted total tariff rate [1/1+(2)] (3)	Degree of liberalization from QRs[c] (4)	Overall degree of liberalization (5)
	Regular[a] (1)	Total[b] (2)			
1965	49.5	52.7	65.5	6.0	35.8
1966	49.5	52.3	65.7	9.3	37.5
1967	49.5	52.6	65.5	52.4	59.0
1968	56.7	58.9	62.9	50.1	56.5
1969	56.7	58.3	63.2	47.1	55.2
1970	56.7	58.5	63.1	46.3	54.7
1971	56.7	57.9	63.3	47.0	55.2
1972	56.7	57.5	63.5	43.4	53.5
1973	48.1	48.2	67.5	44.7	56.1
1974	48.1	48.1	67.5	43.8	55.7
1975	48.1	48.1	67.5	41.6	54.7
1976	48.1	48.1	67.5	44.1	55.8
1977	41.3	41.3	70.8	40.8	55.8
1978	41.3	41.3	70.7	52.2	61.5
1979	34.4	34.4	74.4	56.2	65.3
1980	34.4	34.4	74.4	57.4	65.9
1981	34.4	34.4	74.4	60.7	67.6
1982	34.4	34.4	74.4	62.5	68.5
1983	34.4	34.4	74.4	66.6	70.5
1984	26.7	26.7	78.9	75.0	77.0
1985	26.4	26.4	79.1	78.2	78.7
1986	24.7	24.7	80.2	82.0	81.1
1987	23.9	23.9	80.7	84.1	82.4
1988	22.4	22.4	81.7	86.0	83.9
1989	15.7	15.7	86.4	86.7	86.6
1990	14.1	14.1	87.6	87.5	87.6

Source: Data for 1965–85 are from Kim, K.S. (1987: 33), and the recent data are estimates based on the simple average rate of legal tariffs and the government-announced 'ratio of AA items to total tradable items' for respective years.
[a] The average rate of regular tariffs, weighted by the value of 1975 production.
[b] Includes the average rate of special tariffs on imports in addition to the regular tariffs for the 1965–73 period.
[c] Represents the degree of import liberalization from QRs based on both trade programme and special laws.

liberalization in terms of tariffs rose from about 66 per cent in 1965 to 88 per cent by 1990, as the average rate of legal tariffs declined from 53 per cent to 14 per cent over that period.

Second, the degree of import liberalization from QRs is estimated by consolidating the import-restricting effects of special laws with the QRs based on MTI's trade programme. The degree of import liberalization from the QRs based only on the trade programme, which represents the ratio of automatic approval (AA) items to total commodity items as announced by MTI, is adjusted by the import-restricting effects of special laws that are separately estimated (see Kim, K. S., 1987 for the nature of these special laws). The special laws have provided for additional QRs since 1967 owing to the adoption of a new 'negative-list system' of trade programme in that year.[9]

Finally, an overall degree of import liberalization is obtained by simply averaging the degree of liberalization in terms of tariffs and that from QRs. The overall degree of liberalization so estimated rose sharply between 1965 and 1967, and then after about ten years of no change or minor deterioration started to rise again from 1978, very gradually this time. For instance, the overall degree, which had been only 36 per cent in 1965, jumped to 59 per cent in 1967, and then after ten years of minor deterioration rose again from 56 per cent to 88 per cent between 1977 and 1990. This indicates that in Korea conscious efforts to liberalize imports were actually made during the two periods 1965–7 and 1978–90.

As can be seen from the table, the first episode of import liberalization consisted primarily of a loosening of QRs on imports, whereas the second episode took the form of both a loosening of QRs and a reduction of tariff barriers on imports. The first episode of import liberalization was not successful as it failed to assure continued progress in liberalization, whereas the second episode has been rather successful since it has provided the basis for continued liberalization.

A previous study (Kim, K. S., 1991a: 121–4) indicates that imports of the commodity items liberalized from QRs during 1965–7 and 1978–9 generally accelerated in the same year and the year following the liberalization. In other words, the increase in imports of those items liberalized tended to be much higher than the growth of aggregate imports in one or both of the first two years following liberalization, but tapered off after that. A research report by the Korea Institute for Economics and Technology (1986), and Lee et al. (1988: 44–70) support this finding, although the two reports cover different periods, 1982–4 and 1978–87. Despite the tendency of temporary acceleration in the increasing rate of imports liberalized from QRs, the actual impact of import liberalization has not been so visible, probably because the liberalization has been cautious and gradual. Neither of the two liberalization episodes had any discernible negative impact on the growth rates of important macroeconomic variables for the country: GNP, employment, investment, imports or balance of payments.

In order to analyse the economic impact of import liberalization at the sectoral level, K. S. Kim (1990) conducted a correlation analysis by relating changes in sectoral degrees of liberalization (all QRs and tariffs consolidated) to changes in those sectors' major economic variables over the two periods 1966–70 and 1975–85. The result indicates that although import liberalization had some tendency to increase imports during the two periods, and had an adverse impact on domestic production and employment at the thirty-eight manufacturing sectors level during the earlier period, it had no significant, direct impact during the latter period. There is no clear indication, however, that liberalization had any significant effect on domestic industrial productivity during either period. A main reason for the difference in the impact of liberalization between the two periods may be that the approach to liberalization changed between the two periods. Liberalization in the latter half of the 1960s was essentially made by a one-stage approach in the sense that the degree of liberalization made a sudden jump in 1967 but made no further progress for about ten years, whereas the liberalization begining in 1978 followed a gradual, multi-stage approach by using the system of 'advance notices'.

What are the characteristics of the Korean experience of import liberalization? One basic factor that has directly influenced the Korean policy of import liberalization over the long period has been government concern about the country's balance of payments. The government has not promoted import liberalization actively when the country's balance of payments has been in difficulty (Kim, K. S., 1991a: 128). This factor can be used to explain the sequencing of import liberalization following a separate stage of export promotion; the discontinuance of the first liberalization programme after 1967; the continuous progress made in the second liberalization programme; and the success of a gradual multi-stage approach adopted in the second episode. This experience seems unique to Korea, since the experiences in other countries indicate that a drastic approach tends to be more successful (see Papageorgiou *et al.*, 1990: 15).

Since the government concern about the country's balance of payments determined the speed of liberalization, the success of the second episode was made possible by the success of the economic stabilization programme in stabilizing domestic prices in the 1980s. In the 1960s when the country was pursuing an expansionary policy, domestic inflation and the increasing current account deficits resulting from that policy prevented the continuation of the liberalization policy. It is also noted that the realistic exchange rate, which is an important determinant of a country's external balance, could be more easily maintained in the 1980s when the country achieved relative price stability than in the 1960s when it was under inflationary conditions.

Changes in the structure of protection

Various trade-restricting measures directly or indirectly affect the prices of output and input items subject to such measures. The economic effect of such measures can therefore be estimated first by the nominal rate of protection, which is the price difference between the domestic and world markets, expressed as a percentage of the latter. When legal tariffs are the only instrument of trade restrictions in a country, the legal tariff rate should represent the nominal rate of protection. In Korea, however, legal tariffs are generally not a good measure of nominal protection rates since non-tariff trade barriers have widely been used, as already mentioned. There are other reasons for the unreliability of legal tariffs: first, some tariffs have been prohibitive, although relatively low in absolute magnitude; second, tariff exemptions and reductions have been granted for various purposes; and third, much of Korean industry has been export-oriented even though domestic markets have been protected by tariffs.

Because legal tariffs cannot be used as an indicator of the nominal protection rate, the nominal rates should be estimated by direct price comparisons between the domestic and world markets for tradable items. The nominal rates of protection based on price comparisons do not, however, give a very good indication of the resource-diverting effects of tariffs and QRs, although they are better than the legal tariff rates. A much better measure is the rate of effective protection, because the protection of a certain production activity is affected not only by the nominal protection on the product itself but also by nominal rates on traded inputs. The effective rate of protection is designed to measure the degree of protection afforded to value-adding processes. It is the percentage difference between domestic value added under protection and the value added in world market prices.[10]

The effective rate of protection cannot, however, take into account subsidies in the form of income tax exemptions and preferential low-interest loans to specific activities. Such subsidies provided substantial incentives to exporting activities in Korea, especially in the 1960s and the 1970s. In order to describe the structure of protection for Korea, therefore, it is necessary to introduce the concept of the effective subsidy rate, in addition to the effective protection rate. For calculation of the effective subsidy rate, total direct tax and interest subsidies should be added to value added in domestic prices. This adjusted value added is then divided by value added in world market prices, and the ratio (minus one) is the effective subsidy rate (Balassa and Associates, 1982: 17–18).

Table 10.8 presents the nominal and effective protection rates for domestic sales and effective subsidy rates for exports, all by industry group, for 1968, 1978 and 1988, that have so far been estimated in Korea by different authors. As can be seen from the table, the effective subsidy rates for 1988 are not available. In fact, a separate estimation of the effective subsidy rates was not justifiable in view of the abolition of most of the direct tax reductions and interest-rate preference for export industries by the 1980s.

The presentation in the table represents the average rates of nominal and effective protection and effective subsidy at the level of an eleven industry groups classification, which are properly weighted by the world price value of domestic sales or the world price value added. The estimates given in

Table 10.8 Nominal and effective protection rates for domestic sales and effective subsidy rates for exports, by industry group, Korea, selected years (%)

Industry group	Nominal protection rate for domestic sales			Effective protection rate for domestic sales[a]			Effective subsidy rate for exports[a]	
	1968	1978	1988	1968	1978	1988	1968	1978
Primary industry								
Agriculture, forestry and fishing	17	55	100	19	77	159	−10	16
Mining	9	−20	24	4	26	32	3	11
Primary industry total	17	46	90	18	62	139	−3	15
Manufacturing								
Processed foods	3	40	9	−18	−29	−55	2	32
Beverage and tobacco	2	20	23	19	28	38	15	13
Construction materials	4	7	8	−11	−15	−2	6	19
Intermediate products I	3	−2	11	−25	−38	−27	43	24
Intermediate products II	21	1	7	26	8	14	17	26
Non-durable consumer goods	12	15	−2	−11	32	4	5	17
Consumer durables	39	40	3	64	131	22	2	38
Machinery	30	18	11	44	47	17	5	24
Transport equipment	55	31	14	163	135	54	23	26
Manufacturing total	12	10	5	1	5	1	12	23
All industries	14	18	13	11	31	16	9	18

Sources: Westphal and Kim (1982: 23), for 1968 data; Nam (1981) for 1978 data; and Hong (1992) for 1988 data.
[a] Estimates by the Balassa method. Effective subsidy rates for 1982 are not available.

the table should be taken to indicate the relative magnitudes, not the absolute levels of protection and subsidy rates by industry group.[11] In addition, the nominal and effective protection rates, as well as the effective subsidy rates, are gross figures not adjusted for any overvaluation of the won currency over time.

From the data given in the table, some interesting characteristics of the Korean structure of protection or incentives can be observed. First, the nominal and effective rates of protection for Korea were not only relatively low when compared with those in other developing countries, but also showed a pattern of protection unique among the developing countries, giving much higher protection to the primary sector than to the manufacturing sector (Balassa and Associates, 1971, 1982). In addition, the extent of discrimination in the protection rates between the two sectors widened in the two decades under observation.

Second, the average effective rate of protection for the manufacturing sector's domestic sales was −1 per cent and 5 per cent in 1968 and 1978, respectively, but the average rate of effective subsidy for same sector exports was reasonably high, 12 per cent and 23 per cent, respectively, in the two years. This seems to indicate that, within manufacturing, export incentives were much greater on average than the incentives to import substitution in Korea. However, the estimates of both effective protection and subsidy rates showed much variation among industry groups within manufacturing during the same period, indicating a wide dispersion of incentives even within that sector.

Third, the nominal and effective protection rates for three industry groups, that is, consumer durables, machinery and transport equipment, were generally much higher than those for other industry groups in the two decades, although this pattern of industrial discrimination in protection rates was significantly alleviated by 1988.

Finally, in both 1978 and 1988 the nominal rates of protection were negative for a few industry groups. These negative rates of nominal protection in the two years are unusual ones in view of the fact that the competitive situation in an open economy would not allow such a phenomenon. Nam (1981) argues that the negative rates for 1978 resulted from the government's direct price controls on some of the industrial products belonging to such industry groups.

Foreign investment and technology imports

Although Korea relied heavily on foreign resources for financing its investment until the mid-1980s, direct foreign investment (DFI) was relatively unimportant as a source of investment finance. Korea imported foreign capital mainly in the form of repayable loans; DFI accounted for only about 5 per cent of total capital inflows during the 1962–84 period when a substantial amount of foreign capital was imported each year.

In accordance with the Foreign Capital Inducement Promotion Law first enacted in 1960 and revised thereafter, the government provided various incentives for DFI, including tax holidays, guarantees of profit remittances and withdrawal of principal, tax rebates for technology licences, as well as equal treatment with domestic firms. Despite the incentives, the DFIs approved in the decade of 1962–71 amounted to only US$266 million for 389 cases (Ministry of Finance, 1991). DFI inflows were not very active in this decade due partly to domestic political instability and partly to the domestic firms' preference for foreign debts over equity investment, which was attributable to the large interest rate gap between domestic and foreign loans that existed in that period.

Beginning in 1972, DFI started to increase rapidly as those factors that had been discouraging DFI before were largely removed. The government then introduced more restrictive regulations on DFI. The general guidelines on DFI announced in 1973 included: (i) provisions favouring joint ventures over firms wholly owned by foreign investors; (ii) eligibility criteria that eliminated the DFIs which might be in competition with domestic firms in either domestic or world markets; (iii) basic limitation of the foreign participation rate to 50 per cent; and (iv) a minimum amount requirement for DFI.

Beginning in the early 1980s, the government gradually liberalized foreign investment while reducing tax concessions provided for DFI. As of 1990, about 98 per cent of all manufacturing activities (522 in total) were subject to automatic approval for DFI without any limitation on foreign ownership, foreign remittances, etc. This DFI liberalization of the 1980s was quite consistent with the phase of the country's industrialization that necessitated DFI for acquiring the sophisticated technologies not usually accessible by other means. DFI inflows were greatly accelerated in the 1980s.

Of the total DFI, equivalent to approximately US\$7.9 billion, approved in the last three decades, the actual arrival was about \$5.9 billion, or 75 per cent of the approved amount, as of the end of 1990, due partly to time lags between approval and arrival, and partly due to some cancellations. In terms of DFI arrival in Korea, the country relied very heavily on two countries, Japan and the US, for the source of DFI; Japan accounted for the highest share, 49 per cent of the total, which was followed by the US share of 29 per cent. Only 23 per cent of the total DFI came from other countries (Ministry of Finance, 1991).

DFI in the manufacturing sector occupied about 65 per cent of the total DFI arrivals, while that in the service sector, including hotels and financial institutions, accounted for 34 per cent. DFI in the primary sector was almost negligible, reflecting the country's poor natural resource endowment. Within manufacturing the bulk of DFI went to four technology-intensive industries: electronics and electrical equipment, chemicals, transport equipment, and machinery (Ministry of Finance, 1991). This industrial distribution of DFI shows that they have been channelled mainly to technology-intensive industries so that domestic industries might be given access to the sophisticated new technologies. Koo (1986: 198–201) examines the pattern of DFI in Korean manufacturing during 1962–81 and suggests that the pattern appears to have closely followed the direction of government industrial policy.[12]

The country's imports of disembodied technologies have also been increasing rapidly, particularly since the late 1970s. The average annual import of foreign technologies, which had been limited to only fifty cases during 1962–76, jumped to 245 cases in 1977–81 and continued to accelerate until 1990. This rapid increase in the recent years reflects the ever-increasing demand of domestic industries for disembodied new technologies. This is in contrast to the observation by Westphal et al. (1984), based on the Korean experience in the 1960s and the 1970s, that 'machinery imports and turnkey plant construction have been of much greater consequence in the transfer of technology, and a tremendous amount of know-how has entered with Koreans returning from study or work abroad'. As the country's industrialization progressed, domestic industries in the 1980s and the early 1990s could no longer depend much upon the technologies embodied in imported machinery.

As in the case of DFI, Korea relied very heavily on two countries, Japan and the United States, for the source of disembodied technological licences. The industries that imported disembodied technologies in large number until 1990 were machinery, electronic and electrical equipment, petroleum refining, chemical, metal, chemical fibre, processed food, etc. in the order of the number of cases (Ministry of Finance, 1991).

SELECTIVE POLICY FOR HEAVY AND CHEMICAL INDUSTRIES

Main features of the heavy and chemical industries (HCI)

In 1973 the Korean government adopted an ambitious Heavy and Chemical Industries Promotion Plan (hereafter called the HCI Plan), requiring a total investment of US$9.6 billion, to be implemented during a nine-year period (1973–81).

The plan envisioned the promotion of six key industries: steel, non-ferrous metal, machinery, shipbuilding, electronics and chemicals. It was expected that the plan would increase Korea's per capita GNP and exports to US$1,000 and $10 billion, respectively, by the target year (1981). The corresponding figures for 1972, the year that had just ended when the plan was announced, were only $318 for per capita GNP and $1.6 billion for exports, both in current prices.

Even before the announcement of the HCI Plan, some HCI-related projects had been promoted on a case-by-case basis. The big push on HCI which began in 1973 was, however, significantly different from the past approach to industrial planning and policymaking in Korea. The past plans covering five-year periods had shown the main features of indicative planning in the sense that they only set the direction of government policy regarding private investment in manufacturing. In contrast, the HCI Plan was not an indicative plan, since it not only provided a comprehensive list of HCI projects to be undertaken during the plan period, together with the timetables for their construction, but also envisioned direct government intervention in business sector decision-making to achieve the plan targets. In addition, the HCI Plan attempted to provide for a collective accommodation of related HCI projects in large industrial complexes: for instance, the Changwon Industrial Complex for machinery industry, the Yochon Complex for petrochemical industry, the Kumi Complex for electronics, etc.

Why did Korea adopt such an ambitious plan for the development of

HCI in 1973? We may give three major reasons. First, the development of HCI was promoted for the purpose of constructing the domestic defence industries, which were considered important for enhancing the nation's self-defence capability in the wake of the partial withdrawal of US troops from the country in the early 1970s. Second, the construction of HCI was considered inevitable for a sustained, export-led growth of the economy in view of the expectation that it might soon face a limit to growth through the expansion of labour-intensive, light industry exports.[13] Third, the HCI Plan was considered important for improving the country's balance of payments, since the past strategy emphasizing light industry exports only increased imports for both capital and intermediate goods and was not effective in reducing the current account deficits.

After the announcement of the HCI Plan, the first oil crisis and the consequent recession in Western industrial countries caused substantial difficulties for the Korean economy in 1974–5. The country's GNP growth slowed down significantly while both the rate of domestic inflation and the current account deficit soared. Although some amendment to the plan was attempted when formulating the Fourth Five-Year Economic and Social Development Plan (1977–81), the original HCI Plan was executed without substantial revisions until 1979, when an adjustment of investment in HCI projects was attempted in accordance with a comprehensive economic stabilization programme. By then, however, most of the planned HCI projects had already been either completed or were well underway. For this reason, all of the adjustments made to the HCI projects thereafter mainly reflected government efforts to bail out financially insolvent firms in the HCI sector.

A basic problem in promoting the HCI projects in the early part of the 1970s was how to mobilize and channel the necessary resources, including capital, technology, technical manpower, industrial sites and entrepreneurship, to the HCI sector. There were many constraints to solving this basic problem. First of all, the country's capital market, which should supply long-term investment funds, was still underdeveloped, while banking institutions were mainly engaged in supplying short-term working capital. Domestic educational institutes and vocational training facilities were not producing enough quantity and quality of the technical manpower required for the planned HCI projects. It was also very difficult for private enterprises to secure large industrial sites required for the HCI projects due to complicated laws and regulations concerning land-use. Under these circumstances private enterprises were very reluctant to invest in HCI even if they saw a promising long-run prospect in such ventures (Lee, K. T., 1991: 146). The HCI Plan therefore included various policy measures to eliminate these constraints.

Plan implementation and evaluation

Practically, all of the planned HCI projects were expected to be undertaken by private enterprises. Thus implementation of the HCI Plan actually took the form of taking various policy measures to mobilize and channel necessary resources to the HCI sector. In the early stage of the plan's implementation the government did not hesitate to designate and force certain large business establishments to undertake selected key HCI projects, but it also gave various incentives to those establishments undertaking the HCI projects. Policy measures taken to implement the plan can be summarized as follows:

(i) *Financial support*: In order to procure the necessary financial resources for HCI projects, the government enacted the Law on National Investment Fund (NIF) in December 1973. In accordance with this law, varying proportions of either public funds or increments in savings deposits of various financial institutions were required to be deposited to the NIF. The law also prescribed that the funds deposited into the NIF should be used for lending to HCI and other specified projects. The total amount of funds deposited into the NIF increased from 10.9 per cent of the increase in gross liquidity (M3) to 12.4 per cent between 1974 and 1981. About 55 per cent or more of the loanable funds was allocated to HCI for equipment loans and credit for purchase of domestic machinery (Lee, S. C., 1991: 444–5). Interest rates on equipment loans for HCI projects were generally lower than those on ordinary bank loans by about 2–5 percentage points during the 1973–81 period.

(ii) *Tax incentives*: The Law Concerning Tax Exemptions and Reduction which was amended in 1974 provided a variety of tax incentives for enterprises engaged in HCI. The law allowed the HCI industries to choose one of three options: tax holidays (100 per cent for three years and 50 per cent for the following two years); investment tax credits (8–10 per cent); or accelerated depreciation (100 per cent) (Lee, K. T., 1991: 152). As a result, the marginal effective corporate tax rate for enterprises in the HCI sector ranged, on average, from 15 per cent to 20 per cent during 1975–81, whereas the rate for other industrial enterprises was between 48 and 52 per cent (Lee, S. C., 1991: 448).

(iii) *Technology and manpower policies*: The government established six new research institutes and increased its expenditures for research and development (R&D) in order to reduce gradually the country's dependence on foreign technologies in the fields of HCI. During 1974–9, the government financed about 55 per cent of the total R&D expenditures, which were still less than 1 per cent of GNP (Economic Planning Board, 1982: 260). On the other hand, the government undertook some drastic measures to meet an expected increase in the HCI sector's demand for technical manpower.[14]

(iv) *Construction of industrial complexes*: The government constructed nine industrial complexes between 1973 and 1979 in order to place HCI-related plants. During the 1974–1981 period, government spending for the construction of industrial complexes amounted to 344 billion won, or about 36 per cent of total government expenditures for HCI projects which, in turn, comprised about 2–5 per cent of the total central government budget.

(v) *Increased protection of HCI*: Although one of the major objectives of the HCI Plan was to diversify the country's structure of exports by increasing exports of HCI products, the promotion of the planned HCI projects actually led to emphasizing import substitution in relative terms. The minor deterioration in the country's overall degree of import liberalization between 1968 and 1977, discussed in the previous section, resulted partly from government policy to protect new HCI producers. In addition, the government intensified its control on machinery imports in 1976 by introducing domestic content requirements for major industrial facilities, a licensing system for imports of foreign machinery costing more than US$1 million, and a pre-review system for machinery imports by government agencies and public enterprises. The higher rates of effective protection on the HCI sectors than other sectors that we mentioned in the preceding section reflect this policy direction to protect domestic HCI producers.

Of these five policy measures, only the last one can be taken as the proper instrument of trade policy in a narrow sense. This reflects the fact that the role of trade policy in the implementation of the HCI Plan was relatively small compared with other industrial policy instruments. In any case, these policy measures changed the attitudes of many large business groups who had been initially reluctant to invest in HCI projects to rush for 'a ride on the HCI bandwagon'. This rush resulted in a substantial increase in the HCI's share of investment relative to that of light industry. The total investment in HCI, which had been about 57 per cent of total manufacturing investment during 1971–4, increased to 64 per cent in 1975–9, while that in light industry declined from 44 to 36 per cent. Separating out equipment investment from all manufacturing investment, the HCI's share in that sector's total equipment investment was as high as 76 per cent on average during 1973–9.

In the course of implementing the HCI Plan, the government consistently followed an expansionary fiscal and monetary policy, although inflationary pressures accumulated. When the second world oil crisis began to affect the economy in early 1979, however, the country had no other choice than to follow a strong economic stabilization programme, in view of the rapid increases in both domestic prices and the balance of payments deficit. This sudden shift of policy did not immediately reduce the rate of inflation, but resulted in a drastic slowdown of the economic growth rate (even to a negative rate in 1980) and a sharp decline in capital utilization in the HCI sector. Many of the completed HCI plants could not operate without government assistance, thus necessitating government intervention for investment adjustment or bail-out. Due to the neglect of investment in light industrial sectors, international competitiveness of domestic light industry was also significantly weakened by then.

In 1979–80 the government undertook a few rounds of 'investment adjustment' in the HCI sector. The main purpose of the adjustment was to relieve the major HCI firms of their financial difficulties by promoting mergers among competing HCI firms or by scaling down the planned capacities in some cases. Many of the HCI plants with excess capacity were subject to this kind of investment adjustment, which usually accompanied 'rescue' financing from the government or the government-controlled financial institutions.[15]

Despite the painful adjustment efforts of the government, the general performance of the HCI sectors remained sluggish until around 1985. Although the electronics and petrochemical industries started to take off from the slump in 1983, most of the HCI sectors had to wait until early 1986 when the business environment was dramatically changed by the 'golden opportunity of three lows' (low oil price, low dollar value and low interest rate). Many of the troubled HCI sectors were able to increase their output and exports very rapidly from 1986, thereby increasing both their capacity utilization rates and business profitability. Thus the shares of HCI in both manufacturing exports and value added continuously expanded.[16] This indicates that the HCI became the country's new growth industry by the latter half of the 1980s.

It is difficult to make an *ex post* evaluation of the HCI Plan. The HCI Plan was successful, at least in the long run, in bringing out structural improvement in both the country's exports and manufacturing output as originally envisioned. The country could also achieve its current account surplus during 1986–9, owing, at least partly, to the rapid expansion of HCI exports and the import substitution of some intermediate goods and capital goods realized by the development of the HCI sector. The HCI Plan was, however, not successful in the sense that it resulted in a substantial waste of resources during 1979–85 when the planned capacities of many HCI plants were underutilized. The weakening of international competitiveness of light industry in the 1970s, which was attributable to the HCI Plan, was also a cost to the economy in that it reduced growth potential based on the continuous expansion of light industry exports.

The country's experience of economic difficulties in the late 1970s and early 1980s, which resulted partly from the strong implementation of the

Table 10.9 Contribution to growth rate of all manufacturing output: comparison by different periods, Korea (%)

	1967–73	1973–9	1979–88	1967–77	1977–88	1967–88
A. Contributions in percentage points (annual average basis)						
Total factor productivity	4.16	1.87	0.54	3.42	0.61	1.94
Labour input	1.11	0.91	0.57	1.15	0.52	0.82
Capital input	2.13	3.24	2.07	2.67	2.19	2.42
Intermediate input	15.78	14.77	9.80	16.39	9.85	12.85
All sources total	23.18	20.79	12.98	23.63	13.17	18.03
B. Percentage of output growth						
Total factor productivity	17.95	8.99	4.16	14.47	4.63	10.76
Labour input	4.79	4.38	4.39	4.87	3.95	4.55
Capital input	9.19	15.58	15.95	11.30	16.63	13.42
Intermediate input	68.07	71.05	75.50	69.36	74.79	71.27
All sources total	100.00	100.00	100.00	100.00	100.00	100.00

Source: Kim and Hong (1992).

ambitious HCI Plan, yielded some important lessons to policymakers. In 1979 the government began to shift not only its policy emphasis from growth to stability, but also its industrial policy focus from the previous, industry-specific policies toward a functional approach. The new government that came into power in 1980 reorganized the system of incentives, redirecting tax incentives and financial support to R&D activities and the training of technical manpower, irrespective of industrial branch. In other words, the government began to reduce its role in industrial planning and targeting, and attempted to undertake policy reforms to promote competition in domestic markets. The active promotion of trade liberalization in the 1980s, the enactment of the Anti-trust and Fair Trade Law in 1981, and the replacement of industry-specific promotional laws by a more neutral Industrial Development Law in early 1986 should all be taken as part of such reform attempts.

PRODUCTIVITY GROWTH IN MANUFACTURING

Trends in total factor productivity

The TFP growth rates of Korean manufacturing at the level of the thirty-six subsectors classification are estimated for the period 1967–88 following a growth accounting method.[17] The estimated results aggregated to the level of the whole manufacturing industry are shown in Table 10.9. They have been obtained by measuring output growth on the basis of gross output instead of value added.

As shown in the table, the whole manufacturing industry's TFP grew at an average annual rate of 1.9 per cent during the entire period 1967–88, contributing 10.8 per cent to the output growth of that industry which reached 18 per cent on an average annual basis. During the same period, the growth contributions of labour input and capital input in percentage points were 0.8 and 2.4 respectively, significantly lower than the growth contribution of intermediate inputs, which reached 12.9 in percentage points, or 71.3 per cent of output growth.

The manufacturing industry's TFP growth rate and its contribution to that industry's output growth vary by different period of observation. During the early period of high growth from 1967 to 1973, manufacturing output grew by an average annual rate of 23.2 per cent, and the TFP growth rate was a high 4.2 per cent, equivalent to about 18 per cent of the output growth. The growth rates of both output and TFP declined to 20.8 per cent and 1.9 per cent, respectively, in the following period of 1973–9, during which the first world oil crisis took place and the second one was just beginning to have some impact on the economy. During the last period, 1979–88, which included the years of economic recession and adjustment in the early 1980s, the growth rate of manufacturing output declined sharply to 13 per cent, while that of TFP dropped to 0.5 per cent. This indicates that the growth rates of both manufacturing output and TFP have continuously declined over the last two decades.

The growth rates of both manufacturing output and TFP for the whole period (1967–88) are now broken down to those for two sub-periods, 1967–77 and 1977–88, since 1977 is considered a normal year in terms of the economic growth rate. The TFP for manufacturing grew by an average annual rate of a relatively high 3.4 per cent during the early period of 1967–77, contributing 14.5 per cent to the output growth rate which was as high as 23.6 per cent. During the latter period (1977–88), the growth rates of both output and TFP sharply declined to 13.2 per cent and 0.6 per cent, respectively. The relative contribution of TFP growth to manufacturing output growth also declined sharply between the two periods since the declining rate of TFP was much more drastic than that of output.

The estimated TFP growth rate for the whole manufacturing industry during the entire period (1967–88) is only slightly lower than the previous estimate by K. S. Kim and Park (1988) for the period 1966–83, but significantly lower than the estimate by C. K. Kim et al. (1984) for 1967–79, partly because the latter study measured output growth on the basis of value added. The observed trend of decline in the estimated TFP growth rate over the last two decades, particularly the sharp decline following the first oil shock of 1973–4, is, however, consistent with the results of other studies (Kim, C. K., et al., 1984; Kim, K. S., and Park, 1985, 1988).

The declining trend in the average TFP growth rate of the whole manufacturing industry might be explained by many factors, some of which are dealt with later in this section. But two major factors are considered responsible for the general trend of decline in the TFP growth rate, although it is not possible to provide empirical evidence. One is that the industrial efficiency gains which could be generated through the positive effects of opening-up to semi-free trade in the 1960s was largely spent by the first half of the 1970s (Kim, K. S. and Park, 1985: 173). Another related factor may be that the rapid efficiency gains which were made possible by the domestic industry's efforts to catch up with technical and managerial practices of advanced countries could no longer be expected after the mid–1970s, since the technological gap between Korea and the advanced countries narrowed significantly by that time.

Reviewing the estimated TFP growth rates and their contributions to output growth by major sector and by subsector within manufacturing, one finds that both light industry and heavy-and-chemical industry (HCI) experienced significant declines in their output and TFP growth rates between the two periods 1967–77 and 1977–88, as in the case of the average for all manufacturing. Reflecting progress in the country's industrialization, however, output of its HCI grew much faster than that of light industry. In other words, the annual growth rate of HCI output was about 5–7 percentage points higher than that of light industry on average during the two periods under observation. Despite this significant difference in the output growth rate between the two industries, the growth rate of TFP did not show a wide divergence between those industries. The growth rate of TFP for HCI was 3.6 per cent during the early period (1967–77), only slightly higher than that for light industry. During the latter period, the TFP for heavy industry grew only by an average annual rate of 0.64 per cent, compared with 0.58 per cent for light industry. For this reason, TFP's relative contribution to output growth of HCI turned out to be lower than that of light industry during the two periods, despite the higher growth rate of output in the former industry (Kim, K. S., 1993). This indicates that the rapid growth of HCI during the period under observation can be explained not by TFP growth but mainly by the rapid increases in factor inputs (including intermediate inputs).

Turning to the estimated results of TFP growth rates and their contributions to output growth by subsector, we find that, on the one hand, the subsectors belonging to HCI generally attained higher rates of TFP growth than those of the subsectors belonging to light industry during the entire period (1967–88). The reason may be that their output growth rates were generally higher than those of the light industrial subsectors. In fact, out of the ten subsectors recording the highest rate of TFP growth, all but one belong to HCI. On the other hand, the ten subsectors that recorded the lowest growth rates of TFP mainly included energy-related subsectors (oil refining, other petroleum and coal products) and resource-intensive subsectors (other non-metallic minerals, iron and steel), as well as labour-intensive light industrial subsectors (leather products, wearing apparel, processed food, textile yarn and fabric).

Trade policy and productivity change

The literature on trade and development suggests a possible causation between trade and industrial policy orientation and productivity growth rates. One hypothesis is that an export-oriented industrialization policy may result in better productivity performance than the alternative, import-substitution policy. The reason is that export promotion not only leads to the realization of scale economies through the expansion of the market beyond a narrow domestic market, but also accompanies smaller deviations from a first-best optimal policy of equalized incentives for all industries than under import substitution (Krueger, 1981: 17). The second hypothesis is that import liberalization increases domestic industrial efficiency or productivity, while a protective policy to promote import substitution may adversely affect industrial efficiency. Although the growth of imports that is caused by import liberalization may restrict the domestic market and contribute negatively to attaining scale economies, it is generally accepted that liberalization will contribute positively to domestic productivity since it introduces foreign competition into the domestic economy and stimulates domestic specialization in the industries in which the country may have a comparative advantage.

Based on a similar line of hypothesis, there have been many attempts to investigate the possible links between trade policy and productivity growth empirically as suggested by Pack (1988), Havrylyshyn (1990) and Tybout (1992). It seems that some strong evidence of positive links between trade policy and productivity growth has been found by cross-country studies. But in many cases inter-temporal comparisons within a single country have not shown clear evidence of such positive trade–productivity links. There are, however, a few exceptions. Krueger and Tuncer (1982), and Nishimizu and Robinson (1984) found some significant associations between trade-industrial policy orientation and productivity growth.

In addition to the above hypotheses, we may also empirically test other hypotheses concerning the causes of productivity change. One is the hypothesis of the so-called Verdoorn's law that the productivity growth rate is influenced by the output growth rate. The second is that capacity utilization may directly influence TFP growth rates. The third is that industrial concentration may negatively affect TFP growth. Finally, sectoral R&D expenditures may positively contribute to increasing sectoral TFPs as suggested by Terleckyj (1980).[18]

In order to examine the effects of trade policy and other variables on TFP growth, a correlation matrix among the related variables is first calculated using the cross-section data for thirty-six subsectors for 1967–88, as

353

shown in Table 10.10.[19] Although we have mentioned about five plausible factors that may influence TFP growth, it was necessary to include ten variables altogether in the correlation analysis since trade and industrial policy could be represented not by a single variable but by several alternatives.

Examining the effects of several alternative variables representing trade and industrial policy on subsectoral TFP growth, we first direct our attention to the effect of import liberalization. Although it was expected that progress in import liberalization would positively contribute to increasing TFP growth, Pearson's simple coefficient of correlation between the overall degree of import liberalization (ML) and TFP turned out to be statistically insignificant. The overall degree of import liberalization was estimated by consolidating the degrees of liberalization from both QRs and legal tariffs.[20] The insignificant relationship between import liberalization and TFP seems to result from the fact that, even if progress in import liberalization (ML) contributes to enhancing industrial efficiency, it raises the ratio of imports to gross output (M/X) which is negatively correlated to TFP growth. In fact, the coefficient of correlation between ML and M/X turned out to be positive and statistically significant, indicating that the country's import liberalization was effective in increasing imports at the subsectoral level.

Second, the effects of increases in both nominal and effective protection rates on TFP growth are examined (data on NPR and EPR are from Westphal and Kim, 1982, and Hong, 1992). The coefficient of correlation between the TFP growth rate (TFP) and the nominal protection rate (NPR) or effective protection rate (EPR) turned out to be negative as expected, but the coefficient between TFP and NPR was only marginally significant at the 10 per cent level, while that between TFP and EPR was statistically insignificant. The insignificant relationship between TFP and EPR may be caused by a much wider divergence in the estimated EPRs by subsector than in TFP growth rates. The negative correlation between TFP and NPR or EPR may support the hypothesis that higher protection on domestic industry will adversely affect productivity growth through technological innovation, if it was statistically significant.

Third, the coefficient of correlation between the change in the export/gross output ratio (E/X) and the TFP growth rate was positive but statistically insignificant. It may indicate that the effect of export expansion on TFP growth is not significantly different from that of production for domestic sales on TFP growth. When the export variable is changed to a net export basis, however, the correlation between the net exports/output ratio [(E–M)/X] and TFP growth turned out to be positive and statistically significant since exports could be an offset to the negative effect of imports. The correlation coefficient between E/X and ML was positive and statistically significant as expected, whereas that between E/X and NPR or EPR was negative and statistically significant. These coefficients reflect the fact

Table 10.10 Matrix of correlation between subsectoral TFP growth rates and related variables, Korea, 1967–88 (Pearson's simple correlation coefficients)

	TFP	X/P	ML	NPR	EPR	E/X	E−M/X	M/X	OR	CR
TFP growth rates (TFP)	1.0									
Real output (gross) growth rate (X/P)	0.513	1.0								
Change in overall degree of import liberalization (ML)	-0.053	0.157	1.0							
Rate of increase in 1 plus nominal protection rate (NPR)	-0.268	-0.272	-0.352	1.0						
Rate of increase in 1 plus effective protection rate (EPR)	-0.216	-0.226	-0.257	0.155	1.0					
Change in the ratio of exports to output (E/X)	0.015	0.227	0.520	-0.351	-0.216	1.0				
Change in the ratio of net exports to output (E−M/X)	0.410	0.052	-0.215	-0.038	-0.118	0.271	1.0			
Change in the ratio of imports to output (M/X)	-0.421	0.004	0.337	-0.037	0.075	-0.062	-0.978	1.0		
Rate of increase in capacity utilization index (OR)	-0.040	-0.122	-0.289	0.294	-0.146	0.161	0.164	-0.136	1.0	
Degree of industrial concentration (CR)	0.198	0.104	0.476	0.277	0.046	0.114	0.037	0.013	0.315	1.0

The degree of industrial concentration represents the average concentration ratio for 1970, 1982 and 1988, which was calculated in terms of the three largest enterprises in each industry's sales at the five-digit level of industrial classification. All other variables are given in either percentage rate of increase or percentage point difference between 1967 and 1988.

Except for the variable on capacity utilization (OR), the number of observations for all variables was 36 (subsectors). Coefficients of correlation exceeding 0.32 are therefore statistically significant at the 5 per cent level, while those exceeding 0.27 are significant at the 10 per cent level. Since the number of observations for the OR variable was 29, the coefficient must exceed 0.35 to be statistically significant at the 5 per cent level.

that those subsectors with high export/output ratios are the competitive industries that do not require much protection from imports.

Even if one accepts that such export industries are more competitive than other domestic industries, the above results indicate that those industries did not attain any significantly higher rates of TFP growth than other industries during the period under observation. This implies that the subsectors producing mainly for domestic sales increased their efficiency almost as much as the export industries over the last two decades. This is not unexpected in view of the gradual but substantial reduction in the overall level of industrial protection which resulted from progress in trade liberalization over the past two decades.

The above discussion on the relationship between TFP growth and alternative trade policy variables does not necessarily support all the hypotheses that have been presented. It seems consistent with the general evidences of other countries surveyed by Pack (1988) and Havrylyshyn (1990), but contradictory to the findings of Krueger and Tuncer (1982), and Nishimizu and Robinson (1984). These two studies derived their conclusions from a comparison of TFP growth rates under different trade and industrial policy regimes. But South Korea has maintained roughly the same policy of export-oriented industrialization over the period under observation since it shifted its policy in the first half of the 1960s. Our result is therefore mainly based on comparing the different effects of export expansion, domestic output expansion for domestic sales (or import substitution), and import liberalization on TFP growth under the same policy regime.

Turning to other hypotheses not directly related to trade and industrial policy, it seems clear that Verdoorn's law also applies to the case of Korean manufacturing, as expected. However, the change in the capacity utilization rate (OR) did not have any statistically significant impact on TFP growth, partly because three-year moving average indexes were used to estimate the TFP growth rates, and partly because the subsectoral data on capacity utilization are not very reliable. The coefficient of correlation between the TFP growth rate and the degree of industrial concentration (CR) turned out to be positive, contrary to our expectation, although statistically insignificant.[21]

Finally, some multiple regressions were run to verify the results of the simple correlation analysis so far explained. Many alternative forms of regression equations were estimated using the same cross-section data for 1967–88 used for the simple correlation analysis, but only the most plausible result is reported below (each variable is as defined in Table 10.10).

$$TFP = 2.700 + 0.001 \, (X/P) - 0.287 \, (M/X) - 0.410 \, NPR + 81.819 \, CR$$
$$\quad (0.9) \quad (3.2) \qquad (-3.4) \qquad (-1.7) \qquad (1.7)$$
$$R^2 = 0.51; \, DW = 2.3$$

The above regression equation indicates that the TFP growth rate is influenced positively by the growth rate of real gross output and the degree of industrial concentration, but negatively by the changes in both the import/gross output ratio and the nominal protection rate. All the slope regression coefficients turned out to be statistically significant. The variable representing the degree of industrial concentration turned out to have a statistically significant, positive influence on TFP growth, although the positive coefficient of correlation between the two variables shown in Table 10.10 was statistically insignificant. This unexpected positive influence of industrial concentration on TFP growth was also found in the case of the United States according to Kendrick and Grossman (1980). The positive relation between the two variables is said to occur because the degree of industrial concentration is usually associated positively with the ratio of R&D expenditures to value added in manufacturing. It is, however, not possible to verify this hypothesis on the basis of Korean data since time-series data on R&D expenditures by subsector are not available.

The results of the multiple regression exercise generally support the results of the simple correlation analysis, with the exception of the variable representing the degree of industrial concentration. The inclusion of such important trade policy variables as the changes in the degree of import liberalization (ML) and in the ratio of exports to gross output (E/X) in the regressions did not improve their fits. The reported regression equation can explain only 51 per cent of variations in subsectoral TFP growth rates for 1967–88. This indicates that many of the important variables which may explain the variations are still missing in our analysis.

CONCLUDING REMARKS

From this overview, several points can be derived as to the characteristics of Korean policies and experience in the last three decades.

First, Korea has persistently followed an export-oriented industrialization policy and succeeded in rapid industrialization and growth since the policy shift in the first half of the 1960s. There has not been any reversal of that policy although the policy was relatively weakened during the implementation of the Heavy and Chemical Industry (HCI) Promotion Plan in the 1970s.

Second, the country not only delayed the promotion of import liberalization until it became somewhat confident in export expansion even after the shift to the export-oriented policy, but has also been cautious in the promotion of liberalization. Although it had experimented with the one-stage approach to liberalization in the latter half of the 1960s, it has succeeded in opening up the domestic market by taking a gradual, multi-stage approach since 1978. The speed of the country's trade liberalization has, in general, been greatly influenced by the government's concern about the country's current account balance.

Third, the Korean government has maintained a strong leadership in economic management and business sector decision-making as demonstrated by the experience of the ambitious HCI Plan formulation and implementation. It has not hesitated to intervene selectively in business sector decision-making for achievement of its policy objectives. Thanks to the 'strong state' tradition, it has also had both the willingness and ability to implement its plan and policies once formulated.

Fourth, the country has not experienced any serious shortage of manpower until very recently in the course of rapid industrialization and growth. Ambitious entrepreneurs, competent managers, engineers and many different classes of skilled workers have always been available within the country to satisfy the domestic demand for such manpower that has been constantly increasing in the course of rapid industrialization. It seems that the traditional emphasis on education and the relatively high level of general education in the country have been attributable to the smooth supply of required human capital.

Fifth, the country's export-oriented industrialization strategy did not necessarily bring about an improvement in the country's balance of payments situation until serious efforts were made to achieve domestic price stability. Korea achieved a significant improvement in its current account balance and also some surplus only in the 1980s, during which policy emphasis was placed on stabilization rather than growth.

Sixth, the country's export-oriented industrialization was accompanied by the rapid growth of big business groups or jaebols. Although they have played an important role in increasing the country's exports and diversifying domestic industries into technology and capital-intensive industries, they have resulted in an undesirable concentration of economic power.

Finally, the country has experienced a gradual deceleration in the TFP growth rate of manufacturing, particularly since the early 1970s. An analysis based on Korean data does not necessarily support the hypothesis that export expansion and import liberalization lead to a higher TFP growth than can be achieved by domestic output expansion for domestic sales or import substitution. It is possible that different effects of export expansion and import substitution on TFP growth existed prior to Korea's shift to an export-oriented industrialization policy in the first half of the 1960s, but disappeared thereafter.

NOTES

1 For this reason, free market exchange rates on export dollars developed in the country and were differentiated according to the source of earnings, mainly

because the earnings from exports to a particular foreign country could be used only for importing from that country (Kim, K. S., 1991b; 103–4).

2 By observing the government and business relations during the Park regime (1964–79), Jones and SaKong (1980: 79–140) suggested that 'Koreans are even better at implementation than at planning' and that their ability essentially stems from the government system which can be characterized as a Myrdalian 'hard' state (or 'strong state' in Myrdal's terms).

3 The new exchange rate which was based on a medium value of the purchasing power parity (PPP) ratio calculated at the end of 1963 was considered by many to have undervalued the won slightly at the time of devaluation (Brown, 1973: 139).

4 The special tariffs resulted in about a 2–3 per cent increase in the average legal tariff rate, which had already been raised to nearly 40 per cent by the tariff reform of 1962 (Kim, K. S., 1991a: 40–1).

5 The nominal effective exchange rate for exports is obtained by adding net export subsidies per dollar of exports to the official exchange rate. Similarly, actual tariffs and tariff equivalents per dollar of imports are added to the official rate to obtain the nominal effective rate for imports. The effective exchange rate for exports so estimated may be used as an index of net export incentives compared with a free trade situation, whereas the effective rate for imports may give an index of actual trade protection on domestic industry.

6 The value of manufactured exports in 1965 was still in the region of US$107 million, only about $100 million higher than that in 1960, although the 61 per cent share in total exports may seem quite impressive compared with 15 per cent in 1960.

7 The I–O data for the earlier years (1963–75) shown in the table are in 1968 constant domestic prices while the data for the later years (1975–85) are in 1975 constant prices. Two different figures for 1975 are therefore shown: one in 1968 constant prices and the other in 1975 constant prices.

8 The analytical framework used here is based on Syrquin's method (1976) which represents a modification of the pioneering work of Chenery et al. (1962).

9 The semi-annual trade programme had previously been formulated in the form of a 'positive-list system', under which only those items listed in the programme could be imported with or without government approval. Under the new system, the trade programme lists only those items whose import is prohibited or restricted, implying that all items not listed are AA items.

10 The general formulas for calculation of the effective protection rate are well presented in Balassa and Associates (1971: 315–21). There are two different methods of computing effective protection rates when there are non-tradable inputs: the Corden and Balassa methods (see Balassa and Associates, 1971: 321–4).

11 Since the estimates of nominal protection rates are derived from direct price comparisons between domestic and world markets, reliability of the estimated results is determined by the accuracies of the estimated nominal rates, which cannot be easily tested because of product quality issues involved.

12 During 1974–8, foreign firms exported a slightly higher share of their production than domestic firms in Korea. During the same period, the value added by foreign firms in the manufacturing sector was less than 20 per cent of the total (Koo, 1986: 217–19). More recent data are not available.

13 The growing protectionism in advanced industrial countries against labour-intensive goods, and the rapidly rising wage-rental ratio within the country in

the early 1970s, contributed to pessimism regarding growth based on light industry exports.

14 That is, (i) the enrolment capacities of science and engineering colleges were expanded from 26,000 to 58,000 between 1973 and 1980; (ii) total enrolment in technical high schools was doubled, while that in technical junior colleges was expanded more than fivefold; (iii) twenty-two vocational training centres were established to produce 12,000 additional technicians a year (Lee, S.C., 1991: 448).

15 HCI subsectors for which the investment adjustment was made in 1979–80 included power generators, automobiles, electronic switchboards, heavy electrical equipment, diesel engines and copper refining (Economic Planning Board, 1981: 89–90).

16 That is, HCI exports increased from about 21 per cent of total manufactured exports in 1972 to 42 per cent in 1981 and to 52 per cent by 1989, while value added in HCI increased from 47 per cent of total value added in manufacturing to 55 per cent and to 64 per cent in the same period (Lee, K. T., 1991: 169–70).

17 Assuming that the production is of a transcendental logarithmic (translog) form, translog indexes are used to measure output, various inputs and productivity of each activity or subsector. The methodology, as well as a detailed description of statistical data sources, is given in K. S. Kim and Hong (1992).

18 The effect of R&D expenditures on TFP growth could not be empirically investigated due to lack of consistent data on R&D expenditures at the thirty-six subsectors level of classification.

19 Attempts were made to divide the whole period into two periods (1967–78 and 1978–88) and estimate the correlation matrix separately for each of the two periods. But since the results for the two periods are very similar, only the result for the entire period is reported in the table.

20 The method of estimating the country's overall degree of import liberalization reported by K. S. Kim (1991a: 34–44) was applied to the subsectoral level, and in addition, quantitative restrictions by special laws were consolidated with the QRs by trade programmes. See K. S. Kim (1988: 87) for the subsectoral estimates of the degree of import liberalization for selected years between 1966 and 1985.

21 It is interesting to note that the degree of industrial concentration (CR) is negatively correlated with the overall degree of import liberalization (ML) but positively correlated with nominal protection rate (NPR) and capacity utilization (OR). Since all the relevant correlation coefficients are statistically significant, they seem to suggest that those subsectors dominated by monopoly and oligopoly producers have enjoyed higher protection from imports, and higher capacity utilization rates, than other subsectors.

REFERENCES

Balassa, Bela and Associates (1971) *The Structure of Protection in Developing Countries*, Baltimore: Johns Hopkins University Press.
—— (1982) *Development Strategies in Semi-industrial Economies*, Washington, DC: World Bank Research Publication.
Balassa, Bela, Voloudakis, E., Fylaktos, P. and Suh, S. T. (1989) 'The Determinants of Export Supply and Export Demand in Two Developing Countries: Greece and Korea', *International Economic Journal* 3(1): 1–16.
Bank of Korea (various years) *Economic Statistics Yearbook*.
—— (1984) *National Income Accounts*.
—— (1990) *National Accounts*.

Brown, Gilbert T. (1973) *Korean Pricing Policies and Economic Development in the 1960s*, Baltimore: Johns Hopkins University Press.

Chenery, Hollis B., Shishido, S. and Watanabe, T. (1962) 'Patterns of Japanese Growth, 1914–1954', *Econometrica* 30(1): 98–139.

Cho, Lee-Jae and Kim, Yoon-Hyung (eds) (1991) *Economic Development in the Republic of Korea: A Policy Perspective*, Honolulu: East-West Center.

Choo, Hak-Choong (1987) 'Income Distribution', in Cho S. and H.C. Choo (eds) *The Theory and Practice of the Korean Economy* (in Korean), Seoul: Seoul University Press, pp. 141–79.

Economic Planning Board (1967) *Korea Statistical Yearbook* Economis Planning Board, Seoul.

—— (1981) *Economic White Paper* (in Korean).

—— (1982) *Major Statistics of the Korean Economy*.

—— (1990) *Our Economy Seen in Numbers* (in Korean).

Frank, Charles R. Jr., Kim, Kwang Suk and Westphal, Larry E. (1975) *Foreign Trade Regimes and Economic Development: South Korea*, New York: NBER.

Havrylyshyn, Oli (1990) 'Trade Policy and Productivity Gains in Developing Countries: A Survey of the Literature', *The World Bank Research Observer* 5(1): 1–24.

Hong, Sung-Duck (1992) 'Structural Change in Nominal and Effective Protection Rates in Korea' (in Korean), KDI Policy Research Paper no. 92–01, Seoul.

Hong, Wontack (1979) *Trade Distortions and Employment Growth in Korea*, Seoul: KDI Press.

—— (1988) 'Market Distortions and Trade Patterns: 1960–85', KDI Working Paper no. 88–07, Seoul.

Jo, Sung-Hwan (1991) 'Promotion Measures for General Trading Companies (1975)' in Lee-Jae Cho and Yoon-Hyung Kim (eds) *Economic Development in the Republic of Korea: A Policy Perspective*, Honolulu: East-West Press, pp. 511–25.

Jones, Leroy and SaKong, Il (1980) *Government, Business, and Entrepreneurship in Economic Development: The Korean Case*, Cambridge, Mass.: Harvard University Council on East Asian Studies.

Kendrick, John W. and Grossman, E. S. (1980) *Productivity in the United States: Trends and Cycles*, Baltimore: Johns Hopkins University Press.

Kim, Chuk-Kyo, Yoo, J. S. and Hwang, K. H. (1984) *Analysis of Manufacturing Productivity in Korea, Taiwan and Japan* (in Korean), Seoul: Hanyang University Institute of Economic Research.

Kim, Kwang Suk (1987) 'The Nature of Trade Protection by Special Laws in Korea', Discussion Paper 87–01, Kyung Hee University Graduate School of Business Administration, Seoul.

—— (1988) *Economic Impact of Import Liberalization and Industrial Adjustment Policy* (in Korean), Seoul: KDI Press.

—— (1990) 'Import Liberalization and Its Impact in Korea', in Jene K. Kwon (ed.) *Korean Economic Development*, New York: Greenwood Press, pp. 99–113.

—— (1991a) 'Korea', in M. Michaely, D Papageorgiou and A. Choksi (eds) *Liberalizing Foreign Trade: Korea, the Philippines and Singapore*, vol. 2, Cambridge: Basil Blackwell, pp. 1–131.

—— (1991b) 'The 1964–65 Exchange Reform, Export Promotion Measures and Import Liberalization Program', in Lee-Jae Cho and Yoon-Hyung Kim (eds) *Economic Development in the Republic of Korea: A Policy Perspective*, Honolulu: East-West Press, pp. 101–34.

—— (1993) 'Manufacturing Productivity and Trade Policy in South Korea', Kyung-Hee University, Seoul.

—— and Hong, Sung-Duk (1990) *Sources of Longterm Industrial Growth and Structural Change in Korea (1955–1985)* (in Korean), Seoul: KDI Policy Research Series 90–05.

—— and Hong, Sung-Duk (1992) *Manufacturing Productivity and Its Determinants* (in Korean), Seoul: KDI Press.

—— and Park, Joon-Kyung (1985) *Sources of Economy Growth in Korea, 1963–1982*, Seoul: KDI Press.

—— and Park, Sung-Nok (1988) *Productivity Growth of Korean Manufacturing and Its Causes* (in Korean), Seoul: Korea Institute for Industrial Economics.

Koo, Bohn-Young (1986) 'The Role of Direct Foreign Investment in Korea's Recent Economic Growth', in Joong-Woong Kim (ed.) *Financial Development Policies and Issues*, Seoul: KDI Press, pp. 189–236.

Korea Development Institute (1982) 'The Basic Task of Industrial Policy and Reform Proposals of the Support Measures' (in Korean), KDI Report no. 82–09, Seoul.

Korea Foreign Trade Association (1990a) *Major Indicators on Trade Activities* (in Korean), Seoul: KFTA.

—— (1990b) 'Export and National Economy: Industrial Linkage Effects of Exports' (in Korean), KFTA Research Report no. 90–4, Seoul.

—— (1991) *International Trade* (monthly magazine in Korean), April.

Korea Institute for Economics and Technology (1986) *Analysis of Effects of Import Liberalization* (in Korean), Seoul: KIET.

Korea Trade Research Center (1969) *Measures to Increase Net Foreign Exchange Earnings from Exports*, Seoul: KTRC.

Krueger, Anne O. (1981) 'Export-led Industrial Growth Reconsidered', in W. Hong and L. B. Krause (eds) *Trade and Growth of the Advanced Developing Countries in the Pacific Basin*, Seoul: KDI Press, pp. 3–27.

—— and Tuncer, B. (1982) 'Growth of Factor Productivity in Turkish Manufacturing Industries', *Journal of Development Economics* 11(3): 307–25.

Lee, Kyu-Uk (no date) 'International Trade and Industrial Organization: The Korean Experience', mimeo, Korean Development Institute, Seoul.

—— and Lee, Jai-Hyong (1990) *Business Groups and Economic Power Concentration* (in Korean), Seoul: KDI Press.

Lee, Kyung-Tae (1991) *The Theory and Practice of Industrial Policy* (in Korean), Seoul: Korea Institute for Economics and Technology.

——, Kim, J. S. and Park, H. J. (1988) *Analysis of Economic Impact of Import Liberalization* (in Korean), Seoul: Korea Institute for Economics and Technology, and Korea Foreign Trade Association.

Lee, Suk-Chae (1991) 'The Heavy and Chemical Industries Promotion Plan (1973–1979)', in Lee-Jae Cho and Yoon-Hyung Kim (eds) *Economic Development in the Republic of Korea: A Policy Perspective*, Honolulu: East-West Press, pp. 431–71.

Mason, Edward S., Kim, M. J., Perkins, D. H., Kim, K. S. and Cole, D. C. (1980) *The Economic and Social Modernization of the Republic of Korea*, Cambridge, Mass.: Harvard University Press.

Ministry of Finance (1991) *Fiscal and Financial Statistics* (monthly in Korean), January.

Nam, Chong-Hyon (1981) 'Trade and Industrial Policies, and the Structure of Protection in Korea', in Wontack Hong and Lawrence Krause (eds) *Trade and*

Growth of Advanced Developing Countries in the Pacific Basin, Seoul: KDI Press, pp. 187–211.

Nishimizu, M. and Robinson, S. (1984) 'Trade Policies and Productivity Change in Semi-industrialized Countries', *Journal of Development Economics* 16(1–2): 177–206.

OECD (1991) *OECD Economic Outlook 49*, July.

Pack, Howard (1988) 'Industrialization and Trade', in Hollis Chenery and T. N. Srinivasan (eds) *Handbook of Development Economics*, vol. 1, Amsterdam: North Holland, pp. 333–80.

Papageorgiou, Demetrios, Choksi, A. and Michaely, M. (1990) *Liberalizing Foreign Trade in Developing Countries: Lessons of Experience*, Washington, DC: World Bank.

Rhee, Yung Whee, Ross-Larson, B. and Pursell, G. (1984) *Korea's Competitive Edge*, Baltimore: Johns Hopkins University Press.

Syrquin, Moshe (1976) 'Sources of Industrial Growth and Change: An Alternative Measure', Paper read at the European Meeting of The Econometric Society, August, Helsinki, Finland.

Terleckyj, Nester E. (1980) 'Direct and Indirect Effects of Industrial Research and Development on the Productivity Growth of Industries', in J. W. Kendrick and B. N. Vaccara (eds) *New Developments in Productivity Measurement and Analysis*, Chicago: University of Chicago Press, pp. 359–86.

Tybout, James R. (1992) 'Linking Trade and Productivity: New Research Directions', *The World Bank Economic Review* 6(2): 189–212.

Westphal, Larry E. and Kim, Kwang Suk (1977) 'Industrial Policy and Development in Korea', World Bank Staff Working Paper no. 263, Washington, DC.

—— and Kim, Kwang Suk (1982) 'Korea', in Balassa and Associates, *Development Strategies in Semi-industrial Economies*, Washington, DC: World Bank Research Publications, pp. 212–79.

——, Rhee, Y. W. and Pursell, G. (1984) 'Sources of Technological Capability in South Korea', in M. Fransman and K. King (eds) *Technological Capability in the Third World*, London: Macmillan, pp. 279–300.

11

INDUSTRIAL RESTRUCTURING AND PERFORMANCE IN MALAYSIA

Lim Teck Ghee and Toh Kin Woon

INTRODUCTION

Since independence in 1957, Malaysia's industrialization strategy has undergone several broad changes in direction and emphasis. These may be summarized as follows:

1950s–1960s	generalized import substitution
1970s	export expansion and diversification of the manufacturing sector
1980s	import substitution in heavy and resource-based industries
1986	liberalization of investment rules emphasizing export-oriented industrialization, and
1988	promotion of skill- and technology-intensive industries.

As a result of the state's industrialization push as outlined above, Malaysia experienced rapid growth of its manufacturing sector over the last two decades, averaging 12.0 per cent in 1970–80 and 9.3 per cent in nominal terms in 1980–90 (Tables. 11.1 and 11.3). At the same time, rapid structural changes were also experienced, encompassing both macroeconomic structural shifts between various sectors as well as reallocation of resources within the manufacturing sector.

The purpose of this study is to analyse the sources of structural change in Malaysia, at both the macroeconomic and industry levels. The next section provides an overview of growth and the role of external resources since 1970. The third section describes the industrial restructuring in the overall macroeconomy as well as within the manufacturing and manufactured export sectors. The fourth section decomposes the sources of growth and structural change in the manufacturing sector into their main components on the demand side. Since import substitution was an important

Table 11.1 Gross domestic product by industrial origin, annual growth rate, 1970–90, Malaysia (constant 1978 prices)

	Compound annual growth rate			Share
	1970–80	*1980–5*	*1985–90*	*1980 (%)*
Agriculture, livestock, forestry and fishing	4.7	3.1	3.7	22.9
Mining and quarrying	13.1	5.9	5.2	10.1
Manufacturing	12.0	5.2	13.6	19.6
Transport, storage and communications	9.9	7.6	8.5	5.7
Wholesale, retail trade, hotels and restaurants	6.8	5.1	5.1	12.1
Finance, insurance, real estate, business services	7.7	6.6	8.8	8.3
Government services	7.0	8.7	4.3	10.3
GDP at market price	7.8	5.1	6.8	100.0

Sources: Ministry of Finance, *Economic Report*, various issues; and Bank Negara Malaysia, *Annual Report 1991*.

contributor to growth up to the 1980s, the fifth section examines the changing structure of protection and efficiency in the manufacturing sector. The penultimate section discusses the sources of growth in the manufacturing sector from the supply side, as suggested by trends in factor accumulation and productivity and is followed by some concluding comments.

OUTPUT GROWTH AND USE OF EXTERNAL RESOURCES

Over the last two decades Malaysia stands out as one of the most dynamic economies in Southeast Asia, having experienced rapid economic growth in real terms, enjoyed large increases in real per capita incomes and undergone major structural shifts in its domestic economy. Between 1970 and 1980, Malaysia's real GDP increased at an average annual rate of 7.8 per cent (Table 11.1). This declined to 6.0 per cent during 1980–90, primarily because of the serious recession experienced in the mid-1980s. There was a more than fourfold increase in Malaysia's real per capita income over the 1970–90 period (Malaysia, 1991: 8).

From 1970–90 the manufacturing sector experienced the highest rate of growth, at an average annual rate, in real terms, of 10.7 per cent. It was followed by mining and quarrying (9.3 per cent), transport, storage and communications (9.0 per cent) and financial services (7.7 per cent). Mining and quarrying was, in fact, the faster growing sector during the 1970s as a result of the discovery and exploitation of oil and natural gas during the second half of the decade. The pace of growth of this sector, however, slowed during the 1980s as a result of conservation policies, while manufac-

Table 11.2 Saving and investment rates, Malaysia (% of GNP)

Period	Exports	Imports	Gross national saving	Gross capital formation	Current account balance	Inflation (%)
1971–5	39.6	35.8	21.1	24.2	–3.0	8.5
1976–9	47.8	35.5	29.2	25.3	4.0	6.1
1980	52.85	43.99	28.4	29.7	–1.2	11.2
1981	47.05	46.18	24.2	34.6	–10.4	9.7
1982	44.92	46.38	23.5	37.9	–14.4	6.3
1983	47.11	44.27	25.0	36.7	–11.7	4.3
1984	48.58	41.39	30.7	36.0	–5.3	4.3
1985	49.02	39.25	27.5	29.7	–2.1	0.5
1986	49.64	39.25	27.4	27.8	–0.5	0.7
1987	56.80	40.11	33.6	24.7	8.9	1.0
1988	60.82	47.65	33.0	27.5	5.5	3.2
1989	66.80	59.94	30.0	30.6	–0.6	3.7
1990	69.11	68.74	30.0	34.1	–4.1	4.1
1991	–	–	27.8	37.4	–9.7	4.4

Sources: Bank Negara Malaysia, *Quarterly Economic Bulletin*, various issues; Ministry of Finance, *Economic Report*, various issues.

turing continued to surge ahead, particularly during the last couple of years of the decade.

The rapid real rate of growth of the economy in the 1980s was fuelled by the use of external resources, particularly during 1981–5 and 1990–1. This is evident in the huge current account deficit or savings-investment gap in these two periods (Table 11.2). The savings gap as a proportion of GNP reached an average of 12 per cent over 1981–3, after which it declined over the next three years. This was followed by a large surplus over the next two years, 1987 and 1988, during which net exports constituted an important source of growth in demand. But this was again reversed over the next three years when the current account balance showed a deficit, which increased from 0.6 per cent of GNP in 1989 to 9.7 per cent in 1991. This was a result of a decline in the savings rate from 32.9 per cent of GNP in 1979 to 25.0 per cent in 1983 and again from 33 per cent in 1988 to 27.8 per cent in 1991. At the same time as the rate of savings declined, the investment rate increased from 24.7 per cent of GNP in 1987 to 37.4 per cent in 1991.

The pattern of external resource inflows varied over the course of the 1980s. While the savings gap in the first half of the 1980s was filled primarily through external debt financing, from 1987 to 1991 it was bridged through massive inflows of direct foreign investment (DFI). In fact, from 1987 till 1990, Malaysia experienced a net outflow of official long-term capital on account of the settlement of principal and interest on debt previously accumulated. The massive inflows of DFI, however, more than covered this negative outflow (except for 1987 and 1988), resulting in a surplus on the long-term capital account that more than covered the current account deficit, especially during 1989–90. A concomitant of the large increase in DFI was an increase in demand for capital goods, the bulk of which were imported. As a result, the import to GDP ratio rose rapidly after 1987, outstripping the rise in the export ratio.

Finally, a notable feature of Malaysia's pattern of development has been its relatively low rate of inflation for most years in the 1970s and 1980s. The only periods of high inflation were 1973–5 and 1979–81, both of which coincided with oil shocks. Although Malaysia is a net exporter of oil, the bulk of what she produces is exported while oil for domestic consumption is imported.

STRUCTURAL CHANGE IN OUTPUT, MANUFACTURING, AND EXPORTS

Intersectoral reallocation of resources

Differences in sectoral rates of growth in Malaysia have been reflected in changes in the structure of the economy over time. In 1970, the agricultural sector was the largest single sector, accounting for 30.8 per cent of Malaysia's GDP, while manufacturing contributed only 13.4 per cent. By 1980, there had been a substantial decline in the share of agriculture in total output (to 22.9 per cent) and a concomitant rise in the share of manufacturing (to 19.6 per cent). During most of the 1980s, the share of agriculture continued to fall, albeit at a much reduced pace, while that of manufacturing continued to increase at a faster pace. This led, by 1987, to the manufacturing sector overtaking, for the first time, agriculture as the leading sector of the economy. By 1990, the share of manufacturing in GDP had increased further to 27 per cent while that of agriculture dropped to 18.7 per cent. However, in 1990 employment in agriculture still accounted for 28.4 per cent of total employment while employment in manufacturing accounted for about 20 per cent of the total (Table 11.3). This is quite unlike the experience of the Republic of Korea and Taiwan, where growth in industrial employment closely matched the decline in the agricultural sector's share of labour. This implies that industrialization in both Korea and Taiwan was preceded by a more successful agricultural development strategy which raised both productivity and income in the agricultural sector to much higher relative levels than in Malaysia, where the level and rate of growth of agricultural productivity lagged behind that of manufacturing. The shift in the sectoral composition of total employment in Malaysia was still, however, faster than in the other three ASEAN countries of Indonesia, Philippines and Thailand (ESCAP, 1991).

Table 11.3 Manufacturing share in the Malaysian economy, 1970–90

Year	Gross manufacturing output		Gross manufacturing exports		Employment in the manufacturing sector	
	% change	As a % of GDP	% change	As a % of total exports	% change	As a % of total employment
1970	–	13.4	–	12.2	–	9.0
1971	12.6	14.3	-17.2	10.4	8.3	9.4
1972	10.2	14.4	19.9	12.8	8.3	9.8
1973	32.9	15.8	82.9	15.3	8.2	10.2
1974	1.8	16.1	51.4	16.8	8.4	10.7
1975	3.0	16.4	17.5	21.8	8.2	11.1
1976	18.5	17.4	25.0	18.5	39.1	14.2
1977	10.6	17.9	11.8	18.6	6.4	14.8
1978	13.2	19.0	31.7	21.5	0.3	14.6
1979	11.3	19.3	33.1	20.1	6.3	15.0
1980	9.2	19.6	25.9	21.8	6.8	15.7
1981	4.7	19.2	3.3	23.4	4.2	15.6
1982	5.8	19.2	17.7	26.5	1.5	15.5
1983	7.6	19.5	28.8	20.1	5.3	15.5
1984	12.3	20.3	27.3	31.6	4.5	15.8
1985	–3.8	19.7	–0.4	32.2	–2.7	15.2
1986	7.5	20.9	26.6	43.8	0.7	15.1
1987	29.9	22.5	31.9	45.2	7.0	15.7
1988	2.7	24.2	34.0	49.6	10.0	16.6
1989	12.0	25.1	35.0	53.9	15.6	18.4
1990	17.9	26.9	28.9	59.2	10.2	19.5

Compounded annual growth rate

Period	GDP	Manufacturing	Exports	Manufacturing exports	Employment	Manufacturing employment
1970–80	7.8	12.0	18.8	25.9	3.7	9.6
1980–90	5.9	9.3	11.0	22.7	3.2	5.5
1970–90	6.9	10.7	14.8	24.3	3.5	7.5

Source: Vijayakumari (1990, table 3).

The manufacturing sector

Parallel with intersectoral resource shifts, there occurred intrasectoral reallocation of resources. Within manufacturing, such resource reallocation took place at a fairly rapid pace during the 1970s and 1980s (Vijayakumari, 1990). In 1974, the three major resource-based industries (the food products, wood products and rubber products industries) accounted for 40.9 per cent of value added. However, this ratio had fallen drastically to 25.2 per cent by 1989 (Table 11.4). During the same period, electrical machinery increased its weight sharply, from 9.4 per cent in 1974 to 18.6 per cent in 1989. Its contribution to total manufacturing employment also

Table 11.4 Value added (VA) and employment in manufacturing industries,[a] Malaysia 1974–89 (%)

Sectors	1974 VA	1974 EMP.	1978 VA	1978 EMP.	1982 VA	1982 EMP.	1987 VA	1987 EMP.	1989 VA	1989 EMP.
Food products	17.3	10.7	20.8	8.8	17.3	15.7	14.4	12.9	13.9	10.6
Beverages and tobacco	6.3	4.1	5.3	2.8	–	–	7.1	1.8	3.7	1.5
Textiles	5.3	13.3	8.0	14.7	7.1	12.4	7.9	14.4	6.2	13.3
Timber-based products	10.9	17.0	10.4	15.0	18.6	22.1	5.9	9.7	6.9	12.7
Paper and printing	6.2	7.2	4.8	5.9	–	–	5.0	5.0	4.7	4.5
Chemicals and chemical products	6.8	4.0	5.7	3.4	4.9	3.3	7.7	3.1	11.9	2.9
Petroleum products	1.8	–	3.3	–	2.5	0.3	4.8	4.1	3.4	4.1
Rubber products	12.7	10.3	9.9	8.6	5.9	6.4	7.6	7.8	4.4	7.6
Non-metallic minerals	4.4	5.1	3.9	4.7	6.0	4.5	6.3	4.6	5.2	4.4
Iron and steel basic industries	–	–	–	–	–	–	3.4	2.1	3.9	2.1
Fabricated metals	–	–	–	–	–	–	2.9	2.9	3.7	4.0
Machinery except electrical	–	–	–	–	–	–	2.7	4.1	3.2	2.6
Electrical machinery	9.4	10.6	10.9	17.0	17.1	15.2	18.5	21.3	18.6	23.3
Transport equipment	3.2	1.4	3.0	3.6	4.3	4.2	3.1	2.6	4.7	2.9
Other manufactures	15.7	16.3	14.0	15.5	16.3	15.9	2.6	4.1	5.7	3.5
Total	100.0	100.0	100.0	100.0	100.0	100.0	100.0	100.0	100.0	100.0

Sources: Data for years 1974–82 were taken from Osman-Rani *et al.* (1986: table 1), which was compiled from Department of Statistics, *Survey of Manufacturing Industries* (1974, 1978); *Fourth Malaysia Plan, 1981–1985* (1981); and Department of Statistics, *Industrial Surveys* (1982). Data for 1987 and 1989 were compiled from Department of Statistics, *Industrial Surveys* (1987, 1989).
[a] Peninsular Malaysia

rose rapidly from 10.6 per cent in 1974 to 23.3 per cent in 1989, when it was the largest single employer within the manufacturing sector, followed by textiles at 13.3 per cent. By 1990, electrical machinery accounted for 31.9 per cent of total manufacturing employment (Malaysia, 1991, table 4–3). Again, the textiles and clothing subsector came second, with its employment accounting for 16 per cent of total manufacturing employment by 1990. Together, electrical/electronics and textiles accounted for close to half of the total jobs in the manufacturing sector compared to 35.7 per cent three years earlier. This signifies a substantial shift in the composition of industrial employment away from the traditional sources such as the food, wood and rubber industries. From 1973 to 1987, electrical machinery absorbed about 34 per cent of the incremental growth in manufacturing jobs, while food, wood and the rubber industries, on the other hand, provided only 11.5 per cent, 6.6 per cent and 5.7 per cent of the new jobs respectively (Vijayakumari, 1990: 6). Over the last five years of the 1980s, the electrical/electronics subsector continued to contribute significantly to employment generation within the manufacturing sector, growing by 20.2 per cent per annum during 1985–90. However, the resource-based industries still made up an important component of the Malaysian manufacturing sector. This has been boosted in recent years by the coming onstream of a few giant resource-based industries such as Malaysian Liquefied Natural Gas, Sabah Gas Industries and ASEAN Bintulu Fertilizer.

Despite the rapid pace of industrialization in Malaysia, the industrial base remains small. The electrical/electronics industry remains by far the most dominant, with the textile and garments industry a distant second. One source of potential expansion of the industrial base is in production linkages forged between the electrical/electronics and textile/garment industries and other local firms. This potential may be limited, however, by the high proportion of electrical/electronics and textile firms that are foreign-owned (mainly Japanese) and located in free-trade zones (FTZs) or licensed manufacturing warehouses (LMWs).

A comparison of Japanese and local firms in Malaysia revealed that Malaysian manufacturing firms that produce final consumer goods tended to acquire a larger proportion of their inputs locally (see Osman Rani *et al.*, 1986). Japanese firms that produced electronic components for export generally imported the bulk of their raw materials from foreign sources, notably Japan. Generally, in the electronic components industry, hardly any local raw materials were used in production; when they were used, they constituted less than 5 per cent of total inputs. Only minor process items such as metal taps, trays and trollies made in local foundries were reported as sourced from local vendors. In terms of production equipment, nearly all the electrical/electronic firms in Malaysia chose to import all their machinery requirements. In most cases, production equipment and inputs were purchased through foreign trading companies or parent companies, instead of through Malaysian trading companies.

Among the non-electronic firms, Malaysian-controlled enterprises were more domestic-market oriented than Japanese-controlled firms. As a result, the extent of forward linkage was higher for locally controlled firms. Locally controlled firms also exhibited much higher levels of backward linkage: five out of the six firms which purchased most of their inputs locally were locally controlled firms. Of the other five Japanese-controlled firms, only two sourced as much as 15 – 25 per cent of their inputs locally. In general, the main source of inputs was Japan, and this was true not only of Japanese-controlled firms but also of locally controlled firms. Thus, eight out of the thirteen locally controlled Japanese-minority firms imported more than 60 per cent of their inputs from Japan, and four of these imported almost 100 per cent.

The reasons for not having a higher level of local sourcing were poor quality and delivery unreliability. Japanese firms, in particular, seemed to attach particular importance to both quality and standards. Many Japanese firms producing for the international market actually bring their traditional subcontractors with them or integrate backwards to maintain a much higher level of self-sufficiency. A recent study (Rasiah, 1990) on market-oriented linkages has, however, found that domestic sourcing in electrical/ electronics production activities has grown in the 1980s. Rasiah's sample showed that electrical, consumer electronics and computer peripheral firms sourced between 10 and 70 per cent of their inputs domestically. However, between 5 and 40 per cent of these requirements are supplied either by their own subsidiaries or other foreign subsidiaries in Malaysia. As for semiconductor and telecommunication components, domestic sourcing has increased from 0.5%–2 per cent in the early 1970s to 6–20 per cent in 1990. Between 3 and 10 per cent of these items (for example, lead frameworks and machinery) are supplied by their own subsidiaries or foreign firms operating in FTZs/LMWs.

Rasiah identified several areas, in particular in the semiconductor and telecommunication component industry, where components were being subcontracted to domestic firms. These were metal stamping, tooling, precision turning, automated machinery on jobbing basis (as rapid technological obsolescence and aggressive throughput time targets necessitate frequent modifications and improvisation), and plastic tubing. Both local and foreign firms have expanded production to service such purchasing linkages. Despite growing trends in the forging of backward linkages, Malaysia is, unfortunately, still weak in the plastic, metals fabrication and engineering industries, all of which are key feeder industries to the electrical/electronic industry (Tan, 1991). In the case of plastics, the setting up of a strong upstream raw material supply is in train with the implementation of the Petronas/Shell/Idemitsu and the Titan petrochemical complexes. What remains now is for the downstream plastic manufacturers to upgrade and broaden the scope of activities from daily consumer plastic goods to the higher precision parts required for the electrical/electronic industries. In the case of metal fabrication, Malaysia is not yet at the stage of producing high-quality steel sheets. Even if the China steel project and the Perwaja (Malaysia's government-owned steel mill) flat products mill were to both come onstream, it will be some time before they can supply this requirement. Besides, Malaysia's foundries are both small in number and weak in scope. In addition, growth in metal fabrication is currently retarded by a lack of a strong pool of engineers and technicians.

While backward purchasing links have grown, despite facing serious problems, forward links have not shown any encouraging growth trends (Rasiah, 1990). All semiconductor and telecommunication components are exported, providing no forward linkages with the domestic economy. This is true even in the case of one local semiconductor firm. Japanese producers in Malaysia that sell their output to American and German firms sell them directly in Malaysia, but within the FTZs and LMWs (Rasiah, 1990). Likewise, computer peripherals are exported mainly to sales offices abroad.

Market-oriented linkages between the textile/garment industry and the Malaysian economy are generally also limited and weak (Rasiah, 1990). Most of the chemical inputs and fibres are either imported or acquired from foreign suppliers operating locally. The situation is slightly better in the case of apparel firms. The Gherzi Report (1990) stated that less than 40 per cent of zippers and buttons, less than 20 per cent of labels, but 100 per cent of interlining, rivets/snaps and elastic, were imported in 1989. More than 60 per cent of threads are acquired domestically, while the yarn used in the local production of threads mainly comes from domestic textile firms.

Manufactured exports

At the same time as the structure of the Malaysian economy experienced changes, the composition of exports too underwent major shifts. From making up a mere 12.2 per cent in 1970, manufactured exports as a percentage of total exports increased to 59.2 per cent by 1990, surpassing the share of primary commodity exports (Table 11.3). During the 1970s, manufactured exports grew at a rate of 25.9 per cent, which increased further to 31 per cent during the 1985–90 period (Malaysia, 1991, table 4–2: 130). Gross manufactured exports as a proportion of gross manufactured output also increased rapidly during the 1980s. From 16.5 per cent in 1981, this proportion increased to 45.3 per cent in 1989 (Table 11.5). The rapid increase in this proportion, especially in the latter part of the 1980s, was due to the success of the government in attracting increased investments in export-oriented industries, especially from the newly industrialized economies (NIEs) of Taiwan and Singapore.

Not only did manufactured exports increase their share of total exports, but the structure of manufactured exports also underwent substantial changes (Table 11.6). In 1970, chemicals and petroleum products dominated, with a share of 32 per cent, followed by food, beverages and tobacco (18 per cent) and wood products (14 per cent). By 1980, the largest single share came from electrical and electronic goods (48 per cent), followed by textiles (13 per cent). Throughout the 1980s, electrical and electronic goods continued to increase their dominant share of exports of manufactured goods, reaching 50 per cent by 1985 and 56.2 per cent by 1990. By 1985, the share of textiles and clothing had fallen to about 8 per cent, where it stayed to 1990.

Table 11.7 shows the change in composition of manufactured exports by factor intensity and the implied shift in comparative advantage between 1965 and 1988. Between 1975 and 1985, resource-intensive manufactured

Table 11.5 Gross manufacturing exports as a proportion of gross manufacturing output, Malaysia, selected years

Year	Gross manufacturing output (M$ million)	Gross manufacturing exports (M$ million)	Gross manufacturing exports over gross manufacturing output (%)
1975	10,733	1,978	18.4
1976	13,625	2,472	18.1
1978	18,549	3,640	19.6
1979	25,906	4,844	18.7
1981	38,278	6,302	16.5
1982	37,627	7,417	19.7
1983	41,474	9,554	23.0
1984	46,256	12,164	26.3
1985	45,586	12,111	26.6
1986	42,427	15,329	36.1
1987	50,700	20,216	39.9
1988	74,214	27,085	36.5
1989	80,802	36,567	45.3

Source: Department of Statistics, *Industrial Surveys*, various issues.

Table 11.6 Exports of manufactured goods, Malaysia (% share)

Sector	1970	1980	1990
Food, beverages and tobacco	18	8	4.4
Textiles, clothing and footwear	7	13	8.5
Wood products	14	7	3.3
Rubber products	3	1	2.9
Chemicals and petroleum products	32	6	6.8
Non-metallic mineral products	3	1	1.6
Iron and steel and metal manufactures	4	4	3.5
Electrical and electronic machinery and appliances	3	48	56.2
Other machinery and transport equipment	11	4	4.7
Other manufactures	5	8	8.2
Totals	100	100	100.0

Source: Ministry of Finance, *Economic Report* (1989/90, 1991/92: table 3.5).

exports (mainly processing of primary commodities such as rubber, palm oil and timber) declined dramatically from 80.1 per cent to 45.8 per cent of total manufactured exports. Over the same period, scale-intensive goods (mainly electrical machinery) increased more than threefold from 11.6 per cent to 37.0 per cent.[1] These trends continued throughout the next half of the 1980s as the share of resource-intensive exports continued to fall (to 29 per cent) while that of scale-intensive goods (or labour-intensive ones – see endnote) increased to half of total manufactured exports.

Table 11.7 Changing composition of manufactured exports by factor intensity, Malaysia (%)

Year	Resource-intensive[a]	Labour-intensive[b]	Differentiated goods[c]	Scale-intensive[d]	Science-based[e]	Total
1965	89.0	1.9	1.8	4.9	2.5	100
1970	90.4	2.2	2.1	4.2	1.1	100
1975	80.1	5.5	2.1	11.6	0.7	100
1980	57.9	8.8	2.4	28.1	2.7	100
1985	45.8	8.5	6.1	37.0	2.7	100
1986	32.0	10.3	7.4	48.0	2.3	100
1987	30.3	11.1	8.1	48.2	2.3	100
1988	29.0	11.6	7.1	49.6	2.8	100

Source: ESCAP (1991: table III–28).
[a] Includes SITC categories 41, 42, 43, 61, 63, 641, 251, 334, 335, 661, 662, 663–663.9, 68.
[b] Includes SITC categories 65, 691, 692, 695, 696, 697, 699, 84, 851, 898, 899.
[c] Includes SITC categories 71, 72, 73, 74, 76, 77, 881–885.
[d] Includes SITC categories 51, 52, 53–533, 581, 621, 625, 629, 642, 663.9, 664, 665, 666, 67, 693, 694, 78, 79–792, 892, 893, 894.
[e] Includes SITC categories 533, 54, 55, 75, 792, 87.

The share of labour-intensive exports also rose, more than doubling from 5.5 per cent of total manufactured exports in 1975 to 11.6 per cent in 1988.

DEMAND-SIDE SOURCES OF MANUFACTURING GROWTH

Changes in the sectoral composition of economic activity are the result of the interaction of changes in the composition of demand and variations on the supply side, though initial conditions such as size and resource endowments affect the timing and sequencing, if not the pattern, of such intersectoral resource reallocation (see chapter 2). There are three sources of demand that have led to a shift of resources from agriculture to manufacturing. These are domestic demand expansion (DE), import substitution (IS) and export expansion (EE). Changes in the composition of demand for manufactured goods in turn reflect shifts in comparative advantage which in part are influenced by the trade and overall macroeconomic policy measures that in turn have a bearing on the degree of industrial competition. On the supply side, increases in factor inputs coupled with total factor productivity growth are the sources of increases in manufacturing output.

Table 11.8 presents estimates of the contribution to manufacturing growth of each of the three demand-side sources identified above for the periods 1973–81 and 1982–5. In the first period, the major source of demand for manufacturing sector output was domestic demand expansion, contributing about 143 per cent to total output growth (Table 11.8). This

Table 11.8 Sources of output growth of the manufacturing sector by major groups, Malaysia, 1983–5

	Domestic demand expansion (%)	Import substitution (%)	Export expansion (%)
1973–81:			
Consumer goods	95.99	8.75	−4.74
Intermediate goods	351.41	114.66	−366.07
Capital goods	85.81	27.60	−13.41
Total	143.25	36.19	−79.71
1982–5:			
Consumer goods	63.03	−5.49	−42.45
Intermediate goods	43.26	9.32	47.43
Capital goods	−140.78	−277.72	518.50
Total	−5.53	−31.66	137.19

Source: Vijayakumari (1990: table 8).

was not surprising as the economy achieved an annual real rate of economic growth of 7.3 per cent during the 1970s. Import substitution contributed about 36 per cent while export expansion contributed negatively as a source of growth of manufacturing output. This is not unexpected, given the emphasis on import substitution with its reliance on tariff protection as a mechanism to shift resources out of agriculture into manufacturing during the 1960s. The negative contribution of export expansion shows that despite the export-oriented industrialization drive that started with the promulgation of the Investment Incentive Act in 1968, Malaysia's manufacturing sector was still essentially very much inward-looking up till the early 1980s (Vijayakumari, 1990: 10). However, this demand pattern was completely reversed in 1982–5, when export expansion became the predominant source of growth, partly as a result of the exploitation of plant capacities built up in the 1970s to produce goods for export, particularly by foreigners. Both domestic demand expansion and import substitution were insignificant as sources of growth during this latter period.

The same pattern described above is repeated when the analysis is carried out at a more desegregated level. Domestic demand expansion and, to a lesser extent, import substitution were the major sources of growth of output of consumer, intermediate and capital goods during the 1973–81 period, with export expansion as a negative source of growth. In 1982–5, however, export expansion became an important source of growth, particularly for capital goods, largely consisting of electrical machinery exports by transnational corporations. Domestic demand expansion was still important, however, as a source of growth for both consumer and intermediate goods during the 1980s, signalling the important contribution

375

Table 11.9 Manufacturing unit labour costs of East Asian countries

Year	Malaysia	Korea	Taiwan	Singapore	Hong Kong	Thailand
1980	100.0	100.0	100.0	100.0	100.0	100.0
1981	103.6	96.4	111.3	113.4	96.8	104.0
1982	116.8	104.8	112.2	132.0	107.1	97.9
1984	143.8	98.9	120.7	140.6	73.8	99.6
1985	156.3	101.5	116.2	146.9	84.3	91.6
1986	143.3	101.9	120.4	131.9	81.3	n.a.
1987	132.9	120.4	141.2	n.a.	n.a.	n.a.

Source: Vijayakumari (1990: table 17).

played by continued rising incomes and therefore domestic market expansion to growth of manufacturing output.

The dominance of export expansion as a major source of growth in manufacturing and electrical/electronic goods in manufacturing exports in the 1980s shows that Malaysia is internationally competitive in electrical/electronic goods production. This production primarily involves the assembly of semiconductors (integrated circuits, diodes, transistors, etc.), a stage in the production process that is essentially labour intensive. Given this and the technical possibility of these operations being shifted to overseas production centres that have attractive relative factor price ratios, the future of the electrical/electronic goods industry in Malaysia as a source of export and output growth depends on the maintenance of low unit labour costs. Recent evidence seems to suggest, however, that manufacturing unit labour costs in Malaysia rose at a faster rate between 1980 and 1985 than those of the East Asian countries and Thailand (Table 11.9). Unit labour costs have continued to move up in Korea and Taiwan since 1985, while those of Malaysia and the other countries have fallen. In Malaysia, the fall between 1985 and 1987 reflects the depressed labour market conditions then prevailing. By 1987 unit labour costs in Malaysia were still substantially higher, relative to 1980 values, than the other East Asian countries compared and Thailand. Furthermore, with the pick-up in manufacturing activity between 1987–90 and the labour shortage problem currently faced by the manufacturing sector in Malaysia, unit labour costs are likely to have risen again.

These variations in unit labour costs suggest the existence of a wage-setting system in Malaysia that is fairly responsive to labour market conditions. A crucial contributory factor could be the absence of institutional intervention via trade unions, which are barred in the key electronics subsector, though there is some state intervention through its welfare protection schemes. Malaysia's rising unit labour costs have, however, been mitigated somewhat by a depreciation in the real value of the currency since 1985 and rising labour productivity. Between 1980 and 1984, the real value of Malaysia's currency (vis-à-vis the currencies of its major trading

Table 11.10 Real effective exchange rate, Malaysia, 1960–90

Year	REER index[a]	Year	REER index[a]	Year	REER index[a]
1970	124	1977	125	1984	111
1971	133	1978	132	1985	118
1972	137	1979	121	1986	147
1973	116	1980	122	1987	147
1974	112	1981	125	1988	164
1975	132	1982	122	1989	164
1976	127	1983	115	1990	175

Source: Recalculated from Edwards (1981: table 4).
[a] Based on 1965 = 100. An increase in the index means that the Malaysian ringgit has depreciated and that Malaysia has become more competitive *vis-à-vis* its trading partners.

Table 11.11 Labour productivity and average earnings, Malaysia (% change)

Year	Earnings	Labour productivity	Period	Earnings	Labour productivity
1980	−2.56	–			
1981	6.04	–	1973–9	6.29	3.14
1982	4.96	4.15			
1983	7.05	15.12	1981–4	5.67	9.48
1984	5.01	9.44			
1985	7.81	6.59	1985–7	−1.38	2.70
1986	−0.72	9.05			
1987	−2.03	−3.27	1981–7	3.61	6.70

Source: Vijayakumari (1990: table 13).

partners) had increased consequent upon heavy capital inflows to finance huge budgetary deficits (Edwards, 1991; also see Table 11.10 and Fig. 11.1 in this text). But from 1985 onwards, there has been continuous real currency depreciation, by 48 per cent to 1990. Meanwhile, Malaysia's manufacturing sector has registered continuous annual increases in labour productivity. Between 1973 and 1979, the annual rate of growth in labour productivity in the manufacturing sector averaged 3.14 per cent. This more than doubled in 1981–7 to 6.70 per cent, which exceeded the annual rate of growth in average (wage) earnings (Table 11.11). A major factor contributing to the rise in labour productivity was the rising capital-intensity of production, particularly in the electronics subsector. This shift in the capital-labour ratio was partly in response to the rising unit labour costs referred to earlier.

THE STRUCTURE OF PROTECTION AND EFFICIENCY OF THE MANUFACTURING SECTOR

Several studies have been undertaken on the structure and causes of Malaysian manufacturing sector protection (Power, 1971; Von Rabenau, 1975;

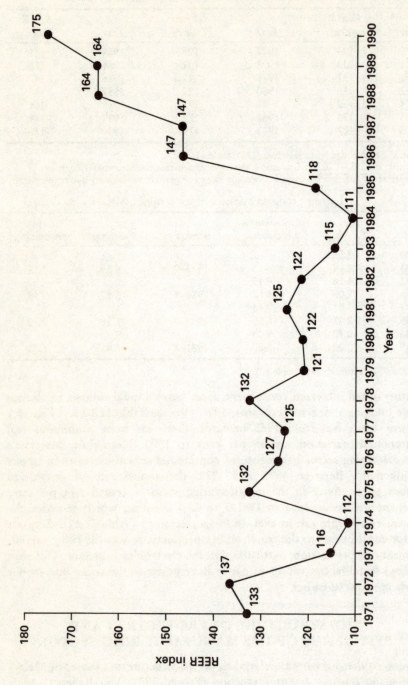

Figure 11.1 Real effective exchange rate

Edwards, 1975, 1990; Ariff, 1975; IMG Consultants, 1984; Lee, 1985). A review of the literature indicates that with the attainment of national independence, tariffs became important as one of several potentially effective policy instruments for the development of Malaysia's manufacturing industries, although other measures to promote industrialization, such as generous tax incentives and the provision of infrastructure, were also adopted. Indeed, between the early 1960s and the early 1970s, there was a substantial rise in the average level of the effective protection rate (EPR) of manufacturing, to between 35 and 40 per cent, which was still moderate compared to other developing countries. However, the rise in the average EPR led to a bias against agriculture, the creation of distortions within the manufacturing sector that led to the establishment of some high-cost industries (mainly textiles for the domestic market, paper boxes, fertilizers, iron and steel, galvanized sheets and pipes, and components of motor vehicles and cycles for assembly), a favouring of products at more finished stages of fabrication, and a bias against exports. The positive relationship between protection and the level of fabrication implies an incentive for resources to flow to finished products rather than to intermediate product industries (Lee, 1985). This prevented the development of strong backward linkages and the deepening of the industrial structure.

When the government realized the limitations of the import-substitution strategy of industrialization and began to shift to a more outward-looking strategy in the early 1970s, there followed a fall in levels of protection. By 1982, the average EPR was down to 23 per cent, although there was a wide dispersion in effective protection rates between, as well as within, industries (World Bank, 1986: 90). The average EPR continued to decline after 1982, to about 17 per cent in 1987 (Edwards, 1990). This downward trend in the average EPR obviously did not imply a total abandonment of the policy of tariff protection.

As described earlier, Malaysia launched into export-oriented industrialization with a high degree of success. While some hidden subsidies might have been provided via FTZ facilities and duty-free imports, most export-oriented industries appear to be efficient, having to sell their output at unprotected world prices. Malaysia may thus be characterized in the 1970s and 1980s as having a kind of dualistic manufacturing sector with respect to economic efficiency, a highly efficient export sector that is mostly located in FTZs, and the domestic market sector operating in a protected environment (Shepherd, 1980: 189; Edwards, 1990).

For an alternative measure of the extent of protection, a recent study found the net subsidy equivalent (NSE) of protection granted to the manufacturing sector to have increased more than fivefold in absolute terms, though it fell sharply as a percentage of manufacturing value added, between 1969 and 1979 (Edwards, 1990). Between 1979 and 1987, the NSE was maintained at more or less the same level (see Table 11.12). As a

Table 11.12 Manufacturing protection and the net subsidy equivalent

	1969	1979	1987
1 Net subsidy equivalent (NSE) of protection (M$ billion) in sample	0.3	1.6	1.5
2 NSE as % of value added at domestic prices	31	24	14
3 NSE as % of value added at free trade prices	45	31	17
4 Estimated NSE for all Malaysian manufacturing (M$ billion)	0.4	2.0	1.9
5 NSE as % of GDP	4.2	4.4	2.6
6 NSE as % of public sector current expenditure	19	17	9

Source: Edwards (1990: table 3.A.2).
Row 1 is obtained from Edwards (1975: 97).
Row 4 is calculated by multiplying row 3 by row 2.

percentage of GDP, the NSE rose slightly between 1969 and 1979, from 4.2 to 4.4 per cent, falling sharply to 2.6 per cent in 1987. However, as a percentage of the public sector current expenditure (PSCE), the NSE declined over the entire period 1969–87 from 19 to 9 per cent. Even at 9 per cent of PSCE, however, the NSE in 1987 was still substantial, considerably exceeding operating expenditure on health (Edwards, 1990: 47).

Both the EPRs and the NSEs measure the incentive effects of protection. While this aspect is important, there is an obvious need to look into the costs of protection. This can be captured by the measure of domestic resource cost (DRC). Edwards (1990) estimated the DRC for sixty-three manufacturing industries at the MIC five-digit level, whose value added collectively make up close to 90 per cent of the value added of the entire manufacturing sector. According to Edwards, the ratio of the real DRC to the foreign exchange savings that separates efficient from inefficient industries is either 0.81 or 0.96 depending on whether the profits accrue to Malaysians or to foreigners. He argues that any Malaysian industry enjoying an EPR above 17 per cent is likely to be socially inefficient. In terms of the nominal protection rate, Edwards argues that, if the protection on inputs is close to the average of 3 per cent, any rate above 15 per cent is likely to create an inefficient industry. Edwards regards these as appropriate cut-offs. After estimating the ratio of real DRCs to foreign exchange savings for sixty-three manufacturing industries, he finds the equivalent cut-off between efficient and inefficient industries in terms of the EPR to be 17 per cent.

Using this criterion, Edwards examined EPRs on an industry-by-industry basis to see if there had been overprotection and hence an excess of costs over benefits (Table 11.13). Here, we merely summarize his findings on a broad industry basis. For the first category, the resource-based industries, Edwards found the level of protection on rubber tyres was excessive. Although the EPR in this industry has declined since the 1960s, the EPR

Table 11.13 Effective protection rates (EPR) and net subsidy equivalents (NSE) by industry

	MIC code	Industry description	1987 EPR (%)	1987 NSE (%)	1979 EPR (%)	1979 EPR ($ million)	1969 EPR (%)	1969 EPR ($ million)
1	31129	Other dairy products	−1	−2	55	28	30	6
2	31131	Pineapple canning	Not est.		Not est.		20	2
3	31140	Canning, preserving and processing of fish, crustacea and similar food	−11	−5	28	12	−	−
4	31151	Coconut oil manufacturing	Not est.		Not est.		NVA	13
5	31152	Palm oil	−23	174	−1	−7	−	−
6	31153	Palm kernel oil	NVA	71	401	51	−	−
7	31159	Other vegetable and animal fats	11	5	−12	−6	100	4
8	31163	Flour mills	1346	71	NVA	0	−	−
9	31169	Other grain milling	Not est.		Not est.		80	7
10	31171	Biscuit factories	70	24	NVA	31	−	−
11	31180	Sugar factories and refineries	NVA	187	52	38	185	13
12	31190	Cocoa, chocolate and sugar confectionery	9	8	91	21	−	−
13	31214	Meehon, noodles and related products	22	8	19	3	−	−
14	31219	Other food products, nec	21	9	94	21	−	−
15	31220	Prepared animal feeds	1	−	−20	−5	−	
16	31330	Malt liquors and malt	146	97	NVA	106	35	11
17	31340	Soft drink/carbonated water industries	−18	−27	38	17	5	1
18	31400	Tobacco	−26	−185	NVA	183	125	44
19	32	Textiles					95	12
20	32111	Natural fibre spinning and weaving mills	12	21	42	44		
21	32112	Dyeing, bleaching, printing and finishing of yarns and fabrics	12	15	62	74		
22	32115	Synthetic textile mills	34	23	69	10		
23	32130	Knitting mills	2	2	59	22		
24	32201	Clothing factories	6	18	45	45	400	7
25	33111	Sawmills	233	197	30	117	50	29
26	33112	Plywood, hardboard and particle board mills	8	15	50	63	15	3
27	33113	Planing mills, window and door mills, and joinery works	4	3	33	15	−	−
28	33200	Furniture and fixtures	43	23	84	22	40	3
29	34120	Containers and boxes of paper and paperboard	32	20	79	17	−	−
30	34190	Pulp, paper and paperboard articles, nec	25	13	52	9	140	5
31	34200	Printing, publishing and allied industries	−9	−38	26	56	−	−
32	35111	Industrial gases	11	21	13	10	−	−
33	35119	Other basic industrial chemicals	16	19	Not est.		160	2
34	35120	Fertilizers and insecticides	8	8	50	38	300	12
35	35210	Paints, varnishes and lacquers	30	17	76	20	0	0
36	35220	Drugs and medicines	−11	−8	32	8	−	−
37	35231	Soap and cleaning preparations	−2	−2	80	39	10	2
38	35239	Perfumes, cosmetics	Not est.		Not est.		55	5

Table 11.13 Continued

	MIC code	Industry description	1987 EPR (%)	1987 NSE (%)	1979 EPR (%)	1979 EPR ($ million)	1969 EPR (%)	1969 EPR ($ million)
39	35290	Chemical products, nec	57	34	50	18	–	–
40	35300	Petroleum refineries	5	12	22	43	–	–
41	35400	Petroleum products	Not est.		Not est.		0	0
42	35510	Tyre and tube (A)	39	58	305	110	140	27
43	35591	Rubber remilling and rubber latex process	–6	–23	–30	–174	–20	–29
44	35593	Rubber footwear	6	12	100	42	–	–
45	35599	Plastic products, nec	18	10	141	16	–	–
46	35600	Other rubber products, nec	163	167	312	99	265	8
47	36100	Pottery, china and earthenware	1	0	25	4	–	–
48	36200	Glass and glass products	30	20	39	19	–	–
49	36910	Structural clay products	69	36	12	10	–5	–1
50	36921	Hydraulic cement	NVA	302	16	28	30	9
51	36991	Cement and concrete products	–12	–29	24	21	40	5
52	37101	Primary iron and steel industries	447	102	25	17	55	5
53	37109	Iron and steel basic industries	131	136	86	32	28	10
54	37209	Other non-ferrous metal basic industries	Not est.		77	13	170	3
55	38130	Structural metal products	1	1	25	14	35	2
56	38191	Tin cans and metal boxes	74	34	11	4	65	4
57	38192	Wire and wire products	22	11	34	17	35	2
58	38193	Brass, copper, pewter and aluminium products	23	10	32	7	25	2
59	38199	Other fabricated metal products	11	7	43	10	–	–
60	38291	Refrigerating exhaust, ventilating and airconditioning machinery (B)	16	20	172	45	1,600	16
61	38299	Machinery and equipment, nec	21	19	6	44	–	–
62	38321	Radio and TV sets, sound reproducing and recording equipment	–8	–25	2	13	–	–
63	38329	Semiconductors and other electronic components and communication equipment and apparatus	–5	–92	Not est.		–	–
64	38391	Cables and wires	50	22	6	3	–	–
65	38392	Dry cells and batteries	Not est.		Not. est.		130	6
66	38410	Shipbuilding and repairing	–3	–1	11	2	–	–
67	38432	Manufacture and assembly of motor vehicles	NVA	174	129	51	125	13
68	38439	Manufacture of motor vehicle parts and accessories	17	9	53	7	–	–
69	38441	Manufacture and assembly of motorcycles and scooters	181	36	43	7	245	2
70	39093	Manufacture of toys	–19	–16	Not est.		–	–
		Subtotals	17	1,500	31	1,623	45	265

Sources: Edwards (1990: table 3.A.3); IMG Consultants (1984).
Figures may not sum precisely due to rounding.
nec: not elsewhere classified.

in 1987 was still as high as 30 per cent. The NSE given to this industry in 1987 was over $50 million, or more than $12,000 per worker employed in the industry. There is thus a case for reviewing the protection on the industry with a view to reducing it or to making it conditional on the achievement of export targets, a strategy adopted in Korea to enhance efficiency of its industrial sector.

In the case of the export-oriented subsector, Edwards found the level of protection to be low since the bulk of the output of this subsector was exported. However, in the import-substituting subsector Edwards found the level of protection to be generally high, particularly for the heavy industries of cement, iron and steel, transport equipment, chemical products and plastics. In the case of cement, the value added at free trade prices was negative. The high price of domestically produced iron and steel has been singled out as a factor that has held back the development of the local engineering industry. High rates of protection were also found for sugar refining and flour within the food, beverages and tobacco industry, as well as for paper and paper products; in many industries in the food and beverages category, however, there was tariff redundancy.

SUPPLY-SIDE SOURCES OF MANUFACTURING GROWTH

Growth in manufacturing output can be brought about through increases in factor inputs and/or increases in factor productivity. This section of the paper analyses both factor accumulation and growth in factor productivity as sources of growth in Malaysia's manufacturing sector. We begin by looking at the inter-temporal changes in the investment ratio in the manufacturing sector. This will be followed by an analysis of changes in factor productivity. The measurement of such changes will be based on the value added to labour ratio, value added to capital ratio, the incremental capital—output ratio (ICOR), and total factor productivity growth (TFPG). The pitfalls arising from using partial factor productivity growth as measures of changes in factor productivity are well known. For instance, a rising value added to capital ratio may be more the result of rising capacity utilization than enhanced capital productivity. Be that as it may, the analysis that follows should suffice since our aim is merely to show broad trends.

Investment

One measure of capital accumulation is gross fixed capital formation (GFCF) in the manufacturing sector. GFCF as a proportion of GDP grew by 14.1 percentage points during the period 1981–7 (Rasiah, 1990: 21). As a proportion of GDP, it increased from 20.5 per cent in 1981 to 37.4 per cent in 1985 but fell marginally to 36.9 per cent in 1986. This again reflects

Table 11.14 Gross domestic investment and incremental capital output ratios, various countries (% of GDP)

	Gross domestic investment		Annual growth of GDI[a]		ICOR
	1965	1986	1965–80	1980–6	1963–85
South Korea	15	29	15.9	9.6	3.6
Taiwan	22	29	12.3	−1.0	3.3
Singapore	22	40	14.4	3.3	4.3
Hong Kong	36	23	8.6	−0.6	n.a.
Malaysia	20	25	10.4	0.8	n.a.
Thailand	20	21	7.5	0.8	n.a.
India	18	23	4.9	4.6	5.1
Brazil	25	21	8.5	−2.7	4.5
Mexico	22	21	7.2	−7.6	4.6
Kenya	14	26	7.1	−5.1	n.a.

Source: Lall (1990: table 9).
[a] 1980 prices.

the generally depressed investment climate prevailing in 1985–6. On a comparative basis, Malaysia ranked behind Singapore, South Korea and Kenya in terms of gross domestic investment (GDI) as a proportion of GDP in 1986, but was ahead of Taiwan, Hong Kong, Thailand, India, Brazil and Mexico (Table 11.14). While half the countries in the table recorded negative annual growth rates of GDI (Taiwan, Hong Kong, Brazil, Mexico and Kenya) between 1980 and 1986 because of the impact of the global recession, Malaysia was among those to register positive annual real rates of growth, albeit only marginally. Thus, in terms of building up the stock of physical capital, Malaysia did moderately well up to the mid-1980s, ahead of most countries but behind Singapore and South Korea.

Productivity

Building up the stock of physical capital, while contributing to manufacturing growth, may be less important than increasing the productivity of the capital stock. Here, several crude measures may be used to measure the changing productivity of Malaysia's capital stock. The first is the incremental capital–output ratio (ICOR).

Malaysia's overall capital productivity seems to have fallen between 1965–80 and 1980–8, with the ICOR increasing from 3.6 during the former period to 7.0 in the latter period (see chapter 2). Massive public-sector investments in social infrastructure, particularly in the early 1980s, with their long gestation periods, enhanced investment by state enterprises in what were long regarded as private-sector (directly productive) activities up to the mid-1980s, and the impact of the recession which led to the build-up of excess capacity all contributed to Malaysia's decline in overall

Table 11.15 Incremental capital-output ratio by sector, Malaysia, 1971–85

Sector	1971–80	1981–5
Agriculture	2.61	2.61
Mining	2.81	3.14
Manufacturing	4.20	4.80
Construction	6.30	5.50
Finance, insurance and real estate	13.37	12.80
Wholesale and retail trade and restaurants	1.23	1.23
Transport, storage and communications	6.78	6.80
Government services	3.53	3.50
Other services	2.80	2.80
Electricity, gas and water	11.68	15.50
Totals	4.36	5.07

Source: National Economic Consultative Council (1991: table 4).

Table 11.16 Capital and labour productivity in the Malaysian manufacturing sector, 1981–7 (1985 prices)

Year	MVA/GFCF	MVA/employment
1981	1.06	0.021
1982	0.93	0.021
1983	0.75	0.024
1984	0.71	0.026
1985	0.57	0.031
1986	0.62	0.033
1987	0.66	0.036

Source: Adapted from Rasiah (1990: tables 2.5, 2.6).

capital productivity. Within the manufacturing sector itself, the ICOR increased marginally from 4.2 during 1971–80 to 4.8 during 1981–5 (Table 11.15). On a cross-country basis, Malaysia's performance in this regard was not unique; the efficiency of the capital stock fell in many other countries during the 1980–8 period below the levels of the earlier period of 1965–80.

The fall in capital productivity as measured by changes in the ICOR is corroborated by another measure, the ratio of manufacturing value added to gross fixed capital formation (MVA/GFCF). For the first half of the 1980s, there was a persistent decline in this measure, though it increased in 1986 and 1987 (Table 11.16). But the increase in MVA/GFCF in the latter two years could be the result of enhanced utilization of capacity built up in the earlier period rather than an increase in the productivity of the capital stock.

Labour productivity as measured by MVA/employment, on the other hand, increased between 1981 and 1987. This movement in MVA per number employed is closely correlated to changes in the capital–labour

Table 11.17 Growth of output and productivity, 1960–89

Period	Annual growth rate of GDP	Rate of growth of TFPG	TFPG's % contribution to output growth
1960–70	6.4	3.0	47.4
1970–82	7.3	3.0	41.5
1980–9	4.9	0.5	10.2

Source: Based on notes received from Moshe Syrquin, Bar-Ilan University, Israel.

ratio which also increased during the same period. Rising capital intensity thus contributed to rising labour productivity in the manufacturing sector during the greater part of the 1980s.

According to Syrquin (chapter 2) TFPG for the entire economy declined from 3.0 per cent in 1960–82 to 0.5 per cent in 1980–9. This implies that TFPG's percentage contribution to real output growth declined from 47.4 per cent in 1960–70 to 41.5 per cent in 1970–82. This fell even further to 10.2 per cent in 1980–9 (Table 11.17). Overall, Malaysia's rate of growth in real output during the 1980s was due primarily to physical increases in factor inputs rather than to overall total factor productivity growth.

CONCLUSION

Our analysis of industrial restructuring and performance in Malaysia has shown that though it attained impressive rates of growth of manufacturing output throughout the 1970s and 1980s, the manufacturing sector remained rather narrowly based, with a dualistic structure made up of a relatively inefficient import-competing sector and a more efficient export-oriented sector with little linkage between them. Industries in the import-substituting sector continued to enjoy high rates of effective protection and hence high net subsidy equivalents, thereby giving rise to high domestic resource costs of saving foreign exchange. The export-oriented subsector, though relatively more efficient, was characterized by a higher degree of foreign ownership and control than was found in the NIEs at a similar stage of development. The dominant electronic components industry, for example, was dominated by a few giant TNCs from Japan, the United States, and a few European countries, with participation by firms from Taiwan and Korea on the rise in more recent years. While Malaysia was successful in persuading the major TNCs to relocate or set up their assembly bases in the country, local participation in the supply of components and in final assembly remained minimal. The question of how Malaysia can forge greater such linkages in order to broaden and diversify the manufacturing base as well as to diffuse technical know-how more widely thus needs to be addressed. The electrical/electronic goods industry in Malaysia's manufacturing sector offers a good base for the country to build upon in its efforts to broaden the industrial base and to increase Malaysian participation in this sector. Of course, the issue of increasing the efficiency of the manufacturing sector, especially the import-competing sector, is equally pressing. Where overprotection has been provided, there is clearly a need to reduce it. Alternatively, protection might only be continued on the condition that the protected industries can meet certain stipulated export targets as was done in South Korea (Edwards, 1990).

NOTE

1 In the factor intensity analysis of the composition of exports, the electrical machinery sector has been categorized as a physical capital-intensive industry that is at the same time scale-intensive. This categorization is due to the standard practice of industrial ranking on the basis of United States manufacturing value added data (Chowdhury et al., n.d.). However, in Malaysia the electronics industry is not generally capital intensive but rather labour intensive, though recent evidence suggests that there has been some increase in the physical and human capital-intensity in electronics production.

REFERENCES

Ariff, Mohamed (1975) 'Protection for Manufactures in Peninsular Malaysia', *Hitotsubashi Journal of Economics* 15(2): 41–53.

Ariff, M. and Hill, H. (1985) *Export-Oriented Industrialization: The ASEAN Experience*, Sydney: Allen & Unwin.

Bank Negara Malaysia (1991) *Annual Report*.

——, *Quarterly Bulletin*, various issues.

Chenery, H. B. and Taylor, L. (1968) 'Development Patterns – Among Countries and Over Time', *Review of Economics and Statistics* 50/4: 391–416.

Chowdhury, A., Kirkpatrick, C. and Islam, I. (n.d.) 'Structural Adjustment and Human Resource Development in ASEAN', mimeo.

Department of Statistics, *Industrial Surveys*, various issues, Kuala Lumpur.

——, *Survey of Manufacturing Industries*, various issues.

Edwards, C. B. (1975) *Protection, Profits and Policy: Analysis of Industrialization in Malaysia*, 2 vols, Norwich: University of East Anglia Press.

—— (1990) 'Protection and Policy in the Malaysian Manufacturing Sector', report prepared for the government of Malaysia, UNIDO, Vienna.

—— (1991) 'Tariff and Trade-Related Policies', paper presented to the conference on Managing Industrial Transition: Policies for the 1990s, Kuala Lumpur: Institute for Strategic and International Studies.

ESCAP, United Nations (1991) *Industrial Restructuring in Asia and the Pacific*, Bangkok: ESCAP.

Gherzi Textile Organisation (1990) *Malaysian Textile Study*, Zurich: Gherzi Textile Organisation.

Hoffman, L. and Tan Siew Ee (1980) *Growth, Employment and Foreign Investment in Peninsular Malaysia*, Kuala Lumpur: Oxford University Press.

IMG Consultants (1984) *Malaysian Industrial Policy Studies*, Sydney: IMG Consultants Pty Ltd.

Jomo, K. S. (1987) 'Economic Crisis and Policy Response in Malaysia', in R.

Robison, K. Hewison and R. Higgott (eds) *Southeast Asia in the 1980s: The Politics of Economic Crisis*, ch.5, Sydney: Allen & Unwin.

Kuznets, S. (1956) 'Quantitative Aspects of the Economic Growth of Nations, Level and Variability of Rates of Growth', *Economic Development and Cultural Change* 5(1): 1–94.

Lall, S. (1990) *Building Industrial Competitiveness in Developing Countries*, Paris: OECD.

Lee, K. H. (1985) 'The Structure and Causes of Malaysian Manufacturing Sector Protection', in C. Findlay and R. Garnaut (eds) *The Political Economy of Manufacturing Protection: Experiences of ASEAN and Australia* Sydney: Allen & Unwin, pp. 99–134.

Malaysia (1981) *Fourth Malaysia Plan, 1981–1985*, Kuala Lumpur: National Printing Department.

—— (1991) *Sixth Malaysia Plan, 1991–1995*.

MIDA (1987) *Malaysia – Investment in the Manufacturing Sector – Policies, Incentives and Procedures*, Kuala Lumpur: Malaysian Industrial Development Authority.

Ministry of Finance, *Economic Report*, various issues, Kuala Lumpur: Ministry of Finance.

National Economic Consultative Council (1991) 'Economic Policy for National Development', Kuala Lumpur: National Printing Department.

Osman-Rani, H., Toh, K. W. and Ali, A. (1986) *Technology and Skills in Malaysia*, Singapore: Institute of Southeast Asian Studies.

Power, J. H. (1971) 'The Structure of Protection in West Malaysia' in B. Balassa and associates, *The Structure of Protection in Developing Countries*, ch. 9, Baltimore: Johns Hopkins University Press.

Rasiah, R. (1990) 'Review of Linkage Development in the Export Processing Manufacturing Sector with Particular Focus on the Electrical/Electronics and Textile/Garment Industries', report prepared for the government of Malaysia, UNIDO, Vienna

Shepherd, G. (1980) 'Policies to Promote Industrial Development', in K. Young, W. Bussink and P. Hasan (eds) *Malaysia: Growth and Equity in a Multiracial Society*, ch. 7, Baltimore: Johns Hopkins University Press.

Tan, T.W. (1991) 'Need to Broaden Industrial Base', *New Straits Times*, 8 June 1991.

United Nations Industrial Development Organization (1985) *Medium and Long Term Industrial Master Plan, Malaysia*, Vienna: UNIDO.

Vijayakumari, K. (1990) 'Industrial Restructuring and its Implications for Employment, Wages and Human Resource Development', Kuala Lumpur: Institute for Strategic and International Studies.

Von Rabenau, K. (1975) 'Trade Policies and Industrialization in a Developing Country: The Case of West Malaysia', Economics Discussion Paper no. 55, University of Regensburg, Regensburg.

World Bank (1986) *Malaysia: Industrializing a Primary Producer*, Washington, DC: World Bank.

12

TRADE AND INDUSTRIAL POLICIES AND EXPERIENCE IN SRI LANKA

Ganeshan Wignaraja

The author is grateful to Gerry Helleiner, Lal Jayawardena, Sanjaya Lall, Ian Little, Lance Taylor, Andrew R. Turesky and Howard White for valuable comments on earlier drafts. The views expressed here remain solely my responsibility.

INTRODUCTION

Since the mid-1970s, Sri Lanka has followed outward-oriented policies to promote rapid industrialization. Sri Lanka's industrial performance lags behind those achieved by the East Asian newly industrializing countries (NICs) in the 1970s and 1980s, despite some successes in manufactured exports and manufacturing growth. This paper investigates some of the factors behind this lacklustre industrial performance – notably, the initial conditions, trade policy, macroeconomic stability and industrial strategy. One conclusion is that the absence of both macroeconomic stability and an industrial strategy may have hindered industrial performance in Sri Lanka.

The paper is organized as follows. The first section discusses Sri Lanka's initial conditions and the previous inward-oriented trade policy and industrial performance of the period 1960–77. The next three sections examine the outward-oriented trade policy, macroeconomic stability and industrial strategy in the post-1977 period, followed by a discussion of industrial performance during the post-1977 period.

INITIAL CONDITIONS AND ECONOMIC ORGANIZATION

Countries adopt outward-oriented policies to foster industrialization in a range of economic, social and political circumstances. Let us first look at how Sri Lanka's initial conditions influenced the outcome. For purposes

389

Table 12.1 Some basic economic data, Sri Lanka, early 1970s

Land area (square kilometres)	65,607
Population (millions) (1971)	12.7
Average annual rate of population growth (1971–6)	2.0
GNP per capita (US$) (1975)	150
Structure of GDP (percentage) (1970–1)ᵃ	
Agriculture	34.3
Manufacturing	13.9
Mining	0.7
Construction	5.7
Services	45.4
Manufacturing employment as percentage of total (1971)	7.6
Exports plus imports as percentage of GDP (1970–1)	30.1
Exports as percentage of GDP (1970–1)	14.7
Manufactured exports as a percentage of total exports (1972)	2.6
Average annual rate of inflation (1971–7)	5.7
Debt service as percentage of GNP (1970–1)	2.1
Debt service as percentage of exports (1970–1)	10.8
Government expenditure as percentage of GNP (1970–1)	29.3
Government revenue as percentage of GNP (1970–1)	20.4
Share of public enterprise investment in gross fixed capital formation (1970–1)	41.3
Share of public enterprises in manufacturing value added (1973–4)	50.0

Sources: World Bank (1977, 1988); International Labour Office (1980).
ᵃ 1959 prices.

of analysis, a country's initial conditions may be classed under several headings: country size, resource endowment, living standards, structure of production, participation in international trade, macroeconomic conditions, the nature of the state and the development strategy (see Chenery *et al.*, 1986; Griffin, 1989). Some data on Sri Lanka's initial conditions, in the early 1970s, are shown in Table 12.1.

Sri Lanka, located about 35 kilometres to the south of India, is a small pearl-shaped island. Its surface area is 65,607 square kilometres, a quarter the area of the United Kingdom. The population, which stood at the 1971 census at 12.7 million, provides for a small internal market. Few minerals have been found apart from large mineral deposits of clay, gems, graphite and mineral sands. Similarly, Sri Lanka lacks energy resources such as oil, natural gas and coal but it has numerous fast-flowing rivers, suitable for hydroelectric power. Sri Lanka's small internal market and limited natural resource endowment has induced specialization and trade.

An analysis of Sri Lanka's initial conditions in the early 1970s shows that it had remarkable living standards for a poor country.[1] Clearly, Sri Lanka had a relatively low level of per capita income – in 1975, Sri Lanka's real GNP per capita was only US$150 (Table 12.1). Four comments can be made about Sri Lanka's living standards in the early 1970s. First, the life expectancy at birth of a Sri Lankan in 1971 (sixty-six years) was amongst the highest recorded for developing countries. Second, Sri Lanka's under-five mortality rate in 1971 (forty-five deaths per 1,000 live births) was equally striking. Third, Sri Lanka's adult literacy rate in 1970 at 71 per cent approached those of South Korea (88 per cent) and Singapore (74 per cent). Fourth, the Sri Lankan combined primary and secondary school enrolment ratio in 1970 (71 per cent) was nearly identical to that of South Korea (76 per cent) and Singapore (77 per cent). A healthy, educated labour force is regarded as one of the fundamental determinants of rapid industrial development (Oman and Wignaraja, 1991; World Bank, 1991). Generally high levels of primary and secondary education in Sri Lanka favoured the adoption of simple manufacturing technologies and the fostering of entrepreneurial talent and managerial ability. A human capital endowment of labour of low skill is not favourable, however, to the adoption of more complex manufacturing technologies.

The economy in 1970 was largely dualistic in structure. A highly organized and productive plantation and related service sector co-existed with a subsistence agricultural sector employing the bulk of the population. Foreign trade played an important role in the Sri Lankan economy – in 1970–1 the trade coefficient (exports plus imports as a percentage of GDP) was 30.1 per cent. There was also a small manufacturing sector accounting in 1970–1 for 13.9 per cent of GDP (see Table 12.1). Manufactured products were, however, only a tiny fraction of total exports (2.6 per cent in 1972). Sri Lanka was fortunate in having fairly favourable macroeconomic conditions – in terms of inflation and foreign debt repayments – in the 1970s (see Table 12.1).

The government of Sri Lanka felt it had to assume the responsibility in promoting economic development in the post-independence period. Government expenditure was 29.3 per cent of GNP in 1970–1. A well-educated civil service, a legacy of British rule during the nineteenth and early twentieth centuries, provided a reasonable administrative capacity.

The origins of inward-oriented trade and exchange controls in Sri Lanka can be traced to the early 1960s and they remained, with some modifications, until the mid-1970s. As in other developing countries, these restrictions were the result of a host of non-economic objectives, a mistrust of private enterprise and deep export pessimism. The inward-oriented trade policies were pursued through an extensive array of *ad hoc* government interventions in product and factor markets. These interventions were not devised to correct for market failures that impeded industry in Sri Lanka from realizing its long-term comparative advantage. A brief description of the nature and impact of these policies follows.

Inward-oriented period: trade and industrial policy

The first exchange controls, affecting capital transfers, foreign travel and finance for educational expenditure, were put into effect in August 1960 by the Sri Lanka Freedom Party (SLFP) government. These were gradually followed by a plethora of restrictions and interventions in foreign trade and private-sector industrial activity, both foreign and local (see Pyatt and Roe, 1977; Wickremasinghe, 1985).

First, a variety of tariffs, ranging from 10 per cent to 300 per cent, were introduced on a large number of imported consumer goods and some raw materials and intermediate goods (especially petroleum products and textiles). Later, quotas (imposing limits on the quantities of goods purchased) were adopted instead of tariffs as the major instrument of protection. By the mid-1960s, stringent quotas covered all imports except basic food items, pharmaceuticals, fertilizers and petroleum products.

Second, the government expanded its domination of trade and industry by nationalizing private enterprises and setting up public manufacturing enterprises (PMEs) and public service enterprises (PSEs). Following the enactment of the State Industrial Corporations Act of 1957, several PMEs were established to develop heavy, capital goods industries. Through quotas and import licensing in the 1960s and 1970s, many PMEs and PSEs were provided with near-exclusive access to imports of construction materials, spare parts and capital equipment. Monopoly power enabled them to reap large quota premiums while remaining inefficient. The growth in the number of PMEs and PSEs was rapid – from nine in the late 1950s to 107 by the mid-1970s (Karunatilake, 1987: 140 and 145).

Third, exchange control regulations, by limiting transfers of dividends and profits, also discouraged foreign direct investment (FDI) in the Sri Lankan economy. Further restrictions on FDI were introduced through legislation.[2]

Thus, the gradual strengthening of import and exchange controls, domestic price controls and the establishment of a large number of public-sector enterprises set in motion a classic import-substitution industrialization (ISI) policy in Sri Lanka. The salient characteristic of the ISI policy was that it tended to bias trade and industrial incentives towards production for the domestic market and against exports. Protectionist measures (such as import licensing, quantitative restrictions on imports and domestic content regulations) coupled with an overvalued exchange rate, imposed a double burden on export firms in Sri Lanka. First, because of high import protection, firms faced increased costs of imported raw materials and machinery.[3] Second, the substitution of excessive administrative regulations for market forces generated a large bureaucracy and corruption that hindered private-sector initiatives. Firms went to considerable efforts and costs in securing licences and permits, classic rent-seeking activity (Bhagwati, 1988) distracting them from productive activity. The net result was that firms were discouraged from exporting and new investment was directed toward high-cost industries (largely in the public sector) manufacturing goods for the domestic market.

A few studies have attempted to estimate the extent of trade bias facing manufacturing in Sri Lanka during the inward-oriented period. These studies use different measures of trade bias and are therefore not strictly comparable. Rajapathirana (1988), relying on the ratio of the nominal effective exchange rate for manufactured exports relative to that for total imports, reports that the trade regime favoured import substitution over export production up to the late 1960s. Pyatt and Roe (1977) calculate trade bias estimates from effective protection data and suggest that a bias against exporting was present in several manufacturing branches in 1970.

There was an attempt at partial liberalization of the system of import controls and the promotion of non-traditional exports (i.e. gems, specie and manufactured exports) during the period 1965–70. Important policy reforms included: devaluation of the rupee in 1967; the adoption of a dual exchange rate system; and the reintroduction of the open general licence system for imports (Wickremasinghe, 1985).

But the preliminary moves towards liberalization were largely abandoned in 1970, following the election of the new United Front government. Over the next seven years there was an intensification of trade restrictions and increased state participation in industry (Lal and Rajapathirana, 1989). The trade regime was tightened significantly as quantitative restrictions were brought back. The open general licence system was aborted and all imports were placed under individual licensing. Moreover, there was a large nationalization programme in the plantation sector (both local and foreign) in which many private industrial firms were also taken over by the state. Consequently, public manufacturing enterprises (PMEs) rapidly increased in their number, size and role in economic activity (see Table 12.1).

Nearly two decades of ISI policy, focused on large PMEs and almost random interventions, left a deep imprint on manufacturing. There is a general consensus that manufacturing in Sri Lanka had the following features during the inward-oriented period: (i) it was highly protected and inefficient; (ii) it was oligopolistic in structure; (iii) it substantially underutilized capacity; (iv) it was dependent on capital-intensive technologies with limited job-creating capacity; (v) it was dependent on imports of intermediates and capital goods and vulnerable to foreign exchange constraints; and (vi) above all, it was biased against exporting.[4]

The combined impact of these features is further reflected in industrial performance during the 1970s (see Tables 12.9 and 12.10). There was only a modest expansion of manufactured exports and output. The share of manufactured exports in total exports increased from a negligible 2.6 per cent in 1972 to 14.7 per cent in 1975–7; real manufacturing output grew at 1.7 per cent per year during 1970–7. Real labour productivity in manufacturing increased at the rate of only 1.9 per cent per year between 1970 and 1977. The size of the manufacturing sector in the economy remained modest, averaging 15.5 per cent of GDP per year during 1970–7.

Despite relatively favourable initial conditions, Sri Lanka's industrial performance was weak, retarded by its inward-oriented trade policy and the massive array of government interventions in product and factor markets. The lack of dynamism of manufactured exports, output and productivity slowly bred disenchantment with the ISI policy. The time was ripe for change.

OUTWARD-ORIENTED PERIOD: TRADE POLICY

The 1977 elections resulted in a United National Party government committed to sweeping reforms to introduce outward-oriented policies. The shift in focus signalled a break with the past: for the first time since independence in 1948, Sri Lanka was set to embark upon a development strategy emphasizing economic growth based on a rapid growth of manufactured exports from private firms and a greater reliance on the price mechanism to allocate resources.

In November 1977, the government of Sri Lanka introduced the following package of policy reforms:[5]

(i) Reduction of direct intervention in foreign trade, exchange and financial markets (removal of most import quotas and replacement of quantitative restrictions by a system of import tariffs, devaluation of the rupee and higher interest rates).

(ii) Elimination of consumption subsidies and other price controls and encouragement for private-sector investment (through tax breaks and infrastructural development, including the setting up of a free trade zone).

(iii) Initiation of a privatization programme for PMEs.

The main objective of the 1977 package was to transform the inward-oriented trade policy into an outward-oriented one, i.e. one that did not selectively discriminate between production for the domestic market and exports (Ministry of Finance and Planning, 1985, 1987). Elimination of the bias against exports involved a shift to policy neutrality, following which, it was hoped, resources would shift away from formerly protected sectors into alternative sectors, and output and exports of the latter sectors would increase. Policymakers in Sri Lanka felt that outward-oriented trade policies had underpinned the superior industrial performance of the East Asian NICs (relative to inward-oriented countries) since the 1960s. By adopting an outward-oriented trade policy, Sri Lanka sought to emulate the industrial success of countries such as South Korea, Taiwan and Singapore.

Table 12.2 Trade bias index (TBI) for manufacturing as a whole, Sri Lanka, 1978–87[a]

	TBI
1978	1.08
1979	1.11
1980	1.20
1981	1.22
1982	1.19
1983	1.16
1984	1.20
1985	1.14
1986	1.29
1987	1.28

Source: Kelegama and Wignaraja (1991).
[a] Nominal effective exchange rate for manufactured exports divided by the nominal effective exchange rate for total imports.

Bias of trade policy

Ultimately, the allocation of resources to export development or import substitution in an economy depends on the net effect of all trade policies (Little *et al.*, 1970; World Bank, 1991). The net effect of the 1977 trade reforms will be examined quantitatively. A convenient measure of the relative returns to exports and import substitution in an economy is the trade bias index (Bhagwati, 1988).[6]

Estimates of the trade bias index for manufacturing as a whole are available from Kelegama and Wignaraja (1991) for the 1978–87 period (see Table 12.2). The data suggest that, for manufacturing, the 1977 trade reforms produced a small bias in favour of exports which remained throughout the period, 1978–87. This is indicated by the trade bias index for manufacturing as a whole being slightly above unity in Table 12.2. The finding is corroborated in other research offering estimates of trade bias for non-traditional agriculture and manufacturing for the period 1978–83: 'The policy package (of 1977) can be viewed as having a marginal bias toward export promotion if the focus is only on non-traditional exports. A comparison of estimates of non-traditional agricultural products and manufacturing suggests that this was mostly a reflection of favoured treatment accorded to manufacturing' (Cuthbertson and Athukorala, 1991: 378).

Sri Lanka's sweeping reforms of trade policy evidently created a slightly more-than-neutral export promotion incentive in manufacturing. Outward-orientation proved a better means for achieving rapid industrial development in Sri Lanka than inward-orientation had been.

Trade liberalization

Sri Lanka adopted a gradual, multi-stage programme of trade liberalization beginning in 1977. The elimination of quotas on 16 November 1977 and their replacement by a system of tariffs was the first stage of trade liberalization. The new tariff system had a duty structure consisting of six bands ranging from 0 per cent for essential consumer goods to 500 per cent for luxury goods.[7] A list of 281 items were retained under specific import licensing while the major part of the import trade was placed under open general licensing.

The first stage of trade liberalization in Sri Lanka was an advance towards a more open trade regime. While tariffs may be theoretically as restrictive as quantitative restrictions in static terms, their greater transmission of external changes implies that the former usually represent a more open trading system.[8] In fact, there was a notable expansion in imports following liberalization (see Table 12.9). Sri Lanka experienced major external shocks – such as the oil price hike of 1979 and the world recession of 1980–3 – in the aftermath of trade liberalization. The effects of external shocks in Sri Lanka are discussed later. The important fact is that quantitative restrictions were not re-deployed in balance of payments management in the post-1983 period.

The objective of the second stage of trade liberalization was to establish more uniform incentives for all activities. The rationale behind uniform tariffs is that without the distortions created by varying levels of protection, resources will be more likely to flow into areas of comparative advantage as revealed by market forces.[9] In November 1980, the Presidential Tariff Commission (PTC) was established to evaluate the tariff structure on the principle of effective protection (taking into account import taxes on both final output and inputs) and to propose reforms.

Estimates of the average level of effective protection in the manufacturing sector in Sri Lanka for the period 1979 to 1985 are shown in Table 12.3. The estimates for 1979, 1981 and 1983 were calculated by the Presidential Tariff Commission (PTC) at the request of the author while the estimate for 1985 is from Edwards (1989). The first stage of trade liberalization, namely the shift from quantitative restrictions to a system of tariffs in 1977, successfully reduced the average level of effective protection accorded the manufacturing sector. In 1979 the industry average of 50 per cent was noticeably lower than those recorded for the previous import-substituting phase.[10] Despite a temporary reversal (the industry average rose sharply to 61 per cent in 1981), the second stage of trade liberalization eventually reduced the average level of effective protection granted to the manufacturing sector to 30 per cent in 1985, the latest year for which data are available.

Averages, including weighted averages, can conceal considerable variation in effective protection across manufacturing branches. Table 12.3 also pro-

Table 12.3 Effective rates of protection in manufacturing, Sri Lanka, 1979–85

	1979	1981	1983	1985
Average ERP in manufacturing (%)	50	61	56	30
Range of ERPs in manufacturing (%)	68→267	53→423	59→198	n.a.
Branch-level ERPs (%)				
Food, beverages and tobacco	1	−34	60	n.a.
Textiles, wearing apparel, etc.	61	0	49	n.a.
Wood and wood products	n.a.	n.a.	79	n.a.
Paper and paper products	80	48	26	n.a.
Chemicals, petroleum, etc.	106	70	95	n.a.
Non-metallic minerals	−31	235	75	n.a.
Basic metal products	72	n.a.	32	n.a.
Fabricated metals products and machinery	99	85	30	n.a.

Source: Presidential Tariff Commission, Sri Lanka for 1979–83 and Edwards (1989) for 1985.
n.a. = not available.

vides information on the pattern of effective protection, at the ISIC two-digit level, from 1979 to 1983. The data show that there was wide variation in the levels of effective protection granted to different branches for which there seems to be no economic rationale. The structure of assistance provided for different branches appears to have been determined arbitrarily and not on the basis of any economic logic.[11]

The shortcoming of Sri Lanka's arbitrarily determined pattern of protection was that it probably hindered systematic capability acquisition in potential new export industries in which Sri Lanka still lacked the requisite technological capabilities, i.e. the specialized engineering and technical skills to set up, master and diversify industrial operations, and to operate them efficiently. As noted earlier, outward-orientation typically stimulates more efficient capability acquisition than inward-orientation. Where there are substantial learning costs (in training, search, experimentation, linkage creation and possibly formal research and development) associated with acquiring technological capabilities, and where product and factor markets are characterized by a variety of imperfections (including anti-competitive behaviour by large firms, underinvestment in training and technology by firms, risk aversion and high transaction costs), carefully targeted intervention may be desirable (Bell *et al.*, 1984; Pack and Westphal, 1986; Vernon, 1989; Grossman, 1990; and Lall, 1990). (Trade interventions, however, may not be an optimal policy instrument; they should be relatively mild, short and relatively uniform across activities to minimize distortions to resource allocation. Other instruments are typically also necessary to address market failures in information, skills, technology and institutions.

Protection is therefore only one component in an industrial strategy designed to promote industrial upgrading.)[12]

Exchange rate policy

The liberalization of trade in November 1977 was accompanied by far reaching revisions of the complicated exchange rate system. First, the dual exchange rate system, in force since 1968, was terminated and the exchange rate was unified and 'freed'; and second, the rupee was thereafter permitted to float, its value being determined largely by market forces in the foreign exchange market. The unification of the Sri Lankan currency was accompanied by a substantial nominal devaluation of the rupee against all foreign currencies. Thus, from 16 November to 31 December 1977, the Sri Lankan rupee depreciated 43 per cent against the US dollar, and a similar amount against other major currencies (Wickremasinghe, 1985). Thereafter, the rupee was to move freely against other currencies on the foreign exchange markets.

Free-floating was, however, short-lived. By 1983, following a period of erratic behaviour of the Sri Lankan rupee, a formal managed floating exchange rate policy was adopted by the Central Bank.[13] Under the new policy, the Central Bank actively intervened on foreign exchange markets to smooth out irregular fluctuations of the real exchange rate.

Was the managed exchange rate policy a success? Table 12.4 provides estimates of the real effective exchange rate indexes of the rupee *vis-a-vis* the currencies of important Sri Lankan trading partners and competitor countries. The trading partner real effective exchange rate (TPREER) indicates that the rupee more or less continuously appreciated in real terms after 1978 (except for a brief period during 1985–6 when the real appreciation was halted). In competitor country terms, the real effective value of the rupee also displayed a tendency to appreciate after 1978 but the CCREER behaved relatively more erratically than the TPREER.

For most of the post-1977 period, Sri Lanka's rate of inflation was above those of its trading partners and competitors and the rate of its nominal currency depreciation was insufficient to offset the inflation differential. The conclusion reached by earlier studies can be reiterated. The real appreciation of the currency had an adverse impact on the production of exportables and import substitutes during much of the post-1977 period (Lal, 1985; EDB, 1989; Cuthbertson and Athukorala, 1991; White and Wignaraja, 1991).[14]

Export subsidies and their administration

Beginning in 1979, the government of Sri Lanka began introducing export subsidies and other measures to promote exports directly. The effects of

Table 12.4 Indices of real exchange rates for trading partners and competitors, 1978–88 (1978=100)

Country	1978	1979	1980	1981	1982	1983	1984	1985	1986	1987	1988[c]
Index of TPREER[a]	100.00	100.00	101.16	101.30	102.78	110.15	126.61	106.47	94.72	94.60	97.79
Index of CCREER[b]	100.00	98.49	100.59	98.36	103.60	111.75	126.18	108.75	102.11	102.73	106.77
Competitors											
South Korea	100.00	91.51	104.90	94.89	99.30	110.63	126.05	114.74	110.63	110.94	104.61
Singapore	100.00	105.35	107.96	98.31	101.30	106.93	130.84	104.77	102.48	102.66	132.35
Thailand	100.00	98.45	94.41	100.06	100.08	104.39	134.33	120.25	112.37	112.01	110.87
Malaysia	100.00	100.28	109.47	109.57	109.33	105.19	111.15	96.44	84.27	80.75	80.50
Philippines	100.00	92.36	91.43	87.38	90.80	122.27	122.59	91.36	85.16	85.73	81.10
India	100.00	96.14	89.47	97.88	103.00	109.00	129.01	108.12	99.33	103.32	111.38
Pakistan	100.00	105.30	106.30	100.50	121.38	123.81	138.32	125.58	120.51	123.67	126.57

Source: Calculated from Central Bank of Sri Lanka, Review of the Economy, various issues, and International Monetary Fund (1989).
[a] Countries included in the TPREER are the United States, the United Kingdom, Germany, Japan and France.
[b] The countries mentioned in the table make up the CCREER.
[c] Provisional.

real currency appreciation together with only gradual tariff reform necessitated export subsidies to maintain the desired encouragement for manufactured exports. These export subsidies were administratively allocated to firms by government organizations or a combination of government and private-sector organizations (e.g. commercial banks). There have been three principal export promotion instruments in Sri Lanka (see De Silva, 1988; EDB, 1989). These were: (i) allowing exporters access to duty-free imported inputs; (ii) granting credit for exporting on more favourable terms than for production for the domestic market; and (iii) providing financial rewards (cash subsidies and tax breaks).

An import duty rebate and a manufacture-in-bond scheme were used to try to ensure that export firms gained access to inputs at prices prevailing in world markets. The Central Bank provided low-interest credit to exporting firms through selected financial institutions (the Development Finance Corporation of Sri Lanka, the National Development Bank, the state banks and a few of the domestic commercial banks) under its Short Term and Medium to Long Term Refinancing Facilities; the World Bank provided such credit under its Small and Medium Industry Programme. Tax concessions and subsidies to increase the returns to export activity relative to import substitution were also offered. A five-year tax holiday on export profits was introduced for all firms exporting non-traditional products. The Export Development and Investment Support Scheme (EDISS), administered by the Export Development Board (EDB), paid outright grants (exempt from tax) to all exporters of industrial products (except garments under quota).

Quantitative estimates of export subsidies are useful to highlight their role in Sri Lanka's trade policy (see Table 12.5). The following items were easy to quantify: tariff exemptions, interest rate subsidy, grants, export insurance and investment in infrastructure (like the establishment of free trade zones). Data constraints prevented us from disaggregating the value of subsidies into those for different export categories. Our estimates show the value of export subsidies as a percentage of gross export receipts rose from a negligible 4.41 per cent in 1979 to 12.27 per cent in 1988. They further show that interest rate subsidies (provided by the Central Bank and the World Bank) dominated total subsidies in Sri Lanka. In 1979, they were a third of all export subsidies. Interest rate subsidies markedly increased to nearly two-thirds of the total from 1985 onwards.

Export subsidies can be an important tool of trade policy if they are administered well, as in the case of South Korea and Taiwan (see Scitovsky, 1990; Helleiner, 1990). Fragmentary evidence suggests that problems may have existed in the administration of export subsidies in Sri Lanka (EDB, 1989; Yapa, 1990). Cases were reported where reimbursement of import duties, under the import duty rebate schemes, for example, were subject to delays ranging from three to six months. Exporters were critical of the

Table 12.5 Subsidies for export development, Sri Lanka, 1979–88

Year	Total subsidies (% export earnings)	Composition of export subsidies (% of the total)				
		Tariff exemptions[a]	Interest rate subsidy[b]	Grants[c]	Export insurance[d]	Infrastructure[e]
1979	4.41	29.67	38.06	n.f.	17.88	17.88
1980	7.81	25.32	56.21	0.12	13.41	13.41
1981	10.43	22.78	49.51	4.39	12.98	12.98
1982	10.76	29.64	48.40	3.93	15.43	15.43
1983	15.19	20.70	57.96	9.19	10.58	10.58
1984	10.81	31.58	48.49	5.64	12.81	12.81
1985	8.43	9.93	62.48	7.05	18.90	18.90
1986	12.61	13.97	65.21	5.07	14.59	14.59
1987	12.52	12.12	68.10	5.62	13.46	13.46
1988	12.27	16.25	62.13	7.67	13.58	13.58

Sources: Calculations based on Central Bank of Sri Lanka, *Review of the Economy*, various issues; De Silva (1988); Ministry of Finance and Planning (1986); and EDB database.
[a] Only the Duty Rebate Scheme.
[b] The Central Bank's two concessional refinance schemes and average annual commitments under SMI 1 and SMI 2.
[c] The EDIS scheme and other financial assistance schemes of the SLEDB.
[d] Export credit insurance policies in force issued by SLECIC.
[e] Investments for the establishment of free trade zones and their infrastructure, excluding running costs.
n.f. = not functioning.

multiplicity of bureaucratic procedures followed, the voluminous documents required and the many agencies to be contacted in connection with an application. Similar charges of bureaucratic delays and discretionary assistance were made against the Central Bank's concessional re-finance schemes to commercial banks. More research at the enterprise level is needed before a firm conclusion can be reached on the efficiency with which subsidies were administered in Sri Lanka.

In sum, during 1978–87, the trade reforms not only eliminated the previous bias against exports, the hallmark of ISI policy, but also produced a mildly pro-export bias in the incentives for the Sri Lankan manufacturing sector. Nevertheless, no targeted protection was provided to encourage capability acquisition in promising new industries.

OUTWARD-ORIENTED PERIOD: MACROECONOMIC STABILITY

A stable macroeconomy enhances the credibility of trade reforms. Credibility, in turn, is likely to promote private saving and investments in new industries. Conversely, macroeconomic instability may undermine a programme of trade reform. Macroeconomic stability in Sri Lanka after 1977 will be examined by reference to inflation and the behaviour of two key relative prices – the real exchange rate and the real interest rate.

Following trade liberalization in 1977, the inflation rate in Sri Lanka accelerated to 15.6 per cent per year in 1978–82, compared to 5.7 per cent per year in 1970–7 (see Table 12.12). Then inflation stabilized somewhat at about 10.3 per cent per year during the 1980s. Sri Lanka was fortunate not to experience the high inflation rates that some developing countries have faced in the aftermath of significant currency devaluation and trade liberalization (see Taylor, 1988). Nevertheless, inflation rates in Sri Lanka during the 1980s have been above those of the East Asian NICs. Annual average rates of inflation between 1980 and 1989 were 10.9 per cent in Sri Lanka whereas they were 5.0 per cent in South Korea, 3.2 per cent in Thailand and 1.5 per cent in Singapore.[15]

As indicated earlier, the persistence of relatively high inflation in Sri Lanka in the late 1970s and early 1980s contributed to an appreciating real value of the rupee and a loss in competitiveness relative to trading partners and competitors. The real exchange rate in Sri Lanka has also been very volatile. The stability of the real exchange rate, measured by the standard deviation of quarterly percentage changes of the rate, was less in Sri Lanka than in the East Asian NICs for the period 1981–8. In Sri Lanka this measure was 5.6; in Thailand it was 3.4, in Singapore 3.0, in Taiwan 2.1 and in South Korea 1.9.[16] Freely fluctuating real exchange rates such as Sri Lanka's indicated uncertain profitability for export enterprises.

Real interest rates in Sri Lanka, though remaining generally positive, were variable. As with fluctuations in real exchange rates, they sent signals of impermanence to enterprises. The real rate of interest on commercial bank deposits averaged 2.4 per cent per year during 1978–82 and 2.5 per cent per year during 1983–8 (see Table 12.12). Meanwhile, the real interest rate on commercial bank lending jumped from 1.3 per cent in 1978–82 to 8.3 per cent in 1983–8.

Trade reforms and macroeconomic stability also require a coherent industrial strategy to ensure industrial success. Industrial strategy in Sri Lanka is examined in the next section.

OUTWARD-ORIENTED PERIOD: INDUSTRIAL STRATEGY

The 1977 policy reforms were accompanied by noteworthy changes in the system of national planning (Gunatilleke, 1991).[17] The changes arose from a deep mistrust of national planning as a bureaucratic operation having little relevance for private firms. The planning function was demoted within economic management. The Ministry of Planning was merged with the Ministry of Finance. Attention switched to short-term macroeconomic management on the one hand and short-term project planning and plan implementation on the other. As noted earlier, private firms were stimulated through a trade policy of generalized export promotion aimed at maximizing gross earnings of foreign exchange.

In the process, the reform of industrial policy was neglected in Sri Lanka, and government intervention to remedy market failures in product and factor markets tended to be *ad hoc* for over a decade. Hardly any functional interventions were undertaken to preserve competitive conditions in product markets or to address market failures in factor markets (e.g. asymmetries of information in capital markets; externalities associated with human capital, on-the-job training, 'learning to learn' and research and development (R&D).[18] The reluctance of capital markets to finance difficult-to-appropriate and risky capability development and the consequent underinvestment in human capital and R&D are widely recognized (for a survey see Grossman, 1990). But the government of Sri Lanka had no policies to promote industrial upgrading, target subsidized credits, build supplies of scientific and technological manpower, provide technological support or encourage technology imports. Furthermore, there was no intervention to manage the rationalization or withdrawal of factors from 'sunset' industries via mergers or adjustment loans.

The first attempt to devise a strategy for industry came in 1987 and was called 'The Industrial Policy Statement' (Ministry of Finance and Planning, 1987). This set out objectives and programmes for reforming trade policy, public manufacturing enterprises (PMEs), taxes and industrial finance. The Ministry of Finance and Planning and the line ministries did not, however, fully implement the Industrial Policy and it was abandoned two years later. In 1989 another attempt was made called 'A Strategy for Industrialization in Sri Lanka' (Ministry of Industries, 1989). The Strategy for Industrialization also emphasized reforms of trade policy, PMEs, taxes and industrial finance. It went further by setting out reforms to regulations governing foreign investment inflows and improvements to physical infrastructure. Moreover, the newly restructured Ministry of Industries was granted the exclusive responsibility of implementing the Strategy for Industrialization.

It is still too early to assess the impact of these strategies on industrial performance in Sri Lanka. It should be noted, however, that both of them were concerned with functional rather than selective policies for industry promotion. The remainder of this section will concentrate on the rather piecemeal industrial policies in the areas of internal competition, research and development and foreign direct investment after 1977.

Competition policy

Recent statistics on changes in seller concentration at the branch level in the manufacturing sector in Sri Lanka are hard to obtain. Although somewhat

Table 12.6 Seller concentration in manufacturing, Sri Lanka, 1979 and 1981

Branch	1979	1981
Meat, fish and dairy products	81.0	92.2
Fruit and vegetable products	63.5	99.3
Confectionery, bakery and cereal products	74.5	88.9
Spirits and alcoholic beverages	84.6	85.1
Other food products and tobacco	99.6	99.0
Textiles	41.7	54.4
Made-up garments	54.5	43.1
Petroleum and petroleum products	43.1	64.3
Salt and salt-based products	98.1	99.4
Other chemicals	58.8	72.5
Pharmaceuticals and cosmetics	69.3	62.5
Soap, vegetable and animal oils and fats	99.5	86.7
Leather and rubber products	64.2	61.6
Wood, paper and pulp products	51.7	43.6
Clay, sand and cement products	80.6	88.3
Basic metal industries and machinery	58.7	59.1
Ferrous and nonferrous metal products	41.7	41.2
Transport equipment and spares	66.5	88.8
Electrical goods	47.5	80.1
Optical and photographic goods	77.8	79.2
Unweighted average	67.9	74.5

Source: Cuthbertson and Athukorala (1991: 308).
Seller concentration = share of the three major firms in total output of each sector.

outdated, Table 12.6 provides information on seller concentration in the form of three-firm concentration ratios in various manufacturing branches. The unweighted average three-firm concentration ratio for Sri Lankan manufacturing increased from 67.9 per cent in 1979 to 74.5 per cent in 1981. This was somewhat higher than the same ratios for South Korea and Taiwan which in 1981 were 62.0 per cent and 49.2 per cent, respectively (Amsden, 1989: 54). In 1981, the largest 100 firms in Sri Lanka controlled approximately 75 per cent of total manufacturing sales (estimated from Department of Census and Statistics, 1985: 42).[19] The fragmentary evidence suggests that seller concentration in the manufacturing sector in Sri Lanka was relatively high.

High concentration in the manufacturing sector in Sri Lanka could have different effects on efficiency in individual markets. On the one hand, non-competitive market structures enable economies of scale to be reaped in production. On the other hand, they can be a disincentive to domestic technological efforts directed at reducing costs and enhancing the productivity of inputs.[20] On balance, authors argue that the disincentive effect was dominant in the Sri Lankan case (e.g. Wijesinghe, 1989).

The high levels of concentration in Sri Lanka are not surprising given that little reference was made to internal competition in the 1977 reforms.

For nearly a decade following the 1977 policy reforms, competition policy in Sri Lanka was defined by the National Prices Commission Law No. 42 of 1975. This law established a weak body with the limited function of undertaking price surveillance and making non-legally binding recommendations. No anti-trust laws – such as India's Monopolies and Restrictive Trade Practices Act which restricted large firms entering into new product lines or expanding – existed to discourage monopolies or collusive oligopolies. It was only in 1987 that a new anti-trust law was passed, signalling a renewed interest in competition policy. The Fair Trading Commission Act No. 1 of 1987 set up an authority to control monopolies, mergers and restrictive business practices as well as continuing with price surveillance.

Research and development policy

A policy on expenditure was missing in Sri Lanka during much of the outward-oriented period. The government did not appear to give much priority to Sri Lanka's R&D effort until the mid-1980s. In 1984 the National Science and Technology Planning Coordination Committee was appointed to develop an integrated science and technology plan for several sectors (including industry). An important recommendation of the final report of the Committee, published in 1986, was to increase gross spending on R&D to about 2 per cent of GNP. The Committee did not, however, recommend tax incentives for technological activities or training at the firm level.

In the absence of a national R&D policy, a trio of dated public R&D institutes were relied upon to support capability acquisition in new ('sunrise') export industries. These institutes – the Ceylon Institute of Scientific and Industrial Research, the Industrial Development Board and the National Engineering, Research and Development Centre – were established in the pre-1977 period to conduct applied R&D work on imported technologies and to diffuse them to firms. Not only did they tend to be rather slow and bureaucratic in their approach to R&D but they also lacked the requisite finance, equipment and technical manpower to perform R&D. In addition, they were unable to provide simple technological services such as quality control, equipment maintenance, process adaptation and product design modifications.

Judging simply by the major indicators, R&D performance in Sri Lanka hardly improved during the outward-oriented period (see Liyanage and De Silva, 1987; Wignaraja, 1990a). On the input side, gross expenditure on R&D (as a percentage of GNP) rose from 0.18 per cent in 1975 to 0.19 per cent in 1984. Moreover, the number of scientists and engineers in R&D (per million population) remained static – in 1985 it was 173 per million population. On the output side, there was a modest upward trend in number of patents granted to nationals – eighteen patents were granted to nationals in 1985 compared with nine in 1976. A comparison of Sri Lanka's R&D performance with that of the East Asian NICs is instructive. South Korea and Taiwan stepped up their investments in gross expenditures on R&D in the mid–1980s and devote 2.3 per cent and 1.1 per cent of GNP, respectively, to such expenditures (see Lall, 1990, 1991). The data on personnel engaged in R&D are equally revealing – South Korea employs 1,283 scientists and engineers in R&D per million population while Taiwan employs 1,426. On the output side, patents granted to nationals numbered 2,581 in South Korea and 5,944 in Taiwan (in 1986).

Our brief examination of the major R&D performance indicators suggests that Sri Lanka's technological effort is poor in comparison to South Korea and Taiwan. There is no simple answer for Sri Lanka's poor R&D performance but further research should focus on appropriate R&D policy and the role of the public R&D institutes.

Foreign direct investment policy

One of the hallmarks of industrial policy during the outward-oriented period was the open-door policy towards foreign direct investment (FDI) in industry. The government turned to FDI in an attempt to meet Sri Lanka's needs for imported manufacturing technologies and overseas markets in export development (see Ministry of Finance and Planning, 1985). This is in marked contrast with the inward-oriented period (1960–77) when the government discouraged FDI. Two types of incentive packages were provided to attract FDI in export-oriented projects: those obtainable under the Greater Colombo Economic Commission (GCEC) and those obtainable under the Foreign Investment Advisory Committee (FIAC).

The GCEC, which managed three export-processing zones (EPZs), sought to promote 100 per cent export-oriented FDI. The EPZs offered the following incentive package: (i) exemption from import duties (for all raw materials and machinery) and exchange control regulations (on overseas transactions and remittances); (ii) tax holidays of 2–10 years on profits and salaries of foreign employees; (iii) relaxed labour laws; and (iv) ready access to land and infrastructure facilities within the zones. There were no limitations on the amount of equity held by foreign firms in projects. The FIAC dealt with foreign investment outside the export promotion zones. Typically, such investments were joint ventures where the foreign firm held a minority of the equity (i.e. up to a maximum of 49 per cent). The FIAC granted fewer incentives than the EPZs. Most notable of these were a fixed five-year tax holiday, exemption from import duties for raw materials at the point of export, and concessional income tax rates for foreign employees for three years.

The Asian NICs attracted far more FDI flows than Sri Lanka. During 1978–87 the annual average FDI inflows in million SDRs were: Singapore,

Table 12.7 Cumulative FDI inflows by manufacturing branch, Sri Lanka, 1978–88

Branch	Number of products	Cumulative FDI inflows	
		Rs million	% share
Food, beverages and tobacco	26	936	14.3
Textiles, wearing apparel and leather	133	1,669	25.5
Wood and paper	22	44	0.7
Chemicals, petroleum, plastics and rubber	72	1,139	17.4
Non-metallic minerals	45	1,019	15.6
Fabricated metal products	59	368	5.6
Manufactured products (nes)	62	1,370	20.9
Total	419	6,545	100

Sources: Calculated from Ministry of Finance and Planning (1986); World Bank (1988); and
Central Bank of Sri Lanka, *Review of the Economy,* various issues.
Cumulative Inflows of FDI = foreign investment in industrial projects contracted by the
GCEC and FIAC.

993.7; South Korea, 148.1; Thailand, 109.1; and Sri Lanka, 34.9 (IMF, 1988).
At the end of 1988, there were 419 manufacturing projects involving
foreign equity participation and the cumulative FDI flows stood at Rs.6,545
million (Table 12.7). Textiles and wearing apparel, a relatively simple industry, at 25.5 per cent of cumulative FDI flows, was the leading recipient.

Clearly, a variety of factors influenced the relative attractiveness of Sri
Lanka (in comparison to the NICs) during 1978–87. First, there was labour
cost. Estimates of EPZ average hourly labour costs (wages and social
payments) provided by UNIDO (1988: 30) suggest that Sri Lanka was
probably the cheapest location in Asia in the 1980s.[21] Second, over and
above labour cost, the high literacy and discipline levels of Sri Lankan
workers translated into high productivity levels in simple industries
(particularly wearing apparel). Third, the prospects for rapid growth were
good. Massive inflows of foreign aid accompanying the 1977 reforms,
signalling multilateral and bilateral donor confidence in Sri Lankan development, seemed likely to relieve foreign exchange constraints to rapid
growth (Levy, 1987). It is worth noting in passing that real GDP accelerated
during the outward-oriented period (see Table 12.12). These advantages
made Sri Lanka appear attractive to export-oriented FDI interested in
simple industries.

Other factors, however, probably acted to reduce Sri Lanka's attractiveness as a low-cost location compared with South Korea, Singapore and
Thailand. The principal disadvantages of Sri Lanka were the relatively small
domestic market (of 16.6 million in mid–1988), the lack of scientific and
engineering manpower (see above) and the inadequate physical infrastructure. The lack of scientific and engineering manpower, in particular, hindered Sri Lanka's ability to attract FDI into more complex industries. The
locational disadvantages were compounded by another factor: political

Table 12.8 Share of foreign and local firms in manufactured exports, Sri Lanka, 1979–88 (%)

Ownership	1979	1980	1981	1982	1983	1984	1985	1986	1987	1988
GCEC firms	4.1	9.3	15.1	20.0	27.4	26.5	25.8	32.7	37.2	40.3
FIAC firms	3.4	6.8	8.0	9.4	18.5	13.4	15.1	18.6	14.8	15.3
Foreign firms[a]	7.5	16.1	23.1	29.4	45.9	39.9	40.9	51.3	52.0	55.6
Local firms[b]	92.5	83.9	76.9	70.6	54.1	60.1	59.1	48.7	48.0	44.4

Source: Calculated from UNIDO (1986) and Central Bank of Sri Lanka, *Review of the Economy*, various issues.
[a] Foreign firms are defined as the sum of GCEC and FIAC firms.
[b] Local firms are defined as the sum of public- and private-sector firms.

instability. Since 1983 Sri Lanka has been suffering from a political crisis that has become increasingly violent. Various World Bank reports emphasize that the crisis has given Sri Lanka an 'image problem' and repelled FDI inflows to the country (see World Bank, 1988, 1989, 1990).

A detailed social cost–benefit analysis of the impact of FDI on industrial performance is beyond the scope of the paper (for a review of this work, see Helleiner, 1989). Therefore, only a few tentative remarks will be made. Important gains to total manufactured exports and employment are visible. Table 12.8 reports data on the share of foreign (GCEC- and FIAC-supported) and local firms in total manufactured exports. The information shows that foreign firms which in 1979 accounted for only 7.5 per cent of total manufactured exports increased their share in 1988 to an extraordinary 55.6 per cent. Thus, much of the increase in manufactured exports during the post-1977 period was driven by foreign firms. Similarly, in 1986, foreign firms provided 66,565 jobs in industry, i.e. 30.7 per cent of total manufactured employment in Sri Lanka (UNIDO, 1988: 23). Set against this, manufactured exports by foreign firms tended to be concentrated in a few simple industries like textiles and wearing apparel and gems and jewellery – in 1988, foreign firms accounted for 54.9 per cent and 42.9 per cent, respectively, of Sri Lanka's exports of these products (EDB, 1988: 26). Moreover, backward linkages generated by foreign firms (gauged by utilization of local inputs) were low. Purchases of local raw materials by EPZ firms accounted for less than 10 per cent of their total raw material purchases in 1981–4 (Vidanapathirana, 1986: 189). Without further research it is difficult to generalize more about the overall impact of FDI on the manufacturing sector in Sri Lanka.

In sum, industrial policy was not emphasized during the outward-oriented period in Sri Lanka. The neglect of potentially productive, if carefully deployed, functional and selective interventions (particularly in internal competition, human capital, R&D and FDI) hampered capability acquisition and industrial upgrading in Sri Lanka. Historically, industrial upgrading and diversification in other countries has been closely connected with an amalgam of incentives, promotion and institutions (see Pack and Westphal, 1986; Vernon, 1989; Grossman, 1990; Wade, 1990; Lall, 1991; Oman and Wignaraja, 1991). In other words, dynamic comparative advantage frequently needs to be created in new export industries.

OUTWARD-ORIENTED PERIOD: INDUSTRIAL PERFORMANCE

Did the adoption of an outward-oriented trade policy in 1977 lead to better industrial performance in Sri Lanka? Tables 12.9–12.11 provide several indicators of the industrial performance of Sri Lanka during the outward-oriented period, 1978–88. The specific indicators are the share of manufactured exports in exports, the share of manufactured output that is exported, the growth rate of real manufacturing output, the growth of real labour productivity in manufacturing, capacity utilization in manufacturing, the share of manufacturing output in GDP and the share of manufacturing employment in the labour force. Tables 12.1, 12.9 and 12.10 provided comparative performance indicators for the previous inward-oriented period, 1970–7.

The data suggest that the industrial performance of the outward-oriented period was better than that of the inward-oriented period in three respects. First, manufactured exports grew rapidly. In 1972, the share of manufactured exports in total exports was only 2.6 per cent. By the end of the inward-oriented period, in 1975–7, this had risen modestly to 14.7 per cent. The share of manufactured exports dramatically expanded during the outward-oriented period, from 14.7 per cent of total exports in 1978 to 48.3 per cent in 1988. Significant increases in the share of manufacturing output that was exported were also recorded for Sri Lanka between 1975–7 and 1988 (see Table 12.9). That is, manufacturing output became more export-oriented over time.

Second, real manufacturing output growth also accelerated sharply during the outward-oriented period to 5.6 per cent per annum in 1978–88 compared with 1.7 per cent per annum in 1970–7. This spurt permitted Sri Lanka to outstrip the manufacturing expansion witnessed in both the OECD countries (3.2 per cent) and the low-income developing countries (3.9 per cent).[22] During the period 1978–88, labour productivity in manufacturing grew at 6.1 per cent per year in comparison with only 1.9 per cent per year during 1970–7. The lack of data at the industry level does not permit us to elaborate very much on the factors (such as output mix, capital–labour ratios, age of capital, labour skills, etc.) that lie behind the gains in labour productivity during 1978–88. Increases in capacity utilization appear to have helped. Capacity utilization in manufacturing, which averaged 63 per cent per year between 1970 and 1977, jumped to 75 per cent per year during 1978–88.

Table 12.9 Trade performance indicators, Sri Lanka, 1975–88

	1975–7	1978	1979	1980	1981	1982	1983	1984	1985	1986	1987	1988
Exports (% of GDP)	27.4	34.8	33.7	32.2	30.5	27.4	26.3	28.8	26	23.7	25.2	26.1
Imports (% of GDP)	32.2	39.9	46.1	55.4	48.2	45.5	41.8	36.6	38.2	35.2	35.9	36.3
Exports + imports (% of GDP)	62.2	74.7	79.8	87.6	78.7	72.9	68.1	65.4	64.2	59.3	61.1	62.4
Manufactured exports (% of manufacturing output)	20.0	22.0	34.7	32.3	32.4	31.9	31.0	36.2	36.9	38.3	41.2	41.9
Manufactured exports (% of total exports)	14.7	14.7	24.5	33.9	35.4	38.6	35.2	34.6	39.6	46.6	48.6	48.3
Selected products (% total manufacturing exports)												
Garments	9.0	23.5	29.5	30.4	39.7	41.7	52.6	57.0	53.9	58.3	61.9	60.0
Leather products	3.5[a]	0.6	0.3	0.1	0.2	0.6	0.9	2.1	1.7	1.7	1.9	2.0
Chemical products	1.7	1.9	1.3	1.2	0.9	2.7	1.3	1.5	2.5	2.9	2.4	3.0
Petroleum products	71.2	48.6	51.5	52.4	45.3	39.7	30.4	25.5	27.1	14.9	13.0	10.0
Diamonds and jewellery	–	–	–	0.1	0.1	0.2	0.5	1.0	2.4	6.9	6.1	7.7
Basic metal products	n.a.	0.3	n.a.	0.4	n.a.	0.3	0.8	0.7	0.9	1.6	1.3	1.5
Machinery	n.a.	1.3	n.a.	1.1	n.a.	1.3	2.4	1.6	1.5	1.7	1.3	1.1

Sources: Central Bank of Sri Lanka, *Review of the Economy*, various issues. The figures for basic metal products and machinery are from EDB (1989).
[a] Leather, rubber, wood and ceramics.

Table 12.10 Manufacturing growth and structural change, Sri Lanka, 1970–88

Item	1970–7	1978	1979	1980	1981	1982	1983	1984	1985	1986	1987	1988
Manufacturing output (% of GDP)[a]	15.5	14.6	14.4	13.7	13.6	13.6	13.0	13.9	14.0	14.5	15.3	15.6
Growth rate of manufacturing output (%)[a]	1.7	7.8	4.6	0.8	5.2	4.8	0.8	12.3	5.2	8.4	6.8	4.7
Capacity utilization in manufacturing (%)	63	70	72	73	74	76	74	75	74	78	79	78

	1970	1976	1978	1982	1988
Composition of manufacturing output (%)					
Food, beverages and tobacco	35.3	28.3	29.5	20.3	27.1
Textiles, wearing apparel and leather	14.5	11.2	11.4	15.0	27.1
Wood and wood products	1.1	2.1	1.4	1.4	1.2
Paper and paper products	3.3	3.4	4.2	2.8	2.8
Chemicals, petroleum, etc.	28.3	38.5	37.0	50.6	25.3
Non-metallic minerals	7.1	5.9	6.7	5.1	4.2
Basic metal products	2.0	2.3	2.5	1.0	0.9
Fabricated metals products and machinery	13.2	7.8	6.7	3.5	4.6
Manufactured products (nes)	0.9	0.4	0.6	0.3	0.3

Sources: Growth rates of manufacturing and its share in GDP are from the World Bank (1988, 1990). The compositon of manufacturing is from Central Bank of Sri Lanka, *Review of the Economy* various issues.
[a] 1970 constant factor prices.
nes: not elsewhere specified.

Table 12.11 Labour productivity and capacity utilization in manufacturing, Sri Lanka, 1978–88 (%)

Branch	Average annual growth in labour productivity,[a] 1977–88	Average annual capacity utilization, 1978–88	Capacity utilization			
			1978	1982	1985	1988
Food, beverages and tobacco	4.1	77	70	77	82	85
Textile and wearing apparel	3.9	88	62	94	96	97
Wood and wood products	3.8	87	78	92	86	85
Paper and paper products	4.2	77	72	70	86	87
Chemicals, petroleum, etc.	n.a.	69	67	77	61	67
Non-metallic minerals	3	77	77	85	70	71
Fabricated metal products and machinery	9.3	76	54	83	89	83
Total manufacturing	6.1	75	70	76	74	78

Sources: Calculated form Kelegama (1990), Department of Census and Statistics (1988); and Central Bank of Sri Lanka, *Review of the Economy*, various issues.
[a] Gross output per employee, 1974 constant prices.

Third, a degree of structural change occurred during this period. Industrialization is typically viewed as a process whereby the share of manufacturing output in total economic activity (GDP) and the share of manufacturing employment in the labour force rises over time. The share of manufacturing in GDP (at constant 1970 prices) averaged 15.5 per cent during 1970–7. The share of manufacturing in GDP fell between 1978 and 1983 and only then started rising again. By 1988, the share of manufacturing in GDP (at constant 1970 prices) had risen only marginally to 15.6 per cent. The share of the labour force employed in manufacturing, however, which was approximately 7.6 per cent in 1971 increased to 12.0 per cent in 1981 (ILO, 1980, 1991); and by 1990, to 14.6 per cent.

These are important industrial successes for Sri Lanka. Nevertheless, Sri Lanka's achievements fall far short of those of the outward-oriented East Asian NICs. The industrial performance of the East Asian NICs after a decade of outward-orientation, between 1960 and 1970, was already ahead of that of Sri Lanka (see Scitovsky, 1990; Amsden, 1989; Griffin, 1989; Wade, 1990; Lall, 1991). During the 1970s and 1980s, the performance gap between the East Asian NICs and Sri Lanka widened even further. In

Table 12.12 Selected macroeconomic indicators, Sri Lanka, 1970–88 (year to year percentage changes and period averages)

Period	Inflation rate[a]	Real commercial bank deposit rate	Real commercial bank lending rate	Real GDP growth rate	Budget deficit (% of GDP)[b]
1978	12.1	5.7	4.2	8.2	13.4
1979	10.8	–0.8	–1.4	6.3	13.9
1980	26.1	0.0	–2.4	5.8	23.1
1981	18.0	0.2	–2.0	5.8	15.6
1982	10.8	6.7	8.0	5.1	17.4
1983	14.0	0.7	3.3	5.0	13.4
1984	16.7	–3.9	0.2	5.1	9.0
1985	1.4	12.9	19.4	5.0	11.7
1986	7.8	5.2	12.3	4.3	12.2
1987	7.7	2.6	10.5	1.5	10.1
1988	14.0	–2.3	4.2	2.7	11.6
1970–7	5.7	n.a.	n.a.	3.1	7.8
1978–82	15.6	2.4	1.3	6.3	16.7
1983–8	10.3	2.5	8.3	3.9	11.3
1978–8	12.7	2.5	5.1	5.0	

Sources: World Bank (1977, 1986, 1988, 1989).
[a] Inflation is measured by the Consumer Price Index, 1970 = 100.
[b] Budget deficit before grants.

comparison with the East Asian NICs, Sri Lanka's industrial performance during the outward-looking period, 1978–88, remained lacklustre in several respects. These were: (i) a narrow commodity composition of manufactured exports; (ii) a lopsided pattern of manufacturing growth; (iii) low rates of labour absorption in manufacturing; and (iv) a highly concentrated pattern of manufacturing regionally.

An examination of the commodity composition of exports indicates that the increase in manufactured exports from Sri Lanka originated largely in simple products rather than more advanced products. Table 12.9 shows the shares of selected manufactured exports (as a percentage of total manufactured exports) during the outward-oriented period. There was a significant expansion of wearing apparel from 23.5 per cent of the total in 1978 to 60 per cent in 1988 and a relatively small decline in machinery from 1.3 per cent to 1.1 per cent. Thus, one industry, wearing apparel, dominated the export structure of Sri Lanka during 1978–88. Even in the case of wearing apparel, a high proportion of the exports originated from new EPZ firms rather than from new local firms. Bearing in mind the fact that EPZ firms had few backward linkages with the domestic economy, the spread effects (especially the diffusion of management skills and technological capabilities) from such activity were likely to be small.

Also, the pattern of manufacturing growth was lopsided. Table 12.10

413

provides data on yearly manufacturing growth rates (constant factor prices) and the composition of manufacturing output for selected years. The pattern of aggregate manufacturing growth has been erratic, fluctuating wildly from year to year. The decomposition of manufacturing output reveals that most industries recorded reduced growth momentum during the outward-oriented period. Only textiles, wearing apparel and leather grew in a sustained manner.

Furthermore, the manufacturing sector was characterized by low rates of labour absorption. A useful yardstick to gauge the absorption rate of labour in the manufacturing sector is the employment–output elasticity (EYE).[23] Econometric estimates of EYEs suggest that the manufacturing sector in Sri Lanka was characterized by low rates of labour absorption per unit of output in the long run in comparison with South Korea, Singapore and Hong Kong during the period 1966–85 (Kelegama and Wignaraja, 1989). The long-run EYEs were: Sri Lanka (0.506), South Korea (0.618), Hong Kong (0.740) and Singapore (0.871). The long-run EYEs at a disaggregated level indicate that some of Sri Lanka's major industries (notably textiles, wearing apparel and leather; chemicals, petroleum, etc.) are not the highest absorbers of labour. The limited capacity of the manufacturing sector to provide jobs was a cause for concern given the country's continuing high unemployment rate during the outward-oriented period.[24]

Finally, manufacturing production exhibited high concentration with regard to regional distribution. Information for 1983 indicates that Colombo and Gampha, two neighbouring districts, accounted for only 16.9 per cent of all industrial firms yet produced a staggering 63.1 per cent of manufacturing output and 59.9 per cent of manufacturing value added (see Department of Census and Statistics, 1985). Two of Sri Lanka's EPZs were also established near Colombo. This high degree of geographical concentration of manufacturing production increased regional disparities during the outward-oriented period.

In sum, industrial performance during the outward-oriented period, 1978–88, improved over the inward-oriented period, 1970–7. However, in a number of respects, it fell short of performance in more successful countries.

CONCLUSION

Sri Lanka introduced outward-oriented policies in 1977, reversing nearly twenty years of inward-oriented policies. The 1977 reforms produced a small bias in manufacturing incentives in favour of exports. This was not accomplished via free trade. Rather, import tariffs and an appreciating real exchange rate were offset by massive export subsidies. The Sri Lankan experience suggests that 'outward-orientation works' in terms of promoting exports in simple industries (where comparative advantage exists or is easily gained). There was some capability acquisition but it was concentrated in simple activities. Such activities are characterized by negligible learning costs, low scale economies, and high involvement of foreign firms.

This did not spill into other activities because upgrading of industrial activities usually have high learning costs for private industry (in terms of training, search, experimentation, linkage creation and sometimes formal R&D activities). The Government of Sri Lanka was reluctant to devise a coherent set of policies in this regard. Few functional interventions were carried out to preserve competitive conditions in output markets or to address market failures in factor markets. There was also a general absence of governmental interventions targeted to promote upgrading of industrial activities through, for instance, measures to help firms overcome learning costs, provision of sufficient supplies of scientific and engineering man-power, technological support and technology imports. In addition, Sri Lanka's industrial upgrading was hampered by macroeconomic instability and political volatility.

Let us not forget Sri Lanka's strengths. As a small island economy with a rich human capital endowment and over fourteen years of experience with an outward-oriented policy, it could be highly amenable and respon-sive to the injection of a forward-looking industrial strategy. This may not be a panacea but it could be a significant step towards Sri Lanka's achieve-ment of its stated goal of becoming an NIC.

NOTES

1 The data on Sri Lanka's living standards are from Anand and Kanbur (1991) and UNDP (1991). For a detailed examination of Sri Lanka's social achievements see Bhalla and Glewwe (1986); Griffin (1989); and Anand and Kanbur (1991).

2 For example, following the passing of the Business Undertakings (Acquisitions) Act in 1970, a programme of nationalization was put into effect. Although most of the nationalizations took place in the Sri Lankan private sector and foreign-owned plantation sector, such actions deterred FDI in industry.

3 Weiss estimates the average effective rate of protection (ERP) in the manufactur-ing sector in Sri Lanka in 1970 at 118 per cent (1988: 192); the corresponding figures for India and Pakistan were 125 per cent and 181 per cent. Sirisena estimates that in 1976, at the end of the ISI period, the average ERP in the manufacturing sector in Sri Lanka was in excess of 200 per cent (1988: 50).

4 For a more detailed explanation of these characteristics see Balakrishnan (1977); Vidanapathirana (1986); Karunatilake (1987); and Cuthbertson and Athukorala (1991).

5 See UNIDO (1986), Jayawardena et al. (1987).

6 This is defined as the ratio of the nominal effective exchange rate for exports (NEER$_x$) relative to that of imports(NEER$_m$). Thus, the trade bias index, B = NEER$_x$/NEER$_m$. The NEER$_x$ is the units of domestic currency that are earned for a dollar's worth of exports, minus export taxes plus export subsidies. Simi-larly, the NEER$_m$ is the units of domestic currency that are paid for a dollar's

G. WIGNARAJA

worth of imports, taking into consideration import tariffs and other related payments.

7 The bands were: 0 per cent on essential consumer goods; 5 per cent on most raw materials, spare parts and machinery; 12.5–25 per cent on intermediate goods; a uniform 50 per cent revenue on goods that were neither essential nor luxuries; a protective rate of 100 per cent on goods being produced locally; a prohibitive rate for luxuries of 500 per cent.

8 Unlike quotas, tariffs are price instruments. Tariffs transmit movements in foreign prices more directly to the domestic economy. In comparison, quotas close the domestic economy to the influences of the international economy.

9 Such an argument, however, assumes that: capital markets function effectively; factor markets, in general, are undistorted; externalities are absent; and learning effects are predictable.

10 See note 3 above.

11 This confirms the findings of a 1981 study that revealed a wide variation in levels of effective protection assigned to different sectors with no clear motivation. 'In fact a striking feature of the pattern of assistance is that highly assisted and lightly assisted activities can be found side by side through different manufacturing sectors. Only in a few cases is the story within a sector consistently the same across all firms or products' (Cuthbertson and Khan, 1981: 104).

12 It is recognized that protection imposes current costs on consumers and producers and can lead to vested interests that are hard to remove. The experience of past interventions is replete with government failures. In many cases, haphazard protection was provided, the wrong firms and technologies were promoted and public ownership was emphasized at the expense of private firms. Past interventions were unsuccessful in most developing countries because they tended to be geared towards a variety of non-economic objectives rather than being selectively used to remedy market failures and achieve efficiency in industry. In addition, the implementation was often poor in practice because of a lack of administrative capacity. The current costs of protection can be offset by outward-orientation, careful monitoring and building up administrative capacity. The potential benefits of intervention are those associated with industrial diversification and growth. The experiences of South Korea and Taiwan suggest that a combination of outward-orientation, targeted protection and interventions in factor markets can work in the sense of creating competitiveness in new industrial activities (Wade, 1990; Westphal, 1990).

13 This appears to have been done at the insistence of the International Monetary Fund (IMF) as one of the conditions for a standby agreement. The Central Bank was required to adjust the exchange rate of the Sri Lankan currency regularly with a view to 'at least maintain its competitiveness in real effective terms' (Jayawardena et al., 1987: 17).

14 Recent theory has shown how a whole range of factors affect movements in the real exchange rate. These factors include fundamental determinants – such as the terms of trade, trade policy investment ratios, or capital inflows – which cause the equilibrium real exchange rate to change, as well as shorter-term influences. An attempt to disentangle these different factors can be found in White and Wignaraja (1992).

15 See World Bank (1991: 204).

16 Calculated from UNESCAP database, Bangkok.

17 Like many developing countries of the 1960s and 1970s, Sri Lanka engaged in comprehensive medium- and long-term national planning. The Ten Year Plan, published in 1959, recommended that structural change should become Sri

416

Lanka's major development priority. Similarly, the Five Year Plan covering the period 1972–6 emphasized the development of the export sector and some selective industrial promotion.

18 For the rationale of government intervention in industry to correct for market failures in developing countries see Caves (1987); Stiglitz (1989); and Grossman (1990).

19 UNIDO (1986: 78–9) provide data on the sales and manufacturing output of thirty leading Sri Lankan enterprises for 1983–4. A comparison with 1981 data (for thirty enterprises) suggests that the level of overall concentration was increasing over time.

20 Evidence from case studies in developed and developing countries indicates that 'competition is the prime motive for managers to cut waste, improve technical parameters of production and allocate resources efficiently' (Frischtak *et al.*, 1989: 1).

21 The figures (for 1983, in US dollars) illustrate the point: Hong Kong, $1.12–2.10: South Korea, $0.75–1.50; Malaysia, $0.65–0.90; Thailand, $0.40–0.60; India, $0.50–0.80; and Sri Lanka, $0.15–0.25.

22 See Wignaraja (1990b: table 2).

23 The employment-output elasticity (EYE) for manufacturing measures the ratio of the percentage change in the manufacturing labour force to the corresponding percentage change in physical output in the manufacturing sector. The manufacturing sector absorbs less labour per unit of output when the EYE is low.

24 Estimates of unemployment are notoriously unreliable in developing countries. Sri Lanka is no exception. Nevertheless, estimates from the Census of Population suggest that the rate of unemployment fell from 18.7 per cent in 1971 to 17.9 per cent in 1981. This indicates that the 1977 policy reforms reduced unemployment to some extent. More recent estimates from the Labour Force and Socio-Economic Survey indicate that the rate of unemployment declined slightly thereafter, from 15.3 per cent in 1980–1 to 14.1 per cent in 1985–6. See Korale (1988: 30).

REFERENCES

Amsden, A. (1989) *Asia's Next Giant*, New York: Oxford University Press.

Anand, S. and Kanbur, S. M. (1991) 'Public Policy and Basic Needs Provision: Intervention and Achievement in Sri Lanka', in J. Dréze and A.K. Sen (eds) *The Political Economy of Hunger*, vol. 3, Oxford: Clarendon Press, pp. 59–92.

Balakrishnan, N. (1977) 'Industrial Policy and Development Since Independence' in K.M. De Silva (ed.) *Sri Lanka: A Survey*, London: C. Hurst and Co., pp. 192–212.

Bell, M., Ross-Larson, B. and Westphal, L. E. (1984) 'Assessing the Performance of Infant Industries', *Journal of Development Economics* 16(1): 101–28.

Bhagwati, J. N. (1988) 'Export-Promoting Trade Strategy: Issues and Evidence', *World Bank Research Observer* 3(1): 27–57.

Bhalla, S. S. and Glewwe, P. (1986) 'Growth and Equity in Developing Countries: A Reinterpretation of the Sri Lankan Experience', *World Bank Economic Review* 1(1): 35–63.

Caves, R. (1987) 'Industrial Policy and Trade Policy: The Connections' in H. Kierzkowski (ed.) *Protection and Competition in International Trade*, Oxford: Basil Blackwell, pp. 68–85.

Central Bank of Sri Lanka *Review of the Economy*, various issues.

Chenery, H. B., Robinson, S. and Syrquin, M. (1986) *Industrialization and Growth: A Comparative Study*, New York: Oxford University Press.

Cuthbertson, A. G. and Athukorala, P. (1991) 'Sri Lanka' in D. Papageorgiou, M. Michaely and A.M. Choksi (eds) *Liberalizing Foreign Trade*, vol. 5, Oxford: Basil Blackwell, pp. 283–426.

—— and Khan, M.Z. (1981) 'Effective Protection to Manufacturing Industry in Sri Lanka', mimeo, Ministry of Finance and Planning, Colombo.

Department of Census and Statistics (1984) *Report on the Survey on Manufacturing Industries, Sri Lanka 1980*, Colombo: Ministry of Plan Implementation.

—— (1985) *Census of Industry, 1983: Preliminary Report*, Colombo: Ministry of Plan Implementation.

—— (1988) *Annual Survey of Industries 1988: Preliminary Report*, Colombo: Ministry of Plan Implementation.

De Silva, K. (1988) 'Bank Support for Small and Medium Industry in Developing Countries: Sri Lanka Country Profile', mimeo, World Bank Operations Evaluation Department.

EDB (Export Development Board) (1988) *Annual Review of Export Performance in Sri Lanka*, Colombo.

—— (1989) *National Export Development Plan, 1989–1993*, vols 1 and 2, Colombo.

Edwards, C. (1989) 'Effective Protection in Industry and Tariff Reforms in Sri Lanka', mimeo, Institute of Policy Studies, Colombo.

Frischtak, C., Hadjimichael, B. and Zachau, U. (1989) 'Competition Policies for Industrializing Countries', Policy Planning and Research Paper no.7, World Bank, Washington, DC.

Griffin, K. (1989) *Alternative Strategies for Economic Development*, London: Macmillan.

Grossman, G. (1990) 'Promoting New Industrial Activities: A Survey of Recent Arguments and Evidence', *OECD Economic Studies*, Spring, 14: 87–125.

Gunatilleke, G. (1991) 'National Planning in an Open Economy – The Challenge for Sri Lanka', *Marga Quarterly Journal* 11(4): 1–26.

Havrylyshyn, O. (1990) 'Trade Policy and Productivity Gains in Developing Countries: A Survey of the Literature', *World Bank Research Observer* 5(1): 1–24.

Helleiner, G. K. (1989) 'Transnational Corporations and Direct Foreign Investment', in H.B. Chenery and T.N. Srinivasan (eds) *Handbook of Development Economics*, vol. 2, Amsterdam: North Holland Press, 1442–80.

—— (1990) 'Trade Strategy in Medium-Term Adjustment', *World Development*, 18(6): 879–97.

ILO (International Labour Office) (1980) *ILO Yearbook of Labour Statistics*, Geneva: International Labour Office.

—— (1991) *ILO Yearbook of Labour Statistics*, Geneva: International Labour Office.

International Monetary Fund (1988) *Balance of Payments Statistics*, Washington, DC: International Monetary Fund.

—— (1989) *International Financial Statistics*, Washington, DC: International Monetary Fund.

Jayawardena, L., Maasland, A. and Radhakrishnan, P.N. (1987) *Stabilization and Adjustment Policies and Programmes: Sri Lanka*, Helsinki: UNU/WIDER.

Karunatilake, H. N. S. (1987) *The Economy of Sri Lanka*, Colombo: Centre for Demographic and Socio-economic Studies.

Kelegama, S. (1990) 'The Consequences of Economic Liberalization in Sri Lanka', unpublished D.Phil. thesis, Oxford University.

—— and Wignaraja, G. (1989) 'Labour Absorption in the Manufacturing Sector in

Sri Lanka: With Special Reference to the Post–1977 Period', *Economic Bulletin for Asia and the Pacific* 40(12): 49–61.

—— and Wignaraja, G. (1991) 'Trade Policy and Industrial Development in Sri Lanka', *Marga Quarterly Journal* 2(4): 27–53.

Korale, R. N. (1988) 'A Statistical Overview of Employment and Unemployment Trends', Institute of Policy Studies Research Studies, Employment Series no. 5, Colombo, Sri Lanka.

Lal, D. (1985) 'Real Exchange Rate, Money Supply and Inflation in Sri Lanka, 1970–82', *Weltwirtschaftliches Archiv* 121(2): 682–701.

—— and Rajapathirana, S. (1989) *Impediments to Trade Liberalization in Sri Lanka*, Thames Essay, London: Gower.

Lall, S. (1990) *Building Industrial Competitiveness: New Technologies and Capabilities in Developing Countries*, Paris: OECD.

—— (1991) 'Explaining Industrial Success in the Developing World', in V.N. Balasubramanyam and S. Lall (eds) *Current Issues in Development Economics*, London: Macmillan, pp. 118–55.

Levy, B. (1987) 'Foreign Aid in the Making of Policy in Sri Lanka', Research Memorandum no.106, Williams College, Massachusetts.

Little, I. M. D., Scitovsky, T. and Scott, M. F. G. (1970) *Industry and Trade in Some Developing Countries: A Comparative Study*, London: Oxford University Press.

Liyanage, S. and De Silva, M. A. T. (1987) *Science and Technology Indicators in Sri Lanka, Part I*, Colombo: NRESA (Natural Resources, Energy and Science Authority).

Ministry of Finance and Planning (1985) *Public Investment 1985–1989*, Colombo: National Planning Division.

—— (1986) *Public Investment 1986–1990*, Colombo: National Planning Division.

—— (1987) *Industrial Policy Statement*, Colombo: National Planning Division.

Ministry of Industries (1989) *A Strategy for Industrialization in Sri Lanka*, Colombo.

Oman, C. and Wignaraja, G. (1991) *The Postwar Evolution of Development Thinking*, London: Macmillan.

Pack, H. and Westphal, L. (1986) 'Industrial Strategy and Technological Change', *Journal of Development Economics* 22(1): 87–88.

Papageorgiou, D., Michaely, M. and Choksi, A. M. (1990) *Liberalizing Foreign Trade in Developing Countries: The Lessons of Experience*, Washington, DC: World Bank.

Pyatt, G. and Roe, A. (1977) *Social Accounting for Development Planning with Special Reference to Sri Lanka*, Cambridge: Cambridge University Press.

Rajapathirana, S. (1988) 'Foreign Trade and Economic Development: Sri Lanka's Experience', *World Development* 16(10): 1143–57.

Scitovsky, T. (1990) 'Economic Development in Taiwan and South Korea' in L.J. Lau (ed.) *Models of Economic Development: A Comparative Study of Economic Growth in South Korea and Taiwan*, San Francisco: ICS Press, pp. 127–181.

Silva, P. M. A. J. (1987) 'Export Processing Zones in Sri Lanka' in Asian Productivity Organization (ed.) *Export Processing Zones and Science Parks in Asia*, Tokyo: Asian Productivity Organization, pp. 69–80.

Sirisena, N. L. (1988) 'The Impact of Trade Liberalization and Industrial Energy Pricing Policy in the Manufacturing Sector in Sri Lanka', *Sri Lanka Economic Journal* 3(1): 38–73.

Stiglitz, J. (1989) 'Markets, Market Failures and Development', *American Economic Review Papers and Proceedings* 79(2): 197–203.

Taylor, L. (1988) *Varieties of Stabilization Experience*, Oxford: Clarendon Press for UNU/WIDER.

UNDP (1991) *Human Development Report 1991*, New York: UNDP.

UNIDO (1986) *Industrial Development Review Series: Sri Lanka*, Vienna: United Nations Industrial Development Organization.

—— (1988) *Metal Working Industries in Sri Lanka*, Vienna: UNIDO.

Vernon, R. (1989) 'Technological Development: The Historical Experience', Economic Development Institute Seminar Paper no.39, World Bank, Washington, DC.

Vidanapathirana, U. (1986) 'Pattern of Industrialization: Strategies and Responses', in W. Rasaputra *et al.* (eds) *Facets of Development in Independent Sri Lanka*, Colombo: Ministry of Finance and Planning, pp. 165–93.

Wade, R. (1990) *Governing the Market*, Princeton: Princeton University Press.

Weiss, J. (1988) *Industry in Developing Countries*, London: Croom Helm.

Westphal, L. (1990) 'Industrial Policy in an Export Propelled Economy: Lessons from South Korea's Experience', *Journal of Economic Perspectives* 4(3): 41–59.

White, H. and Wignaraja, G. (1991) 'Nominal and Real Devaluation During Trade Liberalization: Aid-induced Dutch Disease in Sri Lanka', Centro Studi Luca D'Agliano/Queen Elizabeth House Development Studies Working Papers no.38, Oxford.

—— (1992) 'Real Exchange Rates, Trade Liberalization and Aid: The Sri Lankan Experience', *World Development* 20(10): 1471–80.

Wickremasinghe, W. (1985) *A Theory of Multiple Exchange Rates and Exchange Rate Management in Sri Lanka*, Colombo: Central Bank of Sri Lanka.

Wignaraja, G. (1990a) 'The Role of Technological Capability in Industrialization: Some Lessons for Sri Lanka from the East Asian NICs', in C. Kerkoven (ed.) *Industrial Development in Sri Lanka*, Colombo: Sri Lankan Association of Economists, pp. 82–95.

—— (1990b) 'Trade and Industrialization in Sri Lanka: Facts, Economic Perspectives and a Research Agenda', paper prepared for UNU/WIDER Conference on Trade and Industrialization Reconsidered, 5–7 September, Ottawa, Canada.

Wijesinghe, F.D.C. (1989) 'Competition Policy in the Economic Development of Sri Lanka', *Sri Lanka Economic Journal* 1: 29–36.

World Bank (1977) *Sri Lanka: Country Economic Memorandum*, Washington, DC.

—— (1986) *Sri Lanka: Current Economic Situation and Outlook*, Washington, DC.

—— (1987) *World Development Report*, New York: Oxford University Press.

—— (1988) *Sri Lanka: A Break With The Past: The 1987–1990 Programme of Economic Reforms and Adjustment*, Washington, DC.

—— (1989) *Sri Lanka: Recent Macro-Economic Developments and Adjustment Policies*, Washington, DC.

—— (1990) *Sri Lanka: Sustaining the Adjustment Process*, Washington, DC.

—— (1991) *World Development Report*, New York: Oxford University Press.

Yapa, L. F. (1990) 'Problems of Developing Export-Oriented Industries in Sri Lanka' in C. Kerkoven (ed.) *Industrial Development in Sri Lanka*, Colombo: Sri Lankan Association of Economists, pp. 60–81.

13

TRADE AND INDUSTRIALIZATION POLICY AND PRODUCTIVITY GROWTH IN THAILAND

Narongchai Akrasanee and Paitoon Wiboonchutikula

The manufacturing sector in Thailand has grown rapidly over the past three decades and has increasingly been linked with international trade and investment. Both manufacturing production and exports increased at well above the average rate of all other sectors, implying that the size of the manufacturing sector in the GDP and the contribution of manufactured exports to total exports increased significantly. In fact, since the early 1980s the manufacturing sector has outproduced the traditional agricultural sector in terms of both GDP and exports. Manufactured production and exports also diversified – from primary-product processing industries to industries which were intensifying their use of all types of labour, capital and technical know-how. This study sets out to identify determinants of Thailand's manufacturing growth and structural change by separating the output growth rate into different sources or components, and then analysing how the external environment and domestic policy changes affected them.

The categorization of the industrial growth rates by their different sources enables us to measure relative contributions of various sources of growth to the real output growth of industries. The analysis can be done either from the demand or the supply side. On the demand side the growth rates can be separated by the type of market demand, namely, domestic market, export market, or the demand arising from substituting domestic supply for imports. On the supply side, growth of real output can be classified according to either the accumulation of real factor inputs or the increases of total factor productivity (TFP). Many studies have found that TFP growth has been the primary source of manufacturing growth in industrial countries since the Second World War. In the long term it is crucial for industrializing countries to increase TFP growth in order to sustain high output growth. The unresolved issue is how different growth components, particularly TFP, are influenced by changing world economic conditions and domestic development policies.

Thus, this paper will begin by investigating Thailand's trade and industrialization policy over the past three decades, and then analysing the sources of the output growth in the light of the changing policies and economic environments in some subperiods. The first section of this paper describes the development of the manufacturing sector in terms of production, exports and imports since 1960. The next two sections review the macroeconomic policy environment and examines change in trade and industrialization policy during the period in question. This is followed by an analysis of the factors accounting for the industrial sector's growth and structural change on both the demand and the supply sides, and a discussion of possible linkages between the external and trade policy environment and Thailand's sources of growth, particularly total factor productivity growth. The final section is a conclusion of all findings from this study.

DEVELOPMENT OF THE MANUFACTURING SECTOR

Growth and structural change of manufacturing production

The manufacturing sector has expanded rapidly since the late 1950s when the industrialization and other government policies to promote industrial growth began. Despite a small industrial output base, the growth rate of manufacturing value added was as high as 11 per cent a year in the 1960s. In the early days of industrialization domestic production of a number of consumer goods was protected by tariffs and promotional measures under the import-substitution policy. At the time, the industries with the largest share in total manufacturing production were food processing, beverages and tobacco (together about 50 per cent); followed by textiles and textile products, chemicals and chemical products, and transport equipment. Production growth came from expanding domestic consumption and substituting domestic supply for imports.[1]

In the 1970s the average annual growth rate of manufacturing value added fell slightly to 10 per cent in response to external shocks, including a world economic slowdown and energy price increases (see Table 13.1). Government policy shifted towards export promotion following the saturation of the domestic market for import-substituting consumer goods. Although tariff protection was still available for some industries throughout the decade, exporting industries were given incentives to partially offset the existing policy bias against exports. The incentives were rebates on import duties and taxes on imported inputs used in export production, loans at preferential rates to exporters (provided by the Bank of Thailand) and additional privileges to selected firms producing exports. The export-oriented industries which experienced high growth were natural-resource

Table 13.1 Growth and structural change of manufacturing value added, Thailand (%)

Code	Industry	Share in total value added			Growth rate of real value added		
		1970–80	1980–5	1985–90	1970–80	1980–5	1985–90
311	Food processing	11.35	12.87	10.55	6.42	8.77	7.32
312	Other food processing	3.22	2.49	1.63	13.65	5.00	10.62
313	Beverages	8.37	8.31	7.90	7.75	6.34	10.54
314	Tobacco	6.08	5.30	3.89	6.98	−0.94	5.66
321	Textiles and textile products	11.95	10.44	10.84	14.36	4.19	11.79
322	Wearing apparel	9.37	11.65	13.68	9.48	6.96	15.25
323	Leather and leather products	0.83	1.31	2.73	5.88	14.77	25.87
324	Footwear	1.11	1.06	1.08	6.67	5.20	3.99
331	Wood and wood products	4.56	2.71	1.97	3.11	−2.31	−4.40
332	Furnitures and fixtures	1.93	1.71	1.95	5.43	3.89	10.99
341	Paper and paper products	1.30	1.42	1.44	12.19	3.15	9.63
342	Printing and publishing	1.40	1.61	1.33	11.04	7.22	4.29
351	Basic chemicals	0.58	0.60	0.51	17.07	8.29	8.46
352	Chemicals products	2.78	2.75	2.70	10.41	6.76	10.68
353–4	Petroleum and petroleum products	6.77	6.69	6.21	8.71	3.20	7.88
355	Rubber and rubber products	2.04	1.75	1.64	10.87	2.03	12.73
356	Plastic products	0.86	0.89	1.16	8.67	3.26	18.33
361	Manufacture of pottery	0.36	0.43	0.41	12.92	9.71	19.44
362	Glass and glass products	0.47	0.50	0.62	13.59	8.31	12.73
369	Non-metallic mineral products	2.94	3.51	3.55	7.10	6.31	15.85
371	Iron and steel	1.49	0.97	0.82	6.40	4.05	5.65
372	Non-ferrous metal products	1.20	0.76	0.39	4.51	3.98	−1.04
381	Metal products	2.95	2.74	2.57	4.46	4.50	14.12
382	Non-electrical machinery	2.71	2.95	2.87	10.33	6.61	18.17
383	Electrical machinery	2.15	2.66	3.26	13.74	5.00	17.16
384	Transport equipment	8.18	7.00	7.19	12.98	−9.08	27.19
385	Professional and scientific equipment	0.28	0.42	0.69	17.35	7.05	25.97
390	Other industrial products	2.79	4.50	6.41	19.45	10.90	23.08
	Total value added	100.00	100.00	100.00	9.59	4.74	13.19

Source: National Economic and Social Development Board.

based and included some labour-intensive industries. They were: processing of food products such as sugar, tapioca products, canned fruits and other foods; and textiles, garments, rubber products and electronic goods. As mentioned earlier, trade policy in the 1970s did not totally abandon the protection of some import-substitution industries. In fact, tariff rates were raised intermittently to correct balance of payments deficits following a series of oil price increases. As a result, additional industries grew at above-average rates under protection in the 1970s, including transport equipment, paper and paper products, chemical products, and machinery.

The 1980s began with a second large increase in oil prices, followed by depressed commodity prices, widespread world recession, and, finally, increasing protectionism and rapid technological change. In response to the unfavourable world economic conditions, manufacturing production growth fell to an average annual rate of about 5 per cent. However, the government persisted with its export-promotion policy, and in the second half of the decade, when world economic conditions improved and large foreign investment flowed into Thailand, manufacturing production and exports expanded at double-digit rates for many successive years. Among major industries, food processing, beverages, and the tobacco industries as a group continued to decline in terms of their share in total production. Meanwhile, the production of textiles and textile products, garments and shoes grew the most rapidly. In addition, all other export-oriented industries, particularly those with increased foreign investment (such as electronic goods, jewellery, leather products, plastic products, rubber products and toys), grew more quickly than the average for the manufacturing sector as a whole.[2] Additional industries which also recorded above-average growth (due mainly to domestic demand expansion) were chemical products and transport equipment, which continued to depend on government protection and assistance to compete with imports.

Growth and structural change of exports

Thai exports have been increasing rapidly since the early 1970s, with growth rates in nominal terms averaging about 25 per cent and 15 per cent during the first and the second half of the 1970s respectively. In the early 1980s export growth slowed down in response to recession and rising protectionism in major importing countries. However, the average annual growth rate for 1980–5 was still more than 12 per cent (see Table 13.2). From 1985 to 1990 – with improved world demand and economic conditions favourable to Thai exports – export growth jumped to the spectacular rate of almost 25 per cent a year.

During the past three decades the structure of exports has steadily changed from (mainly) primary commodities to processed commodities and other manufactured products. In the 1960s about half of all exports

Table 13.2 Growth and structural change of manufactured exports, Thailand (%)

Code	Industry	Share of exports			Growth rate		
		1980–5	1985–7	1980–7	1980–5	1985–7	1980–7
311–12	Food and other food processing	49.54	40.39	46.26	8.46	17.12	10.93
313	Beverages	0.18	0.17	0.18	28.71	–7.55	18.35
314	Tobacco	1.24	0.71	1.03	2.96	–10.52	–0.89
321	Textiles and textile products	7.35	9.52	8.20	24.86	26.09	25.21
322	Wearing apparel	5.03	5.97	5.24	40.04	–1.80	28.08
323	Leather and leather products	1.24	1.96	1.55	18.61	42.05	25.31
324	Footwear	0.39	0.37	0.37	31.39	12.63	26.03
331	Wood and wood products	1.83	2.51	2.05	15.39	20.97	16.99
341	Paper and paper products	0.22	0.31	0.27	–26.43	62.37	–1.06
342	Printing and publishing	0.03	0.05	0.04	0.73	57.69	17.01
351	Basic chemicals	0.11	0.16	0.13	51.95	60.60	54.42
352	Chemicals products	0.92	1.07	0.96	33.30	2.91	24.62
353–4	Petroleum and petroleum products	0.56	1.21	0.73	46.95	–5.93	31.84
355	Rubber and rubber products	9.73	10.35	9.99	5.02	25.50	10.87
356	Plastic products	0.67	0.80	0.72	14.78	27.69	18.47
361	Manufacture of pottery	0.33	0.38	0.36	6.69	47.44	18.34
362	Glass and glass products	0.21	0.36	0.26	29.95	20.01	27.11
369	Non-metallic mineral products	0.15	0.07	0.12	1.96	34.53	11.26
371	Iron and steel	0.84	1.11	0.91	14.93	6.13	12.41
372	Non-ferrous metal products	4.26	2.15	3.29	86.17	–39.53	50.26
381	Metal products	1.17	1.97	1.46	11.76	33.60	18.00
382	Non-electrical machinery	0.74	2.12	1.28	55.99	40.43	51.55
383	Electrical machinery	5.93	8.86	7.22	11.40	39.13	19.32
384	Transport equipment	0.23	0.40	0.30	12.31	33.78	18.45
390	Other industrial products	7.08	7.30	7.16	9.19	31.79	15.64
	Total exports	100.00	100.00	100.00	12.81	20.51	15.01

Source: Customs Department, *Foreign Trade Statistics*, various issues.

consisted of food and processed food – mainly rice and maize – produced by either the agricultural or the manufacturing sector. Crude materials made up another 40 per cent, leaving the remaining 10 per cent to manufactured goods. In the 1970s, the share of total primary-product exports (including crude materials) declined, but the share of processed foods (such as sugar, tapioca products, canned fruits and food, and other manufactured products) increased. Manufactured products (such as textiles and textile products, clothing, shoes, precious stones, and other miscellaneous products) increased their share in total exports from less than 10 per cent in the 1960s, to almost 24 per cent in the 1970s, and to over 50 per cent in the mid–1980s. In fact, all manufactured products (including processed food exports) experienced such rapid export growth that, by the middle of 1980s, their contribution to total exports was over 75 per cent (compared to 50 per cent in the 1960s). Among all manufactured exports, those with the most rapid growth during the 1980s were canned foods, textiles and textile products, clothing, shoes, leather products, automobile and automobile parts and components, electronic products, toys, jewellery and plastic products, most of which are considered to be non-traditional exports.

Direct foreign investment, mainly from Japan and the Asian NICs, whose price competitiveness and access to world markets had deteriorated, flowed into Thailand in large amounts in the late 1980s. The contribution of foreign investment to total investment increased from 5 per cent during 1970 to 1986 to about 10 per cent during 1987 to 1990. Of all the foreign investment inflow, about 50 per cent was invested in the manufacturing sector, concentrated in the electronic and the labour-intensive goods industries producing for export. Thailand's relatively low wages, foreign investment promotion, and GSP privileges, added to the already favourable investment climate, made it a major foreign investment recipient.

Growth and structural change of imports

In the 1960s the major imports were consumer goods and capital goods, followed by transport equipment and intermediate and raw material goods. In the 1970s, the contribution to total imports of consumer goods and capital goods declined due to the substitution of domestic non-durable consumer goods production for imports, and the sharp increase in oil prices. During the oil shocks in the 1970s, the share of oil imports in total imports increased significantly. Following marked increases in the utilization of imported inputs by exporting industries (such as textiles and textile products, electronics goods and jewellery), the share of intermediate products in total imports also started to rise in this decade.

In the 1980s, the highest-growth import items were intermediate products and raw materials, capital goods, and vehicles and parts. Durable consumer goods imports increased at about the average rate for all imports, and non-durable goods imports increased at slower rates. In the latter part of the decade fuel imports dropped due to increased local oil and gas production and a decrease in world oil prices.

Imports of both intermediate goods and capital goods experienced accelerated growth after 1985. From the early to the late 1980s the import share in total utilization of intermediate products increased from 27 per cent to 34 per cent, and that of capital goods from 28 per cent to 34 per cent. In the late 1980s intermediate goods imports with accelerated growth rates were mainly raw materials used in the high-growth industries (such as canned food, textile and textile products, paper and paper products, chemicals and chemical products, electronic parts and components, and miscellaneous industries). Most of these industries were export-oriented or industries producing intermediate inputs for the exporting industries. The capital goods imports which grew rapidly in the 1980s were non-electrical and electrical machinery and parts for industrial use. Thus, the growth of imports of both intermediate and capital goods in the second half of the 1980s was largely in response to a rapid increase in production and investment in the exporting industries. The rapid growth of exports and foreign capital inflows under the more open and liberalized trade regime in the 1980s enabled imports of intermediate and capital goods to increase for use as factor inputs in export production.

MACROECONOMIC POLICY ENVIRONMENT

In Thailand, fiscal and monetary policies were cautious from 1960 to 1975. Inflation rates averaged only a few per cent before 1973 (see Table 13.3). From 1975 to 1986 government expenditure grew steadily and the budget deficit increased from 2.5 per cent of GDP in the mid–1970s to a peak of 3.5 per cent in only a decade. While monetary and exchange rate policies sought to keep inflation low and exchange rates realistic, fiscal spending could not easily be brought down in the 1970s and the first half of the 1980s. Moreover, since government deficits were largely financed by borrowing from abroad, they had resulted in both increased current account deficits and a rapid accumulation of foreign debt. In fact, after the rapid rise in world interest rates of the early 1980s, the debt service ratio increased from 18.9 per cent in 1980 to 30.1 per cent in 1986 (see Table 13.3).

Thus in 1986, the government introduced an austerity policy by setting a limit on public foreign borrowing. From 1980 to 1990 defence spending – the government's main expenditure – was also cut considerably. The result was a rapid decline in both government expenditure and interest payments on foreign loans. In the second half of the 1980s, when real GDP grew rapidly and government revenue also rose from the correspondingly large increase in tax collection, the government budget went into surplus and the problems of budget deficits and high public debt disappeared.

The ability of the Thai government to cut spending contributed to stability in the foreign exchange market, and improved the country's credit-

Table 13.3 Basic macroeconomic indicators in Thailand (%)

Period	Annual growth rate			Percentage distribution of GDP on			Proportion in GDP of		Market rate of foreign exchange[a]	Real effective exchange rate	Debt service ratio
	Real GDP	Money supply	Inflation	Capital formation	Imports	Exports	Current account	Government deficit			
1960–70	7.00	8.30	2.00	21.40	19.90	17.80	-0.14	-1.50	20.89	n.a.	n.a.
1970–2	4.42	12.22	2.58	23.24	17.76	11.19	-2.10	-4.26	20.91	83.90	n.a.
1972–4	6.83	14.53	18.12	22.88	20.26	15.19	-0.57	-1.58	20.40	79.93	n.a.
1974–7	7.71	10.61	5.40	23.89	22.16	16.82	-3.42	-2.50	20.37	76.88	n.a.
1977–81	6.48	12.05	11.74	25.25	26.68	18.88	-6.51	-2.97	20.67	88.26	18.75
1981–3	5.49	5.80	4.39	24.04	25.84	18.17	-5.84	-3.43	22.59	94.63	22.18
1983–4	6.88	6.70	0.85	24.27	25.30	16.92	-6.15	-2.97	23.30	92.70	24.81
1984–6	4.13	7.64	2.12	23.27	24.04	19.35	-2.75	-3.45	25.67	105.27	29.24
1986–90	10.59	15.91	4.31	28.80	33.33	26.27	-3.73	2.15	25.70	121.73[b]	19.09

Sources: Bank of Thailand, *Annual Report*, various issues; and the World Bank, *World Debt Tables*, various issues.
[a] Baht per US dollar.
[b] 1986–8.

worthiness. Furthermore, the long government tradition of relying on private (domestic and foreign) loans to finance government spending, rather than borrowing from the Central Bank or printing money, enabled Thailand to avoid high inflation resulting from large budget deficits. Thailand's fiscal policy has therefore been consistent with its monetary policy to satisfy the goals of maintaining both price levels and foreign exchange rate stability. These carefully managed macroeconomic policies created a stable environment favourable for Thailand's industrialization and export competitiveness, and indirectly reinforced the effectiveness of Thailand's trade and industrialization policy, to which we will turn later.

As Table 13.3 shows, Thailand's exchange rate remained stable – at about 20.9 baht to the US dollar – for a long period before 1973. It was revalued nominally in 1974 to about 20.4 baht to the dollar, and stayed at that level through the rest of the 1970s. However, with mounting balance of trade and payments deficits in the late 1970s, the government decided to devalue its currency to 21.8 baht to the US dollar in 1981, and again to about 23 baht per US dollar in 1982. The balance of trade and payments deficits were reduced temporarily as a result. In 1983, however, the deficits returned and foreign reserves further declined. A major (15 per cent) devaluation was therefore carried out in late 1984. The country's exchange rate system was also changed from being pegged to the US dollar to a system that fixed the Thai baht to a basket of currencies, in which the US dollar still held the most weight. Thus, when the US dollar depreciated rapidly against other major currencies in the second half of the 1980s, the Thai baht depreciated dramatically against the currencies of its major trading partners other than the US. From 1985 to 1990 the depreciation rate was approximately 10 per cent a year in real terms.

TRADE AND INDUSTRIALIZATION POLICIES

Industrial development plan

Thailand's trade and industrialization policy has changed over time and the guidelines for indicating the changes in the past three decades can best be found in the National Economic and Social Development Board's (NESDB) National Development Plans. In both the First (1961–6) and the Second (1967–71) Plans, government policy stressed promoting private industrial investment, particularly in industries using domestic raw materials which produced products for import substitution. Towards the end of the Second Plan, Thailand experienced balance of payments deficits and export sector stagnation. Thus industrialization policy emphasis in the Third Plan (1972–6) shifted to the promotion of export-oriented and labour-intensive industries. However, policy to promote import-substitution industries (such as durable consumer and intermediate goods) continued. In the early 1980s the government realized that the persistently high protection of the 1970s had fostered inefficient import-substitution industries and discriminated against export activities, so that Thai exports became less competitive in the world market. Thus, in the Fifth Plan (1982–6) emphasis was placed on restructuring industry and improving efficiency and competitiveness in both the domestic and the world markets. In the mid-1980s, although both the industrial sector and exports outperformed all other sectors, developed country protectionist pressures persisted, and both raw materials and skilled personnel could not expand rapidly enough to keep pace with export growth. Thus, in the Sixth Plan (1987–91), the policy was to persist with the previous Plan's approach to increase the competitiveness of Thai exports by improving production and marketing systems and raising product quality. Further, the Plan included additional policies to increase the efficient development of natural resources, human resources and technological capabilities – the basic inputs of industrial production. The Sixth Plan also continued the policy of previous plans to promote small industries and industries located outside the Bangkok Metropolitan Area in order to improve income distribution.

Use of import restriction instruments

Tariffs and taxation

Tariffs and taxation in Thailand have generally been imposed primarily to generate government revenue or to correct the trade balance deficits; thus, they were not really intended to protect specific industries for industrialization purposes. However, different industrial tariff and tax rates, in effect, provide differential incentives across industries.

From the 1960s to the mid-1970s tariff rates were high for non-durable consumer goods and low for intermediate goods imports. In the late 1970s the rates for non-durable consumer good imports declined, but those for durable consumer goods and transport equipment were increased to correct deficits. However, the average nominal tariff rate of all industries increased and there were rises in the variation of tariff rates across sectors as well. In the early 1980s an attempt was made to lower the nominal tariff rates to a maximum of 60 per cent, and to reduce the dispersion of the rates across industries. This would have reduced distortions of both output and input prices.

However, the attempt had limited success because of conflicts with other objectives, such as government revenue enhancement and reductions in production costs. As a result, the initial tariff rate and schedule changes of the early 1980s were followed by only a few more. By the late 1980s, neither the average nominal tariff rate of manufactured goods, nor the dispersion of the rates across industries, had been reduced (Table 13.4). In

Table 13.4 Effective rates of protection by industry group, Thailand (%)

Industry group	Tariff rate			Nominal rate of protection			Effective rate of protection		
	1981	*1984*	*1987*	*1981*	*1984*	*1987*	*1981*	*1984*	*1987*
Export-oriented	3.57	4.00	4.07	6.60	7.00	8.40	9.40	9.50	11.00
Import-competing	31.30	30.28	40.36	14.20	16.10	19.50	18.00	19.70	26.30
Other industries	11.50	13.35	14.39	10.60	12.10	16.10	18.30	32.50	36.30
Total	19.20	19.30	24.50	10.50	11.70	14.70	15.20	20.60	24.50

Sources: Calculated from the Customs Department, *Foreign Trade Statistics*, various issues; and Wiboonchutikula *et al.* (1989).

fact, the weighted average effective rate of protection in 1987 was increased by more than 50 per cent of the average rate in 1981. Meanwhile, the dispersion of the rates was much greater than it had been in the early 1980s, and tariff structure escalation persisted. At the sectoral level, the effective rates of protection of the import-substitution industries were still higher than the rates of exporting industries. Thus, the bias of the measures against exporting industries still exists.

Although both the legal tariff rates and the effective rates of protection of most industries grew proportionately larger in the mid-1980s than the rates of protection earlier in the decade, the actual tariff rates (measured by collected import duties as a percentage of total imports) of all industries showed little increase in the early 1980s, and even declined in the late 1980s. This is in large part due to the existence of a system of tax and tariff reduction or exemption incentives provided to qualified industries under the various promotional schemes in Thailand (see below).

Both domestic production and imports of manufactured goods in Thailand have also been subject to business taxes. Before late 1973, the business tax schedule for all imports, except passenger cars, was the same as for domestic production and therefore had no protective effect on domestic industry. During the 1960s, the rate on most products ranged from 1.5 to 5.0 per cent. In 1970 the rates were increased across the board to 5 per cent or 10 per cent. In 1973 the schedule was changed: domestic production was subject to lower business taxes, but taxes on imports remained intact. Although this revision generated some protective effect, the effect was lessened by the fact that the business tax was a turnover tax on which domestic production was taxed at every stage of fabrication, whereas imports were taxed only once, as finished products. To reduce the burden from the accumulative effect of business taxes, the value-added tax system has been implemented since early 1992.

Non-tariff barriers

The Thai government has imposed non-tariff barriers on a relatively small number of manufactured products. Currently there are forty-nine products under import quotas (accounting for only 2 per cent of the total number of imported products), and only half of them are subject to import-licensing restrictions to protect domestic production or to save foreign exchange. These protected products are primarily in the transport equipment industry which already had high tariff rates. In fact, both the frequency and duration of these restrictions have been reduced significantly since 1980. Local content requirements are also imposed but only on a limited number of industries such as vehicles and diesel engines.

Export promotion policy[3]

Thailand's export promotion measures involve both investment and trade incentives. Some incentives, such as export credit privileges, and the Board of Investment's (BOI) promotional privileges of income tax holidays, might have elements of export subsidies. However, others such as tax refunds, tax rebates, bonded warehouse facilities, export-processing zones, and the BOI's other privileges such as tax exemptions, mainly serve to reduce distortions against exporting industries, or to neutralize the incentive system across all industries.

Export credit financing

Export credit financing is a measure extensively used for promoting export activities in Thailand. There are two types of export credit financing: (i) long-term credit for financing initial investment in fixed assets; and (ii) short-term credit for financing working capital. The long-term credit for investing in export-oriented projects is provided by the Industrial Finance Corporation of Thailand (IFCT). The scheme started in 1985 and provides long-term loans at an interest rate of about 3.6 percentage points below the market rate. However, the scheme has only a limited amount available for lending. All other export investment projects are financed at market rates just like loans for other purposes.

Short-term credit has been made available through the Bank of Thailand's (BOT) packing-credit facility since the late 1950s. It essentially is trade credit for promoting exports at both the preshipment and postshipment stages. The BOT provides rediscounting of promissory notes from commercial banks at a rate of 5 per cent, and the banks, in turn, charge exporters at a rate not exceeding 7 per cent. This special credit facility provides an interest subsidy equivalent to about 2.5–6 percentage points (varying with changes in commercial short-term loan rates) and the loan matures within 180 days.

Rediscounting facilities are traditionally available in two forms: (i) rediscounting of industrial promissory notes; and (ii) rediscounting of export promissory notes. There was little credit available in the first form in the 1960s (about 8 per cent of the total amount of rediscounting). It increased to reach 21 per cent in the 1970s, but has steadily declined since the early 1980s. On the other hand, the amount of rediscounting for export activities has grown rapidly with the value of exports, increasing over tenfold from 10.2 billion baht in 1975 to 128.6 billion baht (accounting for about 40 per cent of Thailand's total export value) in 1988.

Initially, in the late 1950s, the rediscount facility for exports was available to finance milled rice exports only. Since the early 1960s the facility has been extended to cover exports for a variety of products. For the entire period of the 1960s, loans for agricultural exports accounted for about 80 per cent of all export financing credit, then declined steadily to 34 per cent in the 1970s, and 27 per cent in the 1980s. On the other hand, the share of manufactured goods in total credit for exports has increased steadily over time.

Product items under this export rediscounting facility (packing credit) were traditional commodity exports, namely, rice, maize, rubber, sugar, and tapioca products, accounting together for about 38 per cent of all BOT subsidized credit in 1979. This declined to only 20 per cent in the late 1980s. On the other hand, packing credit for manufactured products such as textiles and clothing, canned fruits and food, steel products, electrical goods, jewellery and leather products, which accounted for 22 per cent of total packing credit in 1979, increased its share to 37 per cent in the late 1980s.

The BOT's rediscounted export credits as a proportion of total exports in the agricultural sector increased from 2.2 per cent in 1979 to a peak of 4.6 per cent in 1983, and steadily declined to 1.65 per cent in 1989. For the manufacturing sector the proportion increased from 4 per cent in 1979 to 5–6 per cent in the mid-1980s, and finally declined throughout the second half of the 1980s to only 1 per cent in 1989. The decline was to avoid possible unfair subsidy charges and countervailing or anti-dumping duties imposed in some developed country markets.

Despite a decline in the amount of BOT's export credit across all industries in the late 1980s, credit was given to an increasing variety of manufactured exports. In fact, the number of industries obtaining the BOT's export credits increased from fifteen industries in 1979 to nineteen and twenty-seven industries in 1985 and 1989 respectively. The new industries with increased export credits in the late 1980s were new exports whose share in total exports was still small but whose actual and potential growth rates were relatively high. These included synthetic fibres, leather products, rubber products, footwear, plastic products and miscellaneous products.[4]

Investment promotion

Tax and promotional incentives for encouraging industrial investment and trade have been provided by the BOI since the late 1950s. The BOI set priorities for firms to obtain promotional privileges according to changing government trade and industrialization policy. In the 1960s priority firms were those using the most domestic raw material inputs in production. Since the early 1970s new objectives have been set – to promote firms producing exports and those located outside the Bangkok Metropolitan Area. The major BOI incentives provided to export-oriented firms were exemption or reduction of import duties and business taxes on intermediate inputs and machinery and equipment, and exemptions from corporate income taxes for up to eight years. Additional incentives were granted to promote firms located in specified investment-promotion zones and industrial estates. Also, the corporate income tax holiday could be extended for another five years after the initial allowance, while business taxes on product sales could be reduced up to 90 per cent over five years.

Most firms under BOI promotion were in the manufacturing sector. In the decades before the 1980s, the industries with the highest number of promoted firms were food processing, textiles and textile products, iron and steel, non-electrical machinery, and transport equipment. Since 1980 the number of BOI-promoted firms has increased more rapidly than previously. The rate of increase averaged 25 per cent a year throughout the 1980s, but the rate of growth was particularly rapid after the mid-1980s, and the majority of the firms were export-oriented industries. In fact over 60 per cent of all promoted projects in the second half of the 1980s were export-oriented and were in industries such as canned fruits and food, garments, footwear, rubber products, electronic products, plastic products, artificial flowers, toys and jewellery. The rest of the BOI-promoted industries concerned vehicles and auto parts, non-electrical machinery, and electrical equipment and appliances.[5]

For all BOI-promoted activities the proportion of import duty exemption to total exports increased from 4 per cent in 1986 to 10 per cent in 1990 (Wiboonchutikula et al., 1991). The industry group with the highest tax exemption proportion was machinery and equipment, followed by chemicals and chemical products. However, the machinery and equipment industry group includes a variety of products ranging from electronic products for export, to non-electrical machinery catering to the domestic market. Firms in the non-electrical machinery and equipment industries, and the chemicals and chemical products industries, obtained BOI promotional privileges for being in targeted import-substitution industries or industries located outside the Bangkok Metropolitan Area. If we assume that only a half of the total BOI tax exemption privileges were for export-oriented activities, then the proportion of import duty exemption in exports might be said to have increased from 2 per cent of total exports in 1986 to 5 per cent in 1989. The industries with the highest proportion of tax exemption in total exports were electronic products (17 per cent), followed by other manufactured products such as food processing, footwear, rubber products, toys and jewellery.

Tax refunds

Other incentives to exporters, besides the tax and tariff privileges given by the BOI, were tax refunds (or tax drawbacks) and tax rebates offered by the Ministry of Finance on imported intermediate inputs used in export production. Exporting firms, whether or not they were getting promotional privileges from the BOI, were eligible for such tax refunds and/or tax rebates from the Customs Department.

The tax refund scheme started in 1973, but the number of exporters applying for the refunds increased most rapidly in the 1980s. From 1983 to 1986 the applicants for tax refunds and the amount of tax exemption under the scheme grew annually at the rates of 24 per cent and 30 per cent respectively. The tax refunds as a proportion of total exports increased from 0.84 per cent in 1983 to 1.60 per cent in 1989.

The industries with the highest tax refund rates (tax refunds as a proportion of exports eligible for the refunds) were synthetic fibres, textile fabric, textile products, wearing apparel, plastic products, artificial flowers, steel products and auto parts. Some rapidly growing export-oriented industries, such as electronic products, had low apparent tax refund rates although the import duties on their intermediate inputs were quite high because they had obtained import duty exemption benefits from other incentive schemes, mostly from the BOI.

Tax rebates

Tax rebates were given to exporters for other taxes in the export-producing process as well. The taxes in the rebate system included import duties, business taxes and excise taxes on the cost of intermediate inputs and machinery and equipment. Exporters could apply for import-duty refunds or tax rebates or a combination of both.

The tax rebate scheme started providing incentives for exporters in 1981. The amount of the rebates increased from 24 million baht in the first year to 6,000 million baht in 1989. The rebates increased most rapidly in the second half of the 1980s when exports also grew at a particularly high rate. In fact, from 1986 to 1989 the number of firms applying for the tax rebates increased at a rate of 25 per cent a year, and the value of the rebates grew at 33 per cent. Exports eligible for the rebates increased across all exporting industries from 14 per cent of total exports in 1986 to 27 per cent in 1989. The tax rebate rate (tax rebates as a proportion of exports eligible for the rebates) was stable at about 4 per cent. However, the value of the rebates as a proportion of total exports increased from 0.36 per cent in 1983 to 1.17 per cent in 1989.

During 1986 to 1990 the industries that obtained the largest value of tax rebates were food processing, textiles and textile products, wearing apparel, wood products and furniture, steel products and electronic products. The industries with the highest rebate rates were electronic products, textiles and wearing apparel, metal products and chemical products; these were industries with high import duties and business taxes on intermediate inputs used in their production.

Other incentives

Export incentives were also provided in the form of bonded warehouse and export-processing zones (EPZ). Taxes on both inputs and outputs of bonded or EPZ factories were exempted as long as the goods were manufactured for export. Firms in EPZs also obtained additional benefits such as physical infrastructural support, and freedom (for foreign investors) to own land, bring in foreign experts, and remit foreign exchange abroad.

The bonded warehouse facilities were first made available in 1977 and expansion was most rapid after 1984. From 1977 to 1984 there were only thirty bonded factories, but the number increased to 116 by 1989. The value of taxes and import duties exempted in the warehouses increased from 12 per cent of exports eligible for the bonded warehouse facilities (or 1.27 per cent of total exports) in 1985 to 17 per cent (or 1.60 per cent of total exports) in 1989.

The industries taking advantage of incentives from the bonded warehouse facilities included footwear, leather and leather products, miscellaneous products, electronic products, wearing apparel, and wood products and furniture. By comparing the industries which benefited from the bonded warehouse facilities between the two subperiods of 1975–86 and 1986–9, one can see that the industries with increased incentives in the second subperiod were footwear, leather and leather products, electronic products, and miscellaneous products such as toys and jewellery.

As for incentives from export-processing zones, of which there are now six in operation, the value of tax and import duties exempted in the EPZs grew at a rate of almost 50 per cent a year from 1986 to 1989. The value of tax exemption relative to the total value of exports increased from 0.14 per cent in 1986 to 2.3 per cent in 1989. Firms located in the export-processing zones were in industries producing electronic products, wearing apparel, footwear, leather and leather products, and miscellaneous products. Almost all of the firms in the EPZs produced labour-intensive goods and they also obtained promotional privileges from the BOI.

Apart from tax incentives of various forms, the government gives export producers a 20 per cent cost reduction on electricity. Exporters also benefit from the Ministry of Commerce's trade-promotion activities. The Department of Export Promotion of the Ministry provides training in export techniques and organizes trade fairs and trade missions.

Summary

Thailand's macroeconomic conditions have been quite carefully managed, maintaining low rates of price inflation and realistic exchange rates. The control of government budget deficits has also contributed to the country's creditworthiness. Undoubtedly these well-disciplined macroeconomic policies created an environment favourable for trade, investment, and for the country's industrial growth.

Within the relatively stable macroeconomic environment, trade and industrialization policy underwent significant changes. During the initial phase of industrial development in the 1960s, trade policy was to promote import-substitution industries. From the early 1970s, the policy shifted towards promotion of export-oriented industries. However, measures to protect import-substitution industries – whereby tariffs were imposed on imported products and promotional privileges were given to encourage investment in targeted industries – still existed. In fact, the legal tariff rates and effective rates of protection of most industries rose proportionately more in the mid–1980s than they had fallen in the early 1980s. Moreover, the dispersion of these rates in the 1980s was wider than in the 1970s, when the effective rates of protection for import-substitution industries were greater than those for exporting industries.

Nevertheless, the industrial tariff rates actually collected showed little increase in the early 1980s, and even declined in the late 1980s. A primary reason was the system of incentives in the form of tax and tariff reductions provided to exporting industries and other industries under BOI promotion. In Thailand, incentives to promote exports were in the form of both fiscal and financial credit measures. The fiscal measures comprised promotional privileges from the BOI, tax refunds, tax rebates, bonded warehouse facilities, and export-processing zones. Financial assistance measures were mainly export credit rediscounting facilities offered by the BOT. All these incentive measures, however, were made available to mitigate the product and factor price distortions resulting from biases in the tax and tariff structures, and helped exporting industries to reduce their production costs to levels that were internationally competitive.

Export promotion incentives can be categorized into three groups according to the source of factor cost reduction. The first group comprises tax and tariff refunds and rebates on imported intermediate inputs used for producing exportables. The second group comprises tax and tariff refunds and rebates on imported machinery and equipment used as factor inputs for export production. The third group comprises credit given at below-market interest rates for exporting firms to finance their working capital. The greatest value of incentives, however, came from the intermediate input tax and tariff reduction (about one-half of the overall amount of given incentives). The value of the second group of incentives was much less than that of the first group in the early 1980s, but increased steadily over the decade. The third group comprised by the end of the 1980s the smallest proportion of total incentives due to a significant decline in the value of credit given from 1986 to 1989 (from 35 per cent in 1986 to only 12 per cent in 1989) (see Table 13.5).

Table 13.5 shows that of all export promotional measures in the late 1980s the BOI gave the most incentives, followed by the Ministry of Finance which provided tax and tariff refunds, tax and tariff rebates, and bonded warehouse facilities. The value of incentives given in the export-processing zones was still minor.

We can conclude from the above findings that, although industrial protection measures still existed in Thailand in the 1980s, incentives given to promote exports increased. By combining a neutralized incentive system with favourable world economic conditions – declining interest rates, an oil price reduction, and the growth of developed countries' economies – Thai exporting industries were able to expand at rapid rates.

Under the existing system, exporters do not all benefit equally from the incentive measures. Policy implementation costs and efficiency problems have arisen from the use of time and resources to implement the measures. The incentives, moreover, are not distributed to all exporting firms. Small and medium-sized firms and indirect exporters (including firms not being promoted by the BOI) are not able to share in benefits from existing export promotion measures. Finally, some measures included in the existing system expose Thailand to the risk of being accused of subsidizing exports. Thai exporters could possibly suffer, therefore, from countervailing duties imposed by Thailand's trading partners. To be sure, the existing trade and industrialization policy in Thailand is not of the first-best type. Nevertheless, the social costs of protection under the present incentives system are lower than the costs of the import-substitution regime in the 1960s which did not include export promotion incentives to offset policy biases against exports.

Table 13.5 Incentives from various export promotion schemes, Thailand

Incentive measures	1986		1987		1988		1989		1990	
	Million baht	%	Million baht	%	Million baht	%	Million baht	%	Million baht	%
Tax rebates	1,387	8.95	2,894	12.96	6,418	15.54	6,048	12.22	3,616	n.a.
Tax refunds	2,259	14.57	3,120	13.55	4,879	11.81	8,109	16.38	4,706	n.a.
Bonded warehouse	2,023	13.05	3,209	13.93	5,247	12.70	5,639	11.39	4,975	n.a.
Export-processing zones	186	1.20	390	1.69	510	1.23	806	1.63	1,236	n.a.
BOI promotion	4,207	27.14	8,058	34.99	16,981	41.10	22,876	46.22	20,804	n.a.
Export credit	5,438	35.08	5,268	22.88	7,278	17.62	6,019	12.16	n.a.	n.a.
Total incentives	15,500	100.00	23,029	100.00	41,313	100.00	49,497	100,00	n.a.	n.a.
Export value	233,383		299,853		403,570		516,315		n.a.	
Incentives/export value	6.64		7.68		10.24		9.59		n.a.	

Sources: Customs Department, Board of Investment, and Bank of Thailand.

Table 13.6 Demand decomposition of manufacturing output growth, Thailand, 1960–80

Period	Domestic demand expansion[a]	Export expansion	Import substitution	Total
1960–6	88.90	24.70	–13.60	100.00
1966–72	64.11	6.46	29.43	100.00
1972–5	91.00	8.50	0.50	100.00
1975–80	76.47	25.79	–2.26	100.00

Sources: Akrasanee (1975a) for the 1960–6 and 1966–72 estimates; Akrasanee (1980) for the 1972–5 estimates; Akrasanee *et al.* (1983) for the 1975–80 estimates.
[a] Domestic demand expansion includes both intermediate and final demand.

GROWTH WITH SLOW PRODUCTIVITY CHANGES

It has been shown in previous sections that Thailand's manufacturing industries have grown rapidly over the past three decades, while trade and industrialization policy also changed from import substitution to export promotion. This rapid growth can be decomposed into the sources of output growth on either the demand or the supply side. The analysis of the sources of growth on the demand side measures the relative contributions of different components of market demand. The analysis on the supply side measures the contributions to real output growth of the various factor inputs and the growth of total factor productivity. The contributions of these growth components vary in response to changes in policy environments.

The decomposition of Thailand's manufacturing output growth from the demand side was carried out by Akrasanee (1975a, 1980) and Akrasanee *et al.* (1983) for varying subperiods during 1960 to 1980, using Chenery's method which classifies real output growth rates according to the domestic demand expansion effect, the export demand growth effect, and the import-substitution effect.[6]

The sources of growth of Thailand's manufacturing output from 1960 to 1972 were mainly from domestic market demand expansion and the substitution of domestic production for imports (see Table 13.6). Domestic demand dominated all other sources of growth in the early stage of industrialization in the first half of the 1960s. During this period industries consisted mostly of small-scale firms producing basic consumer goods for the rural population. However, from 1966 to 1972, when domestic market demand growth slowed down and the industries were protected under high import barriers, the import-substitution effect became more prominent. In fact, the contribution of domestic demand expansion declined from 89 per cent of real output growth for 1960–6 to 64 per cent for 1966–72. Meanwhile, the import-substitution effect increased from –13.6 per cent in the former to 29.4 per cent in the latter period.

After export promotion policy was introduced in the early 1970s, the import-substitution effect declined to 0.5 per cent and the contribution of export expansion to output growth increased from an average of 6.5 per cent for 1960–72 to 8.5 per cent for 1972–5. From 1975 to 1980 the shift of the source of real output growth from import substitution to export expansion continued, although the domestic demand effect still contributed about three-quarters of the real output growth. The import-substitution effect further declined from a low positive value in the first half of the 1970s to –2.3 per cent in the second half of the 1970s. At the same time, the contribution of export expansion to real output growth increased to 25.8 per cent. The decline of the import-substitution effect in the 1970s reflected the rising value of imports relative to domestic supply in response to the less stringent import restrictions in the 1970s than in the 1960s. Meanwhile, the contribution of export expansion to real output increased in the 1970s when export promotion measures were more widely implemented. Given that export promotion policies and efforts persisted and were even intensified, and that Thailand's manufacturing sector became more export-oriented, one may presume that export market expansion continued to increase its contribution to output growth in the 1980s.

On the supply side, the growth of real output can be decomposed into contributions from increases in inputs and total factor productivity growth. Table 13.7 presents estimates of the sources of real output growth on the supply side for three-digit ISIC manufacturing industries from 1963 to 1986.[7]

The methods of measuring these real variables are presented in the appendix. The major source of data was the industrial census conducted by the National statistical Office of Thailand (NSOT),[8] supplemented with data from the Ministry of Industry (MOI), the Ministry of Commerce (MOC), the Bank of Thailand (BOT), the National Economic and Social Development Board (NESDB), and the Federation of Thai Industries.

Real output of all industries grew at the rate of 13.8 per cent per year. When separated into two main sources of growth, namely the accumulation of real inputs and TFP growth, Table 13.7 shows that the latter source was still minor despite the high real output growth. In fact, TFP growth contributed only 0.94 percentage points. In other words, a substantial part of real output growth (92.87 per cent) was due to an increase in total real inputs whereas only about 7 per cent was due to TFP growth. Furthermore, the contribution of TFP growth was less than that of total primary inputs, namely labour and capital, combined, to the growth of real output.[9]

The estimate of TFP growth is low compared to the estimates for many developed countries such as the US and Japan. In the US the estimated rate of TFP growth of the aggregate manufacturing sector was about 1.82

Table 13.7 Annual rates of growth of TFP and factor inputs and their contribution to output growth, Thailand, 1963–86

ISIC code	Industry	Trade category	Annual growth rate of				Annual contribution to output of				
			TFP	Intermediate input	Labour input	Capital input	TFP	Labour input	Capital input	Primary input	Total inputs
311	Food processing	EO	1.18	9.23	6.37	6.53	12.17	3.23	16.34	19.57	87.83
312	Other food processing	NIC	2.18	16.93	8.57	10.24	12.46	2.05	10.47	12.52	87.54
313	Beverages	NIC	−0.26	11.72	9.32	13.01	−2.09	6.84	61.68	68.52	102.21
314	Tobacco	NIC	0.77	2.96	0.06	5.22	16.59	−0.65	28.66	28.01	34.91
321	Textiles and textile products	EO	0.56	10.10	5.58	14.03	4.74	5.55	33.72	39.27	95.35
322	Wearing apparel	EO	−0.42	13.08	3.74	14.57	−3.93	5.06	23.47	28.53	103.93
323	Leather and leather products	EO	0.44	8.98	4.62	8.74	4.97	3.54	27.96	31.50	95.14
324	Footwear	EO	0.37	9.29	5.66	10.13	3.97	9.89	30.54	40.43	96.02
331	Wood and wood products	EO	−0.68	4.41	2.05	5.35	−18.83	6.46	40.97	47.43	118.61
332	Furnitures and fixtures	IC	−2.12	7.67	8.27	15.85	−26.95	16.41	50.13	66.54	126.95
341	Paper and paper products	IC	1.55	13.57	9.06	9.22	11.09	5.69	15.69	21.38	88.83
342	Printing and publishing	NIC	2.07	9.85	5.65	8.95	18.73	7.91	24.00	31.91	81.27
351	Basic chemicals	IC	−1.11	14.16	6.80	13.68	−8.86	3.95	25.54	29.49	108.86

352	Chemical products	IC	1.37	8.75	1.41	8.42	14.48	1.16	24.52	25.68	85.62
355	Rubber and rubber products	EO	1.12	18.07	12.80	20.77	5.74	4.16	32.61	36.77	94.26
361	Non-metallic mineral products	EO	0.75	21.00	12.16	18.41	3.83	11.86	17.89	29.75	96.22
362	Glass and glass products	IC	-1.06	14.45	11.68	16.48	-8.09	13.54	39.73	53.27	108.02
369	Other non-metallic mineral	EO	-0.61	10.05	3.42	11.18	-6.76	3.38	35.66	39.04	106.76
371	Iron and steel	IC	0.36	10.96	5.89	10.18	3.37	5.15	20.04	25.19	96.63
372	Non-ferrous metal products	EO	1.16	22.72	14.82	13.15	5.52	3.91	15.84	19.75	94.48
381	Metal products	IC	0.49	6.99	4.15	8.76	6.39	4.07	23.88	27.95	93.71
382	Non-electrical machinery	IC	-0.72	13.72	9.90	14.49	-5.69	7.32	29.54	36.86	105.61
383	Electrical machinery	EO	2.64	17.11	11.36	14.97	14.11	5.66	18.81	24.47	85.89
384	Transport equipment	IC	-0.73	14.37	10.07	14.45	-5.55	5.47	29.01	34.48	105.55
390	Miscellaneous	EO	0.64	10.96	5.34	11.74	-3.75	6.02	29.49	35.51	103.65
	Total		0.94	12.99	8.04	11.78	7.13	4.70	26.48	31.18	92.87

Source: National Statistical Office of Thailand, Report of the Industrial Census; Whole Kingdom, various issues.

per cent (Kendrick and Grossman, 1980) for the 1960–80 period. In Japan it was 2.04 per cent on average (Nishimizu and Hulten, 1978) for all the disaggregated industries; TFP growth accounted for about 17 per cent of real output growth. The TFP growth comparison with other LDCs is more difficult because not many studies have been done. Although there are some economy-wide estimates, those for the manufacturing sector are very scarce. Moreover, those that are available are usually estimated by different methodologies, for varying periods of time, and for different scopes of the manufacturing sector. Above all, they are mostly at a highly aggregated level of industrial classification.

For example, Chen (1977) estimated the TFP growth rates of the aggregated manufacturing sector of the four-fast growing countries in Asia – Hong Kong, South Korea, Taiwan and Singapore – to be 2.29, 3.47, 3.59 and 3.75 per cent respectively, during the 1960s. All of these, however, accounted for only 12–18 per cent of the rate of growth of real output of the sector, which is also low compared to the developed countries' standard. At a more disaggregated level, Krueger and Tuncer's (1980) estimate of the average TFP growth in the Turkish manufacturing industries was about 2.10 per cent during 1963–76, accounting for about 17 per cent of real output growth. Tsao's (1985) estimate of TFP growth in the Singaporean industries during 1970–9 was about 0.69 per cent, accounting for about 4 per cent of real output growth. Finally, Nishimizu and Robinson's (1984) most recent estimation of TFP growth of the manufacturing industries of South Korea and Yugoslavia was 3.71 per cent and 0.48 per cent, accounting for about 21 per cent and 5 per cent of real output growth respectively.

At the three-digit ISIC level, Table 13.7 shows that TFP growth rates ranged from 2.64 per cent for the electrical machinery industry to –2.12 per cent for furniture and fixtures. The industries with above-average rates of TFP and a high contribution of TFP growth to rates of output growth during 1963–86 were a mixture of exporting, import-competing and non-import-competing industries. The exporting industries were food processing and electrical machinery products. The import-competing industries were paper and paper products and chemical products, and the non-import-competing industry was printing and publishing. On average, exporting industries' rate of TFP growth was higher than that of import-competing industries.

Although the rate of TFP growth of Thailand's manufacturing was low compared to those of the developed countries and the few available estimates of LDCs, it increased, albeit very slowly, over the 1963–86 period. During 1963–70, it was about 0.66 per cent, accounting for 3.4 per cent of the 19.34 real output growth rate. During the 1970s, it increased to 1.22 per cent or about 10 per cent of the 12.05 rate of growth of real output. Finally, from 1979 to 1986 the average TFP growth rate declined to 0.55 per cent. However, it accounted for about 10 per cent of the real output

Table 13.8 TFP growth and increases in energy prices, Thailand

Period	Growth rate of manufacturing output	TFP growth rate	TFP contribution to output growth	Rate of change of oil prices
1963–72	18.52	0.31	1.67	n.a.
1972–4	8.34	−0.78	−9.34	44.33
1974–9	12.63	2.40	19.00	10.61
1979–82	3.35	−1.42	−42.39	20.80
1982–6	7.31	2.25	30.78	−3.21

Sources: Same as Table 13.7, and National Energy Policy Board.

growth rate, which was about the same contribution to manufacturing output growth as in the 1970s period. Thus, although the increase in real inputs as a source of real growth declined over time relative to TFP growth, the increase of the total factor productivity contribution was still very small.

In fact, the TFP growth contribution to real output growth was almost stagnant during the slow output growth period in the first half of the 1980s. Not only did TFP growth slow down during the period of recession in the early 1980s, but the TFP growth of almost all industries (except for a few non-import-competing industries) was also retarded by the increases in energy prices and other raw material prices in both the early and the late 1970s. During the period 1972–4, despite controls on the prices of petroleum products for industrial use, their prices increased more than twofold, or about 44 per cent a year (see Table 13.8). The average prices of other major intermediate products of the industrial sector such as textile materials, pulp and paper, chemical materials, and basic metals (especially the imported ones) increased at a rate of over ¼ per cent per year. These price increases slowed down the TFP growth of some industries quickly, while others responded with a time lag. However, the increase in energy prices alone is unlikely to have had that much impact on the slowdown of TFP growth because the cost of energy made up only a small percentage of the value of production of all industries before 1973 and jumped to a maximum of no more than 5–6 per cent later.[10]

What affected the industries more were, first, accompanying increases in the price of other raw materials whose share in total production was over one-half, especially among the heavier import-substituting industries,[11] and second, a decrease in demand for all products in the first half of the 1970s and the early 1980s. Both shocks made it difficult for industries to expand, as can be seen from the decrease in the growth of industrial output to the average annual rate of 8.34 per cent during 1972–4, and 3.35 per cent during 1979–82. Meanwhile, capital and labour inputs were unable to adjust quickly enough in the short run. For example, during the mid-1970s, some capital stock which was accumulated at a fast rate in the late 1960s and early 1970s was underutilized.[12] On the other hand, due to the rise of labour union pressures in this period, some industries, such as textiles and clothing, had difficulties in lowering employment in response to the decline in production. In fact, the labour input grew at 11.51 per cent and the capital input 13.73 per cent during the 1972–4 period. All this made real output decline faster than real inputs, and the result was a substantial decline in TFP growth in many industries. However, from 1974 to 1979, when aggregate demand increased and inputs had adjusted better to the shocks, TFP growth rose again. During this period, output grew at 12.63 per cent a year, both labour and capital inputs slowed their growth to 2.68 per cent and 10.74 per cent respectively, and TFP growth accelerated to 2.40 per cent a year.

In the late 1970s, when there was another steep increase in energy prices combined with slower growth of demand, TFP growth declined again for the same reason as in the early 1970s. During 1979–82, energy prices increased at more than 20 per cent a year. Output decelerated to 3.4 per cent a year, but total real inputs grew at a higher rate of 4.77 per cent. As a result the TFP growth rate fell to 1.42 per cent. As the Thai economy recovered slowly from the unfavourable world economic conditions, manufacturing output expanded at 7.31 per cent a year and TFP growth increased again to 2.25 per cent from 1982 to 1986.

Comparison of TFP growth of import-substituting and exporting industries

Import-substitution industries in Thailand were protected from foreign competition by the government imposing high tariffs on imports competing with them and, at the same time, imposing low tariffs on raw materials and capital inputs used in their production.[13] The protection was to allow newly established industries to survive during an initial period of production when their costs were higher than the products' imported prices. Advocates of the import-substitution policy believed that over the passage of time, as learning-by-doing and externalities could be realized and indivisibilities overcome, total average costs would decline and the new industries would be viable without any more protection.

In Thailand during the period 1963–84, according to Table 13.9, however, the average annual rate of TFP growth of import-competing industries was negative. The average for all industries was about 0.94 per cent a year, which accounted for about 7 per cent of the growth of real output. For exporting industries, the average TFP growth was about 1.30 per cent, accounting for about 9 per cent of real output growth.

The TFP growth of the import-competing industries steadily declined relative to other industries which experienced an increase in TFP growth over time in the three subperiods of the 1960s, the 1970s, and the first half

Table 13.9 Growth rates of TFP relative to real output of industries by trade category, Thailand, 1963–86 (%)

Period	Import-competing industries			Exporting industries		
	Growth rate of		Ratio of TFP growth to output growth	Growth rate of		Ratio of TFP growth to output growth
	Output	TFP		Output	TFP	
1963–86	11.84	0.04	0.34	13.84	1.30	9.39
1963–70	19.44	0.37	1.90	18.90	0.71	3.76
1970–9	12.96	0.12	0.93	12.33	0.94	7.62
1979–86	3.71	–0.22	–0.54	6.99	0.99	14.16

Source: Same as Table 13.7.

of the 1980s. The percentage contribution of TFP growth to the growth in import-competing industries was lower in the latter subperiods than the first one. This was true, despite the fact that some import-substituting industries such as non-electrical machinery and transport equipment industries continued from the first subperiod to have high effective rates of protection. It seems that protection was not only an ineffective means of promoting TFP growth but also provided a shelter for those industries even when their TFP growth did not increase over time.

The TFP growth rate for exporting industries was higher in the 1970s and the first half of the 1980s than in the 1960s. It increased from 0.65 per cent, which accounted for about 4 per cent of real output growth in the first period of the 1960s, to 0.94 per cent and 0.99 per cent which accounted, respectively, for 8 per cent and 14 per cent of real output growth in the 1970s and the first half of the 1980s. The growth of TFP assisted these industries to compete in the world market. At the same time, increased exports allowed domestic production to grow fast enough to permit the use of better quality raw materials, to more efficiently utilize capital stock, and to employ better skilled workers, all of which, together with the extension of production to the most efficient scale, fostered increases in TFP growth.

CONCLUSION

The pace of growth and the structural change of Thailand's manufacturing sector since 1960 is well above the average for LDCs. Domestic demand and import substitution contributed to high growth in the early decades. The growth was sustained and even accelerated in the late 1980s by increasing reliance on export demand expansion under the export promotion policy, started in the early 1970s. However, at least from 1963 to 1986 the TFP growth contribution to manufacturing sector growth was still minor compared to the record of developed countries and newly industrialized countries. As in other countries, TFP growth of most industries declined during the first half of the 1970s and the 1979–84 period at which times there were increases in energy and raw material prices and mild recessions.

The TFP growth contribution to real output growth increased between 1963–70 and 1979–86. The period of increase in TFP growth coincided with that of changes in industrialization and trade policies from import substitution to export promotion. Thailand's implementation of its import-substitution policies did not reward productivity performance or set a time limit beyond which protection was to be phased out. As a result, the import-substitution industries tended to invest resources to perpetuate the inefficiencies associated with protection instead of seeking productivity-increasing activities to reduce costs over time. On the other hand, export promotion policies tended to encourage industries in which the country had a comparative advantage, and hence probably greater potential for TFP growth.

APPENDIX

This appendix discusses briefly methods of estimating real inputs, real output, and factor shares and the construction of the database. All real inputs and output are in constant 1968 prices. The detailed methods are available from the authors upon request.

Real intermediate inputs The value of intermediate inputs reported in the NSOT's industrial census for individual industries were in an aggregated form without being broken into different types of purchased inputs. We therefore deflated the aggregated purchased input value of each industry by appropriate deflators to obtain real intermediate inputs and then find the growth rates. The deflator of intermediate inputs used in each industry was found by weighted-averaging the deflators of purchased inputs used in the industry where weights were their corresponding value shares in total intermediate inputs. The source of data for the deflators was the Ministry of Commerce's wholesale price indexes of industries. The value shares were computed from Thailand's input–output tables for 1975 and 1982.

Real capital stock The capital stock was classified into two types: first, buildings and structures; second, machinery, equipment and vehicles. For each type at any period, the real capital stock was obtained by adding current gross investment at constant prices to the real capital stock of the previous period, excluding real depreciations in the period.

The estimation of real capital stock needs an estimate of initial real capital stock flows of real investment, and rates of depreciation of different assets. The initial real capital stock by type of asset and by manufacturing industry was estimated using the fixed capital formulation figures in 1949, the earliest year for which data are available. The gross nominal investment at a period was defined to be the change in net book values of fixed assets from the previous period plus the depreciations in that period. The data were from the NSOT's revised industrial census. The methods of measuring investment deflators and economic life of capital are as follows.

Investment deflators The deflators for buildings and structures were from wholesale price indexes of construction materials; those for machinery, equipment and vehicles were from the weighted average of the indexes of machinery and equipment, and transport equipment, whose weights were their value share of total investment in them. The price indexes of all assets were from the Ministry of Commerce.

Economic lives of assets Buildings and structures are more durable than machinery and equipment. We estimated an average structure's life to be about thirty-three years and machinery and equipment life to be about fifteen years. Structure life was assumed to be invariant across industries, whereas machinery and equipment lives were made specific to each industry, based on estimates for US industries (Park, 1973). Because the average life of US machinery and equipment is longer than Thailand's, Park's estimate were scaled down so that the weighted average for the whole manufacturing sector is fifteen years.

Labour input The labour input of an industry is the number of workers employed in that industry during the year. This is because data on man-hours classified by different qualities of labourers, such as age, sex and education, are not available in the NSOT's industrial census.

Real output Real output was obtained by deflating the value of production by output deflators. Production data are based on the NSOT's industrial census. However, there are discrepancies between the growth rates of real output of the three-digit ISIC industries reported by NSOT and those implied by the aggregation of the Ministry of Industry and the Federation of Thai Industry data on commodity output. We therefore adjusted the NSOT production data to be consistent with the growth rates computed from the output data from elsewhere. Data on inputs were also adjusted to correspond with the revised NSOT production data. For output deflators, the data source was the Ministry of Commerce's wholesale price indexes of industries.

Factor shares The share of intermediate inputs was computed by dividing the value of intermediate inputs by the value of total production. The value of intermediate inputs included the cost of raw materials and fuel energy used. To calculate the labour share, expenditures on labour were divided by the value of total production. The labour expenditure consisted of wages and salaries, bonuses, piecework payment, overtime payment, and all other fringe benefits. The share of capital was simply the residual. All the data on value of production and expenditures on intermediate inputs and labour were from the NSOT's industrial census.

NOTES

1 A detailed analysis of the demand decomposition of real production growth is provided on pp. 440–7.
2 Detailed discussion of trade policy in the 1980s is found on pp. 429-39, and the impact of foreign investment on manufacturing growth will be examined in the next topic on growth and structural changes of exports.
3 This section is summarized from Akrasanee et al. (1990) and Wiboonchutikula et al. (1991: ch. 2). See these reports for detailed figures and a full discussion.
4 Since past records show that the major beneficiaries of packing credit were the large exporters of agricultural products, the BOT changed its rules and procedures for granting export credit in September 1988 in order to distribute credit to small exporters of all products. Under these new procedures, the BOT continues charging commercial banks the original discount rate of 5 per cent a year for credit given to exporters in general, but charges the banks only 3–4 per cent of the interest rate provided to small exporters whose working capital does not exceed 10 million baht. However, indirect exporters still do not have access to this credit. An export credit guarantee and insurance scheme has been proposed and is under consideration, but has not yet been implemented.
5 Furthermore, realizing the important function of international trading companies in expanding external demand and marketing export products, the BOI also promoted fifteen such trading companies by giving them tax privileges.
6 The method follows the original work of Chenery (1960) and Chenery et al. (1962).
7 Detailed methods of measuring TFP growth and various real inputs are available from the author upon request. A brief description of measurement methods is presented in the appendix.
8 Report on Industrial Census: Whole Kingdom, various issues.
9 This is also found in Turkey and Yugoslavia during the same period in Nishimizu and Robinson (1984).
10 The figures are computed from the National Statistical Office of Thailand, Report of Industrial Census: Whole Kingdom, various issues.
11 In fact, the industries whose TFP growth was most adversely affected during 1972–4 and 1979–82 were the industries with the highest intermediate input shares, shown in Table 13.8.
12 See Bank of Thailand, Annual Report, various issues.
13 Import–competing industries are defined as industries which import more than 10 per cent of total domestic utilization. Those which export more than 10 per cent of their production are categorized as exportables. The rest are called noncompeting industries.

REFERENCES

Ajanant, J., Chunanuntathum, S. and Meenaphant, S. (1985) *Trade and Industrialization of Thailand*, Bangkok: Social Science Association of Thailand.

Akrasanee, N. (1975a) 'Import Substitution, Export Expansion, and Sources of Industrial Growth in Thailand, 1960–1972', in P. Sondysuvan (ed.) *Finance, Trade, and Economic Development in Thailand: Essays in Honor of Khunying Suparb Yossundara*, Bangkok: Sompong Press, pp. 257–77.

—— (1975b) 'The Structure of Industrial Protection in Thailand During the 1960s', *Economic Bulletin for Asia and the Far East* 24(1): 36–57.

—— (1980) 'Industrial Development Strategy in Thailand', mimeo, Thammasat University, Bangkok.

—— (1981) 'Trade Strategy for Employment Growth in Thailand', in A. O. Krueger, H. B. Lary, T. Monson and N. Akrasanee (eds) *Trade and Employment in Developing Countries, Volume 1: Individual Studies*, ch. 9, Chicago: University of Chicago Press, pp. 393–433.

——, Thamruanglerd, S. and Iamkamala, C. (1983) *Sources of Industrial Growth in Thailand*, Bangkok: Industrial Management Co. Ltd.

——, Wiboonchutikula, P., Wahawisan, T., and Chontanawat, J. (1990) 'Export Financing in Thailand', in Asian Development Bank *Export Finance*, ch. 6, Manila: Asian Development Bank, pp. 253–95.

Bank of Thailand, *Annual Report*, various issues.

Berndt, E. R. (1980) 'Energy Price Increases and Productivity Slowdown in United States Manufacturing', in Federal Reserve Bank of Boston, *The Decline in Productivity Growth*, Boston: Federal Reserve Bank of Boston, pp. 60–89.

Bruno, M. (1984) 'Raw Materials, Profits, and the Productivity Slowdown', *Quarterly Journal of Economics* 99(1): 1–29.

Bruton, H. J. (1967) 'Productivity Growth in Latin America', *American Economic Review* 57(5): 1099–116.

Chen, E. K. Y. (1977) 'Factor Inputs, Total Factor Productivity and Economic Growth: The Asian Case', *The Developing Economies* XV(3 June): 121–43.

Chenery, H. B. (1960) 'Patterns of Industrial Growth', *American Economic Review* 50(4): 624–54.

Chenery, H. B., Shishido, S., and Watanabe, T. (1962) 'The Pattern of Japanese Growth, 1914–54', *Econometrica* 30(1): 98–139.

Chenery, H. B., Robinson, S. and Syrquin, M. (1986) *Industrialization and Growth: A Comparative Study*, New York: Oxford University Press.

Customs Department, *Foreign Trade Statistics*, various issues.

Denison, E. F. (1969) 'Some Major Issues in Productivity Analysis: An Examination of Estimates by Jorgenson and Grilliches', *Survey of Current Business* 49: 1–28.

Elias, V. J. (1978) 'Sources of Economic Growth in Latin American Countries', *Review of Economics and Statistics* 60(3): 362–70.

Ezaki, M. (1978) 'Growth Accounting of Postwar Japan: The Input Side', *Economic Studies Quarterly*, December: 193–215.

Hayami, Y. and Ruttan, V. W. (1979) *Agricultural Growth in Japan, Taiwan, Korea and the Philippines*, Honolulu: University Press of Hawaii.

Helleiner, G. K. (1990) *The New Global Economy and the Developing Countries*, Aldershot, UK: Edward Elgar.

Hulten, C. R. (1973) 'Divisia Index Numbers', *Econometrica* 41: 1017–25.

Jorgenson, D. W. and Grilliches, Z. (1967) 'The Explanation of Productivity Change', *Review of Economic Studies* 34: 249–83.

Kendrick, J. W. and Grossman, E. S. (1980) *Productivity in the United States, Trend and Cycles*, Baltimore: Johns Hopkins University Press.

Kendrick, J. W. and Vaccara, B. N. (eds) (1980) *New Developments in Productivity Measurement and Analysis*, Chicago: University of Chicago Press.

Krueger, A. O. (1984) 'Comparative Advantage and Development Policy Twenty Years Later' in M. Syrquin, L. Taylor and L. Westphal (eds) *Economic Structure and Performance: Essays in Honor of Hollis B. Chenery*, New York: Academic Press, pp. 135–56.

—— and Tuncer, B. (1980) 'Estimating Total Factor Productivity Growth in a Developing Country', World Bank Staff Working Paper no. 422, World Bank, Washington, DC.

—— and Tuncer, B. (1982) 'An Empirical Test of the Infant Industry Argument', *American Economic Review* 72/Dec: 1142–52.

Ministry of Commerce, *Wholesale Price Index for Thailand*, various issues Bangkok.

National Statistical Office of Thailand, *Report on the Industrial Census: Whole Kingdom*, various issues Bangkok.

Nishimizu, M. and Hulten, C. R. (1978) 'The Sources of Japanese Economic Growth, 1955–1971', *Review of Economics and Statistics* 60(3): 351–61.

Nishimizu, M. and Robinson, S. (1984) 'Trade Policies and Productivity Change in Semi-industrialized Countries', *Journal of Development Economics* 16(12): 177–206.

Pack, H. (1988) 'Industrialization and Trade' in H.B. Chenery and T. N. Srinivasan (eds) *Handbook of Development Economics*, vol. 1, Amsterdam: North Holland, pp. 333–80.

Park, W. R. (1973) *Cost Engineering Analysis*, New York: John Wiley & Sons.

Ramangkura, V. and Nidhiprapha, B. (1991) 'The Macroeconomics of the Public Sector Deficit: The Case of Thailand', World Bank Working Paper no. 633, World Bank, Washington, DC.

Solow, R. M. (1957) 'Technical Change and the Aggregate Production Function', *Review of Economics and Statistics* 39(3): 312–20.

Syrquin, M. (1988) 'Patterns of Structural Change' in H. B. Chenery and T. N. Srinivasan (eds) *Handbook of Development Economics*, vol. 1, Amsterdam: North Holland, pp. 203–73.

Tsao, Y. (1985) 'Growth Without Productivity: Singapore Manufacturing in the 1970s', *Journal of Development Economics* 19(1–2): 25–38.

Wiboonchutikula, P. (1982) 'The Total Factor Productivity Growth of the Manufacturing Industries in Thailand, 1963–1976', PhD dissertation, University of Minnesota.

——, Chintayarangsan, R. and Thongpakdi, N. (1989) 'Trade in Manufactured Goods and Mineral Products', background paper no. 4, Thailand Development Research Institute Year-End Conference.

——, Rarueysong, C. and Pongpisanupichit, J. (1991) 'Incentives Policy and Measures for Trade and Industrial Development', background report for the National Economic and Social Development Board's Seventh Economic and Social Development Plan (1992–1997), Thailand Development Research Institute, Bangkok.

World Bank, *World Debt Tables*, various issues.

14

TRADE AND INDUSTRIALIZATION IN TURKEY

Initial conditions, policy and performance in the 1980s

Merih Celasun

The author is most indebted to Gerry Helleiner for encouragement and valuable suggestions. Detailed comments by Huricihan Inan are appreciated. The author would like to thank Halis Akder, Ercan Uygur, Fikret Senses, Hasan Olgun, Okan Aktan, Oktar Turel, Arman Kirim, Hayri Maraslioglu, Ahmet Tiktik, Teoman Akgur, and participants at the UNU/WIDER Conference on Trade and Industrialization Reconsidered (Paris, 31 August–3 September, 1991) for helpful discussions. The able help of Ahmet Tiktik is acknowledged in data processing for the analysis of comparative advantage and productivity patterns. The usual disclaimers apply.

INTRODUCTION

The object of the present study is to provide an assessment of Turkey's post–1980 trade and industrial policy and performance in a long-term perspective. In the aftermath of the external shocks of the mid–1970s, Turkey was the first major non-oil middle-income country to encounter a severe economic paralysis in 1978–80 before the outbreak of wider international debt crisis in the early 1980s. In contrast to the prolonged and agonizing adjustment attempts of other major debtors, Turkey's output recovery has been quite rapid and substantial. Following the foreign exchange stringency and output losses of the 1978–80 crisis episode, Turkish GDP increased at 5.6 per cent per year from 1981 to 1987, accompanied by an annual growth rate of exports of 25 per cent in current US dollars in the same period. The share of manufacturing reached 85 per cent of total exports in the late 1980s from 35–40 per cent levels in the late 1970s. The international creditors perceived Turkey's export boom as a 'restructuring success', and resumed voluntary lending in 1983, quite early in the adjustment process.[1]

453

Turkey's recent export-led expansion is of interest to students of industrialization for a number of reasons. Turkey's post-1980 export performance has been largely structured around existing capacities built in the pre-1980 inward-oriented growth era, which emphasized the import-substitution (IS) motive in trade regimes and investment programming. The Turkish case demonstrates the overall feasibility of switching from IS strategy to outward-orientation in the latter stages of the industrialization process, but the transitional costs involved appear to be substantial.

Turkey's recent experience brings out the strong connections between macroeconomic policy and trade reforms. It shows that a credible trade adjustment needs to be supported by sharp shifts in relative prices and wide-ranging deregulation, which inevitably produce policy conflicts in the achievement of stable distributional and macroeconomic conditions. In Turkey, the macroeconomic instability caused by the unanticipated inter-actions of adjustment policies has worsened the climate for new capital formation in manufacturing, which is central to sustained industrialization in the longer run.

The present study aims to provide focus on two sets of issues connected with (i) the macroeconomic policy context and strategy of post–1980 trade reforms, and (ii) their broad impact on industrial adjustment and perform-ance. Thus, the remainder of the paper is organized in two main sections, the first dealing with policy context and the second presenting an assess-ment of developments in manufacturing. In a final section, the paper concludes and recapitulates policy prospects for the 1990s.

POLICY CONTEXT

Development policy and industrialization, 1950–80

Background and initial conditions

In the wake of the Second World War, Turkey was predominantly a rural country. From the early 1920s to the late 1940s, the new Turkish republic was ruled by a single-party system. In the 1930s, under the official banner of 'étatism', the government began to emphasize industrialization by estab-lishing a number of state enterprises to compensate for the lack of indigen-ous entrepreneurship in the business sector. In the late 1940s, Turkey managed to accomplish a fairly smooth transition to a multi-party system, which brought to power a new (Democratic) party in 1950 with a definite tilt toward liberalism.

Under favourable world trade conditions for primary exports and Mar-shall Aid, the Turkish economy experienced rapid growth and import liberalization from 1950 to 1954. In the mid-1950s, Turkey became a NATO member, and subsequently a staunch ally of the West in the cold war era. The latter foreign policy connection proved to be helpful in the arrangement of well-structured concessional assistance in the 1960s, and emergency lending in the episodes of payments crises.

After a massive crop failure in 1954, the foreign exchange stringency induced sporadic import-substitution activity, and facilitated the emergence of an entrepreneurial class. In this period, rural–urban migration began, and domestic political tensions heightened. In view of widened external imbalances, the government adopted an IMF-supported stabilization programme in 1958 involving a large devaluation (Krueger, 1974). In response to a worsening domestic political situation, the military intervened in 1960, and introduced a highly progressive constitutional framework in 1961.

Turkey's 1961 constitution enlarged the scope for liberal labour legislation and wider political participation. The 1961 constitution also institutionalized development planning. The five-year plans set the guidelines for medium-term macro balances and sectoral expansions in a mixed-economy framework. The annual programmes within the five-year plans coordinated public finance and investment, and specified policy measures. The integral parts of the annual programmes were the yearly import programmes and export regimes. Until the 1980s, Turkey's planning process made heavy use of a restrictive trade regime and financial repression as key policy tools to promote industrialization. In the overall planning context of the 1960s and 1970s, the state enterprise investment programmes were used as an additional instrument of industrial development, particularly in capital-intensive intermediate goods manufacturing.

In sharp contrast to the economic imbalances of the 1950s, the overall economic performance significantly improved during the First (1963–7) and Second (1968–72) Plans, generating a substantial rise of GDP at 6.7 per cent per year from 1963 to 1972 with relatively low inflation, around 10 per cent levels. This steady growth process benefited from concessional capital inflows organized largely by the OECD Aid Consortium, not exceeding cross-country norms for external resources in relation to GDP (Celasun, 1983). Moreover, the outflow of Turkish workers to Western Europe eased the unemployment problem in the face of accelerated rural–urban migration.

Although internal demand management was a relatively balanced one in the 1960s, trade distortions were allowed to grow, leading to a foreign exchange stringency toward the end of the decade (Krueger, 1974). To avert an open crisis, an IMF-supported stabilization package was introduced in 1970, involving a large devaluation. In this context, the government sought a more active drive for export expansion. These initiatives coincided with the world economic boom in the early 1970s, and resulted in a surge of workers' remittances and resource-based export revenues (springing mainly from food-processing and semi-processed cotton textiles). The end result was a current account surplus in 1973.

The 1970 official tilt toward export promotion proved to be unsustainable in the mid-1970s. On grounds of law and order, the military intervened in 1971 in a partial fashion, but dislocated the fragile political process. Subsequently, various coalitions ruled the country, and postponed domestic adjustment to the external shocks of the mid-1970s. Following the rapid decumulation of foreign exchange reserves, huge external borrowing became feasible in the milieu of recycled petro dollars.

The foreign-financed spending boom accelerated GDP growth in the mid-1970s with a substantial rise in industrial investment. The widening trade imbalances and appreciating exchange rate could not be sustained, however, by various destabilizing schemes of short-term borrowing. With the sudden drop in creditors' confidence and lending in mid-1977, Turkey faced a massive debt crisis in 1978–80. As documented by Celasun and Rodrik (1989), a credible adjustment could not be launched in 1978–9, and the economy had to adjust to reductions in external resources via import compression, high inflation, output losses and disrupted markets. Thus, the stage was set for a deeper and comprehensive adjustment effort in the 1980s, which is examined later.

The industrialization process and sources of growth

Before proceeding with the discussion of post–1980 policy and performance, it would be useful to note the basic structural characteristics of Turkey's pre–1980 industrialization process. These characteristics are derived from the earlier structure-focused studies of Celasun (1983) and Yagci (1984), and can be recapitulated around a number of major points:

(i) In the context of the cross-country norms of Chenery and Syrquin (1975) for development patterns, Turkey's output restructuring by major sectors was lagging in the 1950s, but caught up with large country norms in the 1970s. The observed trade ratios (especially the export/GDP ratio) had been markedly and consistently below the predicted values, exhibiting a moderate and short-lived rise in the early 1970s.

(ii) In the pre-1980 era, the sectoral reallocation of labour lagged behind the compositional shifts in output. Despite the substantially reduced share of the primary sector in GDP, the relative proportion of primary (predominantly agricultural) labour in total employment remained exceedingly high by cross-country standards. This is a major source of income inequality, and a key factor behind the rapid pace of rural—urban migration (Celasun, 1989). The low speed of labour reallocation points to the rather limited employment-generating capacity of Turkish industrial policies, reflecting the public planning emphasis on capital-intensive industries and the anti-labour bias induced by factor price distortions under financial repression.

(iii) In relation to the cross-country norms of Chenery and Taylor (1968) for output restructuring *within* manufacturing, Celasun (1983) shows that in the 1950s Turkey lagged substantially behind the predicted shares in all intermediate goods industries, while exceeding the norms in food and textiles. The observed transition in the 1960s and 1970s features a pronounced fall in the share of food processing, and a significant rise in intermediate goods, machinery and transport equipment industries, including consumer durables. Thus, in response to the changing composition of domestic demand as income levels rose, the structure of manufacturing output had 'travelled up the staircase' by gradually shifting to 'middle' and 'late' industries as predicted by cross-country regressions.

(iv) Estimates of the demand-side sources of growth in manufacturing output are summarized in Table 14.1 for Turkey, Mexico and Korea. The estimates for Turkey and Mexico show that domestic demand expansion was the primary engine of manufacturing growth from the early 1950s to the mid-1970s in contrast to the significant reliance of Korea on export expansion in the earlier stages of industrialization. The Turkish data point to the sharp rise of export expansion as the predominant source of growth in the early 1980s, reflecting the large change in the demand structure of manufacturing output and plant capacities built in previous periods.

(v) Another interesting feature emerging from the data in Table 14.1 is that import substitution as a measured source of growth for Turkey was positive in 1953–68, but became insignificant and even negative in the post-1968 periods. The implication is that Turkey's industrialization process became increasingly *import-intensive* in the 1970s, creating a rigid structural dependence on imported inputs. The rigidity in the substitution of manufactured imports for domestic output was a major source of difficulty in adjusting to reduced capital inflows during the 1978–80 crisis, and therefore set the stage for the export drive in the 1980s.

(vi) Turkey's heavily protected inward-oriented industrialization resulted, however, in large domestic resource costs (DRCs) for manufacturing industries. Measured as the ratio of the cost of domestic resources to world value added (a proxy for the cost associated with average best practice), Yagci's DRC estimate for total manufacturing is 2.04 for 1981, with a higher value for the public sector, suggesting substantial domestic inefficiency. The DRC measures for paper, fertilizer, iron and steel, and agricultural machinery are 5.2, 5.1, 3.2 and 2.1, and for electrical machinery, textiles, cement, and glass are 0.9, 0.9, 0.6 and 0.6, respectively. Price comparisons indicated a 32 per cent nominal

Table 14.1 Sources of growth in manufacturing output for Turkey, Mexico and Korea

	Annual average growth rate (%)	Sources (%)[a]				
		Domestic final demand expansion	Export expansion	Import substitution	Change in input–output coefficients	Total
Turkey						
1953–63	6.4	80.1	2.2	9.1	7.7	100.0
1963–8	9.9	75.2	4.5	10.4	9.9	100.0
1968–73	9.4	76.2	10.7	−1.5	14.6	100.0
1973–7[b]	7.0	100.4	−1.0	0.6	0.0	100.0
1977–81	−3.0	−36.7	81.5	−143.9	−1.0	100.0
1981–4	6.5	55.6	55.6	−6.8	−0.2	100.0
Mexico						
1950–60	7.0	71.8	3.0	10.9	14.4	100.0
1960–70	8.6	86.1	4.0	11.0	−1.0	100.0
1970–5	7.2	81.5	7.7	2.6	8.2	100.0
Korea						
1955–63	10.4	57.3	11.5	42.2	−11.0	100.0
1963–70	18.9	70.1	30.4	−0.6	0.1	100.0
1970–3	23.8	39.0	61.6	−2.5	1.8	100.0

Sources: Celasun (1983) and Lewis and Urata (1983) for Turkey; Chenery et al. (1986) for Mexico and Korea.
[a] Measured as a percentage of the total change in manufacturing output.
[b] All sectors.

rate of protection, and an 81 per cent effective rate of protection (ERP) for total manufacturing output in 1981 (Yagci, 1984). These large magnitudes of DRC and ERP measures explain the broad logic of the post–1980 policy actions, which assigned top priority to price corrections to promote an export-led adjustment.

The post-1980 adjustment process

The various facets of Turkey's post–1980 economic experience have been extensively reviewed elsewhere.[2] The present section highlights policy issues and policy linkages not widely nor sufficiently stressed in the recent literature on Turkey. There are three points that will be emphasized. First, trade reforms and their effects did not take place in isolation but in the larger context of macro policy and relative price changes, including exchange rate depreciation combined with wage repression. Second, Turkey's macroeconomic adjustment interacted strongly with a regressive income distribution, which contains politically unsustainable aspects for the 1990s. Third, Turkey's relatively unsuccessful fiscal retrenchment – in the context of financial liberalization – produced high inflation and high interest rates in the late 1980s, hindering capital reallocation toward manufacturing. The latter point has also been stressed by Conway (1988) and Rodrik (1990).

Policy mix and sequence: an overview

In the recent era of international debt crisis, the typical prescription for adjusting countries has been to pursue a certain sequence of policy actions, involving the following successive stages: (i) macroeconomic and fiscal stabilization; (ii) rationalization of the incentive system through trade and domestic financial liberalization, and restructuring of public spending; and (iii) liberalization of capital flows in the external account (Boeri, 1991). On the basis of the Southern Cone experience of the late 1970s, the conventional wisdom now is to recommend the postponement of capital account liberalization to the latter stage of country adjustment to avoid exchange rate appreciation and/or large-scale currency substitution.

An examination of policy measures and their timing in Turkey reveals that its adjustment strategy more or less evolved along the path prescribed by conventional wisdom, with a number of highly distinct and country-specific features.

Table 14.2 summarizes policy measures and supportive actions taken in Turkey over four successive policy stages, namely 1980, 1981–3, 1984–8 and 1989–90. The year 1980 is the first stage, characterized by the introduction of a highly comprehensive policy package; 1981–3 is the period of military rule, and strong conditional lending by the IMF and World Bank; 1984–8 and 1989–90 are periods of the civilian Ozal Administration, where the latter stage, 1989–90, involves capital account liberalization and reversals in key relative prices.

The paramount characteristic of Turkey's adjustment strategy is that the policy measures introduced in 1980 constituted an unusually bold and comprehensive set of high-magnitude price adjustments in product, financial and external markets (Celasun and Rodrik, 1989). Under the initial conditions of severe import compression and high inflation, the civilian government of Demirel chose to pursue the twin objectives of immediate export-led output recovery and macroeconomic stabilization. With sharp price adjustments, the government was willing to take the risk of a higher 'corrective' inflation with the expectation that state enterprise deficits would be removed, parallel markets eliminated, and strong signals given to potential exporters. Indeed, the annual rate of inflation increased to 105 per cent in 1980 from 65 per cent in 1979, but dropped to around 30 per cent in 1981–2.

The initial 'big push' in the exchange rate, interest rates and administered product prices was coupled with quickly implemented unorthodox export incentive schemes. These bold initial moves also proved to be helpful in

Table 14.2 Sequence and mix of policy measures, Turkey, 1980–90

Policy orientation and/or measures	1980	1981–3	1984–8	1989–90
A. Liberalization measures				
Deregulation of product markets (private sector)	x			
Import liberalization				
Removal of quotas		x		
Negative list			x	
Realignment of tariffs			x	x
Export subsidies				
Large	x	x		
Moderate			x	x
Deregulation of external flows				
Partial			x	
Substantial				x
Financial liberalization				
Interest rate deregulation	x			
Bank supervision system			x	
Stock exchange framework				
Introduction		x		
Expansion				x
B. External resources and arrangements				
Policy conditionalities				
IMF Stand-by	x	x		
IBRD Adjustment lending	x	x	x	
External capital				
Debt relief and other concessional lending	x	x		
Resumption of voluntary lending		x		
Rise in debt service			x	x
Rise in foreign direct investment			x	x
Surge in short-term debt				x
C. Price adjustments				
Exchange rate				
Maxi-devaluation	x			
Crawling peg		x	x	
Foreign exchange interbank market[a]				x
Appreciation				x
Interest rates				
Switch to positive rates	x			
Financial crisis		x		
State enterprise prices				
Steep hikes	x			
Flexible pricing		x	x	
Restrained adjustment				x
Urban real wages and agricultural support prices				
Deep cuts	x			
Downward trend		x	x	

Table 14.2 Continued

Policy orientation and/or measures	1980	1981–3	1984–8	1989–90
Upward trend				x
D. Fiscal policy actions				
Expenditure cuts	x	x		
Restructuring of public investment		x		
Reduction in 'fiscal drag'		x	x	
Tax incentives to financial intermediation		x	x	
Introduction to VAT system			x	
Fiscal decentralization			x	
Rapid rise in domestic debt			x	x
Stepped up privatization				x
E. Monetary stance				
Tight stance		x		
Monetary programming by the Central Bank				x
F. Political arrangements				
Military rule		x		
Employment freeze and tightened labour legislation		x		
Restrictive multi-party system			x	
Broad participation				x

Source: Enlarged and updated version of policy sequencing reported in Celasun and Rodrik (1989). For brevity, the specification and timing of some of the policy measures are approximate.
ᵃ The FX interbank market became operational in October 1988 under the aegis of the Central Bank of Turkey. After the removal of most restrictions on external capital flows, the full convertibility of the Turkish lira was introduced in April 1990.

regaining the confidence of international creditors. The IMF Stand-by and World Bank adjustment loans were speedily arranged and disbursed in conjunction with additional debt relief operations. New foreign lending allowed the resumption of intermediate goods imports, and eased the pressures on public finance. From the position of exceedingly low rates of capacity utilization (at 45–50 per cent levels), industrial firms showed a strong export response to the rapidly altered incentive structure.

Besides the highly comprehensive nature of the initial 'big push' in price adjustments, another noteworthy characteristic of the adjustment strategy relates to the political management of income redistribution that was associated with relative price changes. In the general equilibrium price system, the counterpart of the sharp rises in the cost of imports, industrial price and interest rates were the steep fall in agricultural prices and urban real wages as shown in Table 14.3.

The political management of real wage reductions proceeded roughly as follows. The Turkish military ruled the country from September 1980 to

Table 14.3 Relative price movements, Turkey, 1978–88 (1978=100)

	1978	1980	1982	1984	1986	1988
A. Increases						
Real exchange rate[a]	100	116	136	148	149	152
Real interest rate (%)[b]	–25	–38	8	4	12	–2
Real sectoral net prices[c]						
Energy+mining	100	126	160	178	207	195
Manufacturing	100	120	120	120	119	124
B. Decreases						
Terms of foreign trade (US$)	100	77	67	75	82	74
Real product wage[d]	100	61	61	51	41	33
Real consumption wage[e]	100	62	65	61	64	56
Real sectoral net prices[c]						
Agriculture	100	84	79	79	72	68
Government services[f]	100	74	67	48	49	50

Source: Celasun and Rodrik (1989) and Celasun (1989), updated by the author's estimates.
[a] A rise in value indicates a depreciation.
[b] The after-tax rate on one year deposits, deflated by the wholesale price index.
[c] The ratio of sectoral value-added deflators to the GDP deflator. ('Net' refers to value added.)
[d] The gross labour cost deflated by the GDP deflator.
[e] The after-tax wage deflated by the private consumption deflator.
[f] Real civil servant salaries.

November 1983, consolidating the initial realignment of the wage–price structure, and managing to secure additional depreciation of the exchange rate. In this interim period, labour union activity was severely curtailed, and wages were settled by the High Arbitration Board. Under the civilian Ozal Administration (and a new and more restrictive constitution), downward real wage flexibility was maintained during 1984–8 to make room for further exchange rate depreciation as part of a compensation for reduction in export subsidies and import protection. With the increased contestability in the political process, real wages began to recover in 1989–90 in conjunction with currency appreciation under liberalized capital flows in the external accounts.

This sketch of Turkey's post-1980 policy environment brings out quite clearly that trade reforms were implemented in the context of a strongly shifted wage–price structure, and therefore that the overall performance cannot be explained on the basis of trade policy changes alone.

Macroeconomic adjustment and income redistribution[3]

The major indicators of recent macroeconomic adjustment are assembled in Table 14.4. Taking the 1980 policy reforms as a benchmark, the 1975–7

Table 14.4 Indicators of macroeconomic adjustment, Turkey

	Pre-reform		Post-reform	
	1975–7	*1978–80*	*1981–4*	*1985–8*
A. Output growth and inflation: annual change (%)				
Real GNP	6.3	0.5	4.5	6.0
GNP deflator	19.4	71.1	36.5	44.1
B. Merchandise trade (% GNP)[a]				
Imports	21.6	13.4	15.2	19.7
Exports	5.7	5.6	11.3	14.7
C. Saving and investment (% GNP)[a]				
Saving	35.3	27.5	25.3	26.0
Foreign[b]	11.2	4.8	−0.1	0.2
Public	8.5	8.7	12.3	10.8
Private	15.6	14.0	13.1	15.0
Investment				
Public	19.4	15.7	15.1	14.0
Private	16.2	11.8	10.2	12.0
Saving–investment imbalances				
Public	−10.6	−7.0	−2.8	−3.2
Private	−0.6	2.2	2.9	3.0
D. Disposable income (% GNP)				
Current prices				
Public	19.3	19.0	17.9	18.1
Private	80.7	81.0	82.1	81.9
Constant 1988 prices				
Public	16.6	17.8	21.7	19.7
Private	83.4	82.2	78.3	80.3
E. Factor shares (%)				
Agriculturalists	30	25	21	18
Non-agricultural	70	75	79	82
Wage income	34	31	24	17
Non-wage income	36	44	55	65
Memo: Saving/disposable income (%)				
Domestic	24.1	22.7	25.4	25.8
Public	51.2	48.9	56.7	54.8
Private	18.7	17.0	16.7	18.7

Sources: Ozmucur (1990a) for distributional data, and State Planning Organization (SPO) data for other estimates.
[a] At constant 1988 prices.
[b] Equivalent to the current external deficit.

and 1978–80 periods are designated as 'pre-reform' and 1981–4 and 1985–8 periods as 'post-reform' policy phases.

To clarify the nature of internal adjustment to changes in net capital inflows or foreign saving (the current account deficit), part C in Table 14.4

shows saving–investment patterns. In contrast to some studies on Turkey's macroeconomy, saving–investment patterns are examined at constant post-reform prices, rather than at current prices, in order to avoid *understatement* of changes in the volume of foreign saving in the pre–1980 periods when the exchange rate was grossly *overvalued*. These estimates show that the magnitude of internal adjustment was very high in Turkey as the volume of foreign saving dropped from 11 per cent of GNP in 1975–7 to 0.2 per cent in 1985–8.

The burden of internal adjustment during the debt crisis fell mainly on investment rather than on saving. In turn, the 1981–4 export promotion and stabilization phase yielded a strong upward adjustment in domestic saving. The rise in domestic saving in 1981–4 was highly instrumental in reducing inflation and lowering domestic absorption to make room for export expansion.

During 1981–4, the rise in domestic saving was engineered by public-sector resource mobilization, despite the decline in the private saving ratio in this period. To shed light on this issue, part D in Table 14.4 gives estimates for the shares of public and private disposable incomes in GNP both in current price and constant price terms. Public disposable income is the difference between GNP and private disposable income. The estimates show that the GNP share of public disposable income increased in real terms from 1978–80 to 1981–4, while it declined in nominal terms.

The implication is that the terms of trade of the public sector *vis-à-vis* the rest of the economy improved in 1981–4, yielding a redistribution of real income from the private to public sector. Because of the higher saving propensity of the public sector (as a whole), economy-wide saving performance was substantially enhanced at the time when the export drive was launched.

As emphasized by Celasun and Rodrik (1989), the improvement in the public sector's terms of trade in 1981–4 was achieved mainly through a massive reduction in the cost of labour services purchased by the government. In the 1980s, restrictive wage policies were pursued by the private sector as well as by the public sector, generating pronounced shifts in the functional income distribution as shown in part E in Table 14.4.

Under a more rapid growth of income, financial liberalization and distributional shift toward capital, private saving recovered during 1985–8 but public saving performance deteriorated. With the virtual disappearance of foreign saving in the late 1980s, the rising public saving gap could be financed only by the rising private saving surplus. At the macroeconomic level, the principal mechanisms to bring forth a saving surplus in the private sector are high interest rates and/or high inflation, which tend to dampen private investment and increase private saving.

Table 14.5 Share of manufacturing in total fixed investment, Turkey (1988 prices, %)

1968–72	*1973–7*	*1978–83*	*1984–8*
36	38	31	19

Source: Maraslioglu and Tiktik (1991).

Key problem areas: public finance, debt, financial liberalization and industrial investment

As the evaluation of macroeconomic indicators shows, the external component of the post-1980 adjustment process yielded credible results in the way of increasing the trade orientation of the economy, and lowering dependence on capital inflows in import financing. The internal component of the adjustment process was quite effective in 1981–4, but then gradually worsened. On the eve of the 1990s, the widening fiscal imbalances produced instability in the price system and output performance. The annual GNP growth rates were 1.9, 9.2 and 1.5 per cent in 1989, 1990 and 1991 respectively.

Measured in nominal terms as percentage of GNP, the public-sector borrowing requirement (PSBR), which is a larger measure than the public saving gap, increased from 4.8 per cent in 1985–6 to 7 per cent in 1987–9, and further to around 10–12 per cent in 1990–1. The widening of the PSBR at the end of the decade sprang from three sources: (i) higher interest payments; (ii) a rising public sector wage bill; and (iii) a slower rate of price adjustment in the state enterprise sector. The rapid increase in public-sector interest payments partly reflects the termination of external debt relief in the mid-1980s, and an accelerating rise in foreign debt service from 1985 onward.

Financial deregulation also sharply altered domestic conditions for financing fiscal deficits. On the one hand, the liberalization of financial markets had definitely succeeded in promoting financial savings through a major shift from currency holdings to interest-bearing bank deposits and government liabilities. On the other hand, it lowered the real demand for central bank money, and thereby the base for seigniorage revenue.[4] In such a setting, the market financing of fiscal deficits pulled interest rates to higher levels, caused a rapid accumulation of government debt, and crowded out private debt instruments and equities. Moreover, the capital account liberalization in 1989–90 relied strongly on high domestic interest rates to avoid capital flight and to encourage short-term capital inflows in the context of an appreciating currency.

Besides the increased cost of funds for private investment, the variable nature of inflation caused considerable uncertainty in price movements, producing a strongly adverse impact on private capital formation for manufacturing as shown by Conway (1988). The data in Table 14.5 show the

post-1980 break in the long-term trend of Turkish manufacturing investment, which partly reflects reduced government participation in new industrial investments.

Trade reforms in the 1980s

General approach to trade-regime alterations

The policy overview in the previous section suggests that three characteristics of the policy environment facilitated the trade reform process. First,
the exchange rate depreciation was deep and sustainable (until 1989) with
the help of a firm political management of real wage reductions. The
real price of tradables was therefore strongly enhanced. Second, domestic
absorption was significantly lowered in the first half of the 1980s to provide
room for the initial push in export expansion. Third, concessional lending
and debt relief in the earlier part of the 1980s allowed a more rapid
recovery of imported inputs from their depressed levels during the 1978–80
crisis.

The changes in trade (or commercial) policy in its strict sense (export
subsidies and import barriers) evolved in a rather gradual fashion in the
1980s. They may be described in relation to their neutrality aspects and
liberalization characteristics. In the first stage from 1980 to 1983, export
subsidies were substantially increased to achieve a greater neutrality of
incentives between exportables and importables. In this stage, a clear signal
was also given toward liberalization by the removal of import quotas, but
licensing was maintained to control the balance of payments.

In the second stage from 1984 onward, the neutrality of the trade regime
was further enhanced mainly through an almost complete elimination of
direct controls for imports by a switch to a 'negative list' from various
categories of 'positive lists', which constitutes the largest trade-liberalizing
action in Turkey's recent history. In the latter stages, export tax rebates
were lowered, and eventually abolished in 1988. However, in the latter
part of the 1980s, other export incentive schemes gained importance in a
rather *ad hoc* and unstable fashion. Following the switch to the negative
list for imports, nominal tariffs were realigned in several stages.[5]

Togan, *et al.* (1987) give economy-wide estimates for the ratio of the
effective exchange rate (EER) for imports to EER for exports from 1980
to 1986. This ratio drops from 1.62 in 1980 to 1.42 in 1983, and further to
1.29 in 1986, suggesting a notable reduction in (but not complete removal
of) the anti-export bias in the trade regime.

Table 14.6 Structure of subsidies for manufactured exports, Turkey, 1979–90 (% of the value of total manufactured exports)

	Direct payments (1)	Export credits (2)	Duty allowance (3)	Tax allowance (4)	Total subsidies (5:1+2+3+4)
1979	11.0	9.9	0.3	0.0	21.2
1980	5.6	14.9	4.2	n.a.	26.7[a]
1981	9.1	13.0	3.3	n.a.	27.4[a]
1982	15.1	10.8	3.6	n.a.	31.5[a]
1983	17.4	10.5	5.6	n.a.	35.9[a]
1984	17.3	5.9	2.0	2.0	27.2
1985	10.0	2.0	5.1	2.0	19.1
1986	9.9	4.8	8.6	2.6	25.9
1987	8.6	2.9	6.7	4.3	22.5
1988	7.6	4.8	6.6	4.3	22.5
1989	5.5	8.8	7.7	5.9	27.9
1990	4.4	9.2	7.7	6.2	27.5

Source: Uygur (1991).
[a] Tax allowance estimated at 2.0%.

Export incentives and subsidy estimates

In the 1970s, a number of export incentive schemes (such as tax rebates, concessional credits and foreign exchange allocation) were already in operation. The impact of these schemes was limited, however, in the absence of realistic exchange rates and supportive macroeconomic policies.

The 1980 adjustment policy package expanded and consolidated export incentive schemes, improved administrative efficiency, and promoted foreign trade companies. Following Uygur (1991), the post–1980 export incentive schemes may be grouped into the following four major categories:

(i) direct payments through tax rebates and cash premia from extra-budgetary funds;
(ii) preferential and subsidized export credits;
(iii) duty allowances on imported inputs and foreign exchange allocation; and
(iv) corporate tax allowances.

In addition to these major promotional arrangements, other schemes such as foreign exchange retention and freight subsidies were also used, but their subsidy components have been relatively minor. The subsidies associated with these four major categories incentives are estimated by Uygur (1991) and shown in Table 14.6. During 1980–4, direct payments were basically in the form of tax rebates, but cash premia from extrabudgetary funds became significant from 1985 onward after Turkey signed the GATT subsidy code and agreed to phase out tax rebates.

Total subsidies for manufactured exports reached high levels of about

30 per cent of the value of total manufactured exports in the 1981–4 phase of export promotion, declined in 1985–8, and recovered again in 1989–0. The general presumption is that the upward shift in tax rebates during 1982–4 was largely due to an increase in fictitious exports. It is estimated that overinvoicing of Turkish exports to the OECD region averaged around 15 per cent during 1982–5, inducing the authorities to phase out tax rebates in the late 1980s (Celasun and Rodrik, 1989: Table 7.6).

The subsidies were differentiated by product groups, and reached higher than average levels for exports channelled through foreign trade companies (Onis, 1990). In particular, the tax rebates were highest for skill-intensive investment goods, higher than average for capital-intensive intermediate goods, and below average for labour- and resource-intensive consumer goods in manufacturing. However, the share of consumer goods was the highest in direct payments, because the latter product group (including textiles and food processing) comprised the largest portion of total manufactured exports. Baysan and Blitzer (1990) report that variations in export EERs do not seem to explain the observed differences among sectors in export growth performance. However, Milanovic (1986) and Senses (1989a, 1990) stress the favourable effects of higher export subsidies for intermediate goods in Turkey's export expansion to the Middle East in the earlier part of the 1980s.

Import liberalization and the structure of protection

During the 1978–80 period of debt crisis and import compression, the import regime was tightened by non-tariff barriers, including prohibitions, quotas and licensing. As noted earlier, the import liberalizing moves were made in two distinct stages in the 1980s.

In 1981, import quotas were removed, but import licensing continued. Then, between 1983 and 1984, a switch to the negative list was introduced in the import regime, consisting of items requiring prior permission, but the list virtually disappeared in the late 1980s. The negative list then only included a few items such as arms, ammunition and certain drugs.

Nominal tariff rates were realigned in 1984, adjusted in 1988 and considerably lowered in 1989. In 1984, tariffs were increased to compensate for the removal of non-tariff barriers. From 1985 onward, various extra-budgetary fund levies were introduced to generate fiscal revenues and to discipline 'misbehaving' domestic producers. The arbitrary manipulation of fund levies created, however, considerable instability in the structure of actual protection. The 1989 tariff reductions aimed at a greater neutrality of incentives between exportables and importables, and putting 'a brake on inflation'. In conjunction with exchange rate appreciation, the 1989 tariff cuts resulted in an import spree and larger trade deficit in 1990.[6]

Two sets of difficulties surround the precise measurement of post-1980

Table 14.7 Structure of protection, Turkey

| | A. Gross tariffs[a] | | | | B. Actual tariffs[b] | | | |
| | Nominal rates (%) | | Effective rates (%) | | Nominal rates (%) | | Effective rates (%) | |
	1983	1989	1983	1989	1985	1989	1985	1989
Agriculture	24.6	28.7	23.3	29.7	10.3	5.7	13.0	4.4
Mining and oil	56.1	25.6	64.2	32.6	0.7	0.4	7.9	-1.5
Manufacturing	81.8	46.8	93.9	80.2	28.1	11.0	31.8	15.1
Consumption goods[c]	129.1	65.3	165.8	147.4	20.0	13.2	58.6	16.8
Intermediate goods[d]	58.0	32.3	71.8	47.3	32.8	8.1	25.9	10.5
Investment goods[e]	61.5	56.7	66.6	101.3	24.3	14.1	32.0	20.6
Weighted average (all sectors)	65.2	41.2	58.8	53.8	17.8	8.7	23.8	11.3
Standard deviation	63.8	33.6	217.4	110.0	–	33.6	58.2	84.3

Sources: Olgun and Togan (1991) for gross tariffs; Ozhun and Tanrikulu (1989) for actual tariffs.
[a] Before tax concessions, including imputed import expenses.
[b] Collected tariffs, reflecting tax concessions.
[c] Consumption goods: food, tobacco, beverages, textiles, clothing, footwear, furniture.
[d] Intermediate goods: other manufacturing industries.
[e] Investment goods: fabricated metal products, transport equipment, machinery and electronics, including consumer durables.

protection in Turkey. On the one hand, there are no reliable estimates for changes in import premia following the import liberalization moves of 1981 and 1983–4. On the other hand, a wide range of tax concessions (granted to capital goods imports of investors and intermediate goods imports of exporters) are difficult to quantify in an interindustry framework. With this cautionary note, Table 14.7 lists estimates for the sectoral structure of protection in the 1980s.

Panel A in Table 14.7 gives estimates by Olgun and Togan (1991) for nominal rates of protection (NRP) and effective rates of protection (ERP) for the benchmark years 1983 and 1989, which are based on legal tariffs before tax concessions, including imputed import expenses. These data indicate that the NRP for manufacturing shows a large decline, while the manufacturing ERP exhibits a more moderate fall. The movements in protection rates for main manufacturing subsectors point to a shift of protection from lower to higher stages especially in investment goods production. The data also bring out reductions in the inter-industry dispersion of tariffs. It also appears that export expansion in consumer goods industries were achieved under strong protection, which broadly justifies export subsidies given to these sectors.

Panel B in Table 14.7 gives estimated protection rates for the benchmark years 1985 and 1989, which are presumably based on actual (collected) import tax receipts. These data confirm the shift of protection to higher stages of processing.

Price responsiveness of Turkish export performance

In the 1980s, Turkey's trade adjustment was supported by deep and sustained exchange rate depreciation (until 1989) and large export subsidies, which increased price incentives for exports. The rapid rise of total merchandise exports, in current US dollars, from 2.9 billion in 1980 to 8 billion in 1985 and further to 11.7 billion in 1988 has been considered an impressive performance, especially in the inhospitable external environment of the early 1980s. It seems, therefore, apt to review recent econometric evidence on the price-responsiveness of aggregate Turkish exports.

The quarterly regression analysis in Celasun and Rodrik (1989) for the 1978–84 period finds a significant positive effect of the level of the real exchange rate, and negative impact of exchange rate volatility on the volume of exports. A dummy variable for the post-1981:II subperiod seems to have very large explanatory power, possibly reflecting the workings of overinvoicing of exports and/or the impact of the Iran–Iraq war. For the longer 1980–7 period, Arslan and van Wijnbergen (1990) conclude that real exchange rate depreciation contributed in a large way to Turkey's export boom, and the favourable additional effect of export subsidies has been moderate.

Uygur (1991) confirms the positive effect of exchange rate policy on export expansion. Furthermore, Uygur captures the favourable impact of domestic demand decline on exports during 1978:I and 1983:IV as strongly suggested in our discussion of macroeconomic adjustment on pp. 458–66. Tansel and Togan (1987) also report significant price elasticities for export supply and export demand over the longer period from 1968 to 1985.

DEVELOPMENTS IN MANUFACTURING

Trade-orientation and comparative advantage

Export propensity and import penetration

To set the stage for a close look at comparative advantage in the next section, the overall trade orientation of manufacturing may be reviewed on the basis of the data shown in Table 14.8. These data summarize export propensities and import penetration ratios for three major subsectors. (Note: The coverage of these subsectors is given in the footnotes to Table 14.7.)

Table 14.8 shows that the export propensity in total manufacturing was 10 per cent in 1972 (during Turkey's earlier short-lived export promotion

Table 14.8 Export propensity and import penetration in manufacturing,[a] Turkey

	Consumption goods	Intermediate goods	Investment goods	Total manufacturing
A. Export propensity (%)				
Inward orientation				
1972	17.8	3.3	0.6	10.0
1977	12.2	1.0	0.9	5.8
1978	10.6	1.6	1.1	6.0
Outward orientation				
1983	15.6	8.2	7.5	11.3
1988	25.0	14.6	10.0	17.8
1990	27.2	13.6	6.7	17.1
B. Import penetration (%)				
Inward orientation				
1972	0.8	12.8	49.3	14.7
1977	0.6	17.0	46.8	17.6
1978	0.8	15.4	35.0	13.3
Outward orientation				
1983	1.1	15.1	35.6	15.9
1988	4.3	20.4	35.6	19.2
1990	8.4	22.5	35.4	22.4

Source: State Planning Organization, Support Studies for the Fifth and Sixth Development Plans, and 1991 Annual Program. 1972–83 and 1988–90 data are at constant 1983 and 1988 prices, respectively.
[a] Export propensity: ratio of exports to gross output. Import penetration: ratio of imports to (gross output − exports + imports).

phase), but dropped to 6 per cent in the late 1970s. In turn, import penetration increased from approximately 15 per cent in 1972 to 18 per cent in 1977. The latter episode is an outstanding example of foreign-financed inward orientation with negative import substitution, which proved to be an unsustainable policy phase. The import compression associated with the 1978–80 debt crisis reduced import penetration in total manufacturing, and particularly so in the investment goods subsector.

In the initial phases of outward orientation of the 1980s, the recovery of export propensities was rapid while import penetration remained at the initial levels. From 1983 to 1988, export propensities and import penetration showed significant rises in the consumption and intermediate goods subsectors.

It appears that Turkey's export-led industrial expansion during 1983–8 was also connected with increased import intensity in manufacturing. The adverse impact of this development on the external balance was offset by invisible earnings and lower prices of energy imports after 1986. Furthermore, we see that exchange rate appreciation in 1989–90 weakened export propensities in intermediate and investment goods subsectors, with an unfavourable impact on export diversification.

Revealed comparative advantage

Table 14.9 gives a classification of manufactured exports and imports at the 26-industry level of disaggregation for the 1987–9 period. These twenty-six industries are categorized into five major groups, which are differentiated on the basis of their presumed source of competitiveness as suggested by OECD (1990). Following the methodology of the OECD, Table 14.9 gives our estimates for revealed comparative advantage (RCA), where the RCA measure is the logarithmic value of the ratio of a particular industry's export/import ratio to the aggregate export/import ratio for the manufacturing sector as a whole. Hence, a positive (negative) RCA value presumably reflects the relative degree of comparative advantage (disadvantage) of a particular industry.

As shown in Table 14.9, exports originating from three industries – textiles and clothing, food processing, and iron and steel – constituted nearly 70 per cent of total manufactured exports in 1987–9. The export share of textiles and clothing is about 40 per cent, which is the largest among the twenty-six industries reported in the table. The industries with more than 1 per cent export shares having positive RCA values are labour-intensive textiles and clothing, and furniture, scale-intensive ceramics and glass, rubber and plastics, and iron and steel, and resource-intensive food processing and petroleum refining.

In retrospect, it seems that Turkey relied heavily on labour-intensive textiles and clothing in her export expansion, while other developing countries (notably Korea and Taiwan) were lowering the share of textiles in their labour-intensive manufactured exports (OECD, 1990: Table 32). A further analysis by OECD (1991) indicates that the mismatch between the mix of Turkey's exports and mix of OECD import demand tended to rise in the 1980s. The challenging task for the 1990s is to diversify Turkey's manufactured exports with a larger and more focused emphasis on skill-intensive differentiated goods, and certain scale-intensive industries such as industrial chemicals and transport equipment, for which the revealed comparative disadvantage declined in the 1980s (OECD, 1990).

Factor allocation and factor productivity

Factor allocation

Estimates for the sectoral mix of value added, labour and capital stock are given in Table 14.10. The labour reallocation toward manufacturing seems to be much more extensive in 1968–78 than in 1978–88. Within manufacturing, an employment rise from 1978 to 1988 is notable in the consumption and intermediate goods subsectors, which exhibited a rise in export propensity as discussed earlier.

Table 14.9 Structure of manufactured trade and revealed comparative advantage (RCA)ᵃ, Turkey

	1987–9 average (%)		
Industries	Exports	Imports	RCA
A. Resource-intensive (RI)			
1. Food, beverages, tobacco	8.1	6.1	1.09
2. Leather	0.4	0.6	−0.30
3. Forest products, pulp	0.5	2.0	−1.42
4. Petrol refineries	2.8	2.4	0.12
5. Other non-metallic	0.7	1.3	−0.62
6. Non-ferrous	1.8	3.6	−0.68
7. Other (RI)	–	0.3	−1.57
Subtotal (RI)	24.3	16.3	0.41
B. Labour-Intensive (LI)			
8. Textiles, clothing, shoes	38.5	2.4	2.79
9. Furniture	0.1	–	1.75
10. Metal products	1.9	7.3	−1.32
11. Other (LI)	0.2	0.4	−0.73
Subtotal (LI)	40.7	10.1	1.39
C. Scale-intensive (SI)			
12. Paper products, printing	0.6	0.5	0.12
13. Industrial chemicals	8.6	18.9	−0.79
14. Rubber, plastics	1.5	0.6	0.90
15. Ceramics, glass	1.9	0.4	1.57
16. Iron and steel	11.5	10.7	0.07
17. Transport equipment	1.5	5.6	−1.26
Subtotal (SI)	25.6	36.7	−0.36
D. Differentiated goods (DG)			
18. Agricultural machinery	0.3	0.4	−0.32
19. Metal working machinery	0.5	1.7	−1.17
20. Special industrial machinery	2.1	9.7	−1.56
21. Other non-electrical machinery	1.4	7.2	−1.66
22. Electrical machinery, appliances	2.9	9.5	−1.19
23. Optical goods, clocks	–	0.7	−2.80
Subtotal (DG)	7.2	29.2	−1.40
E. Science-based (SB)			
24. Special chemicals	2.1	4.2	−0.70
25. Professional equipment	0.1	1.7	−2.48
26. Aircraft	–	1.9	−6.43
Subtotal (SB)	2.2	7.8	−1.26
Total (%)	100.0	100.0	
Total (billion $)	9.8	11.2	

Source: The author's estimates based on trade data provided by the Undersecretariat of Treasury and Foreign Trade.
ᵃ RCA is measured by $\log((E_i/M_i)/(\Sigma E_i/\Sigma M_i))$, where E_i and M_i are exports and imports of commodity group (i).

Table 14.10 Factor allocation and GDP by major sectors, Turkey, 1968–88

	1968	1978	1988
A. GDP (% of total at 1968 factor cost)			
Agriculture	30.7	22.7	21.5
Energy, mining	2.9	4.8	4.7
Manufacturing	17.1	19.3	21.0
Services	49.3	53.2	52.8
B. Employment (% of total)			
Agriculture	67.7	55.3	50.6
Energy, mining	1.5	1.9	2.1
Manufacturing	9.8	12.3	13.1
Consumption goods	4.9	4.7	5.4
Intermediate goods	2.5	4.1	4.6
Investment goods	2.4	3.5	3.1
Services	21.0	30.5	34.2
C. Capital stock (% of total)			
Agriculture	17.7	13.0	10.5
Energy, mining	13.4	12.3	16.5
Manufacturing	18.2	28.3	25.0
Consumption goods	5.3	7.5	6.0
Intermediate goods	10.3	16.7	15.2
Investment goods	2.6	4.1	3.8
Services	50.7	46.4	48.0

Sources: GDP data is from the State Institute of Statistics; factor allocation is derived from Maraslioglu and Tiktik (1991).

The inter-period shifts in the allocation of capital are sharper and more significant. The share of manufacturing in total capital stock was 18 per cent in 1968, increased to 28 per cent in 1978, but declined to 25 per cent in 1988. During 1978–88, the capital shares of energy and services increased significantly. It is evident that Turkey's post-1980 strategy focused on the more productive use of manufacturing capital stock, while emphasizing import-substituting energy (mainly hydropower) projects and other infra-structure systems in services (notably communications and transport).

Labour and capital productivity

The observations on factor allocation over time are reinforced by the analysis of factor productivity changes. Table 14.11 displays estimates for the growth rates of gross output, factor inputs and partial factor pro-ductivities for three subsectors in manufacturing, covering small as well as large private and public firms. The time periods (1968–77, 1977–80 and 1980–8) correspond to inward-oriented, debt crisis, and outward-oriented phases respectively. The estimates in Table 14.11 are based on semi-official time series that are broadly consistent with the empirical base of the

Table 14.11 Growth of manufacturing output, factor inputs, and productivities, Turkey, 1968–88 (% per year)

Industries	1968–77	1977–80	1980–8
Consumption goods			
Gross output	8.0	1.3	5.3
Labour input	2.7	−0.5	3.1
Capital stock	8.6	4.6	1.0
Labour productivity	5.2	1.7	2.1
Capital productivity	−0.5	−3.2	4.3
Intermediate goods			
Gross output	10.4	−1.9	9.4
Labour input	7.1	−1.6	3.8
Capital stock	10.0	8.1	1.8
Labour productivity	3.0	−0.3	5.4
Capital productivity	0.4	−9.2	7.5
Investment goods			
Gross output	11.2	−6.8	6.7
Labour input	4.3	−1.5	4.2
Capital stock	9.3	10.7	1.8
Labour productivity	6.7	−5.4	2.4
Capital productivity	1.7	−15.8	4.9
Total manufacturing			
Gross output	9.6	−1.7	7.4
Labour input	4.4	−1.1	3.6
Capital stock	9.5	7.5	1.6
Labour productivity	5.0	−0.6	3.6
Capital productivity	0.1	−8.6	5.7
Capital/labour ratio	4.8	8.7	−2.0

Source: Estimates based on Maraslioglu and Tiktik (1991).

official five-year plans and recent annual programmes. Thus, our partial factor productivity data are more credible and robust than the estimates for total factor productivity growth in large manufacturing which are reviewed on p. 476.

During the inward-oriented phase of 1968–77, manufacturing output increased rapidly at 9.6 per cent per year, sustained by a 9.5 per cent annual growth of the capital stock, and a 4.5 per cent growth rate of the labour input. The implied rise in the capital/labour ratio reflects the shift in domestic demand to higher income-elasticity subsectors, which typically feature capital-intensive technologies (Celasun, 1983). During the debt crisis of 1977–80, capital productivity fell sharply, mainly in the investment and intermediate goods subsectors, which experienced severe shortages of imported inputs.

During the outward-oriented phase of 1980–8, total manufacturing output increased at 7.4 per cent per year, despite the pronounced slowdown in the growth of the capital stock to less than 2 per cent per year. An unprecedented growth rate of capital productivity (at 7.5 per cent per year) in intermediate goods pulled capital productivity increases in total manufacturing to an impressively high level (5.7 per cent per year). Labour productivity growth was also high in intermediate goods, but quite low in the consumption goods subsector, which made a large contribution to employment expansion.

In the 1980s, the sharp rise in manufacturing capital productivity definitely reflects the initial conditions of low capacity utilization, but also points to the benefits of greater trade orientation. At the aggregate level, the switch to an outward orientation provided a larger role for exports as a demand-side source of growth, and allowed the resumption of imported inputs on which domestic production depended. At the firm level, higher interest rates and pressures for competitiveness induced a greater emphasis on capital efficiency. It may further be hypothesized that a greater trade orientation provided scope for the diversification of imported inputs with a favourable impact on factor productivity as emphasized by Dornbusch (1990).

Total factor productivity growth in large manufacturing firms

Early studies by Krueger and Tuncer (1982), and Nishimuzu and Robinson (1984) provide estimates for total factor productivity (TFP) growth in large Turkish manufacturing firms (defined as those with ten or more workers) from the mid-1960s to mid-1970s. These studies report significant trade-policy effects on historical TFP performance, with a positive export expansion impact and negative import tightening impact.

Table 14.12 assembles the findings of the major studies on TFP growth in large Turkish manufacturing firms. The TFP estimates for recent periods show a wide variation, possibly due to varying capital stock estimates and different price deflators used for outputs and material inputs.

However, both Uygur (1990) and Foroutan (1990) find negative TFP growth during the debt crisis period (the late 1970s), and positive recovery in the 1980s. In general, Foroutan's orders of magnitudes for post-1980 TFP growth seem to be more consistent with the factor productivity estimates discussed earlier. Foroutan reports that TFP growth in the private sector was favourably affected by the rise in import penetration. An important conclusion emerging from the Foroutan study is that the major explanatory factor for TFP changes is output growth, which may reflect scale effects as well as shifts in capacity utilization.

Table 14.12 TFP growth in large manufacturing, Turkey (% per year)

	Large manufacturing		
	Public	Private	Total
Krueger and Tuncer (1982)			
1963–76	2.65	1.04	2.1
1963–7	–	–	3.2
1967–70	–	–	1.31
1970–3	–	–	2.51
1973–6	–	–	–1.18
Nishimuzu and Robinson (1984)			
1963–76	–	–	1.33
Yildirim (1989)			
1963–7	7.01	3.65	5.94
1968–72	2.23	1.48	1.45
1973–7	2.64	1.15	1.61
1978–83	–3.14	–3.63	–3.93
Uygur (1990)			
1965–76	2.0	1.1	1.4
1976–81	0.0	–3.5	–2.4
1981–8	1.0	2.2	1.7
Ozmucur and Karatas (1990, table 1)			
1973–9	–4.2	–1.5	–2.1
1979–82	9.9	0.5	4.1
1982–5	–3.3	–2.2	–2.7
1979–85	2.8	–0.8	0.6
Foroutan (1990, table 19)			
1976–8	–0.5	1.7	–
1979–80	–18.1	–12.1	–
1981–5	5.7	3.4	–

Industrial organization and non-trade policies

Size structure, firm concentration and price-cost margins

In 1985, the share of small enterprises (with less than ten workers) in total manufacturing stood at 94 per cent for number of establishments, 13 per cent for value added, and 34 per cent for employment. Manufacturing establishments with less than fifty workers generated 46 per cent of total employment, but only 20 per cent of value added. Within the so-called large manufacturing firms (with more than ten workers), the share of private (public) enterprises in total value added was 60 per cent (40 per cent), and in total employment 67 per cent (33 per cent).[7]

It is generally observed that the role of public enterprises and small private establishments in the post-1980 export boom was not significant (Senses, 1989b, 1990). The estimated share of small enterprises in total exports is 8 per cent for the year 1988 (OECD, 1991). The export drive was spearheaded mainly by large private enterprises with a small contribution from firms with officially authorized foreign direct investment (Akder, 1990).[8]

To throw light on the impact of the post–1980 trade deregulation on industrial structure and performance, Katircioglu (1990) provides an analysis of large private manufacturing firms in seventy-one four-digit industries for the benchmark years 1975, 1980 and 1985. Katircioglu shows that the average four-firm concentration ratio (weighted by number of workers) declined from 37 per cent in 1975 to 32 per cent in 1980, and further to 28 per cent in 1985. Concentration has a positive and strong effect on price-cost margins (PCM) in all benchmark years. The effect of import penetration on PCM seems to be weakly positive in 1975 and 1980, but becomes significantly negative in 1985, possibly reflecting the impact of the post–1980 removal of non-tariff barriers on imports.[9]

Non-trade policies for industrial promotion

The assessments presented on pp. 458–70 bring out the policymakers' central concern with export-led recovery, macroeconomic adjustment and liberalization in the 1980s. The post–1980 administrations did not favour official in-depth work on a formal and comprehensive industrial strategy. Nevertheless, the government has attempted to make use of a number of non-trade policy instruments to promote industrial restructuring and adjustment. The principal ones used were the following: (i) issue of investment certificates which provided direct subsidies, concessional credits and tax allowances; (ii) encouragement of foreign direct investment (FDI); (iii) privatization of state enterprises to a limited degree; (iv) promotional schemes, including organized sites, for small and medium enterprises (SMEs); (v) extrabudgetary funds for high-tech defence industries in cooperation with FDI and the private sector; (vi) *ad hoc* programmes for labour training; and (vii) extrabudgetary funds to subsidize the purchase of domestically produced machinery and support industrial R&D.[10]

Since its establishment in the late 1960s, use of investment certificates has been highly popular with the private sector, and has generated lively rent-seeking activity. The eligibility criteria have been related mainly to the scale characteristics of investment projects in designated sectors and to regional locations. The share of manufacturing in the total issue of investment certificates was at 85–90 per cent in 1978–80, dropped to around 40 per cent in the mid-1980s, but began to increase in the late 1980s.[11]

Although the underlying legal framework has been highly liberal, the contribution of FDI to Turkish industrialization has historically remained quite moderate. The government's more enthusiastic FDI stance, coupled with external financial liberalization, has started to pay off, however, in recent years. From 1985 to 1990, the annually authorized FDI increased from US$235 to 1,784 million, accompanied by a rapid rise in realized inflows as well (Uygur, 1991; OECD, 1991). Unlike earlier historical periods, however, the recent FDI activity has not been heavily concentrated in manufacturing. Instead there has been a notable rise in the share of services (tourism, banking, etc.). This is consistent with our earlier observation as to the dampened nature of manufacturing investment in the late 1980s. Despite active administrative work on financial liberalization, FDI authorizations and issue of investment certificates, the share of manufacturing in total economy-wide investment fell from 38 per cent in 1973–7 to 19 per cent in 1984–8. Meanwhile, the capacity utilization rate in total manufacturing increased from 50 per cent levels in 1980 to 78 per cent in 1990.[12] These trends point to the possible emergence of capacity bottlenecks in sustaining industrial expansion in the 1990s.

CONCLUSIONS AND PROSPECTS

Summary and conclusions

The present study has provided a broad evaluation of Turkey's trade and industrial experience in the 1980s in the light of initial conditions and country-specific macroeconomic circumstances. In the earlier periods of the 1960s and early 1970s, it was quite justifiable to assess developing country industrial performance by focusing almost entirely on the effects of trade policy changes, mainly because macroeconomic conditions were quite stable and manageable. Turkey's recent experience illustrates that the macroeconomic policy mix and stance have a close bearing on the choice and efficacy of trade and industrialization policies after the country gets into a debt crisis.

The overall emphasis of the post-1980 Turkish adjustment was on export expansion, which had to be based on manufacturing productive capacities in view of the inhospitable external environment for primary exports. Given the strategic choice between complete fiscal stabilization first and export promotion and liberalization later, and export promotion first with gradual liberalization and fiscal adjustment, the policymakers evidently preferred the latter option. The latter strategy carried considerable risks, but paid off in terms of export-led growth and regained creditworthiness in the international capital markets. The chosen strategy eventually produced, however, macroeconomic instability in the late 1980s. The choice of the former strategic option with a more relaxed emphasis on exports would have also involved substantial risks, possibly prolonging the reliance on import compression with an unfavourable impact on output recovery. Thus, the *management of policy risks* emerges as a critical issue in country adjustment, which merits more focused analytical research in the future.[13]

479

Unlike much of the earlier research on Turkey, the present study attaches a great deal of importance to the policy-effectiveness of the initial 'big bang' on relative factor and product prices. Besides shifting incentives toward tradables production, the realignment of relative prices redistributed real income from low-savers to high-savers, including – surprisingly – the public sector with its vast holdings of state enterprises, employing a large labour force. Turkey's post-1980 regressive income redistribution lowered domestic absorption and made room for export expansion. Real wage reductions rendered feasible the sharp and steady depreciation of the exchange rate (until 1989), and improved 'price competitiveness' of manufactured and service exports. At the enterprise level, real wage restraint allowed private firms to adjust to a higher cost of financing with less pain under financial liberalization. A key point that emerges from our emphasis on relative price changes, income redistribution and demand management is that the effects of trade policy changes should be evaluated in the broader context of shifts in macroeconomic adjustment patterns.[14]

The analysis of factor allocation and productivity patterns shows that the post-1980 adjustment increased the GDP and employment shares of manufacturing, but notably lowered the share of this sector in the total capital stock. This pattern for manufacturing implies high rates of capital productivity growth in the 1980s as confirmed by a more disaggregated look at the growth of output, factor input and factor productivity at the subsectoral level.

Prospects

The present study brings out two sets of policy issues surrounding the sustainability of Turkish industrialization in the 1990s. The first set involves the issues connected with macroeconomic stabilization subject to an *acceptable incomes policy*. The second set relates to the design of a *coherent industrial policy framework*, which facilitates efficient restructuring and capital formation in manufacturing with an eye to enhanced competitiveness in the 1990s.

After the 1989 general elections, the domestic political process has become definitely more open and contestable, and generated social pressures to redress the distributional imbalances accumulated in the 1980s. After liberalizing capital flows in the external account, the authorities allowed a sharp rise in external liabilities, which caused a substantial appreciation in the real exchange rate. Lower domestic prices of imports somewhat dampened the inflationary pressures. This setting provided scope for a real wage rise in 1989–91. However, the large increase in the government's wage bill has further widened the fiscal deficit.

Against the backdrop of the post-1989 distributional reversal in favour of labour and agriculturalists, the government's options for fiscal correction appear to be more limited in the early 1990s than they were in the early 1980s. While searching for additional foreign resources, the policymakers are likely to strive to come up with a politically acceptable mix of privatization, tax hikes and expenditure cuts, perhaps with the help of a more formal incomes policy to restrain additional wage claims in the public sector.

In conjunction with a credible macroeconomic stabilization effort, a large step needs to be taken toward the design of a policy frame for industrial promotion, involving an efficient mix of trade and non-trade policies. The import tariff system needs to be further rationalized and stabilized to avoid adverse effects of arbitrary reversals in import taxes and fund levies. The non-trade incentive system needs overhauling to provide more selectivity in government interventions to upgrade labour skills and to promote skill-intensive industries, the comparative disadvantage of which seems to have a declining trend.

NOTES

1 See Dornbusch (1990) for the identification of recent Turkish adjustment as a 'restructuring success'.
2 See, for example, the recently published books by Celasun and Rodrik (1989) and Aricanli and Rodrik (1990). For further macroeconomic assessments, see Boratav (1986); Taylor (1988: 108–9); Rodrik (1990); Ekinci (1990); Senses and Yamada (1990); Uygur (1990, 1991); and OECD (1990, 1991).
3 The discussion in this section draws on the ongoing work of Celasun and Tansel of METU on saving-investment behaviour in Turkey.
4 For the analysis of the inflation tax base in Turkey, see Anand et al. (1990), Rodrik (1990), and OECD (1991); Akyuz (1990) and Boeri (1991) provide assessments of Turkey's financial adjustment.
5 Turkey's trade policy changes are documented in varying detail by Togan et al. (1987); Baysan and Blitzer (1990); Balkir (1990); Uygur (1991); and Olgun and Togan (1991).
6 See OECD (1991) for provisional estimates of trade performance in 1990.
7 In 1985, the number of establishments stood at 194,000. See State Planning Organization (1989) and Kazgan (1987) on size structures in manufacturing. Kazgan (1989) draws attention to the relatively small size of domestic firms and their fragile organizational structure in the context of Turkey's possible integration with the EC.
8 However, if a wider definition applies to small and medium-sized enterprises (SMEs), their contribution to the export boom becomes more notable. A firm-level survey by Kaytaz (1990) classifies establishments with 0–99 workers as SMEs and finds that 30 per cent of SMEs in his sample (from the Istanbul-Kocaeli region) are producing partly for export markets, mainly in textiles and metal product industries. In a sector-specific study on clothing, Kirim (1990a) points to the need for a sectoral consortium to coordinate design and marketing efforts. See also Kirim (1990b) for the organization of technology aspects in Turkish manufacturing.
9 Ozmucur (1990b) finds a positive correlation between TFP growth and profit/sales ratios in the private sector, but a negative correlation in the public sector.

The author concludes that high rates of increase in state enterprise prices played a significant role in generating high rates of profit in the public sector in the post–1980 period.

10 For a brief discussion of some of these policy instruments, including SME promotion, see OECD (1991). Kjellstrom (1990) provided an assessment of the Turkish privatization experience in the 1980s.

11 Based on estimates provided by the State Planning Organization.

12 Figures for capacity utilization rates are from various issues of the State Planning organization, *Main Economic Indicators*.

13 See Rodrik (1989) for a conceptual analysis of policy issues connected with structural adjustment programmes.

14 See Boeri (1991) and OECD (1991) on financial issues, emphasizing the rising share of short-term debt in total financial debt of private manufacturing firms. The favourable employment effect of real wage flexibility (under trade reforms) is also supported by counterfactual policy model simulations reported in Celasun and Rodrik (1989).

15 For new research perspectives on trade and non-trade policies for industrialization, see Helleiner (1992).

REFERENCES

Akder, H. (1990) *Industrial Organization, Exports and Turkey's Place in the Middle East*, Istanbul: Friedrich Ebert Foundation.

Akyuz, Y. (1990) 'Financial System and Policies in Turkey' in T. Aricanli and D. Rodrik (eds) *The Political Economy of Turkey*, London: Macmillan, pp. 98–131.

Anand, R., Chhibber, A. and van Wijnbergen S. (1990) 'External Balance and Growth in Turkey: Can They Be Reconciled?' in T. Aricanli and D. Rodrik (eds) *The Political Economy of Turkey*, London: Macmillan, pp. 157–83.

Aricanli, T. and Rodrik, D. (eds) (1990) *The Political Economy of Turkey*, London: Macmillan.

Arslan, I. and van Wijnbergen, S. (1990) 'Turkey: Export Miracle or Accounting Trick?', World Bank Working Paper WPS 370.

Balkir, C. (1993) 'Turkish Trade Strategy in the 1980s', in A. Eralp, M. Tunay and B. Yesilada (eds) *The Socio-Economic Transformation of Turkey Since 1980*, Praeger Publications, forthcoming.

Baysan, T. and Blitzer, C. (1990) 'Turkey's Trade Liberalization in the 1980s and Prospects for its Sustainability' in T. Aricanli and D. Rodrik (eds) *The Political Economy of Turkey*, London: Macmillan, pp. 9–36.

Boeri, T. (1991) 'Problems in Implementing Structural Reforms in Developing Countries: The Experience of Turkey in the 1980s', Centro Studi Luca d'Agliano, Development Studies Working Paper no. 35, Queen Elizabeth House.

Boratav, K. (1986) *Stabilization and Adjustment Policies and Programmes: Turkey*, Helsinki: WIDER.

Celasun, M. (1983) *Sources of Industrial Growth and Structural Change: The Case of Turkey*, World Bank Staff Working Paper no. 614.

—— (1989) 'Income Distribution and Employment Aspects of Turkey's Post–1980 Adjustment', *METU Studies in Development* 1(3–4): 1–32.

—— and Rodrik, D. (1989) 'Debt, Adjustment and Growth: Turkey,' in J. Sachs and S. Collins (eds) *Developing Country Debt and Economic Performance: Country Studies*, vol 3, Book IV, Chicago: University of Chicago Press, pp. 615–808.

Chenery, H. B. and Syrquin, M. (1975) *Patterns of Development: 1950–1970*, London; Oxford University Press.

Chenery, H. B. and Taylor, L. (1968) 'Development Patterns: Among Countries and Over Time', *Review of Economics and Statistics* 50(4): 391–416.

Chenery, H. B., Robinson, S. and Syrquin, M. (1986) *Industrialization and Growth: A Comparative Study*, London: Oxford University Press.

Conway, P. (1988), 'The Impact of Uncertainty on Private Investment in Turkey', Department of Economics, University of North Carolina.

Dornbusch, R. (1990) 'Policies to Move from Stabilization to Growth', in *Proceedings of the World Bank Conference on Development Economics*, Washington, DC: World Bank.

Ekinci, N. (1990) 'Macroeconomic Developments in Turkey: 1980–1988', *METU Studies in Development* 17(1–2): 73–114.

Foroutan, F. (1990) 'Foreign Trade and its Relation to Competition and Productivity in Turkish Industry', World Bank-CECTP, Washington, DC.

Helleiner, G. K. (ed.) (1992), *Trade Policy, Industrialization and Development*, Oxford: Clarendon Press.

Katircioglu, E. (1990) 'Competitive Structure and Performance of Turkish Private Manufacturing Industry, 1975–1985', Friedrich Ebert Foundation, Istanbul.

Kaytaz, M. (1990) 'The Role of Small and Medium Industries in Development: A Case Study of Selected Sectors in Turkey', *Journal of Economics and Administrative Sciences* 4(2): 53–68.

Kazgan, G. (1987) *An Overview of the Chemicals and Machinery Industries in Turkey*, Istanbul: Friedrich Ebert Foundation.

—— (1989) *Summary Report of the Manufacturing Sector with Special Reference to Turkey's Integration with the EC*, Istanbul: Friedrich Ebert Foundation.

Kirim, A. (1990a) *Turkiye Hazir Giyim Sektorunun Yeniden Yapilanma Gerekleri (Restructuring Requirements in the Turkish Clothing Sector)*, Istanbul: Friedrich Ebert Foundation.

—— (1990b) *Turkiye Imalat Sanayiinde Teknolojik Degisim (Technological Change in Turkish Manufacturing)*, Ankara: Turkish Union of Chambers.

Kjellstrom, S., 1990, 'Privatization in Turkey', World Bank PRE Working Paper WPS 532.

Krueger, A. O. (1974), *Foreign Trade Regimes and Economic Development, Turkey*, New York: Columbia University Press.

—— and Tuncer, B. (1982) 'Growth of Factor Productivity in Turkish Manufacturing Industries', *Journal of Development Economics* 11(3): 307–25.

Lewis, J. and Urata, S. (1983) 'Turkey: Recent Economic Performance and Medium-Term Prospects, 1979–1990', World Bank Staff Working Paper no. 602.

Maraslioglu, H. and Tiktik, A. (1991) 'Turkiye'de Uretim, Sermaye ve Istihdam, 1968–1988' ('Output, Capital and Employment in Turkey, 1968–1988'), Publication no. DPT: 2271, IPB: 428 State Planning Organization, Ankara.

Milanovic, B. (1986) 'Export Incentives and Turkish Manufacturing Exports, 1980–1984', World Bank Staff Working Paper no. 768.

Nishimizu, M. and Robinson, S. (1984) 'Trade Policies and Productivity Change in Semi-Industrialized Countries', *Journal of Development Economics* 1: 177–206.

OECD (1990) (1991), *Turkey, Economic Survey*, Paris: OECD.

Olgun, H. and Togan, S. (1991) 'Trade Liberalization and Structure of Protection in Turkey in the 1980s: A Quantitative Analysis', *Weltwirtshaftliches Archiv* 127(1): 152–70.

Onis, Z. (1990), 'Organization of Export-Oriented Industrialization: The Turkish

Foreign Trade Companies in Comparative Perspective', Bogazici University, Research Paper ISS/EC 90–14, Istanbul.

Ozhan, G. and Tanrikulu, K. (1989) 'Turkiye Sanayiinde Koruma Oranlari' ('Protection Rates in Turkish Industry'), State Planning Organization (DPT), Ankara, IPB-UVPD.

Ozmucur, S. (1990a) 'Social Aspects of Turkish Liberalization, 1980–1988', Bogazici University, Research Paper ISS/EC 90–04, Istanbul.

—— (1990b) 'Profitability and Total Factor Productivity in Turkey, 1973–1988', Bogazici University, Research Paper ISS/EC 90–10, Istanbul.

Ozmucur, S. and Karatas, C. (1990) 'Total Factor Productivity in Turkish Manufacturing', *Journal of Economics and Administrative Sciences* 4(2).

Rodrik, D. (1989) 'How Should Structural Adjustment Programs be Designed?', *World Development* 18(7): 933–47.

—— (1990) *Premature Liberalization, Incomplete Stabilization: The Ozal Decade in Turkey*, NBER Working Paper no. 3300.

Senses, F. (1989a) 'The Nature and Main Characteristics of Recent Turkish Growth in Exports of Manufactures,' *The Developing Economies* XXVII(1): 19–33.

—— (1989b) *1980 Sonrasi Ekonomi Politikalari Isiginda Turkiye'de Sanayilesme (Industrialization in Turkey in the Light of Post–1980 Economic Policies)*, Ankara: Verso A.S.

—— (1990) 'An Assessment of the Pattern of Turkish Manufactured Export Growth in the 1980s and its Prospects' in T. Aricanli and D. Rodrik (eds) *The Political Economy of Turkey*, London: Macmillan, pp. 60–77.

—— and Yamada, T. (1990) *Stabilization and Adjustment Program in Turkey*, Tokyo: Institute of Developing Economies, JRP Series 85.

State Planning Organization (1989), 'Kucuk Sanayi, VI. Bes Yillik O.I.K. Raporu' ('Small Industry, Special Committee Report for the Sixth Development Plan'), DPT Yayin no. 2169–OIK 340, Ankara.

Tansel, A. and Togan, S. (1987) 'Price and Income Effects in Turkish Foreign Trade', *Weltwirtshaftliches Archiv* 123(3): 521–34.

Taylor, L. (1988) *Varieties of Stabilization Experience: Towards Sensible Macroeconomics in the Third World*, Oxford: Clarendon Press.

Togan, S., Olgun H. and Akder, H. (1987) *Report on Developments in External Economic Relations of Turkey*, Ankara: Foreign Trade Association of Turkey.

Turel, O. (1987) 'Turkiye'de Sanayinin Gelisimine Genel Bakis' ('An Overview of Industrial Development in Turkey'), *1987 Sanayi Kongresi Bildirileri* (*Proceedings of 1987 Industrial Congress*), Chamber of Mechanical Engineering, Ankara, Publication no. 127, pp. 1–22.

Uygur, E. (1990) *Policy, Productivity, Growth and Employment in Turkey, 1960–1989*, Geneva: International Labour Office, MIES 90(4).

—— (1991) 'Policy, Trade and Growth in Turkey: 1970–1990', Expert Group Meeting on Trade Policies in Developing Countries (UNCTAD), Antalya.

Yagci, F. (1984) 'Protection and Incentives in Turkish Manufacturing', World Bank Staff Working Paper no. 660.

Yildirim E. (1984) 'Total Factor Productivity Growth in Turkish Manufacturing Industry Between 1963–83: An Analysis', *METU Studies in Development* 16(3–4): 65–96.

AFRICA

15

TRADE AND MACROECONOMIC POLICIES AND THE INDUSTRIALIZATION EXPERIENCE IN KENYA IN THE 1970s AND 1980s

Francis M. Mwega

INTRODUCTION

Kenya is a typical, small, non-oil country with an average GDP per capita of only $350 and an estimated population of 24 million (1990). The country has, however, received some attention in the Sub-Saharan Africa development literature because of its comparatively good macroeconomic performance which has been achieved within a relatively *laissez-faire* framework. The country, for example, experienced a faster average annual growth in GNP per capita and a lower rate of inflation than in Sub-Saharan Africa in general. However, it experienced a smaller expansion in merchandise trade in the 1960s and 1970s although it did not experience as drastic a collapse in merchandise exports and imports as Sub-Saharan Africa (SSA) in the 1980s.[1]

The country performed best during the first decade of independence. In 1969–73 for example, the real GDP grew at 8.3 per cent while average domestic prices rose by only 4–5 per cent per annum. The external payment balances were also healthy despite a mini balance of payments crisis in 1971. The foreign exchange reserves exceeded the legally stipulated four months' worth of imports and the current account deficit was modest and more than compensated for by net long-term capital inflows to produce a positive basic balance.

Many factors accounted for this generally good macroeconomic performance. These include large (fixed) investment and savings which comprised about 22–25 per cent and 18 per cent of GDP respectively and a prudent fiscal policy. The budget deficit and government borrowing from the banking system were relatively modest at 4.9 per cent and 0.7 per cent of GDP

487

respectively. Domestic credit and money supply did expand rapidly, but they were not too inflationary nor did they severely weaken the balance of payments because of the strong economic growth that increased money demand while most (82 per cent) of the credit accrued to the private sector, facilitating production.

Since then the economy has performed less well, registering an average real growth rate of about 4.5 per cent while the average rate of inflation increased to about 10 per cent in 1974–90. The balance of payments situation has also deteriorated. Except for the 1974–8 period when the country experienced an improvement in the terms of trade following an increase in the prices of coffee and tea, foreign exchange reserves were much less than the legally stipulated four months' worth of imports, declining to only 1.5 months' worth in 1989–90. The current account deficit was large (about 6 per cent of GDP) and, except in 1984–8, was not compensated for by long-term net capital inflows, so that the basic balance was negative, accounting for about –3.7 per cent of GDP in 1989–90.

The decline in economic performance was due to various domestic and external factors. While investment and saving rates remained high, (implying an increase in capital costs and/or a decline in capital productivity) there was a marked relaxation of fiscal discipline. The share of current government revenue increased from 18 per cent in 1972 to 24 per cent of GDP in 1990 and that of expenditure from 21.0 per cent to almost 40 per cent respectively. Consequently, the overall budget deficit expanded substantially, especially in the late 1970s and early 1980s, resulting in increased government borrowing from the banking system, and a crowding-out of credit to the private sector. Among exogenous factors that contributed substantially to the poor performance of the economy were the various negative shocks that the economy experienced. These included the two oil shocks of 1973 and 1979, which hit Kenya very hard with fuel imports comprising about 10 per cent of total imports in the early 1970s; the collapse of the East Africa Community (EAC) in 1977 and the temporary closure of the border with Tanzania, severely curtailing exports of manufactures (total exports to these countries declined from 29 per cent of Kenya's total in 1969–73 to 10.6 per cent in 1979–83); the military coup attempt of 1982 that reduced business confidence and caused some capital flight; and droughts (the worst in the country's recorded history in 1984) which curtailed agricultural output.

The country experienced a serious decline in the terms of trade, of nearly 35 per cent, between the mid-1970s and 1989–90. As a consequence of the resulting pressures on the balance of payments, there was severe import compression, especially in the first half of the 1980s when the volume of imports declined by nearly 10 per cent following the second oil price crisis of 1979. There was an improvement in the situation in 1984–8 due to an increase in coffee export prices in 1986 following a drought in Brazil, while the situation deteriorated in 1989–90 when the volume of imports declined by 1.5 per cent per annum. It is ironic that the poor performance occurred as the government borrowed heavily externally and pursued stabilization and structural adjustment policies. As a result of the heavy external borrowing, the country incurred a heavy debt burden. By 1989, Kenya had an external debt of US$5.7 billion, of which about 70 per cent was long-term public or publicly-guaranteed credit (World Bank, 1991). The debt service charges increased from 4.0 per cent in 1974 to about a third of the export earnings in 1990, severely constraining the development process.

The rest of this chapter is organized as follows: the first section discusses the trade structure and performance in Kenya, and is followed by a section tracing the evolution of trade policies. The next section examines the implementation of trade policies in the 1980s, following which there is a discussion of the role of the other policies and institutions important in the industrialization process. The penultimate section evaluates the relationship between trade/macro policies and the industrialization process. An evaluation and summary is found in the final section.

TRADE STRUCTURE AND PERFORMANCE

The Kenyan economy is very open with the trade ratio (imports plus exports as a proportion of GDP) comprising on average more than 40 per cent in 1969–90, though the ratio fluctuated greatly from period to period. Coffee, tea and petroleum are the dominant commodity exports.[2] Commodity concentration seems to have increased as indicated by the decline in the share of 'non-traditional' commodity exports. These exports individually contribute very little to export earnings, with none contributing more than 5 per cent of total export earnings, although some, like horticultural products, have expanded fast in the 1980s, slightly increasing their shares in total commodity exports. Tourism is an important invisible export and since 1987 has overtaken coffee as the main foreign exchange earner in the country. Manufactured exports account for less than 10 per cent of total commodity export earnings.

The openness of the economy and the heavy reliance on a few primary products means that the country is highly vulnerable to exogenous shocks that influence the volume and the prices that their products face in the international markets. There is therefore a close correlation between the terms of trade and real economic growth.

The main merchandise imports were (Table 15.1) industrial non-food supplies or intermediate inputs; machinery and transport equipment; fuels and lubricants; and food, beverages and other consumer goods. The import-substitution (IS) industrialization strategy pursued in the country had a major influence on the structure of imports. Consumer imports declined

Table 15.1 Composition of imports by broad economic categories, Kenya (%)

	1970	1972	1974	1976	1978	1980	1982	1984	1986	1988
Food and beverages	8.3	9.9	6.6	6.5	5.8	4.3	5.9	11.6	8.7	5.7
Industrial non-food supplies	36.0	34.6	39.9	30.5	27.2	27.3	25.0	26.4	30.5	36.0
Fuels and lubricants	9.3	10.6	21.2	25.5	17.8	33.6	36.9	30.3	17.8	13.9
Machinery and other equipment	14.7	19.1	11.2	17.8	21.1	16.0	17.7	16.9	19.0	23.5
Transport equipment	16.7	14.3	11.6	10.8	19.2	12.6	9.5	10.3	19.4	15.1
Consumer goods nes	11.9	11.0	9.2	8.7	8.4	6.0	4.9	4.3	4.5	5.3
Goods nes	3.0	0.6	0.3	0.2	0.3	–	0.1	0.2	0.1	0.1
	100.0	100.0	100.0	100.0	100.0	100.0	100.0	100.0	100.0	100.0

Source: Statistical Abstract, various issues.
nes: not elsewhere specified.

from an average 25 per cent of total imports in the mid-1960s to about 16 per cent in 1974–90, while the share of intermediate and capital imports rose from 75 per cent to about 84 per cent in 1974–90. With imports now reduced to the 'bare essentials', the demand for imports has become more inelastic, making the economy more vulnerable to unexpected reductions in the supply of foreign exchange.

THE EVOLUTION OF TRADE POLICIES IN KENYA

For about the first decade after independence in 1963, Kenya pursued an import-substitution industrialization strategy. This reflected the prevailing mainstream paradigm which grew out of criticism of the Ricardian comparative advantage theory after the Second World War. The main argument was that the earnings of the primary products that poor countries export are not only highly volatile, making macroeconomic management very difficult, but their terms of trade also tend to have a long-run declining trend.[3] These countries were therefore advised to diversify their economies away from primary products towards the production of industrial products with the help of appropriate trade/macro policies.

The strategy pursued in Kenya was articulated in various publications starting with the first and second five-year Development Plans covering 1966–74. The second plan argued that import-substitution opportunities in the country were not yet exhausted and pledged that the government would continue to pay particular attention to the protection of industries through import tariffs (on goods from outside the EAC), import licensing and quantitative restrictions. It was, however, hoped that the industrialization process would move more deeply rather than concentrate on the more simple manufacturing. An Industrial Protection Committee was established in 1969 to advise on all aspects of industrial protection essential to the development of a 'balanced' industrial sector.

A number of studies were also done in this period on the degree of protection accorded the various industries. Reimer (1970) and Phelps and Wasow (1972) showed that some industries were highly protected and that the system of protection tended to favour finishing touch industries. For example, the latter study indicated that 43 per cent of the sample of consumer goods industries, 36 per cent of intermediate goods industries, and 18 per cent of capital goods industries had negative value added at world prices. This was nevertheless a period when the economy was growing very rapidly and high protection of the industrial sector was not necessary, with import licensing covering only about seventy commodities.

In the 1960s, the economy did not experience a major balance of payments problem, and therefore did not seek high conditionality external finance. The country experienced its first major balance of payments problem in 1971 when there was a drastic rundown of reserves (from thirty to seven weeks' worth of import requirements) following an experiment with expansionary fiscal policies concomitant with a decline in the terms of trade (King, 1979). The government reacted to this crisis by adopting for the first time very restrictive trade policies where some imports were banned, others were placed under quota, and import licensing began to be used extensively for balance of payments support and to protect specific industries. Use of tariffs was, however, still constrained by membership in the EAC.

A number of studies were done at this time highlighting the limitations of the IS industrialization strategy, particularly in ameliorating the balance of payments and in diversifying the economy. Hopcraft (1973) and others put forth the conventional arguments that the domestic market constraint and the import requirements for industrial growth made the growth of industrial exports imperative through an outward-orientation of the industrial structure. The studies advised that while the IS strategy produces a short 'exuberant' period of industrial growth, it is likely eventually to lead to balance of payments problems and other constraints that inhibit sustained industrialization. By encouraging the establishment of a high-cost industrial sector which operates behind a protective wall, it discourages industrial exports by increasing the cost of inputs and by depressing the earnings of the relatively unprotected export-oriented industries. Direct factor earnings repatriated abroad by foreign owned IS industries and the high propensity to use imported inputs would to a large extent offset the savings in foreign exchange. The IS industrialization strategy was therefore anti-export and could exacerbate rather than ameliorate the balance of payments difficulties. According to Hopcraft (1973), if protectionism was not reversed, Kenya would 'increasingly get into a situation of export lethargy, chronic balance of payments disequilibrium, and eventually declining industrialization and growth'. He therefore recommended a liberalization of the trade regime through tariff reforms and the adoption of a market-based product pricing policy; a 'realistic' exchange rate; a value-added tax; and subsidies to industrial exports if the industrial sector was to break from the confines of a small market and to make a contribution to employment, foreign exchange earnings and to the overall growth of the economy. The World Bank (1975) similarly argued that Kenya had completed the first phase of IS industrialization out of which the costlier aspects of the protection policy, such as the establishment of high-cost industries with no clear comparative advantage, were already evident. Though there was some potential for further import substitution in a few specific industries, the Bank study advised that further blanket IS industrialization would inevitably lead to high-cost intermediate and capital inputs for potentially viable exporting industries.

The advice to liberalize the trade regime was heeded by the authorities. In 1973, the system of import controls was partially liberalized with the number of banned import items reduced and the foreign exchange restrictions on about a third of the 300 affected items lifted. There was also a clear change in the trade policies articulated in the third Development Plan (1974–8), which now put some emphasis on export promotion and trade liberalization, and it presented a programme towards the achievement of lower, more uniform tariffs and the provision of a manufactured exports subsidy to replace import duty drawbacks which were cumbersome to operate and involved high administrative costs and delays. In 1974, the Local Manufacturers (Export Compensation) Act was passed by parliament to institute a subsidy to manufactured exports at a rate of 10 per cent. The purpose of the subsidy was to compensate exporters 'for the bias against them caused by import duties which make it easier for manufacturers who substitute for imports to attract labour and capital away from those that produce for export'.

Following the oil crisis of 1973, the country reacted to the ensuing recession by tightening the trade control regime in 1974–5 and by seeking external finances whose general policy conditionalities were spelled out in Sessional Paper no. 4 of 1975.[4] The IMF programme was, however, abandoned when the country experienced an improvement in the balance of payments resulting from a large increase (80–91 per cent) in the world prices of coffee and tea in 1976–7 due to a frost in Brazil that drastically reduced its coffee harvest. The proceeds of this boom were not sterilized (for example by putting some of them in a domestic price stabilization fund) and were fully passed on to the farmers. The resulting expansion in aggregate demand, which was compounded by an expansion in government expenditure, spilled into imports and produced a serious balance of payments crisis beginning in 1978 and exacerbated by the second oil crisis of 1979, during which import bans, quotas, quantitative restrictions and an advance import deposit scheme were used to try to contain the situation. The balance of payments problems again forced the country to seek recourse in international money and capital markets whose general loan conditionalities were published in the fourth Development Plan (1979–83). This document pledged among other things the imposition of duty on imports of capital and intermediate goods to encourage employment creation; gradual phasing out of protective concessions to firms more than five years old; the cessation of the 'no objection certificate' given by local manufacturers to importers of competitive imports; and a whole series of export incentives. These and other policies were incorporated in the following two five-year Development Plans (1984–93) and in other official publications. The 1980s are a period when the country attempted fairly sustained trade liberalization efforts.

These documents argue the case for trade liberalization and pledge that the government will, among other policies, convert quantitative restrictions to tariffs and standardize and rationalize the levels of industrial protection so as to restructure the industrial sector, make it more efficient and competitive, and increase production for the domestic market and for export. Industrial restructuring was to be achieved through greater reliance on domestic market forces and on foreign private investment through the kind of policies described in the next section.

THE IMPLEMENTATION OF TRADE POLICIES
IN THE 1980s

Because of large macroeconomic imbalances, the government was unable to implement structural adjustment programmes (SAPs) successfully in the early 1980s. The IMF/World Bank stand-by and SAPs negotiated in 1979–82 all failed or collapsed, in the case of the IMF programme because the stipulated credit ceilings were exceeded. The government was more successful, however, in implementing later programmes and it was only in 1986, for example, that the government found itself without a programme with the IMF.

Many trade policies were therefore at least partially implemented in the 1980s:

(i) The export credit guarantee and insurance schemes are in the early implementation stages by the central bank.

(ii) Efforts have been made to strengthen various institutions, with the Kenya External Trade Authority (established in 1976 but moribund by 1985), for example, revamped in 1990 to promote Kenyan products abroad. A Green Channel facility has in addition been created to expedite the handling and the processing of the relevant export documents while the Investment Promotion Centre (IPC) was established in 1986 to serve as a one-stop centre to assist potential investors.

(iii) A manufacturing-under-bond (MUB) scheme took off in 1989 and eleven factories (of the fifty or so approved by IPC) were operating in the scheme by mid-1991. Under MUB, production is done exclusively for the export market, simplifying the export documentation processing and facilitating the importation of inputs.

(iv) An act covering the legal and administrative framework for the establishment of export-processing zones (EPZs) was passed by parliament in 1990 and sites have been identified at Athi River near Nairobi and in Mombasa, with development to be funded by the World Bank and the African Development Bank respectively. A private EPZ (Sammeer Industrial Park), a subsidiary of Firestone Ltd., was commissioned in Nairobi in early 1991 and by mid-year three firms were in the process of establishing their operations there.

It is, of course, too early to assess the likely impact of these efforts in increasing industrial exports. Below we discuss in detail some of the progress made towards the implementation of the more traditional trade policies and their impact in reducing the anti-export bias of the Kenyan trade regime.

Tariff reforms

Until 1977 Kenya participated in a customs union with Tanzania and Uganda, first under the East Africa Common Services Organization, during which there was a joint customs adminstration with trade among the three countries virtually tariff-free, and from 1967 under the EAC. Under the latter import duties were assessed at about 30 per cent, with higher rates on luxury goods and lower (or zero) rates on intermediate and capital goods, though with specific and mixed duties to protect local industries such as footwear, textiles and cement (Barve, 1984).

In 1980, a 10 per cent tariff surcharge was imposed on all imports and there were tariff increases in over 200 items. The tariff surcharge was to protect domestic industries from the effects of the relaxation of import controls while the tariff increases were to rationalize the structure of protection (Ng'eno, 1988). These reforms were continued in the following year with tariff increases ranging from 2 to 90 per cent imposed on about 1,400 items. There were also tariff reductions on about twenty items used mainly by export-oriented industries. The tariff reductions started in 1981 have gradually been extended in the 1980s to more import items, particularly in 1983–4 and since 1987 under the support of the World Bank Industrial Sector Adjustment Credit Facility. The number of tariff categories, for example, were reduced from twenty-five to eleven while the

Table 15.2 Collected tariff rates in Kenya in selected years (%)

	1970	1974	1978	1980	1982	1984	1986	1988
Food, beverages, tobacco	34.4	18.7	43.0	34.1	43.1	31.0	26.5	40.0
Textiles and clothing	37.5	34.0	46.5	40.4	24.8	28.9	30.0	24.8
Leather and footwear	20.7	33.9	36.5	41.6	43.3	20.6	41.3	31.8
Wood, cork and furniture	6.0	23.6	25.1	36.2	41.3	25.0	25.5	17.7
Paper and printing	9.3	11.8	15.5	18.1	19.2	23.4	20.2	23.4
Chemicals and rubber	7.4	3.4	10.3	15.8	23.4	23.4	14.1	16.6
Petroleum, coal products	80.8	38.3	15.7	12.6	9.4	9.8	10.7	10.7
Building materials, etc.	15.5	20.2	26.3	30.3	43.3	35.2	24.9	30.3
Basic metal industries	4.5	5.2	14.3	20.9	30.8	24.4	21.1	16.8
Machinery	6.1	13.0	20.3	29.1	32.6	38.6	22.5	22.0
Metal manufactures	9.7	7.5	12.2	–	21.9	23.3	17.3	13.3
Transport equipment	23.9	30.4	19.7	16.9	20.7	23.9	14.9	15.9
Miscellaneous	21.5	22.8	24.8	24.7	19.3	21.9	19.6	18.2
Total manufacturing	17.9	15.2	17.6	27.4	19.6	20.2	16.0	15.6

Source: Statistical Abstract, various issues.

Table 15.3 Import tariffs collected as percentage of imports, Kenya

	1970	1988
Intermediate imports	15.9	17.4
Capital imports	10.3	15.1
Final household imports	35.5	16.2

Source: Statistical Abstract, various issues.

maximum tariff rate was reduced from 170 per cent to 70 per cent in 1987–91.

Although the tariff reforms implemented in the 1980s had some impact in reducing the effective tariff protection accorded the manufacturing sector, tariff rates increased in many industries. Table 15.2 shows the collected tariff rates derived by dividing import duties by retained imports in various industries in selected years.

The average effective tariff rates on retained imports in the manufacturing sector declined in the early 1970s, increased in the late 1970s and declined again in the 1980s from 27.4 per cent in 1980 to 15.6 per cent in 1988. Nine out of the thirteen industries in Table 15.2, however, had higher average tariff rates in 1988 than they did in 1970. Only the major mainly consumer industries – textiles and clothing; petroleum and coal products; and transport equipment – and miscellaneous manufactures had lower average effective rates. There was also some redistribution of the tariff burden from final to intermediate and capital imports between 1970 and 1988 (Table 15.3).

The contribution of intermediate and capital imports to the import tax revenue in the manufacturing sector increased from 60.2 per cent in 1970 to 87.3 per cent in 1988, reflecting change in the import structure and the increase in tariffs on these imports to prevent a too-drastic decline in government revenue from this source. Tariffs typically account for about a fifth of total central government recurrent revenue, down from about a quarter in the 1960s.

Several studies have analysed the average nominal scheduled tariff rates in Kenya. Sharpley and Lewis (1988), for example, estimate that the rate increased from 21.58 per cent in 1970 to 41.02 per cent in 1984 with a standard deviation of 28.74 per cent in 1970 and 27.14 per cent in 1984. They therefore conclude that Kenya experienced a movement towards higher but more uniform average nominal scheduled tariffs although this varied from industry to industry. Ng'eno (1988) estimated that the average unweighted tariff rates increased from 45 per cent in 1981–2 to 51 per cent in 1982–3 and then decreased continuously to 39 per cent in 1986–7. The World Bank (1987) estimated the unweighted average scheduled tariff rate in Kenya to be 40 per cent in the mid-1980s, which, however, varied from 28 per cent for capital goods to 34 per cent for intermediate goods and to 55 per cent for consumer goods. The study concluded that these rates were relatively high by Sub-Saharan African standards although they were relatively more uniform with an average standard deviation of 22 per cent.

These and other studies also analysed the nominal and effective rates of protection accorded the manufacturing sector. Sharpley and Lewis (1988), for example, standardize results from Reimer (1970) and the World Bank (1987) and conclude that the average effective rate of protection increased from 31 to 51 per cent of value added between 1968 and 1985. Keyfitz and Wanjala (1991), tracing the impact of tariffs through input–output tables, estimated the mean effective rate of protection (ERP) of the manufacturing sector to have increased from 66.3 per cent in 1976 to 164.2 per cent in 1987.

According to these studies, therefore, tariff protection has increased at least for the majority of the industries, and many industries in the manufacturing sector still receive very high ERPs. Attempts to make them more outward-looking through a reduction in tariffs have not been very successful. The World Bank study also found that the ERP decreased with firm size so that smaller firms received less protection, while ERPs were positively correlated with profitability. The ERP was 67 per cent for parastatals, 57 per cent for foreign firms, and 35 per cent for local firms, so that parastatals received the most protection and the local private firms the least amount of protection. These results are consistent with estimates by Grosh (1988) who found the ERP in 1984 to vary from 47 per cent for public firms entirely owned by the state, to 3 per cent for quasi-public local—foreign joint-venture firms, and to 22 per cent for private firms, based on a sample of seventy-seven manufacturing firms.[5] All the studies found a close correlation between the nominal and the effective rates of protection.

496

Relaxation of quantitative restrictions

Since the balance of payments crisis of 1971, Kenya has used administrative controls extensively to manage the balance of payments and to provide protection to some industries. Quantitative restrictions (QRs) on imports in Kenya have usually been administered through import licensing, import bans, and the 'no objection' certificate, by which written permission is required from a local producer to import a competing product. Among these the most common is import licensing. This is pervasive. The number of import products under licence increased from 228 in 1972 to 2,737 in 1985 and in the mid-1980s the Import Management Committee was processing an average 2,000 applications for foreign exchange per week (Dlamini, 1987). Essential products are put in the less restrictive licence categories while the non-essential products are put in the more restrictive imports categories or completely banned. Import liberalization essentially involves a shift of items from the more restrictive categories to the less restrictive categories. In 1990–1, for example, imports were allocated to three schedules. Schedule I comprises high priority items such as capital goods, raw materials and intermediate goods. Schedule II, on the other hand, covers priority items which require government approval, mainly because of their technical aspects. Schedule IIIA covers priority items in many ways similar to those in Schedule I; Schedule IIIB lower priority locally produced items; and Schedule IIIC the least priority items. The import schedules are published annually.

In the fourth Development Plan (1979–83), it was stated that 20 per cent of the items in the then less restrictive Schedules IIA and IIB were to be shifted to the less restrictive Schedule I each year. This process was halted, however, by a serious balance of payments problem in 1982 and the entire import licensing programme was temporarily halted. When the new schedules were published in 1983, the process had been reversed with the less restrictive Schedule I having 24 per cent items less than before (Ng'eno, 1988).

Nevertheless, some progress has been made towards trade liberalization, with arbitrary QR mechanisms such as import bans and the 'no objection' certificate eliminated in 1980–2 while the number of import items in the less restrictive categories has increased. In mid-1982, for example, 317 items were moved from Schedule II to I with the value of approved imports under the less restrictive Schedule I increasing from 51.6 per cent of the total in 1982 to 74.9 per cent in 1983 but decreasing to 68.0 per cent in 1986 (Dlamini, 1987). According to the World Bank (1990), the number of import items under quantitative restrictions declined from 40.3 per cent of the total (or 12 per cent of total imports) in 1986/87 to 22.1 per cent (or 5.4 per cent of total imports) in 1990/91 when more items were moved from the more restrictive Schedule IIIC to the less restrictive

IIIB. Overall the import licensing system has been streamlined with the average lag between licence application and foreign exchange allocation reduced from six months to about three weeks, hence curtailing some of the rent-seeking behaviour (World Bank, 1990).

Manufactured exports subsidy

By the late 1970s it was generally agreed that the impact of the subsidy introduced in 1974 on manufactured exports was quite limited because the rate was quite low (at 10 per cent of the FOB value of goods manufactured in Kenya with a local value added of at least 30 per cent) and payments were subjected to much delay, in some cases of several months. There were various attempts to rectify this situation. For example, the rate was increased to 20 per cent in 1980. However, because of balance of payments problems experienced in the early 1980s, the scheme was suspended in June 1982. The subsidy was reintroduced in December 1982 at the rate of 10 per cent with a bonus (incremental) rate of 15 per cent to new exporters and those who increased their exports in the previous year. This bonus rate was abolished in 1985 and the basic rate raised to 20 per cent. In 1986 the number of items eligible for export compensation was reduced from 2,000 to 700 but later increased to 1,260. In 1990, exporters were permitted to process their claims through commercial banks to speed up payments while export firms were given the option to claim duty exemptions on imported inputs rather than export compensation. The scheme has been shifted from the customs department to the central bank to facilitate administration.

Since the manufactured exports subsidy was introduced, there has been no systematic study of its effects on export performance. Low (1982), however, conducted interviews with manufacturing firms eligible for the subsidy and could not find a definitive relationship between the export subsidy and the firms' export performance. He attributed this to the 'delays and uncertainties surrounding disbursement procedures and ... the limited extent to which the subsidy lessened the anti-export bias of a policy structure which has emphasized import substitution'. In effect, the subsidy is treated as a windfall by those few firms that receive it rather than an incentive for increased exportation. In the 1980s, between a third and two-thirds of the total subsidy payments accrued to the top four firms while the payments comprised only about 5 per cent of manufactured exports, so that the subsidy has minimal incentive value (World Bank, 1990).

Exchange rate policy

In the 1960s and 1970s, Kenya adopted a fixed exchange rate policy in which the nominal rate was only occasionally adjusted. Economic observers

Table 15.4 The foreign exchange rate and the real effective indices, Kenya

	Official rate Ksh./$ (average)	Official rate Ksh./SDR (average)	Real effective rate[a] (1982=100)	Nominal effective rate[a] (1982=100)
1979	7.5	9.7	99.3	93.8
1980	7.4	9.7	100.3	92.9
1981	9.0	10.6	103.7	94.6
1982	10.9	12.0	100.0	100.0
1983	13.3	14.2	105.5	108.8
1984	14.4	14.7	98.5	102.7
1985	16.4	16.7	100.0	107.4
1986	16.2	19.0	115.3	120.6
1987	16.5	21.3	127.6	129.7
1988	17.7	23.9	137.9	135.9
1989	20.6	23.4	143.5	136.2

Source: World Bank (1990: 141).
[a] An increase in the index indicates a devaluation.

are generally agreed that the shilling was never grossly overvalued. Quantitative restrictions on imports were only intensively applied since the early 1970s. The official exchange rate changed from Ksh. 7.143 to Ksh. 7.738 against the dollar while the nominal and real effective value of the Kenyan shilling appreciated by 4.0 per cent and 14.9 per cent respectively between 1964–8 and 1974–8 (Ng'eno, 1988). This effective appreciation was, however, more than rectified in the early 1980s. Following several discretionary devaluations in 19812, the country has since 1983 employed a more flexible regime in which the exchange rate is adjusted on a daily basis against a composite basket of currencies of the main trading partners in a crawling peg system. Consequently, the Kenyan shilling has been depreciated significantly both in nominal and in real terms, as the data in Table 15.4 show.

Between 1979 and 1989 the official Kenya shilling/SDR exchange rate was depreciated by 141 per cent while the nominal and the real trade-weighted rate were depreciated by 31 per cent which has perhaps improved the competitiveness of Kenyan producers/exporters. The exchange rate has, however, interacted with other measures, especially import and foreign exchange controls, external borrowing and recessionary stabilization policies in a generally weakened balance of payments situation, so that it is difficult to isolate its impact in reducing the anti-export bias of the Kenyan trade regime. A number of studies (Ng'eno, 1988; Mwamamzingo, 1988; Lesiit, 1990), for example, could not find a significant relationship between total, non-oil or manufactured exports and the effective exchange rate in Kenya. One positive consequence of the adoption of the crawling peg regime, however, is that changes in the exchange rate have been largely depoliticized.

In summary, trade liberalization mainly occurred through efforts to relax the import licensing process and was supported by higher tariffs for the majority of the industries and the depreciation of the Kenyan shilling. It should also be clear from the discussion that the government's attitude toward and success in the implementation of trade reform policies in Kenya, especially the relaxation of QRs, was mainly determined by the state of the balance of payments and the related balance of political forces against reforms; in many cases they were only seriously enforced when the government was implementing SAPs financed from outside. Two types of interests were arrayed against removal of administrative controls: commercial and industrial entities favoured by the historical allocation of import licences, and government agencies with important roles in determining the mix and distribution of production and distribution activities (Hecox, 1988).

The balance of payments situation in turn was significantly influenced by, among other factors, the fiscal position which, as we saw earlier, drastically deteriorated in the late 1970s and in the 1980s; except in the 1960s, when the government pursued a conservative fiscal stance, the budget deficit has been significantly correlated with increases in domestic credit and money supply, whether financed domestically or externally (Mwega, 1990). Domestic credit in turn adversely affected the balance of payments position, forcing the authorities to tighten import restrictions which in turn adversely affected the fiscal position by reducing tax revenues. A general tightening of import restrictions due to balance of payments problems gives more protection to domestic industries, inducing them to be less efficient and less able to export. Hence, while there are few direct effects of general macroeconomic policy on the industrial sector, there are considerable effects which operate through the impact of macro policies on the balance of payments, foreign exchange reserves, and the direction of trade policy (Sharpley and Lewis, 1988). This has produced an unstable policy environment which has no doubt hampered supply responsiveness of exports to the provided incentives.

OTHER IMPORTANT POLICIES AND INSTITUTIONS IN THE INDUSTRIALIZATION PROCESS

Besides trade policies, other policies and institutions are important in determining the performance of the industrial sector. These include the availability of financial capital and its cost as influenced by the financial system; taxes on firms; and price and wage policies.

The financial system

Kenya has a relatively well-developed financial system. In the 1960s and 1970s, the government followed a policy of maintaining low fixed interest rates to promote investment. Hence from the establishment of the central bank in 1966–80, interest rates charged by financial institutions were only adjusted upwards once, and then only by 1–2 per cent. In the 1980s this policy was changed and the rates have been frequently adjusted upwards in an effort to maintain them positive in real terms; interest rates were fully liberalized in July 1991.

The central bank is responsible for implementing the country's monetary policy using instruments such as minimum cash and liquidity ratios, quantitative ceilings on overall credit expansion by commercial banks, and the sectoral allocation of credit in favour of agriculture, which reduces the availability of credit to the industrial sector. Commercial banks allocate about 20 per cent and deposit-taking non-bank financial institutions (NBFIs) about 13 per cent of their credit to the manufacturing sector.

Besides these institutions, Kenya has four state-owned development finance companies (DFIs) that provide medium- and long-term finance to industry and commerce. These are the Industrial Development Bank established in 1973; the Development Finance Company of Kenya (1963), and its subsidiary, the Small Enterprises Finance Company of Kenya (1983); Kenya Industrial Estates; and the Industrial and Commercial Development Corporation (1954). These DFIs approved project loans amounting to US$12.6 million in 1989.

A major problem that has afflicted DFIs in the 1980s is a shortage of local investment funds, and because borrowers have not been willing to take foreign-currency denominated loans which expose them to foreign currency fluctuation risks, the DFIs have ended up with largely unutilized foreign lines of credit. This forced the government to establish an Exchange Risk Assumption Fund at the treasury to absorb the foreign exchange fluctuation risks and hence reduce the risks on the loans that DFIs provide in the domestic market.

While Kenya has a well-developed money and financial system, its capital market is still in its infancy. The market for short-term securities continues to be dominated by government paper. Various short-term drafts and bills of exchange for use by enterprises such as crop finance bills and promissory notes are common even though a secondary market in them has not developed. Commercial banks and NBFIs, however, accept them as security for credit which they keep until the loans are repaid. Other short-term instruments, such as commercial paper, do not exist although there are plans to introduce them as the financial system becomes increasingly liberalized. The central bank has recently permitted commercial banks to issue negotiated certificates of deposits.

The Nairobi Stock Exchange (NSE) was established in 1954 with a listing of twenty companies. Today it deals with fifty-five publicly-quoted companies. The NSE is dominated by six brokers and therefore does not exhibit a high degree of competition in the determination of stock prices. Business firms in Kenya rarely raise capital through public issues of equity and debt securities. The main sources of local equity for new investment continue to be retained earnings, savings of family groups, direct government investment and the development banks. Parastatals and private firms rely to a large extent for debt finance on direct borrowing, largely through bank overdrafts.

Taxation of industrial firms

Taxes collected from industrial firms include the company income tax and indirect taxes. Income taxes were introduced in Kenya in 1937 and their administration combined with those of Tanzania and Uganda two years later. The three countries, however, went separate ways in 1973 and the Income Tax Act no. 16 of 1973 forms the basis of the current direct tax system in Kenya, even though it has undergone many amendments since then. The company income tax was enacted at 45 per cent on the profits of resident companies, but this was reduced to 40 per cent in the mid–1980s and to 37.5 per cent in 1991. In a study of the incidence of the tax, Brent (1986) found that the tax was more than fully shifted forward from profits so that it increases the prices of Kenyan products relative to those of competitors with lower taxes or whose tax burden is less shifted from profits.

The sales tax was introduced in 1973 at equal rates on domestic and imported manufactures. Food, exports, sales of small businesses and some agricultural inputs were exempt from the tax. The tax was enacted at 10 per cent, but by January 1990, when it was replaced by a value-added tax, the basic rate was 17 per cent with higher rates on 'luxuries', although some products – petroleum, beer and electricity – were taxed at specific rates. Sales taxes accounted for 30.7 per cent of total tax revenues in 1989/90, up from 25.9 per cent in 1975/6. Sales taxes on domestic manufactures constituted about 50–60 per cent of total sales tax revenue in the 1980s. With the share of manufactured imports in total sales on the decline (World Bank, 1987), this share was achieved through the imposition of higher sales tax rates on imports, hence providing additional protection to the domestic industry. The excise tax is dominated by three products – beer, cigarettes and sugar – and it accounted for about 6 per cent of total tax revenue in 1990. The new value-added tax has broadened the tax base by including some business services in the tax net.

Brent (1986) and Mwega (1988) found that sales taxes were largely unshifted from profits (value added), especially after accounting for lags in adjustment which reduce the profitability and the long-term growth of the manufacturing sector.

Price and wage policies

Price controls in Kenya are based on the Price Control Ordinance of 1956, although they only started to be extensively applied following the balance of payments crisis of 1971. The number of items affected started to decline in 1987 when ten products were removed from the price control order. In 1988 another twenty products were price-decontrolled and the process has continued so that only thirteen commodities were subject to controls by 1991. The main objectives of price controls were to protect low-income persons and to curb excess monopoly profits. Manufacturers complain, however, about long delays between application and the grant of a price increase while the cost-plus method applied to determine prices does not fully incorporate differences and changes in input structures. The method also does not encourage firms to reduce their costs of production or to be efficient, which is necessary if a firm is to venture into foreign markets. It is hence argued that price controls impede entrepreneurship, investment and growth, with negative effects that are likely to outweigh their positive impact on price stability.

In the 1960s there was a large increase in real wages. Since 1973 the government has used wage guidelines and the Industrial Court to regulate wages. As a consequence of the pursuit of an active incomes policy, real wages have declined drastically. Real average wages received by employees (deflated by the consumer price index) declined by an average 1.6 per cent per annum in 1974–83, but increased by 0.9 per cent per annum in 1984–8. Real wages paid by producers (deflated by the GDP deflator) increased by an average 1.9 per cent per annum in 1974–83, hence reducing profitability; however, paid real wages declined by 1.2 per cent per annum in 1984–8. The same pattern obtains in the manufacturing sector. The decline in employees' average real wages has constrained the demand for manufacturing output, especially from small/micro enterprises.

TRADE/MACRO POLICIES AND INDUSTRIALIZATION EXPERIENCE IN KENYA

Kenya has a relatively large and diversified industrial sector that employed close to 0.2 million people in 1990. Table 15.5 shows that the quantity index of manufacturing production increased about threefold between 1972 and 1990. Industries that expanded fastest (though in some cases from a small base) include printing and publishing, because of expansion in school enrolments; transport equipment; petroleum and other chemicals; plastic products; and rubber products. All of these are highly import-intensive

Table 15.5 The quantity index of manufacturing production, Kenya (1976=100)

	1972	1976	1980	1984	1988	1990
Food manufacturing	69.0	100	110.7	128.2	167.5	173.2
Beverages and tobacco	68.8	100	135.1	137.7	201.9	210.7
Textiles	62.6	100	175.0	166.6	197.2	227.8
Clothing	112.1	100	218.3	369.5	368.3	347.2
Leather and footwear	49.1	100	94.6	81.3	88.1	99.2
Wood and cork products	74.9	100	133.8	91.5	67.1	70.2
Furniture and fixtures	107.4	100	54.3	69.8	72.7	73.7
Paper, paper products	82.0	100	188.5	137.1	189.3	203.9
Printing and publishing	50.2	100	240.0	317.3	389.1	401.8
Basic industrial chemicals	115.7	100	174.6	167.8	182.1	211.3
Petroleum, other chemicals	73.4	100	161.5	245.0	279.0	457.8
Rubber products	67.0	100	192.5	227.5	286.3	325.9
Plastic products	35.5	100	207.7	186.3	202.8	227.4
Clay and glass products	129.2	100	289.9	282.3	306.5	367.2
Non-metallic metals	75.5	100	124.4	108.4	135.0	167.1
Metal products	58.7	100	129.4	89.4	104.4	177.0
Non-electrical machinery	67.1	100	123.8	103.1	138.7	103.8
Electrical machinery	60.4	100	157.8	147.2	189.3	190.3
Transport equipment	91.5	100	658.6	774.9	612.4	673.5
Miscellaneous manufacturing	67.0	100	107.9	157.7	260.1	406.1
Total manufacturing	71.1	100	156.5	170.3	188.7	235.6

Source: Economic Survey, various issues.

and therefore benefited from the import liberalization efforts (and perhaps were adversely affected by the depreciation of the Kenyan shilling) in the 1980s. Only the wood and furniture industries experienced a decline in production over the 1972–90 period because of restrictions on felling trees in the government's conservation efforts. The share of manufacturing increased from about 11 per cent of GDP in the early 1970s to 13 per cent in 1990. Labour productivity decreased in the 1970s and early 1980s but increased in the late 1980s. In the 1980s the manufacturing sector grew at about 5.2 per cent per annum. Employment, however, expanded at 2.9 per cent to give an implicit expansion of labour productivity of 2.3 per cent. The share of wages remained fairly constant at about a third of manufacturing value added. Real investment (at 1982 prices) in the sector declined from a peak of K£157 million in 1978 to K£65 million in 1985, although it partially recovered in the late 1980s to reach K£109 million in 1989.

An IS industrialization strategy may be considered 'successful' if there is: (i) a reduction of the proportion of imports in the total domestic supply of industrial products; (ii) an increase in the proportion of industrial output that is exported to indicate improved access to external markets as industries mature and become competitive; and (iii) an increase in the proportion of domestic value added to gross output in the industrial sector (Sharpley and Lewis, 1988). By these criteria, the Kenyan record is mixed. The share

Table 15.6 Ratio of imports to manufacturing sector supply, Kenya, 1983

–10%	Beverages and tobacco; clothing; leather products and footwear; wood and cork products; furniture and fixtures; rubber products; plastic products; and non-metallic mineral products.
11–20%	Textiles; paper and paper products; printing and publishing; metal products; and miscellaneous manufactures.
21–50%	Petroleum and other chemicals (34%); pottery and glass products (32%); electrical machinery (37%); and transport equipment (31%).
>50%	Industrial chemicals (64%); non-electrical machinery (90%).

Source: World Bank (1987).

Table 15.7 Exports as percentage of production, Kenya

	1979–83	1984–8
Food manufacturing	5.7	2.7
Beverages and tobacco (excl. coffee and tea)	2.0	2.4
Chemicals (incl. petroleum)	7.3	4.6
Machinery and transport equipment	1.5	1.3
Other manufactures	7.5	5.7
Total manufacturing sector	5.9	3.8

Source: Compiled from World Bank (1990).

of imports in the total supply of manufactures decreased from about 44.3 per cent in 1972 to 19.3 per cent in 1985 (World Bank, 1987). Concomitantly, the share of domestic products in the total supply of manufactured goods increased from about 50 per cent in the mid-1960s to 75 per cent in the mid-1980s (Sharpley and Lewis, 1988). The country has therefore become increasingly self-sufficient in the supply of manufactured goods. The proportion of imports, however, varies greatly from industry to industry as Table 15.6 shows for the early 1980s. In six out of nineteen manufacturing industries, the ratio exceeds 20 per cent, indicating some scope for further import substitution.

However, the share of manufactured exports declined drastically from 40 per cent in 1964 to 7.5 per cent in 1985 (World Bank, 1987), and declined still further in the late 1980s. Table 15.7 shows the proportion of manufactured output exported in various subsectors. This decline in manufactured exports has been attributed to a decrease in exports to neighbouring countries, especially Tanzania where the volume of imports from Kenya has not yet reached the levels attained before the break-up of the East African Community in 1977; to growth in domestic demand for such products as paper; to the anti-export bias of trade policies; and to supply constraints, especially the intermittent shortage of foreign exchange to purchase intermediate inputs (Siggel, 1990; Sharpley and Lewis, 1988).

Lastly, the share of value added in gross manufacturing output has

Table 15.8 Gross output and value added in the manufacturing sector, Kenya

	(K£ million)		(%)
	Gross output (1)	GDP at factor cost (2)	(2)/(1)
1975	599.5	127.13	21.2
1976	730.1	151.33	20.7
1977	1091.7	199.31	18.3
1978	1342.7	245.75	18.3
1979	1177.1	249.84	21.2
1980	1453.1	295.14	20.3
1981	1764.6	342.44	19.4
1982	2054.1	391.04	19.0
1983	2281.7	408.26	17.9
1984	2796.9	460.96	16.5
1985	3383.0	518.40	15.3
1986	4097.2	576.37	14.1
1987	4772.7	655.56	13.7
1988	6102.7	797.56	13.1
1989	6960.2	855.36	12.3

Source: Economic Survey, various issues.

declined drastically, as shown in Table 15.8. The value added share decreased from about 20 per cent in the late 1970s to 12 per cent in 1990, partially offsetting the decrease in the gross imports/supply ratio. While this ratio may decline due to structural changes that enhance inter-industry linkages and hence specialization (Siggel, 1990) the decline more likely suggests that the Kenyan industrial sector has not been robust. The ratio declined alongside some import substitution, with the share of imports in total intermediate inputs decreasing from about 30 per cent in the early 1970s to less than 20 per cent in the mid-1980s, perhaps due to an increase in import prices; higher tariffs on intermediate imports; and the non-tariff constraints to importation during foreign exchange shortages (Siggel, 1990).

The protective trade policies pursued in Kenya, by hindering the development of a more competitive environment, have produced a predominantly monopolistic/oligopolistic industrial market structure where firms have earned large profits selling in the domestic markets and hence have little incentive to seek external markets. House (1981) found that there is a significant positive correlation between industrial concentration in Kenya as measured by a 'hybrid' index (the share of employment attributable to the largest three plants in an industry, multiplied by the share of domestic production in total Kenyan sales) and price-cost margins (to measure profitability) for given firm size and a negative correlation between industrial concentration and exports, though the latter relationship was not significant. Utilizing data from the censuses of industrial production, House also concluded that industrial concentration increased in the 1960s,

Table 15.9 Evolution of industrial concentration, Kenya

	Maufacturing employment/sales by market structure (%)		
	1963	1967	1972
Monopoly and concentrated oligopoly	49	51	43
Unconcentrated oligopoly	16	25	36
Competition	35	24	21
	100	100	100
	1976	1980	1985
Monopoly firms	15	6	6
Oligopoly firm	64	68	57
Competitive firms	22	26	38
	100	100	100

Sources: House (1981); World Bank (1987).

although the World Bank (1987) found that the degree of concentration had decreased since the mid-1970s as the data in Table 15.9 show.

The industrial sector hence relied heavily on domestic demand, limiting the scope of the IS industrial strategy. Various studies have analysed the sources of industrial growth in Kenya. Sharpley and Lewis (1988) disaggregated the manufacturing sector into consumer, intermediate and investment industries (distinguishing the petroleum industry, because of its size and because the impact of the various oil price shocks may distort the overall picture) and derived the sources of growth in 1964–84 for each (see Table 15.10).

The data in table 10 show that in 1964–84 the following factors applied:

(i) The consumer goods industry was dominant in explaining the growth of the manufacturing sector. This was followed by chemicals, rubber and petroleum; the investment goods industry; and the intermediate goods industry. The growth of the consumer goods industry was in turn dominated by food, beverages and tobacco, which alone accounted for 42.28 per cent of the growth of the manufacturing sector, raising doubts about the depth and breadth of the growth process. Other important industries were clothes, textiles and leather; metal products; transport equipment; and paper, printing and publishing.

(ii) Growth of the manufacturing sector was overwhelmingly driven by domestic demand (68.7 per cent), followed by import substitution (26.3 per cent). Exports accounted for only 5.0 per cent of total manufacturing growth. This is a poor performance, especially if the chemical, rubber and petroleum industry (2.8 per cent) is excluded. Other important exports were food, beverages and tobacco, and building

Table 15.10 Sources of growth of manufacturing output,[a] Kenya, 1964–84 (%)

	Total	Domestic demand	Export growth	Import substitution
Food, beverages, tobacco	42.28	34.50	1.30	6.48
Clothes, textiles, leather	6.80	2.24	0.14	4.41
Total consumer goods	49.07	36.74	1.44	10.89
Wood and furniture	2.10	1.61	0.07	0.42
Paper, printing, publishing	5.04	3.26	0.11	1.68
Building materials	3.26	2.45	0.53	0.28
Total intermediate goods	10.40	7.32	0.70	2.38
Chemicals, rubber, petroleum	23.71	13.94	2.77	7.01
Metal products	6.73	3.68	0.07	2.98
Machinery	3.89	1.86	0.00	2.03
Transport equipment	5.46	4.94	0.00	0.53
Miscellaneous	0.74	0.25	0.04	0.46
Total investment goods	16.81	10.72	0.11	5.99
Total	100.00	68.72	5.01	26.27

Source: Sharpley and Lewis (1988).
[a] At current prices.

Table 15.11 Sources of growth of the manufacturing sector, comparative results (%)

		Domestic demand	Import substitution	Export expansion
Sharpley and Lewis (1988)	1964–70	76.1	14.6	9.3
	1970–5	73.2	18.6	8.3
	1975–80	95.1	–8.2	13.1
	1980–4	73.7	24.6	1.8
Gulhati and Sekhar (1982)	1963–71	70.0	17.0	13.0
World Bank (1987)	1976–83	40.8	64.0	–4.8
Siggel (1990)	1972–85	64.0	42.0	6.0

materials. Published data, however, underestimate exports growth because of smuggling across the country's borders.

These conclusions are supported by Gulhati and Sekhar (1982); the World Bank (1987), and Siggel (1990), as the data in Table 15.11 show. The first two studies are almost in agreement that industrial growth was overwhelmingly driven by domestic demand in the first decade of independence from the early 1960s to the early 1970s (70–76 per cent), followed by import substitution (15–17 per cent). Exports made a minor contribution, accounting for 9–13 per cent of total manufacturing sector growth. When it comes to the second decade, however, there is a divergence in the results by the World Bank and Siggel, who assign a bigger role to import substitution relative to domestic demand. But the three studies are in

Table 15.12 Average real labour productivity in large firms, Kenya (1973=100)

1973	1976	1979	1982	1985	1988
100	99	96	88	104	109

Source: *Statistical Abstract*, various issues.

agreement that export expansion made a negative or small contribution to manufacturing sector growth (−4.8 per cent to 13 per cent) in this period despite government attempts to promote manufactured exports.

Little research has been done on productivity change in Kenya's manufacturing sector. Table 15.12, however, shows that average real labour productivity in large manufacturing firms and establishments in Kenya declined in the 1970s and increased in the 1980s, perhaps because of the structural adjustment and stabilization policies pursued in this period.

Using a production function approach, Shaaeldin (1989) found that the total factor productivity growth (TFPG) was negative (−54 per cent) during the first decade of Kenya's independence (1964–73) and positive but small (13 per cent) in the second decade (1973–83), perhaps due to the stabilization and liberalization policies pursued in the second decade. The growth of the sector was therefore mainly accounted for by the growth of capital (121 per cent and 68 per cent, respectively) and labour (23 per cent and 19 per cent, respectively).[6] The study explains the poor performance in TFPG by factors such as low capacity utilization caused by import compression and a small domestic market, production inefficiency, excessive product varieties and inadequate incentives to secure technical competence given a monopolistic and oligopolistic industrial structure. Coughlin (1988) reports some very low rates of capacity utilization in some industries such as pharmaceuticals (21 per cent), transport vehicles (23 per cent), steel rolling (22 per cent) and high capacity utilization in other industries such as textiles (86 per cent in 1986) and paper (91 per cent in 1987). The World Bank (1987) estimates a generally higher average capacity utilization rate in Kenya's industrial sector of 79 per cent which varied from 96 per cent for textiles and clothing; 93 per cent for wood and wood products; and 89 per cent for food products; to 42 per cent for electrical and transport equipment; 53 per cent for leather and footwear; and 56 per cent for iron and steel products, perhaps because the year of the study (1986) was buoyant due to a 39 per cent increase in coffee prices.

Capacity utilization in the manufacturing sector, estimated by shortfall from trend-through-peaks in a quantity index of production (1967–90), shown in Table 15.13, increased from about 70 per cent in the 1970s to about 80 per cent in much of the 1980s, perhaps because of the structural adjustment and stabilization policies pursued, or the programme finance associated with them, in this period.

Table 15.13 Capacity utilization in the manufacturing sector, Kenya (%)

1969–73	1974–8	1979–83	1984–8	1989–90
70.1	69.9	80.3	80.2	84.3

AN EVALUATION AND CONCLUDING REMARKS

A conventional interpretation of the relationship between trade/macro policies and the industrialization experience in Kenya is that these policies had a major influence on the structure and the growth of the manufacturing sector. The pattern of manufacturing in turn had a major feedback effect into the general macroeconomic and balance of payments situation of the country. Accordingly the failure of the sector to meet the various policy objectives such as the promotion of exports, generation of employment, development of domestic linkages, etc. is due to the protectionist policies pursued in the past. In the 1960s and 1970s, Kenya's manufacturing sector encountered generally increasing levels of protection by tariffs, quantitative restrictions and an overvalued currency which penalized the other sectors of the economy, especially agriculture and exports. These inherent subsidies had by the early 1980s become unsustainably large, hence justifying the adoption of adjustment policies. The reforms instituted in the 1980s did not, however, significantly reduce the anti-export bias of the past trade/macro policies. The World Bank (1990) for example estimates the bias against non-traditional non-oil (NT) exports to have changed as shown in Table 15.14. These estimates suggest that it was 13 per cent more profitable in shilling terms (ignoring the impact of QRs) in 1980, and 10 per cent more so in 1989, to produce one dollar's worth of an import substitute than one dollar's worth of a non-traditional exportable.

Despite the government's declared intentions to move from IS policies, its institutions and administrative framework still remain biased against export promotion. The implementation of export policies was slow and uneven and proceeded in such a manner that much of their incentive value was lost. This can be attributed to a pervading mistrust between the operators in the industrial sector, which is dominated by Kenya-Asians and multinationals, and the government bureaucracy which does not have major economic interests in manufacturing. The remedy then is to continue

Table 15.14 Real exchange rates and anti-export bias, Kenya, 1980–9

	1980	1985	1986	1988	1989
REER for NT exports ($REER_x$)	8.1	7.4	7.6	7.9	8.3
REER for non-oil imports ($REER_m$)	9.2	8.2	8.3	8.9	9.2
Anti-export bias ($REER_m/REER_x$)	1.13	1.10	1.09	1.13	1.10

Source: World Bank (1990).

the implementation of import and export policies that reduce the anti-export bias until an efficient industrial sector and an export culture are established. Sharpley and Lewis (1988), for example, recommend continued devaluation of the Kenyan shilling with a concurrent general reduction of tariffs alongside a contractionary fiscal policy partly offset by an expansionary monetary policy supportive of the private sector, particularly those industries that would be adversely affected by the restructuring.

This conventional interpretation of the relationship between trade/macro policies and the industrialization experience in Kenya is, however, subject to several caveats. First, appropriate timing and sequencing of industrial policies are important if they are to deepen and extend the industrial sector. This is essential to resolve at least in the short run the tradeoff between maintaining a high-cost protected sector and de-industrialization due to competition from imports during trade liberalization. The sequencing suggested by Kenya's trade policies is the tariffication of import controls followed by a gradual reduction of tariff rates, both supported by the depreciation of the exchange rate and direct export promotion policies. This assumes, of course, that tariffs are not undermined by loopholes in the tariff law; import duty avoidance; and illegal importation. Recent experiences in Kenya and elsewhere also show that a most important determinant of the success of SAPs is macroeconomic stability if such a sequencing is to be perceived as credible. Macroeconomic stability in turn cannot be achieved when the country is incurring large budget deficits that are financed by borrowing from the banking system. Central bank credit to the public sector has a direct negative impact on the balance of payments; accelerates inflation; and constrains economic growth (Mwega, 1990). Reining in the budget deficit is therefore essential to achieving macroeconomic stability. This requires control of overall government expenditure and/or increases in tax revenues, while sustaining or boosting the expenditure components that promote exports and avoiding negative tax incentive effects on exports. This is one area where Kenya has experienced problems.

Second, detailed industry-specific planning is still necessary to exploit the potential of more directly targeted policies to encourage elected industries and firms in the country to break into and to keep foreign markets and to prevent the unnecessary proliferation of the makes and models of similar products resulting from free-for-all industrial licensing. A non-traditional export product that could be targeted in Kenya is horticulture, as it has high potential. Dealing with a perishable product, the industry however faces many problems such as the high cost (and low quality) of packaging material because of import controls, and inadequate handling, cooling, storage and freight facilities which might best be provided by the public sector. Similarly, in a small economy, unnecessary product differentiation ensures that many firms operate with large underutilized capacity and with high overhead costs, especially from the acquisition of dies, moulds and casting patterns. In Kenya, for example, the country's plastics industry produces twenty-seven models of half-litre container plastic bottles; the glass factory makes 105 sizes and designs of glass bottles; the Firestone company makes forty-five tyre sizes, twenty-five for cars and twenty for trucks, some with multiple designs; a motor spare parts company makes seventeen radiator models; the motor industry assembles sixty makes of sedan cars in 200 models and ninety-four models of trucks, buses and pick-ups (Coughlin, 1985). This proliferation results in a low production trap characterized by high production costs, high prices and low sales and is unlikely to be conducive to the development of a dynamic industrial sector with adequate economies of scale to penetrate external markets. Active state involvement in industrial development is therefore needed at least to regulate entry into industries by industrial licensing based on projected demand and the degree of capacity utilization although this may increase the amount of protection provided to the industrial sector, and to rationalize the product makes and models within industries.

NOTES

1 The comparative data are:

	1965–89	
	Kenya	SSA
% GNP per capita growth	2.0	0.3
% inflation rate	7.9	14.2

	1965–80		1980–9	
	Kenya	SSA	Kenya	SSA
% merchandise export growth	0.3	6.6	0.1	–0.7
% merchandise import growth	1.7	4.9	0.6	–5.0

Source: World Bank (1991).

2 The contribution of petroleum to foreign exchange earnings is, however, small with the country mainly re-exporting imported petroleum products after their refining.

3 Kenya, too, has experienced a serious long-term deterioration in its long-run terms of trade. A curve fitted to data on commodity terms of trade for 1964–88 yielded a highly significant trend deterioration of 3.4 points per annum (with 1980=100). By 1988 the import purchasing power of a unit of exports was a mere half of the 1964 level.

4 Kenya became one of the first countries to qualify for the IMF Extended Fund Facility. The loan agreements are discussed in detail by Killick (1984).

5 These results should, of course, be interpreted with caution and are likely to vary with the method used, the assumptions made, and the industry coverage.

6 These results are also likely to be influenced by the methodological shortcomings

of the study, particularly in the measurement of the factors of production and the failure to incorporate changes in capacity utilization of the capital stock.

REFERENCES

Barve, A. G. (1984) *The Foreign Trade of Kenya: A Perspective*, Nairobi: Transafrica Press.

Brent, R. J. (1986) 'Lagged Reactions in the Short-Run Estimates of Tax Shifting on Company Income and Sales Taxes in Kenya', *Journal of Development Economics* 20(3): 15–32.

Coughlin, P. (1985) 'Economies of Scale, Capacity Utilization and Import Substitution: A Focus on Dies, Moulds and Patterns', *Eastern Africa Economic Review* 1(1): 97–106.

—— (1988) 'Towards a New Industrialization Strategy in Kenya?' in P. Coughlin and G.K. Ikiara (eds) *Industrialization in Kenya: In Search of a Strategy*, ch.14, Nairobi: Heinemann Kenya Ltd.

Dlamini, A. T. (1987) 'Management of Foreign Exchange Reserves through Quantitative Controls: The Kenyan Experience', MBA Research Paper, University of Nairobi.

Government of Kenya, *Economic Survey*, various issues.

Government of Kenya, *Statistical Abstract*, various issues.

Grosh, B. (1988) 'Comparing Parastatal and Private Manufacturing Firms: Would Privatization Improve Performance?', in P. Coughlin and G.K. Ikiara (eds) *Industrialization in Kenya: In Search of a Strategy*, ch.12, Nairobi: Heinemann Kenya Ltd.

Gulhati, R. and Sekhar, U. (1982) 'Industrial Strategy for Late Starters: The Experience of Kenya, Tanzania, and Zambia', *World Development* 10(11): 949–72.

Hecox, W. E. (1988) 'Structural Adjustment, Donor Conditionality and Industrialization in Kenya', in P. Coughlin and G.K. Ikiara (eds) *Industrialization in Kenya: In Search of a Strategy*, ch. 10, Nairobi: Heinemann Kenya Ltd.

Hopcraft, P. (1973) 'Outward-Looking Industrialization: The Promotion of Manufactured Imports from Kenya', Institute for Development Studies Discussion Paper no. 141, University of Nairobi.

House, W. (1981) 'Industrial Performance and Market Structure', in T. Killick (ed.) *Papers on the Kenyan Economy*, ch.VII–5, Nairobi: HEB.

Keyfitz, R. and Wanjala, J. (1991) 'Optimal Tariff Reform for Kenya', Ministry of Planning and National Development Technical Paper 91–05.

Killick, T. (1984) 'Kenya, 1975–81', in T. Killick (ed.) *The IMF and Stabilization: Developing Country Experiences*, ch.5, London: HEB.

King, J. R. (1979) *Stabilization in an African Setting: Kenya 1963–1979*, London: HEB.

Lesiit, M.L. (1990) 'Determinants of the Current Account of the Balance of Payments: An Analysis for Kenya, 1973–88', MA Research Paper, University of Nairobi.

Low, P. (1982) 'Export Subsidies and Trade Policy: The Experience of Kenya', *World Development* 10(4): 293–304.

Mwamamzingo, M. H. (1988) 'Determination and Effects of Exchange Rate Changes in Kenya, 1966–1986: A Simultaneous Equation Approach', MA Research Paper, University of Nairobi.

Mwega, F. M. (1988) 'Short-Run Shifting of Manufacturers' Sales Taxes in Kenya: Revisited', *Eastern Africa Economic Review* 4(1): 42–7.

—— (1990) 'An Econometric Study of Selected Monetary Policy Issues in Kenya', ODI Working Paper no. 42, London.

Ng'eno, N. K. (1988) 'Kenya's Export Performance', mimeo, University of Warwick.

Phelps, M. G. and Wasow, B. (1972) 'Measuring Protection and Its Effects in Kenya', IDS Working Paper, University of Nairobi.

Reimer, R. (1970) 'Effective Rates of Protection in East Africa', IDS Staff Paper no. 78, University of Nairobi.

Shaaeldin, E. (1989) 'Sources of Industrial Growth in Kenya, Tanzania, Zambia, and Zimbabwe: Some Estimates', *Africa Development Review* 1(1): 21–39.

Sharpley, J. and Lewis, S.R. (1988) 'Kenya's Industrialization, 1964–84', IDS Discussion Paper no. 242, University of Sussex.

Siggel, E. (1990) 'Recent Industrial Growth and Development in Kenya: Constraints and Prospects for the Future', paper presented to the 9th World Congress of the International Economic Association.

World Bank (1975) *Kenya Into the Second Decade*, Baltimore: Johns Hopkins University Press.

—— (1987) *Kenya: Industrial Sector Policies for Investment and Export Growth*, Washington, DC: World Bank.

—— (1990) *Kenya: Stabilization and Adjustment: Toward Accelerated Growth*, Washington, DC: World Bank.

—— (1991) *World Development Report*, Washington, DC: World Bank.

16

TRADE AND INDUSTRIALIZATION IN TANZANIA

A review of experience and issues

Benno J. Ndulu and Joseph J. Semboja

INTRODUCTION

Tanzania's articulation of the motivations for and the intended process of industrialization are contained in two long-term strategic statements, *The Long-Term Plan: 1964–80* (URT, 1964a) and the *Basic Industrialization Strategy* (URT, 1976a). Three operational documents characterize the phasing of the strategies. The *First Five-Year Plan, 1964–69* (URT, 1964b) proposed a wide range of import-substituting industrial investments, concentrating on the relatively easy 'first stage' of import substitution – predominantly in consumer goods. Although a shift towards intermediates and construction materials was encouraged, the emphasis was on a maximum growth strategy concentrating on quick-high yield areas. The *Second Five-Year Plan, 1969–74* (URT, 1969) emphasized structural change. Relative expansion of sectors producing intermediates and capital goods as well as pre-export processing were emphasized (Wangwe, 1983). The *Third Five-Year Plan, 1967–81* (URT, 1976b), drawing on the *Basic Industrialization Strategy*, emphasized the deepening of domestic resource-based import substitution and the expansion of manufactured exports as an extension of the home market.

Infant industry protection was adopted as a measure to realize the expected benefits from industrialization. In the pre-independence and early independence period, such protection was directly linked to attraction of foreign investment in local industry. Potential investors submitted proposed investment projects and tariff protection was granted against foreign competition to ensure high profit rates. The simultaneous establishment of industrial projects and the granting of tariff protection during this early period led to a tariff structure that was determined by negotiations between investors and public officials (Rweyemamu, 1973: 130–1). With the growth of public-sector participation in the industrialization process, protection

515

was further extended through duty relief (exemption) on imported raw materials, machinery and parts. An escalated tariff structure was subsequently maintained throughout.

Trade and trade-related policies aimed at protecting infant industries generate anti-export bias and negatively affect export performance. Although specific export promotional measures were instituted to (partly) offset this bias, such efforts were only marginally effective. The link between the anti-export bias of the protective structure and the manufacturing sector's export performance is thus an important issue to consider. The high import dependence of this sector and the sensitivity of its performance to the availability of foreign exchange makes this issue even more important.

The next section reviews the industrialization experience in Tanzania and assesses performance and efficiency in the manufacturing sector. The growth performance of the sector and structural changes are reviewed. The assessment of efficiency and performance is done in two parts: first, via trends in productivity and efficiency over time, based on domestic prices under the protected regime; second, using a 1985 'snapshot' analysis of competitive efficiency. In the following section major factors and policies affecting import substitution are reviewed. In so doing, trade and trade-related issues affecting performance are highlighted. This is followed by a review of the export performance of the manufacturing sector and major factors affecting export orientation. Again, trade and trade-related policies are the focus. The last section draws the main lessons from the experience and identifies some issues for further research.

INDUSTRIALIZATION, INDUSTRIAL PERFORMANCE AND EFFICIENCY IN TANZANIA, 1961–90

Industrialization

At independence (1961), the contribution of the industrial sector (manufacturing, construction, mining, power and water) to real GDP was 13 per cent. The manufacturing sector, which we focus on here, contributed 4 per cent to GDP (or 31 per cent of the industrial GDP). More than 60 per cent of the manufactures consumed in the country were imported. Most firms engaged in manufacturing were foreign-owned or had dominant foreign ownership shares (Rweyemamu, 1973). Local manufacturing was dominated by last-stage processing and packaging for local markets, processing for export and first-stage 'simple' substitution for a small range of intermediates and capital goods (Wangwe, 1990). The decision to raise the share of industry in the economy and change its structure and ownership

Table 16.1 Investment and investment productivity in the manufacturing sector, Tanzania (%)

Gross investment	1966–70	1971–5	1976–80	1981–3	1984–8
Real investment rate[a] (gross fixed capital form/MVA)	31.0	28.4	64.6	59.5	63.4
Share of investment in total manufacturing	15.4	13.9	33.4	23.1	18.9
Real MVA growth rate	10.0	4.8	2.7	–7.0	0.9
Gross investment productivity (MVA growth rate/investment rate)	28.0	30.7	4.2	–11.8	0.001
Net investment productivity	48.6	31.6	1.8	–18.4	1.4

Sources: URT, *National Accounts of Tanzania 1966–76* and *1976–88*; URT, *Survey of Industrial Production*, various issues; URT, *Economic Survey*, various issues.
[a] The high investment rates after 1975 reflect resource transfers from the rest of the economy and external sources to this sector.
MVA, Manufacturing sector value added or GDP.

pattern was considered important for a young nation that wanted to assert its independence and achieve longer term economic development.

Industrial expansion, 1966–80

To implement the above strategy, a rapid expansion of the manufacturing sector's capacity was pursued between 1966 and 1980 (Table 16.1). Its real gross investment rate (the ratio of real capital formation in the sector to its value added) rose from 18.4 per cent during 1971–5 to 64.6 per cent during 1976–80.

A spurt of investment to expand simple import-substitution activities that could grow quickly characterized the first five years, 1966–70. A high growth rate of real value added was achieved, averaging 10 per cent annually. A slackening of investment growth in the manufacturing sector was experienced during 1971–5, which was a period of rapid infrastructural build-up, and its share in total investment declined. The real rate of manufacturing growth declined steeply from the previous period, to an average of only 4.8 per cent per annum.

The implementation of the Basic Industrialization Strategy, starting in 1976, ushered in a new investment boom. The strategy was aimed at linking industrialization to the domestic resource base and the home market. It constituted an attempt at the deepening of import substitution to strengthen backward linkages within the economy and to cater increasingly to the domestic market and hence improve forward linkages. The effort to expand capacity particularly emphasized intermediate and capital goods

sectors. Boosted by large inflows of external project finance, real investment rose significantly, with the manufacturing sector taking up 33.4 per
cent of total investment during the period.

Unlike in the previous ten years when a rise or fall in investment was
associated with commensurate changes in real net output, the investment
boom of 1976–80 was actually accompanied by a decline in the sector's
real growth rate. This was the result of unexpectedly long project gestation
periods due to delays in commissioning because of lack of complementary
infrastructural services, particularly water and power, and other implemen-
tational problems.

Between 1965 and 1980 important structural changes did take place
within Tanzanian manufacturing. Initially, consumer goods very much
dominated the manufacturing sector in terms of gross output, value added
and employment. In 1965, for example, the consumer goods subsector
accounted for 72 per cent of gross output, 56 per cent of value added and
68 per cent of employment in the sector (Table 16.2). There was a steady
decline thereafter in the share of consumer goods in gross output as
intermediate and capital goods sectors increased their shares. In value added
terms, a similar trend was registered after 1973 (Table 16.2). In terms of
employment, however, since intermediate and capital goods industries were
more capital-intensive, the consumer goods sector's dominance remained
more or less unchanged.

In brief, this period was characterized by a rapid expansion of industrial
capacity with very high rates of investment. Although actual net output
growth rates remained positive throughout, they were lower than the rate
of expansion of the sector's potential output. The share of the manufacturing sector in the economy rose significantly, from 4 per cent in 1961 to a
peak of 12 per cent in 1977 before dropping slightly to 10 per cent in
1980.

The economic crisis and forced deindustrialization, 1981–5

Three major interrelated factors are key to understanding the severe stagnation of the industrialization process in Tanzania during this period.
They jointly impacted on the sector through generating foreign exchange
scarcities engendering import 'strangulation' and reduction in activity
(Table 16.3). First, the combination of steep decline in commodity prices
and the second oil crisis which triggered a steep rise in import prices significantly reduced the real purchasing power of the already faltering
exports. (The 1979 war with Idi Amin in Uganda which diverted the
equivalent of a full year's export earnings from productive use made this
foreign exchange constraint worse.) Second, a combination of reduced
external inflows between 1981 and 1984 and an increase in the debt servicing burden associated with the rise in real interest rate on foreign debt

Table 16.2 Manfuacturing sector: structure of output, value added, employment and the rate of value added generation,[a] Tanzania (% shares)

	1965	1973	1977	1981	1984	1986	1988
Gross output							
Consumer goods[b]	72.0	57.0	51.0	53.0	51.6	45.1	49.3
Intermediate goods[c]	23.0	33.0	34.0	35.0	36.0	38.0	42.3
Capital goods[d]	1.0	9.0	11.0	11.0	9.0	7.0	8.4
Value added							
Manufacturing VA/GDP							
of which	9.1	12.0	11.8	9.8	9.2	8.0	8.1
Consumer goods	56.0	59.0	55.0	46.0	50.2	41.3	47.6
Intermediate goods	40.0	33.0	36.0	44.0	36.8	40.0	44.4
Capital goods	3.0	7.0	6.0	6.0	9.0	19.0	8.0
Value added/gross output							
Total manufacturing							
sector	20.0	30.0	31.0	29.0	25.0	23.0	22.0
Consumer goods	16.0	31.0	34.0	29.0	27.3	20.3	21.3
Intermediate goods	34.0	31.0	33.0	32.0	26.6	23.3	23.1
Capital goods	42.0	24.0	18.0	19.0	25.0	20.0	20.0
Employment							
Consumer goods	68.0	69.0	64.0	66.0	66.2	69.7	71.1
Intermediate goods	29.0	25.0	26.0	26.0	25.0	23.9	23.2
Capital goods	2.0	4.0	5.0	7.0	9.0	6.0	6.0
Manufacturing sector/							
total employment	8.4	13.4	17.4	16.9	13.6	15.1	17.8

Sources: World Bank (1987); URT, *Survey of Industrial Production, 1980–81*; URT, *Economic Survey*, various issues.
[a] Firms employing ten or more people.
[b] Consumer goods include food and food products, beverages and tobacco, and textiles and apparel.
[c] Intermediate goods include leather and leather products except shoes, wood and wood products, chemicals and fertilizers, rubber and plastic products, iron and steel and metal and metal products, and non-metallic products.
[d] Capital goods include machinery and transport equipment.

reduced the availability of external finance for current use. Third, industrial capacity expansion over the previous period had created capacity that exceeded, on any reasonable assessment, that which Tanzania could use effectively with only its own resources. The availability of non-fungible foreign resources tied to project finance had meant that capacity expansion faced a less stringent financing constraint than capacity utilization; the lopsidedness of the resulting expansion quickly generated bottle-necks.

Both investment and production are import dependent. Import compression quickly hit both as closure of resource gaps was enforced. Gross and net real investment declined at average annual rates of 5.4 and 6.7 respectively. In the public sector this was enforced largely through freezing new development expenditures. Import licensing was used as the main instrument to implement import compression. The decline in availability

Table 16.3 Indicators of macroeconomic performance and resource gaps, Tanzania, 1978–88

	GDP growth rate	Inflation rate	Foreign saving[a]/ GDP	Real imports[b]/ GDP	Nominal imports/ GDP	Nominal exports/ GDP
1977	0.4	11.6	5.7	23.6	24.1	17.4
1978	2.1	12.2	17.2	31.0	30.8	12.8
1979	2.9	13.0	13.3	21.0	27.7	13.9
1980	2.5	30.2	14.2	18.3	27.3	11.1
1981	−0.5	25.7	10.1	16.3	22.2	10.9
1982	0.6	28.9	11.6	13.2	20.0	8.1
1983	−2.4	27.1	7.3	11.8	14.4	6.9
1984	3.4	36.1	6.5	16.2	14.2	8.2
1985	2.6	33.3	8.9	16.9	13.7	6.3
1986	3.0	32.4	13.5	15.7	21.0	9.3
1987	3.6	29.9	30.4	13.3	37.7	13.8
1988	4.1	28.2	33.5	14.3	42.9	16.6
1989	4.5	25.8	37.2		48.0	18.1

Sources: Bank of Tanzania, *Economic and Operations Report*, various issues; URT, *Economic Survey*, various issues.
[a] Foreign saving is defined as the negative of the current account balance plus net transfers.
[b] The real imports to GDP ratio diverges from the nominal one due to differences in the deflators for the two magnitudes, particularly after 1986.

of imported intermediates translated into cuts in output and a fall in capacity utilization. Real value added of the manufacturing sector declined steeply, at a rate of 7 per cent annually between 1980 and 1983 (Table 16.1). The contribution of the manufacturing sector to GDP declined persistently, reaching 7 per cent (compared with the 1977 peak of 12 per cent) in 1985.

As a result of the faster expansion of production capacities for intermediates and capital goods in the second half of the 1970s, their shares of output and value added rose (Table 16.2). By 1986 the intermediate goods sector had increased its share in output to 38 per cent and in value added to 40 per cent. The capital goods sector also registered significant increases in these shares. The consumer goods sector, however, remained the largest in all aspects.

Economic recovery and industrial restructuring, 1986–91

The relaxation of import compression is one of the main features of the economic recovery period (Table 16.3). Although the Own Funds Imports scheme, introduced in the second half of 1984, significantly increased the volume of imports, for the first 18 months of the scheme these were predominantly consumer goods. From 1986 on, two developments helped reduce import compression in the manufacturing sector very significantly.

First, the rapidly increasing own-funds imports shifted in their structure toward capital and intermediate goods, as scarcity rents in the consumer goods category declined with the rapid expansion of supplies. Second, with the official sanctioning by international financial institutions of the Economic Recovery Programme, foreign resource inflows resumed at an increasing rate. A large proportion of these were in the form of import support programmes favouring the manufacturing sector. Total imports increased steadily from US$992.2 million in 1986 to US$1,550 million in 1990.

The other important feature of the recovery period was a restructuring of the incentives affecting the manufacturing sector. This included a steep reduction in output price protection with import and foreign exchange liberalization, and a large cut in input cost subsidization as the official value of the currency was steeply depreciated. The reduction in import compression helped revive growth. However, the pattern of recovery was influenced by the changes in the incentive structure.

Real investment growth rebounded strongly. Gross fixed capital formation increased at an annual rate of 23.6 per cent between 1984 and 1988. Net additions to fixed assets were concentrated in the textiles, beverages, tobacco manufactures, footwear-leather and non-metallic products industries.

Between 1986 and 1989 manufacturing real value added grew by about 5 per cent per annum (4.2 per cent in 1987, 5.4 per cent in 1988 and 5.1 per cent in 1989). Capacity utilization increased from 25 per cent in 1985 to 35 per cent in 1989. Gross real output also increased by 17 per cent between 1985 and 1989 (Table 16.3). The sectors identified as competitively efficient in 1985 by a World Bank industrial survey (World Bank, 1987) dominated the growth revival; notably textiles, tobacco manufactures, wood and wood products except furniture, paper and paper products, rubber products and non-metallic products. Most of the extremely inefficient sectors steeply contracted their output (Table 16.4).

This last observation is corroborated by the results of another unpublished World Bank industrial survey conducted in late 1989, covering the same sample of forty-eight firms in the sector (over 10 per cent of the formal manufacturing sector) as the 1985 survey. Firms which were found to be relatively efficient in 1985 – domestic resource costs (DRCs) less than two – increased their output by 24 per cent between 1985 and 1988. Those with DRCs greater than two contracted their output by 20 per cent over the same period. Those with negative value added in 1984 experienced a 43 per cent contraction of output over the same period. The later survey, however, notes that even the most 'inefficient' firms survived the significantly reduced protection. This could point to some internal restructuring or continued protection in other forms.

From a detailed study of the textile sector by de Valk and Mbelle (1990)

Table 16.4 Real output index of manufacturing industries, Tanzania

Sector	1985	1986	1987	1988	1989	SR DRC	Attainable SR DRCs
Food manufacturing	100	88	86	98	106	0.39	0.27
Beverage industries	100	89	83	83	82	0.58	0.55
Tobacco manufacture	100	102	103	103	111	0.13	0.11
Textiles	100	117	146	167	159	0.87	0.78
Wearing apparel except footwear							
Leather products except footwear	100	75	73	54	51	∞	∞
Footwear – leather	100	87	43	43	35	∞	∞
Wood and wood products except furniture	100	125	171	184	189		
Paper and paper products	100	160	251	228	245	0.53–2.84	0.24–1.30
Printing and publishing							
Industrial chemicals	100	97	66	54	72	∞	∞
Other chemical products	100	100	119	119	122		
Petroleum refineries	100	93	92	109	104		
Rubber products	100	117	162	161	177	0.37–0.79	
Plastic products	100	107	107	92	146	0.21–0.50	0.15–0.39
Pottery, china, glass, non-metallic products	100	117	127	142	144	0.69–2.23	0.35–0.80
Iron, steel and non-ferrous metals	100	57	85	71	100	∞	∞
Fabricated metal products	100	115	175	127	169	0.58	
Machinery except electrical	100	130	142	89	53	∞	∞
Electrical machinery, apparatus and supplies	100	94	105	111	117		
Transport equipment	100	74	69	69	93	∞	∞
Other manfuacturing industries							
Total manufacturing	100	97	107	115	117		

Sources: URT (1990a), *Industrial Commodities Quarterly Report*; World Bank (1987).
SR DRC, Short-run domestic resource cost; where SR DRC is infinity, activity generates
negative value added at world market prices.

it is apparent that some firms compressed the import content of their
products in response to import strangulation and the subsequent steep rise
in the domestic cost of imported inputs attendant on the official exchange
rate depreciation. In the case of textile firms the composition of their
output seems to have shifted towards less-processed products to evade the
more intensive use of imported inputs in the later stages. The study found
a general contraction of profit rates, but they fell much less in the firms
exporting large proportions of their output. It also found much better
profit performance among private firms.

No major changes from the 1981–5 period were evident at this time in
the structure of the manufacturing sector. The consumer goods sector

continued to dominate intermediate and capital goods in contributions to output, value added and employment.

In brief, there is evidence of the revival of the manufacturing sector in response to reduced import compression. The sector's contributions to total GDP increased from 7 per cent in 1985 to 9 per cent in 1989. The pattern of recovery in the industrial sector also suggests some restructuring in response to reduced protection. If a combined increase in the contribution of the sector to GDP and restructuring towards more efficient sectors is sustained, a stronger industrial base may be established.

Trends in productivity and efficiency in the manufacturing sector, 1966–88

Productivity and efficiency trends are evaluated in this sector from two perspectives. First we shall assess developments in factor productivity in terms of domestic prices. This may provide some indication of the 'learning' gains from protection. Second, an evaluation of competitive efficiency will be undertaken to enable the assessment of the domestic resource cost of protection. The welfare loss associated with higher cost sourcing of consumption (from protected domestic producers) will *not* be considered explicitly in this study.

Efficiency trends under protection

Three measures of efficiency under protection are considered here. Partial factor productivity trends are considered first. Labour and investment productivity are assessed for the period 1966–88. In view of the paucity of the available data, total factor productivity is not explicitly estimated; nevertheless, studies that have attempted such productivity estimation for Tanzania's manufacturing sector are reviewed.

Table 16.5 presents labour productivity trends in Tanzania's manufacturing sector. Until 1980, value added per worker remained reasonably stable. It dropped steeply, however, between 1981 and 1986 mainly as a result of a steep decline in real value added while more or less the same number of employees were maintained.

In terms of depicting the 'correct' labour productivity changes, there are two problems with this measure. First, the number of employees does not represent the effective labour time applied. Second, as can be seen in Table 16.5, labour cost's share in total cost and in value added showed a declining trend during the time when value added was declining, partly offsetting the apparent rise in overemployment.

A modified measure of labour productivity was therefore calculated. First, real labour cost per worker was computed. Presumably, this reflects effective labour time more closely and is a better measure of the cost of a

Table 16.5 Labour productivity in the manufacturing sector and subsectoral composition, Tanzania (constant 1976 prices) (%)

	1966–70	1971–5	1976–80	1981	1982	1983	1984	1985	1986	1988
Manufacturing sector										
Value added per worker (shs '000)	35.4	29.9	22.2	11.7	10.8	9.6	17.0	16.3	13.5	19.8
Real labour cost per worker (shs '000)	9.8	9.3	6.4	5.5	5.6	5.2	5.5	5.2	4.3	4.9
Value added per unit real labour cost (shs)	3.6	3.1	3.5	2.1	1.9	1.8	3.1	2.3	3.1	4.0

	1977	1978	1981	1982	1983	1984	1986	1988
Subsectors: Value added per worker (shs '000)								
Consumer goods	19.3	15.3	9.6	8.5	7.6	13.2	7.8	13.2
Intermediate goods	29.8	28.1	19.7	14.8	13.2	23.8	26.0	37.2
Capital goods	31.5	13.2	12.6	14.6	13.0	16.6	24.3	27.9

	1966–70	1971–5	1976–80	1981	1982	1983	1984	1985	1986	1987	1988
Manufacturing sector:											
Labour cost share in total cost	14.0	18.9	16.8	15.8	16.3	14.6	14.5	12.3	12.5	9.1	
Labour cost share in value added	46.1	43.2	34.5	38.6	41.1	41.4	44.3	40.1	42.5	32.4	

Sources: World Bank (1987); URT, Survey of Industrial Production, various issues; URT, Economic Survey, various issues.

unit of labour to the employer (affordability), a determinant of the number of workers he retains. Productivity was then calculated as value added per unit real labour cost. This measure of productivity fluctuated between 1966 and 1980, strongly declined between 1980 and 1984, and rebounded strongly during 1984–8. Using this modified measure, labour productivity faltered badly only during the economic crisis period when value added registered a steep decline. However, no significant productivity gains since 1966–70 are visible.

The next measure of efficiency we review is a simple measure of investment productivity in the manufacturing sector, to enable us to obtain an approximate assessment of capital productivity trends. The ratio of the growth rate in manufacturing value added to the gross investment rate showed a very steep decline between 1966–70 and 1976–80, and turned negative (–11.8 per cent) during 1981–3 (Table 16.1). The trend is more or less similar using net investment. This steep decline is predominantly explained by a rapid decline in capacity utilization after the mid-1970s (Ndulu, 1986). Many new plants could virtually not begin operations; and underutilization of capacity set in for the older plants. The dominant factor explaining the decline in capacity utilization was import compression (Wangwe, 1983; Ndulu, 1986; Mbelle, 1988). This was reinforced by delays in commissioning new plants located in areas without adequate power and water (for regional equity reasons) and deterioration of supportive infrastructure in operational locations. Capacity utilization was estimated to have fallen from well over 75 per cent before 1973 to 29.4 per cent in 1982 and further to 24.8 per cent in 1985 (Ndulu, 1986; World Bank, 1987; Mbelle, 1988). This steep decline in capacity utilization affected not only short-run efficiency, through increased fixed unit costs of production, but, even more, long-run efficiency, measured in terms of returns to capital. The latter, as we shall argue later, needs to be given special attention when assessing the efficiency of the sector, whether static or dynamic, in the context of alternative policies. With partial recovery of capacity utilization after 1985 and the revival of growth in value added, investment productivity marginally improved in gross terms, but still reached only 1.4 per cent. Capital productivity remained at extremely low levels on account of the large overhang of excess capacity.

Two studies have attempted detailed assessments of the dynamic efficiency of the manufacturing sector in Tanzania. In a comparative study (Kenya, Tanzania, Zambia and Zimbabwe), Shaaeldin (1989) estimated total factor productivity growth (TFPG) for Tanzania using the standard sources of growth method for the period 1966–80. The study finds that while TFPG accounted for 24 per cent of total growth during 1966–73, it turned negative during 1973–80. For the whole period (1966–80) TFPG for Tanzania was negligible. The study concludes that increases in factor inputs were the major source of manufacturing growth in Tanzania and not, as required in the argument for protecting infant industries, factor productivity growth. Among the major reasons considered for the poor TFPG performance after 1973 were capacity underutilization, small market size, protective trade and macroeconomic policies, concentrated market structure and low levels of technological capabilities.

Two obvious methodological problems arise with the above analysis. First, capital stock was not adjusted for capacity utilization, potentially biasing the TFPG estimates downward for 1973–80. Second, labour was measured as the number of employees, far overstating effective man-hours relative to the labour cost index, discussed above. Using the same capital stock data adjusted for capacity utilization and real labour costs, Ndulu (1986) found (as did Shaaeldin) that variations in output were totally explained by changes in factor inputs; factor productivity growth was statistically insignificant. A test as to whether excess capacity might have been associated with output growth through the selective discarding of less productive plants as the import constraint tightened yielded results in the negative.

Mbelle (1988) did a very detailed technical study of textile and beverage industries at sectoral and firm level. Having estimated homothetic frontier production functions for the two industries, he estimated generalized Farrel measures of efficiency at firm and sectoral levels. Output was measured in physical terms, capacity adjusted for utilization, labour measured in actual man-hours and intermediate imports in constant 1976 prices. Pooled time-series and cross-sectional data for the period 1974–84 were used. Technical efficiency was measured as the potential output increase for given inputs or potential cost-saving for given output, with the efficiency frontier as reference point. Scale efficiency was measured as the potential cost savings from operating at one level of scale relative to another. These efficiency measures were estimated both for individual firms and for the industry (structural efficiency).

The results showed that at the individual firm level, the distribution of technical efficiency was skewed towards inefficient ones in both industries, much more so in 1984 than in 1976. Scale efficiency measures were much closer to the frontiers than technical efficiency, suggesting greater prevalence of technical inefficiency.

At the industry level, potential input savings for observed textile output were estimated to range between 21 per cent and 66 per cent in the various years, with higher potential after 1978. For beverage industries, these potential input savings were estimated at 57 per cent and 53 per cent for 1976 and 1984 respectively. Potential cost savings from the observed increase in optimal scale was estimated at only 1.3 per cent. Using the Salter technical advance measure, relatively rapid *potential* technical progress, involving 4–8 per cent annual cost reduction at a high shadow price of imported inputs, was estimated for textiles. In actual performance, however, no technical progress was achieved in either industry.

The above set of indicators of productivity and efficiency in the manufacturing sector raise a number of issues for consideration in the industrialization process. The first concerns the pace of capacity expansion relative to utilization of installed capacity. The steep decline in investment productivity points towards wastage of capital resources, losses in productivity growth and a reduction of welfare as the cost of local manufactures increased with capacity underutilization. As argued elsewhere, this problem was largely associated with the non-fungibility of foreign project finance as between use for capacity expansion and use for capacity utilization (Ndulu, 1986; Rattso, 1988). The crisis of capacity underutilization was thus not simply the result of a total import capacity constraint but also of its lopsided allocation.

Second, as Mbelle (1988) shows, returns from the use of the limited available import capacity were significantly lower than the potential. A system of foreign exchange allocation that strived to keep all firms alive in response to import compression ignored efficiency differences in the use of such a scarce resource. Mbelle shows a wide range of substitution possibilities at lower capacity utilization rates that could have improved efficiency through selective allocation of foreign exchange across products and firms within the textile and beverage industries.

Third, the potential for cost reduction via technical and scale efficiencies was created although not realized. Complementary technological capacities for realizing these benefits were inadequate as shown by at best stagnant labour productivity. The structure of installed capacity created potential for better linkages with other sectors. Thus opportunities for realizing greater benefits from protected industrialization did exist if utilization and efficiency would have been enhanced.

The human capacity constraint was a major bottleneck to improvement of productivity in the sector. Industrialization proceeded at a pace not consistent with available technological capabilities and technological learning (Wangwe, 1990). The structure of industries quickly shifted towards activities demanding unavailable advanced skills and know-how. Reliance on foreign technical assistance (which was expensive and had a high turnover rate) supported operation for as long as it was adequately available. Pre-investment assessments done by foreign consulting firms led to technological choices not matched by available capabilities at home. The link between foreign engineering consultants, machinery suppliers and foreign finance systematically operated against local participation and technological learning (Mlawa, 1983: Skarstein and Wangwe, 1986). Foreign finance and foreign personnel, packaged in turnkey projects, though consistent with the output generation objective, militated against technological learning.

Product technology was largely a replica of formerly imported products.

Import substitution took the form of close substitution of the product characteristics of former imports with little or no indigenization such as is critical for building up skills (Wangwe, 1992).

On the home front, although the literacy rate increased very rapidly, secondary and technical education did not receive adequate emphasis. The number of scientists and technologists fell short of the estimated requirements by at least 42 per cent. Established industry-specific training institutes were starved of resources and, where operational, emphasized basic and low-level operative skills not adequate for existing requirements and not conducive to innovation or assimilation of imported technologies (Wangwe, 1990).

The cost of temporary protection for infant industries has partially been justified by the inappropriability of labour skills acquired through learning-by-doing in the absence of mortgages in workers (Rosenstein-Rodan, 1943). Since the benefits of such training are not appropriable by the trainer, socially optimum levels of training may not take place unless firms are compensated for the cost of training (expensive labour) via protection or direct subsidies. However, to realize the benefits and minimize the cost of such protection, a careful assessment of technological capabilities, appropriate choices of technology, and deliberate, careful design of programmes to enhance technological learning are necessary.

Weak infrastructure also constrained potential productivity and output growth. Deterioration of power and water supplies were responsible for a large proportion of the shut-downs of operating plants and long delays in the commissioning of new large plants. As Mbelle (1988) shows, closure of operating firms due to power and water shortages was a very significant cause of capacity underutilization in the textile and beverage industries during the first half of the 1980s. In the effort to establish multiple growth centres to achieve regional equality, a number of major industrial investments were located in areas without adequate power and water supplies. Long delays in commissioning plants or their partial operation in new industrial centres such as Mbeya, Tabora, Mwanza and Musoma accounted for a large share of the responsibility for the very low capacity utilization of new investments.

Competitive efficiency of the manufacturing sector

In a study entitled *Tanzania: An Agenda for Industrial Recovery*, the World Bank (1987) did a very detailed assessment of the competitive efficiency of the manufacturing sector in 1984. Using data from a large survey of firms cutting across all subsectors and accounting for more than 10 per cent of all manufacturing firms in the formal sector, both short-run and long-run DRCs were calculated and efficiency performance across subsectors was assessed. Table 16.6 contains a summary of the DRCs at actual

Table 16.6 Subsectoral competitive efficiency of industry, Tanzania, 1984

Subsector	Actual capacity	Actual S-R	Actual L-R	Operating rate of profit	Actual Ec.RR (%)	Financial profit prot. (%)	Attainable C.U. (%)	Attainable SR DRC	Attainable LR DRC
Food products	30	0.3	0.93	32	2	11	56	0.22	0.59
Beverages and tobacco	50	0.28	0.72	65	11	38	68	0.25	0.65
Textiles and apparel	40	1.34	3.92	47	-23	43	53	1.57	4.35
Tanneries and leather	12	∞	∞	41	-26	31	34	∞	∞
Plastics and pharmaceuticals	19	4.06	20.27	26	-20	13	45	1.43	5.06
Petrol, chemicals and fertilizers	32	∞	∞	40	-21	50	54	1.21	3.73
Rubber, wood, paper and cement	31	1.62	3.24	18	-26	27	65	0.77	1.40
Iron, steel and metal products	33	5.70	16.28	27	-10	17	60	1.11	2.61
Machinery and transport equipment	13	2.01	7.12	34	-19	26	33	4.79	13.10
Total	25.2	0.99	2.91	34	-15	25	52.5	0.71	1.82

Source: World Bank (1987).

Actual capacity: Actual capacity utilization rate (%) measured as the ratio of actual output to technically rated capacity output.

Actual S-R: Short-run domestic resource cost (DRC) at actual capacity utilization rate, measured as labour cost at shadow value added at world prices. Shadow labour cost conversion factor is 0.53.

Actual L-R: Long-run DRC at actual capacity utilization rate. L-R measured as the sum of shadow values of labour and annual capacity costs divided by value added at world prices. The conversion factor for shadow value of capital costs is the same as for foreign exchange, 2.67.

Operating rate of profit: Value added at domestic prices less labour cost, divided by sales revenue at domestic prices.

Actual Ec.RR: Economic return on capital at actual capacity utilization.

Financial profit prot.: Net financial return on capital less economic return on capital.

Attainable C.U.: Capacity utilization rate that could be attained with improved availability of foreign exchange in the near future.

Attainable SR DRC: Short-run DRC at attainable capacity.

Attainable LR DRC: Long-run DRC at attainable capacity.

and attainable capacity utilization rates (the ratio of actual to technically rated capacity output) as well as a comparison of financial and economic rates of return under the two scenarios of capacity utilization. Implied financial profit protection rates for the local manufacturers are also shown.

The weighted average short-run DRC for the manufacturing sector as a whole at the then-current very low capacity utilization rate (25.2 per cent) was just below 1 (0.99). At the attainable capacity rate of 52.5 per cent, short-run DRC fell to 0.71 for the sector as a whole, significantly improving competitive efficiency. The dispersion of competitive efficiency at actual capacity utilization rates across sectors was very wide, ranging from a short-run DRC of 0.28 for beverages and tobacco to infinity (in the case of negative value added at shadow prices) for tanneries and leather as well as chemicals and fertilizers. At attainable capacity, the range was from 0.22 for food products to infinity for leather and tanneries. Consumer goods industries, on the whole, did much better than their counterparts, with more than 80 per cent of their activities estimated as competitive in the short run at attainable capacity.

The long-run DRC which is more sensitive to capacity utilization on the whole performed much worse than the short-run DRC. For the sector as a whole, the average was 2.91 at actual capacity utilization and 1.82 at attainable capacity utilization. Again the consumer goods sector did much better than the rest. At attainable capacity both the food products and the beverage and tobacco subsectors had their long-run DRCs well below 1.

For the manufacturing sector as a whole, at the actual rate of capacity utilization, 37 per cent of the activities generated negative value added at world market prices. Such activities were concentrated in the subsectors producing intermediates and capital goods, particularly tanneries and leather, and transport equipment.

On the basis of these estimates and our knowledge of the likely major factors explaining the observed differences, we can make the following preliminary observations. Sectors with relatively very low capacity utilization rates tended to do very poorly in terms of competitive efficiency. Indeed, the sensitivity of conventionally measured short-run and long-run DRCs to capacity utilization rates seems to be very high. It has been shown elsewhere (Waverman and Murphy, 1992) that cost penalties associated with capacity underutilization are highly non-linear, increasing fastest below 30 per cent. Second, subsectors with relatively high overemployment combined with high imported input content have also tended to do poorly in competitive efficiency terms. Such subsectors have tended to be most inflexible in reducing labour engaged relative to reduced capacity utilization. Moreover, the highest implicit subsidization of imported input, via the overvalued currency, was likely to be concentrated in highly import-dependent sectors.

Using data from the survey for seventy-four activities with positive value added at international prices, we attempted, with a cross-sectional regression equation, to establish the relative importance of capacity utilization (CU), import content (IMPCONT – the ratio of the value of imported to total inputs, a proxy for the relative extent of imported input cost subsidization), and nominal output price protection (NPRCT) in determining competitive efficiency. With the measure of short-run domestic resource cost (SRDRC) as the dependent variable, representing competitive efficiency, the following results were obtained:

$$SRDRC = 2.1 - 0.027CU + 0.022IMPCONT + 0.001NPRCT (R^2=0.34,$$
$$\quad\quad\quad (2.4)\ (-3.1)\quad\quad (3.1)\quad\quad\quad\quad\quad (0.3)\quad\quad DW=2.1,$$
$$\quad\quad\quad\quad\quad\quad\quad\quad\quad\quad\quad\quad\quad\quad\quad\quad\quad\quad\quad\quad\quad F=8.6)$$

('t' statistics are in brackets)

The results confirm the important impact of capacity utilization on competitive efficiency. Higher subsidization of imported input via currency devaluation was also significantly associated with reduced competitive efficiency (higher SRDRCs). Tariff-based protection (via the escalated tariff structure) was not correlated with efficiency across subsectors. A quick glance at Table 16.6 shows that the consumer goods subsectors, most protected both nominally and effectively, tended to do best at world competitive prices.

Table 16.6 also shows that, except for chemicals and fertilizers, those subsectors which were most competitive internationally tended to receive the highest rate of protection of financial profit. This suggests that the basic response of protected firms was to transform efficiency into very high profits under protection. Reduced protection levels in such cases will reduce profit rates but not necessarily make them unprofitable.

IMPORT SUBSTITUTION AND RELATED POLICIES

Performance

Indicators of import-substitution (IS) performance are given in Table 16.7. IS rose continuously over the 1961–83 period. The share of domestic production in total supply of manufactures rose from 38 per cent in 1961 to 50 per cent in 1978, and 69 per cent in 1983.

The apparent sustenance of high levels of IS in spite of a drop in domestic output during the 1979–83 period was a reflection of import compression (particularly of consumer goods) which arose from severe lack of foreign exchange. During this period, manufacturing output (at 1976 constant prices) declined by 7 per cent per annum. The subsequent recorded decline in IS between 1984 and 1988 exaggerates the real change. The apparent large decline was the result of a relatively greater expansion of manufactured imports, more particularly in value terms (due to frequent

Table 16.7 Import substitution and domestic production: manufacturing sector, Tanzania (current prices)

Ratios	1961	1965	1971	1973	1978	1981	1982	1983	1984	1986	1987	1988
Production for domestic market	29.6	36.0	35.4	42.5	46.7	54.3	57.2	58.9	53.9	46.1	29.9	32.4
Total supply of manufactures Manufactured imports	62.2	56.2	54.1	51.1	49.6	40.5	38.3	36.6	41.1	50.4	64.6	63.7
Total supply of manufactures Domestic production	38.1	43.8	45.9	48.9	50.4	59.5	61.8	68.7	66.9	49.6	35.4	36.3
Total supply of manufactures Total supply of manufactures / consumer goods	50.0	59.5	75.6	72.2	66.8	78.1	78.3	89.1	85.6	78.8	76.8	
/ intermediate goods	25.7	32.1	33.8	39.8	72.2	79.6	76.1	76.1	82.6	56.0	47.2	
/ capital goods	16.4	16.6	15.3	21.4	17.4	22.5	24.6	24.6	18.4	13.4	8.1	

Sources: World Bank (1987); URT, 1988s Trade Statistics; URT, Economic Survey, various issues; Bank of Tanzania, Economic and Operations Report (1987, 1986).

The same ratios at constant prices may differ from those at current prices because of different deflators for domestic production, imports and their combination, which make up the total supply of manufactures.

devaluations) but also in volume (due to import liberalization), than the expansion of domestic output which grew at an average annual rate of 5 per cent between 1986 and 1990.

Trade and related policies and protection of industry

Two sources of profit protection for domestic industrial enterprises in Tanzania can be identified, namely, output price protection and input cost subsidization. The combination of higher domestic prices and lower than border-priced input costs yield protected profit levels in excess of those obtainable at world prices. Several protective instruments under each source were actively employed.

Commercial and pricing policies were the key instruments used for providing nominal output price protection to local industrial enterprises. Nominal tariffs on competitive imports directly raised domestic prices of these imports. Quantitative restrictions (implicit tariffs) also limited domestic supplies and generated upward pressure on prices. In a regime where quantitative restrictions and exchange controls were the main instrument for balance of payments management, implicit tariffs could dominate nominal tariffs in output price protection.

Until July 1984, statutory cost-plus pricing with fixed markups was mandatory for most domestic suppliers of manufactures under the Price Control Act (1973). To ensure compliance, most wholesale trade was internally confined to and controlled by state and parastatal bodies. Cost-plus pricing, while on the one hand restricting monopoly profits, on the other, ensured profit margins irrespective of the cost efficiency of domestic suppliers.

Input cost subsidization was provided through several instruments. The escalated tariff structure provided effective protection in excess of the nominal protection. Higher tariffs were levied on import substitutes in contrast to the much lower rates for non-competitive imports of inputs. The overvalued currency provided an implicit cost subsidy on imported inputs, the subsidy per unit of output varying with imported inputs' share in total cost. Draconian wage controls also reduced labour's share in value added and boosted profit shares (see Tables 16.1, 16.3 and 16.4). Negative real rates of interest on credit (subsidized capital) substantially reduced the financial cost of industrial expansion and lowered fixed costs compared to a more realistic pricing of investible resources.

Industrial licensing policies also worked to create and enforce protection and monopolistic tendencies in a number of areas. We take up below in greater detail the role of each of the instruments of profit protection and their changing roles over time.

While tariff protection was dominant prior to 1970, between the mid-1970s and the mid-1980s the role of tariffs in determining the pattern and efficiency of resource allocation was overshadowed by the prominence of quantitative restrictions. Policy instruments and reforms adopted since 1984, however, including the own-funds import scheme, the open general licence (OGL) facility, price decontrol, deconfinement and exchange rate adjustment, considerably reduced the role of non-tariff barriers again, in providing protection to local industries.

Tariffs

During the 1961–7 period, industrial tariff protection was provided through two categories of tariffs, namely the external tariffs and 'transfer taxes'. The external tariffs, which were levied on goods originating from outside the East African common market, were set on a common basis for the three partner states. This introduced inflexibility to the tariff protection policies of the less industrialized partners since, once an industry in one partner state was granted tariff protection, markets in the other partners were automatically protected. And, since Kenya was more industrialized than the other partners, the protective structure was basically determined by the former's industrial protection needs.

As pressure for an East African federation eased, Tanzania initiated changes which increased its flexibility to pursue independent economic policies. As a result, inter-community tariffs (commonly referred to as 'transfer taxes') were introduced in December 1967 to be levied on some goods originating from partner states, with the aim of promoting new industries in less industrialized partners. However, the conditions for imposing transfer taxes were made so stringent that only about 18 per cent of inter-community trade was affected (Mbogoro, 1977: 26–7) and, in Tanzania, the concentration was on five items, namely, soap and soap products, matches, woven cotton fabrics, unknitted clothing, and footwear and parts, which together accounted for 75 per cent of the revenue collected from this source in 1963 and 1969 (Segal, 1971).

The 1970–82 period can generally be considered to be one of uncoordinated developments in tariff-based protection. The tariff structure was designed to reflect multiple government objectives, as determined by Tanzania's declared policy of 'socialism and self-reliance', and in response to the demands of different segments of the society. During this period the tariff structure was determined primarily by revenue targets. The objective of protection was fulfilled mainly by non-tariff instruments. Although one can discern an increasing trend in tariff protection, its significance could not be evaluated by a mere perusal of the tariff schedule. The role of tariff protection was, in fact, heavily reduced by duty exemptions and evasion.

Duty exemptions, measured as the difference between actual collections and what should have been collected if no exemptions were granted, exceeded actual collections by 88 per cent in 1986. Capital goods accounted for 53.9 per cent of total exemptions, followed by intermediates at 27.3 per cent and consumer goods at 18.8 per cent (Ndulu *et al.*,1987). The effect of duty exemptions was to lower the actual (or effective) individual tariff rates relative to those on the schedules. However, the escalated structure of exemptions further strengthened the spread between effective rates of protection and nominal tariff protection for industrial activities.

Duty evasion was also high, especially in high-duty imports. The structure of declared imports responded to the duty rate structure as high scheduled rates either became prohibitive or induced evasion in declaration. For example, luxury consumer goods or intermediates used in the production of luxury goods, which were normally subjected to duty rates of 100 per cent and above, were hardly ever recorded as being imported, an indication that the rates were prohibitive or led to evasion. Moreover, most of the recorded imports under this category were probably made only after exemption was guaranteed; this category of imports registered a collection rate of only 10 per cent compared to a weighted average scheduled rate of 120 per cent in 1986 (Ndulu *et al.*, 1987).

Until mid-1988, Tanzania's tariff structure was relatively complex, with eighteen different rate categories and wide rate dispersions ranging from 0 to 200 per cent. Since then, however, the government has adopted changes which were aimed at rationalizing the tariff structure. In mid-1988, the number of rate categories and their levels were reduced. The structure retained its escalation, with imports of intermediate and capital goods subject to lower tariffs (of 20–25 per cent) and consumer goods subject to a higher basic rate (of 60 per cent) with higher rates for luxuries. Attempts to reduce exemptions to achieve increased transparency, however, met with resistance primarily on account of existing agreements with external agencies which are largely exempt from taxation on imports of goods and services which they finance.

In June 1960, further reforms were made in the tariff structure by reducing the number of rate categories to five, namely 0 per cent, 20 per cent, 30 per cent, 40 per cent and 60 per cent. However, the escalated structure was maintained.

The structure of tariff protection which emerged from the East African external tariffs encouraged resources to flow to the protected Kenyan industries. Moreover, new industries were encouraged to go to Kenya, even in areas which faced insignificant external tariff protection, to take advantage of the positive externalities generated via the tariff-protected industries. Only those industries which, by utilizing natural advantages, operated more efficiently in Tanzania than Kenya were likely to be established in the former partner state. Furthermore, activities which utilized (protected) imported inputs from Kenya had to operate more efficiently than they otherwise would in order to be competitive, especially if they aimed to export their outputs.

Table 16.8 Tariff protection in the manufacturing sector, Tanzania, 1966 and 1984

Industry	1966		1984
	Nominal protection (%)	*Effective protection (%)*	*Effective Protection (%)*
Tobacco	234	528	316
Beer	103	187	1,399
Canned fruit and vegetables	375	184	335
Soft drinks	16	−23	5
Textiles	73	269	240
Tyres and tubes	36	270	59
Soap	27.5	151	5,258
Tanning and leather	30	130	
Footwear	43	123	
Metal products	25	93	
Glass products	30	31	424
Paper products	12.5	26	6,682
Cement	7.5	12	101
Sisal and jute bags	1.5	1	
Pharmaceutical products	0	0	2,952

Sources: Rweyemamu (1973); World Bank (1987).

The main objective of transfer tax protection was to assist infant industries with 'teething problems', not industries which were uneconomic or which attempted to evade competition. Since few items qualified for transfer tax protection and the rates imposed were low, the industrial sector was still exposed to competition for quality and cost effectiveness within the union (Hazlewood, 1966).

The protective structure generated by the combination of external tariffs and transfer taxes remained largely the same until the early 1980s, in spite of the collapse of the East African Community in the second half of the 1970s. The protection structure (shown in Table 16.8) had the following characteristics.

First, with the exception of a few products, effective rates of protection (ERP) were predominantly higher than nominal rates of protection (NRP). Higher ERP than NRP was the result of much lower tariffs for intermediates and capital goods. This encouraged the importation of raw materials and other inputs inducing a bias in favour of import-dependent production techniques. Overvalued currencies only enhanced this tendency through further subsidization of imported inputs. The decrease in the ratio of domestic value added to gross output and the increased vulnerability to instability in import capacity observed after 1978 are partly the product of increased import dependence. Ngiliule (1986) has also shown that the structure of protection encouraged capital-intensive investment.

Secondly, the dispersion of ERPs across activities indicated a structure of protection very much favouring import substitutes, particularly non-durable consumer goods. The dispersion was much higher for ERPs than NRPs, and the range much wider for particular activities than for sectoral averages.

Consumer products were the most tariff-protected, especially liquor and spirits, musical instruments, tobacco and matches, whose rates were fixed at 100 per cent and above. Despite the adoption of the basic industry strategy in the mid-1970s, intermediate and capital goods sectors continued to receive the least tariff protection. The process of import substitution deepening was thus not supported by the tariff structure, although this was more than compensated through other protective measures, particularly the overvalued currency in these generally much more import-dependent sectors. This may be due to the continuing dominance of non-competitive imports in the capital and intermediate goods sectors, the concern for minimizing consumer price increases by lowering producer tax burdens, and the government's objective of loading relatively more on price-inelastic products for revenue collection purposes.

High effective protection allows activities to earn higher value added than under (world) competitive conditions. Rweyemamu (1973: 136–7) and Semboja (1978) found a high correlation between effective protection and profitability. (A Spearman rank correlation of 0.60 was obtained by Rweyemamu.) The fact that even those firms producing at negative value added earned reasonably high profits pointed to some considerable protection of inefficiency. Again, Semboja (1978) found that fifteen out of sixteen firms with very low capacity utilization rates in 1976 nevertheless managed to earn high profit rates under protection. Although the usual concerns in this respect are based on static measures, it is unlikely that the potential dynamic benefits of protection were realized.

The recent reduction of rate categories and ranges harmonized the tariff protection of activities which fall within one or similar groups, increased the neutrality of the protective structure, and reduced the average level of tariff protection in the manufacturing sector.

Industrial licensing

As a result of the Kampala Agreement of 1964 in which certain major industries were to be distributed under the Territorial Industrial Licensing Ordinance, giving each exclusive rights to operate throughout the community, Tanzania was allocated the manufacture of aluminium sheets and foil, tyres and tubes, and radio assembly and parts. The exclusive right to the East African market was not long-lived; nevertheless it prompted the establishment of these industries in Tanzania. Until 1990, when the National Investment (Promotion and Protection) Act was passed, no further serious policy attempt was made to create an enabling environment for industrial development through licensing.

The National Investment Act, 1990 specified new incentives and rules which included:

(i) the granting of exemption from paying import duties and sales tax on all machinery, equipment, spare parts, materials and supplies imported for use by the enterprise (however, for revenue purposes, the practice has been for the treasury to limit exemptions only to machinery and equipment);

(ii) reservation of specified areas exclusively for the public sector and local investors; and

(iii) allowance for the retention of a portion of the foreign exchange for use in acquiring inputs and meeting debt service, profit and dividend payments, and other external obligations (URT, 1990b).

The incentive structure specified by the National Investment Act, 1990 had protection and choice of technology implications. First, by granting tax exemption to imports, the provision encourages import- and capital-intensive technologies. However, since the provision does not discriminate among activities within the major groups, the implications for the structure of protection within groups are neutral. However, between groups, the implications of the practice are to lower protection of capital goods relative to other major groups. Second, by specifying areas for the public sector and local investors, the Act has given room for the creation of monopolies, contradicting the current policy directions towards increased competition. Third, by allowing the retention of foreign exchange earned by the export-ing firms for their own use, the Act will encourage investment in export-oriented activities.

Import controls and exchange rate policy

During the 1961–7 period, two interrelated forms of quantitative restriction were adopted, namely import licensing and quotas. Under the import licensing system, importers were allowed to import only if domestic producers were unable to satisfy local demand. (Sometimes the producer was also given exclusive rights to import or granted permission for importation.) This instrument was used mainly for protective purposes, to give the domestic producer the advantage of a guaranteed market. By 1968, import licensing was applicable to about 160 groups of goods originating from outside East Africa, an additional forty items that came from East Africa, and about forty items which were confined to parastatals. About 20 per cent of the goods subject to import licensing if they originated from outside East Africa were not being produced in Tanzania (Grundmann, 1969: 11).

In general, a licence was not granted if the domestic producer was able to satisfy local demand with comparable quality and price. The administrative requirements for determining if the domestic industry could produce adequate quantity (of good quality and at a competitive price) were greater than could be handled by the Import Licensing Department staff at the Bank of Tanzania and, in the end, the system depended on information provided by the producers themselves. Therefore, in fact, it was the domestic producers who decided whether they were ready for competition or not. The result was that firms were given import licensing protection for an indefinite duration (Grundmann, 1969).

Quotas were also used to limit the inflow of goods whose levels of importation were considered to be undesirably high, either for economic reasons (including balance of payments and industrial protection objectives), political or social reasons. For example, in 1967 special import restrictions were imposed on Japanese goods with the aim of correcting the imbalance of trade between the two countries. And suitcases could only be imported when the Suitcase Manufactures of Tanzania Ltd. (SUMATA) had failed to satisfy domestic demand; that is, the import quota was made subject to its level of production.

Although quotas were imposed mainly for balance of payments purposes, the result was to increase the market advantage of the domestic producer. If the quota system had been administered in such a way as to allow significant amounts of imports to maintain some level of competition, the resulting quota protection could have promoted improved quality and productivity. To ensure that the industries were 'growing up', the quota protection could have been gradually reduced. However, quotas which were fixed subject to domestic producers' production levels and approval tended to generate very high levels of protection over indefinite periods, and the resulting lack of competition probably reduced the quality and productivity of industry.

Starting in the early 1970s, import controls were related mainly to foreign exchange availability. Up to the late 1960s, Tanzania maintained a fiscal surplus, a balanced external account, and a rate of inflation which compared favourably with its trading partners. By 1970–1, however, a trade deficit had already surfaced and between 1966 and 1978 the real value of the shilling appreciated by 29 per cent mainly because of high domestic inflation rates associated with deteriorating terms of trade and increasing external debt. Between 1978 and 1985, the shilling appreciated in real terms by a further 57 per cent as the performance of these variables continued to worsen and the government maintained an inflexible stance in the management of the nominal exchange rate. The tightening of import restrictions contributed to currency overvaluation and reduced the potential transparency of the protective tariff structure.

The majority of imported intermediate and capital goods were purchased at the official exchange rate, effectively costing only a fraction of the border price equivalent at an 'appropriate' exchange rate. This amounted to a significant subsidy to import-intensive local production, with the rest of the economy bearing a much higher cost of the ensuing effective protection. The implied foreign exchange subsidy continued to rise with the rising real overvaluation of the shilling.

Under the administrative system of foreign exchange allocation, importers were supposed to be granted licences according to set priorities. Petrol, medicines, food grains and defence needs were given first priority. Consumer imports were given less priority and were determined on a case-by-case basis. The other criteria included end use (e.g. agricultural inputs, namely fertilizers, bags and tractors, received greater attention), local content, 'essentiality' of the commodity, and export orientation. The foreign exchange allocation was also administered in such a way as to assure the survival of existing firms.

Except for a few users, the guidelines were not clear enough and the eventual allocation was the product of a bargaining process which took into account past import patterns, the need to alleviate short-term crises, political strength and size of firms. It was difficult to ensure that the administrative allocation of foreign exchange did not negatively affect the efficiency of utilization of the scarce foreign exchange. The divergence between intended allocation and actual allocation has been demonstrated by two studies: World Bank (1987) and Mbelle (1988). The World Bank study showed that administrative allocation favoured economically inefficient firms at the expense of efficient ones. For example, 25 per cent of the gross output of firms surveyed in 1984 was produced at negative value added, and this output used 42 per cent of all imported inputs and 50 per cent of foreign exchange allocations. Firms with short-run DRCs greater than 1 (66 per cent of surveyed firms) produced 53 per cent of gross output, using 74 per cent of foreign exchange allocated.

In a detailed study, Mbelle (1988) confirmed the above allocation pattern. Using input–output analysis, he demonstrated the excess usage of scarce foreign exchange by 'inefficient' sectors. He also showed that, contrary to the stated criteria, allocation to net foreign exchange earners and savers did not receive priority as intended. The allocation pattern showed a tendency to spread resources thinly across all industries, in order to keep all alive. In effect allocations were highly correlated with past allocations.

Starting in 1986, Tanzania adopted a more flexible exchange rate policy stance. The exchange rate, which stood at shillings 17 to the US dollar in early 1986, rose to shillings 40 in mid-1986, shillings 120 by the end of 1988, shillings 145 in June 1989, and shillings 230 in mid-1991. As a result, the gap between the official and parallel market rates narrowed, though it still remained significant by June 1991.

Also beginning in 1984, the government permitted importation of a specific list of items on an own-finance basis to be sold at market clearing prices. Own-finance import licences were provided automatically and the list of eligible items increased significantly thereafter. In 1986, own-finance imports accounted for 64.7 per cent, 17 per cent and 40.5 per cent of consumer, intermediate and capital goods imports, respectively.

In early 1988, the open general licence (OGL) system was reintroduced. This set aside a portion of the official (externally funded) foreign exchange to be used for specified imports of intermediate and capital goods on demand (non-administrative allocation). In 1990, the OGL accounted for 10 per cent of total imports and the intention was to raise this proportion steadily.

Recent policy changes to reduce currency overvaluation and other changes in the foreign exchange regime were aimed at improving allocation of resources; but success depends on a number of factors. For example, with relative improvements in the availability of foreign exchange, the availability of local cash cover turned out to be the new binding constraint. This was exacerbated by stringent credit ceilings imposed by the IMF. As we shall see shortly, bank credits were not given purely on the basis of creditworthiness. Furthermore, the treasury tended to bail out loss-making parastatals by providing them with government credits, grants or credit guarantees. Under these conditions, foreign exchange could be given to firms which operated inefficiently as long as they were backed by the government. Recent devaluations also caused financial problems to firms which received priority in obtaining foreign loans during earlier years. Since firms were generally required to assume the foreign exchange risk of loans, devaluations hit firms with large foreign debt and little chance to increase prices amid intense competition from imports.

Pricing and confinement policies

The price control system introduced in 1973 applied initially to 1,000 products. The number of controlled items reached a peak of 3,000 by 1978. Subsequently, the number of price-controlled items was steadily reduced. By the end of 1990, only ten products (namely farm implements, electric cables, cement, sugar, corrugated iron sheets, tyres and tubes, petroleum products, fertilizers, reinforced steel, and beer) were price-controlled. In the 1991–2 budget, only petroleum products and chemical fertilizers remained price-controlled.

Under the policy of confinement, wholesale trade in some domestic and imported commodities was restricted to assigned institutions. Industries were required to sell specified goods and to purchase their inputs (both imported and domestically produced) through these institutions. As early as the late 1960s, state trading corporations were given an import monopoly on tinned milk, safety matches, textiles, sugar, cement, metal window louvres, and sisal fabrics. Some producing enterprises were given an import monopoly over the products they themselves manufactured. By the mid-1980s, over fifty products (mainly consumer goods, building materials and agricultural implements) were subject to internal confinement; all imported goods were deemed confined, unless specifically exempted.

During the period of the Economic Recovery Programme, numerous exemptions were granted in an attempt to move away from monopoly towards diversified confinement. In 1990, only sixteen items, in addition to services, were still confined. The number was reduced in the 1991–2 budget along with additional price decontrol measures.

The cost-plus pricing method which was used to determine maximum prices of manufactured goods suffered from several weaknesses. Since profit margins were based on the costs incurred and capital employed, there was no incentive to reduce costs and use labour-intensive technologies. Price protection arose because efficiency was evaluated on the basis of the average firm insulated from foreign competition (Rice, 1976).

There was, however, some disadvantage to the firms subjected to cost-plus pricing. Since most firms did not revalue their capital employed, historical costs of capital were used in the computations. This provided insufficient funds for capital replacement. Insufficient provision of capital replacement was a non-issue during earlier years when government grants and credit guarantees existed in plenty and bank credits were cheap and available. The situation changed in the mid–1980s as such guarantees were increasingly dismantled.

The protection implications of confinement depend on the institution assigned to administer the instrument for the particular product. When administration was undertaken by a trading company, the protection implications were not clear-cut since they were not directly linked to domestic producers. On the other hand, when such administration was done by the respective producers, they would tend to act in their self-interest. In the late 1960s the Tanzania Shoe Company Ltd. had an import monopoly on footwear and leather uppers, and SUMATA, the sole producer of suitcases, had the exclusive right to import suitcases. Later, producers of textiles, farm implements and fertilizer enjoyed similar rights. The tendency of these producers was to limit importation of the products they manufactured to preserve their profits regardless of their cost efficiency.

Interest rate and credit allocation policies

Prior to the mid-1980s, Tanzania adopted an inflexible stance on interest rates. Throughout the 1970s until 1988, the real interest rate remained negative. Modest adjustments to nominal rates of interest in 1982 and 1983 were insufficient to bring about positive real interest rates because the rates of inflation were still too high and unresponsive to policy prescriptions.

The manufacturing sector received about 9 per cent of commercial bank lending during the first half of the 1980s. This was down from 25 per cent for 1975–9, largely because of the reduced credit demand consequent upon the decline of manufacturing production and the government's change of policy to give priority to agriculture. However, the manufacturing sector still received about 60 per cent of the credit given by development banks (i.e. Tanzania Development Finance Limited and Tanzania Investment Bank).

The systems of credit and foreign exchange allocation were interdependent and reinforcing. Credits were allocated on the basis of 'wrong' signals engendered by macroeconomic, trade and price distortions and with the objective of ensuring the survival of existing firms.

In an effort to raise the real rates of interest during the implementation of the Economic Recovery Programme, measures were taken to raise nominal rates of interest and lower the rate of inflation. By the end of 1988, nominal rates of interest had reached between 25 per cent and 31 per cent. The savings deposit rate was 25 per cent. The rate of inflation, which stood at 28 per cent in 1988, declined to 24 per cent in 1989 and to 19 per cent in 1990, resulting in positive real interest rates in the period beginning in 1989.

Negative real rates of interest tended to discourage savings and promote preferential credit rationing, capital flight and overinvestment in fixed capital (since capital was heavily subsidized). Credit subsidies tended to complement and reinforce the other forms of protection discussed earlier.

MANUFACTURING SECTOR EXPORT PERFORMANCE

Performance

Table 16.9 presents trends in the performance of manufactured exports in Tanzania in the period 1966–88. Manufactured exports showed, on average, a persistent improvement between 1966 and 1980. The high rate of increase of manufactured exports during 1966–70 was spearheaded by exports of petroleum products. With the commissioning of the oil refinery in 1966, exports of these products increased quickly, accounting for more than 50 per cent of total manufactured exports. Non-oil manufactured exports fluctuated during this period with a slight declining trend. Between 1971 and 1980, however, non-oil manufactures dominated export growth and accounted for the significant increase in the contribution of manufactures to total exports. The highest rates of increase were in 1979 and 1980 as a result of a large increase in textile exports. These went up tenfold between 1978 and 1979–80, spurred on by the commissioning of a large increase in capacity and a subsectoral export drive.

Table 16.9 Export performance: manufacturing sector, Tanzania

	Total manufactured exports		Manufactured exports excluding petroleum products			Share of manufactured exports excluding petroleum products in total exports
	Average annual value	Average growth rate	Average annual value	Average growth rate	Share of total manufactured exports	
	(US$ million)	(%)	(US$ million)	(%)	(%)	(%)
1966–70	33.1	20.7	18.6	–1.9	13.5	7.5
1971–5	50.6	13.5	30.7	19.1	14.8	8.9
1976–80	77.0	24.7	58.4	34.3	15.1	11.4
1981–5	54.5	–20.6	39.4	–25.1	14.3	9.9
1985–8	51.1	26.4	46.9	41.9	17.9	16.3
1989	87.0	56.5	71.4	26.8	28.0	22.5

Sources: URT, *Foreign Trade Statistics*, 1989; Bank of Tanzania, *Economic and Operations Report*, various issues.

Manufactured exports faltered badly between 1981 and 1985, declining at an annual average rate of 20.6 per cent for all manufactures and 25.1 per cent excluding petroleum products. The relative contribution to total exports did not decline as steeply because there was a general faltering of exports at the same time.

A strong recovery of non-oil manufactured exports was registered during 1986–9. The recovery was led by the increase of textile exports. In value terms, the peak of 1976–80 was exceeded by 1989. Preliminary data for 1990 show continued improvement in the performance of manufactured exports.

Table 16.10 presents the changing structure of manufactured exports for the period 1978–87. Data availability limited the period of analysis. Tobacco manufacturing (defined here to include factory processing of raw tobacco and cigarette manufactures), food manufactures (including cereal and cereal products), textiles and garments, industrial chemicals and petroleum products (dominated by petroleum products), and pottery, china, glass and non-metallic products (dominated by cement) have been the largest contributors to manufactured exports. The growth in the contribution of textiles and garment exports after 1980 is notable. The relative contribution of manufactured food exports fluctuated widely, mainly as a result of weather-affected supplies of cereals. The significant increase in the contribution by paper and paper products after 1985 is linked to the commissioning of the new large pulp and paper mill. Also of significant note is the rising share of machinery and supplies, dominated by electrical machineries and supplies, as a result of the coming on-stream of new plants. The structure of manufactured exports as seen in the table is quite diversified.

Table 16.10 The structure of manufactured exports, Tanzania (%)

	1978	1980	1982	1984	1985	1987
Food manufacturing	17.8	13.8	10.0	5.3	6.5	10.9
Tobacco manufacturing	24.9	9.3	23.7	14.2	16.4	19.0
Textiles and garments	13.7	27.0	16.8	18.9	10.9	26.2
Wood and wood products	0.3	0.5	0.7	0.2	0.2	0.4
Paper and paper products	0.1	0.1	0.0	0.9	0.4	9.6
Industrial chemicals and petroleum refineries	11.9	17.3	19.0	31.3	34.8	17.3
Pottery, china, glass and non-metallic products	25.7	27.5	23.0	23.1	25.3	8.8
Iron, steel, non-ferrous metals and fabricated metal products	3.8	2.2	2.6	2.4	1.8	3.8
Machinery and supplies	1.3	1.6	3.7	3.2	3.6	3.1
Others	0.5	0.7	0.5	0.5	0.1	0.5

Sources: URT, *Foreign Trade Statistics*, 1989; Bank of Tanzania, *Economic and Operations Report*, various issues.

Table 16.11 Export orientation by sector, exports/gross output, Tanzania (%)

Sector	1978	1979	1980	1984	1985	1986	1987
Food manufacturing	9.6	16.3	9.1	1.7	2.3	4.5	9.7
Tobacco manufacturing		63.6	51.1	32.7	44.0	43.2	70.5
Textiles and garments	5.5	19.3	14.9	8.6	5.5	18.1	25.0
Wood and wood products	2.5	1.7	1.9	0.7	0.9	2.4	3.6
Paper and paper products	6.9	0.7	1.3	3.8	0.5	10.7	27.2
Industrial chemicals and petroleum refineries	13.0	12.2	23.8	20.2	26.8		25.0
Pottery, china, glass and non-metallic products	1.4	97.2		36.5	43.6	17.1	15.5
Iron, steel, non-ferrous metals and fabricated metal products	4.5	2.9	3.6	1.5	1.4	2.9	6.2
Machinery including electrical and supplies	4.7	3.3	7.2	8.5	8.3	9.6	15.8
Transport equipment	0.0	0.0	0.3	0.7	0.2	0.07	1.0
Total manufacturing sector	10.2	14.5	13.2	7.5	8.1	7.08	15.5

Sources: URT, *Foreign Trade Statistics*, 1989; URT, *Survey of Industrial Production*, various issues.

The dominant sectors were largely competitively efficient. Their short-run domestic resource cost ratios, according to the 1984 World Bank survey, ranged between 0.13 and 2.0 at actual capacity utilization rates and 0.11 and 0.87 at attainable capacity utilization.

Table 16.11 shows the changing degree of export orientation (the ratio of exports to gross output) of the manufacturing sector, by industry, for the period 1978–87. The contraction of export orientation across all sectors during 1981–5 and its subsequent recovery after 1986 is notable. By 1987, the export orientation of most sectors exceeded previous highest levels.

Trade and trade-related policies affecting manufactured exports

Two major sets of policies affecting export incentives are considered here: commercial policy and the exchange rate. Commercial policy may give rise to both explicit and implicit taxation of exports. Import duties raise the profitability of domestic sales and indirectly discourage exports. Explicit taxation of exports directly reduces the relative profitability of exports. We shall measure this total taxation of exports (or fiscal anti-export bias) here as $[(1 + t_m)/(1 - t_x)] - 1$, with t_m and t_x recording the effective import duty rate and export tax rate, respectively.

Quantitative restrictions and the related exchange controls have two effects on anti-export bias. Restrictions used for balance of payments management purposes act as implicit tariffs by limiting supplies and raising domestic prices, hence making domestic sales more attractive. With an inactive nominal exchange rate policy, the resultant inflationary pressure leads to real currency appreciation. On the other hand, the associated exchange controls yield currency inconvertibility. Depending on the efficacy of enforcement, a parallel market for foreign currency and imports may develop at a much more depreciated domestic currency value. The resultant dual exchange rate system, while yielding rents to those with access to official import licences, gives rise to taxation of those exports that take place through the official channel. While such exporters surrender their proceeds at the appreciated value of the domestic currency, they purchase imports at the much more depreciated parallel rate or forego the higher return on the black market rate for currency. The wider the margin between the two rates, the higher the marginal taxation rate. This rate here will be measured, following Pinto (1989), at the ratio of the parallel exchange rate premium on foreign exchange to the parallel market rate, i.e. (UOER – OER)/UOER, with UOER and OER being the parallel and official exchange rates, respectively.

Whether a parallel market for imports and foreign exchange exists or not, real appreciation of the official value of the currency constitutes implicit taxation of exports. A passive exchange rate policy that compensates neither for the widening of price differentials with trading partners nor for changes in other fundamentals affecting the real exchange rate both erodes the external competitiveness of exportables and turns the internal terms of trade against exports.

Movements in the real official exchange rate are used as another measure of export incentive changes. The official real exchange rate is here measured such that a rise in the index signifies real depreciation and a decline real

Table 16.12 Trends in anti-export bias, Tanzania

	Explicit taxation[a] (%)	Marginal taxation[b] (%)	Real exchange rate index[c] (%)
1966	16.1	17.0	100
1967	19.06	17.9	93.8
1968	20.0	16.0	79.3
1969	20.8	17.9	69.7
1970	15.8	29.9	72.5
1971	13.0	38.4	74.2
1972	13.7	53.0	76.2
1973	18.4	51.5	80.0
1974	17.2	47.1	80.9
1975	14.6	64.0	72.8
1976	19.6	61.7	77.4
1977	26.3	61.5	76.7
1978	22.3	41.3	74.5
1979	19.3	31.3	80.1
1980	13.5	61.0	70.9
1981	8.9	69.9	53.7
1982	7.1	71.4	44.2
1983	8.0	71.6	39.6
1984	9.6	72.2	37.6
1985	10.0	82.7	32.3
1986	8.3	79.2	58.4
1987	8.7	63.5	89.4
1988	8.2	60.5	132.6

Sources: Kauffman and O'Connell (1991); URT, *Economic Survey*, various issues; Bank of Tanzania, *Economic and Operations Report*, various issues.

[a] $[(1 + t_m/1 - t_x)] - 1$.
[b] (UOER − OER)/UOER, where OER, official exchange rate; UOER, parallel market rate.
[c] The real exchange rate is defined so that an increase in the index indicates real devaluation.

appreciation. The chosen base year, 1965, was characterized by stable macroeconomic balances and a more or less convertible currency (Krumm, 1990; Ndulu, 1991). A fall in the index, other things being equal, signifies penalization of exports.

Table 16.12 presents the three measurements of the evolution of export incentives for the period between 1966 and 1988: those based on explicit taxation, the marginal taxation of exports implicit in dual exchange rates, and the official real exchange rate. The latter two measures seem to move together.

Anti-export bias was reasonably low during 1966–70, rising during the 1970s. Both explicit taxes and exchange rate appreciation significantly discouraged exports during 1966–79. The steep real currency appreciation during 1980–5 swamped explicit taxes as a source of anti-export incentives. Actually, explicit taxation rates during this period declined drastically as export taxes were more or less scrapped. Exchange controls were severely tightened and quantitative restrictions became the main instrument for balance of payments management in the 1970s. The rapid further rise in parallel premium rates and marginal tax rates on exports during 1978–85 was associated with the tightening of quantitative restrictions. While import compression to close the resource gaps during this period was inescapable, implementing it using quantitative restrictions alone exacerbated the problem by discouraging exports.

Several export promotion measures were either intensified or instituted during 1979–85 in an attempt to ameliorate the rise in anti-export bias mentioned above. A duty rebate scheme for exporters was established in 1981 to replace the previous duty drawback for imported inputs used in the production of exports. The rebates ranged from 5 to 25 per cent of export value, depending on import content. The largest beneficiaries were exporters of manufactures, and the rebates averaged 8 per cent of manufactured export values between 1982 and 1984 (World Bank, 1987: 24).

An export retention scheme was instituted in 1983–4. The scheme allowed exporters to retain between 10 and 100 per cent of foreign exchange earnings for purchase of inputs, spares and other goods for resale at non-controlled prices. Non-traditional exports were allowed a higher retention rate. The large difference between official and parallel market exchange rates meant that the retention scheme enabled exporters to realize a much higher implicit exchange rate than the official one, particularly when they imported items for resale at open market prices.

The other export promotion schemes put in place at that time included financial services to exporters at preferential interest rates; an export credit guarantee scheme involving both pre-shipment financial cover (of up to 75 per cent of loss) and a comprehensive shipment guarantee against commercial risk (covering 45–95 per cent of any loss, depending on cause); an export facilitation scheme aimed at reducing various procedural bottlenecks to exporters, including rationalization, harmonization and simplification of documents; an export revolving fund/seed capital revolving fund; a presidential export award; and preferential foreign exchange allocation for export production (Lyakurwa, 1991).

The period from 1987 onwards saw major policy reforms aimed at reversing the anti-export incentive structure and promoting exports. A key measure was the reduction of currency overvaluation through 'maxi' nominal devaluations. The official real value of the currency depreciated by 89 per cent (in US dollar terms) between 1986 and 1990. Although, on purchasing power parity grounds, this had, by 1988, more than compensated for changes since 1965 (see Table 16.12), taking into account changes in other fundamentals affecting the competitiveness of exports, the currency remained slightly overvalued (Ndulu, 1991).

In 1988, tariff reforms were made affecting not only the structure but also the magnitude of rates. The maximum tariff rate was reduced from

200 to 100 per cent. The Finance Bill of 1990–1 further reduced the rates to range from 0 to 60 per cent, lowering the weighted average scheduled tariff rate. The combination of steep real currency depreciation and lower tariffs significantly raised the relative profitability of exports.

Rationalization of various measures instituted during 1980–5 to promote exports was also undertaken during the later reform period to complement the restructuring of incentives. Retention schemes were made more systematic and the dispersion of rates applicable to exporters was reduced. In 1987, the range of applicable rates was reduced from the previous 10–100 per cent to a dual rate 50 per cent for non-traditional exports and 10 per cent for traditional ones. The export rebate scheme was abolished in 1986 and a duty drawback scheme was reintroduced in 1989 in its place. The duty drawback scheme was geared at reducing the disincentives to export caused by import duties on inputs.

The link between policy and performance

The faltering of export performance during 1981–5 (Table 16.9) was closely associated with the changing incentive structure. Both in terms of volume and value, a very rapid decline in manufactured exports was recorded. Although the steepness of the decline was definitely influenced by the decline in manufacturing output, the proportion of output exported also fell drastically across all subsectors, as shown in Table 16.11. Although it is rather early to offer solid conclusions, the post-1986 reforms seem to have at least halted the decline in the export performance of the sector, and preliminary results point toward a recovery of export orientation. From the low level of the 1981–5 period, the proportion of output exported rose sharply in 1986 and 1987.

CONCLUDING REMARKS

Tanzania's industrialization experience over the last three decades was one of a created potential not put to full use. While reasonable success was achieved in terms of expanding output potential, and changing the subsectoral structure through an investment drive, actual utilization of this potential was subject to changing macroeconomic and external conditions. After sustaining a reasonable level until 1975, capacity utilization fell drastically from 75 per cent to only 25 per cent in 1985, before slightly recovering to 35 per cent in 1989. The main reasons for this decline were overexpansion of capacity relative to utilization ability in the 1970s and severe import compression after 1978.

The available evidence suggests that no significant factor productivity growth was achieved in Tanzanian manufacturing. In part this was due to cyclical instability of actual production. The large fluctuations in labour and investment productivity seem to have been mainly influenced by output and value-added variations. Interruptions in the process of learning-by-doing are not conducive to skill formation. However, as argued earlier, a growing gap had set in, particularly since the late 1970s, between skill requirements and available human capacity, as the level of sophistication in the new plants rose.

Different forms of protection provided to local producers enabled them to earn profits in excess of levels consistent with (world) competitive efficiency. During the first one and a half decades, protection was mostly provided through an escalated tariff structure and subsidized imported inputs due to a degree of currency overvaluation. Price controls, quantitative restrictions and exchange controls became much more pronounced in the next fifteen years. In combination with a grossly overvalued currency, protection levels soared in the late 1970s up to the mid-1980s. Trade and trade-related policy reforms since the mid-1980s not only considerably reduced effective protection levels but also shifted the instruments of protection away from non-tariff barriers. The continued survival of grossly inefficient activities during the crisis period was made possible through enhanced protection levels; a steep decline in real labour cost, providing more room for profit's share in value added; cost-plus pricing; and, in the case of public enterprises, budgetary absorption of enterprise losses.

In terms of efficiency, about 40 per cent of manufacturing activities in the mid–1980s generated negative value added. These inefficient activities used up more than their fair share of scarce foreign exchange since they also tended to be on average more import-intensive. Although the very low capacity utilization rates were significantly related to the high domestic resource costs of the sector, the foregoing analysis points towards the (unutilized) potential for industrial restructuring to enable higher returns from the scarce available resources.

Preoccupation with import substitution had, until the early 1980s, resulted in neglect of the importance of the export orientation of the sector. The incentive structure was severely biased against exports. During the first half of the 1980s, the government actively instituted export promotion measures to partly offset the negative effects of the other discouragements to export performance. The second half of the 1980s saw export orientation rising as a result of a combination of real currency devaluation, reduction in anti-export bias and the streamlining of various export promotion measures.

REFERENCES

Bank of Tanzania, *Economic and Operations Report*, various issues.

Bhagwati, J. (1978) *Anatomy and Consequences of Exchange Control Regimes*, Cambridge, Massachusetts: Ballinger Publishing Company.

Dobrska, Z. (1968) 'Criteria for Public Investment in Manufacturing: Five Tanzanian Case Studies', Economic Research Bureau Paper no. 68.28, University of Dar-es-Salaam.

de Valk, P. and Mbelle, A. (1990) 'Textile Industry Under Structural Adjustment in Tanzania (1980–90)', research report, ISS, The Hague.

Grundmann, H. (1963) 'Implications of the Concept of Effective Rate of Protection', Economic Research Bureau Paper no. 68.19, University of Dar-es-Salaam.

—— (1969) 'Towards a More Rational Protection Policy', Economic Research Bureau Paper no. 69.1, University of Dar-es-Salaam.

Hazlewood, A. (1966) 'The East African Common Market: Importance and Effects', *Bulletin of the Oxford University Institute of Economics and Statistics* 28(1).

Helleiner, G. (1989) 'Lessons for Sub-Saharan Africa from Latin American Experience', *African Development Review* 1(1): 3–20.

Kauffmann, D. and O'Connell, S. (1991) 'The Macroeconomics of the Unofficial Foreign Exchange Market in Tanzania', in A. Chhibber and S. Fischer (eds) *Economic Reform in Sub-Saharan Africa*: World Bank, Washington, DC, pp. 39–49.

Kessell, B. (1968) 'Effective Protection of Industry in Tanzania', *East African Economic Review* 4(1): 1–18.

Krumm, K. (1990) 'Medium-Term Framework for Analysis of the Real Exchange Rate, Applications to the Philippines and Tanzania', mimeo, World Bank.

Lyakurwa, W. (1988) 'Tanzania – Confinement Policy and Deconfinement', unpublished report to the World Bank, Dar-es-Salaam.

—— (1991) 'Trade Policy and Promotion in Sub-Saharan Africa: A Review of Experiences and Issues', Special Paper 12, African Economic Research Consortium, Nairobi.

Mbelle, A. (1988) 'Foreign Exchange and Industrial Development: A Study of Tanzania', unpublished PhD thesis, Gothenburg University.

Mbogoro, D. (1977) 'The Common Market Concept and Economic Development: Tanzania's Experience in the East African Common Market', Economic Research Bureau Paper no. 77.8, University of Dar-es-Salaam.

Mlawa, H. (1983) 'The Acquisition of Technological Capability and Technical Change: A Study of the Textile Industry in Tanzania', unpublished DPhil dissertation, University of Sussex.

Ndulu, B. J. (1986) 'Investment, Output Growth and Capacity Utilization in an African Economy: The Case of the Manufacturing Sector in Tanzania', *Eastern Africa Economic Review* 2(1): 14–30.

—— (1993) 'Exchange Rate Policy and Management in the Context of Economic Reforms in Sub-Saharan Africa: Tanzania as an Illustrative Case', in G. Hanson (ed.) *Trade Growth and Development: The Role of Politics and Institutions*, ch. 12, Routledge.

—— and Lipumba, M. (1991) 'International Trade and Economic Development in Tanzania', in J. H. Frimpong-Ansah, S. M. R. Kanbur and P. Svedberg (eds) *Trade and Development in Sub-Saharan Africa*, Manchester: Manchester University Press, pp. 21–61.

—— Lyakurwa, W., Semboja, J. and Chaligha, A. (1987) 'Import Tariff Study – Tanzania', unpublished report to the Ministry of Finance, Dar-es-Salaam.

Ngiliule, P. (1986) 'Effective Rate of Protection in Tanzania's Industry', unpublished MA dissertation, University of Dar-es-Salaam.

Nishimizu, M. and Page, Jr. J. (1986) 'Productivity Change and Dynamic Comparative Advantage', *Review of Economics and Statistics* 68/2: 241–7.

Pack, H. (1992) 'Learning and Productivity Change in Developing Countries', in G. K. Helleiner (ed.) *Trade Policy, Industrialization and Development: New Perspectives*: pp. 21–45, Oxford: Clarendon Press.

Pinto, B. (1989) 'Black Market Premia, Exchange Rate Unification and Inflation in Sub-Saharan Africa', *World Bank Economic Review* 3(3): 321–8.

Rattso, J. (1988) 'Import Compression Macro-Dynamics: Macroeconomic Analysis for Sub-Saharan Africa', mimeo, University of Trondheim.

Rice, R. (1976) 'The Tanzania Price Control System: Theory, Practice and Some Possible Improvements', Economic Research Bureau Paper no. 76.4, University of Dar-es-Salaam.

Rosenstein-Rodan, P. (1943) 'Problems of Industrialization of Eastern and Southern Europe', *Economic Journal* 53: 202–11.

Rweyemamu, J. (1973) *Underdevelopment and Industrialization in Tanzania: A Study of Perverse Capitalist Industrial Development*, East Africa: Oxford University Press.

Segal, M. (1971) 'The Revenue Effects of East African Transfer Taxes: Tanzania', Economic Research Bureau Paper no. 71.5, University of Dar-es-Salaam.

Semboja, J. J. (1978) 'Effective Rate of Protection and Industrialization in Tanzania', Economic Research Bureau Paper no. 78.4, University of Dar-es-Salaam.

Shaaeldin, E. (1989) 'Sources of Industrial Growth in Kenya, Tanzania, Zambia and Zimbabwe: Some Estimates', *African Development Review* 1(1): 21–39.

Skarstein, R. and S. Wangwe (1986) *Industrial Development in Tanzania: Some Critical Issues*, Uppsala: Scandinavian Institute for African Studies; and Dar-es-Salaam: Tanzania Publishing House.

URT (United Republic of Tanzania), *Economic Survey*, various issues.

—— *National Accounts of Tanzania*, various issues.

—— *Survey of Industrial Production*, various issues.

—— (1964a) *Long-Term Plan, 1964–1980*.

—— (1964b) *First Five-Year Plan, 1964–1969*.

—— (1969) *Second Five-Year Plan, 1969–1974*.

—— (1976a) *Basic Industrialization Strategy*.

—— (1976b) *Third Five-Year Plan, 1976–1981*.

—— (1988) *Trade Statistics*.

—— (1989) *Foreign Trade Statistics*.

—— (1990a) *Industrial Commodities Quarterly Report*.

—— (1990b) *National Investment (Promotion and Protection) Act, No. 10*.

Wangwe, S. (1983) 'Industrialization and Resource Allocation in a Developing Country: The Case of Recent Experiences in Tanzania', *World Development* 1(6): 483–92.

—— (1990) 'Industrial Development in Tanzania: Are Infant Industries Maturing?', Paper presented to the Economic Policy Workshop, Dar-es-Salaam.

—— (1992) 'Building Indigenous Technological Capacity: A Study of Selected Industries in Tanzania', in F. Stewart, S. Lall and S. Wangwe (eds) *Alternative Development Strategies in Sub-Saharan Africa*, London: Macmillan, pp. 265–93.

Waverman, L. and Murphy, S. (1992) 'Total Factor Productivity in Automobile Production in Argentina, Mexico, Korea and Canada: The Impacts of Protection'

in G. K. Helleiner (ed.) *Trade Policy, Industrialization and Development: New Perspectives*, Oxford: Clarendon Press, pp. 279–93.
World Bank (1987) *Tanzania: An Agenda for Industrial Recovery*, Vols I and II, Washington, DC: World Bank.

INDEX

financial liberalization, Turkey 465–6
financial system, Kenya 501–2
fiscal reform, Chile: in structural
    reforms 109; and trade liberalization
    111–12
Fischer, S. 107–8, 113
Fitzgerald, E.V.K. 232
FOMEI (Mexico) 172
FOMEX (Mexico) 172
foreign capital, in Brazil 66
Foreign Exchange Regulations Act
    (India, 1973) 302
foreign investment: India 302–3; Korea
    343–5; policies on 22–3; Sri Lanka
    392, 406–9
Foroutan, F. 476
Franco, H.B. 63–95
Frank, C.R. 320, 323–4
free trade zones, Malaysia 370–2
Fritsch, W. 63–95

Garay, L.J. 145
Gelb, A. 107–8
General Agreement on Tariffs and
    Trade (GATT) 16–17, 24; and
    Mexico 192–3
General Trading Companies (Korea)
    328
Ghee, L.T. 364–88
Griffin, K. 390, 412
Gross Domestic Product: Bangladesh
    262; changes, Peru 230; and exports
    and imports, Chile 106; growth,
    Colombia 136; growth rates, as
    macroeconomic performance
    indicators 5; India 306; Kenya 487–8;
    Korea 319; Malaysia 365; and
    manufacturing growth, Peru 237–8;
    Mexico 188–9; and output and
    productivity, growth of 48; Sri Lanka
    390
Gross National Product: as economic
    indicator 40; Korea 319
Grossman, E.S. 357
Grossman, G. 28, 397, 409
Grundmann, H. 538–9
Guimaraes, E.P. 80
Gulhati, R. 508
Gunatilleke, G. 402

Hachette, D. 97
Hallberg, K. 145, 148

Hamann, J. 233
Harberger, A. 111, 114
Harrison, A. 11
Havrylyshyn, O. 29, 353, 356
Hazelwood, A. 536
Hecox, W.E. 500
Helleiner, G.K. 1–36, 400
Helpmann, E. 28
Hernandez Laos, E. 181, 183
Hirschman, A.O. 37, 41
Hong, S.D. 330
Hong, W. 335
Hong Kong: investment and capital
    output ratios 384; unit labour costs
    376
Hopcraft, P. 491
House, W. 506
Hulten, C.R. 444
Hunt, S. 239
Hussain Committee 296
Hutchenson, T.L. 134, 148

IMG Consultants 379
import duties see tariffs
import-substitution industrialization
    8–10; Brazil 65–6; Colombia 132,
    133–4, 136–7; Kenya 489–90, 504,
    507; Malaysia 364; manufacturing
    for export 24; Mexico 173, 177; Peru
    218–23, 232; Sri Lanka 392; Tanzania
    531–43; Thailand 446–7
imports
    coefficients, Brazil 68
    composition of, Kenya 490
    controls, Tanzania 538–41
    dependence on, Peru 235
    duty, exemptions and trade policy
        17–18
    evolution of, Chile 102–7
    foreign investment and technology
        import: Korea 343–5
    and GDP, Chile 106
    liberalization: Korea 336–40; Turkey
        468–70
    and manufacturing, Brazil 67
    penetration of, Turkey 470–1
    Peru 231
    policy, Korea 336–45
    protection: Brazil 71–3; Korea 340–3
    restriction instruments, Thailand
        430–2
    structural change in, Thailand 426–7